Research Anthology on Securing Medical Systems and Records

Information Resources Management Association
USA

Volume II

Published in the United States of America by
IGI Global
Information Science Reference (an imprint of IGI Global)
701 E. Chocolate Avenue
Hershey PA, USA 17033
Tel: 717-533-8845
Fax: 717-533-8661
E-mail: cust@igi-global.com
Web site: http://www.igi-global.com

Library of Congress Cataloging-in-Publication Data

Names: Information Resources Management Association, editor.
Title: Research anthology on securing medical systems and records / Information Resources Management Association, editor.
Description: Hershey, PA : Information Science Reference, [2022] | Includes bibliographical references and index.
Identifiers: LCCN 2022016825 (print) | LCCN 2022016826 (ebook) | ISBN 9781668463116 (hardcover) | ISBN 9781668463123 (ebook)
Subjects: MESH: Medical Records Systems, Computerized | Confidentiality | Security Measures | Internet of Things | Big Data
Classification: LCC R864 (print) | LCC R864 (ebook) | NLM WX 175 | DDC 610.285--dc23/eng/20220527
LC record available at https://lccn.loc.gov/2022016825
LC ebook record available at https://lccn.loc.gov/2022016826

British Cataloguing in Publication Data
A Cataloguing in Publication record for this book is available from the British Library.

List of Contributors

Abdul, Qudrotullaah Bolanle Suleiman / *University of Ilorin Teaching Hospital, Nigeria*............ 775
Acharya, Subrata / *Towson University, USA* 573
Adeleke, Ibrahim Taiwo / *Federal Medical Centre, Bida, Nigeria* 775
Ahmed, Muhammad Mashhood / *De Montfort University, UK* 1
Al Momin, Md Abdullah / *University of Louisiana at Lafayette, USA* 255
Alti, Adel / *LRSD Lab, Computer Science Department, Faculty of Sciences, University of SETIF-1, Algeria* 517
Anastasiou, Athanasios / *AiM Research Team, Biomedical Engineering Laboratory, National Technical University of Athens, Greece* 970
Anderson, Damon P. / *Capitol Technology University, USA* 764
Androutsou, Thelma / *National Technical University of Athens, Greece* 970
Aridi, Amalisha Sabie / *Capitol Technology University, USA* 750
B. R., Yuvaraj / *Anna University, India* 294
Barboza, Marcelo / *Instituto Federal de São Paulo, Brazil & Escola Politécnica da Universidade de São Paulo, Brazil* 238
Barhoun, Rabie / *Hassan II University, Faculty of science Ben M'sik, Casablanca, Morocco* 955
Basu, Abhishek / *RCC Institute of Information Technology, India* 533
Bates, Benjamin R. / *Ohio University, USA* 358
Bhardwaj, Aashish / *Guru Tegh Bahadur Institute of Technology, India* 1012
Bhargava, Nimisha / *AUL Corporation, Napa, USA* 764
Bhatia, Dinesh / *North Eastern Hill University, India* 662
Bhatt, Alekha Parimal / *Capgemini IT India Pvt. Ltd., India* 269
Bhushan, Bharat / *HMR Institute of Technology and Management, Delhi, India* 617
Bhutani, Samarth / *Vellore Institute of Technology, Vellore, India* 833
Bingi, Prasad / *Purdue University, Fort Wayne, USA* 381
Bock, Eduardo G. P. / *Instituto Federal de São Paulo, Brazil* 238
Burmaoglu, Serhat / *Izmir Katip Celebi University, Turkey* 84
Burrell, Darrell Norman / *The Florida Institute of Technology, USA & Capitol Technology University, USA* 750, 764
Burton, Sharon L. / *Grand Canyon University, USA* 764
Buyya, Rajkumar / *The University of Melbourne, Melbourne, Australia* 922
Candereli, Zehra Ozge / *Izmir Katip Celebi University, Turkey* 84
Choi, Young B. / *Regent University, USA* 706
Coats, Brian S. / *University of Maryland – Baltimore, USA* 573
Costarides, Vassilia / *Institute of Communication and Computer Systems (ICCS), Greece* 970

Darra, Eleni / *Center for Security Studies (KEMEA), Greece* 59
Dawson, Maurice / *Illinois Institute of Technology, USA* 750, 764
Dwivedi, Rajendra Kumar / *Madan Mohan Malaviya University of Technology, Gorakhpur, India* 922
Ed-daibouni, Maryam / *Hassan II University, Faculty of Science Ben M'sik, Casablanca, Morocco* 955
Elgujja, Abba Amsami / *University of Salford, UK* 788
Farhadi, Maryam / *Kennesaw State University, USA* 995
Ferrag, Mohamed Amine / *Guelma University, Algeria* 1
Garg, Hitendra / *GLA University, Mathura, India* 903
Gautam, Siddharth / *HMR Institute of Technology and Management, Delhi, India* 617
Giannouli, Dimitra / *Computer Solutions SA, Greece & University of Leeds, UK* 970
Gkotsis, Ilias / *Center for Security Studies (KEMEA), Greece* 59
Govinda K. / *VIT University, India* 843
Grati, Rima / *Zayed University, UAE* 811
Gungor, Dilek Ozdemir / *Izmir Katip Celebi University, Turkey* 84
Gupta, Lalit Mohan / *APJ Abdul Kalam Technical University, Lucknow, India* 903
Haddad, Hisham M. / *Kennesaw State University, USA* 995
Ionescu, Oana Claudia / *Titu Maiorescu University, Romania* 225
Jain, Esha / *The NorthCap University, Gurugram, India* 204
Javid, Tariq / *Hamdard University, Pakistan* 449
Jayaprakasam, Manessa / *Independent Researcher, India* 486
Jinwala, Devesh C. / *S. V. National Institute of Technology, India* 103
John, Naveen / *Nesamony Memorial Christian College, Marthandam, India* 878
Kaddoura, Sanaa / *Zayed University, UAE* 811
Kamoun, Faouzi / *ESPRIT School of Engineering, Tunisia* 726
Karmakar, Ranit / *Tata Consultancy Services, India* 533
Karthick G. S. / *Bharathiar University, India* 150
Kaushik, Ila / *Krishna Institute of Engineering and Technology, India* 617
Khamparia, Aditya / *Lovely Professional University, India* 617
Khandelwal, Brijesh / *Amity University, Raipur, India* 181
Kidak, Levent B. / *Izmir Katip Celebi University, Turkey* 84
Kisku, Dakshina Ranjan / *National Institute of Technology Durgapur, India* 31
Knight, James R. / *The Ohio State University, USA* 381
Kumar, Binod / *JSPM's Rajarshi Shahu College of Engineering, India* 685
Kumar, Rakesh / *Madan Mohan Malaviya University of Technology, Gorakhpur, India* 922
Kumar, Vikas / *Chaudhary Bansi Lal University, Bhiwani-127021, Haryana, India* 1012
Lamba, Jonika / *The NorthCap University, Gurugram, India* 204
Laouamer, Lamri / *Department of Management Information Systems, College of Business and Economics, Qassim University, Saudi Arabia* 517
Leão, Tarcisio F. / *Instituto Federal de São Paulo, Brazil* 238
Li, Yue / *Southwest Jiaotong University, Chengdu, China* 408
M., Vigilson Prem / *R. M. D. Engineering College, India* 294
Maglaras, Leandros / *De Montfort University, UK* 1
Manikis, Georgios C. / *Institute of Computer Science, Foundation for Research and Technology Hellas, Heraklion, Greece* 322

Mantzana, Vasiliki / *Center for Security Studies (KEMEA), Greece* 59
McLester, Quatavia / *The Chicago School of Professional Psychology, USA* 750
Medhekar, Anita / *Central Queensland University, Australia* 428
Muller, S. Raschid / *Capitol Technology University, USA* 750
Namir, Abdelwahed / *Hassan II University, Faculty of Science Ben M'sik, Casablanca, Morocco* 955
Nicho, Mathew / *Zayed University, UAE* 726
Nobles, Calvin / *University of Maryland Global Campus, USA* 750
Novak, Alison Nicole / *Rowan University, USA* 336
Oncioiu, Ionica / *Titu Maiorescu University, Romania* 225
Pal, Parashu Ram / *ABES Engineering College, India* 685
Panchatcharam, Parthasarathy / *VIT University, Vellore, India* 128
Pankajavalli P. B. / *Bharathiar University, India* 150
Pathak, Pankaj / *Symbiosis Institute of Digital and Telecom Management, Symbiosis International University, India* 685
Pepić, Selver / *Higher Technical Machine School of Professional Studies in Trstenik, Serbia* 644
Pitoglou, Stavros / *National Technical University of Athens, Greece & Computer Solutions SA, Greece* 970
Pradhan, Chittaranjan / *KIIT University, India* 464
Prasad, Sheetal B. / *SRM Institute of Science and Technology, India* 685
Punithavathi P. / *VIT Chennai, India* 17
Pushkar, Shashank / *Birla Institute of Technology, Mesra, India* 942
Rakshit, Rinku Datta / *Asansol Engineering College, India* 31
Rangarajan (Ray) Parthasarathy / *University of Illinois at Urbana-Champaign, USA* 381
Rangarajan, Anuradha / *Indiana State University, USA* 381
Reddy, Pradeep / *VIT-AP, India* 853
S., Indra Priyadharshini / *R. M. K. College of Engineering and Technology, India* 294
Sahay, Ajita / *KIIT University, India* 464
Sam, Shatheesh / *Manonmaniam Sundaranar University, India* 878
Samad, Abdus / *University Women's Polytechnic, Aligarh Muslim University, Aligarh, India* 903
Santos, Bruno J. / *Instituto Federal de São Paulo, Brazil* 238
Saracevic, Muzafer H / *University of Novi Pazar, Serbia.* 644
Saxena, V. K. / *Vikram University, Ujjain, India* 942
Selimi, Aybeyan / *International Vision University, North Macedonia* 644
Selvanambi, Ramani / *Vellore Institute of Technology, Vellore, India* 833
Shahriar, Hossain / *Kennesaw State University, USA* 995
Shanmugam, Poonkuntran / *Velammal College of Engineering and Technology, Madurai, India* 486
Sharma, Anand / *Mody University of Science and Technology, Lakshmangarh, India* 269
Sharma, Dhruti P. / *Sarvajanik College of Engineering and Technology, India* 103
Sharma, Nikhil / *HMR Institute of Engineering and Technology, Delhi, India* 617
Sherwani, Shariq I. / *Ohio University, USA* 358
Shuai, Mengxia / *University of Science and Technology of China, Anhui, China* 408
Shufutinsky, Anton / *Cabrini University, USA* 750
Sinha, Amandip / *West Bengal University of Technology, India* 464
Soualmi, Abdallah / *LRSD Lab, Computer Science Department, Faculty of Sciences, University of SETIF-1, Algeria* 517
Spanakis, Emmanouil G. / *Institute of Computer Science, Foundation for Research and*

Technology Hellas, Heraklion, Greece 322
Spanakis, Marios / *Institute of Computer Science, Foundation for Research and Technology Hellas, Heraklion, Greece* 322
Springs, Delores / *Regent University, USA* 764
Subbiah, Geetha / *VIT Chennai, India* 17
Tabacow, Rachel P. / *Instituto Federal de São Paulo, Brazil* 238
Tiwari, Ankita / *Amity University, India* 662
Tripathi, Raghuvendra Pratap / *Amity University, India* 662
Ulaganathan, Pradheeba / *R. M. K. College of Engineering and Technology, India* 294
Vamsi, Desam / *VIT-AP, India* 853
Veauli, Komal / *Vellore Institute of Technology, Vellore, India* 833
Verma, Parul / *Amity University, Lucknow, India* 181
Vivekanandan S. / *VIT University, Vellore, India* 128
Wang, Hongxia / *Southwest Jiaotong University, Chengdu, China* 408
Williams, Christopher E. / *Regent University, USA* 706
Wright, Jorja B. / *The University of Charleston, USA* 764
Wyant, David K. / *Belmont University, USA* 381
Xiong, Ling / *Xihua University, Chengdu, China* 408
Yu, Nenghai / *University of Science and Technology of China, Anhui, China* 408

Table of Contents

Preface xvi

Section 1
Securing Healthcare Systems

Chapter 1
Cyber Threats in the Healthcare Sector and Countermeasures 1
Muhammad Mashhood Ahmed, De Montfort University, UK
Leandros Maglaras, De Montfort University, UK
Mohamed Amine Ferrag, Guelma University, Algeria

Chapter 2
Digital Healthcare Security Issues: Is There a Solution in Biometrics? 17
Punithavathi P., VIT Chennai, India
Geetha Subbiah, VIT Chennai, India

Chapter 3
Biometric Technologies in Healthcare Biometrics 31
Rinku Datta Rakshit, Asansol Engineering College, India
Dakshina Ranjan Kisku, National Institute of Technology Durgapur, India

Chapter 4
Cyber-Physical Security in Healthcare 59
Vasiliki Mantzana, Center for Security Studies (KEMEA), Greece
Eleni Darra, Center for Security Studies (KEMEA), Greece
Ilias Gkotsis, Center for Security Studies (KEMEA), Greece

Chapter 5
Applying Blockchain Technologies in Healthcare: A Scientometric Analysis 84
Zehra Ozge Candereli, Izmir Katip Celebi University, Turkey
Serhat Burmaoglu, Izmir Katip Celebi University, Turkey
Levent B. Kidak, Izmir Katip Celebi University, Turkey
Dilek Ozdemir Gungor, Izmir Katip Celebi University, Turkey

Chapter 6
Multi-Keyword Searchable Encryption for E-Health System With Multiple Data Writers and Readers 103
Dhruti P. Sharma, Sarvajanik College of Engineering and Technology, India
Devesh C. Jinwala, S. V. National Institute of Technology, India

Chapter 7
Internet of Things (IOT) in Healthcare – Smart Health and Surveillance, Architectures, Security Analysis and Data Transfer: A Review 128
Parthasarathy Panchatcharam, VIT University, Vellore, India
Vivekanandan S., VIT University, Vellore, India

Chapter 8
Healthcare IoT Architectures, Technologies, Applications, and Issues: A Deep Insight 150
Karthick G. S., Bharathiar University, India
Pankajavalli P. B., Bharathiar University, India

Chapter 9
IoT-Based Smart and Secure Health Monitoring System 181
Parul Verma, Amity University, Lucknow, India
Brijesh Khandelwal, Amity University, Raipur, India

Chapter 10
Advanced Cyber Security and Internet of Things for Digital Transformations of the Indian Healthcare Sector 204
Jonika Lamba, The NorthCap University, Gurugram, India
Esha Jain, The NorthCap University, Gurugram, India

Chapter 11
Healthcare Security Assessment in the Big Data Era: Lessons From Turkey 225
Ionica Oncioiu, Titu Maiorescu University, Romania
Oana Claudia Ionescu, Titu Maiorescu University, Romania

Section 2
Securing Medical Devices

Chapter 12
Cyber Security in Health: Standard Protocols for IoT and Supervisory Control Systems 238
Bruno J. Santos, Instituto Federal de São Paulo, Brazil
Rachel P. Tabacow, Instituto Federal de São Paulo, Brazil
Marcelo Barboza, Instituto Federal de São Paulo, Brazil & Escola Politécnica da Universidade de São Paulo, Brazil
Tarcisio F. Leão, Instituto Federal de São Paulo, Brazil
Eduardo G. P. Bock, Instituto Federal de São Paulo, Brazil

Chapter 13
Medical Device Security 255
Md Abdullah Al Momin, University of Louisiana at Lafayette, USA

Chapter 14
Quantum Cryptography for Securing IoT-Based Healthcare Systems 269
Anand Sharma, Mody University of Science and Technology, Lakshmangarh, India
Alekha Parimal Bhatt, Capgemini IT India Pvt. Ltd., India

Chapter 15
Constructive Solutions for Security and Privacy Issues at the Edge: Securing Edge Framework – A Healthcare Application Use Case 294
Indra Priyadharshini S., R. M. K. College of Engineering and Technology, India
Pradheeba Ulaganathan, R. M. K. College of Engineering and Technology, India
Vigilson Prem M., R. M. D. Engineering College, India
Yuvaraj B. R., Anna University, India

Chapter 16
Personalized Mobile eHealth Services for Secure User Access Through a Multi Feature Biometric Framework 322
Georgios C. Manikis, Institute of Computer Science, Foundation for Research and Technology Hellas, Heraklion, Greece
Marios Spanakis, Institute of Computer Science, Foundation for Research and Technology Hellas, Heraklion, Greece
Emmanouil G. Spanakis, Institute of Computer Science, Foundation for Research and Technology Hellas, Heraklion, Greece

Chapter 17
"Sensitive but Essential Information": Policy Debates on Fitness Application Privacy and Data Security 336
Alison Nicole Novak, Rowan University, USA

Chapter 18
Role of Wearable Technology and Fitness Apps in Obesity and Diabetes: Privacy, Ownership, and Portability of Data 358
Shariq I. Sherwani, Ohio University, USA
Benjamin R. Bates, Ohio University, USA

Chapter 19
DeTER Framework: A Novel Paradigm for Addressing Cybersecurity Concerns in Mobile Healthcare 381
Rangarajan (Ray) Parthasarathy, University of Illinois at Urbana-Champaign, USA
David K. Wyant, Belmont University, USA
Prasad Bingi, Purdue University, Fort Wayne, USA
James R. Knight, The Ohio State University, USA
Anuradha Rangarajan, Indiana State University, USA

Chapter 20
A Lightweight Three-Factor Anonymous Authentication Scheme With Privacy Protection for Personalized Healthcare Applications 408
Mengxia Shuai, University of Science and Technology of China, Anhui, China
Nenghai Yu, University of Science and Technology of China, Anhui, China
Hongxia Wang, Southwest Jiaotong University, Chengdu, China
Ling Xiong, Xihua University, Chengdu, China
Yue Li, Southwest Jiaotong University, Chengdu, China

Chapter 21
My Health Record and Emerging Cybersecurity Challenges in the Australian Digital Environment 428
Anita Medhekar, Central Queensland University, Australia

Section 3
Securing Medical Images

Chapter 22
Secure Access to Biomedical Images 449
Tariq Javid, Hamdard University, Pakistan

Chapter 23
Medical Signal Security Enhancement Using Chaotic Map and Watermarking Technique 464
Ajita Sahay, KIIT University, India
Chittaranjan Pradhan, KIIT University, India
Amandip Sinha, West Bengal University of Technology, India

Chapter 24
Integer Transform-Based Watermarking Scheme for Authentication of Digital Fundus Images in Medical Science: An Application to Medical Image Authentication 486
Poonkuntran Shanmugam, Velammal College of Engineering and Technology, Madurai, India
Manessa Jayaprakasam, Independent Researcher, India

Chapter 25
Multiple Blind Watermarking Framework for Security and Integrity of Medical Images in E-Health Applications 517
Abdallah Soualmi, LRSD Lab, Computer Science Department, Faculty of Sciences, University of SETIF-1, Algeria
Adel Alti, LRSD Lab, Computer Science Department, Faculty of Sciences, University of SETIF-1, Algeria
Lamri Laouamer, Department of Management Information Systems, College of Business and Economics, Qassim University, Saudi Arabia

Chapter 26
Implementation of a Reversible Watermarking Technique for Medical Images 533
Ranit Karmakar, Tata Consultancy Services, India
Abhishek Basu, RCC Institute of Information Technology, India

Section 4
Securing Patient Data and Medical Records

Chapter 27
Healthcare Information Security in the Cyber World 573
Brian S. Coats, University of Maryland – Baltimore, USA
Subrata Acharya, Towson University, USA

Chapter 28
Applicability of WSN and Biometric Models in the Field of Healthcare.. 617
Nikhil Sharma, HMR Institute of Engineering and Technology, Delhi, India
Ila Kaushik, Krishna Institute of Engineering and Technology, India
Bharat Bhushan, HMR Institute of Technology and Management, Delhi, India
Siddharth Gautam, HMR Institute of Technology and Management, Delhi, India
Aditya Khamparia, Lovely Professional University, India

Chapter 29
Implementation of Encryption and Data Hiding in E-Health Application 644
Muzafer H Saracevic, University of Novi Pazar, Serbia.
Aybeyan Selimi, International Vision University, North Macedonia
Selver Pepić, Higher Technical Machine School of Professional Studies in Trstenik, Serbia

Chapter 30
Advancements in Data Security and Privacy Techniques Used in IoT-Based Hospital Applications 662
Ankita Tiwari, Amity University, India
Raghuvendra Pratap Tripathi, Amity University, India
Dinesh Bhatia, North Eastern Hill University, India

Chapter 31
Quantum Security for IoT to Secure Healthcare Applications and Their Data 685
Binod Kumar, JSPM's Rajarshi Shahu College of Engineering, India
Sheetal B. Prasad, SRM Institute of Science and Technology, India
Parashu Ram Pal, ABES Engineering College, India
Pankaj Pathak, Symbiosis Institute of Digital and Telecom Management, Symbiosis International University, India

Chapter 32
A HIPAA Security and Privacy Compliance Audit and Risk Assessment Mitigation Approach 706
Young B. Choi, Regent University, USA
Christopher E. Williams, Regent University, USA

Chapter 33
A New Perspective on the Swiss Cheese Model Applied to Understanding the Anatomy of Healthcare Data Breaches 726
Faouzi Kamoun, ESPRIT School of Engineering, Tunisia
Mathew Nicho, Zayed University, UAE

Chapter 34
Exploring System Thinking Leadership Approaches to the Healthcare Cybersecurity Environment 750
Darrell Norman Burrell, The Florida Institute of Technology, USA & Capitol Technology University, USA
Amalisha Sabie Aridi, Capitol Technology University, USA
Quatavia McLester, The Chicago School of Professional Psychology, USA
Anton Shufutinsky, Cabrini University, USA
Calvin Nobles, University of Maryland Global Campus, USA
Maurice Dawson, Illinois Institute of Technology, USA
S. Raschid Muller, Capitol Technology University, USA

Chapter 35
Adopting Organizational Cultural Changes Concerning Whistle-Blowing in Healthcare Around Information Security in the "Internet of Things" World 764
Darrell Norman Burrell, The Florida Institute of Technology, USA
Nimisha Bhargava, AUL Corporation, Napa, USA
Delores Springs, Regent University, USA
Maurice Dawson, Illinois Institute of Technology, USA
Sharon L. Burton, Grand Canyon University, USA
Damon P. Anderson, Capitol Technology University, USA
Jorja B. Wright, The University of Charleston, USA

Chapter 36
Opinions on Cyber Security, Electronic Health Records, and Medical Confidentiality: Emerging Issues on Internet of Medical Things From Nigeria 775
Ibrahim Taiwo Adeleke, Federal Medical Centre, Bida, Nigeria
Qudrotullaah Bolanle Suleiman Abdul, University of Ilorin Teaching Hospital, Nigeria

Chapter 37
Impact of Information Technology on Patient Confidentiality Rights: A Perspective 788
Abba Amsami Elgujja, University of Salford, UK

Chapter 38
Blockchain for Healthcare and Medical Systems 811
Sanaa Kaddoura, Zayed University, UAE
Rima Grati, Zayed University, UAE

Chapter 39
Security and Privacy for Electronic Healthcare Records Using AI in Blockchain 833
Ramani Selvanambi, Vellore Institute of Technology, Vellore, India
Samarth Bhutani, Vellore Institute of Technology, Vellore, India
Komal Veauli, Vellore Institute of Technology, Vellore, India

Chapter 40
Geo-Location-Based File Security System for Healthcare Data 843
Govinda K., VIT University, India

Chapter 41
Electronic Health Record Security in Cloud: Medical Data Protection Using Homomorphic Encryption Schemes 853
Desam Vamsi, VIT-AP, India
Pradeep Reddy, VIT-AP, India

Chapter 42
Provably Secure Data Sharing Approach for Personal Health Records in Cloud Storage Using Session Password, Data Access Key, and Circular Interpolation 878
Naveen John, Nesamony Memorial Christian College, Marthandam, India
Shatheesh Sam, Manonmaniam Sundaranar University, India

Chapter 43
TBHM: A Secure Threshold-Based Encryption Combined With Homomorphic Properties for Communicating Health Records 903
Lalit Mohan Gupta, APJ Abdul Kalam Technical University, Lucknow, India
Abdus Samad, University Women's Polytechnic, Aligarh Muslim University, Aligarh, India
Hitendra Garg, GLA University, Mathura, India

Chapter 44
Secure Healthcare Monitoring Sensor Cloud With Attribute-Based Elliptical Curve Cryptography 922
Rajendra Kumar Dwivedi, Madan Mohan Malaviya University of Technology, Gorakhpur, India
Rakesh Kumar, Madan Mohan Malaviya University of Technology, Gorakhpur, India
Rajkumar Buyya, The University of Melbourne, Melbourne, Australia

Chapter 45
Risk Reduction Privacy Preserving Approach for Accessing Electronic Health Records 942
V. K. Saxena, Vikram University, Ujjain, India
Shashank Pushkar, Birla Institute of Technology, Mesra, India

Chapter 46
An Extended Attribute-Based Access Control (ABAC) Model for Distributed Collaborative Healthcare System 955
Rabie Barhoun, Hassan II University, Faculty of science Ben M'sik, Casablanca, Morocco
Maryam Ed-daibouni, Hassan II University, Faculty of Science Ben M'sik, Casablanca, Morocco
Abdelwahed Namir, Hassan II University, Faculty of Science Ben M'sik, Casablanca, Morocco

Chapter 47
Cybercrime and Private Health Data: Review, Current Developments, and Future Trends............... 970
Stavros Pitoglou, National Technical University of Athens, Greece & Computer Solutions SA, Greece
Dimitra Giannouli, Computer Solutions SA, Greece & University of Leeds, UK
Vassilia Costarides, Institute of Communication and Computer Systems (ICCS), Greece
Thelma Androutsou, National Technical University of Athens, Greece
Athanasios Anastasiou, AiM Research Team, Biomedical Engineering Laboratory, National Technical University of Athens, Greece

Chapter 48
Assessing HIPAA Compliance of Open Source Electronic Health Record Applications.................. 995
Hossain Shahriar, Kennesaw State University, USA
Hisham M. Haddad, Kennesaw State University, USA
Maryam Farhadi, Kennesaw State University, USA

Chapter 49
Electronic Healthcare Records: Indian vs. International Perspective on Standards and Privacy 1012
Aashish Bhardwaj, Guru Tegh Bahadur Institute of Technology, India
Vikas Kumar, Chaudhary Bansi Lal University, Bhiwani-127021, Haryana, India

Index... xxiii

Preface

With the influx of internet and mobile technology usage, many medical institutions—from doctor's offices to hospitals—have implemented new online technologies for the storage and access of health data as well as the monitoring of patient health. Telehealth was particularly useful during the COVID-19 pandemic, which monumentally increased its everyday usage. However, this transition of health data has increased privacy risks, and cyber criminals and hackers may have increased access to patients' personal data. Medical staff and administrations must remain up to date on the new technologies and methods in securing these medical systems and records.

Thus, the *Research Anthology on Securing Medical Systems and Records* seeks to fill the void for an all-encompassing and comprehensive reference book covering the latest and most emerging research, concepts, and theories for those working in healthcare. This two-volume reference collection of reprinted IGI Global book chapters and journal articles that have been handpicked by the editor and editorial team of this research anthology on this topic will empower security analysts, data scientists, hospital administrators, leaders in healthcare, medical professionals, health information managers, medical professionals, mobile application developers, security professionals, technicians, students, libraries, researchers, and academicians.

The *Research Anthology on Securing Medical Systems and Records* is organized into four sections that provide comprehensive coverage of important topics. The sections are:

1. Securing Healthcare Systems;
2. Securing Medical Devices;
3. Securing Medical Images; and
4. Securing Patient Data and Medical Records.

The following paragraphs provide a summary of what to expect from this invaluable reference tool.

Section 1, "Securing Healthcare Systems," explains the threats, challenges, and strategies in healthcare system security. The first chapter, "Cyber Threats in the Healthcare Sector and Countermeasures," by Prof. Mohamed Amine Ferrag of Guelma University, Algeria and Profs. Leandros Maglaras and Muhammad Mashhood Ahmed of De Montfort University, UK, presents all cyber threat actors that exist in the healthcare sector, common cyber-attacks that can be launched against all actors, and real incidents that took place during the past years. Based on these, the authors propose in a tabular form a set of recommendations that can be used as countermeasures against any type of attack. The next chapter, "Digital Healthcare Security Issues: Is There a Solution in Biometrics?" by Profs. Punithavathi P. and Geetha Subbiah of VIT Chennai, India, examines how biometric technology can be applied to the digital healthcare services. The following chapter, "Biometric Technologies in Healthcare Biometrics," by Prof. Dakshina Ranjan Kisku of National Institute of Technology Durgapur, India and Prof. Rinku Datta Rakshit of Asansol Engineering College, India, introduces biometrics systems and discusses the essential components of biometrics technologies in the healthcare system. The discussion also includes the state-of-the-art biometrics technologies, selection criteria of a suitable biometrics system, biometrics identity management, and multi-biometrics fusion for healthcare biometrics system. The next chapter, "Cyber-Physical Security in Healthcare," by Profs. Vasiliki Mantzana, Eleni Darra, and Ilias Gkotsis of Center for Security Studies (KEMEA), Greece, presents healthcare critical asset vulnerabilities, cyber-physical threats that can affect them, architecture solutions, as well as some indicative scenarios that are validated during the project. The following chapter, "Applying Blockchain Technologies in Healthcare: A Scientometric Analysis," by Profs. Serhat Burmaoglu, Zehra Ozge Candereli, Levent B. Kidak, and Dilek Ozdemir Gungor of Izmir Katip Celebi University, Turkey, explores blockchain applications in healthcare with an explorative perspective with a scientometrics analysis. With this analysis, the trends and evolutionary relations between health and blockchain technology are examined via the queries in the Web of Science database. The next chapter, "Multi-Keyword Searchable Encryption for E-Health System With Multiple Data Writers and Readers," by Prof. Devesh C. Jinwala of S. V. National Institute of Technology, India and Prof. Dhruti P. Sharma of Sarvajanik College of Engineering and Technology, India, proposes a multi-keyword SE for an e-health system in multi-writer multi-reader setting. With this scheme, any registered writer could share data with any registered reader with optimal storage-computational overhead on writer. The proposed scheme offers conjunctive search with optimal search complexity at server. It also ensures security to medical records and privacy of keywords. The theoretical and empirical analysis demonstrates the effectiveness of the proposed work. The following chapter, "Internet of Things (IOT) in Healthcare – Smart Health and Surveillance, Architectures, Security Analysis, and Data Transfer: A Review," by Profs. Parthasarathy Panchatcharam and Vivekanandan S. of VIT University, Vellore, India, displays the idea of solving health issues by utilizing a recent innovation, the internet of things (IoT). The next chapter, "Healthcare IoT Architectures, Technologies, Applications, and Issues: A Deep Insight," by Profs. Karthick G. S. and Pankajavalli P. B. of Bharathiar University, India, analyzes the applications of IoT in healthcare systems with diversified aspects such as topological arrangement of medical devices, layered architecture, and platform services. This chapter focuses on advancements in IoT-based healthcare in order to identify the communication and sensing technologies enabling the smart healthcare systems. The following chapter, "IoT-Based Smart and Secure Health Monitoring System," by Prof. Parul Verma of Amity University, Lucknow, India and Prof. Brijesh Khandelwal of Amity University, Raipur, India, focuses on how IoT can be integrated with healthcare systems and draw maximum benefits from its ubiquitous presence. The chapter also covers various security concerns of an IoT-based healthcare system and their suggested solutions to overcome those concerns. The next chapter, "Advanced Cyber Security and Internet of Things for Digital Transformations of the Indian Healthcare Sector," by Profs. Esha Jain and Jonika Lamba of The NorthCap University, Gurugram, India, methodically reviews the need for cybersecurity amid digital transformation with the help of emerging technologies and focuses on the application and incorporation of blockchain and the internet of things (IoT) to ensure cybersecurity in the well-being of the business. The final chapter, "Healthcare Security Assessment in the Big Data Era: Lessons From Turkey," by Profs. Ionica Oncioiu and Oana Claudia Ionescu of Titu Maiorescu University, Romania, contributes to the decrease of the shortcomings that exist in the healthcare security assessment by focusing on data mining for public institutions and organizations in Turkey.

Section 2, "Securing Medical Devices," reviews the protocols, challenges, and strategies in medical device security including wearable technologies and apps. The first chapter, "Cyber Security in Health: Standard Protocols for IoT and Supervisory Control Systems," by Profs. Bruno J. Santos and Rachel P. Tabacow of Instituto Federal de São Paulo, Brazil; Prof. Marcelo Barboza of Instituto Federal de São Paulo, Brazil & Escola Politécnica da Universidade de São Paulo, Brazil; and Profs. Tarcisio F. Leão and Eduardo G. P. Bock of Instituto Federal de São Paulo, Brazil, explains that increasing collaboration in terms of medical equipment, artificial organs, and biosensors is a way to facilitate H4.0. As a result, cyber security budgets have increased, new technology has been purchased, and healthcare organizations are improving at blocking attacks and keeping their networks secure. The next chapter, "Medical Device Security," by Prof. Md Abdullah Al Momin of University of Louisiana at Lafayette, USA, provides an overview of these security risks, their proposed solutions, and the limitations on IMD systems which make solving these issues nontrivial. The chapter further analyzes the security issues and the history of vulnerabilities in pacemakers to illustrate the theoretical topics by considering a specific device. The next chapter, "Quantum Cryptography for Securing IoT-Based Healthcare Systems," by Prof. Anand Sharma of Mody University of Science and Technology, Lakshmangarh, India and Prof. Alekha Parimal Bhatt of Capgemini IT India Pvt. Ltd., India, describes that it is necessary to use quantum cryptography system to make sure the security, privacy, and integrity of the patient's data received and transmitted from IoT-based healthcare systems. Quantum cryptography is a very fascinating domain in cyber security that utilizes quantum mechanics to extend a cryptosystem that is supposed to be the unbreakable secure system. The following chapter, "Constructive Solutions for Security and Privacy Issues at the Edge: Securing Edge Framework – A Healthcare Application Use Case," by Profs. Indra Priyadharshini S. and Pradheeba Ulaganathan of R. M. K. College of Engineering and Technology, India; Prof. Vigilson Prem M. of R. M. D. Engineering College, India; and Prof. Yuvaraj B. R. of Anna University, India, explains some of the serious and non-discussed security issues and privacy issues available on edge. The next chapter, "Personalized Mobile eHealth Services for Secure User Access Through a Multi Feature Biometric Framework," by Profs. Emmanouil G. Spanakis, Marios Spanakis, and Georgios C. Manikis of Institute of Computer Science, Foundation for Research and Technology Hellas, Heraklion, Greece, argues how a biometric identification system can greatly benefit healthcare, due to the increased accuracy of identification procedures. The following chapter, "'Sensitive but Essential Information': Policy Debates on Fitness Application Privacy and Data Security," by Prof. Alison Nicole Novak of Rowan University, USA, explores how government representatives, industry leaders, regulators, and politicians discursively constructed and critiqued data privacy in fitness applications in congressional contexts. The next chapter, "Role of Wearable Technology and Fitness Apps in Obesity and Diabetes: Privacy, Ownership, and Portability of Data," by Profs. Shariq I. Sherwani and Benjamin R. Bates of Ohio University, USA, addresses the concerns about health data privacy, personal ownership, and portability. The following chapter, "DeTER Framework: A Novel Paradigm for Addressing Cybersecurity Concerns in Mobile Healthcare," by Prof. Rangarajan (Ray) Parthasarathy of University of Illinois at Urbana-Champaign, USA; Prof. David K. Wyant of Belmont University, USA; Prof. Prasad Bingi of Purdue University, Fort Wayne, USA; Prof. James R. Knight of The Ohio State University, USA; and Prof. Anuradha Rangarajan of Indiana State University, USA, presents a comprehensive framework (DeTER) that integrates all three perspectives through which cybersecurity concerns in mobile healthcare could be viewed, understood, and acted upon. The next chapter, "A Lightweight Three-Factor Anonymous Authentication Scheme With Privacy Protection for Personalized Healthcare Applications," by Profs. Mengxia Shuai and Nenghai Yu of University of Science and Technology of China, Anhui, China; Prof. Hongxia Wang of

Southwest Jiaotong University, Chengdu, China; Prof. Ling Xiong of Xihua University, Chengdu, China; and Prof. Yue Li of Southwest Jiaotong University, Chengdu, China, proposes a lightweight three-factor anonymous authentication scheme with forward secrecy for personalized healthcare applications using only the lightweight cryptographic primitives. The final chapter, "My Health Record and Emerging Cybersecurity Challenges in the Australian Digital Environment," by Prof. Anita Medhekar of Central Queensland University, Australia, discusses the challenges of embracing e-health digital technologies and assurance of advancing cybersecurity of online My Health Record, which will transform e-health provision and empower patients and healthcare providers.

Section 3, "Securing Medical Images," reviews the technologies and techniques involved in ensuring that medical images are protected. The first chapter, "Secure Access to Biomedical Images," by Prof. Tariq Javid of Hamdard University, Pakistan, introduces a framework for secure access to biomedical images. In this chapter, a cryptocompression system is also proposed which integrates both encryption and compression to fulfill the requirements of electronic protected health information records. The next chapter, "Medical Signal Security Enhancement Using Chaotic Map and Watermarking Technique," by Profs. Chittaranjan Pradhan and Ajita Sahay of KIIT University, India and Prof. Amandip Sinha of West Bengal University of Technology, India, explores medical signal security enhancement using chaotic map and watermarking techniques. This new approach provides security to both the medical image and also maintains the confidentially of both the patient and doctor. The following chapter, "Integer Transform-Based Watermarking Scheme for Authentication of Digital Fundus Images in Medical Science: An Application to Medical Image Authentication," by Prof. Poonkuntran Shanmugam of Velammal College of Engineering and Technology, Madurai, India and Prof. Manessa Jayaprakasam, Independent Researcher, India, presents an integer transform-based watermarking scheme for digital fundus image authentication. It is presented under multimedia applications in medicine. The chapter introduces image authentication by watermarking and digital fundus image. The key requirements in developing watermarking scheme for fundus images and its challenges are identified and highlighted. The next chapter, "Multiple Blind Watermarking Framework for Security and Integrity of Medical Images in E-Health Applications," by Profs. Abdallah Soualmi and Adel Alti of LRSD Lab, Computer Science Department, Faculty of Sciences, University of SETIF-1, Algeria and Prof. Lamri Laouamer of Department of Management Information Systems, College of Business and Economics, Qassim University, Saudi Arabia, gives a new secure framework to protect medical data based on blind multiple watermarking schemes. The proposed approach consists of combining LWT (lifting wavelet transform), QR decomposition, and Arnold chaotic map in transform domain for the first watermark, while for the second watermark is encrusted in the spatial domain. The final chapter, "Implementation of a Reversible Watermarking Technique for Medical Images," by Prof. Abhishek Basu of RCC Institute of Information Technology, India and Prof. Ranit Karmakar of Tata Consultancy Services, India, proposes a reversible data hiding algorithm which also is capable of holding a large chunk of data without affecting the cover media.

Section 4, "Securing Patient Data and Medical Records," examines threats to patient's data and strategies for protecting their privacy. The first chapter, "Healthcare Information Security in the Cyber World," by Prof. Subrata Acharya of Towson University, USA and Prof. Brian S. Coats of University of Maryland – Baltimore, USA, presents a cognitive science-based solution by addressing comprehensive compliance implementation as mandated by the Health Insurance Portability and Accountability Act, the certified Electronic Health Record standard, and the federal Meaningful Use program. The next chapter, "Applicability of WSN and Biometric Models in the Field of Healthcare," by Prof. Aditya Khamparia of Lovely Professional University, India; Prof. Bharat Bhushan of HMR Institute of Technology and Management, Delhi, India; Prof. Ila Kaushik of Krishna Institute of Engineering and Technology, India; and Profs. Nikhil Sharma and Siddharth Gautam of HMR Institute of Technology and Management, Delhi, India, presents the role of WSN and biometric models such as two factor remote authentication, verifying fingerprint operations for enhancing security, privacy preserving in healthcare, healthcare data by cloud technology with biometric application, and validation built hybrid trust computing perspective for confirmation of contributor profiles in online healthcare data. The following chapter, "Implementation of Encryption and Data Hiding in E-Health Application," by Prof. Muzafer H. Saracevic of University of Novi Pazar, Serbia; Prof. Aybeyan Selimi of International Vision University, North Macedonia; and Prof. Selver Pepić of Higher Technical Machine School of Professional Studies in Trstenik, Serbia, presents the possibilities of applying cryptography and steganography in design advanced methods of medical software. The next chapter, "Advancements in Data Security and Privacy Techniques Used in IoT-Based Hospital Applications," by Prof. Dinesh Bhatia of North Eastern Hill University, India and Profs. Ankita Tiwari and Raghuvendra Pratap Tripathi of Amity University, India, delves upon understanding the working of a secure monitoring system wherein the data could be continuously observed with the support of MSNs. The following chapter, "Quantum Security for IoT to Secure Healthcare Applications and Their Data," by Prof. Binod Kumar of JSPM's Rajarshi Shahu College of Engineering, India; Prof. Sheetal B. Prasad of SRM Institute of Science and Technology, India; Prof. Parashu Ram Pal of ABES Engineering College, India; and Prof. Pankaj Pathak of Symbiosis Institute of Digital and Telecom Management, Symbiosis International University, India, proposes that there should be a strong mechanism to combat the security gaps in existing healthcare industry. If the healthcare data are available on the network, an attacker may try to modify, intercept, or even view this data stream. With the use of quantum security, the quantum state of these photons changes alert the security pros that someone is trying to breach the link. The next chapter, "A HIPAA Security and Privacy Compliance Audit and Risk Assessment Mitigation Approach," by Prof. Young B. Choi of Regent University, USA and Prof. Christopher E. Williams of Regent University, USA, explores network design in order to meet the complexity standards and unpredictable measures posed by attackers. Additionally, the network must adhere to HIPAA security and privacy requirements required by law. Successful implantation of network design will articulate comprehension requirements of information assurance security and control. The following chapter, "A New Perspective on the Swiss Cheese Model Applied to Understanding the Anatomy of Healthcare Data Breaches," by Prof. Faouzi Kamoun of ESPRIT School of Engineering, Tunisia and Prof. Mathew Nicho of Zayed University, UAE, reveals how Reason's swiss cheese model (SCM) provides a powerful analytic model to explain the human, technical, and organizational factors of healthcare data breaches. The next chapter, "Exploring System Thinking Leadership Approaches to the Healthcare Cybersecurity Environment," by Prof. Maurice Dawson of Illinois Institute of Technology, USA; Prof. Amalisha Sabie Aridi of Capitol Technology University, USA; Prof. Calvin Nobles of University of Maryland Global Campus, USA; Prof. Anton Shufutinsky of Cabrini University, USA; Prof. Quatavia McLester of The Chicago School of Professional Psychology, USA; Prof. Darrell Norman Burrell of The Florida Institute of Technology, USA & Capitol Technology University, USA; and Prof. S. Raschid Muller of Capitol Technology University, USA, explores the nuances and complexities around systems thinking in the healthcare cybersecurity environment. The following chapter, "Adopting Organizational Cultural Changes Concerning Whistle-Blowing in Healthcare Around Information Security in the 'Internet of Things' World," by Prof. Maurice Dawson of Illinois Institute of Technology, USA; Prof. Sharon L. Burton of Grand Canyon University, USA; Prof. Darrell Norman Burrell of The Florida Institute of Technology, USA; Prof. Nimisha Bhargava of AUL Corporation,

Napa, USA; Prof. Delores Springs of Regent University, USA; Prof. Damon P. Anderson of Capitol Technology University, USA; and Prof. Jorja B. Wright of The University of Charleston, USA, presents a foundation to establish techniques and practices for open door policies. The next chapter, "Opinions on Cyber Security, Electronic Health Records, and Medical Confidentiality: Emerging Issues on Internet of Medical Things From Nigeria," by Prof. Ibrahim Taiwo Adeleke of Federal Medical Centre, Bida, Nigeria and Prof. Qudrotullaah Bolanle Suleiman Abdul of University of Ilorin Teaching Hospital, Nigeria, deploys a cross-sectional design to determine perceptions of Nigerian healthcare providers toward medical confidentiality and cyber security in the wake of electronic health records and IoMT. The following chapter, "Impact of Information Technology on Patient Confidentiality Rights: A Perspective," by Prof. Abba Amsami Elgujja of University of Salford, UK, undertakes a general review of the benefits and dangers of embracing these new information technologies and their impact on the confidentiality of sensitive health data. The next chapter, "Blockchain for Healthcare and Medical Systems," by Profs. Sanaa Kaddoura and Rima Grati of Zayed University, UAE, studies the opportunity of blockchain to leverage biomedical and healthcare applications and research. Blockchain also contributes to the medication manufacturing area. The following chapter, "Security and Privacy for Electronic Healthcare Records Using AI in Blockchain," by Profs. Ramani Selvanambi, Samarth Bhutani, and Komal Veauli of Vellore Institute of Technology, Vellore, India, proposes the use of blockchains to store and secure data will not only ensure data privacy but will also provide a common method of data regulation. The next chapter, "Geo-Location-Based File Security System for Healthcare Data," by Prof. Govinda K. of VIT University, India, provides a mechanism to create a secure file storage system that provides two-layer security. The first layer is in the form of a password, through which the file is encrypted at the time of storage, and second is the locations at which the user wants the files to be accessed. The following chapter, "Electronic Health Record Security in Cloud: Medical Data Protection Using Homomorphic Encryption Schemes," by Profs. Desam Vamsi and Pradeep Reddy of VIT-AP, India, explains the homomorphism encryption (HE) method is very suitable for the electronic health record (EHR), which requires data privacy and security. The next chapter, "Provably Secure Data Sharing Approach for Personal Health Records in Cloud Storage Using Session Password, Data Access Key, and Circular Interpolation," by Prof. Naveen John of Nesamony Memorial Christian College, Marthandam, India and Prof. Shatheesh Sam of Manonmaniam Sundaranar University, India, develops a secure data sharing mechanism using the proposed session password, data access key, and circular interpolation (SKC)-based data-sharing approach for the secure sharing of PHR in the cloud. The following chapter, "TBHM: A Secure Threshold-Based Encryption Combined With Homomorphic Properties for Communicating Health Records," by Prof. Abdus Samad of University Women's Polytechnic, Aligarh Muslim University, Aligarh, India; Prof. Hitendra Garg of GLA University, Mathura, India; and Prof. Lalit Mohan Gupta of APJ Abdul Kalam Technical University, Lucknow, India, proposes a novel and secure threshold based encryption scheme combined with homomorphic properties (TBHM) for accessing cloud based health information. The next chapter, "Secure Healthcare Monitoring Sensor Cloud With Attribute-Based Elliptical Curve Cryptography," by Profs. Rakesh Kumar and Rajendra Kumar Dwivedi of Madan Mohan Malaviya University of Technology, Gorakhpur, India and Prof. Rajkumar Buyya of The University of Melbourne, Melbourne, Australia, proposes a security mechanism called attribute-based elliptical curve cryptography (ABECC) that guarantees data integrity, data confidentiality, and fine-grained access control. The following chapter, "Risk Reduction Privacy Preserving Approach for Accessing Electronic Health Records," by Prof. V. K. Saxena of Vikram University, Ujjain, India and Prof. Shashank Pushkar of Birla Institute of Technology, Mesra, India, introduces a novel risk reduction strategy for the healthcare domain so that the risk related with an access request is evaluated against the privacy preferences of the patient who is undergoing for the medical procedure. The following chapter, "An Extended Attribute-Based Access Control (ABAC) Model for Distributed Collaborative Healthcare System," by Profs. Rabie Barhoun, Maryam Ed-daibouni, and Abdelwahed Namir of Hassan II University, Faculty of Science Ben M'sik, Casablanca, Morocco, proposes a new access control model, called Medical-Activity-Attribute-Based Access Control (MA-ABAC), which can effectively enhance the security for healthcare system and produce more perfect and flexible mechanism of access control; order to strongly respond to the requirements of the distributed healthcare environment. The next chapter, "Cybercrime and Private Health Data: Review, Current Developments, and Future Trends," by Prof. Athanasios Anastasiou of AiM Research Team, Biomedical Engineering Laboratory, National Technical University of Athens, Greece; Prof. Stavros Pitoglou of National Technical University of Athens, Greece & Computer Solutions SA, Greece; Prof. Dimitra Giannouli of Computer Solutions SA, Greece & University of Leeds, UK; Prof. Vassilia Costarides of Institute of Communication and Computer Systems (ICCS), Greece; and Prof. Thelma Androutsou of National Technical University of Athens, Greece, provides a historical review of recorded data breaches that resulted in extensive patient data leaks as well as subsequent efforts of monetization via black market structures that utilize the anonymity and counter-tracking environment that the dark/deep web and cryptocurrency provide. It also focuses on the methods and tools used by the villains, the types of vulnerabilities that can result in a successful attack, as well as latest developments and future trends in the field of scientific, technical, and legal/regulatory countermeasures that can be employed in order to prevent sensitive health data from falling into the wrong hands. The following chapter, "Assessing HIPAA Compliance of Open Source Electronic Health Record Applications," by Profs. Hossain Shahriar, Hisham M. Haddad, Maryam Farhadi of Kennesaw State University, USA, identifies HIPAA technical requirements, evaluate two open source EHR applications (OpenEMR and OpenClinic) for security vulnerabilities using two open-source scanner tools (RIPS and PHP VulnHunter) and maps the identified vulnerabilities to HIPAA technical requirements. The final chapter, "Electronic Healthcare Records: Indian vs. International Perspective on Standards and Privacy," by Prof. Aashish Bhardwaj of Guru Tegh Bahadur Institute of Technology, India and Prof. Vikas Kumar of Chaudhary Bansi Lal University, Haryana, India, explores the different aspects of health privacy and health records.

Although the primary organization of the contents in this work is based on its four sections offering a progression of coverage of the important concepts, methodologies, technologies, applications, social issues, and emerging trends, the reader can also identify specific contents by utilizing the extensive indexing system listed at the end. As a comprehensive collection of research on the latest findings related to medical system and record security, the *Research Anthology on Securing Medical Systems and Records* provides security analysts, data scientists, hospital administrators, leaders in healthcare, medical professionals, health information managers, medical professionals, mobile application developers, security professionals, technicians, students, libraries, researchers, and academicians, and all audiences with a complete understanding of the challenges that face healthcare administrators and their patients. Given the need for medical system and record security, this extensive book presents the latest research and best practices to address these challenges and provide further opportunities for improvement.

Chapter 24

Integer Transform-Based Watermarking Scheme for Authentication of Digital Fundus Images in Medical Science:

An Application to Medical Image Authentication

Poonkuntran Shanmugam
https://orcid.org/0000-0002-2778-7937
Velammal College of Engineering and Technology, Madurai, India

Manessa Jayaprakasam
Independent Researcher, India

ABSTRACT

This chapter presents an integer transform-based watermarking scheme for digital fundus image authentication. It is presented under multimedia applications in medicine. The chapter introduces image authentication by watermarking and digital fundus image. The key requirements in developing watermarking scheme for fundus images and its challenges are identified and highlighted. Authors describe a proposed watermarking scheme on integer transform. The experimental results emphasize the proposed scheme's ability in addressing key requirements and its attainment. The detailed results are summarized.

INTRODUCTION

The advent of modern computing techniques and the explosion of the World Wide Web (WWW) are

DOI: 10.4018/978-1-6684-6311-6.ch024

integrated together for providing instant information access to a large percentage of homes and businesses. The development of such integration has stimulated the use of information in the form of text, pictures, graphics, and integrated multimedia applications. Such information is acquired by converting a continuous signal into digital format and it can be viewed by using display devices such as computer monitors and projectors. This information is widely exchanged in digital visual format for its transmission, reception, storage, processing and display. The recent developments on the Internet with the inexpensive digital recording and storage devices have created an environment in which digital information can easily be accessed, replicated and distributed without any loss in quality. This has become a concern for information security. Thus, such information needs to be secured by an efficient method while it is being exchanged (Bovik, 2000) (Cole, 2003). Digital Image Processing (DIP) is a new technological advancement in the areas of digital computation and telecommunication. An image can be defined as two-dimensional function $f(x, y)$, where x and y are spatial coordinates and f is the amplitude at the spatial coordinate pair(x, y), known as grey value or intensity value at that location (x, y). If the spatial coordinates (x, y) and amplitude f are finite, discrete quantities, then the image is called a digital image. The term DIP refers to the processing of digital images by means of digital computers (Gonzalez & Woods, 2002). The DIP incorporates prior knowledge, identification of objects, interpretation of objects, description of objects, pattern classification and pattern recognition.

The applications of DIP acquire a broad spectrum of radiation as shown in figure 1. The ranges of image types can be derived from every type of radiation. The digital image acquisition methods are developed and improved by means of these radiations. For example, the recent developments in medical images come from new sensors that record image data from previously little-used sources of radiation, such as Positron Emission Tomography (PET) and Magnetic Resonance Imaging (MRI) (Bovik, 2000).

FROM CRYPTOGRAPHY TO WATERMARKING

Though security is a general term used in the literature, the way in which security is used in the daily lives of humans is extraordinary. It ranges from passwords that are used for entering the secure computers and electronic wallets, to fingerprint scanning technology that is used for personal identification. Thereby, the security measurements became a part of the daily lives of humans as telephones or automobiles. The human's daily lives are surrounded by a world of secret communication, where people of all types are transmitting information as innocent as an encrypted credit card number to an online store then and as dangerous as a hijacking plan to terrorists. Hence, secure secret communication became essential. The secret communication can be achieved by two techniques. They are cryptography and data hiding (also referred to as information hiding).

- **Cryptography:** It is the science that uses mathematics to encrypt and decrypt the sensitive information. Cryptography transmits sensitive information across insecure networks in an unreadable rubbish format, called *ciphertext*. Hence, the information cannot be read by anyone except the intended recipient. The information to be transmitted is called *plaintext* or *cleartext*. The *plaintext* can be read and understood without any actions. The *encryption* is a process that converts *plaintext* into *ciphertext*. It is used to ensure that the information is hidden from anyone for whom it is not intended, even those who can see the encrypted information. The process of reverting *ciphertext* to its original *plaintext* is called *decryption*. The *encryption* and *decryption* are illustrated in figure 2.

Figure 1. Applications of digital image processing (DIP)

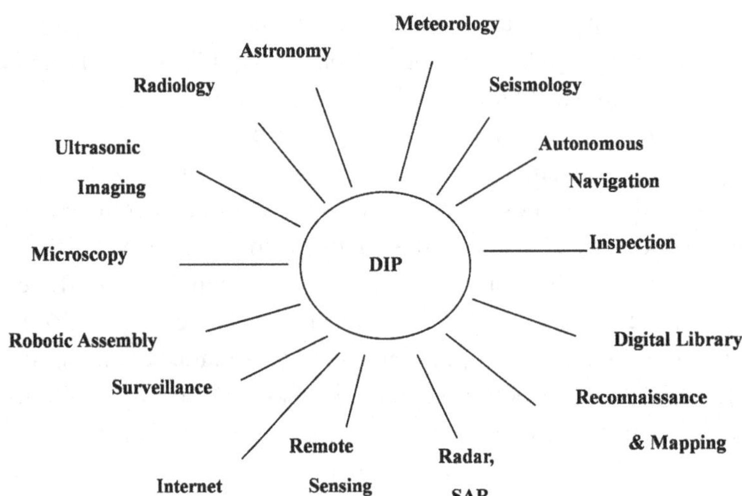

While cryptography techniques are used to prevent unauthorized access to digital information, it is clear that cryptography has its limitations in protecting intellectual property rights. Once the information is decrypted, there is nothing to prevent an authorized user from illegally replicating the information. Hence, another technique is needed to facilitate content authentication, protect ownership rights, track content usage, ensure authorized access and prevent illegal replication (Cox, Miller, Linnartz & Kalker, 1999).

- **Data Hiding or Information Hiding:** The data hiding or information hiding is a general term that encompasses two sub-disciplines. They are steganography and watermarking. Steganography is a process of transmitting the secret information hidden in innocent-looking cover medium so that its existence is undetectable. The secret information is always be hidden in an unseen manner. Watermarking is the process of imperceptibly altering the cover medium to embed the information about the cover medium. Watermarking is closely related to the steganography; however, there are differences between them. In the watermarking, the secret information is related to the cover medium. Steganography relates to secret point to point communications between the two parties where the secret information is not related to the cover medium. Watermarking has additional features. It must have resilience against the attacks that attempt to remove the hidden secret information. The steganography does not have the notion of attacks. Because the secret information is not related to the cover and it is not creating any suspicion to the attackers.

Figure 2. Encryption and decryption

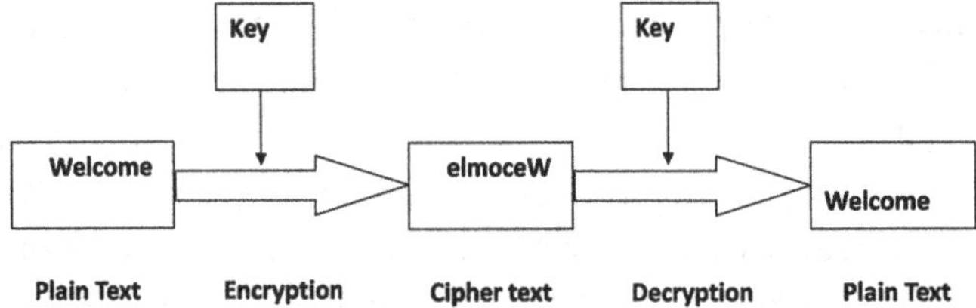

Figure 3. A general watermarking model

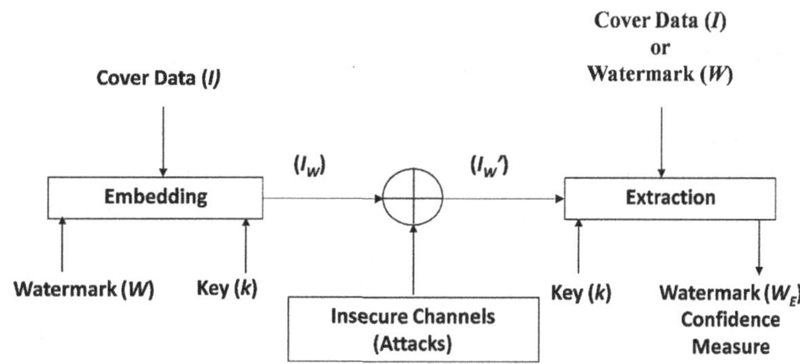

A general watermarking model is shown in figure 3. It involves two processes. They are *embedding* and *extraction*. In this model, the cover medium is referred to as *cover data* (I) and it can be text, audio, image and video. The embedding process inserts the secret information, referred to as *watermark* (W) inside the cover data in an encrypted form using the *key* (k). The key can be either secret or non-secret. The output of the embedding process will be composite data, referred to as *watermarked data* (I_W) containing the encrypted secret information inside the cover data. This watermarked data may be attacked by the hackers to destroy the watermark embedded inside it, to generate the hacked version of the watermarked data (I_W'). Once the watermarked data is hacked, the cover data becomes susceptible to all kinds of fraud. The extraction process separates the cover data and watermark from the watermarked data. The watermark removed from the watermarked data is known as *extracted watermark* (W_E), called a *confidence measure*.

It is used for the verification and validation of the cover data. The extraction process may be carried out with or without the knowledge of the cover data or watermark. Depends on the target application, the extraction process may either be lossy or lossless.

HISTORY OF WATERMARKING

The watermarking is not recent to this century. More than 700 years ago, the watermarking was employed in *Italy* for representing the paper brand and mills that produced it. In the 18th century, watermarking began to be used for anti-counterfeiting measures on money and other documents (Muharemagic & Furht, 2004). The term *watermark* was introduced at the end of the 18th century. Since the marks resemble the effect of water on the paper, the term *watermark* is chosen. In 1954, Emil Hembrook had filed a pattern for his identification towards digital watermarking in music. This was the first work carried out in digital watermarking and the same became an example. In 1988, Komatsu and Tominaga used the term *Digital Watermarking*, first time in the literature. Since 1995, the interest in the watermarking research started growing (Muharemagic & Furht, 2004; Cox, Miller, Linnartz & Kalker, 1999).

RELEVANCE OF WATERMARKING IN MEDICAL IMAGES

Medical Image Processing (MIP) refers to the techniques used to create and manipulate the images of the human body for clinical purposes. The clinical purposes include the medical procedures seeking to reveal and diagnose the disease. The field has research potential that is attempting to understand the processes in humans or animal models. While the general image processing techniques are used for medical images, it requires special treatments due to its special nature. The medical images are derived from different methods of acquisition such as X-Ray, Computed Tomography (CT), Magnetic Resonance Imaging (MRI), Ultra Sound Imaging, Nuclear Imaging, Fundus Imaging etc. Hence, the medical images are differed based on the acquisition methods. The medical images are also differed based on the subject whose images are being acquired. The medical images processed to infer the information about the volume under the skin. It is done exclusively to probe the anatomy of hidden objects below the skin. The medical images can be either as 2-D projection information or as full 3-D mapped information. Medical image protection and authentication are important in an e-healthcare environment where all the visual information and clinical records are stored and exchanged in digital form. Medical image watermarking is a process for enhancing information security, verification and fidelity. At the same time, it is necessary to preserve as much original information as possible in the image, to avoid performance loss for physicians.

SECURITY FEATURES OF MEDICAL IMAGES

The security of medical images is obtained from strict ethics and legislative rules which can be classified in three fixed characteristics: confidentiality, reliability, and availability (Dutta, Singh, Singh, Burget & Prinosil, 2015; Melkemi, Kamal, Singh & Golea, 2017; Hai, Dong Qing, &Ke, 2018; Sliwa, 2019).

- ***Confidentiality*:** It means that only the entitled users have access to the images in the scheduled system.
- ***Reliability*:** It is given by two features. i) Integrity: Ensuring that the images have not been modified by an unauthorized person. ii) Authentication: Ensuring that the image belongs indeed to the correct patient and is issued from the correct source.
- ***Availability*:** It is the capability of an image to be used by the entitled users in the normal scheduled conditions of access and exercise.

In the case of medical image security, the first two characteristics have mainly to be considered. The watermarking scheme has been recognized to control the image reliability by emphasizing its integrity and its authenticity (Coatrieux, Maitre, Sankur, Rolland& Collorec, 2000). A digital watermark is a secret key-dependent signal inserted into digital data and which can be later detected or extracted in order to make an assertion. In medical images, alterations due to the insertion process are not accepted by physicians for diagnosis. Therefore, the requirements in medical images have differed from multimedia applications (Amato, Cozzolino, Mazzeo & Romano, 2018; Wang, Ding & Gu, 2019; Karmakar & Basu, 2019; Bhatt, 2017) .

When the medical images are exchanged in public or private networks, two questions are mainly raised.

1. Whose image is that? It refers to the hospital which sends the image for the diagnosis and associated patient details.
2. Is the image received is genuine? It refers to the authentication of the image.
3. It checks that the image is received from the proper source and ensures that it is not modified.

These two questions can be answered using two different branches of application in watermarking schemes. They are copyright protection and authentication. Copy right protection protects the owner's intellectual property and traces the source of illegal copies of the content. Authentication checks that the received image has been altered or not and localize the tampered regions too. Authentication is the first and basic step in any security architecture whose success prevents other issues in the systems.

This chapter is focusing on developing a watermarking scheme for the authentication of Digital Fundus Image (DFI), a special class of medical images. The next few sections will be discussing on significance of DFI and its security.

DIGITAL FUNDUS IMAGE

The digital fundus images are one particular class of medical images. Ophthalmology is the branch of medicine which deals with the diseases and surgery of the visual pathways, including the eye, brain, and areas surrounding the eye, such as the eyelids. In ophthalmology, the fundus is the interior surface of the eye, including the retina, optic disc and macula. The fundus can be viewed with an ophthalmoscope. The fundus images are taken using a fundus camera. A fundus camera is a specialized low power microscope with an attached camera designed to photograph the interior surface of the eye as shown in figure 4. The optical design of the fundus camera is based on the principle of monocular indirect ophthalmoscopy. A fundus camera provides an upright, magnified view of the fundus. A typical camera views 30 to 50 degrees of retinal area, with a magnification of 2.5 x, and allows some modification of this relationship through zoom or auxiliary lenses from 15 degrees which provides 5 x magnifications to 140 degrees with a wide-angle lens which minimize the image by half. The optics of a fundus camera are similar to those of an indirect ophthalmoscope in that the observation and illumination systems follow dissimilar paths (Coatrieux, Lamard, Puentes& Roux, 2005).

The observation light is focused via a series of lenses through a doughnut-shaped aperture, which then passes through a central aperture to form an annulus, before passing through the camera objective lens and through the cornea onto the retina. The light reflected from the retina passes through the un-illuminated hole in the doughnut formed by the illumination system. As the light paths of the two systems are independent, there are minimal reflections of the light source captured in the formed image. The image forming rays continue towards the low powered telescopic eyepiece. When the button is pressed to take a picture, a mirror interrupts the path of the illumination system allow the light from the flashbulb to pass into the eye. Simultaneously, a mirror falls in front of the observation telescope, which redirects the light onto the capturing medium. Because of the eye's tendency to accommodate while looking through a telescope, it is imperative that the exiting vengeance is parallel in order for an in-focus image to be formed on the capturing medium. The example of fundus images is shown in figure5. The fundus photography is usually taken using a green filter to acquire images of retinal blood vessels. Greenlight is absorbed by blood and appeared a darker color in the fundus photograph than the

Figure 4. A fundus camera
(Source: Creative Common, USA)

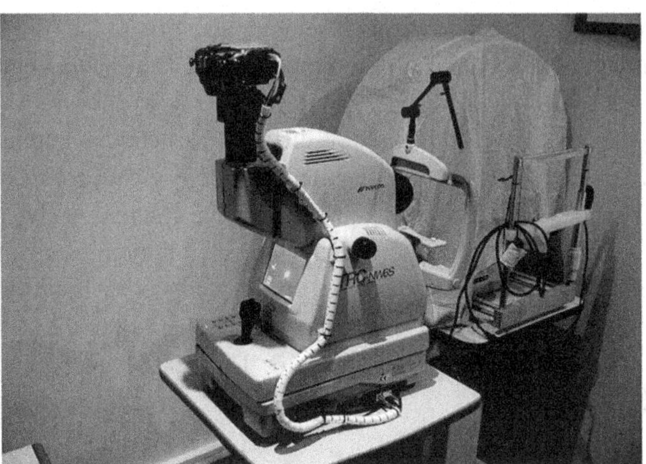

background and the retinal nerve fiber layer. Hence, the green channel of the fundus images possess valuable information for diagnosis than other channels (Hu, GuoHu, &Chen, 2005).

Importance of Digital Fundus Images in Medical Sciences

Fundus images are used by optometrists, ophthalmologists, and trained medical professionals for monitoring the progression of a disease, diagnosis of a disease. It can also be combined with retinal angiography for mass screening, where these images are analyzed first. Retinal fundus images are useful for the early detection of a number of ocular diseases-if left untreated, which can lead to blindness. Examinations using retinal fundus images are cost-effective and are suitable for mass screening. In this view, retinal fundus images are obtained in many health care centers and medical facilities during medical checkups for ophthalmic examinations. The increase in the number of ophthalmic examinations improves ocular

Figure 5. Digital fundus image

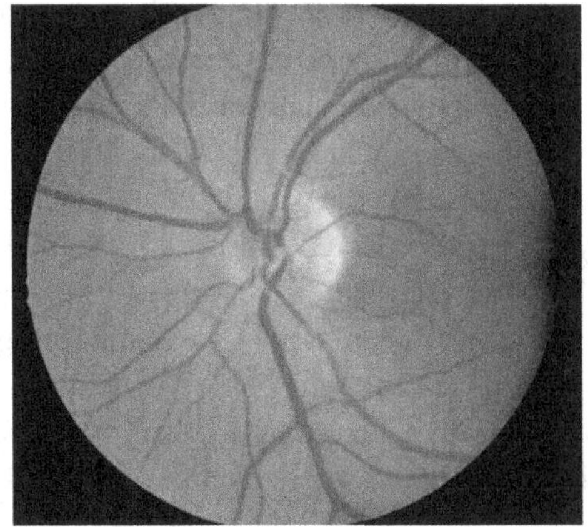

health care in the population but it also increases the workload of ophthalmologists. Therefore, modern health care systems are developed with Computer-Aided Design (CAD) and networking for analyzing retinal fundus images and it can assist in reducing the workload of ophthalmologists and improving the screening accuracy. Such modern health care systems require highly secure communication techniques for exchanging information from one place to another (Wu & Liu, 2003).

Developing user authentication is a challenging task for digital fundus images. Because, when images are sent through a network for getting suggestions and judgments from the medical science experts from various geographical locations, they must be secured against any form of external attacks.

Scope of the Research in Digital Fundus Images

Research on digital fundus image is an emerging area which is having a good scope in the medical sciences. Regular fundus examinations can detect the initial signs of various major diseases like diabetic retinopathy. Thereby, the actual treatment cost of such diseases in the later stages can be reduced drastically. In the security of medical images, the digital fundus images have not been studied in security. Hence, the theme of developing a security scheme for digital fundus image has been taken here.

KEY REQUIREMENTS FOR MEDICAL IMAGE AUTHENTICATION SCHEME

The following are key requirements used to design and develop an authentication scheme for any classes of medical images. The same requirements have been considered for digital fundus images. However, the behavior of the requirements will have differed from one class of images to another.

R1: Reversibility

Reversibility refers to the lossless watermarking scheme that retains the original image after the extraction process. The scheme is said to be irreversible if it is not able to produce the original image without loss of information after the extraction. Since the fundus images are used for diagnosis purposes, the watermarking schemes must be reversible. The loss of information in such cases may lead to an inaccurate diagnosis. Hence, the fundus images use only reversible watermarking schemes (Bovik, 2000; Muharemagic & Furht, 2004; Poonkuntran, Rajesh, & Eswaran, 2008).

R2: Tamper Detection

The tamper detection is an essential feature in the authentication. It detects the unauthorized modifications done in the fundus images, while it is communicated over a network. This requirement can only detect the modifications on the fundus images, not localize the modifications (Bovik, 2000; Gonzalez & Woods, 2002).

R3: Tamper Localization

This is another feature in the authentication. It localizes the modifications in the fundus images. Based on this requirement (R3), the second requirement (R2) is measured. For a given fundus image, if there

Figure 6. Tradeoff among imperceptibility, fragility, and capacity

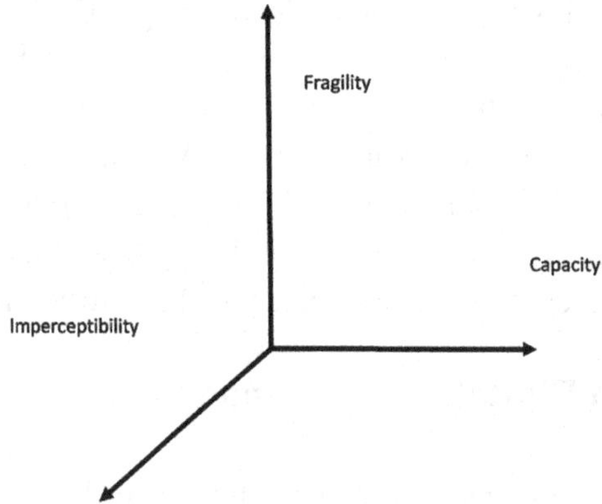

are no modifications, then the image is authentic. Otherwise, it is not authentic (Bovik, 2000; Gonzalez & Woods, 2002).

R4: Imperceptibility

Imperceptibility refers to the level of appearance of watermark in the fundus images under normal observation. Since the investigation is mainly done for authentication, it is to be invisible. The hidden watermark should not create any external artifacts in the images. The external artifacts may create rooms for suspicion to the hackers (Bovik, 2000).

R5: Capacity

The capacity is the amount of message to be embedded inside the fundus image. The capacity is measured in terms of the number of bits. The capacity will be in tradeoff with imperceptibility and fragility as shown in figure 6.

R6: Blind Detection

The extraction process in the watermarking can be done in two ways. They are blind and known detection. In blind detection, the watermark is extracted from the watermarked image without the knowledge of the original image. Only with the help of a secret or non-secret key, a watermark is extracted. In the known detection, the watermark is extracted with the knowledge of the original image. The need for the knowledge of the original image in the extraction process may degrade the security. Moreover, the knowledge of the original images may help the hackers to alter the images without altering the watermark. Thereby, the validity of the authentication process will be failed (Bovik, 2000; Gonzalez & Woods, 2002). Hence, it is decided to use blind detection in this research.

R7: Fragility

The fragility refers to the sensitiveness of the watermarking scheme to the attacks. The scheme must be sensitive to the attacks; thereby the watermark should easily be broken in order to authenticate (Bovik, 2000).

PROBLEM STATEMENT AND CHALLENGES

The primary objective of this work is to perform a detailed investigation of the design and development of watermarking schemes for digital fundus image authentication by satisfying the above mentioned all the key requirements (R1-R7). The second objective of this research is to propose and validate a mathematical based algorithmic scheme for fundus image authentication using watermarking. The proposed scheme will be quantitatively analyzed on a common testbed for the above-mentioned requirements (R1-R7) towards satisfying all the requirements.

From the above discussions, it is found that the digital fundus images have not been studied and analyzed on security in content authentication. It is also found that no specific investigation has been done for digital fundus image authentication by satisfying the above mentioned key requirements (R1-R7). Therefore, the detailed investigation has to be carried out in the design and development of digital fundus image authentication scheme by satisfying all the key requirements (R1-R7). The following are the challenging issues for designing such an authentication scheme.

Digital fundus images are one particular class of medical images. It is acquired through a fundus camera. The characteristics of the fundus images may limit the behavior of the scheme. Thereby, a few key requirements may not be satisfied. In the requirements, the capacity, imperceptibility and fragility are in tradeoff by nature. Complete study of all the requirements of the scheme is very difficult (Muharemagic & Furht, 2004). It is also very difficult to fix the optimal point where all the requirements will be satisfied at the possible maximum level (Muharemagic & Furht, 2004). Only a few works of literature are in the direction of the current area of research. The scheme should be designed with current available network bandwidth requirements. It should not seek the extra bandwidth requirements. (Poonkuntran, Rajesh & Eswaran, 2009a; Poonkuntran, Rajesh & Eswaran, 2009b; Poonkuntran, Rajesh & Eswaran, 2009c; Poonkuntran, Rajesh & Eswaran, 2009d).

PROPOSED SCHEME: MODIFIED INTEGER TRANSFORM WATERMARKING SCHEME

This section presents a Modified Integer Transform Watermarking Scheme (MITWS) for fundus image authentication. MITWS uses the color characteristics of the pixel and integer transform. It classifies the color values of the pixels in the image in to primary and secondary. The secondary colors are only used for embedding through the integer transform. MITWS improves the imperceptibility while increasing the capacity. MITWS could extract the watermark completely at the receiver side.

Related Works

The (Nammer &Emman, 2007) have proposed a High Capacity Steganography Scheme (HCSS) for color Bitmap (BMP) images. It hides the data into unwanted areas of the image that are identified with many color differences. It gives a high capacity rate and robust against visual and statistical attacks. The limitation of HCSS is irreversibility. The fundus image requires a reversible scheme which brings the originality of the image without any loss of information. Hence, the HCSS cannot be applied directly to the fundus image. (Tian, 2003) has proposed a Multiple Layer Data Hiding Scheme (MLDHS) for medical images. It uses the integer transform for embedding the secret data and produces the reversible solutions. It could not able to provide a reliable and confidential communication. The reason is that it generates high distortion when embedding takes place in multiple layers. The above mentioned two schemes cannot be applied to fundus images. As the first scheme HCSS is irreversible and second scheme MLDHS produces high distortion, these two schemes cannot suitable for digital fundus image. Through the literature survey, it is found that the use of color characteristics of pixels may improve the capacity with low distortion. Since the HCSS uses color characteristics for embedding and MLDHS is reversible, a new hybrid watermarking scheme using the HCSS and MLDHS is proposed. The proposed scheme mainly uses color characteristics of the pixels and integer transform. The integer transform in MLDHS uses a sequential pixel selection strategy and it is modified in the proposed scheme by introducing a new pixel selection strategy called "intra plane difference embedding" for reducing the distortion. Since the proposed scheme is given by a modified integer transform; it is called as "Modified Integer Transform Watermarking Scheme (MITWS)".

Color Characteristics of Pixels and Its Relevance to Watermarking

Information hiding inside the image is a popular technique nowadays.

An image with a secret message inside can easily be spread over the World Wide Web.

To hide a message inside an image without changing its visible properties, the cover image can be altered in "noisy" areas with many color variations. So that less attention is drawn to the modifications. The schemes in (Poonkuntran, Rajesh & Eswaran, 2009a; Poonkuntran, Rajesh & Eswaran, 2009b; Poonkuntran, Rajesh & Eswaran, 2009c; Poonkuntran, Rajesh & Eswaran, 2009d) are most common schemes that are altering the images in the above-mentioned way for embedding. In true-color images, each pixel is given by red (R), green (G) and blue (B) components. These three components are referred to as a primary color or RGB color space. Here, each pixel is represented in 24 bits or 3 bytes. Each byte contains a number between 0 and 255. With these three bytes, the computer can generate 256×256×256 = 16777216 combinations. Such a combination is illustrated in figure 7 where R, G and B components are plotted in three different axes. It is very difficult to define a precise color by adjusting these three components.

When a 24-bit color image is used, a bit of each of red, green and blue color components can be used for embedding. In this case, a total of 3 bits of secret information is stored in each pixel. Thus, a 256 × 256 color image can contain a total amount of 524288 bits (65536 bytes). When a bit of each color plane of the pixel is used for embedding, the maximum capacity of the watermark is 196608 bits. It is found that the capacity can be improved if the color variations are used for embedding. It means that more than one bit of information can be embedded in a pixel without any external artifacts if the color variations in the image are vague. In a 24-bits or 3 bytes of RGB color, each byte contains two nibbles.

Figure 7. RGB color space (cube model)

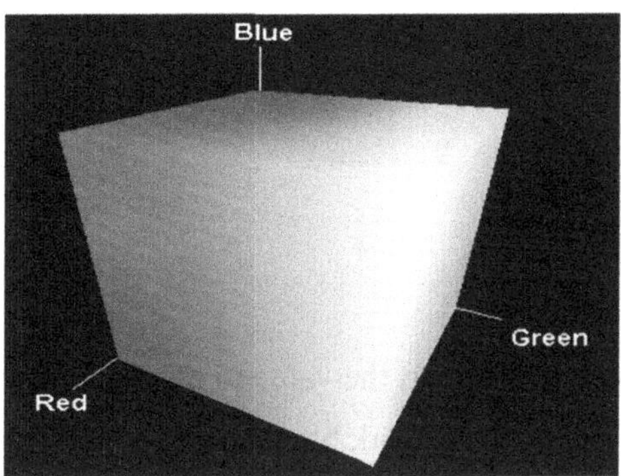

The left nibble contains the highest value in the byte while the right nibble contains the lowest value in the byte. Any changes in the right nibble do not create much impact in a byte value and also minimizes embedding alterations. At the same time, a small change in the left nibble creates much impact in the byte value. The 3 bytes is composed of different proportions of three main colors. This proportion classifies these three main colors into primary and secondary. The color which dominates all other colors in a pixel is known as primary color and other colors are known as secondary color. The primary color plays an important role in making a particular color shade. The secondary colors are added with primary colors to create a particular color shade. It is found that if the secondary colors are modified, it improves the capacity with low distortion. Hence, the proposed MITWS is designed using color characteristics. The MITWS identifies the primary and secondary colors for each pixel of the image and the secondary colors are modified to embed the secret data inside the pixel.

Integer Transform Using Intra Plane Difference Embedding

Integer Transform

The integer transform is also called as integer Haar wavelet transform or S transform. The integer transform satisfies the property of reversibility (Tian, 2002). It works as follows. For an 8-bit grayscale pixel pair (x, y), $0 \leq x, y \leq 255$ the integer transform is given by the pair (m, d). Where m refers integer average and d refers to difference.

The m and d are calculated as follows.

$$m = \left\lfloor \frac{x+y}{2} \right\rfloor \quad (1)$$

$$d = x - y \quad (2)$$

The inverse transform is given by

$$x = m + \left\lfloor \frac{d+1}{2} \right\rfloor \tag{3}$$

$$y = m - \left\lfloor \frac{d}{2} \right\rfloor \tag{4}$$

Where $\lfloor \ \rfloor$ refers floor operation which rounds the value to nearest integer. In the integer transform, the difference *(d)* is modified based on the watermark bit *(b)* to hide the *b* into the pixel pair. The reversible integer transform provides one to one correspondence between *(x, y)* and *(m, d)*.

Here *(x, y)* and *(m, d)* are in integers that represent the pixels in the image.

The *(x, y)* is in the range of [0, 255]. The *(m, d)* should also be in the same range [0, 255] to prevent the overflow and underflow. It means that for a given pixel pair *(x, y)*, $0 \leq x, y \leq 255$ the *(m, d)* should satisfy the following condition.

$$0 \leq m + \left\lfloor \frac{d+1}{2} \right\rfloor \leq 255 \tag{5}$$

$$0 \leq m - \left\lfloor \frac{d}{2} \right\rfloor \leq 255 \tag{6}$$

The above inequalities are equivalent to

$$d \leq 2(255 - m) \tag{7}$$

$$d \leq 2m + 1 \tag{8}$$

By this, the following condition is made easily.

$$\begin{array}{ll} d \leq 2(255 - m) & \mathit{if}\, 128 \leq m \leq 255 \\ d \leq 2m + 1 & \mathit{if}\, 0 \leq m \leq 127 \end{array} \tag{9}$$

Here the secret data bit (watermark) can be embedded by expanding the differences *(d)*. The expanded difference *(d')* is obtained by

$$d' = 2 \times d + b \tag{10}$$

The expanded difference should satisfy the overflow and underflow conditions. Therefore,

$$\left|d'\right| \leq \min\{2 \times (255 - m), 2 \times m + 1\} \tag{11}$$

The *(d')* is said to be expandable, if

$2 \times d + b \leq \min\{2 \times (255 - m), 2 \times m + 1\}$.

Where $b = \{0, 1\}$ represents the watermark (secret information). While these differences are being expanded, the integer average is not expanded. Therefore with this, a new pixel pair is made by using *(m, d')* through the equation 3 and 4.

From equation 10, it is found that the expanded difference is given by the sum of multiples of 2. Therefore, the expanded difference can be rewritten as

$$d' = 2 \times \left\lfloor \frac{d'}{2} \right\rfloor + LSB(d') \tag{12}$$

Where *LSB (d')* returns the least significant bit of integer *d'*. The following example explains how equation 10 is rewritten by equation 12.

Consider a difference *d*=4 and the watermark *b*=*1*. Using equation 10, the *d*=4 is expanded as follows.

From equation 10

$$d' = 2 \times d + b \tag{13}$$

By applying *d*=4 and *b*=1 in equation 13

$$d' = 2 \times 4 + 1 = 9 \tag{14}$$

Now, *d'* is derived from the *d'* using equation 12 as follows.

From equation 12

$$d' = 2 \times \left\lfloor \frac{d'}{2} \right\rfloor + LSB(d') \tag{15}$$

By applying *d'=9* in equation 15

$$d' = 2 \times \left\lfloor \frac{9}{2} \right\rfloor + LSB(9) = 9 \tag{16}$$

Thus, the expanded difference (*d'*) is rewritten. The differences are first checked whether it is expanded or not. For the expandable differences, the expansion is done by the modification of LSB. After this modification, the expandable differences can be changed further to embed another bit of information.

It is known as multi-layer embedding. The expanded differences are changed under the integer average value. The integer average value is not altered in the integer transform. With the help of this integer average value, the original pixel values are restored without any loss of information at the extraction process. Thus, the integer transform performs reversible embedding.

Modified Integer Transform using Intra Plane Difference Embedding

Tian (2003) proposed an MLDHS using the above-discussed integer transform. It is popularly known as the DE method. The scheme works as follows.

***Step 1*:** Form the pixel pair from the consecutive pixels in the image and transform the pixel pair using integer transform. For example, consider the pixel pair (208,203). According to the above discussed integer transform

x=208 y=203

Mean (m) = floor ((208+203)/2) =205

Difference (d) =208-203=5.

Now, the pair (m, d) is obtained from the pair (x, y). It is known as a forward integer transform.

***Step 2*:** Expand the difference for embedding watermark bit (b) inside the pixel pair (x, y). It is done by modifying the difference (d) with watermark bit (b). For example b=1, the modified difference (d') is obtained from equation 10 as follows.

$d' = 2 X d + b = 2 X 5 + 1 = 11.$

***Step 3*:** Generate watermarked pixel using modified difference value. Apply inverse integer transform to get the modified pixel pair. For the example given in step1 and 2,

x'=m+ floor ((d'+1)/2) =205+ (12/2) =211.

y'=m-floor (d'/2) =205-(11/2) =200.

The modified pixel pair (x'=211 y'=200) is obtained. Thus, the watermark is embedded in the image. Now, this (x', y') is sent to the receiver.

***Step 4*:** Once the receiver, receives the (x', y') repeat the step1 for x=x' and y=y'. x'=211 and y'=200

Mean (m) = floor ((211+200)/2) =205

Difference (d) =211-200=11.

***Step 5*:** Read the least significant bit of (d) to get the watermark information.

LSB (d) =LSB (11) =1 →Watermark is extracted here.

***Step 6*:** Retrieve the original pixel pair by modifying the d by $d/2$.

d'=floor ($d/2$) =floor (11/2) =5.

$x=m$+floor ((d'+1)/2) =205+floor ((5+1)/2) =208.

$y=m$-floor ($d'/2$) =205-floor (5/2) =203.

Thus, the watermark and original pixel pair are extracted without any loss of information. It is experimentally found MLDHS is not fragile for smaller size of watermarks. When this scheme is applied to fundus images with various sizes of watermarks, the scheme could make the changes in only one color plane. The rest of the color planes are untouched.

When MLDHS is applied to the fundus image, it changes only the Red color plane of the fundus image for the watermark size from 10000 to 100000 as shown in table 1.

It does not change the other color planes. The watermark could not able to sense the modification done in the other color planes (green and blue). Thus, MLDHS is failed in fragility. However, the size (capacity) can be increased to make the scheme as fragile. Increasing capacity directly affects the imperceptibility. The literature survey shows that the fragility is decided by the way in which the locations of the image are chosen for embedding. Instead of ordered selection, if the locations are chosen randomly, fragility can be improved. This means that the locations are selected in a way by which when an attempt is made to tamper the image, the embedded watermark is also changed (Poonkuntran, Rajesh & Eswaran, 2009e). Therefore, a new location selection strategy has been brought in to the MITWS. It is known as intra plane difference embedding. It selects the pixel pair across the color planes rather than consecutive pixels in the single color plane. Thereby, the MITWS modifies two color planes to improve the fragility, while the watermark is being embedded. It is clearly shown in table 2. Thus, the newly introduced intra plane difference embedding strategy improves the fragility in MITWS.

The capacity, tamper detection, and tamper localization are other limitations found in MLDHS. For a given fundus image of size 256×256, the MLDHS can embed a maximum of 128×128 bits per layer. The reason is that it selects the pixel pair consecutively. In MITWS, the pixel pair is formed across the plane. So, the MITWS can embed a maximum of 256×256 bits per layer. Thus, the capacity is improved by the new pixel selection strategy in the MITWS. However, the tamper localization and detection is not yet addressed by the MITWS. The above-discussed color characteristics and modified integer transform with new pixel selection strategies are chosen as key techniques for the design of the proposed scheme MITWS presented in this chapter.

Table 1. Fragility of MLDHS

MLDHS			
Size of the Watermark	**PSNR at Red**	**PSNR at Green**	**PSNR at Blue**
10000 bits	58.3826	100	100
20000 bits	49.4946	100	100
30000 bits	45.4838	100	100
40000 bits	43.2254	100	100
50000 bits	41.5407	100	100
60000 bits	40.2972	100	100
70000 bits	39.3442	100	100
80000 bits	38.6115	100	100
90000 bits	38.1254	100	100
100000 bits	37.6290	100	100

Modified Integer Transform Watermarking Scheme (MITWS)

The original fundus image (*I*) is given in 24-bits or 3 bytes of RGB color in MITWS. Each byte contains two nibbles. The left nibble contains the highest value in the byte while the right nibble contains the lowest value in the byte. Since, the nibble value is represented in 4 bits, yielding 16 different decimal values in the interval [0, 15].

This interval is used to identify the primary and secondary color of the pixels in the image. For a given pixel in RGB, the color index is calculated as

$$C_{index} = floor\left(\frac{Color\,Value}{16}\right) + 1 \tag{17}$$

Where *Color Value* = {*Red, Green, Blue*}. The color which contains minimum index value is chosen as primary color and others are secondary colors. The primary color of the pixel is untouched and the rest colors of the pixels are taken to integer transform for embedding. The integer transform in MITWS work as follows. For an 8-bit gray scale pixel pair (x, y), $(x, y) \varepsilon Z$, $0 \leq Z \leq 255$, the integer average m and difference d are defined as follows:

$$m=floor\,((x+y)/2) \tag{18}$$

$$d=x-y \tag{19}$$

Table 2. Fragiity of MITWS using intra plane difference embedding

MITWS using Intra Plane Difference Embedding			
Size of the Watermark	**PSNR at Red**	**PSNR at Green**	**PSNR at Blue**
10000 bits	100	65.4757	74.9776
20000 bits	100	52.1807	52.5528
30000 bits	100	41.9646	42.0290
40000 bits	100	38.0520	38.0924
50000 bits	100	35.6311	35.6489
60000 bits	100	33.8596	33.8751
70000 bits	100	32.4007	32.4153
80000 bits	100	31.1363	31.1484
90000 bits	100	30.0566	30.0690
100000 bits	100	29.1001	29.1130

The inverse transform is defined as:

$$x' = m + floor((d+1)/2) \quad (20)$$

$$y' = m - floor(d/2) \quad (21)$$

The difference (d) is expanded by using watermark bit b to create an expanded difference (d').

$$d' = 2 \text{ X } d + b \quad (22)$$

Where d' is modified difference after embedding the watermark bit (b).

The modified difference (d') is calculated by satisfying the following condition in order to prevent the overflow or underflow during the embedding process.

$$|d'| \le 2 \times (255 - m) \text{ If } 128 \le m \le 255$$

$$|d'| \le 2 \times (m + 1) \text{ If } 0 \le m \le 127 \quad (23)$$

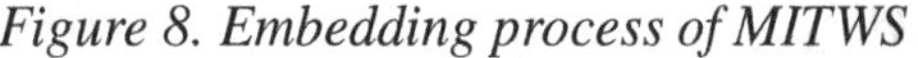

Figure 8. Embedding process of MITWS

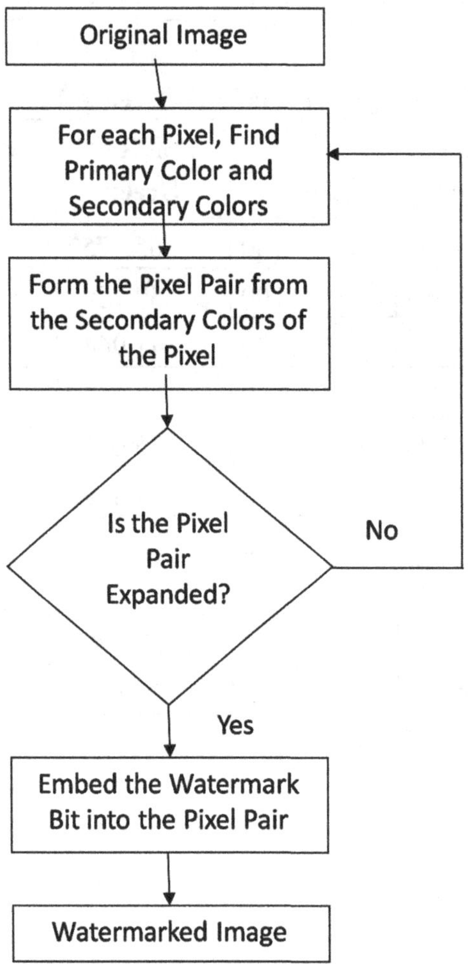

If d' satisfies the equation 23, then d is expandable. Otherwise, d is unexpandable. An expandable difference can be used to hide secret information. If all the expandable differences are selected for data embedding, the capacity rate reaches its maximum limit. Let N and N_e denote the number of different and the number of expandable differences, respectively.

The hiding capacity of an image is defined as:

$$C=N_e/N \tag{24}$$

Therefore, the hiding capacity of the image is proportional to the number of expandable difference. Thus, the MITWS embeds the secret data into the original fundus image to create the watermarked image. The proposed embedding process is illustrated in figure 8.

The extraction process is reversible and it extracts the secret data and original image without any loss of information. For multilayer embedding, the same pixel pair is selected for further data embedding. Here some of the differences may not be expandable for a longer time (Tian, 2003). The extraction process requires information about the primary color of the pixel in the image. The reason is that the primary color of the pixel is not altered in the image for embedding. It means that no information is hidden inside the primary color of the pixel and it is untouched in the process. The secondary colors of the pixel are modified by the integer transform to embed the watermark into it. At this time, the actual color characteristics of the pixel are changed and it is restored at the extraction process after removing the watermark from the watermarked image. It is also difficult to classify the primary and secondary colors in the extraction process without prior information.

To avoid this problem, the Color Classification Map (CCM) is created separately and it is also sent with the watermarked image. The CCM contains binary values {0, 1}. The 0 refers that the color is primary which is not altered in the embedding process. The 1 refers that the color is a secondary color that is altered in the embedding process. For one pixel in the image, a 3-bit code is generated for each of the primary color planes red, green and blue. The expandable pixel pair in the image is also easily identified by this CCM. For non-expandable pixels, the CCM is 000.

Then, the extraction process becomes simple. The extraction process receives the watermarked image and CCM. CCM identifies the secondary colors of the pixel. These pixel values are given to the equation 18 and 19 to find the m and d. Then, the watermark or secret information embedded in the pixel pair is extracted by reading the LSB of a difference value between the pixels in the pixel pair. The other steps are done as discussed in section 4.4.2.

Thus, the embedding and extraction are done using intra plane difference embedding and color characteristics of the pixels in MITWS.

EXPERIMENTAL RESULTS AND ANALYSIS

The MITWS has been simulated using an exclusive common testbed that has been created in this research for the quantitative analysis of the proposed scheme. The details of the testbed are as follows.

- **Test Images:** The test digital fundus images were taken from two public research databases STARE and DRIVE (Poonkuntran, Rajesh & Eswaran, 2014). The database details are as follows.
  - Database Name: Structured Analysis of Retina (STARE)
  - Digital Retinal Images for Vessel Extraction (DRIVE)
  - Address: http://www.ces.clemson.edu/~ahoover/stare/
  - http://www.isi.uu.nl/Research/Databases/DRIVE/
  - Image Format: Tagged Image File Format (TIFF)
  - Size of the image: 565x584x3
  - Color Mode: RGB (Red, Green, Blue).
- **Image Formats:** The test images used in the experiments were given in the Tagged Image File Format (TIFF). Tagged Image File Format (abbreviated TIFF) is a file format for storing images, including photographs and line art. As of 2010, it is under the control of Adobe Systems. Originally created by the company Aldus and called "desktop publishing". The TIFF format is widely applied in medical image processing, image manipulation, publishing, scanning, faxing, word processing, optical character recognition and other applications. Adobe Systems, which acquired Aldus, now holds the copyright to the TIFF specification. The experiment uses 12 test images that are shown in figure 9. The secret message used for embedding is shown in figure 10.

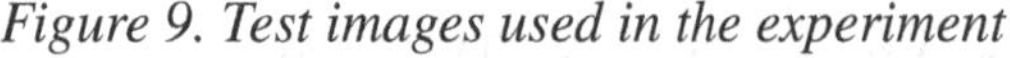

Figure 9. Test images used in the experiment

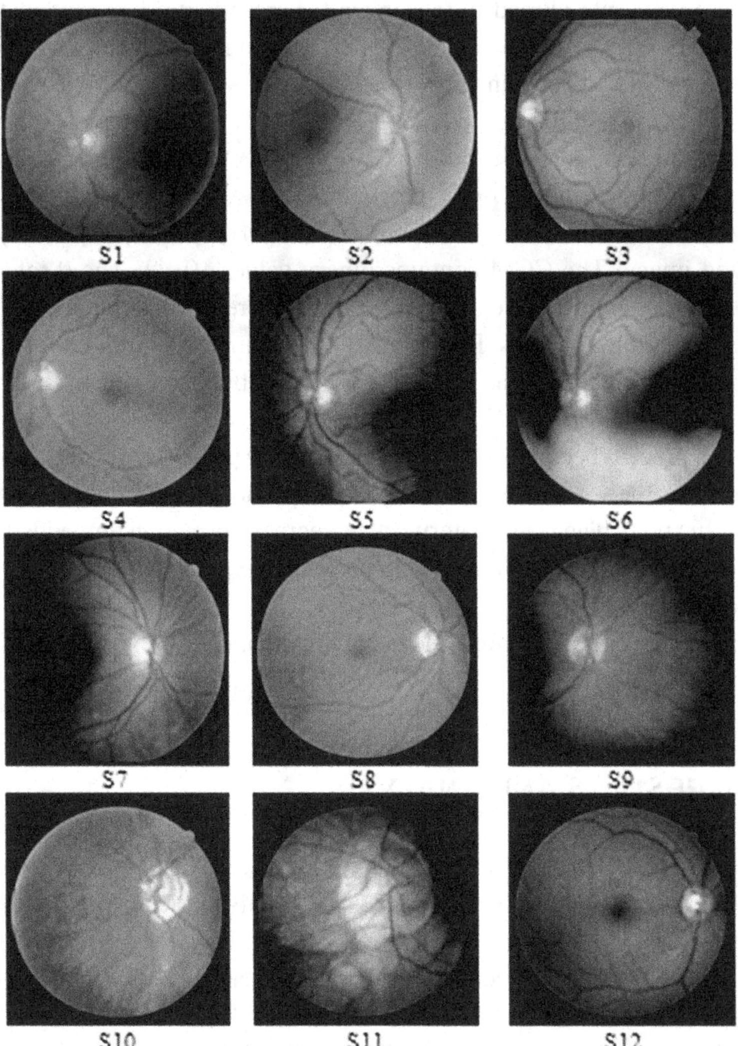

It consisting of 64 bits IIN (Image Identification Number), 160 bits digital signature, 48 bits manifest type that includes codes for various types of alterations in the retina (for example, emboli refers to emboli manifestation) and 128 bits vessel information that includes diameter of optic disc, Cup to Disc Ratio (C/D) and vessel width details. Finally, the total information came to 400 bits (Coatrieux, Maitre, Sankur, Rolland& Collorec, 2000) (Gonzalez & Woods, 2002). Thus, the watermark has been produced as cover independent. The experiments were carried out for all the key requirements mentioned in section 1. The results are analyzed and discussed in forthcoming sub-sections

Figure 10. Secret message used in the experiment

CAY34567 // IIN
SHANMUGAMPOONKUNTRAN
// Digital Signature
EMBOLI // Type of Manifest
0.45 // C/D ratio - Optic Disc
0.33 // Maximum Vessel Width
0.22 // Median Vessel Width
0.44 // Minimum Vessel Width

Reversibility Experiment

To evaluate the reversibility of the MITWS quantitatively, Peak Signal to Noise Ratio (*PSNR*) in decibel (*dB*) between original image (I) and its extracted version image (I_E) were used as a parameter. The PSNR is given by

$$PSNR\ (I, I_E) = 10\ Log_{10}\ [(2^{depth}-1)^2 / MSE] \tag{25}$$

$$MSE(I, I_E) = \frac{\sum_{M,N} \left[I(i,j) - I_E(i,j) \right]^2}{M * N} \tag{26}$$

Where *MSE* is mean square error, $i=0$ to $M-1$ and $j=0$ to $N-1$. It is experimentally found that the MITWS is reversible for any size of watermark (capacity). The MITWS produces PSNR as 100% and thereby it guarantees reversibility. It confirms that the changes done in the original image for embedding is completely recoverable due to the integer transform.

Imperceptibility Experiment

The PSNR described above is again used here to measure the imperceptibility of the scheme. Here, the PSNR is taken between the original image (I) and its watermarked image (I_W). It is found from the experiment that MITWS produces 80.72% as an average PSNR for Imperceptibility. It means that 80.72% of the original images are not altered and it does not produce any external artifacts under normal vision. The lower PSNR will produce the artifacts. However, the imperceptibility is limited by capacity. When, the capacity increases, the imperceptibility decreases. The imperceptibility results are tabulated in Table 3.

Tamper Detection, Tamper Localization, and Fragility Experiment

For this experiment, 11 attacks have been chosen from the literature survey (Muharemagic & Furht, 2004; Poonkuntran & Rajesh, 2014). It includes jittering, geometrical and filtering attacks. These at-

Table 3. Imperceptibility of MITWS

Test Images	MITWS		
	PSNR at Red (in dB)	PSNR at Green (In dB)	PSNR at Blue(in dB)
S1	70.5785	59.8719	59.3724
S2	100.0000	59.5424	59.3338
S3	100.0000	74.0945	100.0000
S4	74.2004	60.2082	59.70214
S5	100.0000	59.1657	58.87464
S6	100.0000	59.2097	58.78281
S7	100.0000	61.7198	61.4854
S8	100.0000	74.0945	93.2853
S9	100.0000	78.0945	100.0000
S10	100.0000	76.3451	100.0000
S11	100.0000	74.0945	100.0000
S12	100.0000	74.0945	100.0000
Average for each plane	95.3982	67.5446	79.2363
Average for all Planes			80.7264

tacks have widely occurred against image authentication (Muharemagic & Furht, 2004). The attacks are explained as follows:

- **Jittering Attack:** The jittering attack is common to attack in any type of watermarking system. It modifies the pixel value of an image either by changing pixel value or duplicates in an unnoticeable manner. Hence, such an attack is not creating any suspicion externally. Under normal vision, these differences could not be noticed by humans. Jittering can be done on various levels. The levels were modeled as multiples of 5 from 5% to 95% in the experiment.
- **Average:** Returns an averaging filtered output of an image. The averaging can be done by using a mask of size (M x N). Where M refers to number of rows and N refers to the number of columns. The mask size of 3x3 is used in the experiment.
- **Disk:** Returns a circular averaging filtered output of an image. It is done by a mask and radius of the circle. The size of the mask is defined based on the radius of the circle used. If the radius of the circle is R, then the size of the mask is (2xR+1) x (2xR+1). The radius of the circle used in the experiment is 5.
- **Gaussian:** Returns a rotationally symmetric gaussian low pass filtered output of an image. It is done by using two parameters mask and sigma value. The mask size of 3x3 and the default value of sigma = 0.5 is used in the experiment.
- **Laplacian:** Operates the image with approximating the shape of the two dimensional Laplacian operator and returns the output. The approximated shape of Laplacian is controlled by the pa-

rameter called alpha. The mask of size 3x3 and the default value of alpha=0.2 were used in the experiment.

- **Log:** Returns a rotationally symmetric Laplacian of gaussian filtered output of an image. The size of the mask used in the experiment is 5×5. The default value of sigma =0.5 is used in the experiment.
- **Motion:** Returns the output of the motion filter. The motion filter approximates the convolved image with the linear motion of a camera by l pixels and an angle of theta degrees in a counter-clockwise direction. The filter becomes a vector for horizontal and vertical motions. The default l is 9 and the default theta is 0, which corresponds to a horizontal motion of nine pixels. The default values of the filter are used in the experiments.
- **Prewitt:** Returns Prewitt edge Filtered output of images.
- **Sobel:** Returns Sobel edge filtered output of images.
- **Unsharp:** Returns a 3x3 Unsharp contrast enhancement filtered output of images.
- **Rotate** Rotates image by angle degrees in a counterclockwise or clockwise direction around its center point. The rotated image is calculated using bilinear interpolation. The final rotated image is cropped to fit in the original image size. The two angle values 25° and 75° are used in the experiment.

For all the above-mentioned attacks, the default values of the parameters are used in the experiment. The reason is that the default values are specifying the stable behavior of all the attacks. Moreover, these are the minimum requirements for the attacks.

If the scheme is fragile against the minimum requirements of the attack, it is sure that the scheme will be fragile for other levels of the requirements of attacks.

The first experiment is done for a jittering attack. In this, the watermarked image is modified from 5% to 95% in the multiples of 5. For the same, the number of bits changed in the corresponding watermark is also measured. From the results, it is found that MITWS changes around 38% at an average of the watermark to authenticate. The results are tabulated in Table 4.

The next experiment is done for geometrical and filtering attacks. It is experimentally found that MITWS changes around 45% of the watermark at an average for the geometrical and filtering attacks. The results are shown in figure 11 and table 5. It is also experimentally found that the MITWS could not detect and locate the tampering in the images. The reason is that the watermark in the MITWS is generated without the knowledge of the cover image.

Capacity Experiment

To identify the optimal size of the watermark with good imperceptibility, the experiment is conducted on a set of test fundus images in the size of 512×512×3 and the corresponding imperceptibility has been calculated using *PSNR* between original image *(I)* and watermarked image (I_W). In this experiment, red and blue color planes of the fundus image are only considered for imperceptibility. The reason is that the green color plane of the fundus image is the primary color and it is not modified during embedding. Only red and blue color planes of the fundus images are modified for embedding.

From table 6, figure 12 and figure 13, the red plane is able to produce good *PSNR* (around 70 dB at an average) values to the watermark size of 100000 bits. At the same time, blue planes are not able to produce good *PSNR*. In the blue plane, for the size of 20000 bits, *PSNR* reaches below 50 dB.

Table 4. MITWS: Results of jittering attack

Percentage of Modification in the Watermarked Image	MITWS	
	Number of bits Modified out of 400 bits of Secret Information	Percentage of Modification in the Watermark
5	40	10.00
10	73	18.25
15	91	22.75
20	108	27.00
25	125	31.25
30	116	29.00
35	160	40.00
40	164	41.00
45	175	43.75
50	161	40.25
55	186	46.50
60	172	43.00
65	190	47.50
70	177	44.25
75	189	47.25
80	188	47.00
85	203	50.75
90	177	44.25
95	217	54.25
Average		38.32

Table 5. MITWS: Results of Geometrical and Filtering Attacks

Name of the Attack	Number of bits modified in 400 Bits of Secret Information	Percentage of Modification in the Watermark
Average	168	42.00
Disk	171	42.75
Gaussian	150	37.50
Laplacian	163	40.75
Log	123	30.75
Motion	311	77.75
Prewitt	321	80.25
Sobel	154	38.50
Unsharp	167	41.75
Rotation by 25°	171	42.75
Rotation by 75°	104	26.00
Average		45.52

Figure 11. MITWS: fragility against geometrical and filtering attacks

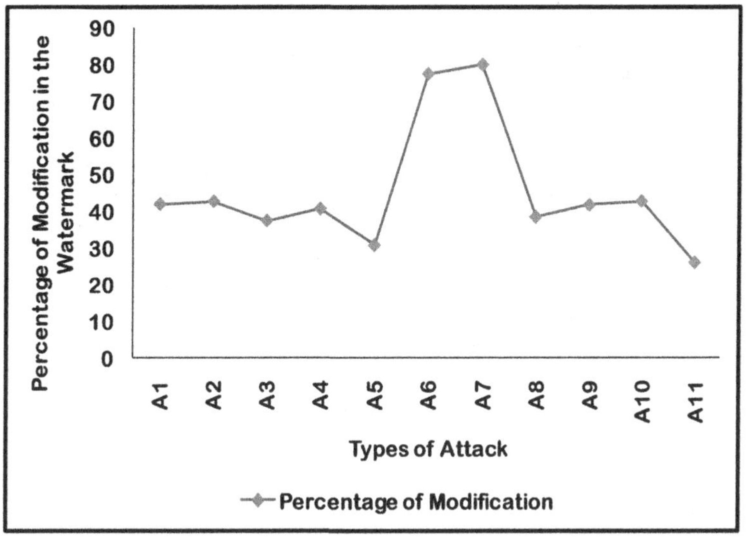

A1 - Average, A2 - Disk, A3 - Gaussian, A4 - Laplacian, A5 - Log, A6 - Motion, A7 - Prewitt, A8 - Sobel, A9 - Unsharp, A10 - Rotation by 25°, A11 - Rotation by 75°.

Therefore, by the number test, it is concluded that 30000 bits is the optimal size of the watermark with good imperceptibility of around 60 dB at an average. It is clearly shown in figure 14. When the size of the watermark is crossing 30000 bits, the visual artifacts are introduced.

Blind Detection Experiment

The MITWS requires knowledge about the watermark for the extraction.

It is experimentally found that MITWS is non-blind.

OBSERVATIONS

This chapter has presented MITWS using color characteristics and integer transform for fundus image authentication. The MITWS first classifies the color values of the pixels of the image in to primary and secondary. The secondary colors of the pixels are modified by integer transform in order to hide the secret information in it. The scheme introduced a new pixel selection strategy called "intra plane difference embedding" which selects the pixel across the plane rather than consecutive pixels in the one plane. This strategy improves the fragility and capacity of the scheme. The MITWS is reversible since it uses the reversible integer transform for embedding. The reversibility is retained for any sizes of the watermark. The MITWS could produce imperceptibility of 80.72% at an average. The MITWS is fragile against jittering, filtering and geometrical attacks.

The fragility rate of MITWS is 38% at an average for jittering attack and 45% at an average for filtering and geometrical attacks. It could not detect the tampering and it could not locate the tampered regions in the images. A watermark of 30000 bits found to be an optimal capacity of MITWS with a

Table 6. MITWS: imperceptibility vs capacity

Size of Watermark in Number of bits	PSNR at Red	PSNR at Blue
10000	81.46387	61.08983
20000	78.06911	50.1236
30000	76.30848	45.73024
40000	74.75822	41.48165
50000	72.99918	37.96801
60000	71.91828	36.63454
70000	70.92042	35.88567
80000	70.40995	35.31327
90000	70.08852	34.86395
100000	69.55787	34.45396

good level of imperceptibility. The MITWS is non-blind. It requires the knowledge of the watermark at the extraction process.

CRITICAL FINDINGS

The tamper detection and localization has not been addressed MITWS. The reason is that the cover independent watermark, i.e. scheme generates the watermark without the knowledge of the cover image.

Figure 12. MITWS: imperceptibility vs capacity for red plane

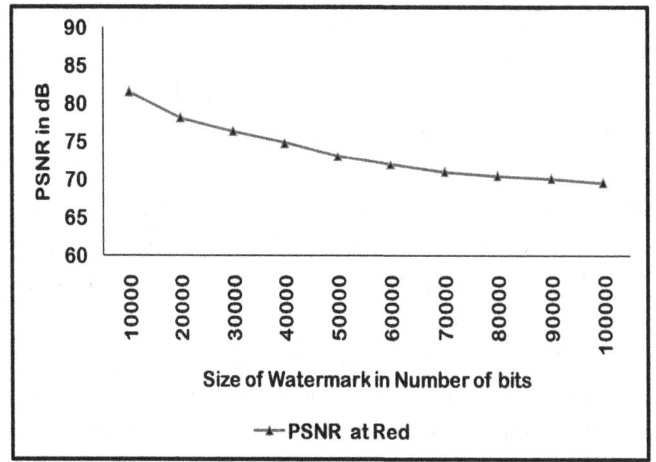

Figure 13. MITWS: imperceptibility vs capacity for blue plane

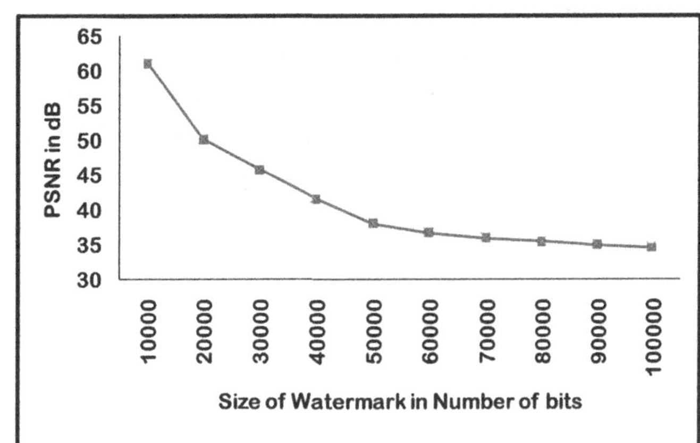

Figure 14. MITWS: imperceptibility vs capacity

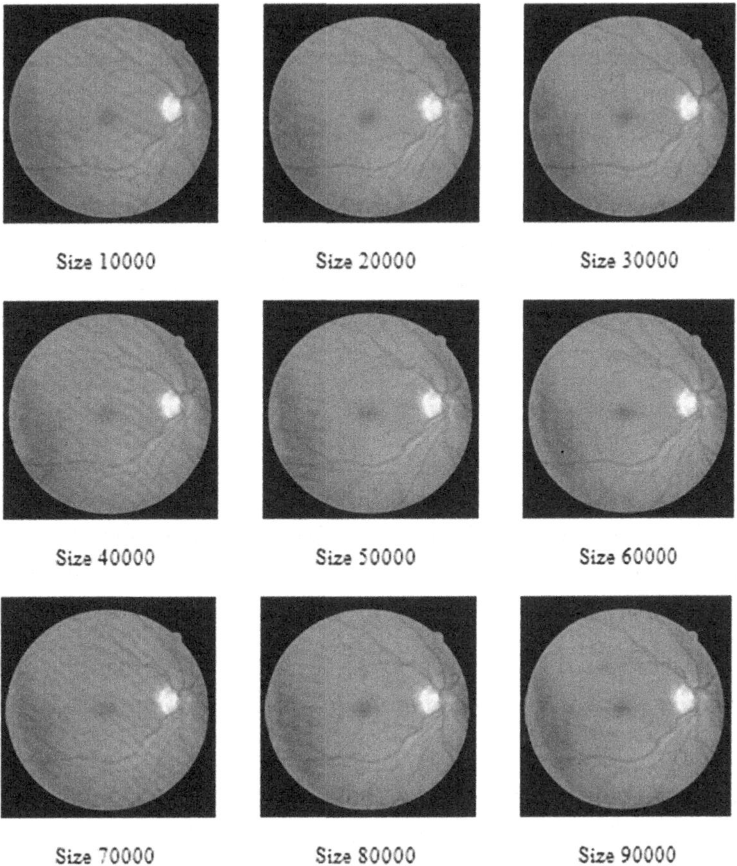

If the watermark is generated using the knowledge of the cover image, any modification in the images can easily be located. Hence, the design of the watermark generation using a cover image is required.

The MITWS is non-blind. It requires the knowledge of the watermark at the extraction process. As per the key requirements of this research given in section 1, the scheme should be blind. The reason is that the watermark is cover independent. If the watermark is a function of the cover image, then the watermark can be known in the extraction process by the function not by sharing any information between the embedding and extraction.

CONCLUSION AND FUTURE ENHANCEMENT

This chapter has explained the Modified Integer Transform Watermarking Scheme (MITWS) for fundus image authentication. It mainly uses color characteristics and integer transforms. The scheme introduces a new pixel selection strategy called "intra plane difference embedding" to form the pixel pair by selecting the pixels across the color planes. The MITWS is reversible, fragile and imperceptible. It could not detect and locate the tampering in the images. The MITWS is non-blind. It requires the knowledge of the watermark at the extraction process. The tamper detection, tamper localization and blind detection are the major issues in the MITWS. If the watermark is generated as a function of the cover image, the two main issues mentioned above can easily be solved. For tamper detection and localization, any changes in the cover lead to change the response of the function used for generating watermark. If the image is tampered, then the watermark is also modified. So, the tampering can be easily detected and located. For blind detection, the function used to generate the watermark can be used to generate the reference watermark for the verification and validation during the extraction process. The actual embedded watermark can be extracted using an integer transform. Thus, the scheme can be designed as a blind scheme.

The future enhancement of this work is to generate watermark as cover dependent using non-linear functions such as chaotic models and hashing techniques. This step will bring tamper detection and localization in the proposed scheme. The marking spaces for embedding will be reviewed further using a pseudo-random process to make the scheme to do extraction in complete blind without the knowledge of the original and secret data.

REFERENCES

Amato, F., Cozzolino, G., Mazzeo, A., & Romano, S. (2018). Intelligent medical record management: A diagnosis support system. *International Journal of High-Performance Computing and Networking*, *12*(4), 391–399. doi:10.1504/IJHPCN.2018.096726

Bhatt, C. M. (2017). Data Protection and Security Issues in Social Media. In C. Bhatt, & S. Peddoju (Eds.), *Cloud Computing Systems and Applications in Healthcare* (pp. 135–162). Hershey, PA: IGI Global. doi:10.4018/978-1-5225-1002-4.ch008

Bovik, A. L. (2000). *Handbook of Image and Video Processing. Academic Press* (pp. 99–69120). Canada: Library of Congress Catalog Number.

Poonkuntran, S., & Rajesh, R. S. (2014). Chaotic model-based semi-fragile watermarking using integer transforms for digital fundus image authentication. *Multimedia Tools and Applications, 68.* doi:10.100711042-012-1227-5

Coatrieux, G., Lamard, M., Lamard, W., Puentes, J., & Roux, C. (2005). A Low Distortion and Reversible Watermark: Application to Angiographic Images of the Retina. *Proceedings of the 27th IEEE Annual Conference on Engineering in Medicine and Biology,* pp. 1-4. Shanghai, China.

Coatrieux, G., Maitre, H., Sankur, B., Rolland, Y., & Collorec, R. (2000). Relevance of Watermarking in Medical Imaging. *Proceedings of the IEEE International Conference on Information Technology Applications in Biomedicine,* Arlington, TX, pp. 250-255, November 2000. 10.1109/ITAB.2000.892396

Cole, E. (2003). *Hiding in Plain Sight: Steganography and Art of Covert Communications.* USA: Wiley Publishing

Cox, I., Miller, M., Linnartz, J. P., & Kalker, T. (1999). A Review of Watermarking Principles and Practices. In K. K. Parhi, & T. Nishitani (Eds.), Digital Signal Processing in Multimedia Systems, pp. 461-485. Marcell Dekker Inc. doi:10.1201/9781482276046-17

Dutta, M. K., Singh, A., Singh, A., Burget, R., & Prinosil, J. (2015). Digital identification tags for medical fundus images for teleophthalmology applications. *Proceedings 2015 38th International Conference on Telecommunications and Signal Processing.* pp. 781-784. Prague, Czech Republic. DOI: 10.1109/TSP.2015.7296372

Gonzalez, R. C., & Woods, R. E. (2002). Digital Image Processing (2nd Ed.), Prentice-Hall Publishers, Upper Saddle River, NJ 07458.

Hai, H., Xie, D. Q., & Ke, Q. (2018). A watermarking-based authentication and image restoration in multimedia sensor networks. *International Journal of High-Performance Computing and Networking, 12*(1), 65–73. doi:10.1504/IJHPCN.2018.093846

Hu, Z., Guo, X., Hu, X., Chen, X., & Wang, Z. (2005). The Identification and Recognition Based on Ocular Fundus, Springer Link Lecture Notes in Computer Science, 3832, pp. 770-776.

Karmakar, R., & Basu, A. (2019). Implementation of a Reversible Watermarking Technique for Medical Images. In S. Bhattacharyya (Ed.), *Intelligent Innovations in Multimedia Data Engineering and Management* (pp. 1–37). Hershey, PA: IGI Global. doi:10.4018/978-1-5225-7107-0.ch001

Melkemi, K., & Golea, N. E. H. (2017). ROI-based fragile watermarking for medical image tamper detection. *International Journal of High-Performance Computing and Networking., 1*(1), 1. doi:10.1504/IJHPCN.2017.10013846

Muharemagic, E., & Furht, B. (2004). Survey of Watermarking Techniques and Applications, Department of Computer Science and Engineering Florida Atlantic University, 777 Glades Road, Boca Raton, FL 33431-0991, USA.

Nammer, N., & Emman, E. L. (2007). Hiding a Large Amount of Data with High Security using Steganography Algorithm. *Journal of Computer Science, 3*(4). pp. 223-232.

Poonkuntran, S., Rajesh, R. S., & Eswaran, P. (2009a). Reversible, Multilayered Watermarking Scheme for Fundus Images Using Intra-Plane Difference Expanding. *Proceedings of the IEEE International Advance Computing Conference,* pp. 2583-2587, Patiala, India.

Poonkuntran, S., Rajesh, R. S., & Eswaran, P. (2009b). Wavetree Watermarking: An Authentication Scheme for Fundus Images. *Proceedings of the IEEE Sponsored International Conference on Emerging Trends in Computing,* pp. 507-511. India.

Poonkuntran, S., Rajesh, R. S., & Eswaran, P. (2009c). A Robust Watermarking Scheme for Fundus Images Using Intra-Plane Difference Expanding. *Proceedings of the IEEE Sponsored International Conference on Emerging Trends in Computing. pp*. 433-436. India.

Poonkuntran, S., Rajesh, R. S., & Eswaran, P. (2009e). Analysis of Difference Expanding Method for Medical Image Watermarking. *Proceedings of 2009 International Symposium on Computing, Communication, and Control,* pp. 30-34. Singapore.

Poonkuntran, S., Rajesh, R. S., & Eswaran, P. (2009d). Imperceptible Watermarking Scheme for Fundus Images Using Intra-Plane Difference Expanding. *International Journal on Computer and Electrical Engineering, 1*(4). 1793-8198.

Shanmugam, P., Rajesh, R. S., & Perumal, E. (2008). A Reversible Watermarking With Low Warping: An Application to Digital Fundus Images. *Proceedings of the IEEE International Conference on Computer and Communication Engineering,* pp. 472-477.

Sliwa, J. (2019). Assessing complex evolving cyber-physical systems (case study: Smart medical devices). *International Journal of High-Performance Computing and Networking, 13*(3), 294–303. doi:10.1504/IJHPCN.2019.098570

Tian, J. (2002). Reversible Watermarking by Difference Expansion. *Proceedings of Workshop on Multimedia and Security: Authentication, Secrecy, and Steganalysis, pp*. 19-22.

Tian, J. (2003). Reversible Data Embedding using a Difference Expansion. *IEEE Transactions on Circuits and Systems for Video Technology, 13*(8), pp. 890-893.

Wang, B., Ding, Q., & Gu, X. (2019). A secure reversible chaining watermark scheme with hidden group delimiter for WSNs. *International Journal of High-Performance Computing and Networking, 14*(3). doi:10.1504/IJHPCN.2019.102126

Wu, M., & Liu, B. (2003). Data Hiding in Image and Video. I. Fundamental Issues and Solutions, *IEEE Transactions on Image Processing, 12*(6), pp. 685-695.

This research was previously published in the Handbook of Research on Multimedia Cyber Security; pages 114-145, copyright year 2020 by Information Science Reference (an imprint of IGI Global).

Chapter 25
Multiple Blind Watermarking Framework for Security and Integrity of Medical Images in E-Health Applications

Abdallah Soualmi
https://orcid.org/0000-0003-2107-8598
LRSD Lab, Computer Science Department, Faculty of Sciences, University of SETIF-1, Algeria

Adel Alti
https://orcid.org/0000-0001-8348-1679
LRSD Lab, Computer Science Department, Faculty of Sciences, University of SETIF-1, Algeria

Lamri Laouamer
Department of Management Information Systems, College of Business and Economics, Qassim University, Saudi Arabia

ABSTRACT

Nowadays, e-health applications carry the most advanced information and communication technologies for ensuring quality, remote healthcare services, and support diagnostics. These applications are sharing and transmitting of medical data over the internet, which makes them serious targets for alteration and illegal access. Image watermarking presents a compelling solution for protecting patient's information and ensures medical image integrity. This paper gives a new secure framework to protect medical data based on blind multiple watermarking schemes. The proposed approach consists of combining LWT (lifting wavelet transform), QR decomposition, and Arnold chaotic map in transform domain for the first watermark, while for the second watermark is encrusted in the spatial domain. During the de-watermarking process, both extracted watermarks are compared to detect any alterations during transmitting. The experimentation results demonstrate that the suggested method achieves good image fidelity and alters detection and robustness contra different kinds of attacks.

DOI: 10.4018/978-1-6684-6311-6.ch025

1. INTRODUCTION

The Telemedicine system is considered as a vital part in health care field, where new mechanisms and information technologies are adopted for the discretion of this sensitive sector. In addition, new generation information attracts more attention of international e-health organizations. Due to their capacity to reduce operations costs as well as gaining time and resources, where physicians are geographically far away from patients. In the other hand, new challenges are raised for researchers, especially in terms of data privacy and security issue.

The data security means the protection of information from not only unauthorized using but also unintentional operation (Agrawal et al., 2019). Cryptography present one of the powerful solutions among others that aims to protect data from threats while being transferred (Gomathikrishnan et al., 2011), which consist of making data accessible only by authorized user (Liu et al., 2018). However, once data are decrypted, this solution couldn't protect the authorship right; ensure the data integrity, or halt their illegal using (Khan et al., 2014).

The digital watermarking technique was raised to complete the cryptography. It consists of encrusting sensitive information into a host document to prove their ownership and authenticates data (Agrawal et al., 2019). It could be categorized into two fundamental domains, namely, spatial or frequency. Spatial techniques encrust the watermark directly in image pixels, to reduce the processing time. However, the robustness with attacks couldn't well granted. The frequency techniques encrust the watermark into a transform of the image using for example: DCT (Discrete Cosine Transform) (Das et al., 2013) or DWT (Discrete Wavelet Transform) (Tao et al., 2014)...etc., it offers more robustness but need high processing time (Kazemi et al., 2020). Moreover, in terms of de-watermarking process, the watermarking schemes could be also grouped into: blind, semi-blind or non-blind approaches (Agrawal et al., 2019). A blind method doesn't require the cover image or the watermark to de-watermark the encrusted information. For the second, it needs the original encrusted data, for the last, the host image is indispensable. The watermarking schemes can be also categorized according to their resistance degree into three types: robust, semi-fragile or fragile (Kamran et al., 2014; prasad et al., 2016). Robust techniques could resist to any attempt practiced to the transferred image (wang et al., 2017; Liu et al., 2019; Xu et al., 2019). Semi-fragile methods could resist minor alteration (Kumar et al., 2020). In fragile schemes, the encrusted bits are erased when the image face the minor operation (Tao et al., 2014).

After the analyzing and studying of several recent schemes (Singh et al., 2015; Falgun et al., 2017; Ustubioglu et al., 2017; Mousavi et al., 2017; Haghighi et al., 2020; Anand et al.,2020), we reveals that for some of this approaches the imperceptibility is poor, while the other doesn't employ any mechanism for image integrity checking or even protect the encrusted data. Therefore, medical image and watermark are transmitted over the untrusted network which could be easily altered by unauthorized part. To this end, it is crucial to keep image fidelity and ensure image integrity. In order to address the above challenges, a new framework based on multiple blind watermarking is proposed. It aims to make the eHealth application more secure from any kind of attacks, enhance imperceptibility for medical image and ensure their integrity. Our approach consists in combing Lifting Wavelet Transform (LWT), QR Decomposition and arnold chaotic map in transform domain for the first watermark, while for the second watermark is embedded in the spatial domain.

The paper remnant: section 2 Presents several medical image watermarking algorithms and recent existing frameworks. section 3 explains some basic foundations. Section 4 details the proposed algorithm framework; section 5 describes experimentation results and performance analysis. section 6 presents the conclusion and future works.

2. RELATED WORKS

Before the developing of the suggested method, several recent watermarking schemes was studied and analyzed (Singh et al., 2015; Falgun et al., 2017; Ustubioglu et al., 2017; Mousavi et al., 2017; Haghighi et al., 2020; Anand et al.,2020).

In (Singh et al. 2015) present a blind scheme using DWT, DCT, and SVD (Singular Values Decomposition), where the DWT is performed on the cover image, Then, the LL band and the cyphered watermark are devolved using DCT and SVD, the DCT-SVD of the watermark are encrusted on DCT-SVD of the LL band, a second watermark is encrusted at HH band. This approach offers good security, embedding capacity and robustness, However, it needs high execution time, and the imperceptibility is mediocre ($PSNR = 33dB$).

Authors in (Falgun et al. 2017) introduced a DWT and SVD based approach, the ROI is decomposed up using DWT, then SVD is practiced on LL band, and the watermark bits are encrusted on the left singular value matrix, This schema grant good resistance with some alteration kinds, However, the execution time needed is long, and the encrusted bits wasn't guaranteed using any mechanism.

In (Ustubioglu et al., 2017), discussed a non-blind watermarking schema that employ Modified Difference Expansion (MDE) and LSB techniques. The host image is segmented into two areas: center and border areas. The first one is used to insert the watermark bits using MDE and LSB techniques, while the second is engaged to encrust the location map and its hash value used as an embedding location. The proposed scheme offers good watermarked image quality and data payload, but it doesn't ensure the integrity, and the data is inserted in ROI (Region of interest) and RONI (Region Of Non Interest); consequently an unauthorized part could add his RONI to make the data extraction difficult or even impossible.

Mousavi *et al.* 2017 conferred a blind schema for medical image in the spatial domain. It consists of encoding the watermark bits referring to ROI pixel, then insert it on the cover image RONI using LSB technique. This method offers good robustness, security, and imperceptibility. However, it was approved only against few attacks, and it doesn't engage any mechanism for integrity checking.

Another work in (Haghighi et al., 2020) present an LWT, DCT, FNN (feed-forward neural network) and SURF (Speed Up Robust Features) based watermarking method. The watermark bits are embedded in DWT-DCT coefficient, while it extracted using FNN and SURF. This technique gives good imperceptibility, robustness with some attacks and alter detection and recovery. However, it requires high computational complexity for watermark encrusting and de-watermarking (exceed the 8 seconds for one image).

In (Anand et al.,2020), authors proposed a multiple schema using DWT-SVD, firstly, apply DWT succeeded by SVD on the host image, then embed the watermark image into the singular values, after that perform invers SVD, encode the watermark text using hamming code and embed it into HH subband. Finally, apply the DWT inverse to obtain the watermarked image, and this last is encrypted and compressed before transferred to the receiver side. This approach offers good resistance to attacks and security; however, it requires high processing time.

As we can note from the schemes cited, some of methods abuse the imperceptibility criteria, does not engage any technique for integrity checking or protect the encrusted watermark data or require high computational complexity. In this paper, conferred a secure and invisible Watermarking-based framework that ensure medical image integrity and gives robustness with some attacks.

3. REQUIRED METHODS

This section introduces the Lifting Wavelet Transform (LWT) and QR Decomposition techniques employed in embedding and extracting processes.

3.1 Lifting Wavelet Transform (LWT)

LWT is a release of the Discrete Wavelet Transform (Tao et al., 2014) in the second generation of wavelets in their fast release (Kabra et al., 2016). LWT is based on three fundamental steps: split, predict and update (Ansari et al., 2016). First, split the signal into even and odd parts, then predict the odd sequence using data correlation between odd and even, and for the last update even value. Figure 1 shows a lifting operation, where H is the high frequency band and L is the low frequency band.

Figure 1. LWT basic operations illustration

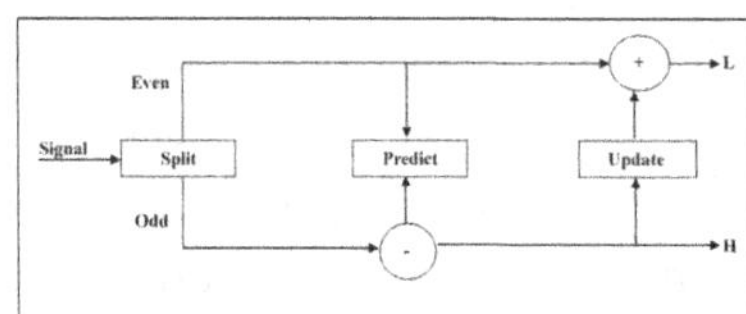

3.2 QR Decomposition

QR decomposition (Su et al., 2017) is a mathematical decomposition, where for a matrix A, the QR is applied as follows:

$$[U, V] = QR(A) \tag{1}$$

where U is an orthogonal matrix of size n×n, and V is a right triangular matrix of size n×n. The QR inverse is simply the multiplication between U and V:

$$QR^{-1} = U * V \tag{2}$$

Figure 2. Proposed framework illustration

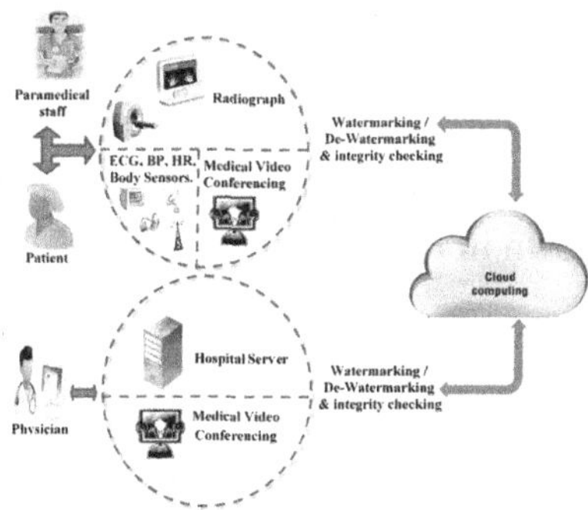

3.3 Arnold Chaotic Map

Arnold Chaotic Map is a technique for scrambling image pixels to produce a novel image with the same original image dimension using the following equation:

$$\begin{bmatrix} i' \\ j' \end{bmatrix} = \begin{bmatrix} 1 & 1 \\ 1 & 2 \end{bmatrix} \begin{bmatrix} i \\ j \end{bmatrix} Mod\left(S\right) \tag{3}$$

where *i, j, i, j* = {0…S-1} denote the anterior pixel and posterior pixel coordinates respectively, while S present the watermark size.

The converse process is retrieved as follow:

$$\begin{bmatrix} i \\ j \end{bmatrix} = \left(\begin{bmatrix} 2 & -1 \\ -1 & 1 \end{bmatrix} \begin{bmatrix} i' \\ j' \end{bmatrix} + \begin{bmatrix} S \\ S \end{bmatrix} \right) Mod\left(S\right) \tag{4}$$

4. PROPOSED FRAMEWORK

The proposed framework mainly shown in Figure 2. In this scheme, we give some principles that enhance the data security threat and make e-health data safer: in the first principle, we consider the medical image integrity from both patient and doctor, in the second principle we provide new multi-domains watermarking technique for medical data protection that includes high impressibility and good robustness. Consequently, the proposed framework preserves the medical image quality and offers high protection to the embedded watermark data. As follow outlining the two major's operations: watermark encrusting and de-watermarking respectively.

4.1 Watermark Encrusting

Watermark encrusting phase works on embedding two watermarks in different domain: frequency and spatial. The embedding process in the first step embeds secret data into a host image using LWT and QR decomposition. While for the second step it embedded in the spatial domain. The watermark encrusting steps are presented as follow and shown in Figure 3.

4.1.1 Preprocessing

Step 1: Select the ROI from the cover image for offering more security (Mousavi et al., 2014). It's noticed that the entire image could be used for watermark embedding process. However, using RONI for watermark data embedding could increase the security threats where an attacker could easily insert his RONI instead of the image RONI and consequently trick the receiver. In the opposite of using only the ROI as an embedding area.

Step 2: Apply Arnold chaotic map on ROI then decompose it up into n x n non-overlapping blocks.

4.1.2 Watermark Encrusting in the Transform Domain (Watermark 1)

Step 3: Select a block (B_i) and adopt LWT on Bi, then QR decomposition on LL sub-band to obtain the QR coefficient block (QB_i) of the orthogonal matrix (U) (see Equation 1).

Step 4. Compute the weight (λ) of QBi by:

$$\lambda = \left(QB_i\left(1,\frac{n}{2}\right) + QB_i\left(\frac{n}{2}+\frac{n}{2}\right)\right) - \left(QB_i\left(1,\frac{n}{2}\right) + QB_i\left(\frac{n}{2}+1\right)\right) \tag{5}$$

Step 5: Embed a watermark bit (W_i) by modifying QB_i according to λ and Wi values:

If W_i =1 && λ <0

Repeat

$$Min\left(QB_i\left(1,\frac{n}{2}\right), QB_i\left(\frac{n}{2},1\right)\right) + \varepsilon$$

Until λ >=0

Else

If W_i =0 && λ >=0

Repeat

$$Max\left(QB_i\left(1,\frac{n}{2}\right), QB_i\left(\frac{n}{2},1\right)\right) - \varepsilon$$

Until λ <0

Else Go to step 6.

where ε is the embedding strength which is a factor used to reinforce the robustness.

Step 6: We obtain the watermarked block by Appling QR^{-1} succeeded by LWT^{-1}.
Step 7: If not all the W_i are encrusted; back to step 3 with i+1, otherwise go to step 8.

An example of embedding two watermark bits in two blocks of size 4x4 (*intensities values are in uint16*) is illustrated in Figure 5.

4.1.3. Watermark Embedding in the Spatial Domain (Watermark 2)

Step 8: Select a Block (B_i) and a watermark bit (W_i).
Step 9: Compute the weight of B_i ($\lambda 1$) by:

$$\lambda 1=\sum_{i=1}^{n-1}\sum_{j=1}^{n-1}\left(B\left(i,j\right)\right)+\sum_{i=2}^{n}\sum_{j=n}^{n-i+2}\left(B\left(i,j\right)\right)-\sum_{i=1}^{n}\left(B\left(i,n-i+1\right)\right) \tag{6}$$

Step 10: Embed W_i into B_i according $\lambda 1$ value:

If $\lambda 1$ mod $2 \neq Wi$ Min=(B(i,n – i +1)+1) {i=1: n*}* (7)

Else
Past to step 11.
Step 11: If all the W_i are encrusted descrambling the watermarked ROI using Arnold chaotic map inverse using the same key used for scrambling and then combine ROI and Region of Non-Interest (RONI) to the watermarked image, otherwise back to step 8.

4.2 Watermark Extracting Process

The extraction process in the first step, comprise the bits de-watermarking from the transform domain (W_1), while in the second step from the spatial domain (W_2). After the bits de-watermarking extracting processes, gauge the differences between the two watermarks: W_1 and W_2 to decide the received image integrity.

4.2.1. Preprocessing

Step 12: Select the ROI from the whole image.
Step 13: Perform arnold chaotic map on ROI and decompose it up into n x n non-extending blocks.

4.2.2. Watermark Extracting From the Transform Domain (Watermark 1)

Step 14: Select a block (B_i) and practice LWT on it, adopt QR decomposition on LL sub-band to attain the QR coefficient block (QB_i) of the orthogonal matrix (U) (Equation 1).
Step 15: Compute the weight (λ) of QBi by Equation 5.

Step 16: Extract a watermark bit (W_i) from QB_i according to λ value:

$$\begin{cases} W_i = 0; if\ \lambda < 0 \\ W_i = 1; else \end{cases} \tag{8}$$

Step 17: If all the W_i are de-watermarked go to step 18. Otherwise back to step 14 with i+1.

4.2.3. Watermark Extracting the Spatial Domain (Watermark 2)

Step 18: Select a Block (B_i) and a watermark bit (W_i).
Step 19: Compute the weight of B_i ($\lambda 1$) by Equation 6.
Step 20. Extract W_i from B_i according $\lambda 1$ value:

$$W_i = \lambda 1 \text{ Mod} 2 \tag{9}$$

Step 21: If all the W_i are de-watermarked compute the Mismatching Rate (MR) between both extracted watermarks watermark1 (W1) and watermark2 (W2) using the following equation to determine whether the watermarked image is altered or not. Else, back to Step 14 where W_n and W_m are the watermarks highs and widths respectively, if the MR exceeds certain threshold T, the watermarked image is altered by an unauthorized person (Figure 4).

5. EXPERIMENTS AND EVALUATIONS

To assess the achievement of the suggested scheme, various assays are executed on MATLAB under Windows using a workstation Intel® Core i5-560 2.67 GHz processor with 4 GB of RAM. Grayscale images of size *256×256* in DICOM Format (Dicom.nema.org, 2019) and a logo of size 16 × 16 taken as watermark are utilized in experimentations. Figure 6 display a number of images used; which are from (Deanvaughan.org, 2019; Dicom.nema.org, 2019), and the watermark logo.

Experiments are performed to measure the imperceptibility, robustness, and integrity checking. Several experiments are presented in the next sections. In all experiments, we take a typical value of the embedding strength ξ =5 and a block size n=4.

5.1 Imperceptibility Measurement

The imperceptibility is how the original image resemble to the watermarked one. Therefore, we measure the similarity of the proposed method using PSNR (Agrawal et al., 2019), which is calculated as follow:

$$PSNR(dB) = 10\log_{10}\left(\frac{255^2}{MSE}\right) \tag{11}$$

Figure 3. The detailed embedding process

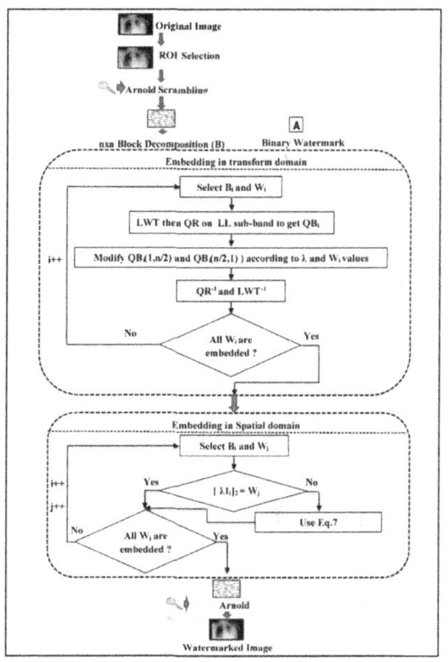

and MSE is defined as follows:

$$MSE = \frac{1}{H_i \cdot W_i} \sum_{n=1}^{H_i} \sum_{m=1}^{W_i} \left(OI\left(n, m\right) - WI\left(n, m\right) \right) \tag{12}$$

Figure 4. The detailed extracting process

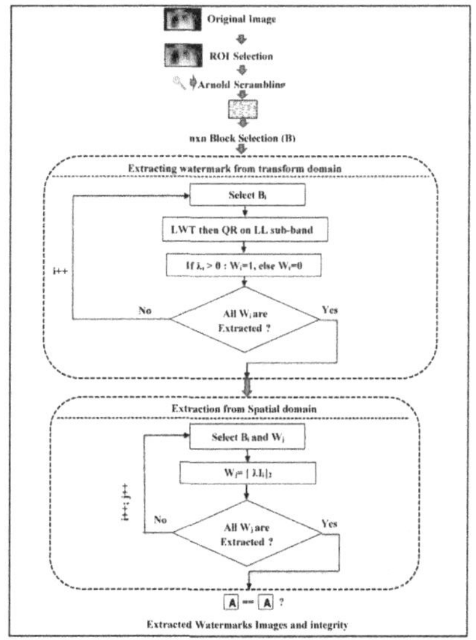

Figure 5. Example of bits embedding

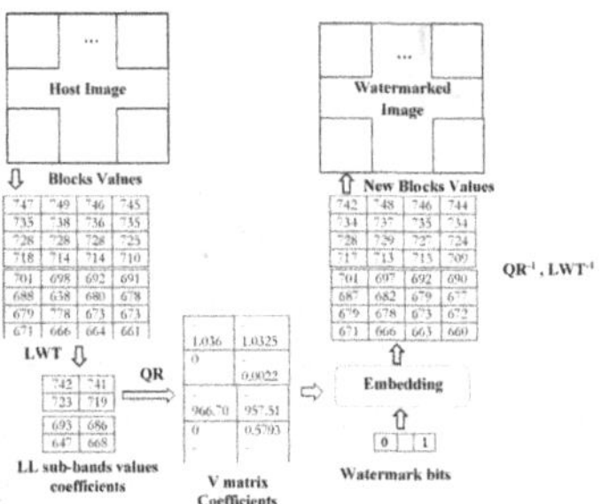

Figure 6. Medical images samples and watermark

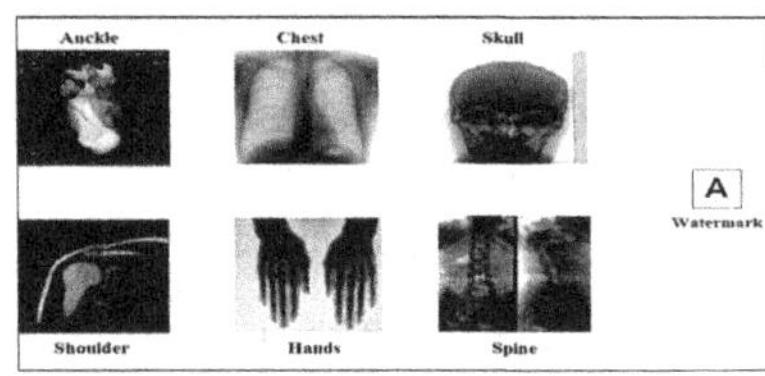

where H_i and W_i are the image height and width respectively, OI and WI are the original and the watermarked images.

The different medical images PSNR (dB) rates are illustrated in Table 1, where we can see that the suggested scheme preserves the medical image aspect even with two embedding watermarks. This result is confirmed by slight modification in the LL sub-bands QR coefficients for the transform domain or in the pixel intensities for the spatial domain which is consists of embedding of a watermark bit.

Table 1. Imperceptibility numeric results (dB)

Images	PSNR(dB)
Ankle	49.71
Chest	52.86
Skull	45.89
Shoulder	44.20
Hands	47.35
Spine	45.27

5.2 Robustness Analysis

The robustness is the hardness of the encrusted data to resist when facing different attempts applied on the watermarked image. In the experimentation, we use the Normalized Correlation (NC) (Mansoori et al., 2016) to measure the robustness of the watermark 1 (the watermark 2 is fragile). Table 2 shows the *NC* rate undermost different attacks.

Table 2. Robustness measurement of the first watermark

Attacks	Ankle	Chest	Skull	Shoulder	Hands	Spine
salt & pepper noise V=0.001	0.855	0.967	0.851	0.855	0.834	0.869
salt & pepper noise V=0.01	0.878	0.971	0.955	0.879	0.978	0.865
White *noise* V=0.0001	0.700	0.78	0.701	0.670	0.655	0.618
speckle noise V=0.0001	0.864	0.800	0.690	0.864	0.801	0.886
DICOM JPEG Lossless	0.850	0.981	0.855	0.853	0.835	0.874
DICOM JPEG Lossy QF=50	0.854	0.981	0.854	0.850	0.832	0.871
DICOM RLE	0.851	0.984	0.855	0.853	0.835	0.874
DICOM JPEG 2000 Lossless	0.854	0.980	0.850	0.850	0.835	0.874
DICOM JPEG 2000 Lossy QF=50	0.846	0.967	0.813	0.815	0.830	0.841
Rotation 0.1°	0.745	0.790	0.695	0.693	0.648	0.685
gamma correction γ=0.95	0.853	0.976	0.857	0.856	0.834	0.876
Translation (1)	0.693	0.742	0.643	0.660	0.640	0.618
Cropping 2%	0.826	0.981	0.806	0.810	0.801	0.804

It is evident that the suggested schema achieves high toughness against attacks since the good, obtained NC rate of the de-watermarked data (watermark 1). Considering, that the watermark is encrusted easily in the orthogonal matrix resulted by applying QR decomposition on the LL sub-bands of LWT.

5.3 Integrity Checking

Integrity is an important factor in the eHealth to secure the access of the applications from the malicious attacks. The integrity checking mechanism could offers to the receiver the possibility to know if the watermarked image was manipulated during their transmission. The Mismatching Rate (MR) generated in the extraction process is compared to a mismatch *Threshold* (T) to provide necessarily the accurate integrity. If MR value overtake the mismatch threshold then the watermarked image is considered as tampered. Table 3 shows the MR values with the desired minor alterations. The slightest alteration of the watermarked images is still detectable with MR values less than 1 and is in opposite of the attacked watermarked images. This improves the good integrity of the proposed technique for alter image detection precision.

5.4 Data Security

The security of the proposed scheme depends on the pixel scrambling operations in the embedding and extracting phases. In addition, each part attempt to de-watermark the encrusted data must know the scrambling key employed in the encrusting process; otherwise, he obtains a wrong watermark data. The key size of the proposed scheme is adequate to confront brute-force attacks. In other words, if an attacker tries to find out the scrambling key used for data encrusted; he needs to perform several operations of (Image High x Image Width). To do this a machine necessitates at least one minute for embedding/extracting operation based on multiple watermarking-based experimentations. Therefore, the attacker

Table 3. Integrity checking using MR values

Alter Types	Ankle	Chest	Skull	Shoulder	Hands	Spine
Without alteration	0.48	0.524	0.63	0.44	0.64	0.42
Salt & pepper noise V=0.0001	1.36	3.00	3.45	1.37	1.52	1.25
White noise V=0.0001	5.03	4.64	5.01	5.03	4.85	5.11
Speckle noise V=0.0001	4.60	4.62	5.03	4.61	4.92	5.42
DICOM JPEG Lossy QF=99	1.28	1.56	1.29	1.28	1.40	1.09
DICOM JPEG 2000 Lossy QF=99	1.81	1.87	1.82	1.83	2.03	2.38
Cropping 1%	3.09	2.54	3.04	3.09	3.05	3.03
Rotation 0.1°	5.31	5.62	5.31	5.31	5.58	4.88
Gamma correction γ=0.95	5.85	4.21	4.33	4.77	5.42	4.57
Scaling 1%	5.81	4.96	5.80	5.60	5.89	5.44

needs years to find out the right scrambling key used with a medical image of size (256x256). To this end, we could conclude that the suggested scheme grants high security for the encrusted data.

5.5 Performances Comparison

To confirm the effectiveness and practicability of the suggested approach, we correlate the obtained results using our approach with some recent schemes. Table 4 exhibit a comparison of the imperceptibility results between the proposed method and related works described in (Singh et al., 2015; Falgun et al., 2017; Ustubioglu et al., 2017; Mousavi et al., 2017; Haghighi et al., 2020; Anand et al., 2020) undermost PSNR (dB).

Table 4. Imperceptibility comparison

Method	(Singh et al., 2015)	(Falgun et al., 2017)	(Ustubioglu et al., 2017)	(Mousavi et al., 2017)	(haghighi et al., 2020)	(Anand et al.,2020)	Proposed method
PSNR (dB)	36.4	44	38	43.2	44	34.04 **48.5**	

Table 5 demonstrate robustness comparison with related works described in (Singh et al., 2015; Falgun et al., 2017; Ustubioglu et al., 2017; Mousavi et al., 2017; Haghighi et al., 2020; Anand et al., 2020) undermost NC metric.

It is undeniable that scheme accord more robustness than the other methods, because the watermark data are embedded in robust place: LWT-QR coefficients of scrambled pixel, this make the embedded data more robust to some *geometric* and *signal processing* attacks.

Table 6 present advantages and drawbacks between the suggested scheme and related works described in (Singh et al., 2015; Falgun et al., 2017; Ustubioglu et al., 2017; Mousavi et al., 2017; Haghighi et al., 2020; Anand et al.,2020).

Table 5. Robustness comparison using NC

Attacks	(Singh et al., 2015)	(Falgun et al., 2017)	(Ustubioglu et al., 2017)	(Mousavi et al., 2017)	(Haghighi et al., 2020)	(Anand et al.,2020)	Proposed method
***salt & peper noise* (V=0.01)**	0.96	**0.99**	-	-	0.83	0.9687	0.96
rotation 1°	0.75	-	-	-	-	0.9221	**0.9673**
cropping	**0.98**	0.82	-	-	0.75	0.5082	0.91
***jpeg compression* Q=50**	0.75	0.91	-	-	0.71	0.9510	**0.97**

Table 6. Comparison results using many criteria

Works	Purpose	Security Degree	Extraction	General Drawbacks
(Singh et al., 2015)	Medical data protection	Good	Blind	Low imperceptibility and require high processing time
(Falgun et al., 2017)	Medical data protection	Mediocre	Blind	require high processing time
(Ustubioglu et al., 2017)	Tamper Localization	Mediocre	Non-Blind	Some data are embedded in RONI: an attacker could easily put his own RONI
(Mousavi et al., 2017)	Medical data protection	Mediocre	Blind	Some important data are embedded in RONI and an attacker could easily put his own RONI
(Haghigh et al; 2020)	Tamper detection and localization	Good	Semi-blind	Require high computational complexity
(Anand et al.,2020)	Medical data protection	Good	Non-Blind	require high processing time
Proposed method	Medical data protection + alter detection	Good	Blind	require high processing time

As this paper focus on medical image security and privacy, we have evaluated security degree which measured the strangeness of the protection mechanism. A high-security degree means more protection of embedded data. For instance, in the proposed scheme, the embedding region is scrambled using Arnold Chaotic Map, and the watermark extraction process necessitates the presence of the key used in the embedding phase. The same thing in (Singh et al. 2015) and (Anand et al., 2020) that used linear encryption and hamming code respectively for protecting the watermark. In the works, (Falgun et al., 2017), (Ustubioglu et al., 2017) and (Mousavi et al., 2017), authors do not use security technique for the watermark data protection. As we can see from Tables 4, 5 and 6 that the suggested technique is surpass other recent methods available in literature. The proposed watermarking scheme is imperceptible, Robust, Secure and Blind this make it effective to protect medical data and detect the medical image Alteration.

6. CONCLUSION

The e-Health applications have a vital role to make healthcare easier. However, it has many security threats that make them unsecure to use. There are many existing frameworks target different security techniques for protecting the eHealth application's data from any kind of attacks. Thus, we suggested a secure framework depend on a new multiple blind watermarking scheme for medical image alter detection. The prime idea is to embed a watermark in the transform domain using LWT and QR decomposition; after scrambling the embedding area using Arnold chaotic map, and then encrust it a second time in the spatial domain using new embedding and extracting processes. The extraction process was achieved only with the presence of the key used in embedding, without the need of the original image or watermark one. Finally, the tow watermarks extracted are compared to decide if the watermarked medical image is tampered or not. Experimentation results proved the good conducts of the suggested scheme in terms of imperceptibility, robustness and alter detection precision. A future enhancement to this work is to extend the proposed method to 3D medical image watermarking.

REFERENCES

Agarwal, N., Singh, A. K., & Singh, P. K. (2019). Survey of robust and imperceptible watermarking. *Multimedia Tools and Applications*, 1–31. doi:10.100711042-018-7128-5

Anand, A., & Singh, K. (2020). An improved DWT-SVD domain watermarking for medical information security. *Computer Communications*, 72–80. doi:10.1016/j.comcom.2020.01.038

Ansari, I. A., Pant, M., & Ahn, C. W. (2016). Robust and false positive free watermarking in IWT domain using SVD and ABC. *Engineering Applications of Artificial Intelligence*, *49*, 114–125. doi:10.1016/j.engappai.2015.12.004

Das, C., Panigrahi, S., Sharma, V.K., & Mahapatra, K.K. (2013). A novel blind robust image watermarking in DCT domain using inter-block coefficient correlation. *International Journal of Electronics and Communications (AEÜ),* 1-10. DOI: . doi:10.1016/j.aeue.2013.08.018

Deanvaughan.org. (2019a). *DICOM Sample Images – Dean Vaughan*. Available at: https://deanvaughan.org/wordpress/2013/07/dicom-sample-images/

Dicom.nema.org. (2019b). *DICOM*. Available at: http://dicom.nema.org.

Gomathikrishnan, M., & Tyagi, A. (2011). HORNS-A Homomorphic Encryption Scheme for Cloud Computing using Residue Number System. *IEEE Transactions on Parallel and Distributed Systems*, *23*(6), 995–1003. doi:10.1109/CISS.2011.5766176

Haghighi, B. B., Taherinia, H. H., & Monsefi, R. (2020). An Effective Semi-fragile Watermarking Method for Image Authentication Based on Lifting Wavelet Transform and Feed-Forward Neural Network. *Cognitive Computation*, 1–28. doi:10.100712559-019-09700-9

Kabra, R. G., & Agrawal, S. S. (2016). Robust Embedding of Image Watermark using LWT and SVD. *International Conference on Communication and Signal Processing*, 1968-1972. DOI: 10.1109/ICCSP.2016.7754516

Kamran, K. A., & Malik, S. (2014). A high capacity reversible watermarking approach for authenticating images. Exploiting down-sampling, histogram processing, and block selection. *Information Sciences*, *256*, 162–183. doi:10.1016/j.ins.2013.07.035

Kazemi, M.F., Pourmina, M.A., & Mazinan, A.H. (2020). Analysis of watermarking framework for color image through a neural network-based approach. *Complex & Intelligent Systems*, 213–220. DOI: doi:10.1007/s40747-020-00129-4

Kumar, S., Singh, B.K., & Yadav, M. (2020). A Recent Survey on Multimedia and Database Watermarking. *Multimedia Tools and Applications*. doi: . doi:10.1007/s11042-020-08881-y

Liu, Y., Zhang, Y., Ling, J., & Liu, Z. (2018). Secure and fine-grained access control on e-healthcare records in mobile cloud computing. *Future Generation Computer Systems*, 1–32. doi:10.1016/j.future.2016.12.027

Liu, J., Huang, J., Luo, Y., Cao, L., Yang, S., Wei, D., Zhou, R. (2019). An Optimized Image Watermarking Method Based on HD and SVD in DWT Domain. *IEEE Access*, 80849- 80860. doi: . doi:10.1109/ACCESS.2019.2915596

Mansoori, E., & Soltani, S. (2016). a new semi-blind watermarking algorithm using ordered Hadamard transform. *The Imaging Science Journal, 64*(4), 204-214.

Mousavi, S., Naghsh, A., & Abu-Bakar, S. (2014). Watermarking Techniques used in Medical Images: A Survey. *Journal of Digital Imaging*, *27*(6), 714–729. PMID:24871349

Mousavi, S.M., Naghsh, A., Manaf, A., & Abu-Bakar, S. (2017). A robust medical image watermarking against salt and pepper noise for brain MRI images. *Multimedia Tools and Applications, 76*, 10313–10342. DOI: . doi:10.1007/s11042-016-3622-9

Prasad, K. L., Rao, T. M., & Kannan, V. (2016). A Novel and Hybrid Secure Digital Image Watermarking Framework Through sc-LWT-SVD. *Indian Journal of Science and Technology*, *9*(23), 1–10.

Singh, A., Dave, M., & Mohan, A. (2015). Hybrid technique for robust and imperceptible multiple watermarking using medical images. *Multimedia Tools and Applications*, *75*(14), 8381–8401. doi:10.100711042-015-2754-7

Su, Q., Wang, G., Zhang, X. F., & Chen, G. L. V. B. (2017). An improved color image watermarking algorithm based on QR decomposition. *Multimedia Tools and Applications*, *76*, 707–729. doi:10.100711042-015-3071-x

Tao, H., Chongmin, L., Zain, J. M., & Abdalla, A. N. (2014). Robust Image Watermarking Theories and Techniques: A Review. *Journal of Applied Research and Technology*, *12*(1), 122–138. doi:10.1016/S1665-6423(14)71612-8

Thakkar, N. F., Srivastava, V. K. (2017). A blind medical image watermarking: DWT-SVD based robust and secure approach for telemedicine applications. *Multimedia Tools and Applications, 76*, 3669–3697. DOI: doi:10.1007/s11042-016-3928-7

Ustubioglu, A., & Ulutas, G. (2017). A New Medical Image Watermarking Technique with Finer Tamper Localization. *Journal of Digit Imaging*, *30*, 665–680. doi:10.100710278-017-9960-y PMID:28243865

Wang, C., Wang, X., Zhang, C., & Xia, Z. (2017). Geometric correction based color image watermarking using fuzzy least squares support vector machine and Bessel K form distribution. *Signal Processing*, *134*, 197–208. doi:10.1016/j.sigpro.2016.12.010

Xu, C., Sun, J., & Wang, C. (2019). A novel image encryption algorithm based on bit-plane matrix rotation and hyper chaotic systems. *Multimedia Tools and Applications*, 1–22. doi:10.100711042-019-08273-x

This research was previously published in the International Journal of Computer Vision and Image Processing (IJCVIP), 11(1); pages 1-16, copyright year 2021 by IGI Publishing (an imprint of IGI Global).

Chapter 26
Implementation of a Reversible Watermarking Technique for Medical Images

Ranit Karmakar
Tata Consultancy Services, India

Abhishek Basu
RCC Institute of Information Technology, India

ABSTRACT

Electronic health records (EHR) contain patients' medical as well as personal details. With the increased use of digital media, these data are stored and transferred through the electronic media all over the world. This makes it vulnerable to unauthorized people. Digital image watermarking can be a useful process of protecting these data from attacker but causes severe and unrecoverable damage to cover media. In the case of highly sensitive images like medical images, this might creates a problem during further diagnosis. In this chapter, a reversible data hiding algorithm is proposed which also is capable of holding a large chunk of data without affecting the cover media. The main cover image is first reconstructed and hidden behind a bigger media and then the extra pixels are used to hide encrypted forms of EHR data along with an authentication signature. As EHR data and the digital signature is passed through various encryption stages while encoding, it is made more secure. The algorithm is developed on the spatial domain adding some cautious measures which made it fragile as well.

INTRODUCTION

The history of imaging dates back in 1826 when a Frenchman Joseph Nicéphore Niépce was able to produce the first picture in the human history, a view through his window. Using the lithographic technique and 8 hours exposure to light, it was possible to capture the first image. Later that century a lot of work has been done for the improvement but it wasn't until late twentieth century when digital imaging was developed. This gave a cheaper and easier solution to the old film-based methods used in photography. In

DOI: 10.4018/978-1-6684-6311-6.ch026

the 1960s, the digital image processing has become a large area of interest in different research facilities around the globe, especially for the applications in satellite imagery, wire-photo standards conversion, medical imaging, videophone, character recognition, and photograph enhancement. However, the cost of processing was fairly high because of low-quality computer equipment available in that era. The scenario soon started changing with the advancement in computer science and in the 2000s, digital images and signal processing have become the most common form of image processing for different applications.

The internet boom of the late 90s and early 2000 allowed this digital media to float all around the globe in real-time. With improvements in technology and digital devices, the amount of digital data started increasing exponentially. A recent paper by IDC, Data Age 2025, predicts that by the year 2025, our world will have 163 ZB (Zetta Byte) of data, almost 10 times than what we have today. But most alarmingly, it suggests that 90% of this data will require some form of security and only about half of this will have it. So, security has become a big concern. For the purpose of securing digital images from different attacks and data theft, a new technique was introduced, named Digital Watermarking. The term digital watermarking was first coined by Andrew Tirkel and Charles Osborne in December 1992 and soon after in 1993 was demonstrated in their paper Electronic Water Mark. Although, watermarking content for IP protection is in use from 13th century, its application in digital media is relatively recent.

- **Digital Watermarking Life-Cycle:** The watermarking of a digital signal is distributed in three steps, Embedding, Attacking and Detecting. In the embedding stage, the watermark signal is embedded under the cover signal or host signal. After transmitting this signal, it may gone through some attacks such as compression, cropping, addition of noise etc. This is known as the attack stage. In the last stage, the watermark signal is tried to be recovered. If the recovered signal is unaltered, it proves that the host signal is not affected anyway. The digital watermarking can be classified in the following ways:

    - **Robustness:** A watermarking algorithm can be called as robust if it can withheld different attacks and transformations. Whereas a fragile watermarking algorithm is easily destroyed with slight modification on the mail signal.
    - **Perceptibility:** Perceptibility deals with the understanding of the signal. If the signal is perceptually indistinguishable even after applying the watermark, it is called perceptible.
    - **Capacity:** Differentiated in two different methods zero-bit and multiple-bit, as the name suggests, capacity determines the size of watermark signal that can be hidden under the host or cover signal.

One of the most widely used application of digital signal processing is on medical images. Medical images contain very sensitive data and can be easily manipulated. Without proper protection, these images are highly vulnerable. The information infrastructure system of modern health care is formed by HIS (Hospital Information System), and its special cases of RIS (Radiology Information System), PACS (Picture Archiving and Communication System). These digitization and recent developments in information and communication technology provide in fact new ways to store, access and distribute medical data. It introduces new practices for the profession, as well as the patient themselves by accessing to their own medical files. Over many advantages these techniques are vulnerable in protecting the Electronic Health Records (EHR), and highly personal documents shared in the open network. The systematized collection of patient and population electronically-stored health information in a digital format is known as Electronic Health Record (EHR), or Electronic Medical Record (EMR). Because of being digital, these information can be shared across different health care settings through network-connected, enterprise-wide information systems or other information networks and exchanges easily. Generally these EHR data includes personal information of the patient's such as demographics, medical history, medication and allergies, immunization status, laboratory test results, radiology images, vital signs, personal statistics like age and weight, and billing information of the patent. A recent study, Medical Identity Theft in Healthcare, shows alarming facts about it as well. So protecting this data from unauthorized access is essential.

If we look closely, we can find that there are two problems that need to be addressed. One, the vulnerability of highly sensitive medical images which can be easily twitched a little to probably misguide the treatment, and two, classified information of the patients that can be stolen. As a solution we can incorporate old watermarking technique to conquer the problems. According to domain based classification, watermarking can be of two types; Spatial Domain and Frequency Domain. Based on human perception it can have Visible and Invisible watermarking where invisible watermarking can again be classified as Robust and Fragile. For the medical images and EHR data to be protected, we require a technique that would both be fragile and robust. This may sound a little contradictory, but we would require a technique that would be fragile enough to destroy the patient's personal information if it faces even a little distortion. On the other hand, it needs to be robust enough to protect the main image after some kind of attack. In the paper "Watermarking Medical Images with Patient Information", A. Deepthi and U.C. Niranjan showed how LSB replacement technique in the spatial domain can be a useful method to find a feasible solution. But the problem with this method was, it made permanent distortion on the cover image. For highly sensitive medical images, this can cause problems. Later in many different research papers scientists have tried to come up with different solutions such as finding the ROI, but the cover image always faced some unrecoverable distortion as the image pixels were modified to hide data. As most cases of data hiding, the cover media experiences some distortion due to hidden data and the exact cover image can never be recovered back to its original form even after extracting out the hidden information from it. In applications like medical diagnosis and law enforcement, it is essential to revert back the hidden media from the original cover media for some legal considerations. On the other hand in applications like remote sensing and high-energy particle physical experimental investigation, the original cover media should be recovered as those contain high-precision data. These type of hiding techniques are famously referred as reversible, invertible, lossless, or distortion-free data hiding techniques. So in reversible data hiding technique the cover media can exactly be recovered even after hiding some important information behind it. But generally lossless data hiding techniques have limitations over the amount of data hidden.

So in this paper we have proposed a data hiding technique specially designed for the highly sensitive images like medical images and to the hide the vulnerable EHR data from attack. First the main image is interpolated to a larger image. The larger image contained image pixels from main image as well as some extra pixels on which the classified data can be hidden. The interpolated image looks almost similar to the main image and can hardly be identified as different by any human being. This made the technique even secure. The text based EHR data is first encrypted with a private key which is only known to the encryption and decryption blocks. Every text bit is then again encoded using UTF-8 standard and divided into 4-bit long blocks. Each 4-bit block replaces the last 4-bits of the extra pixels of the interpolated image. Near the ROI region, the extra pixels are used to hide one doctor's signature. Any try to twitch any pixel near the ROI area will cause a change in the signature image as well. From extracted image we can then find out what type of changes made, if any, and also can predict a form of reverted image.

The algorithm is tested with 40 medical images but it can have a wider scope of implementation. From the results, the algorithm is found to be highly effective and capable of detecting even small attacks. During testing we found that the every time the EHR data is destroyed after any attack and the doctor's signature shows significant proof of that. But even after that, the main cover image can be restored to a certain level and can be used for further evaluation. As the algorithm combines images and data together, it also saves storage space as two different files don't need to be stored separately.

LITERARY SURVEY

According to the data published in http://www.internetlivestats.com/internet-users/, around 40% of the world's population has internet connection now which is about 3.5 billion and still counting. About 20 years back in 1995 it was less than 1%. But in 2005 it reached its first billion, in 2010 the second billion and in 2014 the third billion. This data clearly shows the rapid spread of internet and its high penetration rates even in underdeveloped parts of the world. With the digital revolution and the rapid development in internetwork technology, the health care systems also evolved from its old manual based type to the electronic-based and fully automated type. It led to a new area of technology named telemedicine. In their paper Technology Meets Healthcare: Distance Learning and Telehealth (2001), White LAE, Krousel-Wood MA, Mather F., defined telemedicine as the use of electronic information and communication technologies to provide healthcare to patients who are separated by distance. On a wide geographical scale, this technology is possessing an important role in providing medical sector with the capability of connecting all participants in the healthcare process as well as this information is used for medical related research. However, the paper Learning through telemedicine networks (2003) talks when the data is digitally archived and transferred through any medium of communication, there is one important aspect and that is the security and protection of the EHR. In another paper, Medical Identity Theft (2012), W. Walters, and A. Betz, shows another example of the critical information security crimes is medical identity theft (MIDT).

M. Terry in the paper Medical identity theft and telemedicine security talks about the same. MIDT gets attention from a large number of hackers because this contains the personal and financial information of the patient. Another problem added to it is the alteration of the medical data. If the data is open to the hacker he may change the information of medication, patient's current status and other sensitive details which causes misleading in the further medical diagnostics, and consequently, jeopardizing the patient's life. A report shows that in 2006 approximately 18,000 cases of MIDT reported to Federal Trade Commission (FTC). In 2012, a study conducted at Ponemon Institute shows about 1.5 million victims of MIDT only in America with an estimated total cost of $28.6 billion or approximately $20,000 per victim. This has led an increased awareness over the MIDT protection. In 2014, HHS Budget Makes Smart Investments, Protects the Health and Safety America's Families budget report allocates $80 million for work to spread the adoption and use of health information technology by US govt. is a big proof of this. Digital watermarking can play an important role in protecting this data while transmitting it safely as well as it can play important role in authentication over many other available methods.

L. Xuanwen et al in his paper A lossless data embedding scheme for medical images in application of e-diagnosis, in 2003 showed a lossless data embedding scheme is proposed for medical images where each binary bit- plane is compressed with roughly and later data is embedded to save space. The digital information is integrated prior to embedding process on the medical images. While recovering the data, the first the compressed image is extracted and then decompressed. In the mentioned process, when the data is embedded in the higher bit-plane level, the distortion to the medical image becomes outsized. The data embedding in special domain results less robustness which is another limitation.

In Tamper detection and recovery for medical images using near-lossless information hiding technique (2008), J H K Wu et al. proposed two methods. The first method is based on modulo 256, where initially the medical image was divided into several chunks and each chunk is embedded with the watermarks, which are the combination of an authentication message which is the hash value of the chunk, and the recovery information of other chunk. But as these chunks are too small and extremely compressed, in second method discrete cosine transform (DCT) was introduced with the idea of ROI. From the non-tampered chunks exactly the same image can be obtained but where the chunks are tampered, we can only get an approximately same image. As here only authentication and recovery data are embedded, this method shows a limitation on the watermark hiding capacity. The scheme is non-reversible as well because of the prEHRocessing involved.

In Data hiding scheme for medical images a search based technique was introduced by R. Rodriguez-Colin, C. Feregrino-Urabe, B. G. Trinidiad, where the search started from the center of the image and depending upon the bit to be embedded, the luminance is either increased or decreased. When the embedding bit is 1, the luminance is was changed by adding the grayscale mean value of the block with luminance of block and when it is 0, the luminance is was changed by subtracting the grayscale. The similar search method was implemented while decoding the bits. As some bits are lost in the extraction process, the extracted data is unreadable. Another limitation of this process is, ROI is not implemented which is a big concern in telemedicine.

F. Rahimi and R. Hossein in A dual adaptive watermarking scheme in contourlet domain for DICOM images suggested a blind watermarking technique with an intention of enhancing robustness, confidentiality and authentication. In the ROI the EHR information is hidden which gave them ability to enhance authentication and confidentiality. And a coded digital signature of the physician is hidden in the RONI for the purpose of origin detection. This technique has a high hiding capacity with confidentiality and authentication. However, due to the fact that watermark bit were not scattered in the embedded region, the hidden watermark is not safe and it receive very low protection against various attack which lead to the non-robustness of the technique.

Using the characteristics of ultrasound medical images a 4-rectangle organized as a pyramid was used to locate region ROI in Reversible medical image watermarking for tamper detection and recovery. The rest of the region is assumed to be RONI. Some ROI block holds the watermark bits while the RONI holds the actual LSB values of the ROI for restoration. For this purpose a mapping sequence was used. This technique is fragile and even a small attack on the RONI can destroy the whole image from recovery, however the main limitation is it only can be applied on the ultrasound medical images.

In a paper by A. Deepthi, U.C. Niranjan in Watermarking Medical Images with Patient Information, two data files are used to implement a digital watermarking process into the greyscale level of a medical image using the LSB replacement scheme. The two data files used while watermarking are one test document and an ECG graph. Though this is a realistic model of embedding watermark in medical images, it has limitations because of the permanent distortion on the image. This distortion causes some permanent loss of data. Because of this loss the recovered image can never be used further in telemedicine for diagnosing patient.

In a recent paper on reversible data hiding technique for medical images, A New Reversible and high capacity data hiding technique for E-healthcare applications, authors have introduced interpolation method and then embedded EHR data using LSB replacement technique. Using parity checksum method, the authors have set last two digits of the image pixel to zero. As the main image pixels are still in use and changed some distortions occur on the main image which might be crucial for high sensitive medical images. Also, the EHR data is stored as jpeg pixels which make them less fragile. Even after the attack, in some cases the patient's information is clearly understandable which is not expected.

In the paper A fair benchmark for image watermarking systems, Martin K., and Fabien P. have presented an evaluation procedure of image watermarking systems. On robust digital watermarking systems, a number of papers have been presented, but the criteria has never been discussed clearly. In this paper they tried to address this problem by suggesting a useful benchmark. In another the paper A Benchmark for Medical Image Watermarking, authors, Navas K. A, Sasikumar M and Sreevidya S, have proposed a benchmark for for the evaluation of watermarking techniques used for embedding EHR data on medical images. With a number of medical images available in different modalities and different sizes, the paper tries to talk about the Bounds of capacity, imperceptibility and robustness. Perceptual model based data embedding in medical images, by S. Dandapat, Opas Chutatape and S. M. Krishnan, proposes a perceptual model based technique for embedding patient information in a medical image. The suggested that the distortions in the diagnostic information-content arised due to data embedding can be controlled using a Perceptual Quality Measure (PQM).

In many a different papers different embedding techniques for medical images have been discussed. In A lossless data embedding scheme for medical images in application of e-diagnosis, authors discuss about the data embedding technique but the scheme was still unable to produce a distortionless system. The paper A survey on watermarking application scenarios and related attacks focuses on different applications of digital image watermarking.

SYSTEM IMPLEMENTATION

Watermarking is a very useful technique in hiding EHR data behind a medical image. Among the various methods of watermarking, the hiding of encrypted ERP data using the LSB replacement is very useful. But LSB replacement always causes some irrecoverable damage on the cover media and as medical images are very sensitive this can hamper the quality of image causing loss of data permanently. To avoid this problem we have applied a method which increases the data hiding capacity as well as this method is totally lossless. So even after embedding EHR data behind the cover image the exact main image can be extracted for further use.

As the Fig. 1 suggests, the main image is first interpolated into a bigger image where the main image pixels are distributed through the image. Then on the extra pixels the data is hidden by using LSB replacement technique. We could have used all the pixels for data hiding but that could have resulted in permanent destruction of the main image. The steps are as follow.

1. Pre-Processing

Step 1: First the cover image, say I, of size M x N is taken. If the image is an RGB image, it is converted to a grayscale image of same size. Let the grayscale image be I_{gr}.

Figure 1. Encoding Block

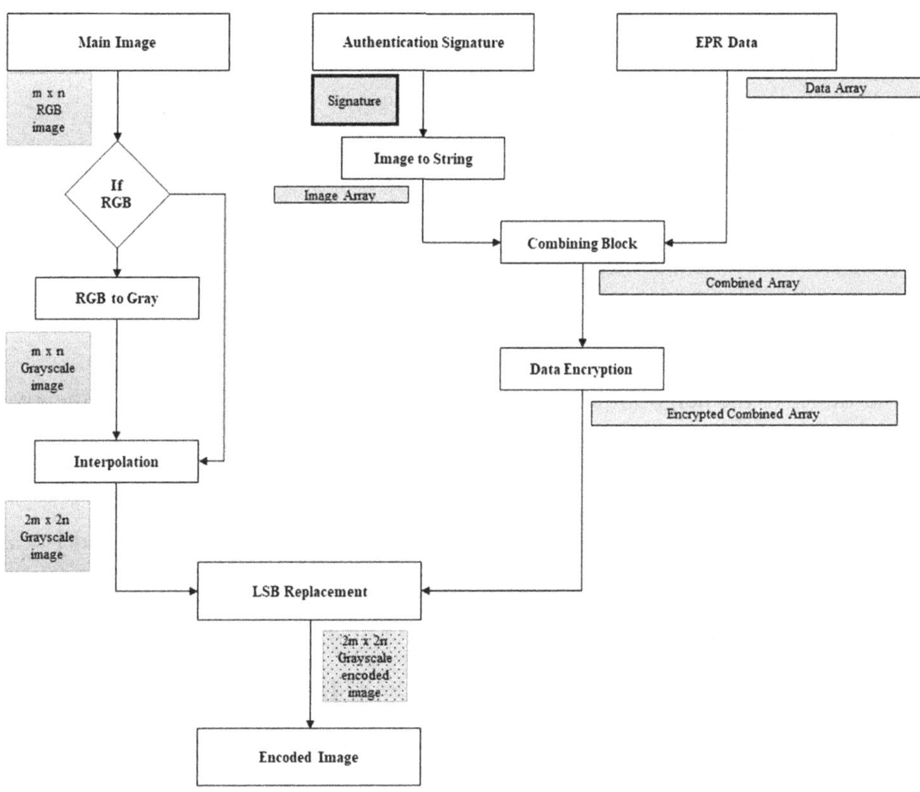

$$I = \begin{bmatrix} i_r(m,n) \\ i_g(m,n) \\ i_b(m,n) \end{bmatrix} | 0 \le m \le M, 0 \le n \le N, i_r(m,n) \in [0,255],$$

$$i_g(m,n) \in [0,255], i_b(m,n) \in [0,255]$$

$$I_{gr} = i_{gr}(m,n) \,|\, 0 \le m \le M, 0 \le n \le N, i_{gr}(m,n) \in [0,255]$$

Step 2: Then the grayscale cover image is interpolated into a bigger image of dimension 2M x 2N. Let the image be I_n.

$$I_n = i_n(m,n) \,|\, 0 \le m \le 2M, 0 \le n \le 2N, i_n(m,n) \in [0,255]$$

The interpolation steps are as followed.

2. Interpolation

Step 3: First a blank image of dimension 2M x 2N is taken.

$$I_n = i_n(m,n) \mid 0 \le m \le 2M, 0 \le n \le 2N, i_n(m,n) = 0$$

Step 4: From the main image I_{gr}, image pixels are replaced in the new interpolated image I_n.

$$I_n(2i-1, 2j-1) = i_{gr}(i,j), where\, i \in 1:m, j \in 1:n$$

Step 5: Now the values of the neighborhood pixels are used to fill the entire image in the given fashion,

$I_n(i,j) = \begin{Bmatrix} I_n(m-1,n-1) + I_n(m-1,n+1) + \\ I_n(m+1,n-1) + I_n(m+1,n+1) \end{Bmatrix} / 4$; for i = 2, 4, 6, …, 2m-2 and j = 2, 4, 6, …, 2n-2

$I_n(i,j) = \{I_n(m-1,n-1) + I_n(m+1,n-1)\} / 2$; for i = 2, 4, 6, …, 2m-2 and j = 2n

$I_n(i,j) = \{I_n(m-1,n-1) + I_n(m-1,n+1)\} / 2$; for i = 2m and j = 2, 4, 6, …, 2n-2

$I_n(i,j) = \{I_n(m-1,n-1)\}$; for i = 2m and j = 2n

$I_n(i,j) = \{I_n(m,n-1) + I_n(m+1,n)\} / 2$; for i = 1 and j = 2n

$I_n(i,j) = \{I_n(m,n-1) + I_n(m+1,n) + I_n(m,n+1)\} / 3$; for i = 1, 3, 5, …, 2m-1 and j = 2, 4, 6, …, 2n-2

$I_n(i,j) = \{I_n(m-1,n) + I_n(m+1,n) + I_n(m,n+1)\} / 3$; for i = 2, 4, 6, …, 2m-2 and j = 1

$I_n(i,j) = \begin{Bmatrix} I_n(m,n-1) + I_n(m+1,n) + \\ I_n(m,n+1) + I_n(m-1,n) \end{Bmatrix} / 4$; for i = 2, 4, 6, …, 2m-2 and j = 1, 3, 5, …, 2n-1

$I_n(i,j) = \{I_n(m,n-1) + I_n(m-1,n)\} / 2$; for i = 2m and j = 1

$I_n(i,j) = \{I_n(m,n-1) + I_n(m,n+1) + I_n(m-1,n)\} / 3$; for i = 2m and j = 1, 3, 5, …, 2n-1

3. Data Encryption

Step 6: The EHR data and the doctor's authentication signature is then taken as input. The EHR data is first encrypted using a private key that is only known to the encryption and decryption blocks. Every alphabet of the EHR data is then converted using UTF-8 conversion to get its binary values. The signature taken is in grayscale, so its each pixel also has an 8-bit value. Between the EHR data, the signature's pixel values are concatenated using some private encryption key. After this process EHR data and the signature rEHResents as a single unit of data. This data is again encrypted using some encryption algorithm before it is passed for the LSB replacement behind the interpolated image. Let the signature be represented as I_L.

$$I_L = i_l(m,n) \mid 0 \le x \le X, 0 \le y \le Y, i_l(x,y) \in [0,255]$$

4. LSB Replacement

Step 7: The main image is only available on the I_n(2i-1, 2j-1) pixels where i ϵ 1:m and j ϵ 1:n. In all the other pixels this encrypted data is hidden in last 4-bits of the image pixels. As every single data unit has an 8-bit value, we needed two pixels to hide one single data unit. The last 4-bits of the first extra pixel is replaced by first 4-bits of the data unit and the last 4 bits of the second pixel is replaced by the last 4 bits of the data unit. After this LSB replacement we get the final image. Let it be I_{en}.

$$I_{en} = i_{en}(m,n) \mid 0 \le m \le 2M, 0 \le n \le 2N, i_{en}(m,n) \in [0,255]$$

During the reconstruction, there are total three things are recovered. Those are-

1. Main medical image,
2. Doctor's authentication signature,
3. EHR data. For this purpose below mentioned steps are followed. The decoding process of the system is shown in Figure 2.

5. Medical Image Reconstruction

Step 8: Let the reconstructed medical image is represented as Ire. Then,

$$I_{re} = i_{re}(m,n) \mid 0 \le m \le 2M, 0 \le n \le 2N, i_{re}(m,n) \in [0,255]$$

Figure 2. Decoding Block

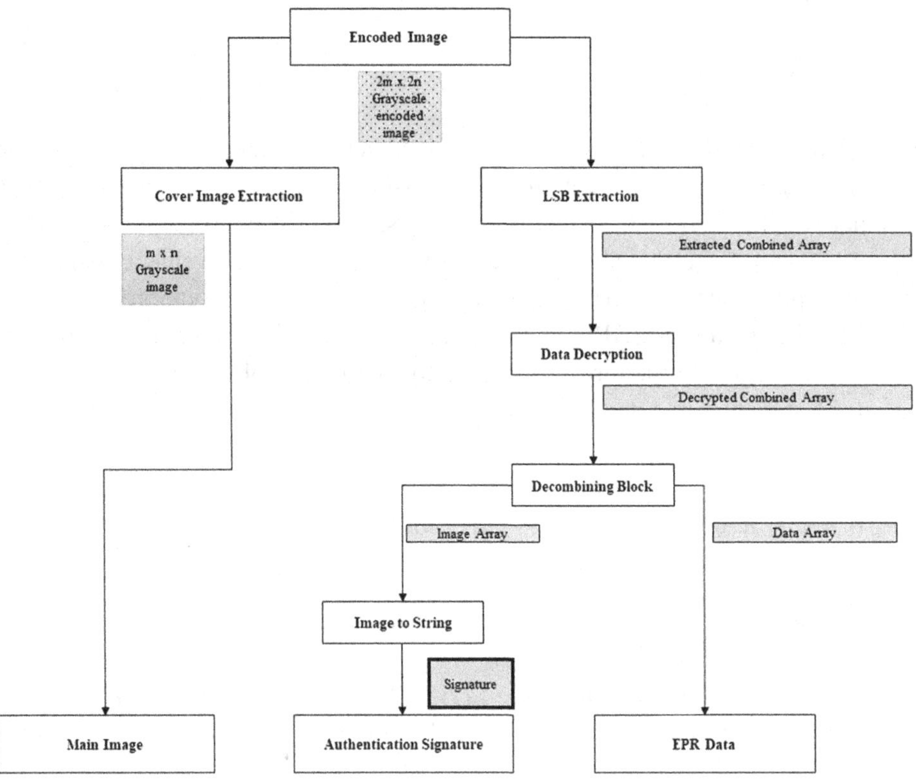

$$I_{re} = I_{en}\left(2i - 1, 2j - 1\right); where\, i = 1 : m\, and\, j = 1 : n$$

Step 9: In LSB extraction block the last 4-bits from the abandoned pixels are extracted and stored in a single array. While encoding, this signature is first concatenated as an 8-bit data with the EHR data array and then encrypted using some private encryption key. So before decoding first the whole data array is decrypted to its real form.

6. Doctor's Authentication Signature

Step 10: Using the known concatenation key, the pixels are first identified and then extracted to construct the signature image. Without the knowledge of this key, reconstruction of the signature is impossible. Let the reconstructed doctor's authentication signature is represented as I_{Lre}. Then,

$$I_{Lre} = i_{Lre}\left(x, y\right) \mid 0 \leq x \leq X, 0 \leq y \leq Y, i_{Lre}\left(x, y\right) \in \left[0, 255\right]$$

7. EHR Data Extraction

Step 11: After the reconstruction of the signature those data are removed from the array which makes it a pure EHR data. This data is then collected and stored for further use.

Figure 3. Data Embedding and Watermarking

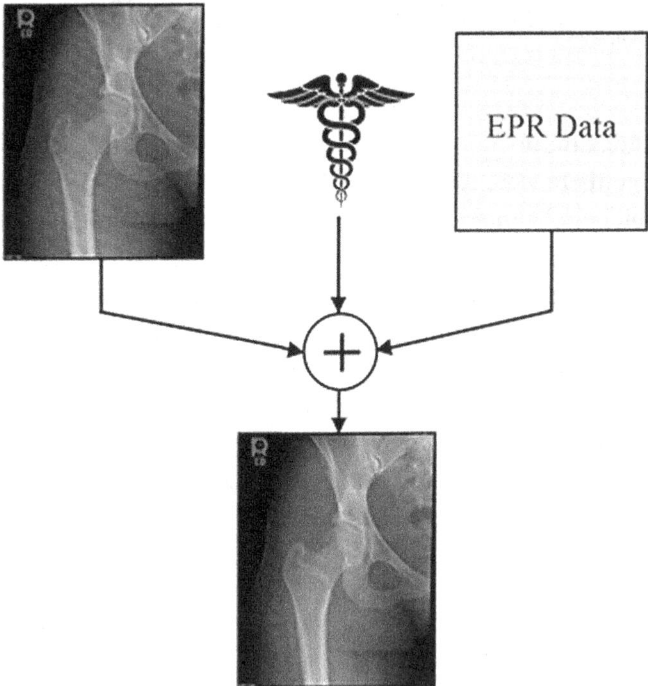

RESULT AND DISCUSSION

Our main motto was to find an efficient algorithm to hide a large chunk of EHR information behind the cover image without effecting it. For this purpose, as mentioned above, we first interpolated the image into a larger image and hide cover image pixel behind them. It gave us extra space for the EHR data to be hidden without even effecting a single bit of the cover image. We took a set a 40 different types of radiological medical images and implemented our algorithm. As the result shows it is fragile in nature which protects the information from attack.

Figure 4 shows the intermediate stages of the image interpolation. The shown image had a dimension of 960x1200 pixels. After the interpolation is performed, the image dimension doubled, increasing it to 1920x2400 pixels. By performing this, we got three times more pixels to hide information behind it without affection the main image.

In Table 1 (A-C) the test result of an image is shown where the main image taken was in dimension 960x1200. After interpolation it is converted into an image of size 1920x2400. Because of this interpolation extra 3,456,000 pixels where created where EHR data and the authenticating logo can be hidden. For authentication any signature of a doctor or the hospital or the medical center can be taken into account. This signature can be the logo of the medical center, any particular symbol or any specific biometric

Figure 4. Intermediate steps of image interpolation

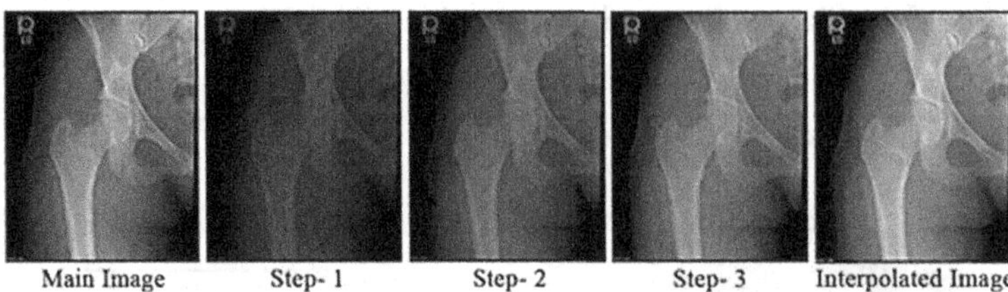

data. In our test-case we took the doctor's logo of dimension 132x117. Fig. 4 shows the encoding stages. Even after hiding the logo there were total 3,417,120 number of pixel left where 1,708,560 number of characters total can be hidden. With a normal margin on an A4 page total 6217 characters can be accommodated approximately with a size 10 font in Times New Roman font style. Which means with a cover image of size 960x1200 approximately a report with 275 pages can be hidden. The hiding capacity increases with the increase of size of the main image. Though the payload capacity of this algorithm is 3, the average PSNR stand at 34.31 with a 13.26% bit error rate. The details is given in Fig. 6.

Fragility is a big concern for medical information. It is better for the information to be destroyed completely than to be obtained by some unknown attacker. As the algorithm is implemented on the spatial domain it was already less tolerant to any external attack. The fragility is further increased by implementing an encryption algorithm to the EHR data and the authenticating signature. As the result in Table II (A-D) shows, it is intolerant to any external attack. After any attack performed the output EHR data is nothing but a garbage. We took a patient's report as our test case data, but the result we got after any attack was some random special characters. The sample is shown in Table 4-7. The whole algorithm is designed in a way so that the image and the data are passed through various encryption techniques along with private key hiding locations. So with even one unknown parameter, there will be no data available. It shows the security of the algorithm. After even a minor attack the signature and EHR data gets affected such a manner that it can be noticed. If the attacker wants to change any information that is also not possible without the knowledge of signature's location. The test data result is shown graphically in Figures 6-8. Though the hidden data is destroyed, the main cover image can be reconstructed to some extent if needed, shown in Table I (A-C).

The result of recovered EHR and watermark against different types of attacks are presented in Table 2 (A to D). To test the efficiency of this proposed scheme, results has been compared with some existing scheme in terms of imperceptibility and hiding capacity and presented in Table 3 The results of Imperceptibility and hiding capacity are respectable and fragility of the proposed scheme has been established. Moreover efficiency the method against other state-of-the-art schemes certifies the supremacy of the projected scheme.

CONCLUSION

In this paper a fragile watermarking technique for highly sensitive medical images has been proposed. The proposed algorithm is useful for its highly fragile nature along with high capacity of hiding EHR (Electronic Patient Record) data. However the technique is also robust when the image authentication is considered. It has been rigorously tested with 40 standard medical images to determine its fragility

Figure 5. Images used for test with their dimension

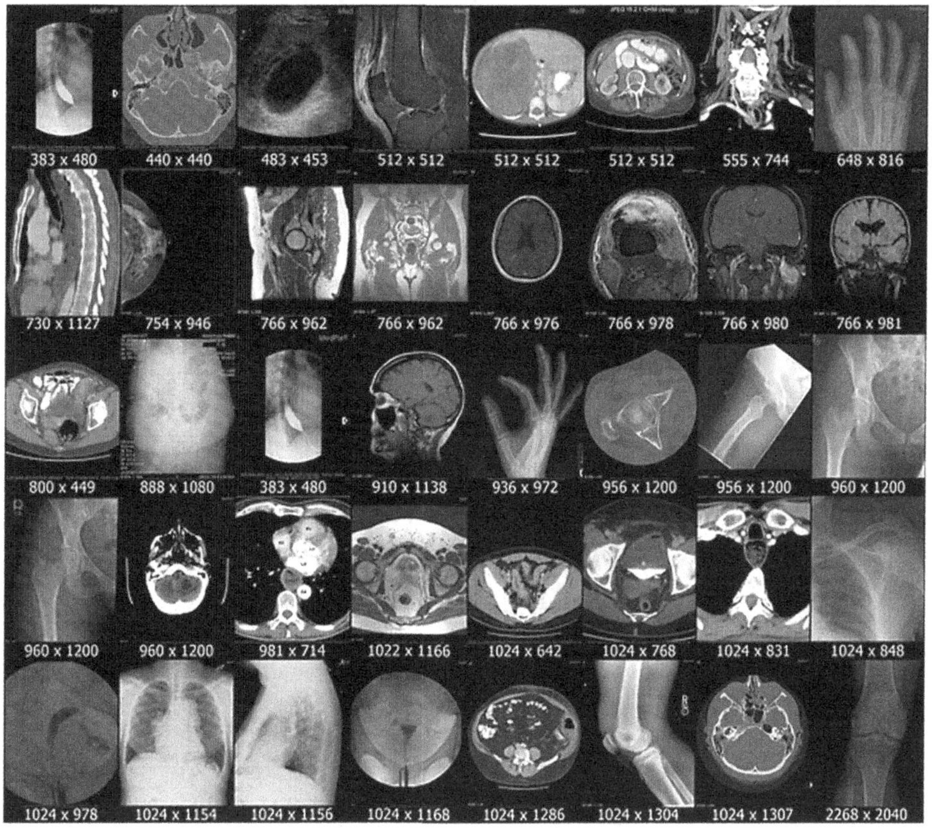

of data and robustness of the authentication watermark. As the result shows it was able to hide large amount of patient's data inside the image without harming even a single pixel of the main image. In the algorithm with the EHR data, an authentication image has been inscribed as well. The image and data were fragile enough to be destroyed with even a small attack. For the test we have used medical images but the algorithm can be used and implemented on any type of highly sensitive images.

Though the suggested algorithm is highly secured with a high data hiding capacity and fragility, the limitation of it comes in case of size. Because of interpolation the image size is increased which can be a concern but as it is designed keeping cloud storage in mind, this limit can be afforded for the better security. In future research we would work on this algorithm to minimize the image size keeping the high security intact.

Table 1. Result against attacks

Attack	Attacked Image	Extracted Image	Testing Data	
No Attack	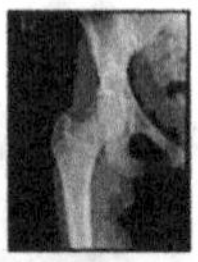	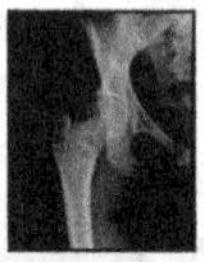	PSNR	Inf
			SC	1
			MI	1
			BERR	0
			JCS	1
			SSIM	1
			WPSNR	Inf
Adjust Filter	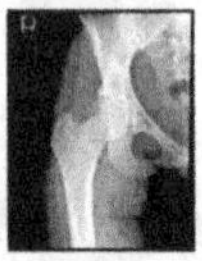	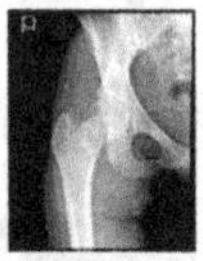	PSNR	15.93294
			SC	0.434355
			MI	0.147926
			BERR	0.409812
			JCS	0.865855
			SSIM	0.899609
			WPSNR	14.89779
Average Blur Filter	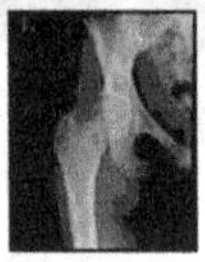		PSNR	36.03213
			SC	0.990457
			MI	0.249055
			BERR	0.231469
			JCS	0.981948
			SSIM	0.866512
			WPSNR	24.62162
Disk Blur Filter	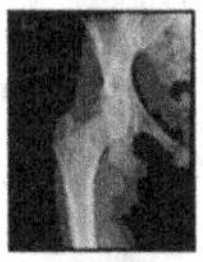	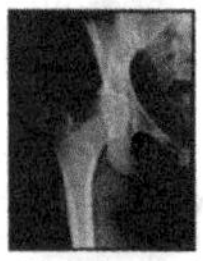	PSNR	32.01688
			SC	0.999251
			MI	0.261129
			BERR	0.236152
			JCS	0.981948
			SSIM	0.836326
			WPSNR	24.62162
Entropy Filter			PSNR	10.54234
			SC	0.001801
			MI	0.762806
			BERR	0.399054
			JCS	0.981948
			SSIM	0.257359
			WPSNR	24.62162
Erode Filter	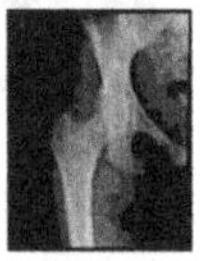	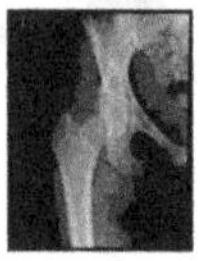	PSNR	30.43538
			SC	0.924124
			MI	0.223587
			BERR	0.172721
			JCS	0.987395
			SSIM	0.927024
			WPSNR	27.49026
Gaussian Filter	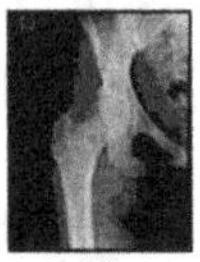	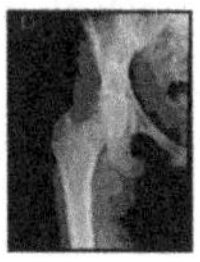	PSNR	44.71956
			SC	0.997238
			MI	0.181837
			BERR	0.155709
			JCS	0.98195
			SSIM	0.96558
			WPSNR	24.62231
Gaussian Noise Filter	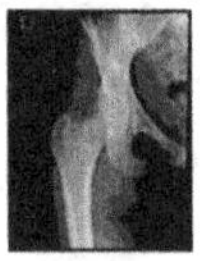	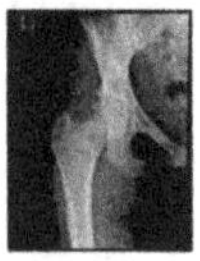	PSNR	20.70157
			SC	0.914377
			MI	0.942072
			BERR	0.380137
			JCS	0.866622
			SSIM	0.130572
			WPSNR	18.21772
GSlid Filter	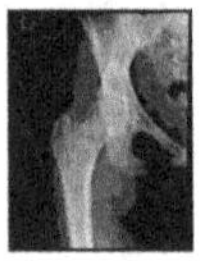	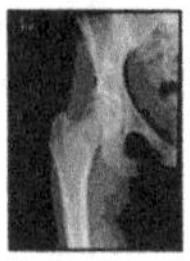	PSNR	36.21941
			SC	0.99309
			MI	0.23291
			BERR	0.176108
			JCS	0.982747
			SSIM	0.864833
			WPSNR	24.86775

Table 2. Result against attacks

Attack	Attacked Image	Extracted Image	Testing Data	
Guided Filter		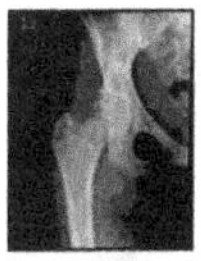	PSNR	39.12411
			SC	0.994291
			MI	0.224282
			BERR	0.21663
			JCS	0.981948
			SSIM	0.899957
			WPSNR	24.62162
Laplacian Blur Filter			PSNR	10.56314
			SC	0.017128
			MI	0.983727
			BERR	0.434199
			JCS	0.611522
			SSIM	0.119174
			WPSNR	11.34216
Log Blur Filter			PSNR	10.65159
			SC	0.036499
			MI	0.96109
			BERR	0.437888
			JCS	0.612738
			SSIM	0.107432
			WPSNR	11.2901
Motion Blur Filter	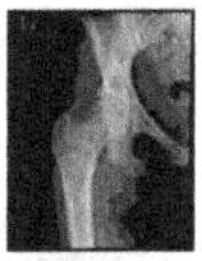	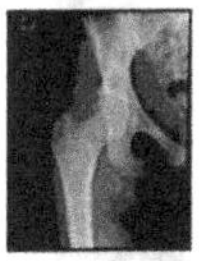	PSNR	32.63777
			SC	0.999297
			MI	0.259161
			BERR	0.232341
			JCS	0.981948
			SSIM	0.848915
			WPSNR	24.62162
Median Blur Filter	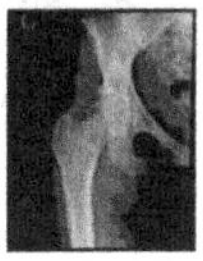	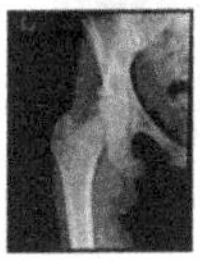	PSNR	36.1909
			SC	0.993291
			MI	0.234442
			BERR	0.17642
			JCS	0.98277
			SSIM	0.863933
			WPSNR	24.88879
Order Filter	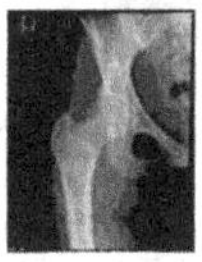	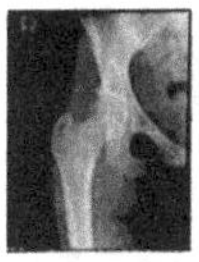	PSNR	25.69851
			SC	0.824716
			MI	0.318193
			BERR	0.314695
			JCS	0.981948
			SSIM	0.744835
			WPSNR	24.62162
Poisson Noise Filter	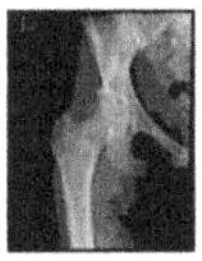	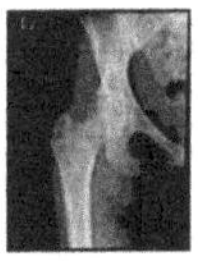	PSNR	30.1453
			SC	0.989745
			MI	0.383754
			BERR	0.295682
			JCS	0.948162
			SSIM	0.638632
			WPSNR	22.62786
Prewitt Filter			PSNR	10.53923
			SC	0.013297
			MI	0.0711
			BERR	0.388469
			JCS	0.463216
			SSIM	0.194419
			WPSNR	11.09414
Sobel Filter			PSNR	10.56765
			SC	0.018634
			MI	0.07882
			BERR	0.388564
			JCS	0.464954
			SSIM	0.194935
			WPSNR	11.02777

Table 3. Result against attacks

Attack	Attacked Image	Extracted Image	Testing Data	
Scaling			PSNR	37.37021
			SC	0.992764
			MI	0.236941
			BERR	0.214577
			JCS	0.981987
			SSIM	0.891605
			WPSNR	24.6469
Speckle Noise			PSNR	23.23075
			SC	0.953547
			MI	0.423346
			BERR	0.3304
			JCS	1
			SSIM	0.44848
			WPSNR	Inf
Salt-Pepper Noise Filter			PSNR	21.55007
			SC	0.921233
			MI	0.148829
			BERR	0.010015
			JCS	0.989888
			SSIM	0.523359
			WPSNR	34.91221
Standard Filter			PSNR	10.61324
			SC	0.004054
			MI	0.483577
			BERR	0.395069
			JCS	0.981906
			SSIM	0.231262
			WPSNR	24.61988
Wiener Filter			PSNR	25.23489
			SC	0.951851
			MI	0.524682
			BERR	0.35738
			JCS	0.981948
			SSIM	0.373462
			WPSNR	24.62162

Table 4. Result of EPR and watermark against attack

<table>
<tr><th>Attack</th><th>Sample Data</th><th>Extracted Image</th><th colspan="2">Testing Data</th></tr>
<tr><td rowspan="7">No Attack</td><td rowspan="7">This is a 43 year
:. Saccadic eye mov
;aze to the right,
;ide. Bidirectional
:orsion swing test
ıead hanging, left
appropriate direct
ıtin. ANALYSIS OF P</td><td rowspan="7"></td><td>PSNR</td><td>Inf</td></tr>
<tr><td>SC</td><td>1</td></tr>
<tr><td>MI</td><td>1</td></tr>
<tr><td>BERR</td><td>0</td></tr>
<tr><td>JCS</td><td>1</td></tr>
<tr><td>SSIM</td><td>1</td></tr>
<tr><td>WPSNR</td><td>Inf</td></tr>
<tr><td rowspan="7">Adjust Filter</td><td rowspan="7">|z$¦v$vy©.$|$|©|1$
|y|.$|¦v¦|$v|y|.$v
XYYZbWy$Z$$v$*)$©|
$$|$|.$v«|$$|$.$vz
zy|vz|y/yv$«v$©v
ILdXF^bVWF_$WLdbWZ
z.$¦y$v¦|$w||$|z$$
$y|v|$$||y©1$Z¦$|z</td><td rowspan="7"></td><td>PSNR</td><td>5.311014</td></tr>
<tr><td>SC</td><td>0.365763</td></tr>
<tr><td>MI</td><td>0.944419</td></tr>
<tr><td>BERR</td><td>0.431163</td></tr>
<tr><td>JCS</td><td>0.877981</td></tr>
<tr><td>SSIM</td><td>0.078664</td></tr>
<tr><td>WPSNR</td><td>17.85829</td></tr>
<tr><td rowspan="7">Average Blur Filter</td><td rowspan="7">□)□+(□+*□□+)□*□;;;
□□*□+:*+□□□)□□:
□+*(□:)□))□*□)□+*□
,+□
□(□□++*+<□++□*□+,*
*)□)□
□*(+□)□'□+
□*□)(□)□)*□(□ ¬ª□.</td><td rowspan="7"></td><td>PSNR</td><td>4.871865</td></tr>
<tr><td>SC</td><td>0.331791</td></tr>
<tr><td>MI</td><td>0.775617</td></tr>
<tr><td>BERR</td><td>0.47707</td></tr>
<tr><td>JCS</td><td>0.878901</td></tr>
<tr><td>SSIM</td><td>0.048648</td></tr>
<tr><td>WPSNR</td><td>16.15405</td></tr>
</table>

Table 5. Result of EPR and watermark against attack

Attack	Sample Data	Extracted Image	Testing Data	
Disk Blur Filter	:::::::::::::::::::: %®J:::::::;_³Õ :::::))**:::*:::*: :::::::::::*::::::: ÏZ::::::::;pÔç=Ä õã))))))))))))))))*** ::::::))*::::::::*: :::::<Ö		PSNR	4.144873
			SC	0.326375
			MI	0.530686
			BERR	0.534941
			JCS	0.862519
			SSIM	0.010745
			WPSNR	15.4858
Entropy Filter	))))))))))))))))))):))))))))))))))))))))))))))))))))))))))))))))))))))))))))))))))))))))))))))))))):))))))))))))))))))):)))))))))))))))))))))))))))▯))))))))))▯		PSNR	2.325885
			SC	0.038016
			MI	0.180211
			BERR	0.62636
			JCS	0.719907
			SSIM	0.022446
			WPSNR	14.01108
Erode Filter	▯]▯Y)▯8▯▯&▯H'▯G▯▯ \▯V▯)▯▯9▯F▯H' ▯▯N(3▯▯J▯&▯▯I6▯F▯)▯ h▯V▯6▯H▯▯▯9▯8▯H▯ ▯▯H▯▯▯▯&▯X▯Y▯ ▯V▯6▯H6▯L▯9▯H6▯H▯ ▯▯W▯▯▯Vw▯▯V▯ /▯6▯H6▯L▯9▯K▯H▯	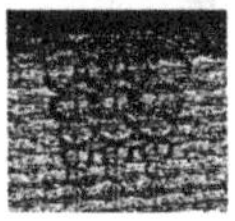	PSNR	3.362764
			SC	0.222408
			MI	0.558244
			BERR	0.554123
			JCS	0.756751
			SSIM	0.053693
			WPSNR	14.21912
Gaussian Filter	QMA??IOXQQ-?IQI_QP. HQAOQXJ`YPI@QZAO?LI PI>MHXMX,LQGQK>QAP. M,@A;;>@H*B\RPQ`^] QOQZPNPJ]OPZNJ`N[^` RRLMN`QAI[N_QXJ^QP(Q``]QAOPO]POYNIQ?KI NWQMIPNPRPLHQXAOY.I		PSNR	12.19521
			SC	0.616529
			MI	0.736436
			BERR	0.359104
			JCS	0.898458
			SSIM	0.332082
			WPSNR	17.67683
Gaussian Noise Filter	m¦Ø æ C Á¶ ▯ F&å(▯v ▯V R ▯v v ëZv(▯ ¶6ã r ▯& ▯ ! o▯ ▯n6 @Ê▯ θ F▯)æ F_å 2 ì »p/o -F vf ©f ▯Vθ~V▯æ ¦▯ ▯ ¢▯ c E & :a▯ ▯ ▯v21 ¼▯ ¶ 2▯		PSNR	4.437733
			SC	0.360862
			MI	0.595233
			BERR	0.527778
			JCS	0.841157
			SSIM	0.018555
			WPSNR	16.1354
GSlid Filter	J▯ ▯ ▯ ▯ 9(▯(▯ ▯ ▯ ▯(▯))(▯)▯(▯ :>89 n½\é^M?ß>▯i▯9*J ▯ 'x1m())▯ Z▯)9		PSNR	3.96664
			SC	0.318259
			MI	0.53579
			BERR	0.534083
			JCS	0.824409
			SSIM	0.018645
			WPSNR	14.45511
Guided Filter	::::::::::9);::::; ;KKKJKK:K:::::;;:: ;::::::::::;::::;:: ::::;::;:::;KK;::; ;::;KKKKKKK;;KK::: ;;:::<K::;:;;:;::: :***;:);;::::::::; :;KL		PSNR	4.309671
			SC	0.316843
			MI	0.607664
			BERR	0.524419
			JCS	0.875909
			SSIM	0.021366
			WPSNR	16.05964
Laplacian Blur Filter	▯Xã VÆ & í▯Ć ▯ & | & ▯ & 5 ▯ & 6 & ▯ ▯ F▯ ▯ ▯ & ▯ ▯ ▯		PSNR	0.911608
			SC	0.053854
			MI	0.865058
			BERR	0.859889
			JCS	0.101188
			SSIM	0.080714
			WPSNR	6.805706
Log Blur Filter	6 | 6 & ▯ ▯F V ▯ 6 ▯6 F F V ▯ ▯ F V V ▯ ▯F ▯ F ▯ 6 6 F V ▯ V		PSNR	0.895973
			SC	0.060916
			MI	0.857452
			BERR	0.860342
			JCS	0.102493
			SSIM	0.087327
			WPSNR	6.819588

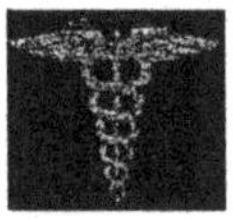

Table 6. Result of EPR and watermark against attack

Attack	Sample Data	Extracted Image	Testing Data	
Disk Blur Filter	::::::::::::::::::::: %®J::::::::;_³Ö :::::))**:::*:::*: ::::::::::*::::::: ÏZ::::::::;pÔç=Ä õã))))))))))))))))*** ::::::))*:::::::*: :::::<Ö		PSNR	4.144873
			SC	0.326375
			MI	0.530686
			BERR	0.534941
			JCS	0.862519
			SSIM	0.010745
			WPSNR	15.4858
Entropy Filter	)))))))))))))))))))))))))))))))))))))))))))))))))))))))))))))))))))))))))))))))))))))))))))))))))))))))))))))))))))))))))))))))))))))))))))))▯))))))))))▯		PSNR	2.325885
			SC	0.038016
			MI	0.180211
			BERR	0.62636
			JCS	0.719907
			SSIM	0.022446
			WPSNR	14.01108
Erode Filter	▯]▯Y)▯8▯&▯H'▯G▯ \▯V▯)▯9▯F▯H' ▯N(3▯J▯&▯I6▯F▯)▯ h▯V▯6▯H▯9▯8▯H▯ ▯H▯&▯X▯Y▯ ▯V▯6▯H6▯L▯9▯H6▯H▯ ▯W▯VW▯V▯ /▯6▯H6▯L▯9▯K▯H▯		PSNR	3.362764
			SC	0.222408
			MI	0.558244
			BERR	0.554123
			JCS	0.756751
			SSIM	0.053693
			WPSNR	14.21912
Gaussian Filter	QMA??IOXQQ-?IQI_QP. HQAOQXJ`YPI@QZAO?L PI>MHXMX,LQGQK>QAP M,@A;;>@H*B\RPQ`^] QOQZPNPJ]OPZNJ`N[^ RRLMN`QAI[N_QXJ^QP(Q``]QAOPO]POYNIQ?KI NWQMIPNPRPLHQXAOY.		PSNR	12.19521
			SC	0.616529
			MI	0.736436
			BERR	0.359104
			JCS	0.898458
			SSIM	0.332082
			WPSNR	17.67683
Gaussian Noise Filter	m¦Ø æ C Á¶ ▯ F&å ▯v ▯V R ▯v v ëZv(▯ ¶6â r ▯& ▯ ! o▯ ▯n6 @Ê▯ 0 F▯ ▯æ F_å 2 ì »p/o -F vf ©f ▯V0~V▯æ ¦▯ ▯ ¢▯ c E & :a▯ ▯ ▯v21 ¼▯ ¶ 2▯		PSNR	4.437733
			SC	0.360862
			MI	0.595233
			BERR	0.527778
			JCS	0.841157
			SSIM	0.018555
			WPSNR	16.1354
GSlid Filter	J▯ ▯ ▯ ▯ 9(▯(▯ ▯ ▯ ▯(▯))(▯)▯(▯ :>89 n½\é^M?ß>▯i▯9*J ▯ x1m())▯ Z▯)9		PSNR	3.96664
			SC	0.318259
			MI	0.53579
			BERR	0.534083
			JCS	0.824409
			SSIM	0.018645
			WPSNR	14.45511
Guided Filter	:::::::::::9);::::; ;KKKJKK:K:::::;;:: ;::::::::::;::::;:: ::::;::;:::;KK;::; ;::;KKKKKKK;;KK::: ;;:::<K::;:;;:;::: :***;:);;:::::::::; :;KL		PSNR	4.309671
			SC	0.316843
			MI	0.607664
			BERR	0.524419
			JCS	0.875909
			SSIM	0.021366
			WPSNR	16.05964
Laplacian Blur Filter	▯Xã VÆ & í▯ ▯ & & ▯ & ▯ & 6 & ▯ ▯ F▯ ▯ ▯ & ▯ ▯ ▯		PSNR	0.911608
			SC	0.053854
			MI	0.865058
			BERR	0.859889
			JCS	0.101188
			SSIM	0.080714
			WPSNR	6.805706
Log Blur Filter	6 6 & ▯ ▯F V ▯ 6 ▯6 F F V ▯ ▯ F V V ▯ ▯F ▯ F ▯ 6 6 F V ▯ V		PSNR	0.895973
			SC	0.060916
			MI	0.857452
			BERR	0.860342
			JCS	0.102493
			SSIM	0.087327
			WPSNR	6.819588

Table 7. Result of EPR and watermark against attack

<table>
<tr><th>Attack</th><th>Sample Data</th><th>Extracted Image</th><th colspan="2">Testing Data</th></tr>
<tr><td rowspan="7">Standard Filter</td><td rowspan="7">▯+,,**-+,+++--▯,*,,
,,,++,,,,,,+)+)+,7-
;+*-,*+*--+,*▯++,,;
+,**9*,,+*-+,+,,,,,'
<+,*▯,+,++*,+▯',+;,
+<,*+-,,*,,*+,,-,)'
,-)▯,*-,++*,+,,*,*,
·+-++▯,+-▯+-,*,,-,)+</td><td rowspan="7"></td><td>PSNR</td><td>3.02158</td></tr>
<tr><td>SC</td><td>0.073582</td></tr>
<tr><td>MI</td><td>0.489356</td></tr>
<tr><td>BERR</td><td>0.598169</td></tr>
<tr><td>JCS</td><td>0.874049</td></tr>
<tr><td>SSIM</td><td>0.065961</td></tr>
<tr><td>WPSNR</td><td>17.65505</td></tr>
<tr><td rowspan="7">Wiener Filter</td><td rowspan="7">ð]+m1¼m▯H%_I▯+▯j]£▯ð
Ꝭ{£▯åâÈM% ▯#|>V▯ #Ñ`
•]9h 9%▯▯ 6^Â¯½T"▯ðÀ(
?W:*Ïz#ßZ´ôÕ0▯ç▯)Tæ
:8IðQ Z▯³▯X▯ VÒ▯®7Ñ▯ ▯
^A'$ d^jm,4·~á§åÈ
U
ZÔQ Ô×ôÒ▯â°ó¶µ¯YBv9</td><td rowspan="7"></td><td>PSNR</td><td>4.93287</td></tr>
<tr><td>SC</td><td>0.429224</td></tr>
<tr><td>MI</td><td>0.626097</td></tr>
<tr><td>BERR</td><td>0.500251</td></tr>
<tr><td>JCS</td><td>0.866874</td></tr>
<tr><td>SSIM</td><td>0.005669</td></tr>
<tr><td>WPSNR</td><td>15.49666</td></tr>
</table>

Table 8. Comparison with different defined techniques

Sl. No.	Technique	PSNR (dB)	Payload (bits)
1.	A New Reversible And High Capacity Data Hiding Technique For E-Healthcare Applications	46.51	196,608
2.	A high capacity reversible watermarking approach for authenticating images: Exploiting down-sampling, histogram processing, and block selection	52.71	700
3.	A blind and fragile watermarking scheme for tamper detection of medical images preserving ROI	57.95	35,000
Proposed Technique			
4.	On the Implementation of a Reversible Watermarking Technique for Hiding in Medical Images	Inf†	13,824,000

†Discussion: While comparing the watermarked image with the interpolated image we found PSNR as 34.31 but the main image pixels in the interpolated image remained untouched. Hence the PSNR for main image and watermarked image will be infinite.

Figure 6a. Imperceptibility of main images with data hiding capacity: PSNR vs. WPSNR

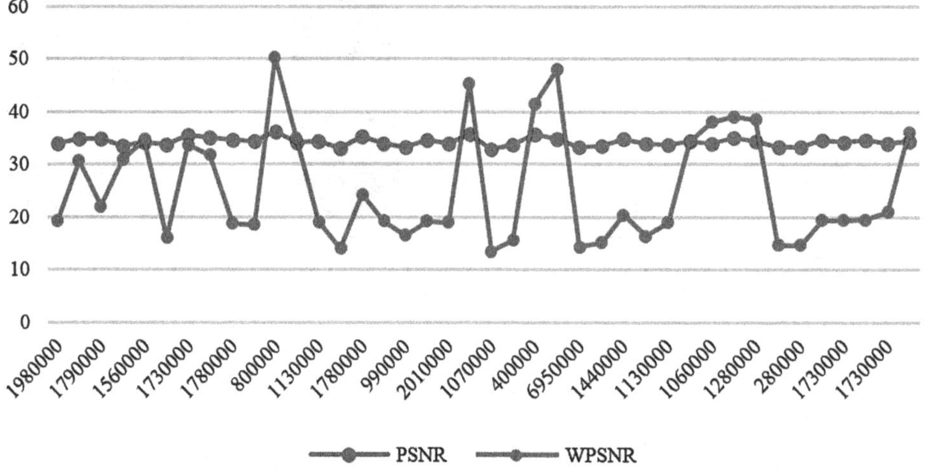

Figure 6b. Imperceptibility of main images with data hiding capacity: JCS vs. MI

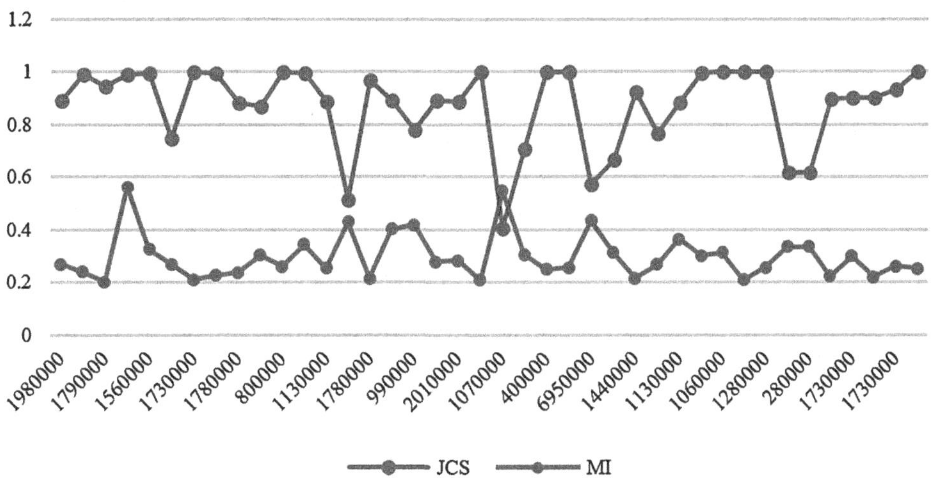

Figure 6c. Imperceptibility of main images with data hiding capacity: SSIM vs. BERR vs. SC

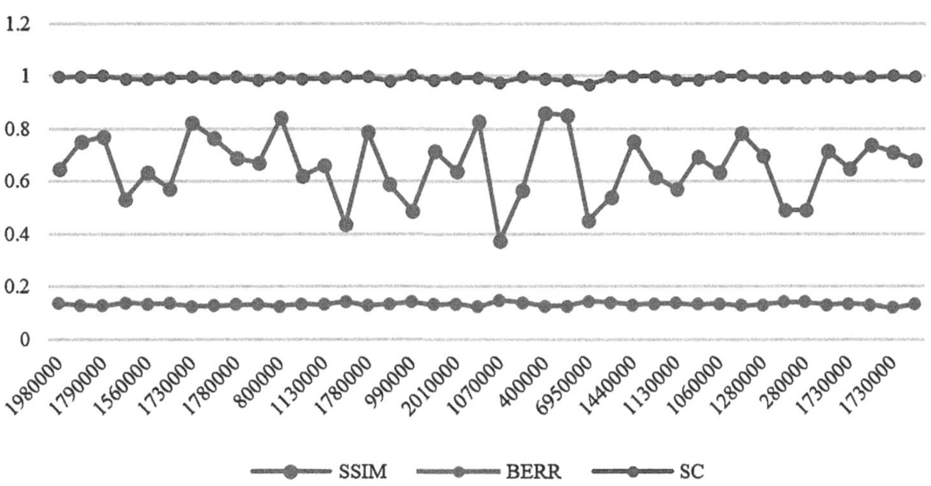

Figure 7a. Fragility of cover image: PSNR vs. WPSNR

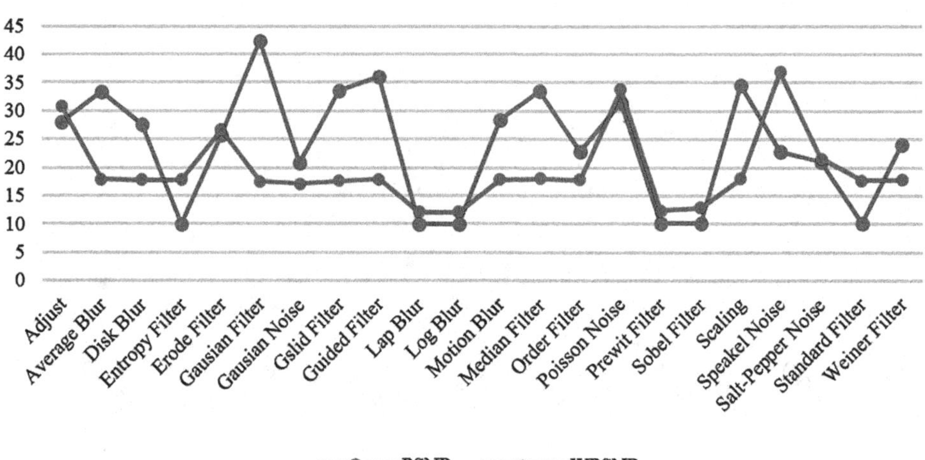

Figure 7b. Fragility of cover image: JCS vs. MI

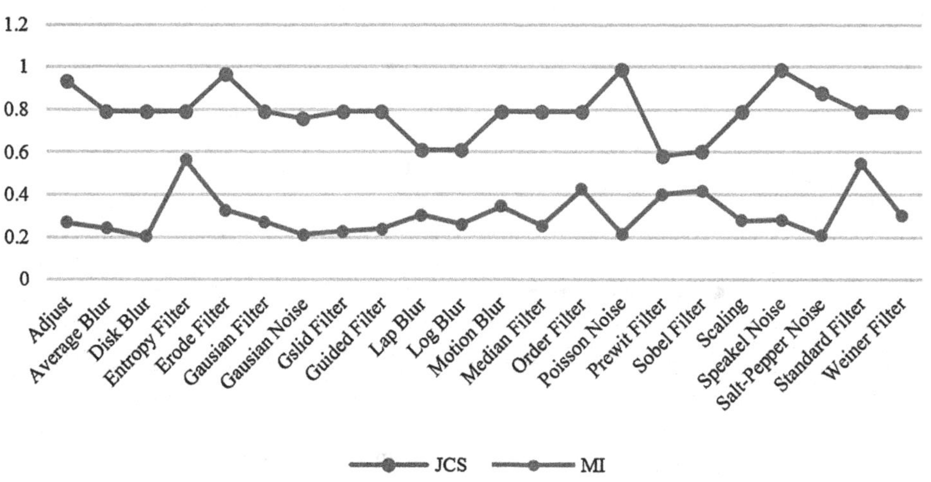

Figure 7c. Fragility of cover image: SSIM vs. BER vs. SC

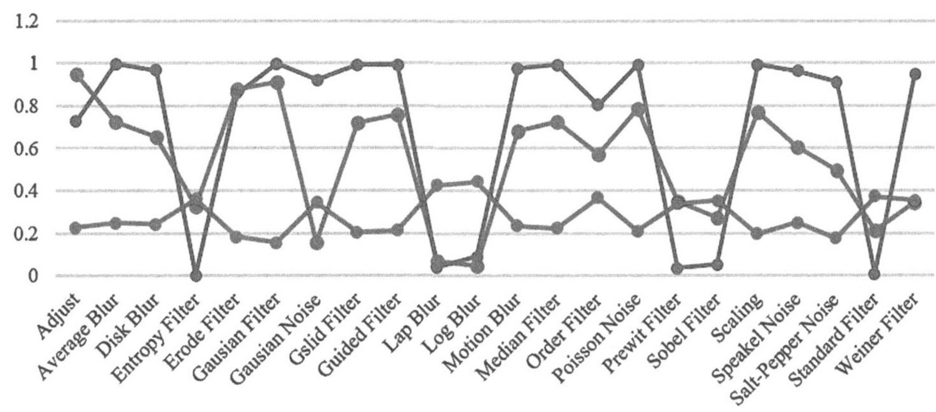

Figure 8a. Fragility of signature

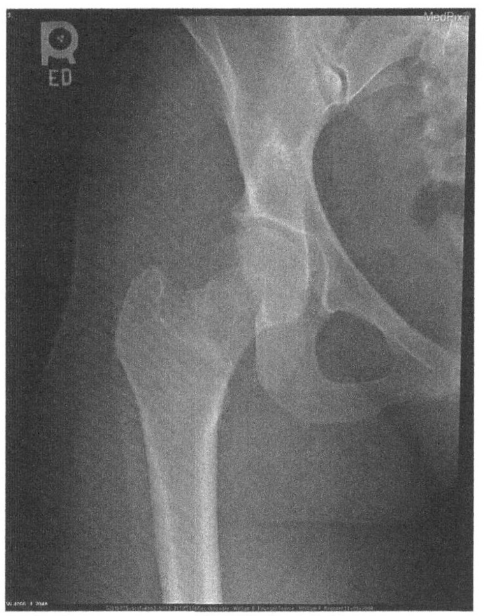

Figure 8b. Fragility of signature: PSNR vs. WPSNR

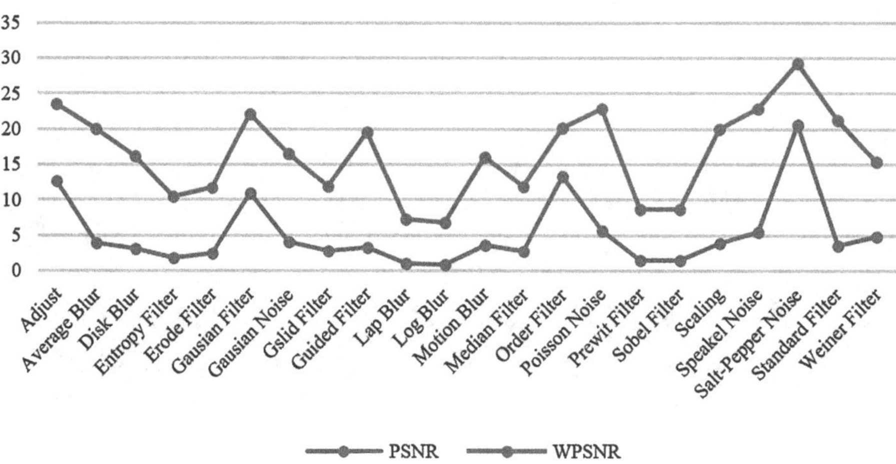

Figure 8c. Fragility of signature: JCS vs. MI

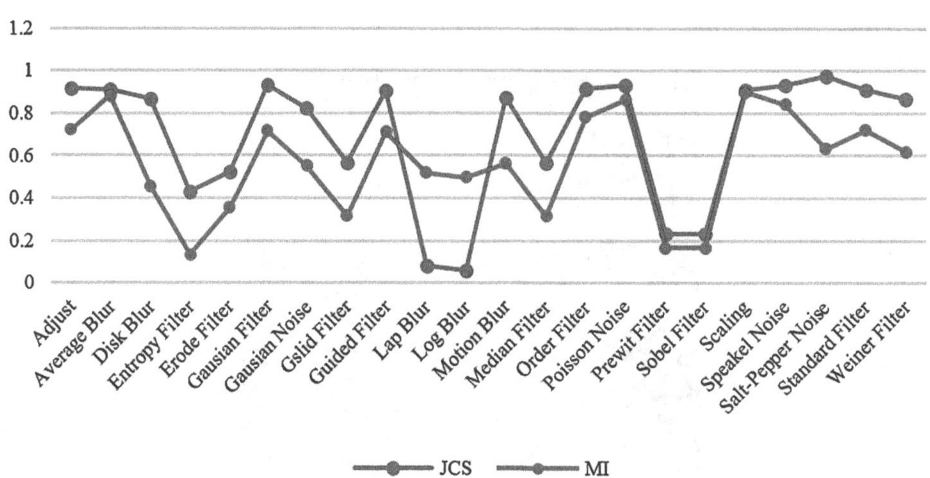

Figure 8d. Fragility of signature: SSIM vs. BER vs. SC

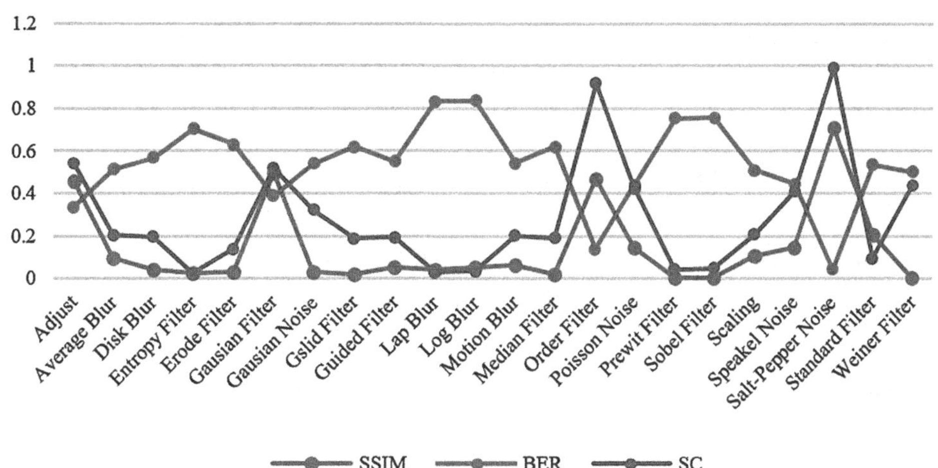

REFERENCES

Latham, A. (1999). *Steganography*. Retrieved from http://linux01.gwdg.de/ alatham/stego.html

Leon-Garcia, A. (1994). *Probability and random processes for electrical engineering*. Addison-Wesley.

Aamodt, A., & Plaza, E. (1994). Case-based reasoning: Foundational issues, methodological variations, and system approaches. *AI Communications*, *7*(1), 39–59.

Acharya, R., Bhat, P. S., Kumar, S., & Min, L. C. (2003). Transmission and storage of medical images with patient information. *Computers in Biology and Medicine*, *33*(4), 303–310. doi:10.1016/S0010-4825(02)00083-5 PMID:12791403

Acharya, R., Niranjan, U. C., Iyengar, S. S., Kannathal, N., & Min, L. C. (2004). Simultaneous storage of patient information with medical images in the frequency domain. *Computer Methods and Programs in Biomedicine*, *76*(1), 13–19. doi:10.1016/j.cmpb.2004.02.009 PMID:15313538

Acharya, U. R., Acharya, D., Bhat, P. S., & Niranjan, U. C. (2001). Compact storage of medical images with patient information. *IEEE Transactions on Information Technology in Biomedicine*, *5*(4), 320–323. doi:10.1109/4233.966107 PMID:11759838

Alattar, A. M. (2004). Reversible watermark using the difference expansion of a generalized integer transform. *IEEE Transactions on Image Processing*, *13*(8), 1147–1156. doi:10.1109/TIP.2004.828418 PMID:15326856

Al-Qershi, O. M., & Khoo, B. E. (2011). Authentication and data hiding using a hybrid ROI-based watermarking scheme for DICOM images. *Journal of Digital Imaging*, *24*(1), 114–125. doi:10.100710278-009-9253-1 PMID:19937363

Anand, D., & Niranjan, U. C. (1998, October). Watermarking medical images with patient information. In *Engineering in Medicine and Biology Society, 1998. Proceedings of the 20th Annual International Conference of the IEEE* (*Vol. 2*, pp. 703-706). IEEE.

Annadurai, S. (2007). *Fundamentals of digital image processing*. Pearson Education India.

Antani, S., Kasturi, R., & Jain, R. (2002). A survey on the use of pattern recognition methods for abstraction, indexing and retrieval of images and video. *Pattern Recognition*, *35*(4), 945–965. doi:10.1016/S0031-3203(01)00086-3

Artz, D. (2001). Digital steganography: Hiding data within data. *IEEE Internet Computing*, *5*(3), 75–80. doi:10.1109/4236.935180

Avcibas, I., Bayram, S., Memon, N., Ramkumar, M., & Sankur, B. (2004, October). A classifier design for detecting image manipulations. In *Image Processing, 2004. ICIP'04. 2004 International Conference on* (Vol. 4, pp. 2645-2648). IEEE.

Badran, E. F., Sharkas, M. A., & Attallah, O. A. (2009, March). Multiple watermark embedding scheme in wavelet-spatial domains based on ROI of medical images. In *Radio Science Conference, 2009. NRSC 2009. National* (pp. 1-8). IEEE.

Bao, F., Deng, R. H., Ooi, B. C., & Yang, Y. (2005). Tailored reversible watermarking schemes for authentication of electronic clinical atlas. *IEEE Transactions on Information Technology in Biomedicine*, *9*(4), 554–563. doi:10.1109/TITB.2005.855556 PMID:16379372

Barni, M., & Bartolini, F. (2004). Data hiding for fighting piracy. *IEEE Signal Processing Magazine*, *21*(2), 28–39. doi:10.1109/MSP.2004.1276109

Barni, M., Bartolini, F., & Piva, A. (2002). Multichannel watermarking of color images. *IEEE Transactions on Circuits and Systems for Video Technology*, *12*(3), 142–156. doi:10.1109/76.993436

Barre, S. (n.d.). *DICOM Medical image samples*. Retrieved from http://barre.nom.fr/medical/samples/

Barreto, P. S., Kim, H. Y., & Rijmen, V. (2002). Toward secure public-key blockwise fragile authentication watermarking. *IEE Proceedings. Vision Image and Signal Processing*, *149*(2), 57–62. doi:10.1049/ip-vis:20020168

Basu, A., Chatterjee, A., Datta, S., Sarkar, S., & Karmakar, R. (2016, October). FPGA implementation of Saliency based secured watermarking framework. In *Intelligent Control Power and Instrumentation (ICICPI), International Conference on* (pp. 273-277). IEEE. 10.1109/ICICPI.2016.7859716

Basu, A., Karmakar, R., Chatterjee, A., Datta, S., Sarkar, S., & Mondal, A. (2017, March). Implementation of salient region based secured digital image watermarking. In *Computer, Communication and Electrical Technology: Proceedings of the International Conference on Advancement of Computer Communication and Electrical Technology (ACCET 2016)* (p. 9). CRC Press. 10.1201/9781315400624-4

Bayram, S., Avcibas, I., Sankur, B., & Memon, N. (2005, September). Image manipulation detection with binary similarity measures. In *Signal Processing Conference, 2005 13th European* (pp. 1-4). IEEE.

Beer, G. (1992). Topological completeness of function spaces arising in the Hausdorff approximation of functions. *Canadian Mathematical Bulletin*, *35*(4), 439–448. doi:10.4153/CMB-1992-058-1

Boncelet, C. G. (2006). The NTMAC for authentication of noisy messages. *IEEE Transactions on Information Forensics and Security*, *1*(1), 35–42. doi:10.1109/TIFS.2005.863506

Boucherkha, S., & Benmohamed, M. (2004). A Lossless Watermarking Based Authentication System For Medical Images. In *International Conference on Computational Intelligence* (pp. 240-243). Academic Press.

Bounkong, S., Toch, B., Saad, D., & Lowe, D. (2003). ICA for watermarking digital images. *Journal of Machine Learning Research*, *4*(Dec), 1471–1498.

BW, T.A., & Permana, F.P. (2012, July). Medical image watermarking with tamper detection and recovery using reversible watermarking with LSB modification and run length encoding (RLE) compression. In *Communication, Networks and Satellite (ComNetSat), 2012 IEEE International Conference on* (pp. 167-171). IEEE.

Cao, F., Huang, H. K., & Zhou, X. Q. (2003). Medical image security in a HIPAA mandated PACS environment. *Computerized Medical Imaging and Graphics*, *27*(2-3), 185–196. doi:10.1016/S0895-6111(02)00073-3 PMID:12620309

Cao, P., Hashiba, M., Akazawa, K., Yamakawa, T., & Matsuto, T. (2003). An integrated medical image database and retrieval system using a web application server. *International Journal of Medical Informatics*, *71*(1), 51–55. doi:10.1016/S1386-5056(03)00088-1 PMID:12909158

Cauvin, J. M., Le Guillou, C., Solaiman, B., Robaszkiewicz, M., Le Beux, P., & Roux, C. (2003). Computer-assisted diagnosis system in digestive endoscopy. *IEEE Transactions on Information Technology in Biomedicine*, *7*(4), 256–262. doi:10.1109/TITB.2003.823293 PMID:15000352

Celik, M. U., Sharma, G., Tekalp, A. M., & Saber, E. (2002). Reversible data hiding. In *Image Processing. 2002. Proceedings. 2002 International Conference on* (Vol. 2, pp. II-II). IEEE. 10.1109/ICIP.2002.1039911

Chamlawi, R., Usman, I., & Khan, A. (2009, December). Dual watermarking method for secure image authentication and recovery. In *Multitopic Conference, 2009. INMIC 2009. IEEE 13th International* (pp. 1-4). IEEE. 10.1109/INMIC.2009.5383118

Chao, H. M., Hsu, C. M., & Miaou, S. G. (2002). A data-hiding technique with authentication, integration, and confidentiality for electronic patient records. *IEEE Transactions on Information Technology in Biomedicine*, *6*(1), 46–53. doi:10.1109/4233.992161 PMID:11936596

Chen, J., Shan, S., He, C., Zhao, G., Pietikainen, M., Chen, X., & Gao, W. (2010). WLD: A robust local image descriptor. *IEEE Transactions on Pattern Analysis and Machine Intelligence*, *32*(9), 1705–1720. doi:10.1109/TPAMI.2009.155 PMID:20634562

Chen, K., & Ramabadran, T. V. (1994). Near-lossless compression of medical images through entropy-coded DPCM. *IEEE Transactions on Medical Imaging*, *13*(3), 538–548. doi:10.1109/42.310885 PMID:18218529

Cheng, S., Wu, Q., & Castleman, K. R. (2005, September). Non-ubiquitous digital watermarking for record indexing and integrity protection of medical images. In *Image Processing, 2005. ICIP 2005. IEEE International Conference on* (Vol. 2). IEEE. 10.1109/ICIP.2005.1530242

Chiang, K. H., Chang-Chien, K. C., Chang, R. F., & Yen, H. Y. (2008). Tamper detection and restoring system for medical images using wavelet-based reversible data embedding. *Journal of Digital Imaging*, *21*(1), 77–90. doi:10.100710278-007-9012-0 PMID:17333416

Coatrieux, G., Huang, H., Shu, H., Luo, L., & Roux, C. (2013). A watermarking-based medical image integrity control system and an image moment signature for tampering characterization. *IEEE Journal of Biomedical and Health Informatics*, *17*(6), 1057–1067. doi:10.1109/JBHI.2013.2263533 PMID:24240724

Coatrieux, G., Le Guillou, C., Cauvin, J. M., & Roux, C. (2009). Reversible watermarking for knowledge digest embedding and reliability control in medical images. *IEEE Transactions on Information Technology in Biomedicine*, *13*(2), 158–165. doi:10.1109/TITB.2008.2007199 PMID:19272858

Coatrieux, G., Lecornu, L., Sankur, B., & Roux, C. (2006, August). A review of image watermarking applications in healthcare. In *Engineering in Medicine and Biology Society, 2006. EMBS'06. 28th Annual International Conference of the IEEE* (pp. 4691-4694). IEEE. 10.1109/IEMBS.2006.259305

Coatrieux, G., Maitre, H., & Sankur, B. (2001, August). Strict integrity control of biomedical images. In *Security and watermarking of multimedia contents III* (Vol. 4314, pp. 229–241). International Society for Optics and Photonics. doi:10.1117/12.435403

Coatrieux, G., Maitre, H., Sankur, B., Rolland, Y., & Collorec, R. (2000). Relevance of watermarking in medical imaging. In *Information Technology Applications in Biomedicine, 2000. Proceedings. 2000 IEEE EMBS International Conference on* (pp. 250-255). IEEE. 10.1109/ITAB.2000.892396

Coatrieux, G., Montagner, J., Huang, H., & Roux, C. (2007, August). Mixed reversible and RONI watermarking for medical image reliability protection. In *Engineering in Medicine and Biology Society, 2007. EMBS 2007. 29th Annual International Conference of the IEEE* (pp. 5653-5656). IEEE. 10.1109/IEMBS.2007.4353629

Coatrieux, G., Puentes, J., Lecornu, L., Le Rest, C. C., & Roux, C. (2006, April). Compliant secured specialized electronic patient record platform. In *Distributed Diagnosis and Home Healthcare, 2006. D2H2. 1st Transdisciplinary Conference on* (pp. 156-159). IEEE. 10.1109/DDHH.2006.1624820

Coatrieux, G., Puentes, J., Roux, C., Lamard, M., & Daccache, W. (2006, January). A low distorsion and reversible watermark: application to angiographic images of the retina. In *Engineering in Medicine and Biology Society, 2005. IEEE-EMBS 2005. 27th Annual International Conference of the* (pp. 2224-2227). IEEE.

Coltuc, D., & Chassery, J. M. (2007). Very fast watermarking by reversible contrast mapping. *IEEE Signal Processing Letters*, *14*(4), 255–258. doi:10.1109/LSP.2006.884895

Cox, I. J., Kilian, J., Leighton, F. T., & Shamoon, T. (1997). Secure spread spectrum watermarking for multimedia. *IEEE Transactions on Image Processing*, *6*(12), 1673–1687. doi:10.1109/83.650120 PMID:18285237

Crespi, M., Delvaux, M., Schaprio, M., Venables, C., & Zwiebel, F. (1996). Working Party Report by the Committee for Minimal Standards of Terminology and Documentation in Digestive Endoscopy of the European Society of Gastrointestinal Endoscopy. Minimal standard terminology for a computerized endoscopic database. Ad hoc Task Force of the Committee. *The American Journal of Gastroenterology*, *91*(2), 191. PMID:8607482

Criminisi, A., Pérez, P., & Toyama, K. (2004). Region filling and object removal by exemplar-based image inpainting. *IEEE Transactions on Image Processing*, *13*(9), 1200–1212. doi:10.1109/TIP.2004.833105 PMID:15449582

Dandapat, S., Chutatape, O., & Krishnan, S. M. (2004, October). Perceptual model based data embedding in medical images. In *Image Processing, 2004. ICIP'04. 2004 International Conference on* (Vol. 4, pp. 2315-2318). IEEE. 10.1109/ICIP.2004.1421563

De Vleeschouwer, C., Delaigle, J. F., & Macq, B. (2003). Circular interpretation of bijective transformations in lossless watermarking for media asset management. *IEEE Transactions on Multimedia*, *5*(1), 97–105. doi:10.1109/TMM.2003.809729

Delp, E. J. (2005). Multimedia security: The 22nd century approach. *Multimedia Systems*, *11*(2), 95–97. doi:10.100700530-005-0193-4

Deng, L., & Poole, M. S. (2003, January). Learning through telemedicine networks. In *System Sciences, 2003. Proceedings of the 36th Annual Hawaii International Conference on* (pp. 8-pp). IEEE.

Dong, C., Chen, Y. W., Li, J., & Bai, Y. (2012, May). Zero watermarking for medical images based on DFT and LFSR. In *Computer Science and Automation Engineering (CSAE), 2012 IEEE International Conference on* (Vol. 1, pp. 22-26). IEEE. 10.1109/CSAE.2012.6272540

Ekici, O., Coskun, B., Naci, U., & Sankur, B. (2001, November). Comparative assessment of semifragile watermarking techniques. In *Multimedia Systems and Applications IV* (Vol. 4518, pp. 177–189). International Society for Optics and Photonics. doi:10.1117/12.448202

Farid, H., & Lyu, S. (2003, June). Higher-order wavelet statistics and their application to digital forensics. In *Computer Vision and Pattern Recognition Workshop, 2003. CVPRW'03. Conference on* (Vol. 8, pp. 94-94). IEEE. 10.1109/CVPRW.2003.10093

Farid, H. (2009). Image forgery detection. *IEEE Signal Processing Magazine*, *26*(2), 16–25. doi:10.1109/MSP.2008.931079

Fridrich, J., Goljan, M., & Du, R. (2001, April). Invertible authentication watermark for JPEG images. In *Information Technology: Coding and Computing, 2001. Proceedings. International Conference on* (pp. 223-227). IEEE. 10.1109/ITCC.2001.918795

Fridrich, J., Goljan, M., & Du, R. (2001, August). Invertible authentication. In *Security and Watermarking of Multimedia contents III* (Vol. 4314, pp. 197–209). International Society for Optics and Photonics. doi:10.1117/12.435400

Fu, D., Shi, Y. Q., & Su, W. (2006, November). Detection of image splicing based on hilbert-huang transform and moments of characteristic functions with wavelet decomposition. In *International workshop on digital watermarking* (pp. 177-187). Springer. 10.1007/11922841_15

Garimella, A., Satyanarayana, M. V. V., Kumar, R. S., Murugesh, P. S., & Niranjan, U. C. (2003, January). VLSI implementation of online digital watermarking technique with difference encoding for 8-bit gray scale images. In *VLSI Design, 2003. Proceedings. 16th International Conference on* (pp. 283-288). IEEE.

Ghosh, S., Kundu, B., Datta, D., Maity, S. P., & Rahaman, H. (2014, February). Design and implementation of fast FPGA based architecture for reversible watermarking. In *Electrical Information and Communication Technology (EICT), 2013 International Conference on* (pp. 1-6). IEEE. 10.1109/EICT.2014.6777819

Giakoumaki, A., Pavlopoulos, S., & Koutouris, D. (2003, September). A medical image watermarking scheme based on wavelet transform. In *Engineering in medicine and biology society, 2003. Proceedings of the 25th annual international conference of the IEEE* (*Vol. 1*, pp. 856-859). IEEE. 10.1109/IEMBS.2003.1279900

Giakoumaki, A., Pavlopoulos, S., & Koutsouris, D. (2006). Multiple image watermarking applied to health information management. *IEEE Transactions on Information Technology in Biomedicine*, *10*(4), 722–732. doi:10.1109/TITB.2006.875655 PMID:17044406

Guo, X., & Zhuang, T. G. (2009). Lossless watermarking for verifying the integrity of medical images with tamper localization. *Journal of Digital Imaging*, *22*(6), 620–628. doi:10.100710278-008-9120-5 PMID:18473141

He, H. J., Zhang, J. S., & Tai, H. M. (2009, June). Self-recovery fragile watermarking using block-neighborhood tampering characterization. In *International Workshop on Information Hiding* (pp. 132-145). Springer. 10.1007/978-3-642-04431-1_10

Hilbert, M., & López, P. (2011). The world's technological capacity to store, communicate, and compute information. *Science, 332*(6025), 60-65.

Honsinger, C. (2002). Digital watermarking. *Journal of Electronic Imaging*, *11*(3), 414. doi:10.1117/1.1494075

Hrsa.gov. (2014). *HHS Budget Makes Smart Investments, Protects the Health and Safety America's Families*. Available at: http://www.hrsa.gov/about/news/pressreleases/2010/100201a.html http://www.internetlivestats.com/internet-users/ https://pulse.embs.org/january-2017/electronic-health-records-data-delivers-better-patient-outcomes/

Hu, M. K. (1962). Visual pattern recognition by moment invariants. *I.R.E. Transactions on Information Theory*, *8*(2), 179–187. doi:10.1109/TIT.1962.1057692

Huang, H., Coatrieux, G., Shu, H., Luo, L., & Roux, C. (2012). Blind integrity verification of medical images. *IEEE Transactions on Information Technology in Biomedicine*, *16*(6), 1122–1126. doi:10.1109/TITB.2012.2207435 PMID:22801523

Huang, H., Coatrieux, G., Shu, H. Z., Luo, L. M., & Roux, C. (2010, July). Medical image tamper approximation based on an image moment signature. In *e-Health Networking Applications and Services (Healthcom), 2010 12th IEEE International Conference on* (pp. 254-259). IEEE. 10.1109/HEALTH.2010.5556561

Huang, J., & Shi, Y. Q. (1998). Adaptive Image Watermarking Scheme Based on Visual masking. *Electronics Letters, 34*(8), 748–750. doi:10.1049/el:19980545

Huang, Y., Lin, S., Stan, Z., Lu, H., & Shum, V. (2004). Face Alignment under Variable Illumination. *IEEE International Conference on Automatic Face and Gesture Recognition.*

Huang, Y., Lin, S., Stan, Z., Lu, H., & Shum, V. (2004). Noise removal and impainting model for iris image. *International Conference on Image Processing.*

Hussain, N., Wageeh, B., & Colin, B. (2013). A Review of Medical Image Watermarking Requirements for Teleradiology. *Journal of Digital Imaging, 26*(2), 326–343. doi:10.100710278-012-9527-x PMID:22975883

Hwai-Tsu, H., & Ling-Yuan, H. (2016). A mixed modulation scheme for blind image watermarking. *International Journal of Electronics and Communications, 70*(2), 172–178. doi:10.1016/j.aeue.2015.11.003

Imran, U., Asifullah, K., Rafiullah, C., & Abdul, M. (2008). *Towards a Better Robustness-Imperceptibility Tradeoff in Digital Watermarking.* Innovations and Advanced Techniques in Systems, Computing Sciences and Software Engineering.

İsmail, A. (2001). *Image Quality Statistics And Their Use In Steganalysis and Compression* (PhD Thesis). Institute for Graduate Studies in Science and Engineering, Uludağ University.

Ismail, A., Bulent, S., & Khalid, S. (2002). Statistical Evaluation of Image Quality Measures. *Journal of Electronic Imaging, 11*(2), 206–223. doi:10.1117/1.1455011

Itti, L., & Koch, C. (2000). A saliency-based search mechanism for overt and covert shifts of visual attention. *Vision Research, 40*(10-12), 1489–1506. doi:10.1016/S0042-6989(99)00163-7 PMID:10788654

Itti, L., & Koch, C. (2001). Computational Modeling of Visual Attention. Nature Reviews. *Neuroscience, 2*(3), 194–203. doi:10.1038/35058500 PMID:11256080

Jalal, F., Jalil, F., & Peter, W. (1999). *Digital Certificates: Applied Internet Security* (Vol. 1). Addison-Wesley.

Janeczko Paul, B. (2006). *Top Secret: A Handbook of Codes, Ciphers and Secret Writing.* Candlewick Press.

Jaseena & John. (2011). Text Watermarking using Combined Image and Text for Authentication and Protection. *International Journal of Computer Applications, 20*(4).

Jianquan, X., Qing, X., Dazu, H., & Duosi, X. (2010). Research on imperceptibility index of image Information Hiding. *Second International Conference on Networks Security Wireless Communications and Trusted Computing (NSWCTC).* 10.1109/NSWCTC.2010.148

Jiansheng, Q., Dong, W., Li, L. C. D., & Xuesong, W. (2014). Image quality assessment based on multi-scale representation of structure. *Digital Signal Processing*, *33*, 125–133. doi:10.1016/j.dsp.2014.06.009

Jianzhong, L., & Xiaojing, C. (2009). An adaptive secure watermarking scheme using double random-phase encoding technique. *2nd International Congress on Image and Signal Processing, CISP '09.*

Johnson, N. F., Duric, Z., & Jajodia, S. (2001). *Information Hiding: Steganography and Watermarking-Attacks and Countermeasures: Steganography and Watermarking: Attacks and Countermeasures* (Vol. 1). Springer Science & Business Media. doi:10.1007/978-1-4615-4375-6

Karthigaikumar, P., & Baskaranc Anumol, K. (2011). FPGA Implementation of High Speed Low Area DWT Based Invisible Image Watermarking Algorithm. *International Conference on Communication Technology and System Design.*

Kaushal, S., Upamanyu, M., Manjunath, B. S., & Shiv, C. (2005). Modeling the Print-Scan Process for Resilient Data Hiding, Security, Steganography, and Watermarking of Multimedia Contents. *SPIE*, *5681*, 418–429.

Kautilya. (1992). *The Arthashastra* (L. N. Rangarajan, Trans.). Penguin Books India.

Keskinarkaus, A., Pramila, A., & Seppänen, T. (2012). Image watermarking with feature point based synchronization robust to print–scan attack. *Journal of Visual Communication and Image Representation*, *23*(3), 507–515. doi:10.1016/j.jvcir.2012.01.010

Kester, Q. A., Nana, L., Pascu, A. C., Gire, S., Eghan, J. M., & Quaynor, N. N. (2015, June). A Security Technique for Authentication and Security of Medical Images in Health Information Systems. In *Computational Science and Its Applications (ICCSA), 2015 15th International Conference on* (pp. 8-13). IEEE. 10.1109/ICCSA.2015.8

Khan, A., & Malik, S. A. (2014). A high capacity reversible watermarking approach for authenticating images: Exploiting down-sampling, histogram processing, and block selection. *Information Sciences*, *256*, 162–183. doi:10.1016/j.ins.2013.07.035

Kharittha, T., Pipat, S., & Thumrongrat, A. (2015). Digital Image Watermarking based on Regularized Filter. *14th IAPR International Conference on Machine Vision Applications.*

Ki-Hyeok, B., & Sung-Hwan, J. (2001). A study on the robustness of watermark according to frequency band. *IEEE International Symposium on Industrial Electronics.* 10.1109/ISIE.2001.932024

Kim, B. S., Kwon, K. K., Kwon, S. G., Park, K. N., Song, K. I., & Lee, K. I. (2002, July). A robust wavelet-based digital watermarking using statistical characteristic of image and human visual system. In *Proc. of ITC-CSCC* (*Vol. 2*, pp. 1019-1022). Academic Press.

Kim, C. Y. (1998). Compression of color medical images in gastrointestinal endoscopy: A review. *Studies in Health Technology and Informatics*, *52*, 1046–1050. PMID:10384620

Kobayashi, L. O., & Furuie, S. S. (2009). Proposal for DICOM multiframe medical image integrity and authenticity. *Journal of Digital Imaging*, *22*(1), 71–83. doi:10.100710278-008-9103-6 PMID:18266035

Kong, X., & Feng, R. (2001). Watermarking medical signals for telemedicine. *IEEE Transactions on Information Technology in Biomedicine*, *5*(3), 195–201. doi:10.1109/4233.945290 PMID:11550841

Kundur, D., & Hatzinakos, D. (1998, May). Digital watermarking using multiresolution wavelet decomposition. In *Acoustics, Speech and Signal Processing, 1998. Proceedings of the 1998 IEEE International Conference on* (*Vol. 5*, pp. 2969-2972). IEEE.

Kundur, D., & Hatzinakos, D. (1998). Improved robust watermarking through attack characterization. *Optics Express*, *3*(12), 485–490. doi:10.1364/OE.3.000485 PMID:19384399

Kundur, D., & Hatzinakos, D. (1999). Digital watermarking for telltale tamper proofing and authentication. *Proceedings of the IEEE*, *87*(7), 1167–1180. doi:10.1109/5.771070

Kutter, M., & Petitcolas, F. A. (1999, April). Fair benchmark for image watermarking systems. In *Security and Watermarking of Multimedia Contents* (Vol. 3657, pp. 226–240). International Society for Optics and Photonics. doi:10.1117/12.344672

Le Guillou, C., Cauvin, J. M., Solaiman, B., Robaszkiewicz, M., & Roux, C. (2000, November). Information processing in upper digestive endoscopy. In *Information Technology Applications in Biomedicine, 2000. Proceedings. 2000 IEEE EMBS International Conference on* (pp. 183-188). IEEE. 10.1109/ITAB.2000.892383

Lee, H. K., Kim, H. J., Kwon, K. R., & Lee, J. K. (2005, June). Digital watermarking of medical image using ROI information. In *Enterprise networking and Computing in Healthcare Industry, 2005. HEALTHCOM 2005. Proceedings of 7th International Workshop on* (pp. 404-407). IEEE.

Lehmann, T. M., Güld, M. O., Thies, C., Fischer, B., Spitzer, K., Keysers, D., ... Wein, B. B. (2004). Content-based image retrieval in medical applications. *Methods of Information in Medicine*, *43*(4), 354–361. doi:10.1055-0038-1633877 PMID:15472746

Li, C., & Liu, L. (2008, May). An image authentication scheme with localization and recovery. In Image and Signal Processing, 2008. CISP'08. Congress on (Vol. 5, pp. 669-673). IEEE. doi:10.1109/CISP.2008.374

Li, C. T., & Yang, F. M. (2003). One-dimensional neighborhood forming strategy for fragile watermarking. *Journal of Electronic Imaging*, *12*(2), 284–292. doi:10.1117/1.1557156

Li, M., Poovendran, R., & Narayanan, S. (2005). Protecting patient privacy against unauthorized release of medical images in a group communication environment. *Computerized Medical Imaging and Graphics*, *29*(5), 367–383. doi:10.1016/j.compmedimag.2005.02.003 PMID:15893452

Liew, S. C., & Zain, J. M. (2010, July). Reversible medical image watermarking for tamper detection and recovery. In *Computer Science and Information Technology (ICCSIT), 2010 3rd IEEE International Conference on* (Vol. 5, pp. 417-420). IEEE.

Lim, Y., Xu, C., & Feng, D. D. (2001, May). Web based image authentication using invisible fragile watermark. In *Proceedings of the Pan-Sydney area workshop on Visual information processing-Volume 11* (pp. 31-34). Australian Computer Society, Inc.

Lin, C. Y., & Chang, S. F. (2000, May). Semifragile watermarking for authenticating JPEG visual content. In *Security and Watermarking of Multimedia Contents II* (Vol. 3971, pp. 140–152). International Society for Optics and Photonics. doi:10.1117/12.384968

Lin, E. T., Podilchuk, C. I., & Delp, E. J. (2000, May). Detection of image alterations using semifragile watermarks. In *Security and Watermarking of Multimedia Contents II* (Vol. 3971, pp. 152–164). International Society for Optics and Photonics. doi:10.1117/12.384969

Lu, C. S., & Liao, H. Y. (2001). Multipurpose watermarking for image authentication and protection. *IEEE Transactions on Image Processing*, *10*(10), 1579–1592. doi:10.1109/83.951542 PMID:18255500

Luo, X., & Cheng, Q. (2003, October). Health information integrating and size reducing. 2003 IEEE nuclear science symposium,'medical imaging conference, and workshop of room-temperature semiconductor detectors'. In *Nuclear Science Symposium Conference Record, 2003 IEEE* (*Vol. 4*, pp. 3014-3018). IEEE.

Luo, X., Cheng, Q., & Tan, J. (2003, September). A lossless data embedding scheme for medical images in application of e-diagnosis. In *Engineering in Medicine and Biology Society, 2003. Proceedings of the 25th Annual International Conference of the IEEE* (*Vol. 1*, pp. 852-855). IEEE.

Macq, B., & Dewey, F. (1999, October). Trusted headers for medical images. In DFG VIII-D II Watermarking Workshop (Vol. 10). Erlangen.

Madsen, M. T., Berbaum, K. S., Ellingson, A. N., Thompson, B. H., Mullan, B. F., & Caldwell, R. T. (2006). A new software tool for removing, storing, and adding abnormalities to medical images for perception research studies. *Academic Radiology*, *13*(3), 305–312. doi:10.1016/j.acra.2005.11.041 PMID:16488842

Maeder, A. J., & Eckert, M. P. (1999, July). Medical image compression: Quality and performance issues. In *New Approaches in Medical Image Analysis* (Vol. 3747, pp. 93–102). International Society for Optics and Photonics. doi:10.1117/12.351629

Me, L., & Arce, G. R. (2001). A class of authentication digital watermarks for secure multimedia communication. *IEEE Transactions on Image Processing*, *10*(11), 1754–1764. doi:10.1109/83.967402 PMID:18255516

Medical Identity Theft in Healthcare. (2010). Retrieved 09, July, 2013. https://www.securetechalliance.org/publications-medical-identity-theft-in-healthcare/

Medical Image Database. https://medpix.nlm.nih.gov/home

Meerwald, P., & Uhl, A. (2001, August). Survey of wavelet-domain watermarking algorithms. In *Security and Watermarking of Multimedia Contents III* (Vol. 4314, pp. 505–517). International Society for Optics and Photonics. doi:10.1117/12.435434

Miaou, S. G., Hsu, C. M., Tsai, Y. S., & Chao, H. M. (2000). A secure data hiding technique with heterogeneous data-combining capability for electronic patient records. In *Engineering in Medicine and Biology Society, 2000. Proceedings of the 22nd Annual International Conference of the IEEE* (*Vol. 1*, pp. 280-283). IEEE.

Mohanty, S. P., Ranganathan, N., & Namballa, R. K. (2003, August). VLSI implementation of invisible digital watermarking algorithms towards the development of a secure JPEG encoder. In *Signal Processing Systems, 2003. SIPS 2003. IEEE Workshop on* (pp. 183-188). IEEE. 10.1109/SIPS.2003.1235666

Mohanty, S. P., Ranganathan, N., & Namballa, R. K. (2005). A VLSI architecture for visible watermarking in a secure still digital camera (S/sup 2/DC) design (Corrected). *IEEE Transactions on Very Large Scale Integration (VLSI) Systems, 13*(8), 1002–1012.

Mostafa, S. A., El-Sheimy, N., Tolba, A. S., Abdelkader, F. M., & Elhindy, H. M. (2010). Wavelet packets-based blind watermarking for medical image management. *The Open Biomedical Engineering Journal, 4*(1), 93–98. doi:10.2174/1874120701004010093 PMID:20700520

Moulin, P., & Ivanovic, A. (2003). The zero-rate spread-spectrum watermarking game. *IEEE Transactions on Signal Processing, 51*(4), 1098–1117. doi:10.1109/TSP.2003.809370

Mukundan, R., & Ramakrishnan, K. R. (1998). *Moment functions in image analysis-theory and applications.* World Scientific. doi:10.1142/3838

Mwangi, E. (2007, December). A geometric attack resistant image watermarking scheme based on invariant centroids. In *Signal Processing and Information Technology, 2007 IEEE International Symposium on* (pp. 190-193). IEEE. 10.1109/ISSPIT.2007.4458073

Nambakhsh, M. S., Ahmadian, A., Ghavami, M., Dilmaghani, R. S., & Karimi-Fard, S. (2006, August). A novel blind watermarking of ECG signals on medical images using EZW algorithm. In *Engineering in Medicine and Biology Society, 2006. EMBS'06. 28th Annual International Conference of the IEEE* (pp. 3274-3277). IEEE. 10.1109/IEMBS.2006.259603

Navas, K. A., & Sasikumar, M. (2007, March). Survey of medical image watermarking algorithms. In *Proc. Internation Conf. Sciences of Electronics, Technologies of Information and Telecommunications* (pp. 25-29). Academic Press.

Navas, K. A., Sasikumar, M., & Sreevidya, S. (2007, June). A benchmark for medical image watermarking. In *Systems, Signals and Image Processing, 2007 and 6th EURASIP Conference focused on Speech and Image Processing, Multimedia Communications and Services. 14th International Workshop on* (pp. 237-240). IEEE. 10.1109/IWSSIP.2007.4381197

Nayak, J., Bhat, P. S., Acharya, R., & Niranjan, U. C. (2004). Simultaneous storage of medical images in the spatial and frequency domain: A comparative study. *Biomedical Engineering Online, 3*(1), 17. doi:10.1186/1475-925X-3-17 PMID:15180899

Nayak, J., Bhat, P. S., Kumar, M. S., & Acharya, U. R. (2004, December). Reliable and robust transmission and storage of medical images with patient information. In *Signal Processing and Communications, 2004. SPCOM'04. 2004 International Conference on* (pp. 91-95). IEEE. 10.1109/SPCOM.2004.1458363

Nayak, J., Bhat, P. S., Kumar, M. S., & Acharya, U. R. (2004, December). Reliable transmission and storage of medical images with patient information using error control codes. In *India Annual Conference, 2004. Proceedings of the IEEE INDICON 2004. First* (pp. 147-150). IEEE. 10.1109/INDICO.2004.1497726

Ni, Z., Shi, Y. Q., Ansari, N., & Su, W. (2006). Reversible data hiding. *IEEE Transactions on Circuits and Systems for Video Technology, 16*(3), 354–362. doi:10.1109/TCSVT.2006.869964

Nikolaidis, A., Tsekeridou, S., Tefas, A., & Solachidis, V. (2001). A survey on watermarking application scenarios and related attacks. In *Image Processing, 2001. Proceedings. 2001 International Conference on* (Vol. 3, pp. 991-994). IEEE. 10.1109/ICIP.2001.958292

Oh, G. T., Lee, Y. B., & Yeom, S. J. (2004, June). Security mechanism for medical image information on PACS using invisible watermark. In *International Conference on High Performance Computing for Computational Science* (pp. 315-324). Springer.

Osada, M., & Tsukui, H. (2002, August). Development of ultrasound/endoscopy pacs (picture archiving and communication system) and investigation of compression method for cine images. In *Electronic Imaging and Multimedia Technology III* (Vol. 4925, pp. 99–103). International Society for Optics and Photonics. doi:10.1117/12.481574

Parah, S. A., Ahad, F., Sheikh, J. A., Loan, N. A., & Bhat, G. M. (2017). A New Reversible and high capacity data hiding technique for E-healthcare applications. *Multimedia Tools and Applications*, *76*(3), 3943–3975. doi:10.100711042-016-4196-2

Parameswaran, L., & Anbumani, K. (2008). Content-based watermarking for image authentication using independent component analysis. *Informatica, 32*(3).

Pereira, S., Voloshynovskiy, S., Madueno, M., Marchand-Maillet, S., & Pun, T. (2001, April). Second generation benchmarking and application oriented evaluation. In *International Workshop on Information Hiding* (pp. 340-353). Springer. 10.1007/3-540-45496-9_25

Piva, A., Barni, M., Bartolini, F., & De Rosa, A. (2005). Data hiding technologies for digital radiography. *IEE Proceedings. Vision Image and Signal Processing*, *152*(5), 604–610. doi:10.1049/ip-vis:20041240

Planitz, B., & Maeder, A. (2005, February). Medical image watermarking: a study on image degradation. In *Proc. Australian Pattern Recognition Society Workshop on Digital Image Computing*. WDIC.

Podilchuk, C. I., & Delp, E. J. (2001). Digital watermarking: Algorithms and applications. *IEEE Signal Processing Magazine*, *18*(4), 33–46. doi:10.1109/79.939835

Prokop, R. J., & Reeves, A. P. (1992). A survey of moment-based techniques for unoccluded object representation and recognition. *CVGIP. Graphical Models and Image Processing*, *54*(5), 438–460. doi:10.1016/1049-9652(92)90027-U

Puech, W., & Rodrigues, J. M. (2004, September). A new crypto-watermarking method for medical images safe transfer. In *Signal Processing Conference, 2004 12th European* (pp. 1481-1484). IEEE.

Qi, X., & Qi, J. (2007). A robust content-based digital image watermarking scheme. *Signal Processing, 87*(6), 1264-1280.

Quellec, G., Russell, S. R., & Abramoff, M. D. (2011). Optimal filter framework for automated, instantaneous detection of lesions in retinal images. *IEEE Transactions on Medical Imaging*, *30*(2), 523–533. doi:10.1109/TMI.2010.2089383 PMID:21292586

Queluz, M. P. (2001). Authentication of digital images and video: Generic models and a new contribution. *Signal Processing Image Communication*, *16*(5), 461–475. doi:10.1016/S0923-5965(00)00010-2

Radharani, S., & Valarmathi, M. L. (2010). A study on watermarking schemes for image authentication. *International Journal of Computers and Applications*, *2*(4), 24–32. doi:10.5120/658-925

Rahimi, F., & Rabbani, H. (2011). A dual adaptive watermarking scheme in contourlet domain for DICOM images. *Biomedical Engineering Online*, *10*(1), 53. doi:10.1186/1475-925X-10-53 PMID:21682862

Rey, C., & Dugelay, J. L. (2002). A survey of watermarking algorithms for image authentication. *EURASIP Journal on Applied Signal Processing*, (1): 613–621.

Ritenour, E. R., & Maidment, A. D. (1999). Lossy compression should not be used in certain imaging applications such as chest radiography. *Medical Physics*, *26*(9), 1773–1775. doi:10.1118/1.598783 PMID:10505862

Rodriguez-Colin, R., Claudia, F. U., & Trinidad-Blas, G. D. J. (2007, February). Data hiding scheme for medical images. In *Electronics, Communications and Computers, 2007. CONIELECOMP'07. 17th International Conference on* (pp. 32-32). IEEE. 10.1109/CONIELECOMP.2007.14

Schneier, B. (1997). *Applied Cryptography* (2nd ed.). Paris: International Thomson Publishing.

Schneier, B. (1996). *Applied cryptography: protocols, algorithms, and source code in C*. Wiley.

Schou, C. D., Frost, J., & Maconachy, W. V. (2004). Information assurance in biomedical informatics systems. *IEEE Engineering in Medicine and Biology Magazine*, *23*(1), 110–118. doi:10.1109/MEMB.2004.1297181 PMID:15154266

Sebald, D. J., & Bucklew, J. A. (2000). Support vector machine techniques for nonlinear equalization. *IEEE Transactions on Signal Processing*, *48*(11), 3217–3226. doi:10.1109/78.875477

Seitz, J. (2005). *Digital watermarking for digital media*. IGI Global. doi:10.4018/978-1-59140-518-4

Shih, F. Y., & Wu, Y. T. (2005). Robust watermarking and compression for medical images based on genetic algorithms. *Information Sciences*, *175*(3), 200–216. doi:10.1016/j.ins.2005.01.013

Singh, A., & Dutta, M. K. (2014, November). A blind & fragile watermarking scheme for tamper detection of medical images preserving ROI. In *Medical Imaging, m-Health and Emerging Communication Systems (MedCom), 2014 International Conference on* (pp. 230-234). IEEE. 10.1109/MedCom.2014.7006009

Solachidis, V., Tefas, A., Nikolaidis, N., Tsekeridou, S., Nikolaidis, A., & Pitas, I. (2001). A benchmarking protocol for watermarking methods. In *Image Processing, 2001. Proceedings. 2001 International Conference on* (Vol. 3, pp. 1023-1026). IEEE. 10.1109/ICIP.2001.958300

Srinivasan, Y., Nutter, B., Mitra, S., Phillips, B., & Ferris, D. (2004, June). Secure transmission of medical records using high capacity steganography. In *Computer-Based Medical Systems, 2004. CBMS 2004. Proceedings. 17th IEEE Symposium on* (pp. 122-127). IEEE. 10.1109/CBMS.2004.1311702

Tagliasacchi, M., Valenzise, G., & Tubaro, S. (2009). Hash-based identification of sparse image tampering. *IEEE Transactions on Image Processing*, *18*(11), 2491–2504. doi:10.1109/TIP.2009.2028251 PMID:19635704

Terry, M. (2009). Medical identity theft and telemedicine security. *Telemedicine Journal and e-Health, 15*(10), 928–933. doi:10.1089/tmj.2009.9932 PMID:19908998

Tian, J. (2002, April). Wavelet-based reversible watermarking for authentication. In *Security and Watermarking of Multimedia Contents IV* (Vol. 4675, pp. 679–691). International Society for Optics and Photonics. doi:10.1117/12.465329

Unser, M., & Aldroubi, A. (1996). A review of wavelets in biomedical applications. *Proceedings of the IEEE, 84*(4), 626–638. doi:10.1109/5.488704

Van Leest, A. R. N. O., van der Veen, M., & Bruekers, F. (2003, September). Reversible image watermarking. In *Image Processing, 2003. ICIP 2003. Proceedings. 2003 International Conference on* (Vol. 2, pp. II-731). IEEE. 10.1109/ICIP.2003.1246784

Voloshynovskiy, S., Pereira, S., Iquise, V., & Pun, T. (2001). Attack modelling: Towards a second generation watermarking benchmark. *Signal Processing, 81*(6), 1177–1214. doi:10.1016/S0165-1684(01)00039-1

Wakatani, A. (2002, January). Digital watermarking for ROI medical images by using compressed signature image. In *System Sciences, 2002. HICSS. Proceedings of the 35th Annual Hawaii International Conference on* (pp. 2043-2048). IEEE. 10.1109/HICSS.2002.994129

Walia, E., & Suneja, A. (2013). Fragile and blind watermarking technique based on Weber's law for medical image authentication. *IET Computer Vision, 7*(1), 9–19. doi:10.1049/iet-cvi.2012.0109

Walia, E., & Suneja, A. (2014). A robust watermark authentication technique based on Weber's descriptor. *Signal, Image and Video Processing, 8*(5), 859–872. doi:10.100711760-012-0312-6

Walters, W., & Betz, A. (2012). Medical identity theft. *Journal of Consumer Education*, 75.

Watson, A. B. (1993, September). DCT quantization matrices visually optimized for individual images. In *Human vision, visual processing, and digital display IV* (Vol. 1913, pp. 202–217). International Society for Optics and Photonics. doi:10.1117/12.152694

White, L. A. E., Krousel-Wood, M. A., & Mather, F. (2001). Technology meets healthcare: Distance learning and telehealth. *The Ochsner Journal, 3*(1), 22–29. PMID:21765713

Woo, C.S., Du, J., & Pham, B.L. (2005). *Multiple watermark method for privacy control and tamper detection in medical images*. Academic Press.

Wu, J. H., Chang, R. F., Chen, C. J., Wang, C. L., Kuo, T. H., Moon, W. K., & Chen, D. R. (2008). Tamper detection and recovery for medical images using near-lossless information hiding technique. *Journal of Digital Imaging, 21*(1), 59–76. doi:10.100710278-007-9011-1 PMID:17393256

Wu, M., & Liu, B. (1998, October). Watermarking for image authentication. In *Image Processing, 1998. ICIP 98. Proceedings. 1998 International Conference on* (Vol. 2, pp. 437-441). IEEE.

Wu, X., Liang, X., Liu, H., Huang, J., & Qiu, G. (2006). Reversible semi-fragile image authentication using zernike moments and integer wavelet transform. In *Digital Rights Management. Technologies, Issues, Challenges and Systems* (pp. 135–145). Berlin: Springer. doi:10.1007/11787952_11

Xin, Y., Liao, S., & Pawlak, M. (2007). Circularly orthogonal moments for geometrically robust image watermarking. *Pattern Recognition*, *40*(12), 3740–3752. doi:10.1016/j.patcog.2007.05.004

Xu, B., Wang, J., Liu, X., & Zhang, Z. (2007, August). Passive steganalysis using image quality metrics and multi-class support vector machine. In *Natural Computation, 2007. ICNC 2007. Third International Conference on* (Vol. 3, pp. 215-220). IEEE. 10.1109/ICNC.2007.544

Yadav, N., Pahal, N., Kalra, P., Lall, B., & Chaudhury, S. (2011, February). A Novel Approach for Securing Forensic Documents Using Rectangular Region-of-Interest (RROI). In *Emerging Applications of Information Technology (EAIT), 2011 Second International Conference on* (pp. 198-201). IEEE.

Yang, H., & Kot, A. C. (2006). Binary image authentication with tampering localization by embedding cryptographic signature and block identifier. *IEEE Signal Processing Letters*, *13*(12), 741–744. doi:10.1109/LSP.2006.879829

Yang, M., Trifas, M., Chen, L., Song, L., Aires, D. B., & Elston, J. (2010). Secure patient information and privacy in medical imaging. *Journal of Systemics, Cybernetics and Informatics*, *8*(3), 63–66.

Yeung, M. M., & Mintzer, F. (1997, October). An invisible watermarking technique for image verification. In *Image Processing, 1997. Proceedings., International Conference on* (Vol. 2, pp. 680-683). IEEE. 10.1109/ICIP.1997.638587

Zain, J., & Clarke, M. (2005). Security in telemedicine: issues in watermarking medical images. Sciences of Electronic, Technologies of Information and Telecommunications, Tunisia.

Zain, J. M., & Fauzi, A. R. (2006, August). Medical image watermarking with tamper detection and recovery. In *Engineering in Medicine and Biology Society, 2006. EMBS'06. 28th Annual International Conference of the IEEE* (pp. 3270-3273). IEEE. 10.1109/IEMBS.2006.260767

Zhao, X., Ho, A. T., Treharne, H., Pankajakshan, V., Culnane, C., & Jiang, W. (2007, November). A novel semi-fragile image watermarking, authentication and self-restoration technique using the slant transform. In *Intelligent Information Hiding and Multimedia Signal Processing, 2007. IIHMSP 2007. Third International Conference on* (Vol. 1, pp. 283-286). IEEE. 10.1109/IIH-MSP.2007.50

Zhou, X. Q., Huang, H. K., & Lou, S. L. (2001). Authenticity and integrity of digital mammography images. *IEEE Transactions on Medical Imaging*, *20*(8), 784–791. doi:10.1109/42.938246 PMID:11513029

Anand, D., & Niranjan, U. C. (1998). Watermarking medical images with patient information. *Proceedings of the 20th Annual International Conference of the IEEE Engineering in Medicine and Biology Society,* 20, 703-706. doi: 10.1109/IEMBS.1998.745518

This research was previously published in Intelligent Innovations in Multimedia Data Engineering and Management; pages 1-37, copyright year 2019 by Engineering Science Reference (an imprint of IGI Global).

Section 4

Securing Patient Data and Medical Records

Chapter 27
Healthcare Information Security in the Cyber World

Brian S. Coats
University of Maryland – Baltimore, USA

Subrata Acharya
Towson University, USA

ABSTRACT

Integrity, efficiency, and accessibility in healthcare aren't new issues, but it has been only in recent years that they have gained significant traction with the US government passing a number of laws to greatly enhance the exchange of medical information amidst all relevant stakeholders. While many plans have been created, guidelines formed, and national strategies forged, there are still significant gaps in how actual technology will be applied to achieve these goals. A holistic approach with adequate input and support from all vital partakers is key to appropriate problem modeling and accurate solution determination. To this effect, this research presents a cognitive science-based solution by addressing comprehensive compliance implementation as mandated by the Health Insurance Portability and Accountability Act, the certified Electronic Health Record standard, and the federal Meaningful Use program. Using the developed standardized frameworks, an all-inclusive technological solution is presented to provide accessibility, efficiency, and integrity of healthcare information security systems.

INTRODUCTION

Healthcare providers and payers have been attempting to achieve HIPAA compliance for nearly a decade. In 1998, shortly after HIPAA's signing, the research firm Gartner Group estimated the implementation of HIPAA would collectively cost healthcare providers $5 billion and health plans $14 billion. By 2005, HHS was estimating that the costs could be at least 3 times the original amount for providers and as much as 10 times the original amount for health plans (HIPAA Security Rule, 2008). In 2009, HIMSS sponsored research suggested that the actual implementation costs for providers would be closer to $40 billion (Title 45-Public Welfare, 1996). This trend indicates a considerable cost increase that in some

DOI: 10.4018/978-1-6684-6311-6.ch027

cases could prove crippling, especially for smaller entities. The costs of these implementations have deviated even more than their timelines and creating financial burdens drastically higher than originally anticipated. Surmounting costs aside, the original schedule set by the Privacy and Security Rules required compliance by 2003 and 2005 respectively (EHR Adoption Trends, 2004). Clearly these compliance goals have not been met by most healthcare organizations around the country. While the road to HIPAA compliance is proving elusive and costly, organizations clearly understand the importance and necessity of completing the undertaking. HIPAA will ultimately ensure better privacy and security of ePHI data. Organizations have both ethical and financial motivations to provide their customers the guarantees that HIPAA requires and are spending massive amounts of time and money on their implementations. It is critical for these organizations to have clear and comprehensive guidelines to follow for maximum efficiency in their efforts.

There are a variety of reasons why HIPAA implementations have proved more expensive and taken considerably longer than originally anticipated by federal regulators and healthcare organizations alike. The biggest hurdle to overcome is simply the creation of an assessment, testing, and implementation plan. While many government agencies, private foundations, and industry consortiums have established high level guidelines and recommendations of how to address each of the HIPAA Rules, there is no nationally mandated implementation plan or standardized framework for organizations to follow. Each entity is responsible for reviewing the guidelines and determining the appropriate solution. The published recommendations are at a very abstract level and require much interpretation to formulate an actual implementation strategy. With a lack of clear direction, many entities have difficulty determining the best path for them to follow to satisfy each requirement. Furthermore, without an apparent plan or timeline, it becomes extremely difficult for organizations to generate realistic cost estimates for their compliance efforts and likewise secure the necessary budgetary commitments. This point has been demonstrated consistently since the first HIPAA implementations began. National cost estimates of HIPAA efforts are approaching a factor of ten higher than what regulators estimated when the law was first enacted (Coats, Acharya, Saluja, and Fuller, 2012).

One of the major steps towards fully meeting the HIPAA regulations is the implementation of an EHR system. With over 90% of healthcare providers in some stage of an EHR solution, HIMSS indicates that as of December 2011, only 66 hospitals, just over 1% nationally, have actually achieved Stage 7 – the final EHR adoption stage (Blumenthal and Tavenner, 2010). Furthermore, even with the federal government offering anywhere from $100,000 to over $2 million per provider, per year just to demonstrate the 'meaningful use' of a partial EHR implementation, only about 41% of providers have cashed in. Over $5.5 billion has already been paid to healthcare providers participating in the Meaningful Use program, but almost another potential $8 billion is being left unclaimed. Clearly providers are being given the proper motivation to implement EHR systems but are finding themselves ill-equipped to take the necessary steps to accomplish the task.

EHR systems will afford significant cost savings to healthcare providers by streamlining and standardizing their exchange and storage of ePHI. These systems will also enable better access to patient data by all parties - providers, insurers, and patients themselves. But with this improved access, healthcare providers are presented with the challenge of ensuring both privacy and security are preserved. Additionally, providers have the daunting task of making the process of patients gaining electronic access to their data simple and straightforward. The healthcare industry, like all industries, entered the digital age with each provider creating its own silos of data stores and corresponding security frameworks to access that data. As such, they are finding themselves poorly positioned to enable the distributed access to

Figure 1. Standardized model

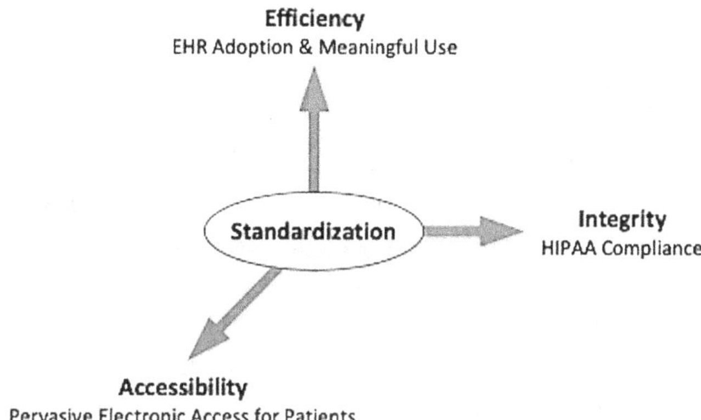

their data that EHR systems facilitate. The regulations and programs, including HIPAA and Meaningful Use, that are driving EHR adoption, provide almost zero guidance on how to address these enormous usability issue. The federal program NSTIC is singularly tasked with creating an "Identity Ecosystem" of interoperable technology standards and policies to provide increased security and privacy, but most importantly ease of use for individuals (EHR Incentive Programs, 2012). The Department of Health and Human Services, the agency responsible for HIPAA and Meaningful Use, is intimately involved in the development of NSTIC. This strategy will force the healthcare entirely restructure their approaches to identity access and management from centralized to distributed models.

The recognition of the need for a standardized framework for healthcare information security is widespread throughout the healthcare industry and federal government, all the way to the White House. Whether it be HIPAA compliance, EHR systems and Meaningful Use, or distributed electronic patient access, every healthcare entity is approaching these issues independently. This approach is continuing to prove both costly and timely, and ultimately the general public feels the impact. The fundamental objectives of all these regulations and programs provide for valuable improvements to the overall health care in the United States. Unfortunately, these benefits can only be realized when the programs are completed and at present that necessary steps are proving extremely challenging for healthcare organizations.

To this effect, the goal of this research is to bridge the gap from regulation to practice in a number of key technological areas of healthcare information security. Using standardized frameworks, this research proposes how accessibility, efficiency, and integrity in healthcare information security can be achieved. This research will converge on these issues by addressing HIPAA compliance, EHR Adoption and the federal Meaningful Use program, and pervasive electronic access for patients; all from the healthcare provider's perspective as shown in Figure 1.

The salient contributions of this research are:

- *The creation of the Healthcare Information Security Framework (HISF) to offer direction for organizations to plan and execute their overall HIPAA compliance projects including attestation,*
- *The creation of the Healthcare Information Security Plan (HISP) to provide comprehensive implementation level guidance for satisfying HIPAA regulations,*
- *The creation of the Healthcare Information Security Testing Directive (HISTD) and a collection of open source security testing software for organizations to assess and mitigate their systems.*

- *The creation of the Healthcare Federated Identity Framework (HFIF) that will position healthcare providers to enable distributed electronic access to patient data.*

Background and Related Work

Information security has perpetually been a hot topic for all industries. The specific subject of healthcare information technology (HIT) and healthcare information security (HIS) has sparked a vast amount of research over the last few decades and is reflected in a wide array of peer-reviewed scholarly papers and journal articles. Furthermore, much attention has been given to the difficulties faced in HIT and HIS related to Health Insurance Portability and Accountability Act (HIPAA) implementation and assessment, EHR adoption, and patient accessibility. After a thorough examination of a substantial amount of the related literature, clear shortcomings became evident in the technological solutions as many researchers lamented some common problems and searched for answers.

Healthcare providers and payers have been attempting to achieve Health Insurance Portability and Accountability Act (HIPAA) compliance for nearly a decade. In 1998, shortly after HIPAA's signing, the research firm Gartner Group estimated the implementation of HIPAA would collectively cost healthcare providers $5 billion and health plans $14 billion nationally. As early as 2003 when the final regulations for both HIPAA rules had been released, healthcare legal expert George Annas (Annas, 2003) was already predicting HIPAA implementations to be "costly, inconsistent, and frustrating". Annas went on to state that "HIPAA consultants" were quickly becoming necessary for hospitals, health plans, and physician practices in order to understand how to comply with "long, complex" unclear regulations. By 2009, researchers still echoed that sentiment by offering that providers have pressure to hire external consultants as "there is a high degree of uncertainty associated with the interpretation of regulations and organizations lack adequate in-house resources" (Appari, Anthony, and Johnson, 2009). The Department of Health & Human Services (HHS) was already estimating that the costs could be at least 3 times the original amount for providers and as much as 10 times the original amount for health plans (HIPAA Return on Investment, 2005). By 2009, HIMSS sponsored research suggested that the actual nationwide implementation costs for providers would be closer to $40 billion. Most recently, the Department of Health and Human Services had re-estimated this figure to have grown to a national average of $114 million to $225 million in the first year and a recurring annual cost of $14.5 million, per healthcare provider (HIPAA Final Rule, 2013). This trend indicates a considerable cost increase that in some cases could prove crippling, especially for smaller entities. The costs of these implementations have deviated even more than their timelines and are creating financial burdens drastically higher than originally anticipated. Many providers and researchers argue the HHS is still significantly underestimating the actual compliance costs (Hirsch, 2013).

Surmounting costs aside, the original schedule set by the Privacy and Security Rules required compliance by 2003 and 2005 respectively (Regulations and Guide, 2014). Unfortunately, these compliance goals were not met by most healthcare organizations around the country. In 2008, the Centers for Medicare and Medicaid Services performed a review of HIPAA covered entities (CEs) and their compliance only with the Security Rule. This review demonstrated that CEs continued to struggle with meeting all aspects of the regulations, specifically in the areas of risk assessment, currency of policies and procedures, security training, workforce clearance, workstation security, and encryption (HIPAA Compliance Review Analysis and Summary of Results, 2008). Even in 2013, Solove (2013) discusses the still present gap in HIPAA compliance by all CEs and offers that "in addition to the dynamism of

HIPAA, compliance is not something that is ever completely solved". He continues that it is not a one-time implementation but rather a daily challenge to maintain. As such, healthcare entities are faced not only with just becoming HIPAA compliant at single point in time, but they must achieve and maintain compliance perpetually. Therefore, it is critical for these organizations to have clear and comprehensive guidelines to follow for maximum efficiency in their efforts.

Fichman, Kohli and Krishnan (2011) note that because ePHI is personal by nature this compounds public fears and concerns related to data breaches. Healthcare providers must work hard to gain the trust of their patients and work even harder to maintain that trust. Data breaches have severe consequences for providers ranging from fines, embarrassment, reputational damage, and remediation costs (Kwon and Johnson, 2013). HHS, as part of the Health Information Technology for Economic and Clinical Health (HITECH) Act, has implemented a new data breach notification process that requires healthcare entities to publicly post breach announcements for cases involving 500 or more individuals (Breach Notification Rule, 2009). Similarly, HITECH also increased the severity of the fines up to $1.5 million for HIPAA violations related to both inadvertent and willful disclosure of patient data. While the penalties are dramatically increasing and organizations are investing in security protection and assessment tools, the reality is there is still a significant gap between the regulations and practice. In the first two years since the HHS installed the Breach Notification Rule, over 10 million patients' data were inappropriately disclosed (Enforcements Results per Year, 2010). A number of issues have been identified as the reason for healthcare organization's limited success with implementing security practices that are effective and compliant with the HIPAA directives. These issues include superficial implementations that don't align technology and business practices (Kayworth and Whitten, 2010), the tendency to be reactive instead of proactive due lack of active, established security programs and security measures being implemented piece meal instead of a comprehensive, complimentary approach (Xia and Johnson, 2010). Compliance as "a snapshot of security about whether an organization exhibits controls". They offer that organizations are more driven by compliance than true data security. Johnson, Goetz and Pfleeger (2009) cautioned that organizations that employ security assessment models with a "check-the-box" mentality do not have true assurance their security measures are effective; it is only through comprehensive testing and auditing that the measures are vetted. Aral and Weill (2007) make the apt distinction that actual security is defined by how well the security controls used for compliance are deployed and function.

As much of the published literature confirms, the core challenge that healthcare providers face with meeting Health Insurance Portability and Accountability Act (HIPAA) compliance, while also ensuring effective security, is simply the creation of a plan to assess and test their environments. Further, once the assessments and tests are complete, the organizations also need a remediation plan in the form of an implementation guide to react to any issues discovered. In an effort to provide organizations a standardized approach for addressing the HIPAA regulations, the National Institute for Standards and Technology (NIST) produced special publication 800-66 that focused on the implementation of the HIPAA Security Rule. This guide gets closer to the concept of mapping regulation to implementation but still does not provide specific actionable recommendations. While many government agencies, private foundations, and industry consortiums have established high level guidelines and recommendations of how to address each of the HIPAA rules, there is no nationally mandated implementation plan or standardized framework for organizations to follow. Each entity is responsible for reviewing the guidelines and determining the appropriate solution.

The idea of having actionable plans based off these various publications as well as other industry best practices is not a novel concept in of itself (Acharya, Coats, Saluja, and Fuller, 2014). The Health

Information Trust (HITRUST) Alliance has created their *Common Security Framework (CSF)* to serve as a holistic solution to this significant need. HITRUST presents their CSF as a "comprehensive and flexible framework that remains sufficiently prescriptive in how control requirements can be scaled and tailored for healthcare organizations of varying types and sizes". Furthermore, the CSF includes federal regulations and standards such as HIPAA, Payment Card Industry Data Security Standards (PCI DSS), and Control Objectives for Information and Related Technology (COBIT) as well as recommendations from NIST, the Federal Trade Commission (FTC), and the International Organization for Standardization (ISO). The scope of the CSF in fact exactly matches the need of a prescriptive, standardized solution for healthcare organizations to follow. As such, it is not surprising that the CSF is the most widely adopted security framework by the healthcare industry in the United States. Unfortunately, the CSF like the consulting firms, comes with a substantial price tag for an annual subscription to access their framework content and information and have very limited (ranges from 10-20 annually depending on subscription tier) 'tickets' for working with a knowledgeable professional about how to implement the CSF.

Outside of healthcare, the concept of establishing standardized frameworks is very common. NIST has established the Risk Management Framework (RMF) to provide a systematic approach for managing organizational risk across all industries and sectors. The framework can be applied to either new or existing information systems to evaluate risk as well select, implement, assess, and monitor mitigating controls to risk. Similarly, the Financial Services Roundtable, a collaborative body made up of the leadership of the nation's largest financial institutions, saw the need to create a standardized approach for information security within the financial industry. As a result, the verbose Banking Industry Technology Secretariat (BITS) Security Program was created that shared information security best practices and successful strategies.

Up to this point a comprehensive solution, like the CSF, RMF, or BITS Security Program, has not been presented in an open academic format for the healthcare industry such that organizations can perform both the abstract style assessment using questionnaires and surveys as well as conduct the active penetration testing themselves. What is also missing from the current commercial offerings is the ability to see specifically the derivation of the all the assessment mechanisms so that they can be updated and adapted if and when regulations are added or changed. This mapping information, tying regulation to practice and assessment, is proprietary to the commercial offerings as it effectively constitutes the entire value of their engagements aside from the man-hours to perform the assessment. Therefore, as it stands today, 2 basic options have developed, either 'pay to play' by contracting with one of the private security assessment firms that specialize in HIPAA compliance or establish a subscription to HITRUST's CSF, or alternately use the NIST guideline and muddle through alone. With many organizations' considerable budget constraints, the latter option of proceeding independently using the existing guidance tends to become the common option. Additionally, without an apparent plan or timeline to follow, it becomes extremely difficult for organizations to generate realistic cost estimates for their compliance efforts and likewise secure the necessary budgetary commitments. This results in enormous wastes of capital, time, and energy for the healthcare provider. This point has been demonstrated consistently since the first HIPAA implementations began. Consequently, national cost estimates of HIPAA efforts have well eclipsed a factor of ten higher than what regulators estimated when the law was first enacted.

Only further complicating the HIPAA compliance landscape, the final rules of the Health Information Technology for Economic and Clinical Health (HITECH) Act of 2009 introduced significant changes to the prior HIPAA regulations. While designed to encourage the development of health information exchanges these changes are still requiring additional attention and therefore cost and effort to be extended to HIPAA compliance. As part of these changes, the rules expanded the types of entities that are covered by HIPAA. Previously, HIPAA only dealt with healthcare providers, health plans, and healthcare clearinghouses. The final rules released in January 2013 now defines covered entities as any vendor that creates, transmits, receives, or maintains ePHI. Furthermore, these additional entities can now be held civilly and criminally liable. Aside from new entities being covered, even those entities that had achieved or were close to achieving HIPAA compliance coming into 2013 are now having to evaluate and accommodate the considerable additions and changes to the regulations. The result of these recent changes has even more entities scrambling to become HIPAA compliant and effectively taking the cumulative percentage of all covered entities' compliance further away from the hundred percent target.

When examining the potential solutions for providing electronic patient access to EHRs there are numerous existing models to consider although this research submits that a viable solution has yet to be developed that is scalable, cost-effective, and easily available to virtually everyone. This electronic identity situation has many healthcare providers finding themselves poorly positioned to enable the types of distributed access that EHR systems are supposed to facilitate. The regulations and programs that are driving EHR adoption, including HIPAA and Meaningful Use, provide virtually no direction on how to tackle these enormous usability and efficiency challenges. The federal program National Strategy for Trusted Identities in Cyberspace (NSTIC) is aggressively working to establish interoperable technology standards and policies for sharing identity information potentially anywhere in the public or private sectors. The Department of Health and Human Services, the agency responsible for HIPAA and Meaningful Use, is intimately involved in the development of NSTIC. This strategy will compound the need for healthcare entities to entirely restructure their approaches for identity and access management from centralized to distributed models.

Framework and Methodology

Organizations have both ethical and financial motivations to provide their customers the guarantees and benefits that the Health Insurance Portability and Accountability Act (HIPAA) and EHR systems afford. As a result, healthcare providers are spending massive amounts of time and money on their implementations. When considering the 3 basic goals of this research - integrity, efficiency, and accessibility in healthcare - it became clear that any technology solution would require a delicate balance of these 3 areas in order to be viable for practical application. As such, integrity and accessibility quickly became the 2 pillars and motivations of the solutions, while efficiency became the measure of success. Integrity (or compliance) was the first of the 2 foundational elements tackled. In a very basic sense, the design approach was to determine how an organization could measure and achieve compliance (ensure integrity) in an efficient manner. Once integrity had been addressed, the research's attention shifted to how to make healthcare access more easily attainable and efficient. These efforts resulted in the creation of 2 unique frameworks that aim to bring together integrity, accessibility, and efficiency for a healthcare provider's organization. The process is included as a step-by-step manner in the Figure 2.

Healthcare Information Security Compliance Framework

A federal grant from the Department of Health & Human Services (HHS), that begun in early 2011, connected Towson University and a large federally-funded regional trauma center and national healthcare provider located in central Pennsylvania national healthcare provider (specific identity of the hospital

Figure 2. Conceptual view of proposed Framework

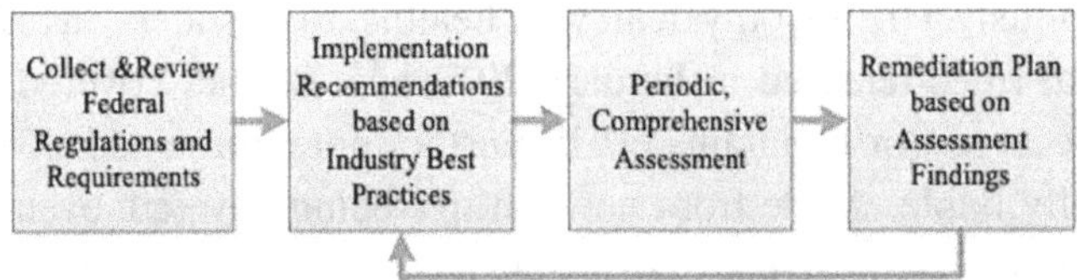

has been suppressed due to non-disclosure agreement of grant). Part of the deliverables of this grant was to assess the Pennsylvania Hospital's HIPAA compliance and to respond to any shortcomings. As a result of this original need, the Healthcare Information Security Compliance Framework (HISCF) concept was first developed with the very specific goal of creating a HIPAA compliance assessment plan for a hospital. During the early discovery and research stage of the grant, it became very apparent that there was a clear lack of implementation level guidance on how to achieve HIPAA compliance and furthermore how to assess it. It became equally evident that the research and work associated with bringing this large national hospital into compliance could be leveraged to create and propose a standardized, reusable model that other organizations could potentially benefit from.

Framework Creation Process

With the goal of creating a standardized method for assessing an organization's HIPAA compliance and addressing any findings, it became apparent there were key steps to accomplish this task. The first step was to create a comprehensive set of all the HIPAA regulations, consisting of the Security and Privacy Rules, as well as any other requirements laid out by HHS related to HIPAA, including the revisions to HIPAA spelled out in the Health Information Technology for Economic and Clinical Health (HITECH) Act. Once all the requirements had been defined, the next step was analyzing their technical implications and what implementation decisions would have relevance to compliance. Following this general analysis, research was done on what guidance NIST, HHS, and other federal agencies had provided to date, and what guidance private organizations like the Healthcare Information Management Systems Society (HIMSS) had produced both from a regulation and implementation perspective (Acharya, Coats, Saluja, and Fuller, 2013). At this point, all the regulations and requirements had been documented, their technical implications identified, and the existing guidance reviewed. It was during this step that the gap of actual implementation guidance was continually observed.

The next steps were to perform an examination of how HIPAA and other types of security and privacy assessments were being accomplished at other healthcare organization as well as and non-healthcare entities. This research formed the basis for the creation of the HISCF. The HISCF at its very core is an internal information security audit using the HIPAA regulations as the effective measurement of success or failure.

Starting with the conceptual basis shown in Figure 2, each step of the process was expanded into phases of actual tasks. The result was the formation of the framework shown in Figure 3. The proposed compliance framework consists of three primary phases enabling complete HIPAA compliance at its conclusion. The framework is designed to take an organization from the initial recognition of the need for compliance all the way through to implementation of any necessary changes to their environment. Further, the framework provides a post-compliance phase to ensure the healthcare provider maintains

Figure 3. Healthcare information security compliance framework

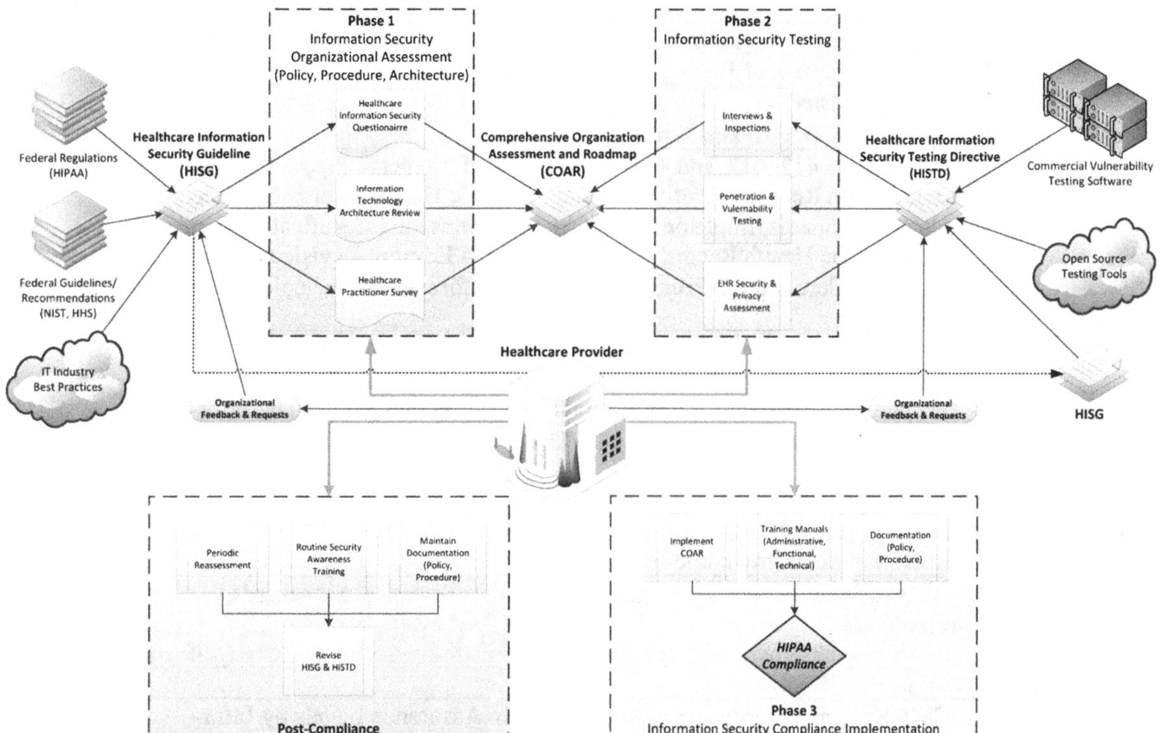

their compliance perpetually. While the phases and associated tasks are performed sequentially, there are feedback loops at almost every stage to reflect findings and feedback of successive steps to the preceding steps to ensure the assessment guides and instruments are organizationally relevant. NIST acknowledges a well-documented and repeatable compliance framework will greatly speed up the assessment and testing process, yield more consistent results, present less risk to the normal business operations of the organization, and minimize the resources needed to perform the testing. This research offers a comprehensive solution to organizational assessment and information security testing by providing step-by-step instructions for how to plan and perform information security compliance assessment and testing, how to analyze the results of the tests, and ultimately how to correct and mitigate any findings.

Healthcare Information Security Guide (HISG)

Many of the various activities laid out in the framework rely on the creation of the Healthcare Information Security Guide (HISG). The HISG is an invention of this research to serve as the cumulative, comprehensive reference manual for healthcare providers to use both for implementation assistance as well as later for assessment. In conjunction with the research performed while creating the HISCF, the basic content of the HISG was likewise compiled. The HISG is the culmination of the actual HIPAA regulations, federal recommendations from the National Institute for Standards and Technology (NIST) and the Department of Health and Human Services (HHS). Once the regulations were documented, research was performed to determine actual implementation suggestions that meet those regulations. The specific implementation recommendations incorporate standards and best practice guides provided

Figure 4. Regulations and requirements for information security compliance

Federal Government Agencies
National Archives and Records Administration
Federal Register, Vol. 78, No. 17, Part II – 45 CFR Parts 160 and 164
Department of Health and Human Services
42 CFR parts 412, 412, and 495: Medicare and Medicaid Programs; Electronic Health Record Incentive Program Stage 2; Health Information Technology: Standards, Implementation Specifications, and Certification Criteria for Electronic Health Record Technology, 2014 Edition; Revisions to the Permanent Certification Program for Health Information Technology; Final Rules
45 CFR parts 160 and 164: Modifications to the HIPAA Privacy, Security, Enforcement and Breach Notification Rules Under the Health Information Technology for Economic and Clinical Health Act and the Genetic Information Nondiscrimination Act: Other Modifications to the HIPAA Rules: Final Rule
Center for Medicare and Medicaid Services
"Regulations and Guidance," available at https://www.cms.gov/home/regsguidance.asp
"HIPAA Security Series – Security Standards: Technical Safeguards," available at http://www.hhs.gov/ocr/privacy/hipaa/administrative/securityrule/techsafeguards.pdf
"CMS System Security and e-Authentication Assurance Levels by Information Type," available at http://www.cms.gov/Research-Statistics-Data-and-Systems/CMS-Information-Technology/InformationSecurity/Downloads/System-Security-Levels-by-Information-Type.pdf
"CMS EHR Meaningful Use Overview," available at https://www.cms.gov/Regulations-and-Guidance/Legislation/EHRIncentivePrograms/Meaningful_Use.html
"Logical Access Controls and Segregation of Duties," available at http://www.cms.gov/Research-Statistics-Data-and-Systems/CMS-Information-Technology/InformationSecurity/downloads/WP02-Logical_Access.pdf
Office of Management and Budget
"M-04-04: E-Authentication Guidance for Federal Agencies," available at http://www.whitehouse.gov/sites/default/files/omb/memoranda/fy04/m04-04.pdf
National Institute of Standards and Technology
An Introductory Resource Guide for Implementing the Health Insurance Portability and Accountability Act (HIPAA) Security Rule (SP800-66 rev1)
"Risk Management Framework (RMF)" available at http://csrc.nist.gov/groups/SMA/fisma/framework.html

by NIST, the National Security Agency (NSA), the Department of Homeland Security, and a myriad of public guides and private industry whitepapers.

Once the information, guidelines, and requirements from all these sources was compiled, they were distilled into a concise, comprehensive guide that covers four key policy areas - disaster recovery and

Figure 5. Implementation recommendations and practices

Federal Government Agencies
Department of Homeland Security - Federal Network Security Branch
"Continuous Asset Evaluation, Situational Awareness, and Risk Scoring Reference Architecture Report (CAESARS)," available at http://www.dhs.gov/xlibrary/assets/fns-caesars.pdf
National Institute of Standards and Technology
Guide for Conducting Risk Assessments (SP800-30 rev1)
Risk Management Guide for Information Technology Systems (SP800-37 rev1)
Managing Information Security Risk: Organization, Mission, and Information System View (SP800-39)
Creating a Patch and Vulnerability Management Program (SP800-40 ver2)
Guidelines on Firewalls and Firewall Policy (SP800-41 rev1)
Guidelines on Securing Public Web Servers (SP800-44 ver2)
Guide to Securing Legacy IEEE 802.11 Wireless Networks (SP800-48 rev1)
Guide for Assessing the Security Controls in Federal Information Systems and Organizations (SP800-53A rev1)
Recommendation for Key Management, Part 1: General (Draft SP800-57 part1 rev3)
Electronic Authentication Guide (SP800-63 rev1)
Guide to Intrusion Detection and Prevention Systems (IDPS) (SP800-94)
Technical Guide to Information Security Testing and Assessment (SP800-115)
Guidelines for Securing Wireless Local Area Networks (WLANs) (SP800-153)
National Security Agency – Central Security Service
"Security Configuration Guides" available at http://www.nsa.gov/ia/mitigation_guidance/security_configuration_guides/index.shtml
Office of Government-wide Policy
"Federal Identity, Credential, and Access Management," available at http://www.idmanagement.gov/pages.cfm/page/ICAM
Private Organizations
Healthcare Information Management Systems Society (HIMSS)
"Guidelines for Establishing Information Security Policies at Organizations with Computer-based Patient Record Systems," available at http://www.himss.org/content/files/CPRIToolkit/version6/v7/D38_CPRI_Guidelines-Information_Security_Policies.pdf
"HIMSS Application Security Questionnaire (HIMSS ASQ)," available at http://www.himss.org/content/files/ApplicationSecurityv2.3.pdf
Medical Universities
Johns Hopkins University
"Information Technology Policies," available at http://www.it.johnshopkins.edu/policies/itpolicies.html
University of California
"Guidelines for HIPAA Security Rule Compliance University of California," available at http://www.universityofcalifornia.edu/hipaa/docs/security_guidelines.pdf
State Governments
State of California. Office of Information Security
"California Information Security Risk Assessment Checklist (CA ISRAC)," available at http://www.cio.ca.gov/OIS/Government/documents/docs/RA_Checklist.doc
State of Maryland. Department of Information Technology
"Information Security Policy," available at http://doit.maryland.gov/support/Documents/security_guidelines/DoITSecurityPolicyv3.pdf
State of North Carolina. Statewide HIPAA Assessment Team
"North Carolina HIPAA Impact Determination Assessment (NC HIDA)," available at http://hipaa.dhhs.state.nc.us/hipaa2002/amicovered/doc/ImpactDeterminationQuestionnaire-Step2-2.doc

business continuity; risk mitigation; operations management; and logical access - and four major technical areas of information technology - network; database; applications; and infrastructure. The HISG then serves as the emblematic ruler that the healthcare organization is evaluated against and appropriate recommendations are derived from for the organization as a remediation plan for any shortcomings. Figure 4 and Figure 5 depict the key sources of regulations and requirements, as well as implementation recommendations and practices respectively.

Phase 1: Information Security Organizational Assessment

The goal of Phase 1 is to carry out a high-level assessment involving a thorough review of all policies, procedures, practices, and architectural designs. This stage is broken into three parts - the Healthcare Information Security Questionnaire, the Information Technology Architecture Review, and the Healthcare Practitioner Survey. These three instruments are designed to measure information security compliance from both technical and functional perspectives. The grant's project director provided quality checks on the instruments to ensure their appropriateness and completeness for the areas the instruments were designed to assess - no external quality evaluation was performed.

Healthcare Information Security Questionnaire (HISQ)

Computing environments by their nature have intrinsic risks that require some form of mitigating action to minimize the potential for harm. These vulnerabilities are essentially any attribute or characteristic of the environment that can be exploited to violate established security policies or cause a deleterious effect. Organizations therefore should have vulnerability assessment plans that are executed routinely to detect, identify, measure, and understand the risks present in their information technology environments. The Healthcare Information Security Questionnaire (HISQ) is designed to comprehensively assess the organization's information security policies, procedures, and practices. The HISQ represents the bulk of the Phase 1 assessment as it evaluates the organization's compliance with the baseline requirements of the HISG. The questionnaire itself was designed by creating sets of dichotomous and semantic differential questions to determine how the organization's policies, procedures, and practices compared to those laid out in the HISG. The assessment is divided into the same 4 key policy subjects as well as 4 overarching technical areas described in the HISG.

There are four key policy areas that the HISQ examines in specific detail: Disaster Recovery and Business Continuity; Risk Management; Operations Management; and Logical Access. These aspects of information technology cut across an organization's strategic and operational practices. Both HIPAA and Meaningful Use clearly lay out numerous requirements in these critical areas. The policy sections of the HISQ are presented in the form of a questionnaire that in most cases asks straightforward, single choice answers. This area is typically completed by the healthcare provider's IT leadership or their representative as it covers the overall organization's IT policies and established procedures.

The technical assessment is likewise divided into the areas of Network, Application, Database, and Infrastructure. In contrast to the policy review, the technical sections are best completed by IT engineers or someone intimately familiar with the technical configuration of the organization IT environment. The technical sections allow for much more free form answers to accommodate and capture environment-specific details. Many of the questions posed in the technical section are directed at specific implementation choices and details compared to the more general inquiries of the policy and procedure sections.

The results assist in providing a comprehensive evaluation of the entire technical architecture, policies, and practices of the healthcare provider.

The HISQ is designed as a questionnaire, not a survey, and it is expected to be filled out in its entirety just once, but collaboratively, using the appropriate technical and leadership resources from across the organization. It is also recommended that the questionnaire be completed through a series of iterative drafts whereby there are active discussions about both the questions and answers. This will ensure there is good understanding of both the question be asked and the response given.

Information Technology Architecture Review (ITAR)

In addition to the completing the HISQ, the organization submits to a full examination of their IT architecture. This review involves obtaining network diagrams, data center diagrams, network device configurations, and other documents that depict how the network and infrastructure architecture is implemented. The topology of the environment is scrutinized specifically for appropriate isolation and segregation of ePHI data on the organization's network.

The HIPAA regulations specifically address transmission security in §164.312(e) (1) by the following statute, "implement technical security measures to guard against unauthorized access to electronic protected health information that is being transmitted over an electronic communications network" (Title 45-Public Welfare, 1996). The regulation goes on to state that there are 2 key components of ensuring the security of ePHI during transit: integrity controls and encryption. The primary purpose of integrity controls is to ensure the ePHI data isn't modified in any way during transmission. Encryption serves to disguise the true content of data such that it is not easily readable or decrypted without proper authorization. These 2 security measures are the basic foundation of providing secure transmissions (Acharya, Coats, Saluja, and Fuller, 2013). If an unauthorized entity can't read the contents of a transmission or alter or delete any portion of it, the authenticity and confidentiality of the transmission is ensured. While the concepts are straightforward, successfully achieving them can be challenging.

There are a number of fundamental approaches that are effective across almost all environments. It is important to acknowledge that before making architectural decisions related to the technical aspects of transmission security, it is imperative that operational needs, functional and financial, be considered. It is easy for the technical staff typically tasked with the implementation of the HIPAA technical safeguards to lose sight of how the technology will actually be used in practice. If the chosen measures provide the appropriate levels of security but are impractical to utilize, the overall solution is ineffective. Further, in such cases the likelihood of both intentional and accidental misuse or circumvention of the organization's security will increase dramatically. The ITAR performs a thorough analysis of the IT architecture and provides an evaluation using the following considerations: Usability, Security and Dependability.

- **Usability:** The verification is to ensure if the systems are functional as needed for normal business operations and if the users can reasonably reach the data, they need from the operational locations.
- **Security:** The verification is to ensure that the entire ePHI data is appropriately isolated and segregated on the network.
- **Dependability:** The verification to check for single points of failure within the architecture that will adversely affect business continuity in a disaster recovery situation.

Healthcare Practitioner Survey (HPS)

The last assessment in Phase 1 is the Healthcare Practitioner Survey. This assessment evaluates the organization's human-technology interaction by the healthcare practitioners. The survey covers the healthcare personnel's perception of the current IT practices, their understanding of requirements and procedures in place, and their specific interactions with ePHI data. It is not uncommon for an organization's published and intended IT security practices to not directly correspond to how their users are actually functioning (Johnson, Goetz and Pfleeger, 2009). This assessment's purpose is to provide a check and balance for established policy and procedures that were examined in the HISQ. The survey is designed to be short but engaging, consisting of 25 'yes-no' questions related to the practitioners' awareness of the healthcare provider's IT policies and practices. The survey should be presented electronically and completed anonymously to encourage honesty and frankness. Once the survey has been completed, the results are compiled and evaluated. The findings of each of the assessments are combined to produce a cumulative Phase 1 summary, presented as the Comprehensive Organization Assessment and Roadmap (COAR). After creating the COAR, Phase 2 performs a practical evaluation of the areas covered in the first phase and amends and expands the COAR as necessary.

Comprehensive Organization Assessment and Roadmap (COAR)

The COAR is effectively the framework's master report of the results of both Phase 1 and Phase 2. At the conclusion of Phase 1, an initial draft of the COAR is produced that contains the results of the all the Phase 1 assessments, along with any recommended mitigating actions. A thorough organization review of the COAR is very useful at this stage, prior to beginning Phase 2. Each question of each questionnaire and survey for all Phase 1 assessments contains a cross-reference to both the HIPAA statute and the corresponding section of the HISG. As such, the recommendations from the Phase 1 assessments can be easily combined with the guidelines laid out in the HISG, to produce a clear set of actionable tasks. Phase 2 shifts the assessment style from abstract to practical. Following the completion of Phase 2, the COAR will be revised to include the results from those assessments as well. Once the results of Phase 2 are included, the COAR will serve as a detailed implementation guide for the organization to follow in order to achieve HIPAA compliance.

Healthcare Information Security Testing Directive (HISTD)

When considering an evaluation of information security, an organization must first establish what the actual objectives are for the environment being examined. After the security objectives have been established, the actual test plan or methodology can be drafted. It is important to recognize that an effective testing plan must be easily repeatable. It is in the repetition of the security tests and surveys that many issues can be identified using comparative analysis of prior test results. Many times, issues or vulnerabilities are not immediately obvious during the course of normal examination but when compared to prior test results, anomalous conditions can be much more readily recognized.

The proposed security testing plan, the HISTD, divides the testing techniques into five key areas: target identification and analysis; target vulnerability validation; password cracking; business process testing, and application assessments. The identification and analysis testing are centered on network discovery, port and service identification, and vulnerability scanning. The vulnerability validation category consists of a variety of penetration tests on the different components of the organization information

Figure 6. Security testing configurations

VM 1		
Operating System - Ubuntu 11.10		
Testing Tools		
	Nessus 5.0	*Vulnerability Scanning*
VM 2		
Operating System - BackTrack 5 R3		
Testing Tools		
	NMap	*Network Enumeration and Port Scanning*
	THC-AMap	*Protocol Detection*
	Enum4Linux	*Windows Enumeration*
	Swaks	*SMTP Testing*
	SSLScan	*Encryption Testing*
	Bluediving	*Bluetooth Penetration Testing*
	AirCrack	*Wireless Penetration Testing*
	SMAP	*SIP Scanning for VoIP*
	OneSixtyONe	*SNMP Scanning*
	SQLMAP	*SQL Injection and Database Takeover Testing*
	Armitage	*Exploitation testing*
	THC-Hydra	*Password Cracking*
	W3af	*Exploit testing*
	Uniscan	*Website Vulnerability Scanning*
	Nikto	*Web Application Testing (White box, Black box)*
	Burpsuite	*Web Application Testing (White box, Black box)*

technology environment. The password cracking area is focused very specifically on testing the strength of passwords within the organization. The business process testing portion, much like the Healthcare Practitioner Survey, provides an examination of how technology is actually being used in normal business operations to ensure security controls are not being circumvented in actual practices. The final testing technique of application assessments is intended to provide in-depth application security testing beyond typical penetration testing.

Unfortunately, no single security test can be used to validate all systems and services from all perspectives. As such, it is necessary to use an assortment of tools to achieve a truly complete assessment. This research has focused on creating a collection of testing tools that can provide a comprehensive set of tests with the minimal amount of overlap. The collection of tools configured and preloaded on the two Tester Virtual Machines (VMs) are depicted in Figure 6. Additionally, the tests have been preconfigured and automated as much as possible to minimize the amount of effort necessary to conduct the testing.

Since security testing is a very fluid and changing process, it is recommended that all organizations establish an information security testing environment to become acquainted with the testing tools and run simulated tests to perfect the organization's testing plan. Figure 7 depicts a basic testing environment that was created by this research and can be utilized by any healthcare organization. Having a dedicated testing sandbox environment can be helpful to show how each type of test is performed and understand their impact to the systems being tested. It is important to perform all types of security testing from both an internal and external perspective. In order to truly validate adequate security exists within the environment the conditions of the tests must match or be relevantly comparable to the scenario being tested.

Figure 7. Security testing environment

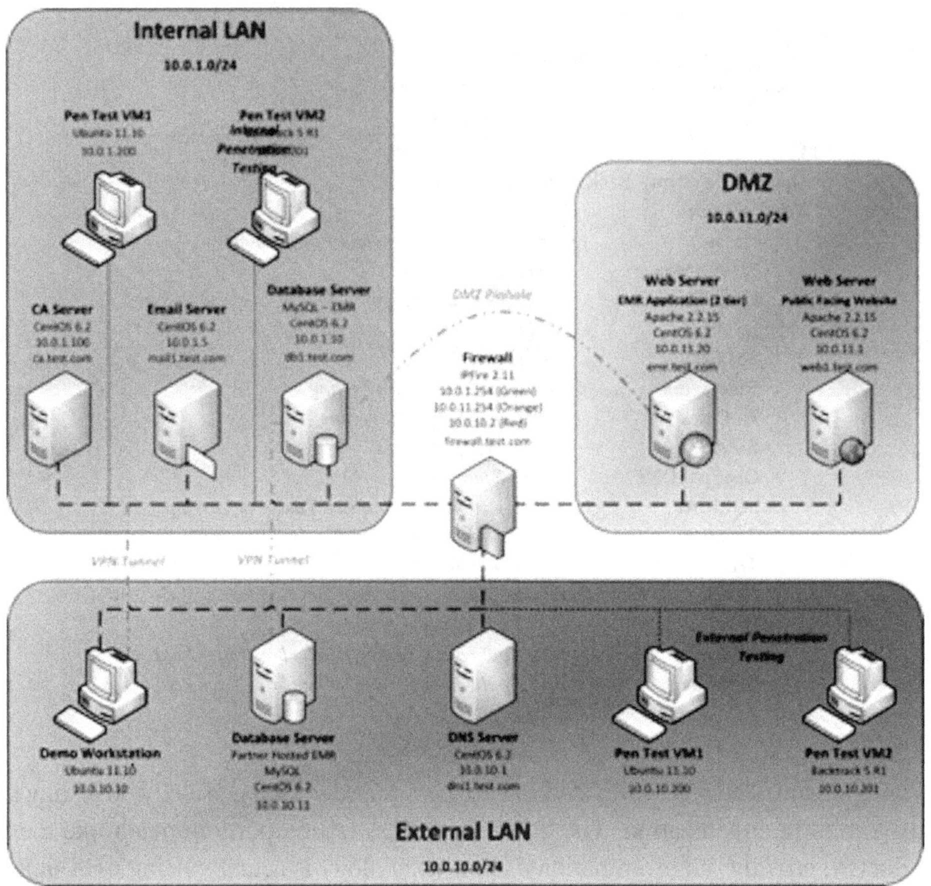

Target Identification and Analysis

For the target identification and analysis tests, the systems on the network segment being tested will be cataloged including each system's operating system (OS) information and patching status as well as any open ports or active services. Network discovery can be performed using either an active scanning tool or passively using a network sniffer. While the passive approach tends to make the lesser impact to the performance of the network or scanned machine, it takes considerably longer, and the results are bound by what events are actually taking place. Active scanning usually yields but more comprehensive results and allows the scans to be targeted to look for specific characteristics, regardless of a system's current activity.

It is important to recognize that discovery scanning can be an intensive process and potentially have significant impact on the systems it is scanning and in cases of older systems, cause system failures. Network discovery can be helpful to detect unauthorized systems present on an organization's network. It is important to note that scanning should not be limited just to the wired network. A number of wireless scanners exist that can very effectively collect relevant data about wireless devices and the local wireless network that wouldn't normally apply to a traditional wired network. The wireless scanning should not only include all 802.11 channels but also Bluetooth and a general radio frequency (RF) spectrum analyzer.

Once the connected systems have been identified for a particular network segment, these hosts are further examined using a port scanner to see which ports open and what services are are running on those ports. The port scanning process can also perform OS fingerprinting. The last test of this group is to perform vulnerability scanning. The types of checks vulnerability scanners can perform depends on the tool, but they typically can identify out of date software, missing patches, and various errors with configurations. Unfortunately, vulnerability scanning has a number of limitations that are important to recognize. First, vulnerability scanning is much like virus scanning as it relies on a repository of signatures and therefore can only detect documented issues. This requires frequent updating of the repository to be able to discover the latest vulnerabilities. Secondly, these scans usually have a high false positive error rate and thus require an experienced information security individual to effectively interpret the results. These weaknesses ultimately limit the scanning process as there are considerable portions of these tests that are labor intensive and cannot be automated. The network-based scans generate significantly more network traffic that network discovery and port/service scanning and can prove harmful to the hosts being scanned. When the vulnerability scanning is complete, the tests in first stage of the security testing plan will have produced a comprehensive report of the organization's connected systems and including information about their OS, active services, and any vulnerability they have.

Penetration Testing

With the information generated in the first round of the testing, the next stage will continue to search for vulnerabilities and demonstrate the exposures created when they are exploited. Penetration testing will simulate real-world attacks and provide information about how the system, application, or network will respond to malicious attacks. Penetration testing also can help provide information about effective countermeasures to attacks, how to detect an attack, and the appropriate response. Penetration testing is very labor intensive, much like vulnerability scanning, and as such typically requires a professional with considerable skill to conduct the testing successfully without damaging the targeted system. The majority of the tests performed as part of this security testing framework fall into the penetration testing category.

Password Cracking

After the penetration testing stage is complete, a series of password cracking tests are performed. There are a couple general approaches for password attacks: dictionary attacks, brute force, and rainbow table attacks. Typically, password cracking involves obtaining the hash of the actual password, either from the target system directly or using a network sniffer. Once the hash is obtained, the attacks take different approaches in an attempt to generate a matching hash to discover the actual password. While an attack could be directed at a system service or application, these attacks are typically not as efficient and take considerably longer to conduct. Using this approach, you are limited to response times of the target system or application per attempt, as well as the round-trip network time, to determine if the attack was successful. While the time associated with a single attack is extremely small, when millions of credentials are being attempted, the compounded time usually makes this approach unattractive. By having a copy of the hash, you are trying to recreate, the attack is only limited to the processing capabilities of the system performing the attack. Different from penetration testing, password cracking can be effectively performed offline to remove the possibility of any impact on the target system, network, or application. The objective of password cracking is to determine how predisposed an organization's password policies are being compromised. In cases where passwords are determined to be vulnerable, their respective strength can be augmented to achieve appropriate entropy.

Business Process Testing

While examining each component of an IT environment is a critical exercise, it is also important to examine entire processes to verify each component is being used appropriately during normal business practices. It is possible that not all security capabilities of each component are actually employed in practice or exceptions have been 'built-in' to processes that circumvent the safeguards the components could normally exert. Clearly, EHR security is a crucial element of any healthcare organization's overall security framework. To this end, the ways in which EHR systems are used in normal practice serve as excellent candidates for process testing scenarios. From a process perspective, EHR security can be examined in three key areas: access, transmission, and storage.

- **Access:** This category deals specifically with the functional areas related to authentication, authorization, and delegation. More specifically this area handles who can have access to data, which data they can access, what type of actions they can take on that data, and who they can provide some degree of access to the data as well.
- **Transmission:** This category covers how data is moved in an electronic medium. This area covers where data can be access from, where that data can be sent to, how the data is formatted while being moved, how data is presented to the user, and what mechanisms can be used to send the data.
- **Storage:** This category accounts for how data is captured and preserved. This area deals with how data can be added, modified, or deleted, how the data is validated upon entry, the format of how data is stored electronically, how the data is preserved, and how data integrity is ensured.

Application Review and Testing

This part of the HISTD involves an extensive review, categorization, and analysis of all enterprise applications. Each application is examined to determine if it interacts with ePHI and if so, in what way and for what function or purpose. This final type of testing is directed specifically at an organization's applications that capture, access, or transmit ePHI. This type of testing involves both *white box* and *black box* approaches. White box testing takes the perspective of an internal user such that the tests assume a working knowledge of how the application works. Conversely, Black box testing assumes the attacker has no familiarity with application or how it is designed and implemented. These types of tests and attacks include injection attacks, file descriptor attacks, data corruption attempts, and intentional misuse of the application beyond the organization's published policies and procedures. Application testing, along with all the other parts of the vulnerability validation-testing phase are used to evaluate systems during actual use. Therefore, the closer the tests are to normal conditions, the more useful the results of the tests will be in discovering potential risks.

Phase 2: Information Security Testing

Phase 2 is a detailed, hands-on technical review and assessment of the IT environment. This phase measures and analyzes the actual performance of the systems and practices both against the theoretical goal of the HISG and the reported state of the organization provided in the assessment stage of Phase

1. The variances found in this effort are reflected in the COAR with appropriate mitigating actions. The technical review includes onsite visits, penetration and vulnerability testing, and a comprehensive review and assessment of all enterprise applications.

Interviews and Inspections

The interviews and inspections stage of Phase 2 is aimed at providing an opportunity to inspect various components of the IT environment including physical security controls for the data center and other locations where ePHI data is stored. While this was evaluated in Phase 1, these inspections should serve as the effective penetration tests of the physical computing environment. The onsite visits should involve interviews with all appropriate personnel of the organization, both within the IT department, and administration, and leadership.

Penetration and Vulnerability Testing

In addition to the onsite visits, the IT staff is engaged to conduct penetration and vulnerability testing on the network and infrastructure portions of the organization. All associated testing is documented in the Healthcare Information Security Testing Directive (HISTD). The HISTD ensures the testing is standardized and easily repeated not only during the current review period but in the future as part of the organization's continued compliance efforts. This stage will simulate real-world attacks and provide information about how the system, application, or network will respond to malicious attacks. The penetration and vulnerability testing also can help provide information about effective countermeasures to attacks, how to detect an attack, and the appropriate response. Business process testing is an important aspect of this stage. This aspect examines entire processes to verify each technological component is being used appropriately during normal business practices. Many information security breaches are actually caused by a failure to use a system as designed or the procedure doesn't match the policy.

EHR Security and Privacy Assessment

The last task of Phase 2 is to perform an in-depth review of the organization's EHR systems specifically. This assessment examines both the security and privacy policies and practices. The evaluation instrument is a survey that is completed by the leadership responsible for the technical support of the EHR system. The survey is broken into 3 main sections - organization policies and practices, functional implementation, and technical implementation. The first part, organizational policies and practices, covers topics such as how staff is trained on HIPAA privacy requirements, security awareness training, the presence and application of acceptable use policies, how ePHI releases are handled, and how data alteration/deletion is guarded against. The functional implementation section covers how the EHR system is used in normal operations. Questions for this section cover how the business practices for how ePHI is captured, accessed, and transmitted. The last area of the survey, technical implementation, examines how the EHR system was deployed technically including the system architecture, how patch management is addressed, presence of intrusion detection and prevention, and finally network location and safeguards. The information captured within this survey provides a complete portrayal of whether the organization has enacted adequate security and privacy controls for their EHR systems. Once each of the technical reviews is complete, the final task of this phase is to update the COAR report with all the findings and corrective actions identified in this phase. At the conclusion of this phase, the organization's entire IT environment has been methodically examined and evaluated.

Phase 3 – Implementation

The final phase involves taking the findings of the first two phases and performing corrective actions as appropriate. Phase 3 is the implementation stage including changes related to technical configurations, policy, procedures, training, and documentation. At the start of the implementation phase, an implementation plan will be drafted, based off of the final COAR. While the findings and recommendations laid out in the COAR will provide specific tasks to complete, a plan needs to be developed of how to put those changes into operation. Meetings with stakeholders, IT staff, and administrative staff will be necessary to create an effective plan including an appropriate timeline. Once the plan has been developed, the actual implementation can be scheduled and started. In addition to the technical, policy, and procedural changes covered in the COAR implementation plan, this phase will also ensure that necessary documentation is created for both the impending changes and the preexisting environment. Further, this phase will include any necessary training – administrative, technical, or functional – related to the changes implemented, new procedures, and general security awareness training of the organization moving forward.

Post-Compliance

With the completion of the third phase, the entire framework will likewise be completed. The designed result of the framework will first and foremost be the achievement of HIPAA compliance for the organization. In the efforts to attain compliance, there will also be the potential for a number of other tangible accomplishments. This framework will create a standardized Healthcare Information Security Guide that can be referenced and updated for perpetuity. The HISG will serve as a critical resource for evaluating future enhancements and changes to the environment and ensure compliance is maintained. Additionally, the framework will produce a series of valuable tools for periodic testing of the security configurations. These tools will provide important actionable information as well as save time and effort in regard to the ongoing penetration and vulnerability testing procedures. Lastly, this framework will afford extremely useful training and awareness of security to the organization at all levels. The assessment exercises alone will orient the healthcare providers, technical staff and administration alike on the current updated state of their IT environment. It is often the case in HIPAA compliance efforts, that the simple lack of knowing how to measure compliance can greatly delay the entire effort. This research educates organizations as to what compliance requires, how these requirements translate into their specific environment, and how to satisfy them quickly, efficiently, and at a significantly reduced cost compared to tackling this effort alone.

Evaluation

In order to validate the effectiveness of this research, it was vital that both frameworks be implemented in an actual healthcare provider's environment. This research was fortunate to have cooperative agreements with 2 national healthcare providers to provide that opportunity. The large central Pennsylvania hospital was engaged for evaluation of the Healthcare Information Security Compliance Framework (HISCF). Both entities are national hospitals with the PA hospital having over 500 licensed beds and more than 400,000 patient admissions (combined inpatient and outpatient) every year, while the Maryland healthcare provider has over 800 beds and more than 350,000 patient admissions (combined inpatient and outpatient) each year. Each of these hospitals interact with a significant number of patients annually and are both faced with the daunting and costly challenges of achieving Health Insurance Portability and Accountability Act (HIPAA) compliance and providing patient access to electronic health records.

Case Study of Healthcare Information Security Compliance Framework

Since the HISCF was largely borne out of a federal grant of which a key deliverable was compliance assessment, the PA hospital was very eager to participate in its implementation even though they had already obtained certification as a HIMSS Stage 6 Hospital. This partnership between the Pennsylvania hospital and Towson University started in 2011 and promised the hospital would be provided a comprehensive assessment of their entire IT environment, including specific, actionable tasks to remedy any deficiencies uncovered. The partnership was scoped for a 3-year engagement, with roughly 1 year allocated per phase of the larger information technology assessment framework. The HISCF, depicted in Figure 3, is designed to take an organization from the initial recognition of the need for Health Insurance Portability and Accountability Act (HIPAA) compliance all the way through to implementation of any necessary changes to their environment. Along the way to compliance, specifically in Phase 2, a comprehensive security audit is performed that partially satisfies the necessary attestation for Meaningful Use.

HISCF: Phase 1

Starting with Phase 1, a high-level assessment, involving a thorough review of all technology practices and architectural designs, was performed. The information technology staff was engaged to assist in the completion of both the HISQ and ITAR.

Healthcare Information Security Questionnaire (HISQ) Execution

The HISQ was presented to a single point of contact in the Pennsylvania hospital's IT group. This individual, a senior security engineer, then worked with the appropriate staff within the 52-member IT department to complete each part of the questionnaire. Once the initial draft of the HISQ responses was completed, a series of interviews were conducted to review the responses for clarity and consistency. The responses were also reviewed by the hospital's Chief Information Officer (CIO) for additional validation. The measurement scale used to quantify the responses is based on the percentage the organization is in compliance with the guidelines laid out in the HISG with is directed based on the HIPAA guidelines and National Institute for Standards and Technology (NIST) recommendations or HIPAA implementations.

HISQ: Policy Assessment Findings

The policy and procedure review results for each of the 4 policy areas had a number of similarities that cut across many of the technology areas of the organization. The common theme was that the healthcare provider had addressed most of the needed areas to some degree but not completely, seemed to emerge very quickly from the results.

Figure 8. Disaster recovery & business continuity outcomes

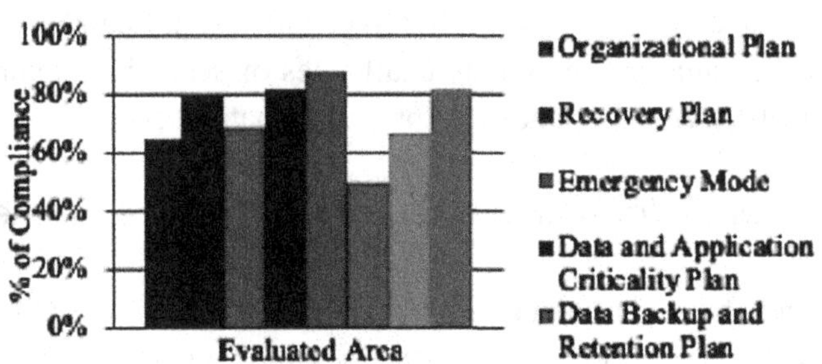

Disaster Recovery and Business Continuity

In the area of Disaster Recovery and Business Continuity, the organization had only partially implemented a DRP plan and the portions that did exist need significant updating. The hospital had been rapidly growing over the last few years and their patient counts had been equally increasing. As such, disaster recovery and business continuity planning had not been given the appropriate degree of attention. Based on the assessment findings shown in Figure 8, the organization's overall compliance with disaster recovery and business continuity rated 77% adequate. As expected, some areas were more complete than others. The organization scored over 80% in compliance for their recovery plan, their data and application criticality plan, their data backup and retention plan, and testing and revision process. However, the organization DRP policy, their emergency mode plan, DRP training, and documentation were all below 70% compliance with training only rating 50%. Some of the specific key findings in this area included the lack of backup copies of data being kept at an off-site facility. There was also no documentation for DRP training and the training that did exist was pretty limited. Another issue uncovered was that fact that there are single points of failure within both the recovery and emergency mode plans. Specific key responsibilities had no delegation accommodations therefore if a specific person is not available, those responsibilities and functions cannot be performed. This was a significant flaw in the organization's current DRP procedures.

Risk Management

The results for Risk Management shown in Figure 9 were considerably worse than the other 3 areas. Overall the organization rated just 52% in compliance. The ongoing risk management activities were by far the least adequate area, scoring just 18%.

The hospital had very little proactive risk monitoring in place. Most risk mitigation efforts were reactive once an issue has been uncovered. Similar to DRP, the organization had partially developed plans for risk analysis and assessment as well as mitigation. Unfortunately, none of these programs were fully implemented nor were they comprehensive enough to be in compliance all HIPAA guidelines.

Operations Management

The healthcare provider had considerably more comprehensive policies and procedures related to operations management as shown in Figure 10. The antivirus program was 100% compliant and both media handling and data disposal had only very minor deficiencies. Security monitoring was in fact the only aspect of this area that had inadequacies of any significant degree. One of the main factors creating

Figure 9. Risk management outcomes

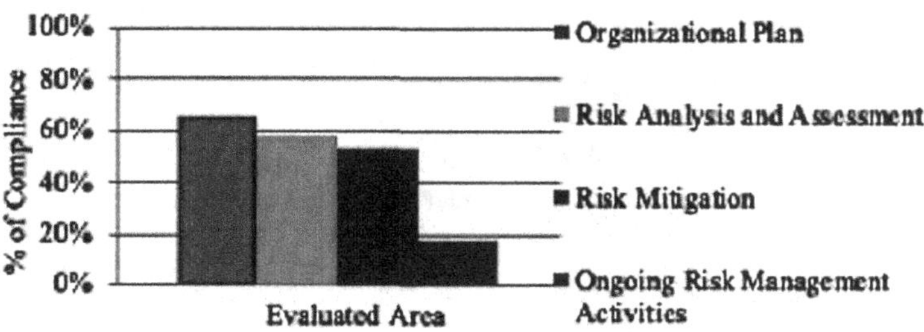

the issues related to security monitoring was that while they had a commercial intrusion detection and prevention system (IDPS) implemented, it had only been configured to monitor a very small segment of the organization's environment. Once the IDPS was fully configured this aspect should have come into compliance.

Logical Access

Logical access, shown in Figure 11, was measured at being 80% compliant overall. As with most areas assessed, plans for the various aspects of logical access had been developed and implemented but they were not comprehensive and were not up to date. It was discovered that many of the hospital's practices were not reflected in the policy nor were all the procedures mentioned in the policies actually in practice. Another key finding was that data could not be easily shared with external entities. While security of this data was sufficient, the logical access practices being employed created usability barriers and deficiencies. Further, due to the inflexible logical access issues, access to ePHI was not possible remotely. This situation also created an issue related to emergency access for business continuity during a disaster scenario.

HISQ: Technical Assessment Findings

In addition to reviewing the policies and practices of the organization, the HISQ is designed to perform a technical assessment of information security. This portion of the questionnaire is divided into 4 main IT areas: Network, Applications, Database, and Infrastructure. The relevant members of the healthcare's organization completed the questionnaire and those responses are denoted below. Only potential actionable issues were mentioned in this assessment. For any portion of the IT environment that is managed or hosted by a third-party, the assumption was made that those aspects of the environment were implicitly

Figure 10. Operations management outcomes

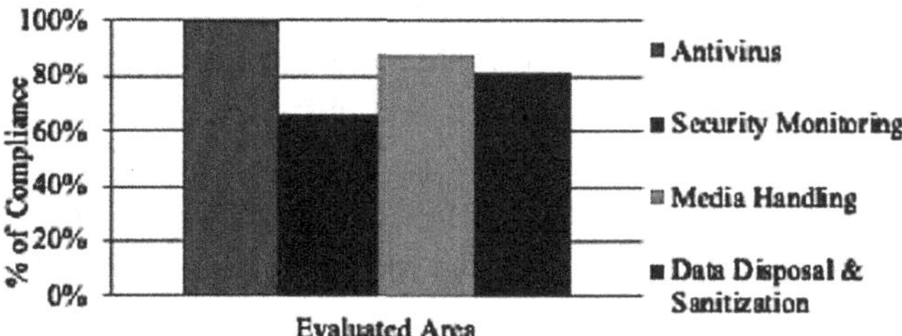

Figure 11. Logical access outcomes

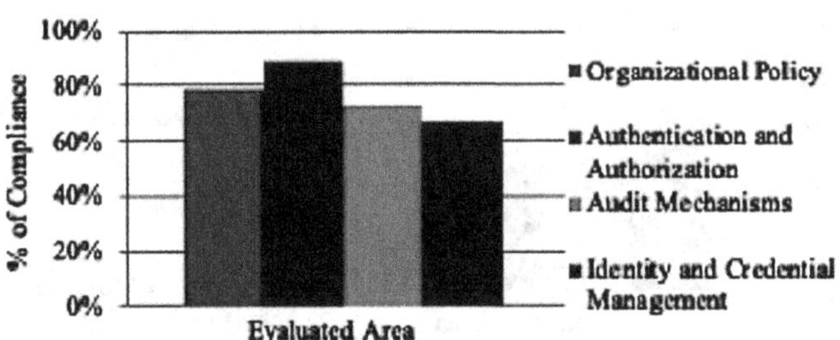

satisfactory and in compliance with all HIPAA regulations. A review of all third-party systems and management practices is out of scope for this assessment. For those potential issues that were identified, a description of the finding and the recommended corrective action to mitigate or remove the issues are provided. Regardless of whether a specific finding was cited with an actionable mitigating response, each area was scored based on how thoroughly and effectively it is being addressed within the current environment. The scoring determination was made from the series of responses given to each question, supplemental comments made in the Healthcare Practitioner Survey, and the general understanding of the environment based on all information provided.

Network

- **Policies and Procedures:** The response to the questionnaire indicated policies and procedures related to network operations and disaster recovery had not been adequately addressed. There seemed to be an indication that policies and procedures were once in place, but they were no longer up to date with the current environment. Having comprehensive policies and procedures established, documented, and published for review would have addressed a number of HIPAA guidelines – §§164.308(a)(1), 164.308(a)(2), 164.308(a)(5), 164.308(a)(7) – related to the security management process, assigned security responsibilities, security awareness and training, and contingency planning. The questionnaire response indicated that acceptable use polices (AUP) were in existence but were not up to date. It is important to have documented and published acceptable use policies that all users agree to and this consent is recorded. Having an AUP in place further satisfies HIPAA guidelines – §§164.308(a) (1), 164.308(a) (5) – related to security management process as well as security awareness and training. The questionnaire response indicated that staff members were regularly receiving security alerts and advisories and likewise took the appropriate actions. That practice in part satisfies HIPAA guidelines related to security awareness and training - §164.308(a) (5).
- **Practices:** The response to the questionnaire indicated that administrative credentials for network devices and applications were in some cases shared and, in some cases, unique to the staff member. The sharing of credentials, especially for administrative accounts with elevated privileges, is strongly discouraged. Without unique credentials the audit logging effectiveness is greatly reduced with respect to identity. The HIPAA technical safeguard guidelines related to access control – §164.312(a) (1) – clearly requires unique identifiers and credentials.

Since non-institutionally owned devices and PCs were allowed to access both the internal wired and wireless networks, it was critical that those machines had been scanned for risks prior to allowing full access to the network resources. Network access protection (NAP) and network admission control (NAC) software can provide the necessary safeguards required for security awareness and training – §164.308(a) (5). The response indicated that software to perform NAP/NAC was licensed but not implemented. The response further indicated that vulnerability scanning was performed but infrequently. It was crucial to regularly check the network for vulnerabilities and problems, and then address them in order to minimize the opportunity for accidental or malicious exploitation. The transmission security and regular evaluation requirements of HIPAA – §§164.308(a) (8), 164.312(e) (1) – necessitate regular penetration and vulnerability testing.

Database

- **Policies and Procedures:** The response to the questionnaire indicated policies and procedures related to database operations and disaster recovery had not been adequately addressed. The responses indicated policies and procedures had either not been created or had not been completed. Having comprehensive policies and procedures established, documented, and published for review would have addressed a number of HIPAA guidelines – §§164.308(a)(1), 164.308(a)(2), 164.308(a)(5), 164.308(a)(7) – related to the security management process, assigned security responsibilities, security awareness and training, and contingency planning. The questionnaire response indicated that staff members were regularly receiving security alerts and advisories but were not taking the appropriate actions. Responding to security notices is a required practice to satisfy in part HIPAA guidelines related to security awareness and training - §164.308(a) (5).
- **Architecture:** The response to the questionnaire indicated in some cases the database, application server, and web server all resided on the same physical machine. ePHI related applications that utilize databases should have use either a 2- or 3-tier architecture such that the database does not reside on the same physical server as either the application or web server. All efforts should be made to minimize the exposure each server has to non-administrative users and networks. Since all applications must inherently be accessed by internal and/or external users, some amount of exposure is necessary. Through a 2 or 3-tier architecture, the only way users can access ePHI data is via proxy through the web or application servers. This minimizes the impact of a breach at a web server since no actual ePHI data resides on those servers.

The response further indicated that there was no redundancy for databases within the environment. Redundancy should exist for databases as appropriate to the sensitivity or criticality of the data they hold. Having redundancy for databases that hold ePHI will assist in providing business continuity and satisfy the HIPAA regulations related to contingency planning – §164.308(a)(7).

Data encryption is critical for protection of ePHI. The response to the questionnaire denoted that encryption occurred only in some cases. In order to satisfy the HIPAA technical safeguards related to access control – §164.312(a) (1) – all ePHI data must be encrypted while at rest.

- **Practices:** The response to the questionnaire indicated there was no monitoring or alert mechanism in place for databases. The indication was that activity logging was in place and was referenced reactively as required when an issue occurred. Having monitoring for database activity is crucial to ensuring the security of ePHI data and knowing what is happening within the database. The monitoring should have the ability to alert the appropriate staff as well as either automatically or manually responding to events. HIPAA regulations – §164.312(b) – require adequate audit controls be in place for both non-repudiation and exception notification.

Administrative credentials for databases were shared among staff members according to the response. The sharing of credentials, especially for administrative accounts with elevated privileges, was strongly discouraged. Without unique credentials the audit logging effectiveness was greatly reduced with respect to identity. The HIPAA technical safeguard guidelines related to access control – §164.312(a) (1) – clearly requires unique identifiers and credentials.

Applications

- **Policies and Procedures:** The response to the questionnaire indicated policies and procedures related to application operations and disaster recovery had not been adequately addressed. The response indicated policies and procedures had either not been created or had not been completed. Having comprehensive policies and procedures established, documented, and published for review would have addressed a number of HIPAA guidelines – §§164.308(a)(1), 164.308(a)(2), 164.308(a)(5), 164.308(a)(7) – related to the security management process, assigned security responsibilities, security awareness and training, and contingency planning. The questionnaire response indicated that staff members were not regularly receiving security alerts and advisories and likewise were not taking the appropriate actions. Distributing and responding to security notices is a required practice to satisfy in part HIPAA guidelines related to security awareness and training - §164.308(a)(5).
- **Functionality:** The response to the questionnaire indicated ePHI related applications had audit logging capabilities that produce easily reviewable logs. However, it was stated that the logs were not easily searchable and there was no central management of these logs. Audit logs that are centrally managed and searchable enable monitoring and alert functionality for proactive security. Adequate audit controls are a HIPAA requirement – §164.312(b) – including the ability to review and search exception reports.

The response further indicated that encryption was not used when ePHI data was transmitted between applications. Encryption is an effective way to safeguard the integrity of data while at rest and in transit. All methods used to transmit ePHI data between applications or within the application itself should use secure channels and some form of encryption. HIPAA regulations related to access control and transmission security – §§164.312(a) (1), 164.312(e)(1) – require encryption to be used when reasonable and appropriate.

All ePHI related applications should have the ability to check their data for accuracy, completeness, and validity. The response indicated that not every relevant application had this capability and furthermore SQL injection vulnerabilities had been identified for some applications. Invalid data can create both intentional and unintentional data pollution. Application and/or database level data checks should be used to mitigate the risk of compromised data integrity and address HIPAA regulations related to audit controls and integrity – §§164.312(b), 164.312(c)(1). The possible methods of ePHI data extraction and transmission were not readily known according to the questionnaire response. It is a fundamental HIPAA requirement – §164.308(a) (8) to have an accurate understanding of how ePHI can be accessed and moved within the electronic environment of an organization. Without an adequate understanding of how users and applications interact with ePHI data it is impossible to take sufficiently secure measures to safeguard said data. All ePHI relevant applications should have all possible methods of ePHI data extraction or transmission secured and documented including aggregations of ePHI data outside of enterprise applications and databases.

- **Practices:** The response to the questionnaire indicated that it was unknown whether administrative credentials for applications were shared or unique to the staff member. The sharing of credentials, especially for administrative accounts with elevated privileges, was strongly discouraged. Without unique credentials the audit logging effectiveness is greatly reduced with respect to identity. The HIPAA technical safeguard guidelines related to access control – §164.312(a) (1) – clearly requires unique identifiers and credentials.

Infrastructure

- **Policies and Procedures:** The response to the questionnaire indicated policies and procedures related to infrastructure disaster recovery had not been adequately addressed. The response indicates policies and procedures had either not been created or had not been completed. Having comprehensive policies and procedures established, documented, and published for disaster recovery would have addressed HIPAA contingency planning – §164.308(a) (7). The questionnaire response also indicated that an accurate inventory of all institutional hardware had not been created or was incomplete. Having a complete, accurate inventory of the organization's hardware will address in part the HIPAA regulations related to workstation use and security and device and media controls – §§ 164.310(a)(1), 164.310(b), 164.310(c).
- **Architecture:** The response to the questionnaire indicated that there was redundancy for servers in some cases but not for all servers within the environment. Redundancy should exist for all servers as appropriate to the sensitivity or criticality of the data they hold, they interact with, or transmit. Having redundancy for servers and therefore the services or applications they hold will assist in providing business continuity and satisfy the HIPAA regulations related to contingency planning – §164.308(a)(7).

The response also indicated that servers were not located on segregated networks from both external hosts and internal user workstations. Network segmentation in conjunction with 2 or 3 tier application architecture allow for greater security through minimizing exposure. Managing information access and exposure is a HIPAA requirement – §164.308(a) (4). No intrusion detection/prevention systems (IDS/IPS) was in place in the environment according to the responses. IDS and IPS provide many tools and techniques to monitor and react to intrusion events, detect and mitigate attacks, and provide notification of unauthorized system use. Most operating systems have some degree of IDS capabilities built-in but may need to be configured and enabled to provide the functionality. An effective IDS/IPS strategy utilizes both the delivered capabilities of the operating systems as well as a stand-alone IDS/IPS application. Monitoring the servers and workstations of potential intrusions both electronic and physical is a requirement of providing adequate security – §164.310(a) (1).

- **Practices:** The response to the questionnaire indicated that unregistered devices/machines were permitted to use NOS resources such as file and print sharing. This type of access implied NOS resources allow anonymous access which was not a secure practice. HIPAA regulations related to workstation security - §164.310(c) – require methods of access to be documented. Anonymous access greatly complicates the accurate recording of access activity.

The response further indicated that users had the ability to modify their PC/device configurations as well as install additional software. In such cases, it is important that users be trained on appropriate security best practices to help guard against unintentional compromises through the installation of malware or other hostile applications. For PCs and devices that have access to ePHI data, users' ability to modify the configuration and install software should be limited as operationally practical. The greater the capacity for users to modify their workstations increases the risk for compromise and likewise must be addressed as part of HIPAA regulations for workstation security – §164.310(c).

There were no measures in place to address ePHI data loss in the event a PC or mobile device was lost or stolen according to the response. At a minimum file encryption and strong device authentication should have been used to safeguard ePHI data if the device it was stored on was no longer in possession or control of the user originally authorized to access it. Many mobile devices have the ability to complete delete their contents remotely if they are attempted to be broken into with brute force or other attacks. Data loss prevention (DLP) measures satisfy in part the HIPAA regulations related to device and media controls – §164.310(d) (1).

Server hardening is an industry best practice that was not being performed according to the response. Hardening ensures only the minimally necessary access and exposure for a server and the services or applications that it hosts. Many malicious attacks exploit unused, accessible resources on servers to compromise those systems.

Information Technology Architecture Review (ITAR) Findings

A number of phone interviews and exchange of emails were performed to gather information about the organization's IT architecture. Network diagrams, system configuration documents, and hardware specifications were examined as part of the architecture review. In contrast to the HISQ where the IT staff answered questions about the organization's policies or technical implementation decisions, the ITAR and subsequent analysis was performed by the team at Towson. Certainly, in subsequent reassessments, the organization could perform this step themselves. The ITAR revealed there were a number of critical areas not addressed in the network design. The network topology was analyzed in detail and determined to be flat in crucial areas which indicates redundancy was not present in all areas. Further, network paths were not optimally designed for enhanced performance. The review also pinpointed a number of single points of failure within the network design thereby not sufficiently satisfying the HIPAA guidelines for contingency planning and business continuity – §164.308(a) (7).

It was documented that VLAN segmentation was not present throughout the network. VLAN segmentation is an essential technique to securing communications within an organization. One part of network segmentation is creating a DMZ in which all publicly accessible web servers are located. According to the review interviews, a DMZ existed but was not effective. Furthermore, it was indicated that not all publicly accessible servers were located within the DMZ implying that portions of the internal network were reachable directly from external hosts. It was also indicated that internal VLANs were not always appropriately segregated from each other thereby enabling unnecessary accessibility to secure resources and data. VLAN segmentation is one aspect of ensuring systems and data is not unnecessarily accessible by internal and/or external hosts – §164.308(a) (4).

The review further determined that all applications and databases could have been accessed directly using a wireless connection. Wireless networks are inherently insecure due to the nature of the transmission medium and the inability to control where the transmission travels and therefore who can receive or intercept it. While there are measures possible to minimize wireless networks' vulnerabilities, they should be regarded as an insecure medium and only used for such applications and services that are tolerant to the intrinsic risk or required for operational necessity.

According to the interview responses, there was an absence of stand-alone intrusion detection/prevention systems (IDS/IPS) within the environment. IDS and IPS provide many tools and techniques to monitor and react to intrusion events, detect and mitigate attacks, and provide notification of unauthorized system use. Many network devices have some degree of IDS capabilities built-in but may need to be configured and enabled to provide the functionality. An effective IDS/IPS strategy utilizes both the delivered capabilities of the network devices as well as a stand-alone IDS/IPS application. Monitoring the network is a requirement of providing adequate transmission security – §164.312(e) (1).

Figure 12. HPS - ePHI access outcomes

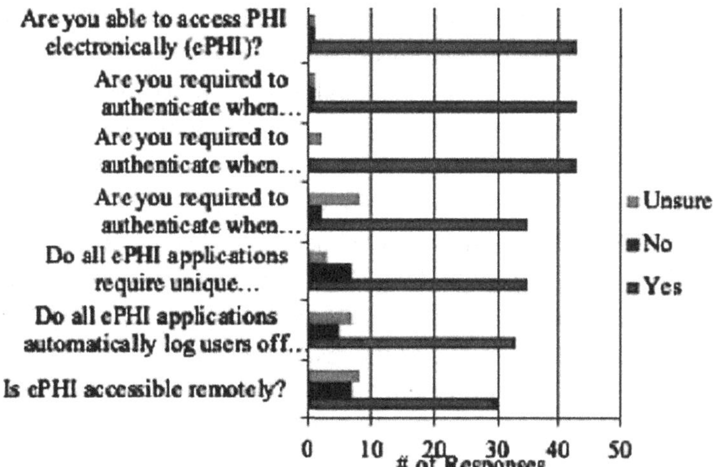

Healthcare Practitioner Survey (HPS) Findings

The focus group used for this survey was approximately 400 healthcare staff from the Pennsylvania hospital and its partner clinical practices. The group's population is diverse in gender, race, ethnicity, and creed.

All members of the focus group were qualified physicians or physicians' assistants at the hospital or clinical practices and appropriately familiar with the policies and practices of the hospital. The survey was completed anonymously to ensure honest, accurate responses as well as remove any undue bias from the analysis of said responses. The survey had a little over 10% response rate, resulting in 45 total responses received as detailed in Figure 12.

The first 7 questions of the HPS were all relevant to the HIPAA Security Rule. The purpose of these questions was to provide a set of baseline questions to ensure the respondents did indeed work with ePHI and had a basic familiarity the hospital's computing environment. Over 95% confirmed this familiarity in questions 1-3 and this only dipped as low as 70% as the complexity of the questions increased about general accessibility of ePHI at the healthcare provider. It is significant that almost 20% of the respondents were unsure whether authentication was needed for imaging applications. Federal regulations require authentication for all access to any application that holds ePHI. The responses of this question suggest that the organization was meeting this requirement satisfactorily and a significant part of the population was unfamiliar and potentially uninvolved with imaging applications. It was also noteworthy that 16% of the survey responses stated that shared accounts were in use to some degree for ePHI-relevant applications. Federal regulations mandate user accounts for ePHI applications be unique per individual for auditing and non-repudiation. The responses suggest that the majority of ePHI applications were using unique user accounts but not all. It is critical for the healthcare provider to review the authentication model for each ePHI application and implement user-specific accounts for any application that doesn't already employ that scheme. Similarly, around 12% of the responses stated automatic log offs did not occur for all ePHI applications. HIPAA regulations clearly require all applications that interact with ePHI to automatically log users off after a period of inactivity. According to the responses, a comprehensive review of all ePHI relevant applications was needed to ensure each application had this capability enabled. There was a specific comment that some applications within the hospital kept the original user logged in indefinitely.

The next group of questions had to do with how ePHI is controlled, including how it can be replicated, where it can reside, and security around its transmission. Based on the range of responses, it was not universally clear whether ePHI data could be saved on mobile and/or personal devices or included in emails. The responses were somewhat split across the board as to the perceived or actual capability of taking ePHI data outside of the organization's data center or including it in email messages.

While the capacity to perform either activity is allowable within the HIPAA regulations, it becomes increasingly more challenging to maintain and demonstrate control of that data. Furthermore, if the organization does allow ePHI data to be included in and/or attached to emails, it is recommended that measures be taken to ensure its integrity. Digital signatures, encryption, and Data Loss Prevention systems are possible mechanisms that can be used for increasing the security of ePHI data included in email. As to the location of ePHI storage, about 74% of the respondents stated all ePHI data was stored within the organization's data center and none of the other responses contradicted the assertion. Control of all ePHI data is required to satisfy HIPAA regulations and having a common, centralized location to store all data makes the control of that data manageable. Similarly, the range of responses about how ePHI is captured suggests that there is not a clear, organizational understanding of all methods for capturing and storing ePHI data.

HIPAA regulations mandate that ePHI be stored in electronic format for interoperability with other healthcare providers and payers. 26% of the responses indicated that there were non-electronic methods being used and a number of additional comments expanded upon this assertion noting that there was considerable data storage using paper. One comment described the environment as half paper and half 'scanned' paper, which may in of itself not have been a completely accurate portrayal of the entire organization, but it did suggest improvements may have been necessary to achieve the electronic storage requirements.

Figure 13HPS - ePHI data control outcomes

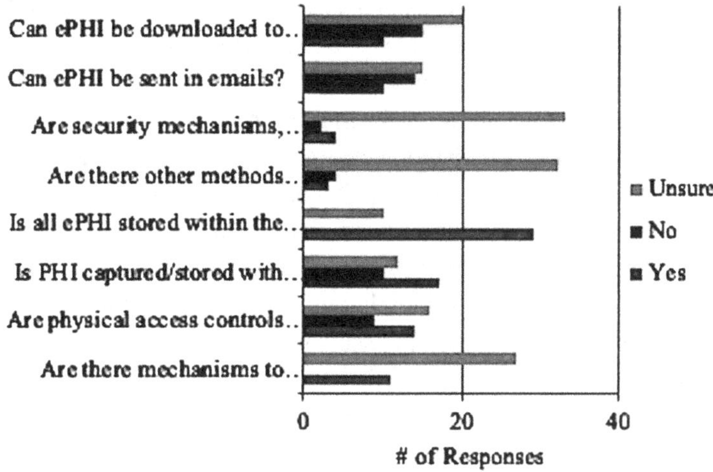

Furthermore, the responses indicated that many locations that store ePHI data were secured physically but not all locations had been adequately addressed. With almost 23% of the respondents stating that physical controls were not present in all ePHI relevant locations that indicated some areas either had no or insufficient controls for ingress/egress. HIPAA regulations require physical access be secure and monitored. Any areas that did not have these controls in place had to be corrected.

Figure 14. HPS - ePHI integrity & privacy outcomes

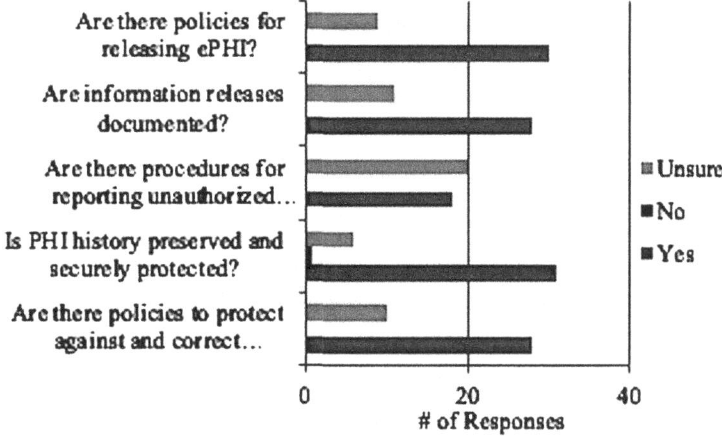

Following the questions related the security of how ePHI was controlled, there were a section of questions related to the healthcare provider's privacy practices and policies as detailed in Figure 13 and Figure 14. Almost 77% of the respondents stated policies and procedures were in place for each of the proposed situations related to ePHI data releases and none of the other responses contradicted the assertion. Additionally, 72% of the respondents stated ePHI data releases were documented and securely recorded and none of the other responses contradicted the assertion. HIPAA regulations clearly require such policies and procedures to exist and require ePHI data releases to be documented and securely stored.

Based on the responses the indication was the organization was satisfactorily meeting this requirement. Similarly, about 82% of the respondents stated ePHI data history was preserved and protected and there was only 1 response contrary to the assertion. Nearly 74% of the respondents stated policies and procedures existed to address ePHI data being changed or deleted and there were no responses that contradicted the assertion. HIPAA regulations require history to be securely stored for all ePHI data and safeguards be in place to ensure the integrity of ePHI data to include any changes or deletions. Based on the responses the indication was the organization was satisfactorily meeting that requirement. Finally, just less than half of the responses stated that procedures existed for reporting unauthorized or inappropriate releases of ePHI data and no responses contradicted the assertion. The other half of the responses were unsure whether such procedures existed or not. HIPAA regulations mandate procedures be established to report and react to ePHI data being released unintentionally. While no responses indicated procedures didn't exist, the lack of understanding by the staff about such procedures in of itself created an implied deficiency.

Figure 15. HPS - policy outcomes

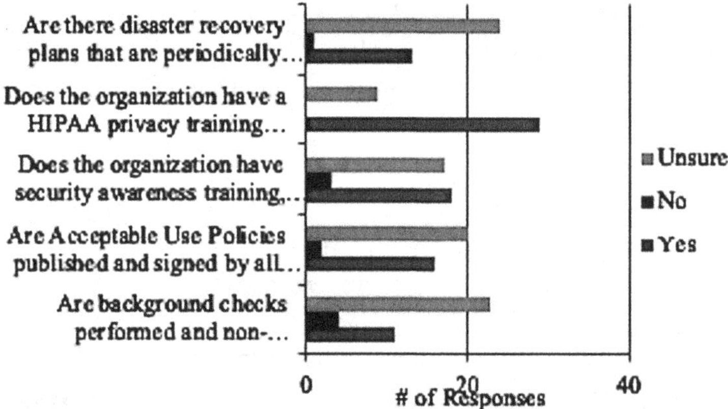

The last group of questions related to the organization's policies and their staff's knowledge and awareness of those policies. Only a third of the respondents definitively stated that disaster recovery and emergency plans existed and were periodically tested. The majority, 63%, of the responses indicated that it was unclear whether plans existed or were tested. Business continuity is a HIPAA regulation of which disaster recovery and emergency plans are a critical component. Almost 78% of the respondents stated a HIPAA privacy training program existed and none of the other responses contradicted the assertion. Privacy training is a requirement of the HIPAA regulations and based on the responses the indication was the organization was satisfactorily meeting that requirement. Just under half of the respondents stated security awareness training was provided on a regular basis although almost as many responses indicated they were unsure if such training existed. Likewise, about 42% of the respondents stated acceptable use policies were published and signed by all users with access to ePHI data. However, almost 53% of the responses indicated they were unsure if such policies existed or were signed by ePHI relevant users. HIPAA regulations clearly require routine security awareness training and acceptable use policies be created, users agree to them, and this agreement must be documented prior to accessing ePHI data.

Based on the responses the indication was while privacy training and acceptable use policies existed within a portion of the organization, they were not pervasive through all units. Roughly 29% of the respondents stated background checks and non-disclosure agreements were signed prior to access being granted to ePHI data. About 11% indicated those practices were not present within the organization and 60%, the majority of responses, were unsure as depicted in Figure 15. HIPAA regulations require all personnel, business associates, and contractors to be adequately screened prior to gaining access to ePHI data. Based on the responses, the indication was that some units were performing the necessary screening, and some were not.

After all assessments were completed and reviewed, each area was rated based on the organization's degree of compliance. Compliance scores were provided for each section and sub-section to give indications where technical and organizational changes may be necessary. For each assessment, an initial draft, with any potential findings, was presented to the organization for their review and acceptance. The healthcare system either accepted the findings or disputed them and provided supporting documentation that demonstrates the finding was not valid. Following the review and acceptance process, the complete COAR report was produced and submitted to the organization for final review and acceptance.

Phase 1 Critical Findings

The three assessments in Phase 1 yielded a significant number of critical findings within the organization's environment. Considering the partner healthcare system is a HIMSS Analytics Stage 6 Hospital, the findings were non-trivial and representative of typical hospitals in the United States. The top critical findings based on organizational impact are detailed below – in decreasing order of criticality – along with their recommended corrective actions.

- **Single Points of Failure:** Analysis of the network topology determined the organization had six significant single points of failure related to how the various buildings on campus were connected both to the institution's data center and the Internet. In some of the cases those single points of failure were due to a single physical transmission medium existing between buildings.

The other cases were that not all buildings had redundant network paths to the internet or the data center. There were three instances where a disaster scenario in one building would segregate one or more buildings by extension from all other networks – internal or external. While a disaster scenario at a particular building is expected to directly impact that building's connectivity, such an impact should not be entirely debilitating to ancillary buildings. Single points of failure create an organizational risk to both contingency planning and business continuity, both of which are required – §164.308(a) (7) – within the HIPAA regulations. Redundancy within the network can be achieved using a variety of hardware and/or software solutions that was detailed in the COAR.

Disaster Recovery (DR) and Emergency Plans: Only a Third of the Healthcare

Practitioner Survey respondents definitively stated that disaster recovery and emergency plans existed and were periodically tested. The majority, 63%, of the responses indicated that it was unclear whether plans existed or were tested. This was reiterated by the responses provided to the HISQ by the organization's technical staff. The lack of awareness of a DR plan is akin to not having a plan altogether since the majority of personnel have not reviewed or tested the plan. Business continuity is a HIPAA regulation – §164.308(a) (7) – of which disaster recovery and emergency plans are a critical component. Disaster recovery plans must be established and periodically tested in order to be fully compliant.

- **Undue Exposure in Application Architecture:** It was discovered that not all applications that interact with ePHI data utilized a 2 or 3-tier architecture. Numerous applications were not configured such that web services, application services, and database services were segregated from one another. In many cases all these services resided on the same physical machine and were directly accessible by internal and external hosts. The final COAR recommended that all ePHI data that would be accessed by users should be done via a 2 or 3-tier application architecture with the data store on an internal, inaccessible network segment. All efforts should have been made to minimize the exposure each server has to non-administrative internal and external networks. Since all applications must inherently be accessed by internal and/or external users, some amount of exposure is necessary on generally accessible networks. Through a 2 or 3-tier architecture, the only way users can access ePHI data is via proxy through the web or application servers. This design minimizes the impact of a breach at a web server since no actual ePHI data resides on those servers.
- **Undue Exposure in Network Architecture:** The organization did not have an adequate demilitarized zone (DMZ) configuration that contained all publicly accessible web servers. Many of the application's web servers resided in the same network subnets where the application and database servers were located. In order to minimize exposure, any web server that is publicly accessible should reside in the DMZ and there should be no publicly accessible machines outside of the DMZ. The DMZ should be segregated from all internal network segments and resources that hold ePHI data. Further all network segments besides the DMZ should be inaccessible from external networks. Network segmentation, such as a DMZ or in conjunction with a 2 or 3-tier application configuration, is an approach for decreasing exposure and ensuring systems and data is not unnecessarily accessible by internal and/or external hosts. Information access management is a specific requirement of the HIPAA administrative safeguards – §164.308(a) (4).
- **Use of Shared Accounts:** 16% of the Healthcare Practitioner Survey respondents stated that shared accounts were in use to some degree for ePHI-relevant applications. HIPAA regulations – §164.312(a) (1) – mandate user accounts for ePHI applications be unique per individual for auditing and non-repudiation. The responses suggest that the majority of ePHI applications were using unique user accounts but not all. It was critical to review the authentication model for each ePHI application and implement user-specific accounts for any application that didn't already employ that scheme.
- **Automatic Logoff:** About 12% of the survey responses stated automatic log offs did NOT occur for all ePHI applications. HIPAA regulations – §164.312(a) (1) – require all applications that interact with ePHI to automatically log users off after a period of inactivity. According to the survey responses, a comprehensive review of all ePHI relevant applications was needed to ensure each application had this capability enabled. There was a specific comment that some applications within the hospital kept the original user logged in indefinitely, which precluded compliance.
- **Security Awareness Training:** Just under half of the survey respondents stated security awareness training was provided on a regular basis although almost as many responses indicated they

were unsure if such training existed. The HIPAA regulations – §164.308(a) (5) – requires routine security awareness training and based on the responses the indication is while training exists within a portion of the organization, it is not present within all units. A security awareness and training program needed to be established and implemented across the organization.

- **Acceptable Use Policies:** Almost 53% of the Healthcare Practitioner Survey responses indicated they were unsure if such policies existed or were signed by ePHI relevant users. HIPAA regulations – §164.308(a) (1) – mandate that acceptable use policies be created, users agree to them, and this agreement is documented prior to accessing ePHI data. Based on the responses the indication was while acceptable use policies existed within a portion of the organization, they were not pervasive through all units. Such policies need to be established that comprehensively define appropriate and inappropriate use, access, and disclosure of ePHI including sanctions for not following the policies.
- **Reporting of Unauthorized or Inappropriate ePHI Release:** Just less than half of the survey responses stated that procedures existed for reporting unauthorized or inappropriate releases of ePHI data and no responses contradicted the assertion. The other half of the responses were unsure whether such procedures existed or not. The HIPAA regulations – §164.308(a) (6) – mandate procedures be established to report and react to ePHI data being released unintentionally. While no responses indicated procedures didn't exist, the lack of understanding by the staff about such procedures in of itself created an implied deficiency. Any staff member that interacts with ePHI must understand how to identify an incident and what to do if and when they occur.
- **Physical Access Controls:** Almost 23% of the Healthcare Practitioner Survey respondents stated that physical controls were not present in all ePHI relevant locations. That indicated some areas either had no or insufficient controls for ingress/egress. The HIPAA regulations – §164.310(a) (1) – require physical access be secure and monitored. Any areas that did not have these controls in place had to be corrected.

HISCF:Phase 2

Phase 2 of the framework included an intensive technical review and assessment of the organization's IT environment. This phase measured and analyzed the actual performance of the systems and practices both against the theoretical goal presented in the HISG and the reported state of the organization provided in the assessment stage of Phase 1. It was critical for the success of this phase to identify the key IT staff within the hospital that could facilitate the exhaustive testing performed as part of the penetration and vulnerability testing. Once this staff was pinpointed, initial interviews were arranged to walk through the testing process and obtain contextual information about the environment to ensure the testing was indeed thorough but wouldn't interrupt normal business operations. It was also very important that we were able to engage directly with the manager of the EHR system to complete the EHR security and privacy assessment. Since the assessment covers a range of areas – policy, functional, and technical – it is impractical for one individual or even one group in a department to adequately respond to all questions. As such, the manager of the EHR system was able to facilitate the completion of this assessment survey. It is important to note that all systems in the organization that were hosted offsite, were considered out of scope for this phase. The technical implementation and likewise testing of those systems were implicitly regarded as meeting all compliance standards by obtaining certification from the hosting entity that their systems are compliant with the appropriate federal regulations, such as HIPAA. This is consistent with the federal government's treatment of hosted systems for audit purposes. This phase's assessments included technical interviews and inspections, penetration and vulnerability testing, and a comprehensive evaluation of security and privacy related to their EHR system. By the conclusion of Phase 2, the organization's complete IT environment had been methodically examined, tested, and documented.

Penetration and Vulnerability Testing Results

Penetration testing and vulnerability scanning by their very nature are an exhaustive, iterative process that many times requires analysis from both operational and security perspectives. One of the most common issues that lead to vulnerabilities or exploitation is merely an ignorance that a particular host is present on the network or a host is running unnecessary or unexpected services. The first step in any penetration test is to create a survey of the hosts that are present on the network and what services that are running. Many of these services are intentional and are functioning as expected. It is those hosts and related services that are unintentional that are of most significance for this initial survey. The survey portion of the security testing discovered the presence of 5,967 unique systems on the organization's production network. These hosts were running a variety of services, amongst which were SMTP, SNMP, SSL, and HTTP, which are protocols that are commonly compromised or exploited. While many of these services may serve an operational purpose, it is important to verify there are no extraneous or unexpected services operating on these ports. The partner hospital's information technology staff did examine these results and confirmed that all hosts discovered were known and the services each host was running, was intentional. An intensive battery of penetration tests and vulnerability scans were performed on the Pennsylvania hospital's production computing environment. Initially the organization's primary server subnet, subnet A, was examined exhaustively and 98 unique hosts were discovered with 799 issues ranging from critical to low risk.

Following this assessment, the decision was made to expand the network range being tested to include other subnets that held other production and development servers as well as clients and workstations. The expanded subnets included subnets B through I. After the expanded testing was completed a total of 1,012 unique systems had been identified across the organization and 13,037 total issues of critical, high, medium, or low risk.

Based on the high number of critical and high-risk issues exposed in subnets A through I, the organization decided that a full examination of all their subnets, including those throughout the main campus that only contained workstations, would be beneficial. Following this last round of testing, 5,967 unique systems had been scanned cumulatively between all three testing exercises. In total, there were 14,448 issues found, 5,846 of which posed either a critical or high risk to the organization. The summary of the findings from all the security testing exercises are depicted in Figure 16.

Discussions and Implications

The core goal of this research was to develop potential solutions for improving accessibility, efficiency, and integrity in healthcare delivery. While this research proposes standardized approaches for evaluating and ensuring Health Insurance Portability and Accountability Act (HIPAA) compliance and for providing electronic patient access to EHR systems, these solutions needed to be tested and legitimized through actual application in a real-world environment. Chapter 4 detailed the case studies of the framework implementations with 2 national healthcare providers and the results borne out of those efforts. While

Figure 16. Security issues per severity ranking

	Subnet	Unique Hosts	Unique Hosts with an ...	Critical	High	Medium	Low	Totals
Data Center	A	100	98	66	234	406	93	799
Servers and Workstations (Hospital)	B	175	171	1583	2155	1611	415	5,764
	C	15	11	97	15	95	36	243
	D	205	179	24	43	1025	195	1,287
	E	205	192	0	10	1114	187	1,311
	F	209	198	15	15	1146	196	1,372
	G	183	87	126	291	603	92	1,112
	H	143	26	359	436	219	50	1,064
	I	123	50	0	54	13	18	85
	J	252	20	0	6	146	41	193
	K	40	35	38	89	253	107	487
Workstations (including Partner Practices)	L	254	18	6	33	105	30	174
	M	254	6	3	19	27	6	55
	N	254	1	0	2	7	1	10
	O	254	5	0	0	25	6	31
	P	254	3	0	0	16	3	19
	Q	254	2	0	0	12	3	15
	R	254	0	0	0	0	0	0
	S	254	0	0	0	0	0	0
	T	254	9	0	6	18	8	32
	U	254	11	0	2	51	7	60
	V	254	13	8	5	38	8	59
	W	254	0	0	0	0	0	0
	X	254	10	0	3	27	4	34
	Y	254	8	38	49	42	4	133
	Z	254	13	0	16	59	10	85
	AA	253	0	0	0	0	0	0
	BB	254	6	0	0	20	4	24
	Totals	5,967	1,172	2,363	3,483	7,078	1,524	14,448

the initial review of those results seems very positive, this chapter aims to delve deeper into what the results actually mean and what possible wider implications they may have for other hospitals.

The HISCF was applied with the Pennsylvania hospital, a 500-bed HIMSS 6 national hospital that admits over 400,000 patients per year. Phase 1 of the HISCF did a systematic review of the organization's policies and procedures. This phase also analyzed the hospital's technical architecture and surveyed healthcare practitioners to get a perspective on how technology was actually being used in day-to-day practice. Phase 2 of the HISCF did a thorough battery of security testing on every aspect of the Pennsylvania hospital's computing environment. Even though considered in the upper tier of hospitals in the United States with regard to information security, there were significant findings that indicated areas where Health Insurance Portability and Accountability Act (HIPAA) compliance was not being met.

Figure 17. Overall compliance performance

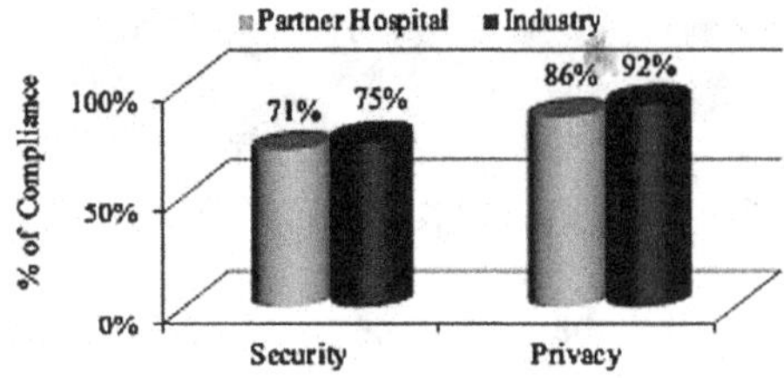

Phase 1 Inferences

While a significant number of findings were made related to the current policies, practices, and architecture of the organization' IT environment, the partner health system's level of compliance was on par with the industry averages as detailed in Figure 17.

Figure 18. Compliance per functional category

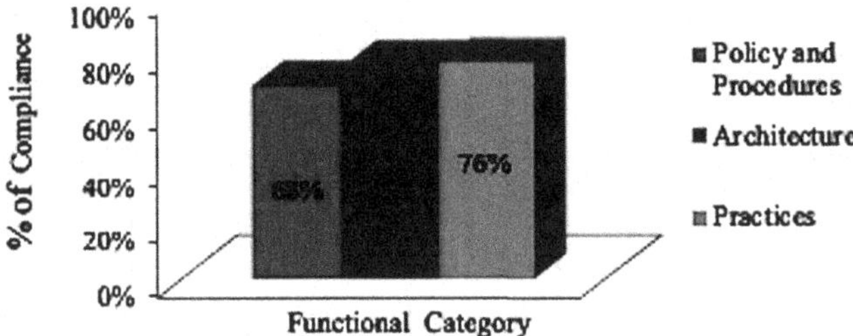

The industry averages, derived from HIMSS sponsored research (Appari, Anthony, and Johnson, 2009), indicated most organizations are closer to full compliance to privacy than security. The partner hospital mirrored this pattern with Privacy Rule compliance at 86% while the Security Rule compliance was approximately 71%. Similar to many healthcare entities, the organization was relatively close to compliance but not at the federally mandated 100% compliance as depicted in Figure 18. The functional area that required the most improvement by the organization was policy and procedures. This deficiency is fairly common throughout all industry with respect to IT and is one of the hardest areas to correct.

Changing policy and procedure requires changes to business practices and it is typically challenging for organizations to secure the leadership commitment and stakeholder buy-in to enact this type of change. Similarly, the organization had the most compliance issues with regard to the human-technology interaction element of IT compared to the four solely technical areas, as depicted in Figure 19. This was actually a good indicator for the organization that their workforce had an increasing propensity for compliance beliefs. In larger healthcare providers, over 300 beds, a high proclivity for compliance is typically indicative of a high level of intervention by management through training, meetings, policy implementation, and enforcement. Having leadership buy-in and involvement in compliance efforts is a critical factor for an organization's compliance programs to be successful.

Even though Phase 1 yielded significant gaps in functional and technical areas that spanned the Pennsylvania hospital's computing environment, none were unsurmountable to remediate. Arguably the

Figure 19. Compliance per technical category

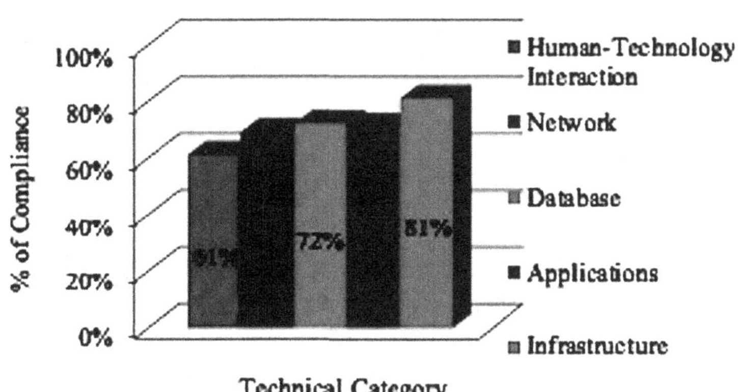

hardest step in compliance is simply the recognition of a requirement and corresponding discrepancy in meeting it. Ignorance through a lack of understanding and awareness is oft times the main reason for organizations be out of compliance (Kwon and Johnson, 2013). Once the issue has been identified, many times remediating the technical problem is not that difficult and can very done very quickly. This was demonstrated by the hospital's ability to respond to the majority of all of Phase 1's findings within a matter of weeks of when they were brought to their attention. Additionally, as the HISG could be leveraged for implementation level guidance, the Pennsylvania hospital's IT staff did not have to go searching for remediation solutions as they were readily available. The fact that the application of the HISCF was directly responsible the realization of the gaps in compliance and facilitated the remediation efforts suggests that the HISCF is an effective tool and was more comprehensive than the compliance program previously instituted at the Pennsylvania hospital. This claim was offered by the organization themselves after having gone through the assessment exercises laid out in Phase 1.

Phase 2 Inferences

While Phase 1 performed a passive examination of the organization's computing environment and practices, Phase 2 did an active evaluation through a series of targeted tests and inspections. Phase 2 identified 5,846 critical and high-risk issues. Undoubtedly the presence of this many elements of increased risk throughout the environment was unfortunate and disappointing to the organization. On the other hand, it was fortunate for the organization that these issues were found so they could be mitigated before the risks turned into compromises. Through analysis of the security testing results, it was discovered that many of the specific critical and high-risk vulnerabilities were found repetitively throughout the environment. Of the 5,846 critical and high-risk issues found, they are made up only 483 unique vulnerabilities.

This finding demonstrated the product of the organization not having a formal security assessment program that performed periodic testing. At a minimum it was recommended that an enterprise wide patching process and schedule be established. Additionally, it was recommended that a standardized deployment configuration for servers and workstations be developed. These fairly simple steps could mitigate many of these issues very quickly and reliably.

Furthermore, the routine testing would bring to light any poor implementation choices or mistakes that were made when a new system or application is brought online. The Pennsylvania hospital's technical staff was able to validate these findings and corresponding mitigation steps to resolve nearly 90%

Figure 20. Security issues per operational host

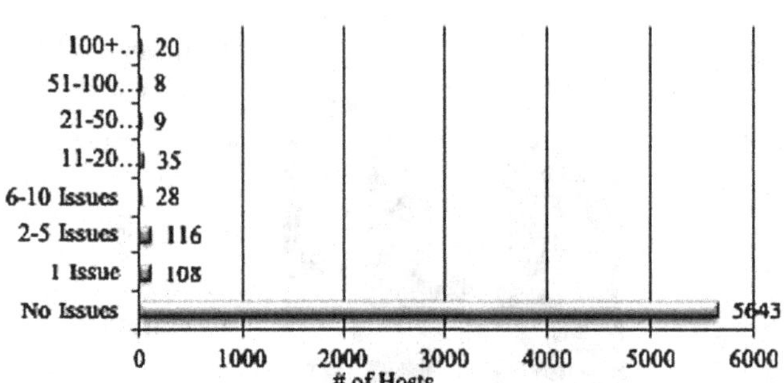

of the findings in about 1 month. Following this analysis, the results were then examined to determine how many issues each individual host had to see if there were any trends or high concentration areas of increased risk. The complete breakdown of the number of issues per host is depicted in Figure 20.

Of the 5,967 hosts present in the healthcare provider's production environment, 324 of these systems had at least 1 issue of critical or high risk. In contrast, 5,643 of the 5,967 hosts, about 95%, had no critical or high-risk issues at all. When looking only at the 1,012 machines at the hospital's main campus - subnets A through K, 725 of these machines, 72%, had no critical or high-risk issues at all. This percentage is notably similar to the organization's approximate 71% overall compliance with the HIPAA Security Rule measured in Phase 1. This similarity in results using different testing methods provides a measure of validation for the evaluation process itself as it produced comparable results between both Phases.

It is significant to note that there were 20 systems that had 100 or more unique elevated risk concerns. In fact, these 20 machines account for 4,153 of the 5,523 total critical or high-risk issues present at the main hospital campus. Which is to say just fewer than 2% of the organization's computing environment represented about 75% of its increased risk exposure. This is a common condition in most organizations as it is typical for the majority of an organization's computing environment is operating at an adequate security level and there is just a small fraction of the systems that are not.

It is concerning however that the data center, subnet A, which housed only servers (production, testing, and development), exhibited 300 critical and high-risk issues. Furthermore, only 16 of the 100 systems in this vital area of the organization and where all the storage of ePHI resided did not have at least 1 issue of critical or high risk. This means 84% of all the systems in effectively sensitive area of the environment had an elevated level of risk.

The crux of the organization's condition was a lack of true patch management program and periodic security assessment program within their computing department. As such a complete periodic security assessment program was proposed for the Pennsylvania hospital that included recommendations for all critical and high-risk issues to be measured and addressed within 30 days. It is industry-recognized that a patch management and vulnerability assessment process is a key element to mitigating risk.

This was a significant realization that came out of the testing that provided an impetus for the organization's leadership to move swiftly and decisively to correct these issues. Similarly, to Phase 1, the fact that the Pennsylvania hospital going through Phase 2 of the HISCF generated the volume and significance of results that it did, coupled with the healthcare provider's size and reputation in the industry, seems to support the claim of the effectiveness and usefulness of the HISCF.

Overall Implications of HISCF's Validity and Future Recommendations

The outcomes of applying the HISCF at the Pennsylvania hospital are very compelling and seem to suggest the framework is comprehensive and effective, at least within the scope of that hospital. Prior to applying the HISCF, the Pennsylvania hospital had failed an external audit, being cited for numerous violations related to HIPAA.

Following the HISCF implementation, the hospital was audited again, and no significant findings were reported. This suggests the HISCF was instrumental in the organization's improvement. This research recommends that further application of the HISCF is needed to strengthen the premise that it can be an effective tool for other hospitals as well. While the simple number of times the framework is applied needs to be increased, so does the variety in hospital sizes. The HISCF may not be a 'silver bullet' solution for every type of healthcare entity but the results from the case study with the Pennsylvania hospital seem indicate the potential that it could benefit other organizations around the nation and also similar healthcare organizations worldwide.

CONCLUSION

Accessibility is a pillar of healthcare delivery. However, as soon as access is afforded, it is the ethical, legal, and financial responsibility of healthcare providers to ensure the integrity of the care delivery is upheld. The Health Insurance Portability and Accountability Act (HIPAA) and EHR systems lay the foundation for satisfying these concerns. Unfortunately, these endeavors have proved challenging to accomplish with the absence of standardized, freely available, implementation plans. Each HIPAA covered entity has been forced to approach these tasks from their localized, individual perspective and hence the figurative wheels are being reinvented again and again. Further, each one of these entities is spending vast amounts of time, resources, and money trying to determine multiple paths towards the same goals. With a lack of direction, it takes significant effort to determine what needs to be done and how to do it even before organizations can get to the point of actual implementation. As such, most healthcare organizations are expending significant and superfluous effort in the assessment and planning stages. Technology has long thrived on the adoption of standards and this research contends that the issues of accessibility, integrity, and efficiency in healthcare information technology are no exception.

There is overwhelming consensus in the healthcare industry that the spirit of HIPAA is positive and beneficial to both patients and providers. Likewise, the move from paper and film to EHR systems is clearly the natural evolution of health information storage and data exchange. It has not been so much of a struggle for most healthcare providers to find answers to the why, it has been the how that has kept these issues at the forefront of the healthcare industry for over a decade. The complexity and reach of HIPAA and the Meaningful Use programs across the entire United States has provided a seemingly endless parade of motivations for finding better methods to ensure their implementation. The guides and tools this research has produced offer promise for assisting healthcare providers with the initial implementation of these initiatives as well as better equip organizations to maintain their ongoing compliance.

REFERENCES

Acharya, S., Coats, B., Saluja, A., & Fuller, D. (2013). A Roadmap for Information Security Assessment for Meaningful Use. *Proceedings of the 2013 IEEE/ACM International Symposium on Network Analysis and Mining for Health Informatics, Biomedicine and Bioinformatics.*

Acharya, S., Coats, B., Saluja, A., & Fuller, D. (2013). Secure Electronic Health Record Exchange: Achieving the Meaningful Use Objectives. *Proceedings of the 46th Hawaii International Conference on System Sciences*, 46, pp. 253-262. 10.1109/HICSS.2013.473

Acharya, S., Coats, B., Saluja, A., & Fuller, D. (2014). From Regulations to Practice: Achieving Information Security Compliance in Healthcare. *Proceedings of the 2014 Human Computer Interaction International Conference.*

An Introductory Resource Guide for Implementing the Health Insurance Portability and Accountability Act (HIPAA) Security Rule. (2008). National Institute of Standards and Technologies. Retrieved from http://csrc.nist.gov/publications/nistpubs/800-66-Rev1/SP-800-66-Revision1.pdf

Annas, G. (2003). HIPAA Regulations - A New Era of Medical-Record Privacy? *The New England Journal of Medicine*, *348*(15), 1486–1490. doi:10.1056/NEJMlim035027 PMID:12686707

Appari, A., Anthony, D. L., & Johnson, M. E. (2009). *HIPAA Compliance: An Examination of Institutional and Market Forces.* Healthcare Information Management Systems Society.

Aral, S., & Weill, P. (2007). IT assets, organizational capabilities, and firm performance: How resource allocations and organizational differences explain performance variation. *Organization Science*, *18*(5), 763–780. doi:10.1287/orsc.1070.0306

Bharadwaj, S., Bharadwaj, A., & Bendoly, E. (2007). The Performance Effects of Complementarities Between Information Systems, Marketing, Manufacturing, and Supply Chain Processes. *Information Systems Research*, *18*(4), 437–453. doi:10.1287/isre.1070.0148

Blumenthal, D., & Tavenner, M. (2010). The Meaningful Use Regulation for Electronic Health Records. *The New England Journal of Medicine*, *363*(6), 501–504. doi:10.1056/NEJMp1006114 PMID:20647183

Breach Notification Rule. (2009). United States. Department of Health and Human Services. Office for Civil Rights. Retrieved from http://www.hhs.gov/ocr/privacy/hipaa/administrative/breachnotificationrule/index.html

CFR parts 160 and 164: Modifications to the HIPAA Privacy, Security, Enforcement and Breach Notification Rules Under the HITECH Act and the Genetic Information Nondiscrimination Act: Other Modifications to the HIPAA Rules: Final Rule. (2013). The United States Health and Human Services. Retrieved from http://gpo.gov/fdsys/pkg/FR-2013-01-25/pdf/2013-01073.pdf

CMS EHR Meaningful Use Overview. (2012). Center for Medicare and Medicaid Services. Retrieved from https://www.cms.gov/Regulations-and-Guidance/Legislation/EHRIncentivePrograms/Meaningful_Use.html

Coats, B., Acharya, S., Saluja, A., & Fuller, D. (2012). HIPAA Compliance: How Do We Get There? A Standardized Framework for Enabling Healthcare Information Security & Privacy. *Proceedings of the 16th Colloquium for Information Systems Security Education.*

Data and Reports. (2012). Center for Medicare and Medicaid Services. Retrieved from http://www.webcitation.org/6EMwIm36I

EMR Adoption Trends. (2014). *HIMSS Analytics*. Retrieved from http://www.himssanalytics.org/stagesGraph.asp

Enforcement Results per Year. (2010). Center for Medicare and Medicaid Services. Retrieved from http://www.hhs.gov/ocr/privacy/hipaa/enforcement/data/historicalnumbers.html

Fichman, R., Kohli, R., & Krishnan, R. (2011). The Role of Information Systems in Healthcare: Current Research and Future Trends. *Information Systems Research*, *22*(3), 419–428. doi:10.1287/isre.1110.0382

Health Reform in Action. (2010). United States White House. Retrieved from http://www.whitehouse.gov/healthreform/healthcare-overview

Helms, M. M., Moore, R., & Ahmadi, M. (2008). Information Technology (IT) and the Healthcare Industry: A SWOT Analysis. *International Journal of Healthcare Information Systems and Informatics*, *3*(1), 75–92. doi:10.4018/jhisi.2008010105

HER Incentive Programs. (2012). The Office of the National Coordinator for Health Information Technology. Retrieved from http://www.healthit.gov/providers-professionals/ehr-incentive-programs

HIPAA Administrative Simplification. (2006). United States. Department of Health and Human Services Office of Civil Rights. Retrieved from http://www.hhs.gov/ocr/privacy/hipaa/administrative/privacyrule/adminsimpregtext.pdf

HIPAA Compliance Review Analysis and Summary of Results. (2008). Center for Medicare and Medicaid Services. Retrieved from http://www.hhs.gov/ocr/privacy/hipaa/enforcement/cmscompliancerev08.pdf

Hirsch, R. D. (2013). Final HIPAA Omnibus Rule brings sweeping changes to health care privacy law: HIPAA privacy and security obligations extended to business associates and subcontractors. *Bloomberg Bureau of National Affairs Heath Law Reporter*, *415*, 1–11.

Johnson, M. E., Goetz, E., & Pfleeger, S. L. (2009). Security through Information Risk Management. *IEEE Security and Privacy*, *7*(3), 45–52. doi:10.1109/MSP.2009.77

Kayworth, T., & Whitten, D. (2010). Effective Information Security Requires a Balance of Social and Technology Factors. *MIS Quarterly Executive*, *9*(3), 163–175.

Kwon, J., & Johnson, M. E. (2013). Healthcare Security Strategies for Regulatory Compliance and Data Security. *Proceedings of the 46th Hawaii International Conference on System Sciences*. 10.1109/HICSS.2013.246

Regulations and Guidance. (2004). Center for Medicare and Medicaid Services. Retrieved from https://www.cms.gov/home/regsguidance.asp

Return On Investment, H. I. P. A. A. (2005). *Blue Cross Blue Shield Association. National Committee on Vital Health Statistics*. Subcommittee on Standards and Security.

Solove, D. (2013). HIPAA Turns 10: Analyzing the Past, Present, and Future Impact. *Journal of American Health Information Management Association*, *84*(4), 22–28.

Title 45 – Public Welfare, Subtitle A – Department of Health and Human Services, Part 164 – Security and Privacy. (1996). United States. National Archives and Records Administration. Retrieved from http://www.access.gpo.gov/nara/cfr/waisidx_07/45cfr164_07.html

United States Department of Commerce, National Institute of Standards and Technology. (2012). *About NSTIC*. Retrieved from http://www.nist.gov/nstic/about-nstic.html

Xia, Z., & Johnson, M. E. (2010). Access Governance: Flexibility with Escalation and Audit. *Proceedings of the 43rd Hawaii International Conference on System Sciences*.

KEY TERMS AND DEFINITIONS

HFIF: The Healthcare Federated Identity Framework aimed at positioning the healthcare providers to enable distributed electronic access to patient data.

HIPAA: The Health Insurance Portability and Accountability Act of 1996 is United States legislation that provides data privacy and security provisions for safeguarding medical information.

HISF: The Healthcare Information Security Framework aimed for organizations to plan and execute their overall HIPAA compliance projects including attestation.

HISP: The Healthcare Information Security Plan is aimed to provide comprehensive implementation level guidance for satisfying HIPAA regulations.

HISTD: The Healthcare Information Security Testing Directive and a collection of open source security testing software for organizations to assess and mitigate their systems.

Meaningful Use: The U.S. government introduced the Meaningful Use program as part of the 2009 Health Information Technology for Economic and Clinical Health (HITECH) Act, to encourage health care providers to show “meaningful use” of a certified Electronic Health Record (EHR).

This research was previously published in Machine Learning and Cognitive Science Applications in Cyber Security; pages 1-56, copyright year 2019 by Information Science Reference (an imprint of IGI Global).

Chapter 28
Applicability of WSN and Biometric Models in the Field of Healthcare

Nikhil Sharma
https://orcid.org/0000-0003-4751-2970
HMR Institute of Engineering and Technology, Delhi, India

Ila Kaushik
Krishna Institute of Engineering and Technology, India

Bharat Bhushan
https://orcid.org/0000-0002-9345-4786
HMR Institute of Technology and Management, Delhi, India

Siddharth Gautam
HMR Institute of Technology and Management, Delhi, India

Aditya Khamparia
https://orcid.org/0000-0001-9019-8230
Lovely Professional University, India

ABSTRACT

Health is considered as the most important ingredient in human life. Health is wealth is the most frequent used proverb. A healthy person can perform its entire task with full enthusiasm and great energy and can solve all problems as mind is a powerful weapon, which controls all our functioning. But now due to change in our lifestyles, we are becoming prone to all kinds of health hazards. Due to unhealthy mind, we are not able to perform any tasks. Humans are becoming victims of many diseases and one of the most common reason for our degradation in health is stress. In this chapter, the authors present role of WSN and biometric models such as two factor remote authentication, verifying fingerprint operations for enhancing security, privacy preserving in healthcare, healthcare data by cloud technology with biometric application, and validation built hybrid trust computing perspective for confirmation of contributor profiles in online healthcare data. A comparison table is formulated listing all the advantages and disadvantages of various biometric-based models used in healthcare.

DOI: 10.4018/978-1-6684-6311-6.ch028

INTRODUCTION

Health is one of the most essential state in human life. No task is carried out without being healthy, whether it is personal or professional life. In order to have proper functioning in all aspects one must be mentally and physically fit. Healthy living has the opportunity, motivation and capability to perform and act in all aspects. Some common factors such as specific diet requirements must be considered important for being healthy (Barbara et al.,2016). Proper diet plan, exercise, sound sleep are main ingredients of healthy life. But now a days, due to excessive work load and eating habits humans are becoming more vulnerable to diseases. Due to advancement in field of technology no physical work is carried out by humans due to which they are becoming unhealthy and prone to diseases. As increase in the number of humans visiting hospitals, taking appointments from doctors, lot of time is being wasted. Now as people have less time, they are not interested to have long span of time. For that purposes biometric have done tremendous work in health sector (Alpaslan, 2016). Everything is now automated which saves time. If person needs to visit doctor, patients' card is created which acts as a smart card having all the details of the patient such as his id, name, age, phone number, gender, address. Using this card, authenticity of the patient is being maintained and every time he need not have to get all his details entered. Just during his next visit card is being scanned and all the updates are being carried out. For treatment of iris and retina, biometric techniques are used which in very less amount of time are used for doing any eye surgery (Khosrowjerdi,2016). Laser based techniques are also used for this purpose. Security plays a very crucial role in any type of secure system. Main features of security such as secrecy which means the intended message must be kept secret during transmission, integrity which means there must be no modification in between while sending and receiving messages, availability which means the message must be available in future for further references (Amjad et al.,2017). In order to have security in the system, many biometric systems are being installed which uses face, palm recognition techniques to have authentication within the system and the outside intruders cannot steal any confidential information from the system (Bakke,2017). In the later section of the chapter, different biometric models such as two factor remote authentication, for security purposes effective fingerprint technique using biometric is adopted, privacy preserving in healthcare, Healthcare information using cloud technology with biometric application & Biometric Validation (Chattopadhyay,2016) based combined technique for trust computing perspective for authentication of providers profile in online healthcare data are studied. A comparison table is designed listing all the Merits and Demerits of the biometric system used in health care.

Internet of Things (IoT) plays a vital role in today's era. Almost each and every product which we use in our day to day life is being mapped with latest use of technologies which is concerned with IoT. With the use of this technology we are becoming advanced in every field (Athanasiou & Lymberopoulos, 2016). IoT applications are used in every field of different sectors which reduced human intervention, saves time and the work is carried out in a very healthy environment. The bridge that binds the gap between user's behaviour and software is known as Natural User Interfaces (NUIs) (Chen et al., 2019). Many recent features are used under this emerging technology. Using smart windows and refrigerators concept online information, can be accessed. Various biometric applications such as gestures on touch screen and touch pads, voice recognition used in homes and cars by using home automation and operations on smartphones. With recent trends and innovations in technologies where mouse and keyboard working are considered time consuming, natural user interfaces came into picture (Din et al., 2019). As the use of natural interfaces increases, risk to sensitive information also increases. The key features of security such as secrecy which means the important information must be made confidential to unauthorised users, integrity which means the information received must be consistent to both the ends i.e. sending and receiving, availability which means information must be made available to the users (Roy et al., 2017). One of the common examples for secure transaction is to enable e payment transactions. Innovative technology of user interface uses ability to capture high dimensional data. Earlier days, only few mouse clicks, mouse movements and key strokes with keyboard were captured and analysed (Premarathne et al., 2015). Whereas with recent technology a multiple key strokes, mouse clicks, touch area, touch locations, touch pressure etc. Users information can be extracted using natural interface. The captured information using biometric captures all information like palm detection, face detection, iris detection, fingerprint etc. (Sae-Bae et al., 2019) which can be used over the internet along with on a local device. Various studies have been done to access the uses of authentication mechanisms. For that reason's various authentication-based algorithms came into picture (Challa et al., 2017). Many techniques were proposed for the patterns which changes over time and various threats and vulnerabilities existing during that period were not addressed. In order to overcome all these above stated drawbacks, various security-based methods were introduced such as cryptography-based techniques, public key-based cryptosystem, authentication methods, dynamic key exchange etc. (Chatterjee et al., 2018). Security is considered as one of the most important concerns in any security-based model. The key elements of security such as availability, integrity and confidentiality must be preserved for carrying out any successful security model (Beldad et al., 2010). Patient's data is considered as one of the most important factors in any health-related system. Health information system is becoming more powerful these days where information is to be shared between patient and providers in order to provide diagnostics, self-care (Singhal et al., 2016). Computer based models were introduced for feeding patient's necessary details such as name, phone number, address, age, gender etc. Now in direction to preserve the privacy and integrity of the information certain security-based models were introduced such as cryptography-based models, setting up of firewalls, access management, backup policies etc. (Mohan et al., 2016). In order to have successful health information system one of the adopted methods is systematic mapping technique which maps certain set of steps such as analysing of health-related problem, types of research conducted for the disease, solution to the problem, recovery time. Some of the security properties comprises of no password verifier table which explains that no table is maintained for storing user password, friendliness of password gives the ease to user to have a user friendly password according to their comfort, no derivation of password by server administration, no loss of smart card attack means that unauthorized user have no access to the patient's card (Jaswal et al., 2019), resemblance to known key attack implies all the necessary combinations of password to have illegal access to the password, pairing of smartcards without having change in the identities of the user, user key agreement defines secret channel of data transfer using a key value between sender and receiver, no synchronization of clock explains that for verification of any patient's data clock must not be synced (Sodhro et al., 2018), means at any point of time patient's record can be maintained, when login is to be accessed, if user enters wrong password it can be easily notified, mutual authentication between user and server, in order to have proper tractability user activities can be properly traced (Gope et al., 2016). Natural user identification technique uses concept of authentication using actuators and sensors.

Three main components in this method are: sensors, actuators, and credentials (Krasteva et al., 2017).

There are three major components such as Actuators, Sensors and Credentials which are explained as follows:

SENSORS

The different types of NUI sensors are explained as follows:

- *Touch Surface:* It is used for capturing information using touch screens which captures fingerprints, hand motion in a two-dimensional plane. The output is shown in form of time line graphs, timestamp values. The touch surfaces are now days used in smartphones, tablets, and smart watches large interactive displays etc.
- *Camera:* It act as sensor node for capturing an image or for displaying videos from different input sets gathered from different locations. Brain-computer interface, microphone and Motion sensor. A 3D sensing camera captures highly sensitive image with more precision and reflects each small point with high sensitivity (Pirbhulal et al., 2018). For using control device, an eye tracking interface, user requires to change gaze direction which is hands on operation. These are commonly used in user based electronic devices.
- *Motion Sensor:* These sensors are used for capturing person's gestural information. These types of sensor are frequently embedded with various electronic gadgets like Instrumented gloves, smartphones, smartwatches, tablets, and increased-reality headsets to wireless game controllers etc. In any three-dimensional coordinated system, these are used to locate position, orientation and space of the object.
- *Microphone:* This device allows hand free operation which the device and captures voice. The interface has been embedded in many electronic devices and is used as an interface between user and devices (Dubey et al., 2016).
- *Brain Computer Interface:* It act as a bridge between user and machine which does not require any interaction between the physical movements. To measure electrical of brain's activity, one of its application is used. The activity can be seen in form of waveform with varying timelines. The waveform pattern can be sent in smart phone using recent technologies. **Figure 1** shows the different types of NUI Sensors.

Actuators

In any communication model, different human parts can be used as positioned for interacting between natural user interface. **Figure 2** shows the different types of positioners used in the process of communication are body, eye, head and brain (thought), finger, hand, vocal fold (voice) (Son et al., 2009).

- *Finger:* Any type of non-verbal communication carried out by finger in the communication process. The interaction process can be deceived using touch surface, camera, or motion sensor. Using different locations of fingers such as in fingertips different sensors are recorded over timeline series with different instant of time.
- *Hand:* This is also a type of non-verbal communication, where the message is being exchanged using hand gesture. Mainly hand gestures are of two types: moving motion and stationary motion. The signs can be captured using red green blue colour spectrum or can also be used with touch surface or motion sensors (Devi et al., 2017).

Figure 1. The different types of NUI Sensors

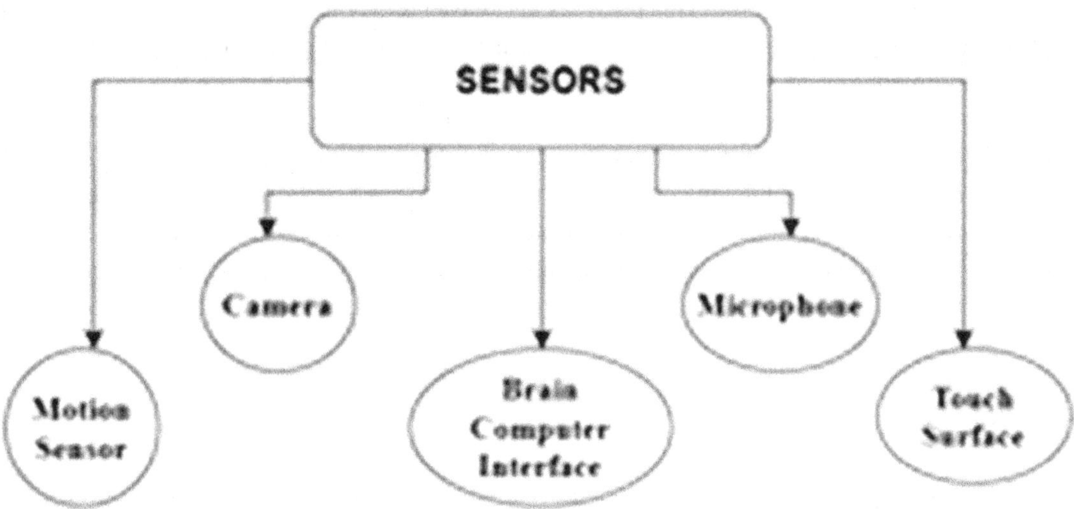

- *Head:* This is another type of non-verbal communication involving movement of head which can be captured by a camera, motion sensor, or touch surface. When a motion sensor is connected via head it captures head orientation and velocity. The intensity of velocity can be measured via using video streaming algorithms.

Figure 2. Types of Positioners used in the communication process

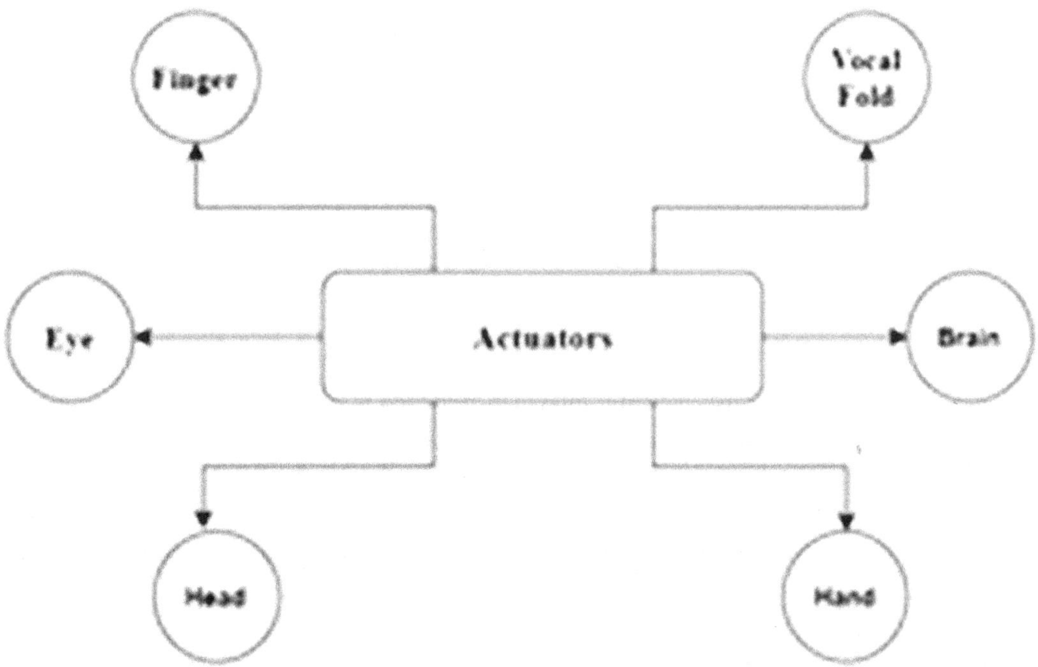

- *Eye:* Applications of eye used in biometric such as iris pattern, retina pattern, eyeball tracking is captured using special cameras. This provides fast, easier and convenient method for user to interact with the system. All the important information can be tracked on two-dimensional coordinate axis using timeline series with varying parameters.
- *Vocal Fold:* On daily basis communication, we use natural mechanism for communicating, by use of vocal cords. Voice recognition system is the technology which uses software programs which have the ability to decode human voice is used to operate device, perform tasks or write something without involvement of mouse, keyboard, or press any button (Alaiad et al., 2017).
- *Brain:* Any unintentional thought or intentional thought with any specific characteristics can be used to authenticate users. Recording of any neural activity can be recorded using electroencephalography.

Credentials

Credentials are some qualities, experiences that add meaning to something or it provides authenticity to the data. In order to have exchange of any confidential information, authenticity is required which states that only authorize users have the right to access information. Validation identifications that do not need a user to carry anything can be classified into one of the following classes: Physiological Biometrics, Secrets, Behavioural Biometrics, and combination (Abdulnabi et al., 2017). **Figure 3** shows different types of Credentials.

Figure 3. Different types of Credentials

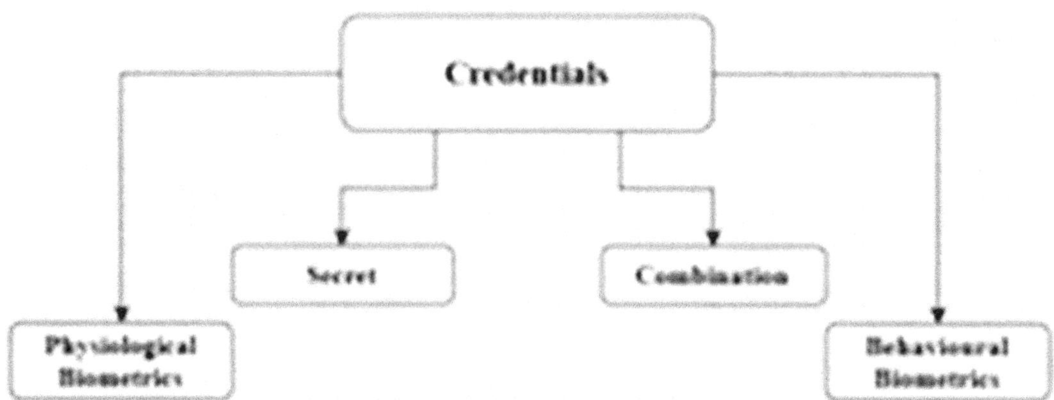

- *Secret:* it is defined as any user specific information which is used as an important credential for authenticity. One of its recent examples is entering of text password using physical keyboard. This specification with natural user interface can be used as an input with other mechanisms.
- *Behavioural Biometrics:* New types of users are enabled using this technique. Characteristics such as signatures, gestures, speech, swipes are distinct among individuals and act as behaviour biometric.
- *Physiological Biometrics:* Some of the biometric applications do not take into consideration use of behaviour, rather they rely on physiological biometric information such as iris, face, fingerprint.

- *Combination:* Different combinations of a behavioural biometric, physiological biometric and secret are used in any authentication system.

The rest of the chapter is organised as follows: Section 2 shows the literature review, Role of Wireless Sensor Networks in Healthcare Applications describes in Section 3, Section 4 discussed various Security Measures Using Biometric Fingerprint Schemes, Section 5 explain the role and utilization of Cloud Technology with Biometric Applications for healthcare records, Two Factor Remote Authentication In Healthcare illustrated in Section 6, Section 7 elucidated role of Biometric Authentication Based System For Validating Online Healthcare Information followed by the conclusion in Section 8.

LITERATURE REVIEW

In order to have secure communication and confidentiality between data transfer, various security-based mechanisms were introduced. One of the used security mechanisms is password-based authentication technique. In this technique an additional database is maintained for storing password of various authenticated users. From the table where the password is being saved is matched, if it is matched then the user is considered authenticated otherwise no information is being shared. In order to decrease the overhead of maintaining an additional database one of the alternative solutions used is using of fingerprint (Patil et al., 2017). Applications of biometric are widely used in all security-based models. One of the loop hole in any security-based model is different types of attack such as key impersonation, man in middle attack, replay etc which decreases the overall efficiency of the system (Venkatesan et al., 2018). Some of the cryptographic based techniques such as hashing, public key and private key are used to provide authentication in the system. In wireless based network many outside adversaries affect the sensor node by capturing its necessary information (Sodhro et al., 2018). An elliptic based cryptography for light weighted authentication protocol is being used. One of the main concerns in wireless network is energy constraint. As wireless nodes have limited energy resources, it is very important to preserve the energy (Sodhro et al., 2018). For this purpose, many energy-based routing protocols were introduced. For any IoT based application, mutual authentication-based protocol was introduced (Kalaivani et al., 2016). This technique provides authenticity of message on both sides i.e. sender and receiver (Kalid et al., 2018). IoT based medical care decreases the replay and disclosure attack frequency occurring in the system. In order to increase the reliability, scalability, efficiency and readability, IoT based technologies can be merged with cloud-based technology (Car et al., 2017).

While designing a Wireless sensor network for healthcare and multimedia applications, power consumption will be the essential factor. Multiple techniques are used to minimize the power consumption in WSNs. A wake-up radio in multimodal sensing that automatize sensor nodes proposed by (Jelicic et al., 2014). In WSNs, it helps to reduce the power consumption as well as response latency to manage. This methodology gets applied for high power consumption sensors in two tier Wireless sensor network for video/camera monitoring applications using low power consuming infrared sensor nodes. The big health application system presented by (Ma et al., 2017), based on health internet of things and big data. The author proposed the cloud to terminates fusion big health application system. The system comprised of multiple layers such as transport, perception and big health cloud layer. The major challenge between these layers is the power consumption for the shorter distance wireless communication.

Wireless multimedia sensor networks (WMSNs) is an infrastructure less implanted gadgets that permits retrieving audio, video streams, scalar sensor information and still images from the physical environments. (Mekonnen et al., 2017) suggested a combination of different methods multilevel WMSNs prototype which comprises of low power hardware systems. WMSN uses a network structure which includes different modes i.e. a shutdown mode, a sleep mode, and wake up mode. (Wong et al., 2006) presented a hash based dynamic authentication strategies to counter different attacks such as Key impersonation, forgery, Denial of Service (DoS), password disclosure, replay and man in the middle etc.

The secret password-based authentication system suggested by (Lamport, 1981). By applying elliptic curve cryptosystem, (Chang et al., 2016) devised a lightweight authentication system. For attaining the possession of forward confidentiality, (Chang et al, 2016) devised an ECC-based authentication. (Yeh et al., 2011) build a two-factor system based on ECC authentication. Based on DH and RHA, (Watro et al., 2004) presented a secure authentication protocol for WSNs. (Yoon et al., 2013) suggested a biometric based user authentication strategy to mitigate security vulnerabilities like DoS, poor repairability and sensor impersonation attack. For handling the data integrity in IoT based WSNs using the knowledge of base stations, (Hameed et al., 2018) introduced a security system based on integrity techniques. For supporting Cloud computing, mobile edge and IoT services like feature adaptability, scalability and reliability, (Al-Turjman et al., 2018) build a cloud desegregated structure. For context aware IoT, a hash-based RFID authentication devised by (Deebak et al., 2019). For IIoT domain, an ECC based authentication system devised by (Li et al., 2018) which uses biometrics characteristics to authenticate the service approach. For IoT networks, secure lightweight authentication scheme which employs password, biometric and smart card as three components to satisfy with key agreements possession introduced by (Wazid et al., 2018). To prove the authenticity of dosage forms, a newly authentication techniques gets devised by (Wazid et al., 2017) for medical spurious systems. For IIoT, a seamless mutual authentication strategy suggested by (Al-Turjman et al., 2018). **Table 1** shows security techniques suggested by different authors and their limitations.

ROLE OF WIRELESS SENSOR NETWORKS IN HEALTHCARE APPLICATIONS

Wireless sensors network also play key role in healthcare applications. Sensors are directly placed to the patient body for monitoring them. In emergency cases, like heart attacks, sudden falls, temperature (by transferring secured signals), low oxygen levels, video or images to the appointed unimpeachable unit, sensors are employed to identify these kinds of serious situation because even few seconds might save any human's life. Thus, for transmission, information gathering and reception real time monitoring requires energy sources (Jain et al., 2016). In WSNs all gadgets are operating using batteries, thus power is the challenging condition almost in every application of WSNs. The total energy utilization of the entire network gets minimized when the energy consumptions of sensors gets reduced which extends the durations of entire networks. Compressive sensing is an approach in which before transmission the information's such as video, signals or images gets compressed and transfer to the reception where this data decompressed.

The clustering is another effective approach where WSN gets split up into a group of clusters. Each group is having a cluster Head (CH). Cluster Heads liaises with each other to share the collected information from forbearing's sensors to Base Station (BS) that liaises with server. All these communication approaches introduced above are based on Binary Transmissions schemes. Instead of using binary trans-

Table 1. Various Security Techniques and Their Limitation. (Deebak et al., 2019)

Ref.	Security Techniques Employed	Formal Analysis Model	Simulation Used	Limitations
(Car et al.,2017)	Seamless Key Agreement Framework [For Mobile-Sink and IoT-Based Cloud-Centric Network]	Partial	No	Difficulty in recovering from different prospective attacks such as key impersonation, password disclosure, DoS (Denial of Service), and official password guessing.
(Wong et al., 2006)	Secure Authentication for Medicine Anti-Counterfeiting System	Yes	No	Difficulty in recovering from different prospective attacks such as message eavesdropping, Denial of Service (DoS), and Smartcard forgery.
(Roy et al., 2018)	Anonymous User Authentication Using Chaotic Map [With Biometrics and Fuzzy Extractor]	Yes	No	Several loopholes were address during working of this mechanism such as storage cost, large computation and partial perfect confidentiality.
(Li et al., 2017)	Improved Secure Authentication [With Data Encryption and User Anonymity]	No	No	Difficulty in recovering from different prospective attacks such as key impersonation, Denial of Service (DoS), and privileged insider.
(Al Turjman et al., 2018)	Seamless Identity Provisioning Framework [With Mutual Authentication Approach]	No	No	Difficulty in recovering from different prospective attacks such as Message Eavesdropping, Denial of Service (DoS), smartcard forgery, and man in the middle.
(Gope et al., 2018)	Lightweight Privacy Preservation Protocol [Using Physically Uncloneable Functions (PUFs)]	Yes	No	Several loopholes were address during working of this mechanism such as storage cost, perfect confidentiality, and large computation.
(Li et al., 2018)	Lightweight RFID Mutual Authentication [Reader with Cache]	No	No	Difficulty in recovering from different prospective attacks such as message eavesdropping, reader impersonation, and tag forgery.
(Li et al., 2018)	Secure 3PAKE Protocol Using Chebyshev Chaotic Maps [With Random Oracle Model]	No	No	Difficulty in recovering from different prospective attacks such as key impersonation, password disclosure and offline password guessing.
(Wazid et al., 2017)	Secure Lightweight Three-Factor Remote User Authentication [Using Smartcard, Password and Personal Biometrics]	Yes	No	Difficulty in recovering from different prospective attacks such as DoS, smartcard forgery and message eavesdropping.
(Deebak et al., 2019)	Hash-Based RFID Authentication [For Context-Aware IoT]	Yes	Yes	Difficulty in recovering from different prospective attacks such as data forgery, DoS, and privileged insider.

missions schemes, the quaternary schemes can be used effectively so that energy can be more efficiently utilized. Using this scheme, instead of using a binary logic, multi valued logic gets employed through which energy efficient structure of WSNs can be build. In (Saleh et al., 2018), the design of sensor networks gets modified so that instead of using binary (two symbols), the quaternary (four symbols) can be manipulated by the sensor networks (SNs). **Figure 4** shows WSNs architecture based on quaternary.

Figure 4. WSNs Architecture based on Quaternary

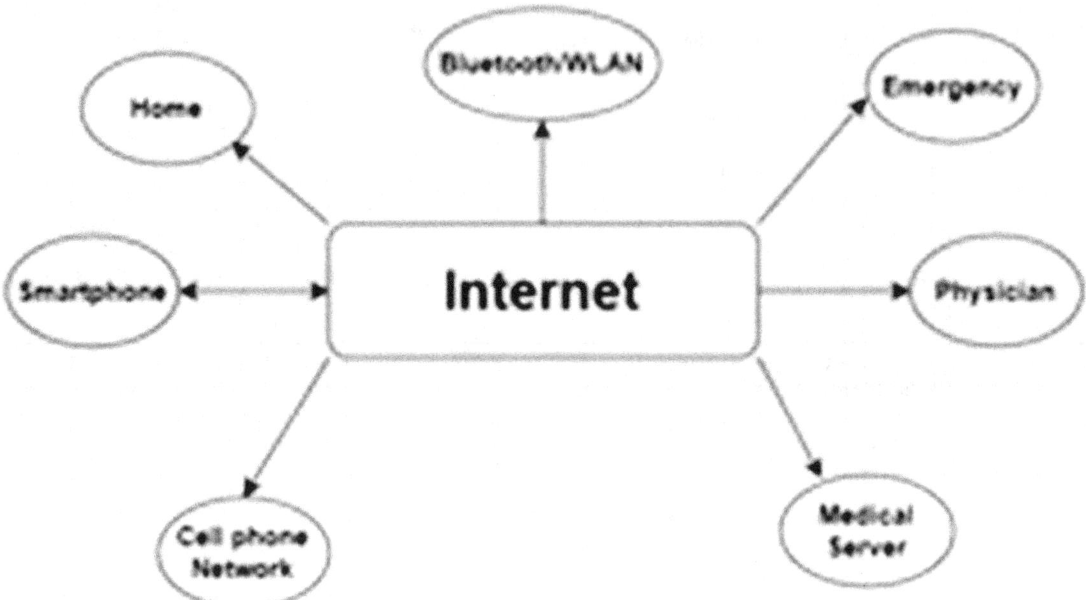

(Saleh et al., 2015) suggested a quaternary architecture through which the transmission of information in WSNs can be modified from binary symbols to the quaternary symbols for healthcare and multimedia applications. The two main modules are used for converting a binary link into a quaternary interconnecting link i.e. a binary to quaternary modulator and quaternary to binary demodulator as shown in **Figure 5**.

In WSNs, LEACH protocol is used to reduce the energy consumption. It contains only meaningful information while transferring data. In LEACH Protocol, the clustering approach used which divides the whole Wireless sensor network into a group of clusters. Each cluster is having a cluster head (Hussain et al., 2006). The author also designed the Neural Network Static RAM (NN-SRAM) architecture for gathering and storing data. The NNSRAM used to store binary information and remains valid till the power is supplied in the network. NN-SRAM helps in improving the lifetime of the system in WSNs as it reduces the energy consumption in the network (Lee et al., 2016). Sensor networks are stored data temporarily that leads in power consumption in wireless sensor network system. Therefore, instead of storing data temporarily in Sensor networks, NN-SRAM (Neural network storage units) (Haider et al., 2015) used which helps in decreasing the power consumption in a network and improves its life span. In WSNs, the energy utilization in NN-SRAM-CBEES (Neural network static random-access memory with clustering-based energy efficient systems) will be minimized by limiting the storage cost that get increased because of using neural network and also by limiting the transferring/receiving cost between sensor nodes and their cluster heads. The non-cluster head of sensor networks must be turned off as long as possible.

Figure 5. WSNs Architecture with the Quaternary Transceiver

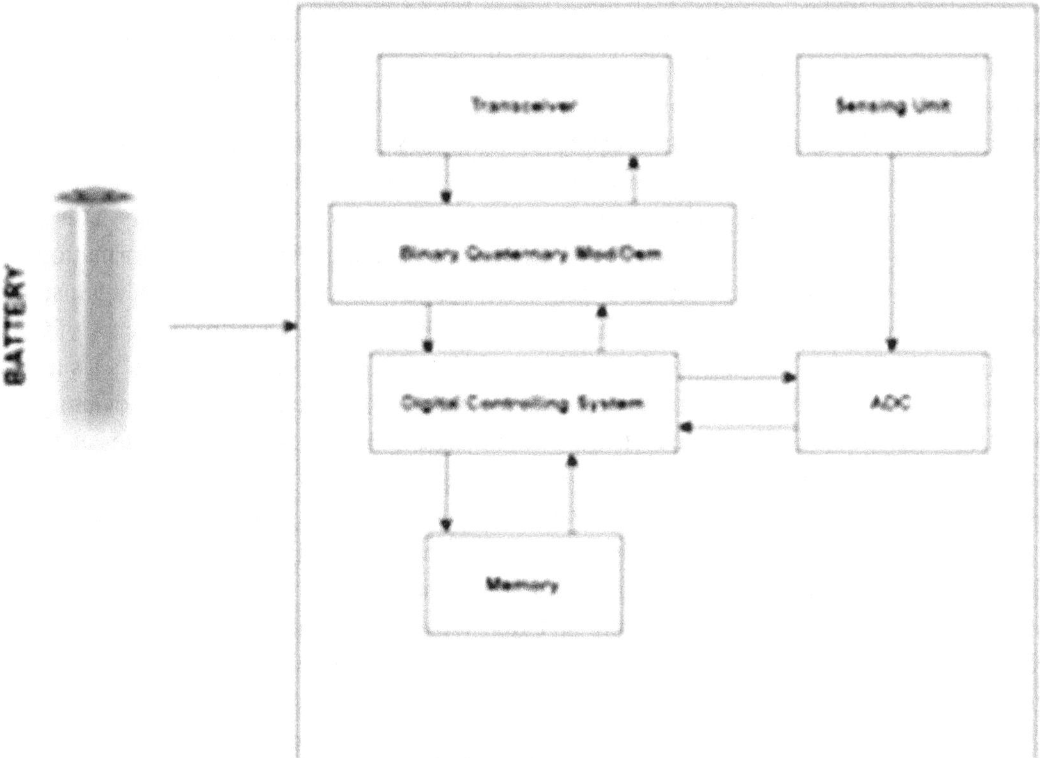

SECURITY MEASURES USING BIOMETRIC FINGERPRINT TECHNIQUE

In today's world as health-related issues are increasing rapidly due to change in the lifestyle, unhealthy eating habits etc. In order to avoid the time pressure of standing in queue for routine check-ups everywhere in health sector, biometric applications are used like recording the personal information of the patient in smart cards which reduces the time burden, and authenticity of the user is maintained. In order to avail authenticity of the user, certain security-based parameters are introduced Nowadays, secrecy, safety& security in electronic healthcare system effect our health Rapidly-Health Records procedure a good communication between patients & any person of the Medical, pharmacy or nursing profession. The secrecy and safety issues recently arising e-Health area are primarily focused around user validation, user information privacy, and patient secrecy protection. Biometric technology has a good opportunity to deal successfully privacy problem by providing trusted & assured user validation and permission to obtain the health information (Jain et al., 1997).

The emergency of electronic health has transformed the health care industry to deliver better health care and service at affordable price, eHR is a digitally archived health care with the aim of looking after a person's lifetime. Supporting the consistency of education and research, and always make certain privacy. Issues of secrecy and security in the eHealth area primarily focus about user validation, data integrity, information privacy and patient's privacy security. Because of conscious nature of health data, dignity, data privacy and patient security. With the conscious nature of health information of patients, the greatest task is toward the enhancement of the effective safety model that can give assurance of information confidentially and dependability, substantiating that only undertaking employees can access their respective health information (Lin et al., 2016). Old validation and access control measure may not match the eHealth record system where roles are not properly addressed to all stakeholder (administrations, patients, health professionals). Presenting healthcare professional needed access to all information as possible that helps in supporting decision making. Forbearing also wanted to gain the access over their personal data related to eHealth records with data privacy. SURF (Speeded Up Robust Features) aims at providing loop variant, technique for descripting and detecting points. This technique is also considered as advanced description of SIFT (Scale Invariant Feature Transformation). SURF aims its popularity in speediness, robustness and different orientation transformation against different locations. For finding space of different scale Gaussian space is calculated using difference of Gaussian. Combination of difference of Gauss and box filter goes beyond expectations in SURF. Using integral images convolution with box filter can be easily calculated, which is one of the major advantages of this approximation technique. For both the metrices such as scale and location, a fixed value calculation i.e. determinant is calculated of Hessian matrix. (Jahan et al., 2017) in his work concluded that biometric has its applications in every field due to its advancing feature in security. One of its application used in healthcare can be used at low cost and is highly secure. Traditional applications lack important security matrices such as authentication, integrity and confidentiality which is provided in biometric systems. Biometrics technology can be integrated into an extensive variety of healthcare applications to assure security and privacy. **Figure 6** shows Schemes used for Verification of users using fingerprint biometric for access control.

To defend the solitude and freedom of the patient's materials a secure verification system must be used to ingress health reports. Any person or institutions wishing to ingests a second hand health record will require a definite approval of that victim. Including freedom perils and reclaiming health history in the EHR arrangement has expanded the demand for a trusted buyer certification in the E-Health realm plan. Certification is considered an important aspect of security in the Healthcare realm which intension to clarify the user's integrity. The user wants to desire maintenances from the cloud. Universal verification methods like usernames, passwords and avenue cards are not useful in the E-Health situation. The incident is being adrift, lifted, erased and mistaken. Secondly, biometric based authentication and approach control have proven capability of providing the crucial safety and confidentiality E-Health applications. This paper presents an extensive audit of biometrics techniques addressing e-security. In the paper, we nominate a potent and active biometric plan to use user authentication and authority fingerprint biometrics to hike confidentiality and safety eHealth system.

Conventional authentication system was based On ID card. It May include badge or encryption that can be off-track, or shattered, on the other hand, attributes can't be misplaced or forgotten. They are hard to hand up dispense. In Addition, the database is needed to authenticate the persons presence, it is crucial to Produce and it is unlikely for the user to cancel it. In order to need HIPAA guidelines, patients and health Executive both required to have approach to medical records. Keeping in mind the demands of health professionals both and patients, biometric validation is capable of meeting security and privacy necessity.in confirmation method, it demonstrates the legitimacy of an individual by their Finger print in the identity method, it provides the recognition of the individual among the enrolled in a database. Without the judgement of an individual, the fingerprint recognition system bid to match it with fingerprint in the entire fingerprint record. Among all the others biometrics characters, fingerprints biometrics attend a vital and very important part in the field health due to its exclusivity and accessibility.

Figure 6. Schemes used for Verification of users using fingerprint biometric for access control

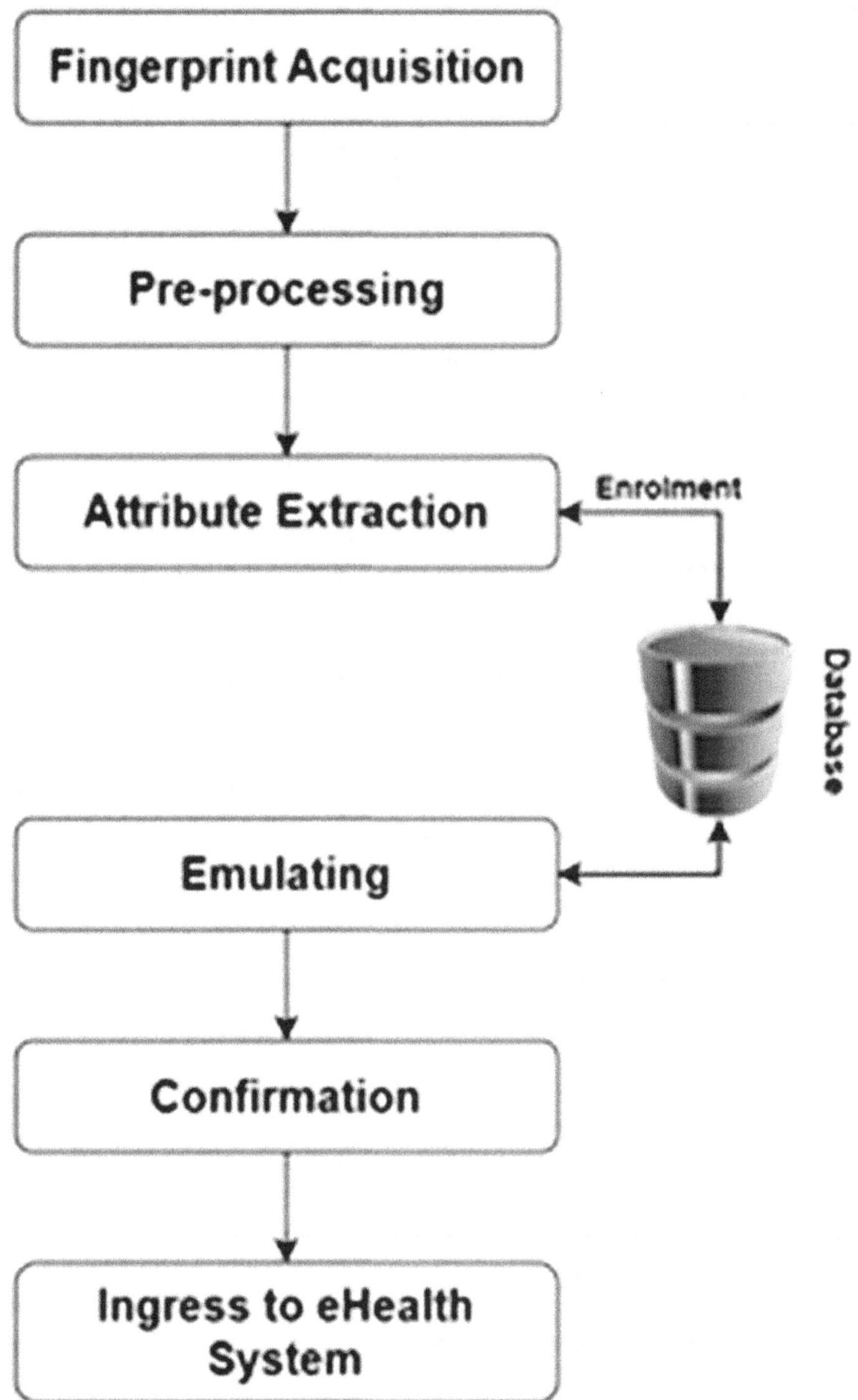

The first step of the fingerprint validation process for catching the traces of fingers pattern using a sensor of digital copy. The catcher picture is called a live scan. The live scan is an electronically managed factor to generate a biometric prototype.

USE OF CLOUD TECHNOLOGY WITH BIOMETRIC APPLICATION FOR HEALTHCARE RECORDS

Healthcare records are prerequisite to each medical professional and patient too, a technique called biometric safety system in health-related sector for availability via the use of programs connected via internet rather than system will be reviewed. By the use of cloud technology as a protected storage means to hoard essential healthcare data have an important part. Currently, this technology is majorly used for storage of data so it may well impregnate wherever and anytime. Security based on biometric is a significant aspect in this technology so that data supremely vital data cannot be retrieved by anyone except you have been acknowledged contact by the system by registration. Biometrics offer improved safety in are zones to which it is required. Healthcare nevertheless, is also in requirement of safety when it deals with storage of data and further essential data. Biometrics offers security and agreeableness anywhere this technology is used (Haghighat et al., 2015). In the field of healthcare, the records and data about patient's health are one of the greatest valued personal information, doctor needs to access them quickly, and they have to be precise and faultless. A failure in security and appropriate counting of information can mean a great variation amongst timely and precise analysis or permit health falsification. Biometrics though can be the response to all those breaches. **Figure 7** shows use of Cloud technology with biometric application for Healthcare records (Choi et al., 2015).

Applications based on use of biometric- Identification and Validation are the two most significant areas of security. Breaching of any of these two factors are not considered secure for any security-based system. The different types of authentication process in any secure system are: something you have (e.g. token device, badge), something you are and something you know (e.g. password). Different applications of biometric includes: Fingerprint biometric system, face recognition system, palm recognition, smart card for containing all the details of the patient.

- *Cloud Technology:* Cloud based computing technology which is based on internet connections, also called demand technology, where user can access and share data and resources to computers connected on wide range. For a shared pool of computing resources this model act as enabling technology. It orders to have effective utilization of resources; this technology is used to scale its expenditure.
- *Cloud Security and Privacy:* Three important aspects of security: Confidentiality, integrity and availability must be ensured in any security-based model. Confidentiality implies that information must be kept confidential while transferring from one source to another. Integrity implies that the content of information must be preserved while reaching at receiver side. No alteration can be done in between the content of the data. Availability implies that data or information must be available for future use.
- *Cloud storage:* For storage of any digital data over the network, cloud storage is used. The physical environment is operated by company, physical storage spans over multiple servers located at different locations where data is being stored and retrieved from the server. The responsibility of

Figure 7. Use of Cloud technology with biometric application for Healthcare records

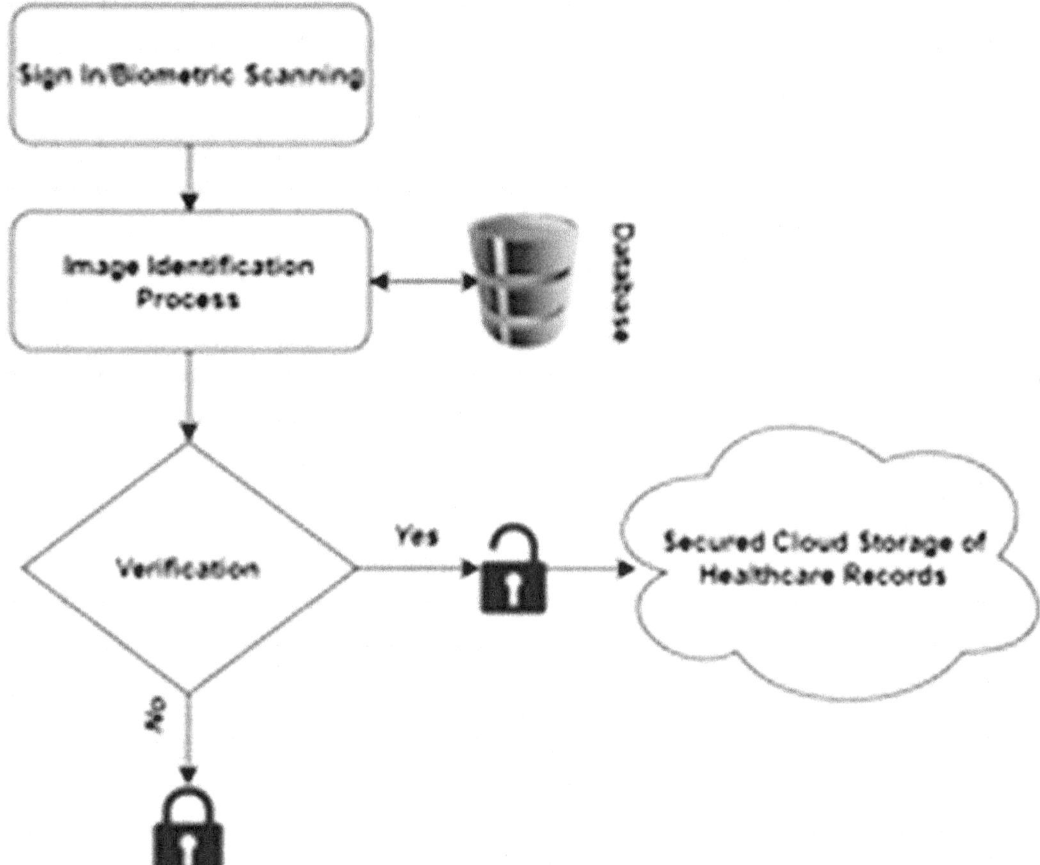

storage provider is to keep data available, authenticated and protected from unauthorized users. Individuals and management purchase or rent storage quantity from the providers to keep data of users, association, or application. In order to have security in the system, many biometric systems are being installed which uses face, palm recognition techniques to have authentication within the system and the outside intruders cannot steal any confidential information from the system Using the technology which uses programs from net rather than system for storing data and additional safety, and the biometric system for user testimony, it will enhance the safety on retrieving important health related data online. Medical experts and health staffs from several healthcare services can access this data online.

For use of security in health care-based sector, biometric applications are being widely used. For accessing patient's data, it is very much difficult to keep track records of all the information. For these reasons, biometric applications are used. They reduce the time boundations and involves less human intervention. Patient now uses smart cards provided by the hospitals which comprises of their unique id, name, gender, sex, address, phone number etc., which provides more authenticity to the patient (Huang et al., 2016).

TWO FACTOR REMOTE AUTHENTICATION IN HEALTHCARE

On procedure to command approach of health accompany info stocked in general database, effective confirmation structure want to be deliberate. The early influence need easy & efficient observable biometrics key-stroke scrutiny exemplary although the next influence need undisclosed PIN system. In influence first confirmation, key-stroke determination is expected where basic info is calm early; then treated info are stocked and trustworthy record are producing certainly (Das, 2011). Conduct determination of the projected system exhibition its ability to validate end-users. Assistance worker may not be efficient to get back delicate health info reserved in server in its infant mode to control secrecy of info. Biometrics certification is one of the possible explanations in server rule being it handle alone trait of end-customer for testimony & approach authority. Biometrics feature may be corporal or observable. Physiological info involves few countenances that endure hardly for several particular such as vein, DNA, fingerprint, nails, iris, teeth pattern etc. (Apama et al., 2017). Biometrics confirmation over key-stroke examine is an accurate procedure for integrity facts. Key-stroke motion boost its demand between the observable biometrics' confirmation approach in assigned atmosphere, because of its clarity & expense influence. Use of key-stroke disclose the classify method of an entity by using alone regular keyboard & easy program. It measures that the exclusive custom are developing in period, ensuing the ability with console, mental status or physical & more container. Reputation of the method could also be ordered as average that means that crowd are not efficiently curious by the way of biometrics info association. Several protection alive systems should tool two-factor confirmation, which underrate defy of info crack caused by illegal approach to delicate info at distant health scheme (Pirbhulal et al., 2015). Couple cause of confirmation is planned attending to improve safety matched with basic attempt & charge in the server. both patients & health specialist want to contribute confirmation evidence before pervade isolated health info of patients. The extensive offering of the paper is to suggest a two-factor confirmation system using key-stroke inquiry & PIN that can be used to remote core. **Figure 8** shows Flowchart of Pin Generation (Bhattasali & Saeed, 2014).

The equitable of this effort is to resolve some of the dominant objection in great free content-based key-stroke inquiry & to suggest two element faraway confirmation core as a possible explanation. It contains examine on extant remote healthcare ideal, access control system & key-stroke gesture procedure for verification. Server established sensor system permit early conclusion of subject. Healing handler have to genuine themselves to notice health status of patients (Azeta et al., 2017). In server based isolated health core, server utility provider manages biometric info where info is stocked in encode plan. Key-stroke study is located on the usual analytical determination or arrangement recognition method. Arrangement has been erected from entity typing style. All of these analysis target on the key-stroke motion input from a measure console (Zhao et al., 2015). In pressure- located user confirmation scheme, the distinct time outstanding is convert into the frequency territory. Typing method is also evaluate during use of hand-held electronic gadget just like wireless cell-phone. After examine differing current entirety on key-stroke gesture, it is projected to be used in server located faraway health core along with privacy PIN approach to diminish expectation of false disclosure. main dispute of key-stroke confirmation is wrong positives & wrong negative that either chunk connection to legal consumer or allocation access to illegal consumer. Key-stroke biometrics can also margin deviation in the typing manner due to occasional classify, using sweaty hand, single hand for typing after a long period. False agreement gives ascent to zero-effort charge, where hypocrite can calmly enter into the rule. False refusal opposes accurate user to come into the organisation which may disturb order ability obliquely. The fair of planned effort is to

Figure 8. Flowchart of Pin Generation

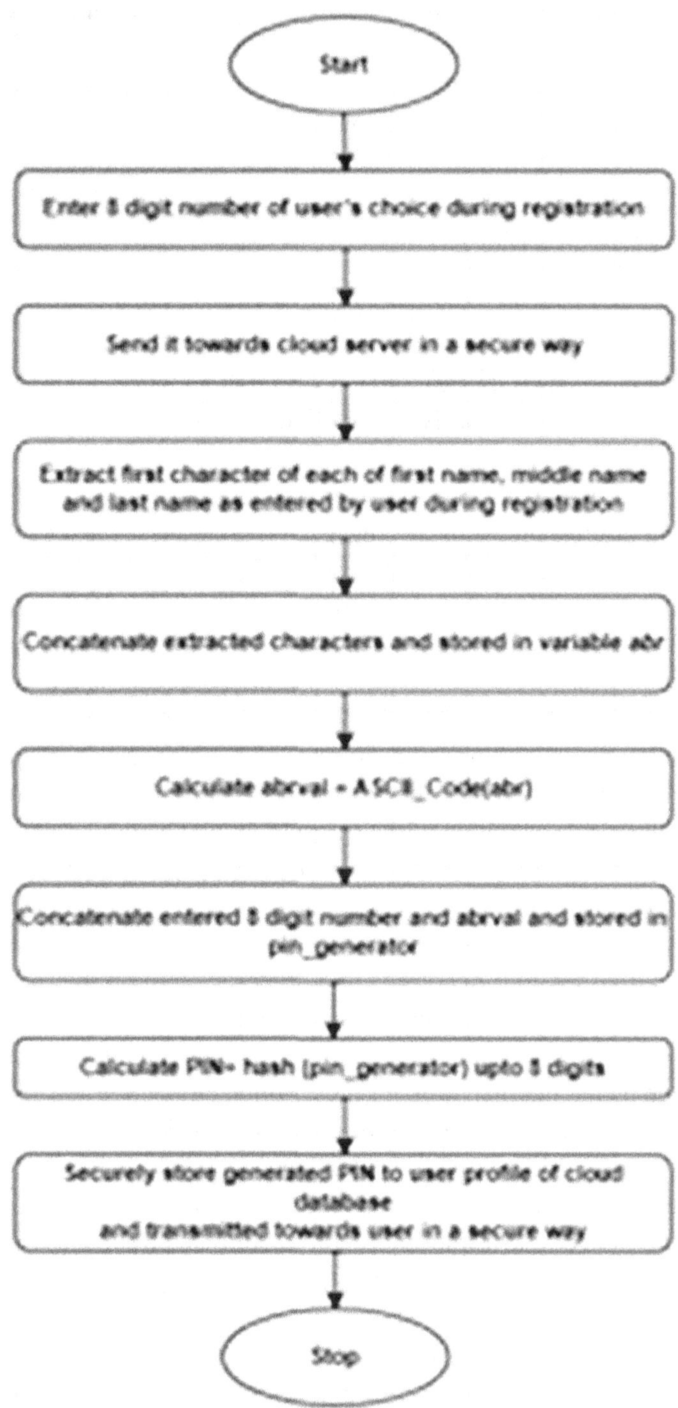

command access of EHR/EMR of patients in a simple technique (Zhang et al., 2014). Faraway health core arranges dissolve biometric confirmation to cut the mistreat of ability within the system. Usual procedure of verification is much more performing exhaustive and may be mistreat by any hypocrite in server condition. It is pretended that assistance support by server provider is assure give to service level compromise.

The journalist has recommended here the custom of key-stroke motion for scheme approach, which does not charge & needs no extra tools except the console. The two major causes confirmation is advised here, where hidden proof is linked with key-stroke inquiry to improve precision level of confirmation. The conclusion show that correctness level is improve in two factor confirmation distinguished to using only one factor key-stroke. The projected key-stroke sense is being changed by considering various operation particular limit & healthy info bent.

BIOMETRIC AUTHENTICATION BASED SYSTEM FOR VALIDATING ONLINE HEALTHCARE INFORMATION

Onset of the Internet and the rise in the usage of cyberspace by clients for online healthcare Information (OHI), various analyst in discrete protocols are engaged on protest and risk of cyberchondria, which is relevant to cyber psychological condition of indecision, concern, superiority, and reliability. OHI-based faith analysis has not once used biometrics to confirm multi-dimensional trust constructions, together with visualization, influence, awareness, and social status. Moreover, this study path is not handled by proof of OHI prospect at provider level through proof institutional Profile and relationship. Accordingly, in order to boost accuracy through proof at trust level, this paper expectation a conception and nominate an offbeat trust-computing model, motorized by visual acknowledgment-based biometric verification of medical profiles. Introductory proof of theory prototype for the proposed approach, an observation is executed that establish the viable execution of the trust-computing pattern. The investigational reaction implementation gather over this model are joint as part of this paper. This model will offer more new researches with the trust-computing model, and will form the support for outlook conviction related research at OHI to address cyberchondria. The Internet has an intellectual shock on the way people pursuit for health care data, and transmission. According to a domestic audit on Internet usage, eight in seven American adults examine networked for health data. The idea of the online fact expectation is specifically crucial in the situation of fitness advice obtaining. While record numbers of American adults are unstable to self-diagnose on the Internet, look for prescription alternative and select a physician, many people face many disputes. Crisis arising from information seeking incapability to discover correct data, irregular instruction or report, inability to find health data, and psychological emotion processes are all samples of some of these disputes. For example, cyberchondria maturity increased concern associated with health litter ensuing from online health information. Study in this area advise that few individuals are mainly liable to online-related trouble to find data. On the clone moment, position of health worry is easily relevant to the regularity and the event of online health information exploration. This seasonal design of agony in facts looking have damaging belonging on the singular, who is in most cases earlier agony outside of a deeply perceptive or Incessant health circumstance that incite the primary seeking to find something. One valuable constituent of trustworthy has to act with consumer refusal or option of a specific place of activity, its opinion to logic such user will imply with place of activity they vision as trustworthy and refuse those, they doubtfulness.

The connection among the handling of images and consumer trustworthy of health web-sites. The analysis in (Chattopadhyay et al., 2017) desire that images boost trustworthy by discover a sensibility of intimacy or advocacy. Consumer occurs to be affected by the trait of the spot or by the occupancy of well-known statue or trustworthy icons. OHI desire that the feature of facts ready for use on a user-based site plays act ahead with the seen profile added knowledge of the physicians. They again acumen that OHI assurance is compelled by the range to which the breadwinner emerges to be weak-known with connectable accomplished a joint public integrity (He et al., 2015). Cyberchondria is not plainly hypochondriacs adopting the Internet, but a bit an obvious shape of online data looking for and develop increase health worry (Awasthi et al., 2013). Cyberchondria has been deliberate as an obvious spiritual clutter and a complex idea with doubtfulness of medical artist as one of its key characteristics. Current analysis has form that cyberchondria is existent additional carefully line up with other mode of dubious Internet purpose than usual hypochondria. Cyberchondria includes an analytical answer to a scarcity of data. Additional Individually, behavioural proof of hypochondria and cyberchondria are where the key dissimilarity halfway the two become seeming. As Vice-versa, hypochondriacs assure themselves they are agony from an exact medical situation, clear material response to their seen problem, and employ in conduct that accomplish their matter. The basic stimulus for hypochondria is the opinion that one has a particular medical situation, the cyberchondria is generally compelled by a want to receive greater data around an explicit circumstance.

The subject of cyberchondria hand-over produce base for social-science researcher, and also particularly, for giving critic. The brunt of cyberchondria can be verified from an informative outlook over the lens of mechanics expertise, health ideas, and social analysis. Some model of tricky or driving need of the Internet has social shock. Therefore, there are entity usually looking for out health data online only to be mistaken or mislead. The basic mater is a wry or faulty idea of private prospect outstanding to online misreport and misleading (Wu et al., 2012). Present-day consumer ability has produced approach toward health concerns as a behaviour prime that is privately trained and keep up. The result cyberchondria be able have on the connection ship and giving of a patient and a health care worker extend the shock straighter to social interplay. the opportunity of online health data and how people select to use up it is basically dynamic how patients communicate with their health care worker. Cyberchondria can be evaluated from the technology outgoing via social network (Chattopadhyay et al., 2017). It is very much difficult to analyse the important points going on via the online sources. Growth in health-related sector will address the in habitats resulting from degradation of health to improvement in health status. The prototype exercise of the singular biometric validation based OHI hope model, as expected in paper, perform the initiate of a much best project hold in OHI hope evaluation. These exertions have grace into the user believe, courage and integrity horizontal level utilising public figure over method similar machine training located allocation & study by cross-confirmation planted certification & validation via trustworthy expert. Actual literature dispute that look to is a multi- dimensional body & want to be extend to a deep situation by seeing trustworthy encourage cause at the corporate level (Pauer et al., 2016). Linking hard & soft trustworthy aspect in the define hybrid access to regulate devotion is an extra extensive & potent indicator of prospect in OHI. Profitable situation of biometrics contain fingerprint examine, voice recognition & retina identification enforce in new technological utilisation and established protected bent. The modern analysis, as given here, follow to address the raised appeal of the OHI trustworthy rule & boost the modern case of the art effort. Furthermore, the Analysis on handle in this paper survey the aspect of trustworthy in OHI gain separating a particular combination position, & suggest a professional explanation to diminish the probable worry correlate with the deal with searching careful & appropriate OHI. Firstly, American Board of Internal Medicines (ABIM) organisation, is a renowned & healing certified website with panel nomination & pro confirmation. These connotations show an aspect in establishment of user assumption chief to user conviction. The health-care services have to decide on their dominate if they will believe the credibility & efficiency of these consumer info as possible on these links. Grant to the biometric trustworthy-estimate exemplary, as planned in this thesis, the specialist profiles in these links can be ascertain the truth opposite to one additional utilizing biometrics on the ocular details. Favourable precedent of biometrics carry fingerprint examine; voice identification & retina recognition achieve in progressive professional function &honoured safe ability. The restricted is then worn to inspect form captured against the OHI links & recovery an identical rate for every image. All these images provide toward the building of the specific image rank wanted for the analysis. A combination of two together pharmaceutically recognised sites & friendly data collection sites were recycled in plan to handling the engaged analysis test. The aspires database is always against with HealthGrades.com as well as cross-checked which is the first set that obtained. It should be eminent that whole of the portrait form support on the Health Grades website exist of naturally little aspect than those hauls precisely from the Aspirus data collection. After adaptation of image verdict & size adjustment for together the Aspirus form & the Health Grades picture figure confirmed to be useless as it was erect to have no enforce on the develop match record. Outstanding to the image condition of the approve Aspirus figure, IBM Watson was capable to even the outer characteristics of the doctor while browse over the figure with distinct culture & distant rendering of age plus attire. The projected biometric confirmation located trustworthy gauge model will support data promise over confirmation of the doctor outline connected with the third member OHI that user is review or pursuing Expected analysis & growth performance be going to also include outline & growth of a real OHI trustworthy metric that develop also relevant & complete trustworthy points for networked health users. **Table 2** presents the Merits and Demerits of various biometric based models used in Healthcare.

CONCLUSION

The chapter presents the importance of health in human life. Health is the most essential and important key element in human life. Life is very difficult for the people who are unhealthy. In order to have happy living, one must inculcate all healthy habits in their lives. But now a days, due to changing lifestyle we are becoming victims of many diseases. In fast going pace of life we are not finding time for ourselves, by which we have to spend large amount of our earnings in doctors and medicines. In order to save time for all these purposes, biometric applications have played a very crucial role. Various applications of biometrics such as patients' smart cards, face recognition system, palm recognition, retina and iris detection are widely used. In this chapter, we have presented four different biometric based models used in health care such as role of WSNs in healthcare, two factor remote authentication, robust fingerprint authentication for improving security, privacy preserving in healthcare, Biometric Validation based hybrid trust computing approach for authentication of providers profile in online healthcare information, Healthcare records using cloud technology with biometric system. The different models possess different characteristics features along with certain disadvantages. Further the work can be extended by using comparative analysis of various models based on different parameters and combining any of the two models and using hybrid approach by comparing new proposed system with existing system.

Table 2. Merits and Demerits of various biometric based models used in Healthcare

S.No	TITLE	AUTHORS	ADVANTAGES	DISADVANTAGES
1.	Robust Fingerprint Verification for Enhancing Security in Healthcare System	(Jahan et al., 2017)	1. Large number of opportunities or information sharing. 2.Preservation of privacy and security for information management system. 3. Authentication and Authorization for security-based systems.	1. Lack of person recognition, if he changes physically. 2. Leading of false rejection and acceptance by fingerprint scanner. 3. More cost incurred in designing hardware and software for fingerprint scanner.
2.	Healthcare records using cloud technology with biometric application	(Choi et al., 2015)	1.Collaboration between different doctor, departments and institutes. 2.No cost involved for maintaining physical serves. 3.Extensibilty to increase or decrease storage of data depending on number of patients count.	1.Less control over the infrastructure as it is completely managed by service provider. 2.Troubleshoot and supporting challenges because of multiple clients at same time. 3.Huge risk involve in storing data because of involvement of third party.
3.	Two factor remote authentication in healthcare.	(Bhattasali & Saeed, 2014)	1. Decrement in password reliancy. 2. Lower management costs and help desk. 3.Healthy online transactions by reducing fraud transactions.	1.More vulnerable to attacks such as phishing etc. 2.No full proof verification of strong passwords. 3. Level of security is being exaggerated.
4.	Biometric Authentication based hybrid trust computing approach for verification of providers profile in online healthcare information	(Chattopadhyay et al., 2017)	1.Assured privacy and security-based systems. 2. Ease of use and high quality of information. 3.Improved trust-based system.	1. Requirement of additional hardware. 2. Difficult to reset once connected. 3. Usage and environment get affected due to external measurement.

REFERENCES

Abdulnabi, M., Al-Haiqi, A., Kiah, M. L., Zaidan, A. A., Zaidan, B. B., & Hussain, M. (2017). A distributed framework for health information exchange using smartphone technologies. *Journal of Biomedical Informatics*, *69*, 230–250. doi:10.1016/j.jbi.2017.04.013 PMID:28433825

Al-Turjman, F., & Alturjman, S. (2018). Context-sensitive access in industrial internet of things (IIoT) healthcare applications. *IEEE Transactions on Industrial Informatics*, *14*(6), 2736–2744. doi:10.1109/TII.2018.2808190

Al-Turjman, F., Hasan, M. Z., & Al-Rizzo, H. (2018). Task scheduling in cloud-based survivability applications using swarm optimization in IoT. *Transactions on Emerging Telecommunications Technologies*, 3539.

Alaiad, A., & Zhou, L. (2017). Patients' Adoption of WSN-Based Smart Home Healthcare Systems: An Integrated Model of Facilitators and Barriers. *IEEE Transactions on Professional Communication*, *60*(1), 4–23. doi:10.1109/TPC.2016.2632822

Alpaslan, A. H. (2016). Cyberchondria and adolescents. *The International Journal of Social Psychiatry*, *62*(7), 679–680. doi:10.1177/0020764016657113 PMID:27358345

Amjad, M., Afzal, M., Umer, T., & Kim, B. (2017). QoS-Aware and Heterogeneously Clustered Routing Protocol for Wireless Sensor Networks. *IEEE Access: Practical Innovations, Open Solutions*, *5*, 10250–10262. doi:10.1109/ACCESS.2017.2712662

Aparna, P., & Kishore, P. V. (2017). An Efficient Medical Image Watermarking Technique in E-healthcare Application Using Hybridization of Compression and Cryptography Algorithm. *Journal of Intelligent Systems*, *27*(1), 115–133. doi:10.1515/jisys-2017-0266

Athanasiou, G. N., & Lymberopoulos, D. K. (2016). A comprehensive Reputation mechanism for ubiquitous healthcare environment exploiting cloud model. *2016 38th Annual International Conference of the IEEE Engineering in Medicine and Biology Society (EMBC),* 5981-5984.

Awasthi, A. K., & Srivastava, K. (2013). A Biometric Authentication Scheme for Telecare Medicine Information Systems with Nonce. *Journal of Medical Systems*, *37*(5), 1–4. doi:10.100710916-013-9964-1 PMID:23949846

Azeta, A.A., Iboroma, D.A., Azeta, V.I., Igbekele, E.O., Fatinikun, D.O., & Ekpunobi, E. (2017). Implementing a medical record system with biometrics authentication in E-health. *2017 IEEE AFRICON*, 979-983.

Bakke, A. (2017). *Ethos in E-Health: From Informational to Interactive Websites*. Academic Press.

Barbara, A. M., Dobbins, M., Haynes, R. B., Iorio, A., Lavis, J. N., Raina, P., & Levinson, A. J. (2016). The McMaster Optimal Aging Portal: Usability Evaluation of a Unique Evidence-Based Health Information Website. *JMIR Human Factors*, *3*(1), 3. doi:10.2196/humanfactors.4800 PMID:27170443

Beldad, A., Jong, M. D., & Steehouder, M. F. (2010). How shall I trust the faceless and the intangible? A literature review on the antecedents of online trust. *Computers in Human Behavior*, *26*(5), 857–869. doi:10.1016/j.chb.2010.03.013

Bhattasali, T., & Saeed, K. (2014). Two factor remote authentication in healthcare. *2014 International Conference on Advances in Computing, Communications and Informatics (ICACCI).* 10.1109/ICACCI.2014.6968594

Car, J., Tan, W. S., Huang, Z., Sloot, P. M., & Franklin, B. D. (2017). eHealth in the future of medications management: Personalisation, monitoring and adherence. *BMC Medicine*, *15*(1), 15. doi:10.118612916-017-0838-0 PMID:28376771

Challa, S., Wazid, M., Das, A. K., Kumar, N., Alavalapati, G. R., Yoon, E., & Yoo, K. (2017). Secure Signature-Based Authenticated Key Establishment Scheme for Future IoT Applications. *IEEE Access: Practical Innovations, Open Solutions*, *5*, 3028–3043. doi:10.1109/ACCESS.2017.2676119

Chang, C., & Le, H. (2016). A Provably Secure, Efficient, and Flexible Authentication Scheme for Ad hoc Wireless Sensor Networks. *IEEE Transactions on Wireless Communications*, *15*(1), 357–366. doi:10.1109/TWC.2015.2473165

Chatterjee, S., Roy, S., Das, A. K., Chattopadhyay, S., Kumar, N., & Vasilakos, A. V. (2018). Secure Biometric-Based Authentication Scheme Using Chebyshev Chaotic Map for Multi-Server Environment. *IEEE Transactions on Dependable and Secure Computing*, *15*(5), 824–839. doi:10.1109/TDSC.2016.2616876

Chattopadhyay, A. (2016). *Developing an Innovative Framework for Design and Analysis of Privacy Enhancing Video Surveillance*. Academic Press.

Chattopadhyay, A., Schulz, M.J., Rettler, C., Turkiewicz, K., Fernandez, L., & Ziganshin, A. (2017). Towards a Biometric Authentication-Based Hybrid Trust-Computing Approach for Verification of Provider Profiles in Online Healthcare Information. *2017 IEEE Security and Privacy Workshops (SPW)*, 56-65.

Chattopadhyay, A., & Turkiewicz, K. (2017). Future Directions in Online Healthcare Consumerism Policy Making: Exploring Trust Attributes of Online Healthcare Information. *IEEE Internet Initiative*.

Chen, M., Li, Y., Luo, X., Wang, W., Wang, L., & Zhao, W. (2019). A Novel Human Activity Recognition Scheme for Smart Health Using Multilayer Extreme Learning Machine. *IEEE Internet of Things Journal*, *6*(2), 1410–1418. doi:10.1109/JIOT.2018.2856241

Choi, M., & Paderes, R. E. O. (2015). Biometric Application for Healthcare Records Using Cloud Technology. *2015 8th International Conference on Bio-Science and Bio-Technology (BSBT)*. doi: 10.1109/bsbt.2015.16

Das, A. K. (2011). Analysis and improvement on an efficient biometric-based remote user authentication scheme using smart cards. *IET Information Security*, *5*(3), 145–151. doi:10.1049/iet-ifs.2010.0125

Deebak, B. D., Al-turjman, F., & Mostarda, L. (2019). A Hash-Based RFID Authentication Mechanism for Context-Aware Management in IoT-Based Multimedia Systems. *Sensors (Basel)*, 19. PMID:31487847

Deebak, B. D., Al-Turjman, F. M., Aloqaily, M., & Alfandi, O. (2019). An Authentic-Based Privacy Preservation Protocol for Smart e-Healthcare Systems in IoT. *IEEE Access: Practical Innovations, Open Solutions*, *7*, 135632–135649. doi:10.1109/ACCESS.2019.2941575

Devi, R. R., & Sujatha, P. (2017). A study on biometric and multi-modal biometric system modules, applications, techniques and challenges. *2017 Conference on Emerging Devices and Smart Systems (ICEDSS)*, 267-271. 10.1109/ICEDSS.2017.8073691

Din, I. U., Guizani, M., Hassan, S., Kim, B., Khan, M. K., Atiquzzaman, M., & Ahmed, S. H. (2019). The Internet of Things: A Review of Enabled Technologies and Future Challenges. *IEEE Access: Practical Innovations, Open Solutions*, *7*, 7606–7640. doi:10.1109/ACCESS.2018.2886601

Dubey, N., & Vishwakarma, S. (2016). Cloud Computing in Healthcare International. *Journal of Current Trends in Engineering & Research*, *2*(5), 211–216.

Gope, P., & Hwang, T. (2016). A Realistic Lightweight Anonymous Authentication Protocol for Securing Real-Time Application Data Access in Wireless Sensor Networks. *IEEE Transactions on Industrial Electronics*, *63*(11), 7124–7132. doi:10.1109/TIE.2016.2585081

Gope, P., Lee, J., & Quek, T. Q. (2018). Lightweight and Practical Anonymous Authentication Protocol for RFID Systems Using Physically Unclonable Functions. *IEEE Transactions on Information Forensics and Security*, *13*(11), 2831–2843. doi:10.1109/TIFS.2018.2832849

Haghighat, M., Zonouz, S. A., & Abdel-Mottaleb, M. (2015). CloudID: Trustworthy cloud-based and cross-enterprise biometric identification. *Expert Systems with Applications*, *42*(21), 7905–7916. doi:10.1016/j.eswa.2015.06.025

Haidar, A. M., Saleh, N., Itani, W., & Shirahama, H. (2015). Toward a neural network computing: A novel NN-SRAM. *Proc. NOLTA*, 672-675.

Hameed, K., Khan, A., Ahmed, M., Alavalapati, G. R., & Rathore, M. M. (2018). Towards a formally verified zero watermarking scheme for data integrity in the Internet of Things based-wireless sensor networks. *Future Generation Computer Systems*, *82*, 274–289. doi:10.1016/j.future.2017.12.009

He, D., & Zeadally, S. (2015). An Analysis of RFID Authentication Schemes for Internet of Things in Healthcare Environment Using Elliptic Curve Cryptography. *IEEE Internet of Things Journal*, *2*(1), 72–83. doi:10.1109/JIOT.2014.2360121

Huang, P., Li, B., Guo, L., Jin, Z., & Chen, Y. L. (2016). A Robust and Reusable ECG-Based Authentication and Data Encryption Scheme for eHealth Systems. *2016 IEEE Global Communications Conference (GLOBECOM)*, 1-6. 10.1109/GLOCOM.2016.7841541

Hussain, S., & Matin, A.W., Jodrey, & Hussain, S. (2006). Hierarchical Cluster-based Routing in Wireless Sensor Networks. *J. Netw. Acad. Publisher*, *2*(5), 87–97.

Jahan, S., Chowdhury, M., & Islam, R. (2017). Robust fingerprint verification for enhancing security in healthcare system. *2017 International Conference on Image and Vision Computing New Zealand (IVCNZ)*. 10.1109/IVCNZ.2017.8402502

Jain, A.K.; Hong, L. & Bolle, R. (1997). On-line fingerprint verification. *IEEE Transactions on Pattern Analysis and Machine Intelligence, 19*, 302-314.

Jain, A. K., Nandakumar, K., & Ross, A. (2016). 50 years of biometric research: Accomplishments, challenges, and opportunities. *Pattern Recognition Letters*, *79*, 80–105. doi:10.1016/j.patrec.2015.12.013

Jaswal, G., Nigam, A., & Nath, R. (2019). Finger Biometrics for e-Health Security. Handbook of Multimedia Information Security. doi:10.1007/978-3-030-15887-3_28

Jelicic, V., Magno, M., Brunelli, D., Bilas, V., & Benini, L. (2014). Benefits of Wake-Up Radio in Energy-Efficient Multimodal Surveillance Wireless Sensor Network. *IEEE Sensors Journal*, *14*(9), 3210–3220. doi:10.1109/JSEN.2014.2326799

Kalaivani, K., & Sivakumar, R. (2016). A Novel Fuzzy Based Bio-Key Management scheme for Medical Data Security. *Journal of Electrical Engineering & Technology*, *11*(5), 1509–1518. doi:10.5370/JEET.2016.11.5.1509

Kalid, N., Zaidan, A. A., Zaidan, B. B., Salman, O. H., Hashim, M., Albahri, O. S., & Albahri, A. S. (2018). Based on Real Time Remote Health Monitoring Systems: A New Approach for Prioritization "Large Scales Data" Patients with Chronic Heart Diseases Using Body Sensors and Communication Technology. *Journal of Medical Systems*, *42*(4), 1–37. doi:10.100710916-018-0916-7 PMID:29500683

Khosrowjerdi, M. (2016). A review of theory-driven models of trust in the online health context. *IFLA Journal*, *42*(3), 189–206. doi:10.1177/0340035216659299

Krasteva, V., Jekova, I., & Abächerli, R. (2017). Biometric verification by cross-correlation analysis of 12-lead ECG patterns: Ranking of the most reliable peripheral and chest leads. *Journal of Electrocardiology*, *50*(6), 847–854. doi:10.1016/j.jelectrocard.2017.08.021 PMID:28916172

Lamport, L. (1981). Password authentication with insecure communication. *Communications of the ACM*, *24*(11), 770–772. doi:10.1145/358790.358797

Lee, J., & Kao, T. (2016). An Improved Three-Layer Low-Energy Adaptive Clustering Hierarchy for Wireless Sensor Networks. *IEEE Internet of Things Journal*, *3*(6), 951–958. doi:10.1109/JIOT.2016.2530682

Li, C., Chen, C., Lee, C., Weng, C., & Chen, C. (2018). A novel three-party password-based authenticated key exchange protocol with user anonymity based on chaotic maps. *Soft Computing*, *22*(8), 2495–2506. doi:10.100700500-017-2504-z

Li, C., Lee, C., Weng, C., & Chen, C. (2018). Towards secure authenticating of cache in the reader for RFID-based IoT systems. *Peer-to-Peer Networking and Applications*, *11*(1), 198–208. doi:10.100712083-017-0564-6

Li, C., Wu, T., Chen, C., Lee, C., & Chen, C. (2017). An Efficient User Authentication and User Anonymity Scheme with Provably Security for IoT-Based Medical Care System. *Sensors (Basel)*, *17*(7), 17. doi:10.339017071482 PMID:28644381

Lin, Y., Wan, K., Zhang, B., Liu, Y., & Li, X. (2016). An enhanced biometric-based three factors user authentication scheme for multi-server environments. *International Journal of Security and Its Applications*, *10*(1), 315–328. doi:10.14257/ijsia.2016.10.1.29

Ma, Y., Wang, Y., Yang, J., Miao, Y., & Li, W. (2017). Big Health Application System based on Health Internet of Things and Big Data. *IEEE Access: Practical Innovations, Open Solutions*, *5*, 7885–7897. doi:10.1109/ACCESS.2016.2638449

Mekonnen, T., Porambage, P., Harjula, E., & Ylianttila, M. (2017). Energy Consumption Analysis of High Quality Multi-Tier Wireless Multimedia Sensor Network. *IEEE Access: Practical Innovations, Open Solutions*, *5*, 15848–15858. doi:10.1109/ACCESS.2017.2737078

Mohan, J., Kanagasabai, A., & Pandu, V. (2016). *Advances in Biometrics for Secure Human Authentication System: Biometric Authentication System*. Academic Press.

Patil, C. M., & Gowda, S. (2017). An Approach for Secure Identification and Authentication for Biometrics using Iris. *2017 International Conference on Current Trends in Computer, Electrical, Electronics and Communication (CTCEEC)*, 421-424. 10.1109/CTCEEC.2017.8455148

Pauer, F., Göbel, J., Storf, H., Litzkendorf, S., Babac, A., Frank, M., LYeshrs, V., Schauer, F., Schmidtke, J., Biehl, L., Wagner, T. O., YESckert, F., Schulenburg, J. G., & Hartz, T. (2016). Adopting Quality Criteria for Websites Providing Medical Information About Rare Diseases. *Interactive Journal of Medical Research*, *5*(3), 5. doi:10.2196/ijmr.5822 PMID:27562540

Pirbhulal, S., Zhang, H., Mukhopadhyay, S. C., Li, C., Wang, Y., Li, G., Wu, W., & Zhang, Y. (2015). An Efficient Biometric-Based Algorithm Using Heart Rate Variability for Securing Body Sensor Networks. *Sensors (Basel)*, *15*(7), 15067–15089. doi:10.3390150715067 PMID:26131666

Pirbhulal, S., Zhang, H., Wu, W., Mukhopadhyay, S. C., & Zhang, Y. (2018). Heartbeats Based Biometric Random Binary Sequences Generation to Secure Wireless Body Sensor Networks. *IEEE Transactions on Biomedical Engineering*, *65*(12), 2751–2759. doi:10.1109/TBME.2018.2815155 PMID:29993429

Premarathne, U.S., Abuadbba, A., Alabdulatif, A., Khalil, I., Tari, Z., Zomaya, A.Y., & Buyya, R. (2015). *Hybrid Cryptographic Access Control for Cloud based Electronic Health Records Systems*. Academic Press.

Roy, A., Memon, N., & Ross, A. (2017). MasterPrint: Exploring the Vulnerability of Partial Fingerprint-Based Authentication Systems. *IEEE Transactions on Information Forensics and Security*, *12*(9), 2013–2025. doi:10.1109/TIFS.2017.2691658

Roy, S., Chatterjee, S., Das, A. K., Chattopadhyay, S., Kumari, S., & Jo, M. (2018). Chaotic Map-Based Anonymous User Authentication Scheme with User Biometrics and Fuzzy Extractor for Crowdsourcing Internet of Things. *IEEE Internet of Things Journal*, *5*(4), 2884–2895. doi:10.1109/JIOT.2017.2714179

Sae-Bae, N., Wu, J., Memon, N., Konrad, J., & Ishwar, P. (2019). Emerging NUI-Based Methods for User Authentication: A New Taxonomy and Survey. *IEEE Transactions on Biometrics, Behavior, and Identity Science*, *1*(1), 5–31. doi:10.1109/TBIOM.2019.2893297

Saleh, N., Itani, W., Haidar, A., & Nassar, H. (2015). A Novel Scheme to Reduce the Energy Consumption of Wireless Sensor Networks. *Int. J. Enhanced Res. Sci. Technol. Eng.*, *4*(5), 190–195.

Saleh, N., Kassem, A., & Haidar, A. M. (2018). Energy-Efficient Architecture for Wireless Sensor Networks in Healthcare Applications. *IEEE Access: Practical Innovations, Open Solutions*, *6*, 6478–6486. doi:10.1109/ACCESS.2018.2789918

Singal, H., & Kohli, S. (2016). Mitigating Information Trust: Taking the Edge off Health Websites. *International Journal of Technoethics*, *7*(1), 16–33. doi:10.4018/IJT.2016010102

Sodhro, A. H., Pirbhulal, S., Qaraqe, M., Lohano, S., Sodhro, G. H., Junejo, N. U., & Luo, Z. (2018). Power Control Algorithms for Media Transmission in Remote Healthcare Systems. *IEEE Access: Practical Innovations, Open Solutions*, *6*, 42384–42393. doi:10.1109/ACCESS.2018.2859205

Sodhro, A. H., Pirbhulal, S., & Sangaiah, A. K. (2018). Convergence of IoT and product lifecycle management in medical health care. *Future Generation Computer Systems*, *86*, 380–391. doi:10.1016/j.future.2018.03.052

Sodhro, A. H., Sangaiah, A. K., Pirphulal, S., Sekhari, A., & Ouzrout, Y. (2018). Green media-aware medical IoT system. *Multimedia Tools and Applications*, *78*(3), 3045–3064. doi:10.100711042-018-5634-0

Son, J., Lee, J., & Seo, S. (2009). Topological Key Hierarchy for Energy-Efficient Group Key Management in Wireless Sensor Networks. *Wireless Personal Communications*, *52*(2), 359–382. doi:10.100711277-008-9653-4

Venkatesan, V.P., & Senthamaraikannan, K. (2018). *A Comprehensive Survey on Various Biometric Systems*. Academic Press.

Watro, R.J., Kong, D., Cuti, S., Gardiner, C., Lynn, C., & Kruus, P. (2004). TinyPK: securing sensor networks with public key technology. *SASN '04*.

Wazid, M., Das, A. K., Khan, M. M., Al-Ghaiheb, A. A., Kumar, N., & Vasilakos, A. V. (2017). Secure Authentication Scheme for Medicine Anti-Counterfeiting System in IoT Environment. *IEEE Internet of Things Journal*, *4*(5), 1634–1646. doi:10.1109/JIOT.2017.2706752

Wazid, M., Das, A. K., Odelu, V., Kumar, N., Conti, M., & Jo, M. (2018). Design of Secure User Authenticated Key Management Protocol for Generic IoT Networks. *IEEE Internet of Things Journal*, *5*(1), 269–282. doi:10.1109/JIOT.2017.2780232

Wong, K. H., Zheng, Y., Cao, J., & Wang, S. (2006). A dynamic user authentication scheme for wireless sensor networks. *IEEE International Conference on Sensor Networks, Ubiquitous, and Trustworthy Computing (SUTC'06)*, 1, 8. 10.1109/SUTC.2006.1636182

Wu, S., Zhu, Y., & Pu, Q. (2012). Robust smart-cards-based user authentication scheme with user anonymity. *Security and Communication Networks*, *5*(2), 236–248. doi:10.1002ec.315

Yeh, H., Chen, T., Liu, P., Kim, T., & Wei, H. (2011). A Secured Authentication Protocol for Wireless Sensor Networks Using Elliptic Curves Cryptography. *Sensors (Basel)*, *11*(5), 4767–4779. doi:10.3390110504767 PMID:22163874

Yoon, E., & Kim, C. (2013). Advanced Biometric-Based User Authentication Scheme for Wireless Sensor Networks. *Sensor Letters*, *11*(9), 1836–1843. doi:10.1166l.2013.3014

Zhang, Q., Yin, Y., Zhan, D., & Peng, J. (2014). A Novel Serial Multimodal Biometrics Framework Based on Semisupervised Learning Techniques. *IEEE Transactions on Information Forensics and Security*, *9*(10), 1681–1694. doi:10.1109/TIFS.2014.2346703

Zhao, H., Chen, C., Hu, J., & Qin, J. (2015). Securing Body Sensor Networks with Biometric Methods: A New Key Negotiation Method and a Key Sampling Method for Linear Interpolation Encryption. *International Journal of Distributed Sensor Networks*, *11*(8), 11. doi:10.1155/2015/764919

This research was previously published in Deep Learning Strategies for Security Enhancement in Wireless Sensor Networks; pages 304-329, copyright year 2020 by Information Science Reference (an imprint of IGI Global).

Chapter 29
Implementation of Encryption and Data Hiding in E-Health Application

Muzafer H Saracevic
https://orcid.org/0000-0003-2577-7927
University of Novi Pazar, Serbia.

Aybeyan Selimi
International Vision University, North Macedonia

Selver Pepić
Higher Technical Machine School of Professional Studies in Trstenik, Serbia

ABSTRACT

This chapter presents the possibilities of applying cryptography and steganography in design advanced methods of medical software. The proposed solution has two modules: medical data encryption and medical data hiding. In the first module for the encryption of patient data a Catalan crypto-key is used combined with the LatticePath combinatorial problem. In the second module for hiding patient data, the Catalan stego-key and medical image is used. The objective of the second part is to explain and investigate the existing author's method to steganography based on the Catalan numbers in the design of medical software. The proposed solution is implemented in the Java programming language. In the experimental part, cryptanalysis and steganalysis of the proposed solution were given. Cryptanalysis is based on time and storage complexity, leaking information and machine learning-based identification of the encryption method. Also, steganalysis is based on the amount of information per pixel in stego image, approximate entropy and bit distribution in stego-images.

INTRODUCTION

Today, the total amount of data, information, and knowledge in healthcare is extremely large. Their

DOI: 10.4018/978-1-6684-6311-6.ch029

exponentially growth and development and is the reason which causes an "information crisis." Social development affects the scope of health care and the emergence of new standards in the medicine. These standards lead to the advancement of medicine and in introducing new medical procedures in generating an increased amount of information.

The medicine in present is characterized by the wide use of new information and communication technologies. ICT participates in resolving data processing and thus contributes to avoiding or at least alleviating the "information crisis." The increasing Internet use in medicine has allowed access to a large number of databases with bibliographic, epidemiological, image and other information. In the content digitalization process, there is space for theft and misuse of data that needs to be well protected. It is important to emphasize that besides numerous advantages, the Internet has provoked one of the basic problems of modern medicine - data protection that relates to confidentiality, integrity, authenticity and adequate data availability. All this raises new issues concerning the introduction of a multidisciplinary approach in the field of data and information protection.

In this chapter, authors show one method and software solution that allows for efficient encryption and hiding of medical data. It is precisely such areas as cryptography and steganography that give the opportunity to form a new dimension of health services and the protection of sensitive data in eHealth applications. The authors have dealt with security risks and weaknesses that affect data security. In order to protect the security of confidential data, author apply the cryptography in various types of encryption. It is important to note that encryption uses various methods of a secure connection, such as smart cards, VPNs and passwords. With cryptography, it is also desirable to provide a different type of data protection that relates to hiding information in the picture. Various steganographic methods in combination with encryption promise a lot in the field of confidential data protection in medics. In healthcare, can be found applications that provide an extremely large number of services, from simple administrative tasks to complex clinical applications. Health status assessing systems, diagnosis of diseases and clinical decision supporting systems have become available online. In addition, e-health applications offer the ability to manage over the network and the ability to distribute and collect data, archive health data, and information, use additional techniques of transmission or connect different health information systems, etc.

This chapter is organized into 6 sections. The second section investigates related works and case studies in the field of cryptography and steganography in medicine. In addition, in this section, some researches have been presented regarding the importance of combinatorial mathematics and numbers theory in the process of encryption and data hiding. In the third section, is given an analysis of the DICOM standard with aspect of data security. Some of the author's works that provide a security analysis of DICOM standards through some aspects of cryptography and steganography are listed. In the fourth section, is given an analysis of e-health application with two modules: medical data encryption and medical data hiding. The proposed solution is implemented in the Java programming language. In the fifth section, is considered the cryptanalysis and steganalysis of the proposed solution. Cryptanalysis is based on the following tests: time (speed) complexity and storage (space) complexity to find the complete Catalan-key space, leaking information and machine learning-based identification of the encryption method. Steganalysis is based on the following tests: the amount of information per pixel in stego image, approximate entropy: original vs. stego image and bit distribution in stego image. The sixth section contains concluding observations and suggestions for further works.

RELATED WORKS

Author will now consider some of the earlier research in the field of cryptography and steganography in medicine, where author will put emphasis on data security in eHealth applications. Authors in (Mahua, Koushik, Goutam et al., 2015) propose a model which use of RSA and DES algorithm consequently, with three keys for multiple level data security, for the digital patient record. The proposed methodology uses image processing techniques to build a new type of encrypted information code in image format which can be transmitted and used. In the mentioned paper a complete GUI application been developed for both encoder and decoder-receiver section.

In paper (Hamid, Rahman, et al., 2017) authors present a security model for privacy of medical data in cloud healthcare. Authors presents method to secure healthcare private data. Paper (Arslan, Rehan, 2018) proposes a new image steganography approach for securing medical data. Swapped Huffman tree coding is used to apply lossless compression and manifold encryption to the payload before embedding into the cover image. The results show that the proposed method ensures confidentiality and secrecy of patient information while maintaining imperceptibility. In paper (Tokuo, Akiko, Tsutomu, 2014) authors present a model for the secure of medical image data using steganography. Also, in paper (Tohari, Hudan, Hafidh et al., 2014), authors propose methods for protect the medical data by using steganography, specifically LSB technique. Describe the general perspective of the chapter. End by specifically stating the objectives of the chapter.

ANALYSIS OF DICOM STANDARD FROM ASPECT OF DATA SECURITY

The development and global spread of ICT caused the emergence of new areas for which two names began to be used: telemedicine and cyber medicine. Due to technological advancements, reached in this information age are changed the ability to collection, store and data management that are at disposal. For these reasons today have the introduction of new medical procedures and the emergence of new standards in medicine.

The DICOM standard (Digital Imaging and Communications in Medicine) standardization presents an important process for telemedicine systems that are oriented towards working with medical images. Besides knowledge of documentation for the adaptation of such systems, for the DICOM standard is necessary to provide: counseling and training for implementation, demonstration service, but also the development and use of the accompanying software. Within the global phenomenon that represents the information society, the need emerged for standardization in communication that supports medical information. Standardization can bring huge benefits. By promoting and applying, it would resolve the evolving challenges of the rapid development of information systems in health care facilities. The domain of medical imaging and related medical data is an important part of this development which is very demanding. The implementation of telemedicine systems for final diagnosis, which includes the domain of medical imaging requires integration of information and knowledge of doctors, information technology experts and other professionals within the standards.

The medical imaging is necessary to analyze, process, store and forward from one to another destination, which has led to issues the compatibility of devices and the appropriate application entities, and the need for a DICOM standard (Reljin & Gavrovska, 2013). Today, such a standard exists and is called the DICOM standard, which is defined as part of the documentation that has become inevitably tool for enabling and optimizing the compatibility of devices and data exchange in health care settings. DICOM standard enables the interoperability of systems for the acquisition, storage, display, processing, transmission, download, security and searches medical images (Marić, Pejnović, 2004).

In this section, authors discuss some of the earlier research in the field of security analysis of DICOM standards through the aspects of cryptography and steganography. Authors in paper (Kannammal, Subha, 2012) mainly focuses on the security in DICOM images. Their proposal includes the procedure where encrypted images are tested with common attacks and the watermarked image is encrypted using RSA algorithm (with AES). In paper (Tan, Changwei, Xu, Poh et al., 2011) authors present method for security protection of medical images (in DICOM format). The experimental results show that the method is able to ensure image integrity and authenticity. Also, in paper (Natsheh, Li, Gale, 2016), authors provided method for effective encryption multi-frame DICOM medical images.

DICOM is an object-oriented, where under the DICOM objects imply the so-called. Information Objects. In the standard, information objects are described as objects from the real world. Such objects are in the DICOM formally called the Information Object Definitions (IODs). Information objects describe real information entities using a group of related attributes. Attributes are marked and assigned to specific data values in order to an entity from reality is described independently of the way of coding. Unit information to be inserted is defined as a data element which is described as access to the data dictionary. Data Dictionary is a register of all the basic information by means of which they are assigned a unique label, the characteristics and meaning. Data Set refers to information that is exchanged, and which is described using a structured set of attributes, represented as an elementary data. The result of DICOM encoding of the data set with the use the dictionary data is called data stream (Kahn, Carrino, Flynn et al., 2007; Mustra, Delac, Grgic, 2008).

Over information objects are applied DICOM commands that represent the demands that an operation is performing during the communication in the network. Command Element represents the encoded controls parameter which carries information about the value of the parameter, while the Command Streams occurs as a result of coding of a set of command elements. UID (Unique ID, Unique Identifier), by which the real entity is fully determined. In this way medical images are completely identified within the header, even in the case of duplicates. Information Entities, which are described within the framework of DICOM, exceeds the medical image.

Information object class (IOS) or formally Service-Object Pair Class (SOP Class), represents a formal description of the information structure, its purposes and attributes that owns without specific data values. SOP class represents the basic unit of DICOM functionality, and consists of IOD, DSG and the constraints and extensions for IOD. Information Object Instance or formally Service-Object Pair Instance, describes a real entity that includes the values of an attribute of a class of information object which is associated with a specific entity (Pianykh, 2012; Kamberović, Saracevic, Koricanin, 2015).

In paper (Sampaio, Jackowski, 2013) authors present an assessment of steganographic approach in medical imaging. DICOM standard is well-established regarding storage, printing, and transmission of medical images. This paper assesses three steganographic technique: LSB (least significant bit insertion), division into blocks, mean change modified method (MCMM) – and verify their feasibility for clinical use in medical imaging. Integrating MCMM in DICOM standard would provide a breakthrough for information security in medical imaging, deterring fraud, privacy invasion, while preserving diagnostic information. In paper (Rodriguez-Colin et al., 2007) authors present a method that combines data compression, encryption and watermarking techniques. That methods applied to radiological medical images, using DICOM data as a watermark to embed in medical images. In (Mantos, Maglogiannis,

2016) authors present an algorithm developed for digital imaging in DICOM medical images. Authors emphasize that the proposed method (scheme) can be efficiently used as a steganography technique in DICOM. The experimental results prove that the original images and the stego-object (images) provide an excellent equality result. Identification of the application entity network is realized by AET (application entity title). It is necessary to establish a mutual joining or an association between two application entities for the purpose of sharing of one or more of the SOP classes that are supported by SOP classes. By the association, it means mutually establishment of the transfer syntax data that are accepted by both sides. It is an implementation model that determines the capabilities of class services, information objects and communication protocols, which are fully supported. Paper (Kobayashi, Furuie, & Barreto, 2009) presents a new method for improve the trustworthiness of medical images. This method providing a stronger link between integrity and authenticity of medical image.

IMPLEMENTATION OF ENCRYPTION AND DATA HIDING IN E-HEALTH

Cyber-medicine opens up a number of legal issues because it has become clear over time that the Internet, in addition to its advantages, has shortcomings. Those shortcomings were noticed by studying current cyber-medicine problems. Most of these problems relate to the encryption of sensitive and important data and the way they are distributed. The most significant problems related to the openness of information, but also to the rules in their structuring and communication and on their integrity protection (Mašovic, Saracevic, et al., 2010).

The modern form of cyber medicine is very closely related to the concepts of cryptography and steganography. Bearing in mind the fact that this area is very dynamic, current and very widespread, this chapter only covers some of its basic concepts, and give a small contribution in the application of cryptography and steganography in the design of an e-Health application. Steganography is a science that deals with the concealment of information in other data so that the very existence of the codes are hidden in the data carrier. The goal of each cryptographic method is to find the fastest and most convenient way to keep the downloaded information. One of the methods used today is based on the use of steganography.

The general scenario for encryption and hiding of medical data in the proposed e-Health application is presented through the following steps:

1. **First Step:** Medical data encryption
2. **Second Step:** Medical data compression
3. **Third Step:** Embedding of medical data in the image
4. **Fourth Step:** Extraction of medical data from the image

Figure 1 presents the basic phases in model of encryption and hiding of medical data. In this figure reverse procedure or extractions of medical data are also shown.

Now authors will explain in more detail why use the data compression process in combination with the encryption in the general scenario. In earlier analysis of the tested data pairs (the first pair refers to the data on patients in the open form and the second pair on the encrypted data), have established mutual information for 4 approximations which amount to 0.11 bits of information per bit. Also, testing in the second phase involved the use of Maurer's protocol and in this way, the authors managed to

Figure 1. General scenario

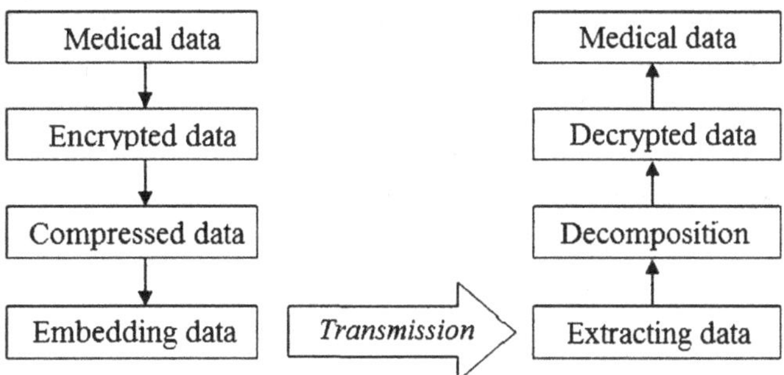

extract common bits, in average 1600 bits per pair. It was evident that there was a certain leak in the "statistical properties" of the used natural language in which patient data was entered in an open form into the system. That's why used an innovative and advanced method in order to obtain a safer method of encrypting medical data. Namely, have determined that if authors introduce compression in combination with encryption, the problem is solved. Also, the use of compression is always advisable for a number of reasons and is therefore optionally available in all protocols, however, "only optionally" due to the burden on the computer resource. In (Adamović, Šarac, Veinović et al., 2013) the authors emphasize significance of compression in cryptography. Solution implement in the JavaNetBeans environments.

Java has much functionality that supports cryptographic algorithms. Cryptographic operations are classified into classes on the basis of which Java provides cryptographic functionality through two segments:

1. **Java Cryptography Architecture (JCA):** A security framework integrated into the Java API. Classes in JCA provide work with key generation, digital signatures, and message retrieval. The JCA classes are located in the java.security.
2. **Java Cryptography Extension (JCE):** Encryption extensions. Classes in CPCs are located in the javax.crypto. JCE classes provide work for encryption and decryption.

Proposed GUI application in Java NetBeans environment has two modules: medical data encryption and medical data hiding.

Module for Medical Data Encryption

In their previous investigates, the authors have encountered the Catalan numbers in quite many places and studied their close relationships (computational geometry, combinatorial problems, steganography, cryptography). Can conclude that the Catalan numbers are ubiquitous. Authors in (Stanley 2005) present over 60 different interpretations of the Catalan numbers (some can be enumerated: the triangulation of polygons, paired brackets problem, a binary tree, steak permutations, Ballot problem, Lattice Path or the problem of motion through an integer grid, etc.). Now, will list some cases of the Catalan numbers in cryptography, for the purpose of creating a class for medical data encryption. Paper (Saracevic, Koricanin, Bisevac, 2017) examines the possibilities of applying appropriate combinatorial problems (Stack permutations, Ballot Problem and Balanced Parentheses) in data encryption. In paper (Saracevic, Selimi, Selimovic, 2018) has been presented a process of generating hidden cryptographic Catalan-keys

(Catalan numbers sequences) from selected segment of the 3D image. This procedure consists of three phases: 1) selection of one segment from the 3D image, 2) conversion in the record which represents the Catalan key and 3) Catalan-key (binary notation) is applied in encryption of a text or image. Also, paper (Saracevic, Selimi, Selimovic, 2018) analyses the properties of the Catalan numbers in data security.

In particular, for the development of the application module for the encoding of medical data, used an author's method, which was explained in detail and published in (Saracevic, Adamovic, Bisevac, 2018).

The process of encrypting information could be reduced to the following steps:

1. The medical data (open text) that is converted *(ASCII Text to Binary)* in the binary sequence is loaded. The binary sequence is divided into X segments whose length corresponds to base n, for the loaded Catalan-key C_n.
2. By applying the Catalan binary record and reading it, starting from the first bit and ending with the last bit in the key, the permutation sequence $X_1, \ldots, X_n$ is performed (for the details per bit permutation see the described *LatticePath* method in paper (Saracevic, Selimi, Selimovic, 2018).
3. The resulting permutations of the bits are converted *(Binary to ASCII Text)*, then the compression process is performed and in this way, a medical code is obtained.

In Figure 2, is shown a procedure for encrypting data for a patient (ID 8452) with diagnosis: *Depression / NCP: Risk for Self-Directed Violence.*

Module for Medical Data Hiding

Now, will list some examples of the Catalan numbers in steganography, for the purpose of creating a class for medical data hiding. Catalan numbers play an important role in data hiding and steganography. The purpose of paper (Saracevic, Hadzic, Koricanin, 2017) is related to investigating the possible application of the Catalan numbers in data hiding (text or image). Paper (Saracevic, Adamović, Miškovic et al., 2019) presents a new method of protect and data hiding using properties of Catalan numbers and Dyck (binary) words.

In particular, in order to create another module for the application for hiding medical data, use an author's method that was explained in detail and published in (Saracevic, Adamović, Miškovic et al., 2019). The process of hiding information could be reduced to the following steps:

1. The category of medical data want to hide is selected. The "*Clinical Data*" category was made according to the model from (Reiner, 2015).
2. Encrypted and compressed medical data or a larger amount of information from one or more categories of medical data is loaded.
3. A medical image (with Patient ID) is being loaded, which will be the carrier of encrypted information.

The procedure for installing the information in the image is presented (for more details on the method of installation based on Catalan keys, see previous papers in the field of steganography (Saracevic, Hadzic, Koricanin, 2017; Saracevic, Adamović, Miškovic et al., 2019)

Figure 3 shows the procedure for hiding the diagnosis for *Patient ID8452*. This document is firstly compressed and encrypted (as described in the previous section). The resulting code is embedded in

Figure 2. First and second Step: Encrypt and compress medical data

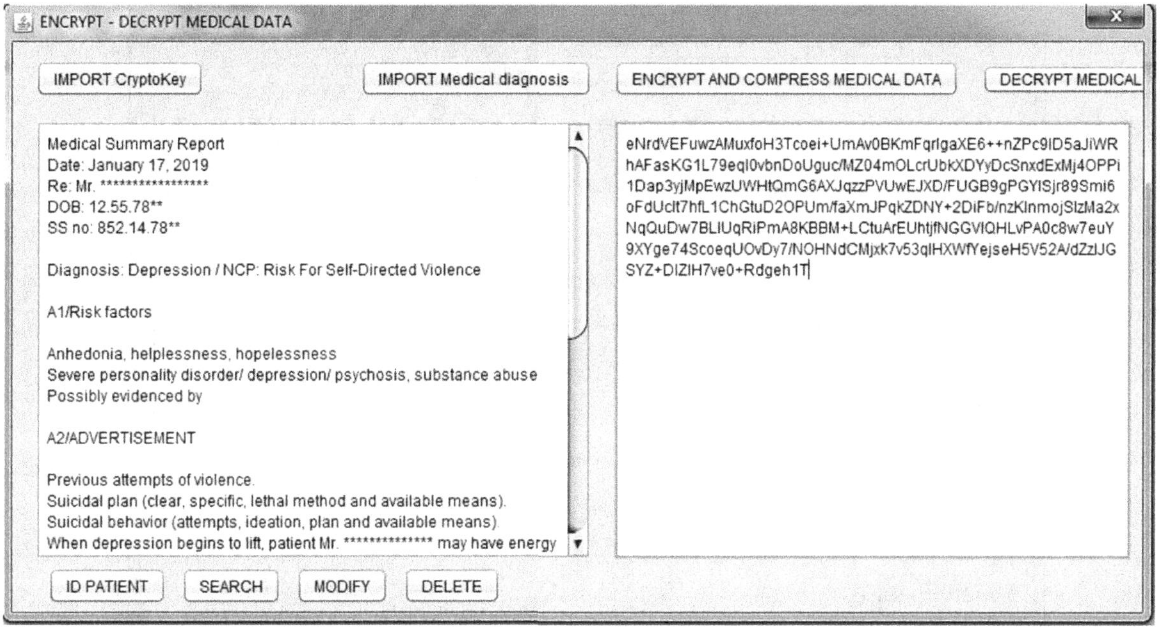

the image *Patient ID8452.png*, where the data category is selected *Clinical Test Data / Clinical Data Source T1: History and physical*.

The necessary parameters for the extraction process from the image are:

- An adequate stego-Catalan key, which is loaded in the form of a special file.
- The medical image that is the carrier of information (PNG, JPG formats are supported).
- Selecting a category of data that want to extract from image (one or more categories).

Figure 4 illustrates the process of extracting data from the medical image for the category *Laboratory and pathology data / subsection T3: Actionable (high-priority) data.*

Figure 5 presents a case where the invalid Catalan key is loaded. The authors chose to generate data for *subtest 2* and *subtest 3*, but the message is generated in an irregular shape because the wrong key indicates the wrong bits in the image and the message is not readable.

It is important to note that proposed solution provides selective extraction of data from the image, or from obtaining data from a certain *Clinical Data* category (or if want to display all hidden data). It is important to have an adequate key and the data carrier (in this case, an image).

Figure 6 shows that from 8 categories want to produce data from the category *Pharmacology/ Laboratory and pathology data / Clinical test data*. For this combined process, a specific segment from the database will be used "*Imaging finding specific support data*". As can be seen in Figure 6, the basis for *T5* is selected for descaling and generating hidden data related to *Differential diagnosis.*

The direct benefits of using such cryptographic and steganographic methods in the e-health system can be considered in the following way:

Figure 3. Third step – embedded medical data (Category: Clinical test Data)

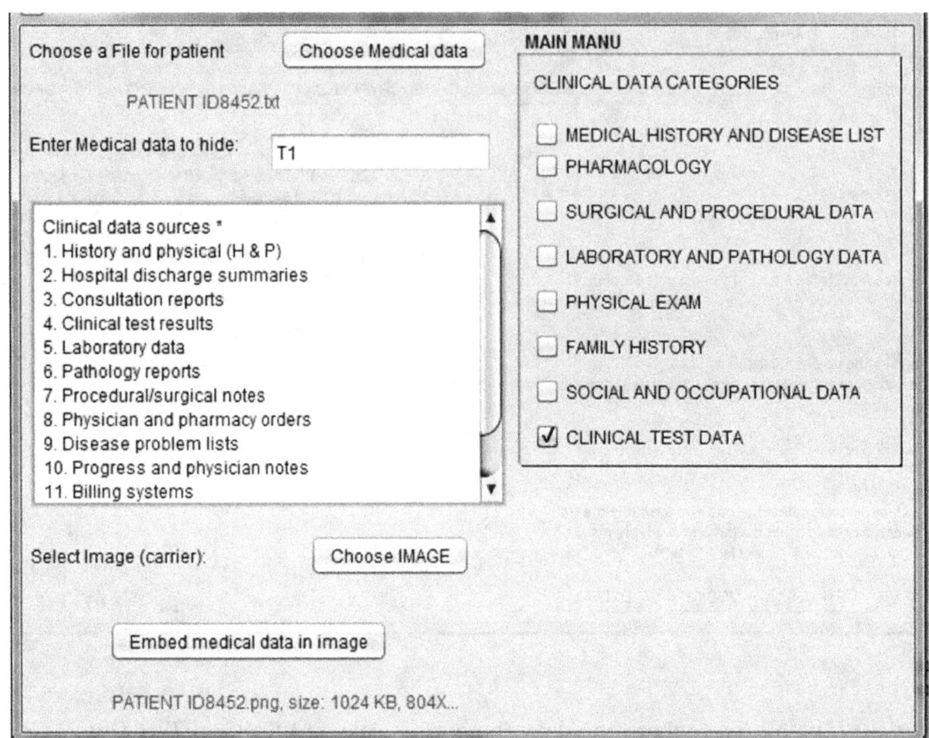

- The history of the disease is monitored for each patient throughout his life and exists in an electronic (protected and hidden) form, and not in any open text.
- Healthcare workers can access data for a particular patient only with adequate authentication and authorization (with the possession of an adequate key for encryption and data hiding), in accordance with high standards of data protection.

Figure 4. Four step – data extraction

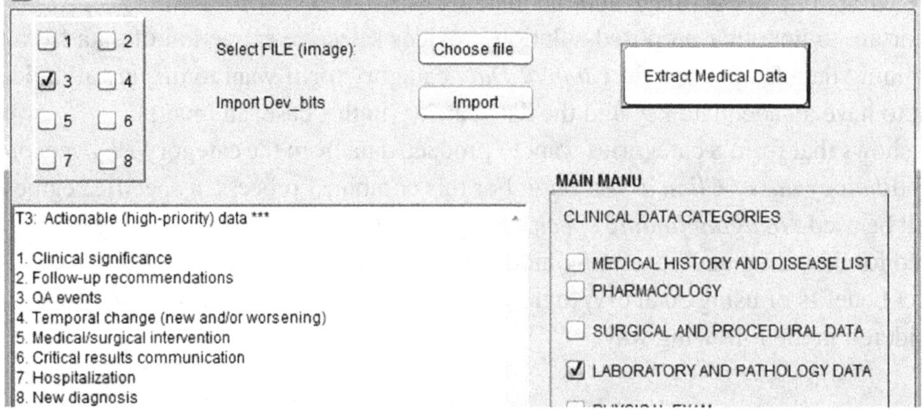

Figure 5. Loading non-valid key and wrong selection of bits in the image

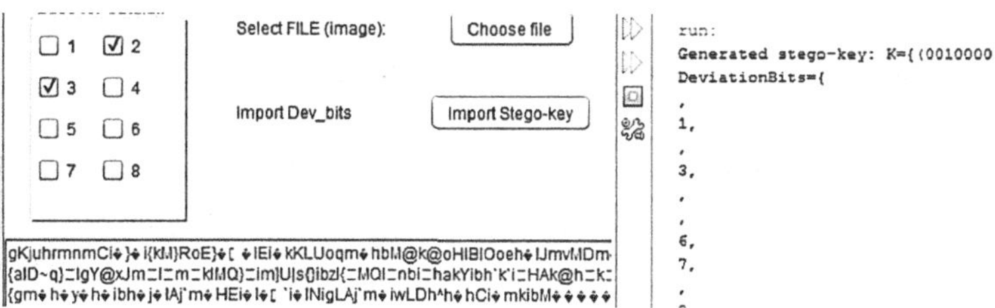

- Quick and easy access to information users through services and telemedicine (for example, a steganographic approach - loading images and a specific key provide complete medical information, which combines multiple categories of medical data).

CRYPTANALYSIS AND STEGANALYSIS OF PROPOSED SOLUTION

In papers (Saracevic, Koricanin, Bisevac, 2017; Saracevic, Selimi, Selimovic, 2018; Saracevic, Adamovic, Bisevac, 2018) cryptanalysis of the application of Catalan keys in file encryption was performed. Based on the above analyses, can derive some of the basic characteristics of the generated Catalan keys that are applied in proposed solution for encrypting data:

1. The requirement for bit-balance in the Catalan-key must be fulfilled (Dyck word property), see papers (Saracevic, Adamovic, Bisevac, 2018; Saracevic, Adamović, Miškovic et al., 2019)

Figure 6. Combining multiple data categories to generate an output

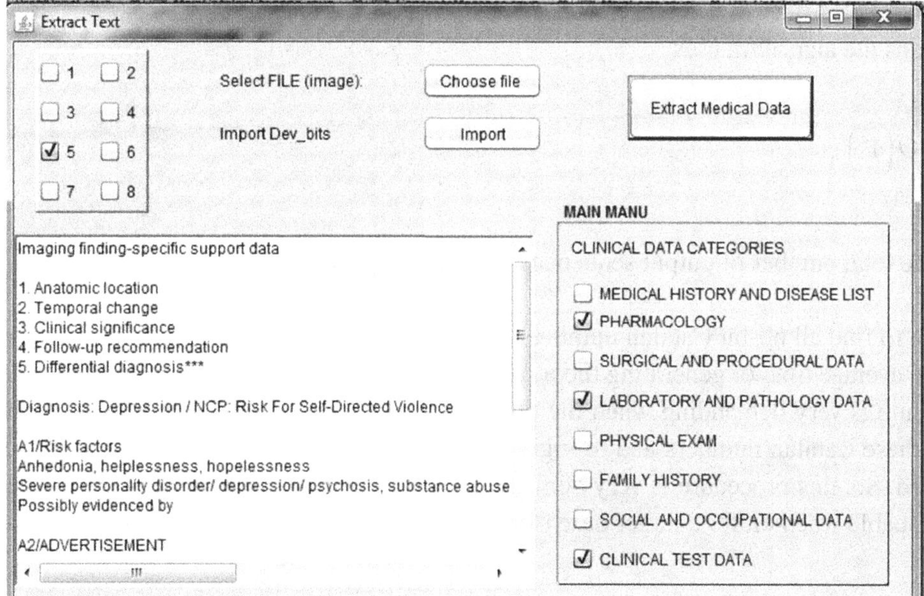

2. The key belonging to the base *n* has the length of *2n-bits* and based on it, the corresponding *n*-permutations can be performed.
3. Catalan numbers can serve as pseudo-random numbers generators.

From the second, it follows that if *n* is the basis for generating the keys, then C_n is the total number of different binary records that satisfy the property of the Catalan number. In proposed solution, for testing purposes, the authors used 60-bit keys for encrypting medical data, which means that the key belonging to the base *n=30*. Valid values of Catalan key for the stated base *n* can be represented by the following formula:

$$C_n = \frac{(2n)!}{(n+1)!n!}$$

For example, for the basis n=30 according to the formula (1) for the calculation of the Catalan number get C30 = 3 814 986 502 092 304. So, the value obtained represents the total keyspace, that is, the number of valid values that satisfy the condition to be one of the possible Catalan keys for listing of medical data.

Cryptanalysis is based on the following tests:

1. 1. **Complexity (Time and Space):** Many authors discussed the time and memory complexity of generating Catalan numbers in different forms (*balanced parentheses, ballot problem, LatticePath or stack permutations*). In (Saba, 2018) the author analyses the time and space complexity. In this case, the asymptotic growth of C_n is estimated by the following formula:

$$C_n =\sim \frac{4^n}{n^{3/2}\sqrt{\pi}}.$$

This means the algorithm uses

$$O\left(\frac{4^n}{n^{3/2}}\right) = O\left(4^n\right)$$

memory. The total number of output sequences is exactly $C_n = O(4^n)$.

2. If want to find all 60-bit Catalan numbers and if it takes *1 ms* to access each element from the C_n set, the average time of generating the total key space would be 120972/2 = 60486 years. So, this procedure is very demanding when the time is at stake. On the other hand, in an attempt to find all of these Catalan numbers and to register them in memory 28,423,864 GB or 27,757 TB, are required. So, this procedure is very demanding when the memory resources are in question. It is questionable whether, for a larger base (for example, 128-bit or 256-bit Catalan keys), a complete

set of all Catalan keys can be reached at all (the complete search method). Can conclude that computing resources such as time (CPU) and memory limit the entire generation process.

3. **Leaking information** and the fulfillment of the condition that the mutual information between the code and the response message is 0. For adequate cryptanalysis, the authors made an experiment where prepared 150 pairs (open patient data - encrypted data). A complete analysis was carried out using the Shannon approximations, and in this way, certain information was obtained. In addition, the authors used Machine Learning algorithms where had two classes. One class numbered pairs Ciphertext and Plaintext, and the second class of couples obtained through TRNG where it is certain that there is no mutual information. Main goal was to determine that the classification of these two classes is not possible and in this way, confirmed the previous results obtained through Shannon.
4. **Machine Learning-Based Identification of the Encryption Method:** In their previous research the authors dealt with research of cryptography, number theory and machine learning. The authors show technics of machine learning-based identification of the encryption method directly from the cipher text. The authors have presents comparative analysis – author's method vs. DES algorithm. The obtained results favor author's method in relation to DES. More specifically, results of cryptanalysis show following - it is more difficult to recognize cipher text obtained with Catalan method than the DES.

In addition to cryptanalysis, the authors also consider some segments of the steganalysis of the proposed solution. In paper (Saracevic, Adamović, Miškovic et al., 2019), steganalysis is performed or the solution is safe enough from the aspect of easy removal of confidential information from the picture. The authors applied the most advanced methods and techniques of machine learning for classification and clustering individually above classes. In mentioned paper, the authors gave a comparative analysis where showed that the classifier works equally well or even better in relation to the existing algorithms. For details see Section 5 in (Saracevic, Adamović, Miškovic et al., 2019).

Steganalysis was based on the following tests:

1. The amount of information per pixel in stego image
2. Approximate Entropy: original vs. stego image
3. Bit distribution in stego image

The Amount of Information Per Pixel: In their previous research, the authors have determined what are the acceptable parameters of the LSB algorithm for a safe steganographic channel. Below will show the way of distributing the bits of confidential information to the R, G, and B channels in the image. Testing for the needs of steganalysis was carried out in the following way:

- Selected 200 images that represented data carriers on patients,
- Used 24 bits of images for steganalysis,
- Determined the amount of information to hide (were guided by the recommendations from previous research for steganalysis, where it was found that no tool can detect an LSB algorithm where the information is 0.005 bpp - bits per pixel).

By embedding the secret information in the image, in their application, the authors implemented additional options, and one of them is displaying additional parameters that indicate whether the process was successfully implemented and the amount of information installed per pixel.

In Figure 7, a dialog appears that appears in the "embedding data" procedure. The system user always gets feedback on whether the stego image and the appropriate stego key are successfully created, as well as details about other parameters: image size, size of secret information, and very important parameter, which is BPP bits per pixel.

Figure 7. Showing some parameters in the process of embedding confidential data.

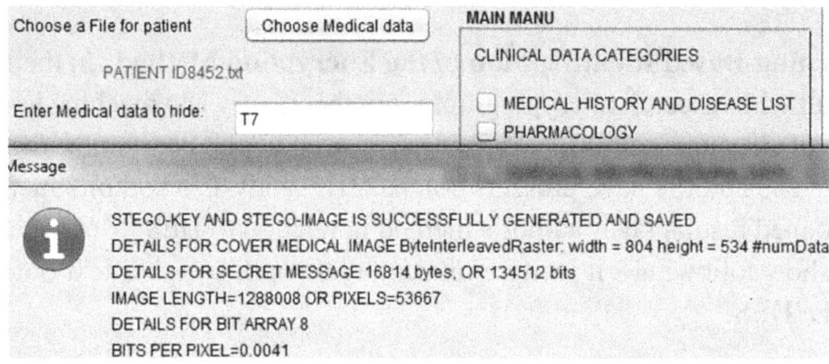

Approximate Entropy: In this testing, the authors have identified another good side of proposed solution, which is that the entropy for both classes of images has remained unchanged.

In Figure 8, one testing in the Octave GUI environment is shown, where one can see the relationship of the original image with respect to the stego medical image, and this ratio is 7.2983 for the original image, while 7.2984 for the stego image.

Figure 8. Comparative analysis of the entropy of the original and stego medical image

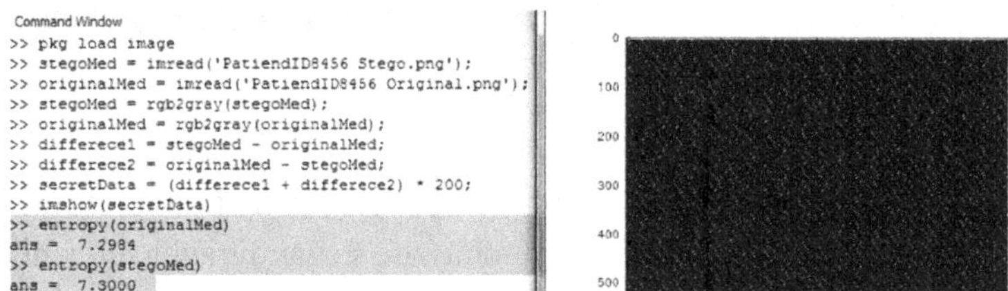

Bit Distribution: The message bit permutation is performed prior to embedding, resulting in uniform bit distribution (with CatalanStego). Popular steganography tools based on LSB differ significantly in the approach of information concealment.

Figure 9 shows the distribution of the bits for a single selected image where secret information is embedded with the LSB algorithm (left) and the distribution of the bits for a single selected image where secret information is embedded with CatalanStego method (right). In this case, only showed built-in bits for the value of 1, while the message bits are represented by the zero-omitted (Octave GUI environment).

For this reason, can conclude that the proposed method gives a good distribution of the bits in the image. This certainly makes it difficult for steganalysis.

Figure 9. Distribution of bits in the medical image

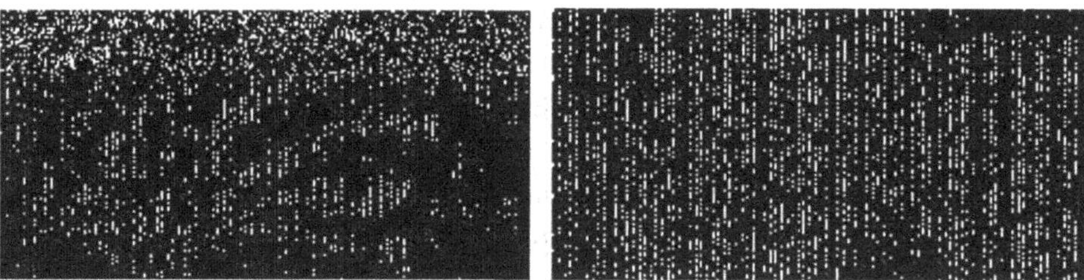

The authors will now show that the proposed method meets another condition, which is to load the three channels on the medical image (R, G, B) evenly. Figure 10 shows the distribution of bits in R, G, B channels, and it can be seen to be fairly even, which means that all channels are equally burdened (the right image is the zoomed part from the left picture). This feature in hiding medical data in the image goes hand in hand with proposed solution for encryption and hiding data in the eHealth application.

Figure 10. Uniform distribution on R, G, B channels

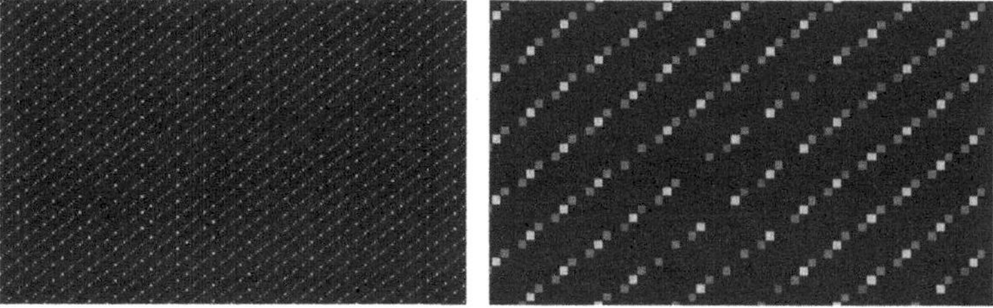

In the process of display of medical images are to be achieved the most realistic display of medical images in order to better quality of stego-image compared to the original. In thier paper (Saracevic, Masovic, et al., 2013), the authors have presented an algorithm for performing optimal triangulation on three-dimensional image data which enables a better reflection of medical images. In mentioned paper presents designed Java software solution which provides good results in terms of execution speed of extract medical data and savings of memory space. The importance of present method can be considered from two aspects: speed and effective storage.

CONCLUSION AND FURTHER WORKS

It's visible that the specialized area of data security and cyber-medicine is becoming a very challenging area that will probably drastically change medical practice. The openness, integrity, authenticity, and availability of medical information and procedures in cyberspace is a sensitive issue of cyber medicine and medical application of the Internet in general.

Health data according to all European regulations are very sensitive data, while their processing can have a major impact on the lives of individuals. Disposing of real and protected information makes it possible to prepare reliable reports. At the same time, these reports simplify the treatment and check the information exchange with emphasis on security and reliability. The development and introduction of new communication technologies that enable global networking and the use of cryptographic and steganographic methods in the eHealth system enable the change of the health care system. They improve security in the data flow, boost healthcare system users, and reduce costs and time. Protection and security of data in the e-health system are of great importance for the development of the healthcare system of one country.

With this chapter, the authors gave several applications of encryption and the hiding of medical data. The authors create an interesting combination of cryptography and steganography in order to efficiently design an application for security, authenticity, and protection of the integrity of sensitive medical data. Their theoretical bases of research are followed by experimental testing. More specifically, the authors provide a case study which includes encryption and hiding modules and implementing in the Java programming language.

A GUI eHealth application implement that has all the necessary elements for easy and efficient encryption and hiding patient data. Cryptanalysis of the proposed solution done through the following aspects: time (speed) and storage (space) complexity to find the complete Catalan-key space, leaking information and machine learning-based identification of the encryption method.

In addition, also the authors stage steganalysis of the proposed solution in the following aspects: the amount of information per pixel in the stego image, approximate entropy - original vs. stego image and bit distribution in stego image.

Bearing in mind the fact that cryptography and steganography are very dynamic areas, that they are current and that they are very widespread, this chapter covers only some of their basic concepts and give a small contribution in the application of medical data protection. The proposed method can be further improved and adapted to more contemporary approaches in steganography and cryptography. In many scientific studies, works, and monographs, when it comes to the future of cryptography, quantum cryptography has emerged as a result of discovery in the field of quantum computing (Koscielny, Kurkowski, Srebrny, 2013). It is important to note that quantum and DNA cryptography, in the near future, will be the basis for protecting confidential documents in medics. Accordingly, the proposal for future work could relate precisely to the application of such methods based on combinatorial mathematics in quantum cryptography and the improvement of existing algorithms and methods in cryptology and steganography.

REFERENCES

Adamović, S., Šarac, M., Veinović, M., Jevremović, A., & Milosavljević, M. (2013). *An add-on for networking CrypTool 2 simulation environments.* Faculty of computing and informatics, Singidunum University, Belgrade, Serbia. (in Serbian)

Ahmad, T., Studiawan, H., Ahmad, H. S., Ijtihadie, R. M., & Wibisono, W. (2014, October). Shared secret-based steganography for protecting medical data. *Proceedings of the 2014 International Conference on Computer, Control, Informatics and Its Applications (IC3INA)* (pp. 87-92). IEEE.

Arslan, M. U., & Rehan, M. U. (2018). Using Image Steganography for Providing Enhanced Medical Data security. Proceedings of the *15th IEEE annual consumer communications & networking conference,* Las Vegas, NV. IEEE.

Hamid, H. A., Rahman, S. M. M., Hossain, M. S., & Almogren, A. (2017). A Security Model for Preserving the Privacy of Medical Big Data in a Healthcare Cloud Using a Fog Computing Facility with Pairing-Based Cryptography. *IEEE Access*, *5*, 22313–22328. doi:10.1109/ACCESS.2017.2757844

Kahn, C. E. Jr, Carrino, J. A., Flynn, M. J., Peck, D. J., & Horii, S. C. (2007). DICOM and Radiology: Past, Present, and Future. *Journal of the American College of Radiology*, *4*(9), 652–657. doi:10.1016/j.jacr.2007.06.004 PMID:17845973

Kamberović, H., Saracevic, M., & Koricanin, E. (2015). The standard for digital imaging and communications in medicine – DICOM. *University Journal of Information Technology and Economics*, *2*(1), 1–4.

Kannammal, A., & Subha, R. S. (2012). DICOM Image Authentication and Encryption Based on RSA and AES Algorithms. In *Trends in Intelligent Robotics, Automation, and Manufacturing*. Berlin: Springer. doi:10.1007/978-3-642-35197-6_39

Kobayashi, L. O. M., Furuie, S. S., & Barreto, P. S. L. (2009). Providing Integrity and Authenticity in DICOM Images: A Novel Approach. *IEEE Transactions on Information Technology in Biomedicine*, *13*(4), 582–589. doi:10.1109/TITB.2009.2014751 PMID:19244022

Kościelny, C., Kurkowski, M., & Srebrny, M. (2013). *Modern Cryptography Primer: Theoretical Foundations and Practical Applications*. Berlin, Germany: Springer. doi:10.1007/978-3-642-41386-5

Mahua, B., Koushik, P., Goutam, G., & … . (2015). Generation of Novel Encrypted Code using Cryptography for Multiple Level Data Security for Electronic Patient Record. *Proceedings of the IEEE International Conference on Bioinformatics and Biomedicine*, Washington, DC (pp. 916-921). IEEE.

Mantos, L. K., & Maglogiannis, I. P. (2016). Sensitive Patient Data Hiding using a ROI Reversible Steganography Scheme for DICOM Images. *Journal of Medical Systems*, *40*(6), 1–17. doi:10.100710916-016-0514-5 PMID:27167526

Marić, N., & Pejnović, P. (2004). Digital imaging and communication in medicine. *Proceedings of the IX Scientific Conference - Information Technology - Present and Future,* Montenegro. Academic Press.

Mašovic, S., Saracevic, M., Kamberovic, H., & Milovic, B. (2010). Information and communication technology as a tool for establishing e-health. *Proceedings of the 10th International Conference -Research and Development in Mechanical Industry RaDMI 2010* (pp. 624-632). Academic Press.

Mustra, M., Delac, K., & Grgic, M. (2008). Overview of the DICOM Standard. *Proceedings of the 50th International Symposium*, Zadar, Croatia (pp. 39–44). Academic Press.

Natsheh, Q. N., Li, A. B., & Gale, G. (2016). Security of Multi-frame DICOM Images Using XOR Encryption Approach. *Procedia Computer Science*, *90*, 175–181. doi:10.1016/j.procs.2016.07.018

Pianykh, O. S. (2012). *DICOM Security: Digital Imaging and Communications in Medicine*. Berlin, Germany: Springer. doi:10.1007/978-3-642-10850-1

Reiner, B. (2015). Strategies for Medical Data Extraction and Presentation Part 2: Creating a Customizable Context and User-Specific Patient Reference Database. *Journal of Digital Imaging*, *28*(3), 249–255. doi:10.100710278-015-9794-4 PMID:25833767

Reljin, I., & Gavrovska, A. (2013). Telemedicine. Belgrade, Serbia: Academic Thought. (in Serbian)

Rodriguez-Colin, R., Claudia, F., & Trinidad-Blas, G. J. (2007). Data Hiding Scheme for Medical Images. *Proceedings of the 17th International Conference on Electronics, Communications and Computers*, Cholula, Puebla (pp. 32-32). Academic Press.

Saba, S. (2018). *Generating all balanced parentheses: A deep dive into an interview question,* Retrieved from https://sahandsaba.com/interview-question-generating-all-balanced

Sampaio, R. A., & Jackowski, M. P. (2013). Assessment of Steganographic Methods in Medical Imaging. *Proceedings of the XXVI SIBGRAPI Conference on Graphics Patterns and Images*, Arequipa, Peru. Academic Press.

Saracevic, M., Adamovic, S., & Bisevac, E. (2018). Applications of Catalan numbers and Lattice Path combinatorial problem in cryptography. *Acta Polytechnica Hungarica: Journal of Applied Sciences*, *15*(7), 91–110.

Saracevic, M., Adamović, S., Miškovic, V., Maček, N., & Šarac, M. (2019). A novel approach to steganography based on the properties of Catalan numbers and Dyck words. *Future Generation Computer Systems,* 100, 186 – 197.

Saracevic, M., Hadzic, M., & Koricanin, E. (2017). Generating Catalan-keys based on dynamic programming and their application in steganography. *International Journal of Industrial Engineering and Management*, *8*(4), 219–227.

Saracevic, M., Koricanin, E., & Bisevac, E. (2017). Encryption based on Ballot, Stack permutations and Balanced Parentheses using Catalan-keys. *Journal of Information Technology and Applications*, *7*(2), 69–77.

Saracevic, M., Masovic, S., Milosevic, D., & Kudumovic, M. (2013). Proposal for applying the optimal triangulation method in 3D medical image processing. *Balkan Journal of Health Science*, *1*(1), 27–34.

Saracevic, M., Selimi, A., Selimovic, F. (2018). Generation of cryptographic keys with algorithm of polygon triangulation and Catalan numbers. *Computer Science – AGH, 19*(3), 243-256.

Stanley, R. (2005). *Catalan addendum to Enumerative Combinatorics*. Massachusetts Institute of Technology. Retrieved from http://www-math.mit.edu/~rstan/ec/catadd.pdf

Tan, C. K., Changwei, N. J., Xu, X., Poh, C. L., & … . (2011). Security Protection of DICOM Medical Images Using Dual-Layer Reversible Watermarking with Tamper Detection Capability. *Journal of Digital Imaging*, *24*(3), 528–540. doi:10.100710278-010-9295-4 PMID:20414697

Tokuo, U., Akiko, O., & Tsutomu, G. (2014). Security Model for Secure Transmission of Medical Image Data Using Steganography. In *Integrating information technology and management for quality of care*. IOS Press.

This research was previously published in the Handbook of Research on Intelligent Data Processing and Information Security Systems; pages 25-42, copyright year 2020 by Engineering Science Reference (an imprint of IGI Global).

Chapter 30

Advancements in Data Security and Privacy Techniques Used in IoT-Based Hospital Applications

Ankita Tiwari
Amity University, India

Raghuvendra Pratap Tripathi
Amity University, India

Dinesh Bhatia
North Eastern Hill University, India

ABSTRACT

The risk of encountering new diseases is on the rise in medical centers globally. By employing advancements in medical sensors technology, new health monitoring programs are being developed for continuous monitoring of physiological parameters in patients. Since the stored medical data is personal health record of an individual, it requires delicate and secure handling. In wireless transmission networks, medical data is disposed of to avoid loss due to alteration, eavesdropping, etc. Hence, privacy and security of the medical data are the major considerations during wireless transfer through Medical Sensor Network of MSNs. This chapter delves upon understanding the working of a secure monitoring system wherein the data could be continuously observed with the support of MSNs. Process of sanctioning secure data to authorized users such as physician, clinician, or patient through the key provided to access the file are also explained. Comparative analysis of the encryption techniques such as paillier, RSA, and ELGamal has been included to make the reader aware in selecting a useful technique for a particular hospital application.

INTRODUCTION

A medical application necessitates treating patient care beyond the healthcare continuum. The healthcare

DOI: 10.4018/978-1-6684-6311-6.ch030

Figure 1. IoT healthcare network (IoThNet) issues

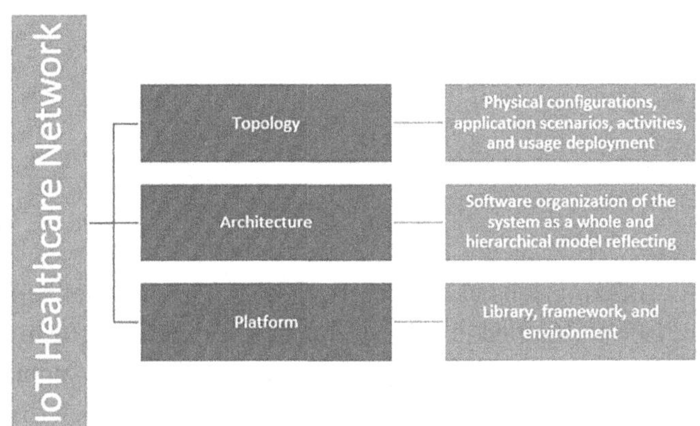

continuum includes homecare, hospital, and long-term care facility. The medical devices which are connected through the Internet are referred as Internet of Things (IoT) applications. IoT applications have been widely investigated, forecasted for widespread future use even located on small scale. Any hospital that starts "smart beds" programme, can detect whether the hospital bed is occupied or not, analyses when the patient requires assistance to use the lavatory or move around and send desired information to the available nurse or nearest hospital staff for patient support (R. Babu, 2015). This smart bed has self-adjustable features, according to the appropriate patient load and nature of support required which can be provided without manual assistance. Some other areas where smart management is being used are home medication dispensers to automatically upload patient data to a cloud server when medication should be avoided or any other health symptoms which require immediate attention of the nursing staff or at home medical care personnel (Chouffani, 2016).

The definition of IoT given by IEEE is: "...a self-configured and adaptive system consisting of networks of sensors and smart objects whose purpose is to interconnect "all" things, including every day and industrial objects, in such a way as to make them intelligent, programmable and more capable of interacting with humans" (Internet of Things, 2018). The information provided by Gartner (Garthner, 2018) is that excluding cell phones, tablets, and computers, there are more than 8.5 billion devices connected through internet frequently which is a large number of devices connected online.

Nowadays, advancement in the proliferation and bioengineering of body sensor platforms has authorized the recognition of mobile health and pervasive systems. In this system, sensors are placed on the patient's body. These sensors record the data and send it to end user. Data transfer and collection must be private and secured because of using open network environment and mobile system considering patient safety aspects (Halperin, Heydt-Benjamin, Fu, Kohno, & Maisel, 2008) (Kumar & Lee., 2013). Some medical devices in present market are unguarded to attacks (Halperin, Heydt-Benjamin, Fu, Kohno, & Maisel, 2008) (Radclliffe., 2011). We contemplate a comprehensive system architecture where some specified technologies are combined to support the crucial patient's data security aspects in MSN based mobile health system.

This security approach depends on standardized protocol i.e. Host Identity Protocol (HIP) (Gurtov, Komu, & Moskowitz., 2009). Till now, HIP has succeeded some promising security algorithms for IoT devices and mobile networks (Heer, 2007) (Moskowitz., 2012) (Olivereau., 2012) (Urien., 2013). In this chapter, review of advancement in data security and privacy technologies by employing IoT in the medical world has been mentioned.

RELATED WORK

Medical Sensing

There is a long history of utilizing sensors in prescription and general wellbeing (Aberg, Togawa, & Spelman, 2002) (Wilson, 1999). Installed in an assortment of restorative instruments for use at doctor's facilities, center, and homes, sensors give patients and their human services suppliers understanding into physiological and physical wellbeing states that are basic to the location, determination, treatment, and administration of infirmities. A lot of present day solution would basically not be conceivable nor be practical without sensors, for example, thermometers, pulse screens, glucose screens, EKG, PPG, EEG, and different types of imaging sensors. The capacity to quantify physiological state is likewise basic for interventional gadgets, for example, pacemakers and insulin pumps.

Restorative sensors consolidate transducers for recognizing electrical, warm, optical, compound, hereditary, and different signs with physiological starting point with flag handling calculations to appraise highlights demonstrative of a man's wellbeing status. Sensors past those that specifically measure wellbeing state have additionally discovered use in the act of prescription. For instance, area and closeness detecting advancements (Khan & Skinner, 2002) are being utilized for enhancing the conveyance of patient consideration and work process productivity in doctor's facilities (Emory & Lenert, 2005), following the spread of maladies by general wellbeing organizations (Hanjagi, Srihari, & Rayamane, 2007), and observing individuals' wellbeing related practices (e.g., movement levels) and introduction to negative natural components, for example, contamination (Patrick, 2007). There are three particular measurements along which progresses in therapeutic detecting advancements are occurring. We expound on every one of the three in the following passages that pursue.

Sensing Modality

Growth and advancement in modern day technologies, for example, MEMS, imaging, and microfluidic and nano-fluidic lab-on-chip are prompting new types of synthetic, organic, and genomic detecting and investigations accessible outside the bounds of a research center at the purpose of-care. By empowering new modest indicative abilities, these detecting advances guarantee to upset human services both regarding settling general wellbeing emergency because of irresistible illnesses (Yager, et al., 2006) and furthermore empowering early location and customized medicines.

Size and Cost

Most therapeutic sensors have customarily been too expensive and complex to be utilized outside of clinical situations. Be that as it may, ongoing advancements in microelectronics and registering have made numerous types of restorative detecting all the more easily available to people at their homes, work places, and other living spaces.

The first to rise (Aberg, Togawa, & Spelman, 2002) were convenient therapeutic sensors for home utilization (e.g., circulatory strain and blood glucose screens). By empowering, continuous estimations of basic physiological information without expecting visits to the specialist, these instruments upset the administration of illnesses, for example, hypertension and diabetes.

Next, walking medicinal sensors, whose little frame factor enabled them to be worn or conveyed by a man, came into existence (Aberg, Togawa, & Spelman, 2002). Such sensors empower people to constantly gauge physiological parameters while connected with routine life exercises. Models incorporate wearable pulse and physical movement screens and Holter screens. These gadgets target wellness lovers, wellbeing cognizant people and watch heart or neural occasions that may not show amid a short visit to the specialist.

All the more as of late implanted medicinal sensors incorporated with assistive and prosthetic gadgets for geriatrics (Wu, et al., 2008) and orthotics (Dunkels, Gr¨onvall, & Voigt, 2004) have been developed in recent past.

At last, we are seeing the development of implantable restorative sensors for persistently estimating inner wellbeing status and physiological signs. At times the reason for existing is to consistently screen wellbeing parameters that are not remotely accessible, for example, intraocular weight in glaucoma patients (Dresher & Irazoqui, 2007). The objective in different cases is to utilize the estimations as triggers for physiological intercessions that avoid approaching unfavorable occasions (e.g., epileptic seizures (Raghunathan, Ward, Roy, & Irazoqui, 2009)) and for physical help (e.g., mind controlled engine prosthetics (Linderman, et al., 2008)). Given their implantable nature, these gadgets confront serious size requirements and need to impart and get control remotely.

Connectivity

Driven by advances in data innovation, medicinal sensors have turned out to be progressively interconnected with different gadgets. Early therapeutic sensors were to a great extent confined with incorporated user interfaces (UIs) for showing their estimations.

In this way, sensors wound up fit for interfacing to outer gadgets by means of wired interfaces, for example, RS 232, USB, and Ethernet. All the more as of late, restorative sensors have joined remote associations, both short-run, for example, Bluetooth, Zigbee, and close field radios to convey remotely to close-by PCs, PDAs, or cell phones, and long-extend, for example, WiFi or cell correspondences, to discuss specifically with distributed computing administrations. Other than the accommodation of tether less activity, such remote associations allow sensor estimations to be sent to parental figures while patients experience their day by day work life far from home, hence proclaiming a time of universal ongoing therapeutic detecting. We take note of that with compact and mobile sensors, the wired or remote availability to distributed computing assets is irregular (e.g., network might be accessible just when the sensor is in cell inclusion territory or docked to the client's home PC).

Accordingly such sensors can likewise record estimations in non-volatile memory for transferring at a later time when they can be imparted to medicinal services staff and further investigated.

Wireless Sensor Platforms

Late years have seen the development of different implanted figuring stages that incorporate preparing, stockpiling, remote systems administration, and sensors. These inserted figuring stages offer the capacity to detect physical wonders at fleeting and spatial constancies that were already unfeasible. Installed processing stages utilized for medicinal services applications extend from cell phones to specific remote detecting stages, known as bits, that have considerably more stringent asset limitations as far as accessible figuring power, memory, organize data transfer capacity, and accessible vitality.

Existing bits regularly utilize 8 or 16-bit microcontrollers with several KBs of RAM, many KBs of ROM for program stockpiling and outer stockpiling as Flash memory. These gadgets work at a couple of milliwatts while running at around 10 MHz (Polastre, Szewczyk, & Culler, 2005). A large portion of the circuits can be controlled off, so the backup power can be around one microwatt. In the event that such a gadget is dynamic for 1% of the time, its normal power utilization is only a couple of microwatts empowering long haul activity with two AA batteries. Bits are normally furnished with low-control radios, for example, those agreeable with the IEEE 802.15.4 standard for remote sensor systems. Such radios as a rule transmit at rates between 10-250 Kbps, expend around 20-60 milliwatts, and their correspondence extend is normally estimated in several meters. At last, bits incorporate various simple and computerized interfaces that empower them to associate with a wide assortment of ware sensors.

These equipment developments are paralleled by advances in installed working frameworks (Dunkels, Gr¨onvall, & Voigt, 2004) (Hil, Szewczyk, Woo, Hollar, Culler, & Pister, 2000), segment based programming dialects (Gay, Levis, Von Behren, Welsh, Brewer, & Culler, 2014), and organizing conventions (Gnawali, Fonseca, Jamieson, Moss, & Levis, 2009) (Buettner, Yee, Anderson, & Han, 2006). Rather than asset compelled bits, cell phones give all the more great microchips, bigger information stockpiling, and higher system data transfer capacity through cell and IEEE 802.11 remote interfaces to the detriment of higher vitality utilization. Their corresponding attributes make cell phones and bits integral stages appropriate for various classifications of medicinal services applications, which is discussed in following sections of this chapter.

MEDICAL SENSOR NETWORK

When sensors are implanted within patient body or wearable, these sensors web to form a network. This network is called as medical sensor network (MSN). These sensor webs receive the information from its surrounding and save in its personal information space. The saved data is sent to remote monitoring systems or prescription systems with information sent to the physician. Figure 3 shows the basic architecture of MSN. The MSN refers to the positioning of different sensors of an IoT medical network and designate representable outline of seamless medical environments. In figure 2, it is shown that a heterogeneous computing network receives and collects a huge amount of sensor data and vital signs such as body temperature, blood pressure (BP), oxygen saturation, and electrocardiograms (ECG) and generates a general IoT medical topology.

At the time of data transmission through wired or wireless medium, there may be a probability of data or information loss. Wireless data transmission is used for sending data from sensors to other place. At the time of wireless data transmission, there are some encryption methods available, which are used to secure data to maintain patient confidentiality. When the sensor web connects with network, it forms a body sensor network (BSN).

Figure 2. Sensor web on human body or patient's body

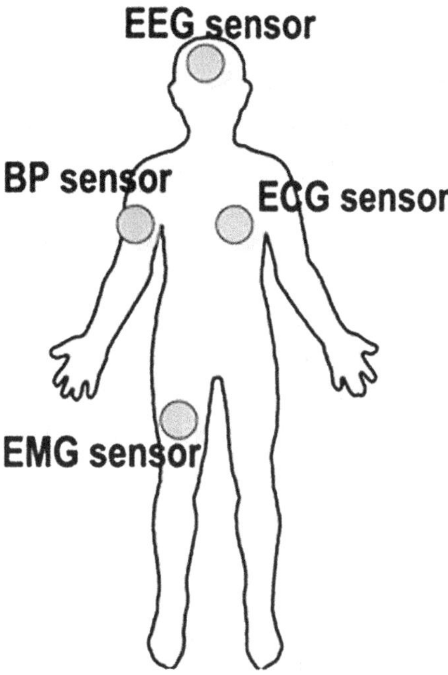

Architecture of MSN

The MSN architecture alludes to a frame for the description of MSN physical elements, its working principles, techniques, and their functional organization. In figure 3, the basic architecture of ambient assisted bio device and telehealth endorsed by Continua Health Alliance has been explained. The main key issues that have been recognized for MSN architecture (Shahamabadi, Ali, Varahram, & Jara, 2013) include multimedia streaming, reliable interaction between caregivers and IoT gateways, and the inter-

Figure 3. Medical sensor network or body sensor network and its backend services

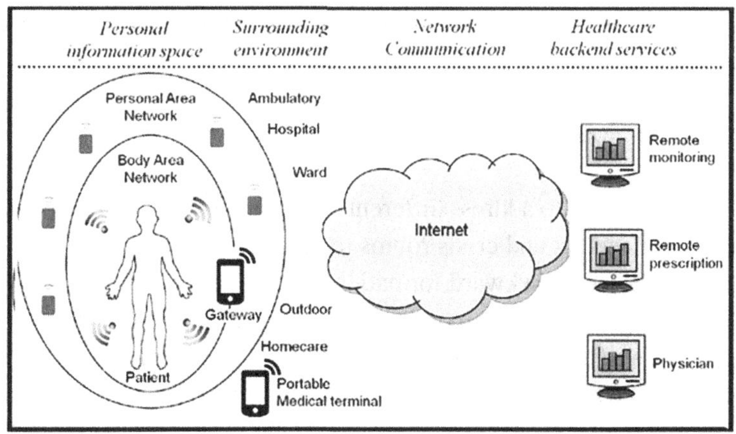

functionality of IoT gateway and wireless personal area network (WPAN)/ wireless local area network (WLAN).

6LoWPAN is based on IPv6, and used for designing MSN architecture (Imadali, Karanasiou, Petrescu, Sifniadis, Veque, & Angelidis, 2012) (Jara, Zamora, & Skarmeta, Jun. 2012) (Maglogiannis, 2012). In (Bormann, 2009), the layer structure of 6LoWPAN is defined which is shown in figure 4. According to the MSN concept, body sensor applications of IPv6 and 6LoWPAN, and the sensor devices for data sending over 802.15.4 protocol. With the help of transmission line protocol (UDP: user datagram protocol), data is received at sensor nodes.

Medical systems have been surveyed for vehicular networks. The medical data, which is captured, have been evaluated with IPv6 application protocol (Imadali, Karanasiou, Petrescu, Sifniadis, Veque, & Angelidis, 2012). Moreover, mobile IPv6 (MIPv6) is not supported by 6LoWPAN, it is a subset of IPv6 protocol versatility. For introducing mobility to 6LoWPAN, there is a protocol proposed in (Shahamabadi, Ali, Varahram, & Jara, Jul. 2013), and data is transferred among base networks, mobile patient nodes and visited networks.

Healthcare Applications

Remotely organized sensors empower thick spatiotemporal testing of physical, physiological, mental, subjective, and social procedures in spaces running from individual to structures to significantly bigger scale ones. Such thick inspecting crosswise over spaces of various scales is bringing about tangible data based social insurance applications which, dissimilar to those portrayed in Section-Medical Sensing, circuit and total data gathered from numerous dispersed sensors. Also, the modernity of detecting has expanded immensely with the advances in shabby and small scale, yet excellent sensors for home that individuals can utilize, the improvement of refined machine learning calculations that empower complex conditions, for example, stress, sadness, and dependence on gathered information from tactile data, lastly the rise of unavoidable Internet availability encouraging convenient spread of sensor data to guardians.

In what pursues, we present a rundown of medicinal services applications empowered by these advancements. Observing in Mass-Casualty Disasters, while triage conventions for crisis therapeutic administrations as of now exist (Hodgetts & Mackaway-Jones, 1995). Their adequacy can rapidly corrupt with expanding number of exploited people. In addition, there is a need to enhance the evaluation of the people on call's wellbeing status amid such mass-loss catastrophes. The expanded compactness, adaptability, and quickly deployable nature of remote detecting frameworks can be utilized to naturally report the triage levels of various unfortunate casualties and ceaselessly track the wellbeing status of people on call at the fiasco scene all the more viably.

Vital Sign Monitoring in Hospitals

Remote detecting innovation helps to address different disadvantages related with wired sensors that are regularly utilized in healing centers and crisis rooms to screen patients (Ko, 2010). The natural scatter of wires appended to a patient isn't awkward for patients prompting confined portability and more uneasiness, but on the other hand is difficult to oversee for the staff. Very normal are consider separations of sensors by tired patients and disappointments to reattach sensors legitimately as patients are moved around in a doctor's facility and gave off crosswise over various units. Remote detecting equipment, those are less recognizable and have diligent system availability to backend restorative record frameworks help lessen the tangles of wires and patient tension, while additionally diminishing the event of mistakes.

At-Home and Mobile Aging

As individuals age, they encounter an assortment of subjective, physical, and social changes that test their wellbeing, autonomy and personal satisfaction (Wood, Fang, Stankovic, & He, 2006). Illnesses, for example, diabetes, asthma, perpetual obstructive pneumonic sickness, congestive heart disappointment, and memory decay are trying to screen and treat. These sicknesses can profit by patients playing a functioning job in the observing procedure. Remotely arranged sensors implanted in individuals' living spaces or carried on the individual can gather data about close to home physical, physiological, and social states with examples progressively and all over. Such information can likewise be associated with social and natural setting. From such "living records", valuable deductions about wellbeing and prosperity can be drawn. This can be utilized for mindfulness and individual examination to help with rolling out conduct improvements, and to impart to parental figures for early location and mediation. In the meantime such techniques are successful and financial methods for checking age-related diseases.

Figure 4. Protocol stack of different layers in 6LoWPAN
Source: Bormann, 2009

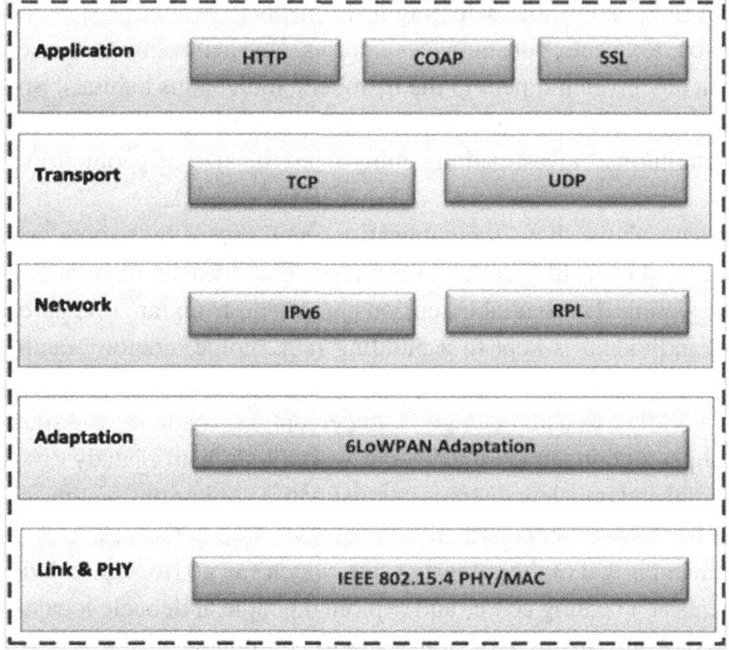

Assistance With Motor and Sensory Decline

Another utilization of remote arranged detecting is to give dynamic help and direction to patients adapting to declining tactile and engine capacities. We are seeing the development of new sorts of shrewd assistive gadgets that make utilization of data about the patient's physiological and physical state from sensors worked in the gadget, worn or even embedded on the client's individual, and installed in the environment. These clever assistive gadgets cannot just tailor their reaction to singular clients and their present setting, yet in addition give the client and their guardian's essential criticism for longer-term preparing. Conventional assistive gadgets, for example, sticks, props, walkers, and wheel seats can combine data from implicit and outer sensors to furnish the clients with nonstop customized input and direction towards the right use of the gadgets. Such gadgets can likewise adjust the physical qualities of the gadget regarding the unique situation and an endorsed preparing or recovery regimen (Wu, et al., 2008). Moreover, remote arranged detecting empowers new sorts of assistive gadgets, for example, way-discovering (Coughlan, 2007) and strolling route (Bohonos, 2007) for the outwardly debilitated.

Large-Scale In-Field Medical and Behavioral Studies

Wearable sensors together with sensor-prepared Internet-associated cell phones have started to change restorative and general wellbeing research thinking by empowering conduct and physiological information to be persistently gathered from an extensive number of dispersed subjects as they lead their everyday lives. With their capacity to give understanding into subject expresses that can't be repeated in controlled clinical and lab settings and that can't be estimated from PC helped review self-report techniques, such detecting frameworks are getting to be basic to restorative, mental, and social research. In reality, a noteworthy objective of the Exposure Biology program under NIH's Genes and Environment Initiative (GEI) is to grow such field deployable detecting instruments to evaluate exposures to condition (e.g., psychosocial push, habit, toxicants, consume less calories, physical action) unbiased, consequently, and for quite a long time at any given moment in the members' indigenous habitats. Specialists, both inside the GEI program and somewhere else, have additionally perceived the utility of such detecting in making estimations for longitudinal investigations going from the size of people to substantial populaces (Krumm, 2007).

As the four precedents above show, the applications empowered by remote organized detecting innovations are disseminated over different measurements. One measurement is the spatial and fleeting extent of circulated detecting. The spatial extension can extend from tangible perceptions of wellbeing status made when an individual is kept to a building (e.g., home, doctor's facility) or an all-around characterized locale (e.g., fiasco site) to perceptions made as an individual moves around throughout day by day life. The worldly extension can go from perceptions made for the span of a sickness or an occasion to long haul perceptions made for dealing with a long haul malady or for general wellbeing purposes. Diverse spatial and transient degrees put distinctive limitations on the accessibility of vitality and correspondences framework, and distinctive necessities on ergonomics.

A second measurement is that of the gathering size, which can go from an individual patient at home, to gatherings of patients at a healing center and exploited people at debacle locales, and the distance to vast scattered populace of subjects in a medicinal report or a plague.

The last basic measurement is the kind of remote systems administration and detecting advances that are utilized: on-body sensors with long range radios, body-territory systems of short-run on-body sensors with a long-go portal, sensors embedded in-body with remote correspondence and power conveyance, remote sensors inserted in assistive gadgets conveyed by people, remote sensors implanted in the earth, and sensors installed in the omnipresent versatile cell phones. Unmistakably, there is a rich decent variety of remote detecting innovation with correlative qualities and obliging diverse applications. Ordinarily, in excess of one kind of detecting innovation gets utilized for a solitary application.

TECHNICAL CHALLENGES

In the sections that tail we portray a portion of the center difficulties in planning remote sensor systems for social insurance applications. While not comprehensive, the difficulties in this rundown length an extensive variety of subjects, from center PC frameworks topics, for example, versatility, unwavering quality, and productivity, to vast scale information mining and information affiliation issues, and even lawful issues.

Trustworthiness

Medicinal services applications force strict necessities on end-to-end framework dependability and information conveyance. For instance, beat oximetry applications, which measure the levels of oxygen in a man's blood, must convey no less than one, estimation at regular intervals (Intille, 2006). Besides, end-clients require estimations that are sufficiently exact to be utilized in restorative research. Utilizing a similar heartbeat oximetry model, estimations must go astray at most 4% from the real oxygen fixations in the blood (Intille, 2006). At long last, applications that consolidate estimations with activation, for example, control of mixture pumps and patient controlled absence of pain (PCA) gadgets, force imperatives on the conclusion to-end conveyance inertness. We term the blend of information conveyance and quality properties the dependability of the framework and guarantee that therapeutic detecting applications require elevated amounts of reliability.

Various components confuse the frameworks' capacity to give the dependability that applications require. To begin with, restorative offices, where a portion of these frameworks will be conveyed, can be exceptionally unforgiving conditions for radio recurrence (RF) correspondences. This brutality is the consequence of auxiliary factors, for example, the nearness of metal entryways and dividers and also consider exertion to give radiation protecting, for instance in working rooms that utilization fluoroscopy for orthopedic techniques. Truth be told, Ko et al. as of late found that parcel misfortunes for radios following the IEEE 802.15.4 standard is higher in healing facilities than other indoor conditions (Liao, Fox, & Kautz, 2005). Also, gadgets that utilization 802.15.4 radios are powerless to impedance from WiFi systems, Bluetooth gadgets, and cordless telephones which are all intensely utilized in numerous healing centers.

The effect of hindrances and impedance is exacerbated by the way that most remote sensor organize frameworks utilize low power radios to accomplish long framework lifetimes (i.e., expanding the battery re-charging cycle). The other ramifications of utilizing low-control radios are that the system throughput of these gadgets is restricted. For instance, the hypothetical most extreme throughput of IEEE 802.15.4 radios is 250 Kbps and much lower by and by because of imperatives presented by MAC conventions also, multi-bounce interchanges. Considering that applications, for example, movement and action observing catch many examples every second, these throughput limits imply that a system can bolster few gadgets or that just a subset of the estimations can be conveyed progressively.

Sometimes the nature of the information gathered from remote detecting frameworks can be endangered not by sensor blames and breakdowns, but rather by client activities. This is genuine notwithstanding for cell phone based detecting frameworks for which huge numbers of the previously mentioned RF challenges are less serious. Considering that remote detecting frameworks for social insurance will be utilized by the elderly and medicinal staff with small preparing, misfortune in quality because of administrator abuse is a major concern. In addition, since remote detecting empowers persistent accumulation of physiological information under conditions not initially imagined by the sensors' engineers, the gathered estimations might be dirtied by an assortment of antiquities. For instance, movement antiques can affect the nature of pulse and breath estimations. In this manner, assessing the nature of estimations gathered under questionable conditions is a noteworthy test that WSNs for human services must address. Thus, this test implies that WSNs need to utilize methods for mechanized information approval and purifying and interfaces to encourage and check their right establishment. To wrap things up, WSNs in social insurance ought to give metadata that illuminate information shoppers of the nature of the information conveyed.

Privacy and Security

Remote sensor arrangements in human services are utilized to decide the exercises of every day living (ADL) and give information to longitudinal examinations. It is then simple to see that such WSNs additionally present chances to disregard protection. Besides, the significance of anchoring such frameworks will keep on ascending as their appropriation rate increments.

The main protection challenge experienced is the ambiguous determination of security. The Heath Insurance Portability and Accountability Act (HIPPA) by the U.S. government is one endeavor to characterize this term. One issue is that HIPPA and in addition different laws characterize protection utilizing human dialect (e.g., English), consequently, making a semantic bad dream. The protection detail dialects have been produced to determine security arrangements for a framework formally. Once the protection details are determined, medicinal services frameworks must authorize this security and furthermore have the capacity to express clients' solicitations for information get to and the framework's arrangements. These solicitations ought to be assessed against the predefined approaches with the end goal to choose on the off chance that they ought to be conceded or denied. This structure offers ascend to numerous new research moves, some extraordinary to WSNs, as we depict in the passages that pursue.

1. Since setting can influence security, approach dialects must have the capacity to express extraordinary kinds of setting from nature, for example, time, space, physiological parameter detecting, ecological detecting, and stream based loud information. Also, the greater part of the setting must be gathered and assessed continuously. Since setting is so focal it should likewise be available in a protected and precise way.
2. There is a need to speak to various kinds of information proprietors and demand subjects in the framework and in addition outside clients and their rights when diverse areas, for example, helped living offices, doctor's facilities, and drug stores cooperate. One of the more troublesome protection issues happens while collaborating frameworks have their own security strategies. Therefore, irregularities in such strategies may emerge crosswise over various frameworks. Hence, on-line consistency checking and notice alongside goals plans are required.
3. There is a need to present to abnormal state collecting solicitations, for example, questioning the normal, greatest, or least perusing of determined detecting information. This security capacity must be bolstered by anonym zing accumulation capacities. This need emerges for applications identified with longitudinal examinations and person to person communication.

4. There is a need to help not just adherence to protection for information inquiries (e.g., information pull demands), yet additionally the security for push setup solicitations to set framework parameters (e.g., for private utilize or arranging particular restorative actuators).
5. Because WSNs screen and control a huge assortment of physical parameters in various settings, it is important to endure a high level of elements and conceivably even permit impermanent security infringement with the end goal to meet practical, wellbeing or execution prerequisites. For instance, an individual wearing an EKG may encounter heart arrhythmia and the continuous announcing of this issue outweighs some current protection prerequisites. At the end of the day to send a crisis caution rapidly it might be important to avoid different security assurances. At whatever point such infringement happen, center medicinal services staff individuals must be advised of such occurrences.

Notwithstanding strategy and database question protection infringement, WSNs are helpless to new side channel security assaults that gain data by watching the radio transmissions of sensors to find private exercises, notwithstanding when the transmissions are encoded. This physical layer assault needs just the season of transmission and the unique finger impression of each message, where a unique mark is an arrangement of highlights of a RF waveform that are exceptional to a specific transmitter. Along these lines, this is known as the Fingerprint and Timing-based Snooping (FATS) assault (Srinivasan, Stankovic, & Whitehouse, 2008).

To execute a FATS assault, a foe records stealthily on the sensors' radio to gather the timestamps and fingerprints of every radio transmission. The enemy at that point utilizes the fingerprints to connect each message with an extraordinary transmitter, and utilizations various periods of induction to derive the area and sort of every sensor. When this is known, different private client exercises and wellbeing conditions can be deduced.

For instance, Srinivasan et al. present this exceptional physical layer security assault and propose arrangements regarding a savvy home situation (Srinivasan, Stankovic, & Whitehouse, 2008). Three layers of surmising are utilized in their work. To begin with, sensors in a similar room are grouped dependent on the closeness of their transmission designs. At that point the general transmission example of each room is passed to a classifier, which consequently distinguishes the sort of room (e.g., washroom or kitchen). Once the kind of room is recognized, the transmission example of every sensor is passed to another classifier, which consequently distinguishes the sort of sensor (e.g., a movement sensor or a cooler entryway). From this data, the foe effortlessly recognizes a few exercises of the home's inhabitants, for example, cooking, showering, and toileting, all with reliably high exactness. From such data it is then conceivable to derive the occupants' wellbeing conditions. Luckily, numerous arrangements with various tradeoffs are feasible for this kind of physical layer assault. Such arrangements incorporate (i) weakening the flag outside of the home to build the bundle misfortune proportion of the spy, (ii) occasionally transmitting radio messages regardless of whether the gadget has information to be sent, (iii) haphazardly postponing radio messages to shroud the time that the relating occasions happened, (iv) concealing the unique mark of the transmitter, and (v) transmitting counterfeit information to copy a genuine occasion.

Sadly, a foe can join data accessible from many (outside) sources with physical layer data to make deductions considerably more precise and intrusive. New arrangements that are practical, address physical layer information, secure against derivations dependent on accumulations of related information, and still allow the first usefulness of the framework to work successfully are required.

A related essential issue, yet unsolved in WSNs is managing security assaults. Security assaults are particularly dangerous to low-control WSN stages in view of a few reasons including the strict asset requirements of the gadgets, negligible openness to the sensors and actuators, and the inconsistent idea of low-control remote correspondences. The security issue is additionally exacerbated by the perception that transient and changeless arbitrary disappointments are regular in WSNs and such disappointments are vulnerabilities that can be misused by assailants. For instance, with these vulnerabilities it is workable for an aggressor to misrepresent setting, adjust get to rights, make disavowal of administration, and, as a rule disturb the task of the framework. This could result in a patient being denied treatment, or more regrettable, accepting the wrong treatment.

Having as a primary concern with one such kind of difficulties, new lightweight security arrangements that can work in these open and asset constrained frameworks are required. Arrangements that adventure the extensive measure of excess found in numerous WSN frameworks are being sought after. This excess makes awesome potential for outlining WSN frameworks that constantly give their objective administrations regardless of the presence of disappointments or assaults. At the end of the day, to meet reasonable framework prerequisites that get from extensive and unattended activity, WSNs must have the capacity to keep on working tastefully and adequately recoup from security assaults. WSNs should likewise be sufficiently adaptable to adjust to assaults not foreseen amid outline or organization time. Work, for example, the one proposed by Wood et al. gives a case of how such issues are tended to, by proposing to plan a self-recuperating framework with the nearness and discovery of assaults, as opposed to attempting to fabricate a totally secure framework (Wood, Fang, Stankovic, & He, 2006).

Data Security

Now a day's data security is one of the basic needs in every sector which include medical, bank, education, defense etc. In almost every field data is transmitted and received through various mediums. There are several encryption algorithms available which provides security to this transmitted data or information. In medical data, the confidential information is in the form of patients name, age, blood group, weight, height etc. which needs to be made secure to prevent its misuse or theft. This is the time to store the data with Internet of Things (IoT), because it is one of the secure place to store patient data for long time duration.

When we talk about data security the first question arises that, "what is the need of data security in medical information?" As it is well know that the identity and privacy breach thefts including medical information are on growth. Ponemon Institute reported (Ponemon Organization, 2015) that since 2010, there is 125 percent increase in criminal attack on medical data which is the main leading cause of information breaches. In the research (Ponemon Organization, 2015), it is also observed that 91 percent of medical organizations have suffered from minimum one data breach, which leads to the loss of more than $2 million.

According to American action forum (Hayes, 2015), it is found that since 2009, medical data breaches have cost the health care system more than $50 billion which is a huge cost. Moreover, medical data cannot be wracked easily, whereas other records such as bank cards can be cancelled quickly. Medical breaches are not only caused by theft, this may also cause by an inadvertent error. Therefore, preventing the data from theft and breaches there is a need to apply specialized data encryption algorithms which have been explained in the section "Data Encryption Techniques".

Figure 5. Cost of data breach per record compromised
Source: Ponemon Organizaztion, 2015

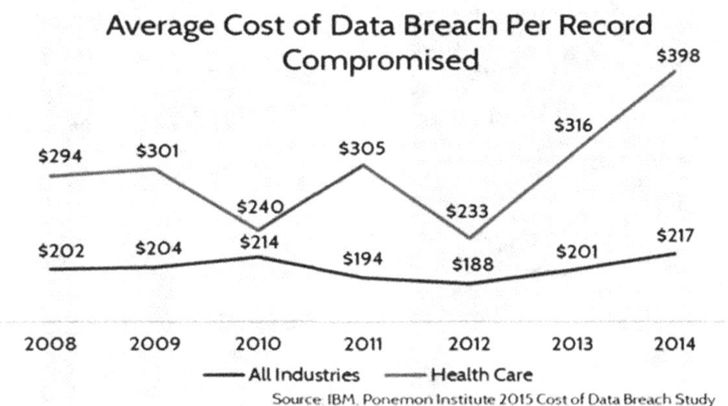

Resource Scarcity

With the end goal to empower little gadget sizes with sensible battery lifetimes, normal remote sensor hubs make utilization of low-control segments with unobtrusive assets. Figure 1 demonstrates a run of the mill wearable sensor hub for therapeutic applications, the SHIMMER stage (Ngoc, 2008). The SHIMMER contains an implanted microcontroller (TI MSP430; 8 MHz clock speed; 10 KB RAM; 48 KB ROM) and a low-control radio (Chipcon CC2420; IEEE 802.15.4; 2.4 GHz; 250 Kbps PHY information rate). The aggregate gadget control spending plan is roughly 60 milliwatts when dynamic, with a rest control deplete of a couple of microwatts. This outline allows little, re-chargeable batteries to keep up gadget lifetimes of hours or days, contingent upon the application's obligation cycles.

There is a great degree constrained calculation, correspondence, and vitality assets of remote sensor hubs prompt various difficulties for framework plan. Programming must be outlined precisely in view of these asset requirements. The insufficient memory requires the utilization of lean, occasion driven

Figure 6. Number of record breaches per year
Source: Hayes, 2015

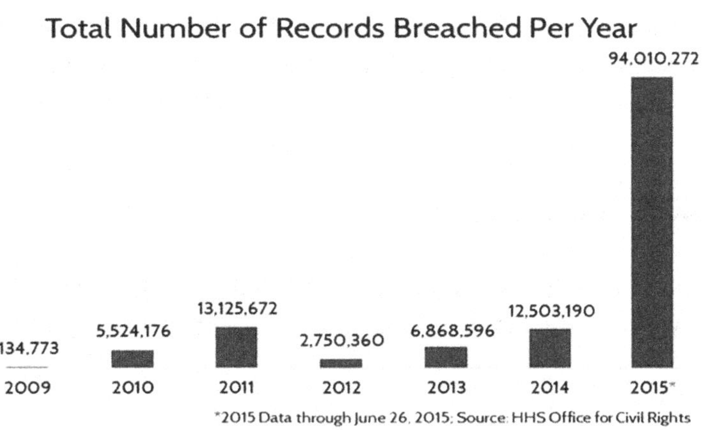

Figure 7. SHIMMER wearable sensor platform

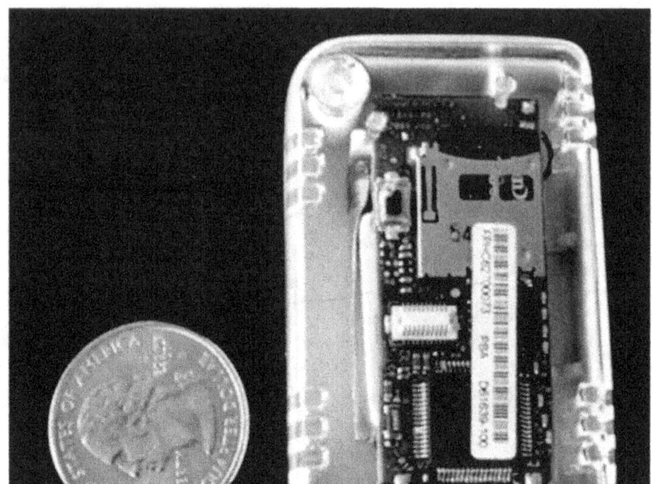

simultaneousness models, and blocks customary OS plans. Computational strength and radio transfer speed are both restricted, necessitating that sensor hubs exchange off calculation and correspondence overheads, for instance, by playing out an unassuming measure of on-board preparing to diminish information transmission prerequisites. At last, application code must be to a great degree cautious with the hub's constrained vitality spending plan, restricting radio correspondence and information handling to broaden the battery lifetime.

While cell phone based frameworks regularly appreciate all the more handling force and remote transmission capacity, the way that they are less adaptable contrasted with adjustable bit stages, confines their ability to forcefully preserve vitality. This prompts shorter re-charge cycles and can restrict the kinds of utilizations that cell phones can bolster.

Another thought for low-control detecting stages is the variance in the asset stack experienced by sensor hubs. Contingent upon the patient's condition, the sensor information being gathered, and the nature of the radio connection, sensor hubs may encounter a wide variety in correspondence and handling load after some time. For instance, if sensor hubs perform multihop directing, a given hub might be required to forward bundles for at least one different hubs alongside transmitting its very own information. The system topology can change after some time, because of hub portability and natural variances in the RF medium, actuating erratic examples of vitality utilization for which the application must be readied.

DATA ENCRYPTION TECHNIQUES

Encryption is a process of encoding an information or data in order to allow only a sanctioned person to access it. The encryption doesn't avert interference, but contradict the comprehensible content to a future interceptor.

Paillier Cryptosystem

This cryptosystem was invented by Pascal Paillier. It was invented in 1999. It is the probabilistic asymmetric cryptographic algorithm for the public key cryptography (Paillier, 1999). The nth residue classes' computation is accepted to be computationally complex. Paillier cryptosystem is an intractability assumption based on decisional composite residuosity assumption (DCRA) (Paillier, 1999). This cryptography scheme is an additive homomorphic encryption method. The homomorphic cryptosystem means that, the encryption of m_1 and m_2 is m_1+m_2.

There are so many encryption algorithm based on additive homomorphic methods. It is most efficient among all of them. Paillier encryption method is an augmentation of Okamoto-Uchiyama scheme (Okamoto & Uchiyama, 1998). As the security parameter is n. Two n bit prime values a and b are selected randomly $N=ab$. It $x \in B$ is an unsystematic base. To cipher any information $m<N$, one selected a random number $y \in \mathbb{Z}_N^*$ calculates the encrypted text as:

$$c = x^m y^N \bmod N^2 \tag{1}$$

When receiving an encrypted text c, it is examined that $c<N^2$. If the condition is true then the message m is decrypted as:

$$m = L\left(c^{\lambda(N)} modN^2\right) / L\left(x^{\lambda(N)} modeN^2\right) modN \tag{2}$$

Paillier cryptosystem has useful properties like product of coded information results in the summation of the real information mod n:

$$D\left[E\left(m_1\right) * E\left(m_2\right) modn^2\right] = m_1 + m_2 modn \tag{3}$$

It is also raising an encrypted text to constant power output in multiple of original message text:

$$D\left[E\left(m\right)^k modn^2\right] = k * mmodn \tag{4}$$

RSA (Rivest-Shamir-Adleman) Cryptosystem

In 1977, the concept of RSA encryption method was first introduced by Ron Rivest and his team (Rivest, Shamir, & Adleman, 1978). In 1983, RSA cryptosystem founded RSA Data Security which was publically released in 2000. This algorithm is widely used for encrypting messages. The key size of private key is around 1024 to 4096 bit. The basic principle of RSA cryptosystem is to find three large non-negative integers e, d and n i.e. modular exponentiation of all integers m (with $0 \leq m < n$):

$$(m^e)^d \equiv m (\bmod n) \tag{5}$$

As we have the knowledge of e, n and m, it is very difficult to find the value of d from above given expression. Moreover, in some operations the above equation can be written as:

$$(m^d)^e \equiv m(\text{mod } n) \quad (6)$$

This cryptosystem includes the private and public key, where public key is universal and used for encryption. The private key is used for decrypting as well as encrypting the information in a reasonable time frame. That is the reason; this algorithm has become universally applied asymmetric cryptosystem (Diffie & Hellman, 1976). This algorithm provides a system of assuring the integrity, confidentiality, non-reputability and authenticity of electronic information transmission and data storage. RSA algorithm works on different protocols such as OpenPGP (Open and free version of Pretty Good Privacy), SSH (Secure Shell), SSL/TLS (Secure Socket Layer/ Transport Layer Security), and S/MIME (Secure/ Multipurpose Internet Mail Extensions) for digital signature and encrypting the information. Signature verification is one of the most common operations performed by RSA cryptosystem in IT applications (Cormen, Leiserson, Rivest, & Stein, 2001).

ELGamal Cryptosystem

This is an asymmetric key encryption system algorithm, generally used for public key encryption. This encryption system is designed on the basis of Diffie-Hellman key exchange model. In 1985, Taher Elgamal explained that, the system creates another layer of security by using an asymmetrically encryption keys, which were previously used only for symmetric information encryption (ElGamal, 1985). This encryption system is used in recent version of PGP (Zimmermann, 2010), GNU Privacy Guard software (Hansen, 2012) and other encryption methods. ELGamal signature scheme (Nyberg & Rueppel, 1996) is different from ELGamal encryption and it is the root for Digital Signature Algorithm (Digital Signature Standard (DSS), 1994)

ELGamal cryptography can be explained as a cyclic group G (Hazewinkel & Michiel, 1994). Its security is influenced by a particular problem in G, this problem is related to computing discrete logarithms. This cryptosystem consists of three steps: key generation, encryption and decryption algorithm.

Key Generation

"The key generation algorithm includes following steps:

- Alice initiates an efficient explanation of the cyclic group G with generator g and order n.
- Alice selected a p randomly from $\{1,\ldots,q-1\}$.
- Alice computes $h{:=}g^p$
- Alice issues h, associated with the explanation of G, g, q as the public key. Alice kept p as the private key, which need to be secure" (ElGamal, 1985).

Encryption

"The algorithm includes following steps to encryption the original information m in form of Alice public key G, g, q

- Bob selected r from $\{1,\ldots,q-1\}$, and then compute $c_1{:=}g^r$
- Bob computed the split secret $s{:=}h^r{:=}g^{pr}$
- Bob plans to convert his message m into m' of G.
- Bob computes $c_2 := m' * s$.
- Bob transmits his cipher text to Alice $\left(c_1c_2\right) = \left(g^r, m' * h\right) = \left(g^r, m' * g^{pr}\right)$

In this encryption method it is easy to calculate h^r, if new message m' is known. This is the reason to generate a new r for every other message. That is the reason to call r as an ephemeral key (Ephemeral Key, 2018)."

Decryption

The algorithm works in following steps to decode the cipher text (c_1c_2) with the Alice's private key p.

- Alice computes the shared encrypted message $s := c_1^p$
- After first step Alice calculates $m' := c_2 * s^{-1}$. Now Alice retrieves the plain text information m, where G group is having s.

This decryption algorithm forms the message which was send, since:

$$c_2s^{-1} = m' * h^r * \left(g^{pr}\right)^{-1} = m' * g^{pr} * g^{-pr} = m' \tag{7}$$

This cryptosystem is generally used in hybrid encryption to encode the message with symmetric cryptosystem. The algorithm is used to encrypt the message using symmetric key encryption. This is the reason that ELGamal like asymmetric cryptosystems are generally slower that symmetric cryptosystems for a same level of security (ElGamal, 1985).

DISSCUSSION AND CONCLUSION

The IoT has demonstrated its presence in our lives, from dealing at an essential level to the social relationship. It has included a new prospective into internet by authorizing communications among objects, livings and non-livings, and building an intelligent and smart world. The IoT has conducted with a vision of "anywhere, anything, anytime, anyway" interactions in real sense. It is perceived that it should be contemplated as the fundamental part of the prevailing internet depending on IoTs future ways, and it is obvious to become different from the available levels of internet compared to what we use and see in our daily lives. Therefore, the conceptual frame comes in the limelight. The Architecture is a substructure of technology that authorizes things to connect each other and communicate with same or different objects by striking human being to be the layer on it. In reality, it is understandable that the present IoT paradigms, which encourages in the direction machine to machine (M2M) interactions, is now getting restricted by so many factors.

In this chapter, the essential components for the IoTs community were examined. The parameters of IoT devices, is requisite to offer established multimedia data transfer. The present module is able to offer the requisite bitrate of text data streaming and transmission were chosen. Furthermore, the bitrate interval dependency was examined for systems working on Bluetooth and Wi-Fi technologies. These analysis were held as a generalised form of the algorithms being advanced for instinctive connection of the IoT modules. The algorithms allow the encryption of the data file with the use of three different algorithms: Paillier cryptosystem, RSA cryptosystem and ELGamal cryptosystem. The performance is checked after the encryption and decryption of data files using these algorithms. The concluding results show that every algorithm has different ability and status to make the data safe. Hence, it is required to decide and finalise the algorithm based on the type of data. However, the results vary depending on the property and size of data file.

FUTURE SCOPE

Wireless Senor Network (WSN) is a conventional technology formed of small size battery operated "motes" with radio communication and limited calculation capabilities. This methodology has the ability to study of resuscitative care and impact the delivery by permitting the device to be fully automated and automatically collect the vital signs from the patient care unit. This collected data would be used for correlation with hospital records, long term observation of the patient and real-time triage. These automated networks would help to provide a better observation environment to the post-operative patient, provide continuous monitoring during neuro-rehabilitation period in ambulatory atmosphere, monitor elderly person at home and patient suffering from lung diseases such as chronic obstructive pulmonary disease (COPD). This work can be extended by including artificial intelligence to the WSN, which is helpful in exploring data robustness, distributed storage, parallel distribution computation and automatic sensor reading classification. The automatic sensor reading classification would assist the physicians in early detection of diseases.

This work can also be extended by designing architecture of remote patient monitoring system. In this system wireless sensor nodes would be able to detect various other environment factors and add to the security of the system. It can be used in home, hospitals, and ambulatory, where it would implement a real time patient monitoring, by which the doctor can watch the patients on remote location and provide the first aid advice to patients.

REFERENCES

Aberg, P. A., Togawa, T., & Spelman, F. A. (2002). Sensors in Medicine and Healthcare. *Wiley-VCH, 15*(3), 152-169.

Babu, A. K. (2015). A Survey on the Role of IoT and Cloud in Health Care. *International Journal of Scientific Engineering and Technology Research, 4*(12), 2217–2219.

Bohonos, S. L. (2007). Universal real-time navigational assistance (URNA): an urban bluetooth beacon for the blind. In *1st ACM SIGMOBILE international workshop on Systems and networking support for healthcare and assisted living environments* (pp. 83-88). New York: ACM.

Bormann, Z. S. (2009). *6LoWPAN: The Wireless Embedded Internet* (1st ed.). London: Wiley.

Buettner, M., Yee, G. V., Anderson, E., & Han, R. (2006). X-MAC: a short preamble MAC protocol for duty-cycled wireless sensor networks. In *4th international conference on Embedded networked sensor systems* (pp. 307-320). ACM.

Chouffani, R. (2016, November). *Can we expect the Internet of Things in healthcare?* Retrieved from http://internetofthingsagenda.techtarget.com/feature/Can-we-expect-the-Internet-of-Things-in-healthcare

Cormen, T. H., Leiserson, C. E., Rivest, R. L., & Stein, C. (2001). Introduction to Algorithms (2nd ed.). MIT Press and McGraw-Hill.

Coughlan, J. (2007). Color targets: Fiducials to help visually impaired people find their way by camera phone. *EURASIP Journal on Image and Video Processing*, *12*(1), 96–111.

Diffie, W., & Hellman, M. (1976). New directions in cryptography. *IEEE Transactions on Information Theory*, *22*(6), 644–654. doi:10.1109/TIT.1976.1055638

Digital Signature Standard (DSS). (1994, May 19). Retrieved from FIPS PUB 186: csrc.nist.gov

Dresher, R., & Irazoqui, P. (2007). A Compact Nanopower Low Output Impedance CMOS Operational Amplifier for Wireless Intraocular Pressure Recordings. In *29th Annual International Conference of the IEEE* (pp. 6055-6058). Engineering in Medicine and Biology Society. 10.1109/IEMBS.2007.4353729

Dunkels, A., Gr¨onvall, B., & Voigt, T. (2004). Contiki - a lightweight and flexible operating system for tiny networked sensors. In *First IEEE Workshop on Embedded Networked Sensors (Emnets-I)* (pp. 15-26). IEEE. 10.1109/LCN.2004.38

ElGamal, T. (1985). A Public-Key Cryptosystem and a Signature Scheme Based on Discrete Logarithms. *IEEE Transactions on Information Theory*, *31*(4), 469–472. doi:10.1109/TIT.1985.1057074

Emory, F. A., & Lenert, L. A. (2005). MASCAL: RFID Tracking of Patients, Staff and Equipment to Enhance Hospital Response to Mass Casualty Events. In *The AMIA Annual Symposium* (pp. 261-265). AMIA.

Ephemeral Key. (2018, June 7). Retrieved from Wikipedia: https://en.wikipedia.org/wiki/Ephemeral_key

Garthner. (2018, May). *Gartner Technical Research.* Retrieved from Internet of Things: http://www.gartner.com/technology/research/internet-of-things/

Gay, D., Levis, P., Von Behren, R., Welsh, M., Brewer, E., & Culler, D. (2014). The nesC language: A holistic approach to networked embedded systems. *ACM SIGPLAN Notices*, *49*(4), 41–51. doi:10.1145/2641638.2641652

Gnawali, O., Fonseca, R., Jamieson, K., Moss, D., & Levis, P. (2009). Collection tree protocol. In *7th ACM conference on embedded networked sensor systems* (pp. 1-14). ACM.

Gurtov, A., Komu, M., & Moskowitz, R. (2009). Host Identity Protocol (HIP): Identifier/locator split for host mobility and multihoming. *Internet Protocol Journal*, *12*(1), 27–32.

Halperin, D., Heydt-Benjamin, T. S., Fu, K., Kohno, T., & Maisel, W. H. (2008). Security and privacy for implantable medical devices. *IEEE Pervasive Computing*, *7*(1), 30–39. doi:10.1109/MPRV.2008.16

Hanjagi, A., Srihari, P., & Rayamane, A. (2007). A public health care information system using GIS and GPS: A case study of Shiggaon. *Springer: GIS for Health and the Environment*, *5*(1), 243–255.

Hansen, R. (2012, Jan.). *Gnu Privacy Guard.* Retrieved from GnuPG: https://www.gnupg.org/faq/gnupg-faq.html#compatible

Hayes, T. O. (2015, August 6). *American Action Forum.* Retrieved from https://www.americanactionforum.org/research/are-electronic-medical-records-worth-the-costs-of-implementation/

Hazewinkel & Michiel. (1994). Cyclic group. In *Encyclopedia of Mathematics.* Springer Science+Business Media B.V. / Kluwer Academic Publishers.

Heer, T. (2007). LHIP lightweight authentication extension for HIP. *IETF*, *12*(3), 290–230.

Hil, J., Szewczyk, R., Woo, A., Hollar, S., Culler, D., & Pister, K. (2000). System architecture directions for network sensors. *Operating Systems Review*, *34*(5), 93–104. doi:10.1145/384264.379006

Hodgetts, T., & Mackaway-Jones, K. (1995). *Major Incident Medical Management and Support, the Practical Approach.* BMJ Publishing Group.

Imadali, S., Karanasiou, A., Petrescu, A., Sifniadis, I., Veque, V., & Angelidis, P. (2012). eHealth service support in IPv6 vehicular networks. In *IEEE Int. Conf. Wireless Mobile Comput., Netw. Commun. (WiMob)* (pp. 579-585). London: IEEE Digital eXplore. 10.1109/WiMOB.2012.6379134

Internet of Things. (2018, May). Retrieved from IEEE: http://iot.ieee.org/about.html

Intille, S. S. (2006). Using a live-in laboratory for ubiquitous computing research. In *International Conference on Pervasive Computing* (pp. 349-365). Berlin: Springer. 10.1007/11748625_22

Jara, A. J., Zamora, M. A., & Skarmeta, A. (2012). Knowledge acquisition and management architecture for mobile and personal health environments based on the Internet of Things. In *IEEE Int. Conf. Trust, Security Privacy Comput. Commun. (TrustCom)* (pp. 1811-1818). IEEE Digital eXplore. 10.1109/TrustCom.2012.194

Khan, O. A., & Skinner, R. (2002). *Geographic Information Systems and Health Applications.* IGI Globa.

Ko, J. L.-E., Dutton, R. P., Lim, J. H., Chen, Y., Musvaloiu-E, R., Terzis, A., ... Selavo, L. (2010). MEDiSN: Medical emergency detection in sensor networks. *ACM Transactions on Embedded Computing Systems*, *10*(1), 89–101. doi:10.1145/1814539.1814550

Krumm, J. (2007). Inference attacks on location track. In *International Conference on Pervasive Computing* (pp. 127-143). Berlin: Springer. 10.1007/978-3-540-72037-9_8

Kumar, P., & Lee, H. (2013). Security issues in healthcare applications using wireless medical sensor networks: A survey. *Sensors (Basel)*, *12*(1), 55–91. doi:10.3390120100055 PMID:22368458

Liao, L., Fox, D., & Kautz, H. (2005). BLocation-based activity recognition using relational Markov networks. *19th Int. In Joint Conf. Artif. Intell.*, 773-778.

Linderman, M. D., Santhanam, G., Kemere, C. T., Gilja, V., O'Driscoll, S., Yu, B. M., ... Meng, T. (2008). Signal processing challenges for neural prostheses. *IEEE Signal Processing Magazine*, *25*(1), 18–28. doi:10.1109/MSP.2008.4408439

Maglogiannis, C. D. (2012). Bringing IoT and cloud computing towards pervasive healthcare. In *Int. Conf. Innov. Mobile Internet Services Ubiquitous Comput. (IMIS)*, (pp. 922-926). Academic Press.

Moskowitz, R. (2012). HIP Diet EXchange (DEX): Draft-moskowitz-hip-dex-00. *Standards Track*, *19*(5), 120–135.

Ngoc, T. V. (2008). *Medical applications of wireless networks*. Washington, DC: Recent Advances in Wireless and Mobile Networking.

Nyberg, K., & Rueppel, R. A. (1996). Message recovery for signature schemes based on the discrete logarithm problem. *Designs, Codes and Cryptography*, *7*(1-2), 61–81. doi:10.1007/BF00125076

Okamoto, T., & Uchiyama, S. (1998). A new public-key cryptosystem as secure as factoring. Advances in Cryptology — EUROCRYPT'98 Lecture Notes in Computer Science, 1403, 308–318.

Olivereau, Y. B. (2012). D-HIP: A distributed key exchange scheme for HIP-based Internet of Things. *IEEE Int'l Symp. on a World of Wireless, Mobile and Multimedia Networks (WoWMoM): IEEE Computer Society*, 1-7.

Paillier, P. (1999). Public-Key Cryptosystems Based on Composite Degree Residuosity Classes. *EUROCRYPT*, 223–238.

Patrick, K. (2007). *A tool for geospatial analysis of physical activity: Physical activity location measurement system (palms).* San Diego, CA: NIHGEI project at the University of California.

Polastre, J., Szewczyk, R., & Culler, D. (2005). Telos: Enabling Ultra-Low Power Wireless Research. *4th International Conference on Information Processing in Sensor Networks: Special track on Platform Tools and Design Methods for Network Embedded Sensors (IPSN/SPOTS)*, 57-62.

Ponemon Organization. (2015, May 7). Retrieved from Ponemon Institute: https://www.ponemon.org/news-2/66

Radclliffe, J. (2011). *Hacking medical devices for fun and insulin.* Retrieved from Breaking the human scada system: http://media.blackhat.com/bh-us-11/Radcliffe/BH US 11 Radcliffe_Hacking Medical Devices WP.pdf

Raghunathan, S., Ward, M., Roy, K., & Irazoqui, P. (2009). A lowpower implantable event-based seizure detection algorithm. In *4th International IEEE/EMBS Conference* (pp. 151-154). IEEE.

Rivest, R., Shamir, A., & Adleman, L. (1978). A Method for Obtaining Digital Signatures and Public-Key Cryptosystems. *Communications of the ACM*, *21*(2), 120–126. doi:10.1145/359340.359342

Shahamabadi, M. S., Ali, B. B., Varahram, P., & Jara, A. (2013). A network mobility solution based on 6LoWPAN hospital wireless sensor network (NEMO-HWSN). In *7th Int. Conf. Innov. Mobile Internet Services Ubiquitous Comput. (IMIS)* (pp. 433-438). IMIS. 10.1109/IMIS.2013.157

Srinivasan, V., Stankovic, J., & Whitehouse, K. (2008). Protecting your daily in-home activity information from a wireless snooping attack. In *10th international conference on Ubiquitous computing* (pp. 202-211). ACM.

T., H. (2007). *LHIP lightweight authentication extension for HIP.* Draft-heer-hip-lhip-00, IETF.

Urien., P. (2013, Oct). *HIP support for RFIDs.* draft-irtf-hiprg-rfid-07.txt.

Wilson, C. B. (1999). Sensors in Medicine. *The Western Journal of Medicine*, *11*(5), 322–335. PMID:18751196

Wood, A. D., Fang, L., Stankovic, J. A., & He, T. (2006). SIGF: a family of configurable, secure routing protocols for wireless sensor networks. In *4th ACM workshop on Security of ad hoc and sensor networks* (pp. 35-48). ACM. 10.1145/1180345.1180351

Wu, W., Au, L., Jordan, B., Stathopoulos, T., Batalin, M., & Kaiser, W. (2008). The smartcane system: an assistive device for geriatrics. In ICST (Institute for Computer Sciences, Social-Informatics and Telecommunications Engineering) 3rd international (pp. 1-4). BodyNets '08.

Yager, P., Edwards, T., Fu, E., Helton, K., Nelson, K., Tam, M. R., & Weigl, B. H. (2006). Microfluidic diagnostic technologies for global public health. *Nature*, *442*(7101), 412–418. doi:10.1038/nature05064 PMID:16871209

Zimmermann, P. (2010, June). *Where to Get PGP*. Retrieved from Phil Zimmermann & Associates LLC: https://philzimmermann.com/EN/findpgp/

This research was previously published in Medical Data Security for Bioengineers; pages 185-207, copyright year 2019 by Medical Information Science Reference (an imprint of IGI Global).

Chapter 31
Quantum Security for IoT to Secure Healthcare Applications and Their Data

Binod Kumar
https://orcid.org/0000-0002-6172-7938
JSPM's Rajarshi Shahu College of Engineering, India

Sheetal B. Prasad
SRM Institute of Science and Technology, India

Parashu Ram Pal
ABES Engineering College, India

Pankaj Pathak
https://orcid.org/0000-0002-5875-0387
Symbiosis Institute of Digital and Telecom Management, Symbiosis International University, India

ABSTRACT

Quantum computation has the ability to revolutionize the treatment of patients. Quantum computing can help to detect diseases by identifying and forecasting malfunctions. But there's a threat associated here (i.e., healthcare data among the most popular cybercriminal targets, IoT devices notoriously lacking in effective safeguards, and quantum computers on the brink of an encryption/decryption breakthrough). Health agencies need a security prognosis and treatment plan as soon as possible. Healthcare companies recently worry more about the quantum security threats. The biggest threat of healthcare data breaches has come in the form of identity theft. There should be a strong mechanism to combat the security gaps in existing healthcare industry. If the healthcare data are available on the network, an attacker may try to modify, intercept, or even view this data stream. With the use of quantum security, the quantum state of these photons changes alert the security pros that someone is trying to breach the link.

DOI: 10.4018/978-1-6684-6311-6.ch031

INTRODUCTION

The Internet of Things (IoT) is a communication system that defines a future in the day-to-day relation of physical objects to the Internet and the capacity to locate and interact locally or remotely (Coetzee, 2011). IoT grows rapidly and changes any technological area through the delivery of smart services, including healthcare. Such smart technologies to boost the standard of living and effectively drive healthcare sector development at the moment. These smart systems monitor numerous computer-based data and state-of-the-art IoT tools such as wearables, networks, etc. To answer the vast volume of knowledge gathered over the last two decades properly.

The concept of the Internet of Things (IoT) is clear: it requires the artifacts to create their own social networks and holds the two layers apart; it makes it possible for individuals to implement rules to preserve their privacy and to view only certain contact outcomes that take place on a social network (Atzori, Nitti, & Marche., 2016).The IoT has been a subject of global concern for a couple of decades. Nevertheless, the healthcare industry has just begun to understand the enormous potential and benefits offered by the implementation of new and more advanced healthcare equipment and services as well as links between several sectors of the industry. The Internet of Things has re-evaluated the healthsector with its numerous applications in the framework. IoT introduced health care to help doctors and nurses take improved medical decisions and reduce human contact by retrieving information from bedside devices to help them reduce error rates (Rao, 2019). The contribution of this chapter is as follows:

- For the healthcare environment, we offer a holistic perspective on IoT fundamentals. Various IoT views for the medical domain are outlined based on various types of relationships in an IoT to the healthcare system, and IoT's for the healthcare domain are discussed in detail.
- We addressed IoT healthcare architecture and technologies. We addressed in this article the 3-layer IoT structure consisting of the perception tier, network layer and application layer. We explained the idea and then demonstrated the way it operated.
- We also studied various research papers that provide approaches to various IoT healthcare problem areas. We evaluated the advantages and disadvantages of each research paper.
- This chapter sums up the importance of IoT in healthcare and offers a solution in Healthcare to design and implement IoT.

This is the rest of the book. Section 2 analyses similar IoT research in the healthcare sector, which increases healthcare productivity through healthcare alignment with other IoT fields. Remaining Sections discusses about Quantum Cryptography Fundamentals,, The Security of QKD, Secure Communications Using Quantum Key Distribution, Quantum Security, Post Quantum Cryptography, Asymmetric Versus Symmetric Encryption, Functions Quantum Cryptography, The Quantum Security for Remote Healthcare Data, IoT Application in Healthcare, Cost and Features of IoT Solutions for Healthcare. Finally conclusions are presented in section 8.

QUANTUM SECURITY FOR IOT

Security requirements of IoT devices can be very complex and it cannot be achieved by a single technology. There are many aspects of security in IoT devices has to be considered. For example secured software development, secure patch management, protection against various attack, and secure communication. Recently many companies started to implement chip-based quantum security mechanisms. In these mechanisms the applicability and practical implementation of quantum security cryptographic methods for embedded systems is the main concern. The quantum security cryptographic techniques ensures the confidentiality, authenticity, and integrity of the multiple data traveling in the IoT ecosystem, both the consumer and industrial one. If the cryptographic methods used in an IoT device can be broken by an attacker, this would expose it to a lot of vulnerabilities. With quantum-safe cryptography, provides security in the long term and against very powerful attackers. The development of post-quantum cryptography that should withstand quantum computing power. The defender could still be implementing cryptography on classical computers and machines, while the attacker may use a quantum computer in the near future. Current approaches for so-called quantum-key distribution [QKD], where quantum technology is used to achieve confidentiality, are currently too expensive or too constraining, whereas current assessments of post-quantum cryptography prove that it could be quantum-safe as well as affordable. Researchers have indicated that information protection will be particularly alarming, as modern quantum encryption techniques might be helpful, however quantum computing may be used to bust up traditional encryption systems and outdated certain established computer security protections.

We foresee other cyber security implications because of quantum computation. Current public key cryptography algorithms like Diffie-Hellman, RSS [Rivest-Shamir-Adleman] and elliptic curve cryptography rely on mathematical problems that are difficult for conventional computers to overcome. It is the basis of the protection of such algorithms. The problem is that a man named Peter Shor at MIT already showed that a quantum computer is able to deal with such mathematical problems within a reasonable period of time. It suggests that if we have a completely functional, realistic quantum machine now, it will be able to crack the RSA, the elliptical curve and the Diffie-Hellman in a fair period of time, not immediately, but in a reasonable amount of time. Each vpN will then be vulnerable, e-commerce, and more (Sharon Shea, 2020). Quantum cryptography is a methodology very relevant that utilizes quantum mechanics' principles in order to create a cryptosystem which is meant to be the securest. This can not be violated by anyone without the sender or receiver of the communication having heard. Quantum cryptography is focused around the usage of photons and their basic quantum properties in order to create an indestructible cryptosystem since the quantum state in every device can't be determined without informing the machine. The essence of quantum cryptography is the idea that it requires the smallest particles, i.e. photons, in existence. Such photons have a function that appears concurrently in more than one condition and that only affects their statuses as counted. It is the fundamental property of quantum cryptography algorithms. If a message travels from the sender to the receiver through a conduit and any hostile party wants to interrupt communications, the sender / receiver is automatically clear through the shift in state of the photon.

RELATED WORK

The IoT provides many opportunities for developing services and delivery of healthcare. IoT promotes a holistic commitment to health care by considering the population's health needs and not people, and promoting policies that minimize illness prevalence, impairment and accidental injury. The convergence of healthcare systems with other areas of IoT thus improves the efficacy of healthcare. The Internet of Things can change people's lifestyle (Rghioui & Oumnad, 2017).

Numerous independent studies have recently examined the potential to use IoT technology in healthcare. IoT may bring many advantages to improve the quality of life of people and provide safety advice on lifestyle. To clarify that the IoT refers to several good studies, each Healthcare protection display problem has been discussed recently. There are several papers publishing a study of different aspects of IoT innovation in health care. For example, the survey (Kwak, Kabir, Hossain, & Kwak, 2015) covers the core technology that allows wireless network and wireless network (WSN) components to be communicated. Jaime Lioret and her colleagues have proposed among these studies a smart communication system for Ambient Assisted Living (Lioret, Canovas, Sendra, & Parra, 2015). Inspired by (Ma, Wang, Yang, Miao, & Li, 2016), the big health model based on the Internet, the big data, was introduced in a recent study.

In elderly and disabled patients, several tools have been built to monitor human activity. This system's purpose is to continuously monitor physiological parameters (Khanna & Misra, 2013) (Riazul, Kwak, Humaun, Hossain, & Supkwak, 2015). The health monitoring system is largely dependent on the wireless sensor network and therefore benefits from lower energy consumption and increased coverage of communication (Singh, 2016). Themes such as less innovative technology, the low availability of smart devices and smart products that are highly required for intelligent healthcare must be addressed by developing countries (Mathew, Amreen, H.N & Verma, 2015) . IoT implementation in intelligent homes offers complex solution services and technology for customized healthcare (Yu & Lu, 2012). IoT is a smart healthcare architecture which uses sensors such as temperature sensors, barometric pressure and ECG sensors (Sreekanth & Nitha, 2016).

The state-of - the-art approaches for efficient and safe eHealth management is studied. They generally gave a detailed eHealth monitoring model by explaining the entire life cycle of monitoring in depth. The key service elements were also illustrated with a focus on data collection on the patient side. We have defined and analyzed the key issues to be resolved in order to develop an efficient and stable patient-centered monitoring system (Sawand, A., Djahel, S., Zhang, Z., & Abdesselam, 2015).

The paper then explains the security and privacy issues of the healthcare implementations of the Body Sensor Network (BSN). Earlier, they found that while the security issue was acknowledged in most popular BSN research projects, strong security services were not implemented which could protect the privacy of the patient. Eventually, BSN was introduced for a safety IoT-based system of healthcare that can efficiently satisfy various BSN healthcare safety requirements (Gope & Hwang, 2016).

To have end-to - end support for IoT applications from an IoT platform, there is a stable IoT program deployed. IoT's framework includes IoT applications, an IoT broker and IoT devices. Typically speaking, in real-time healthcare facilities intermediate protection concerns will be addressed as medical patient knowledge is one of the most important safety details. Growing IoT platform uses a specific identifier as one of its attributes. And if the IoT Broker is an intermediary node, it decrypts and shows data only if the conditions have been fulfilled. (Choi, In, Park, Seok, Seo, & Kim, 2016).

Patient information and health records have been provided with a Secure Patient Profiling System (Ko & Song, 2015). The patient and doctor exchange up-to-date data simultaneously. Data can be leaked while exchanging and transmitting. In order to resolve security problems, there should be established a safe communication network and a one-time key between a patient and a hospital and a dual hash should be used to generate an OTP output value. This work offers a dual-hash method for generating a one-time password that guarantees safe contact with a secure password.

FUNDAMENTAL OF QUANTUM CRYPTOGRAPHY

Quantum cryptography in the broadest context is a sub-set of quantum information processing, including quantum computing and quantum computation. The research for information retrieval functions that can be done utilizing quantum mechanical devices is quantum computation and quantum information. Quantum Mechanics is a conceptual framework or a set of theories for physical growth. Quantum mechanics have basic principles that remain counter-intuitive among scholars, and the early precedents of quantum physics and quantum knowledge can be found in physicists' lifelong need to grasp quantum mechanics more thoroughly. Perhaps the most important of these is a quantum quantum coherence analysis. Entanglement is a distinctly quantum mechanical phenomenon that plays a crucial role in many of the most significant applications of quantum computation and quantum information; entanglement is iron in the conventional bronze age of the world. A great deal of work has been made in recent years to further grasp the properties of entanglement called a fundamental property of Nature, of equal value to energy, information, entropy or some other fundamental tool.

Although there is no full quantum coherence theory yet, some progress has been made in the understanding of this unusual function of quantum mechanics. Most researchers expect that more study of the properties of the interference would include insights that will promote the creation of new technologies for quantum computation and quantum information.

It is important to remember, as we know, about a decade before a quantum computers were discovered to break public key cryptography, a workaround had already been created for that attack – QKD. QKD offers an unconditionally secure way of communicating random keys across insecure networks, focused on the fundamental principles of quantum mechanics. In addition, the protected key created by QKD may be used to improve information protection in the OTP scheme or other encryption algorithms. It chapter lays out the fundamental ideas behind the various QKD or QSS and discusses state-of-the-art techniques for quantum cryptography.

THE SECURITY OF QKD

The safety proof is essential because (a) it provides a QKD protection base, (b) it provides a specification for the QKD protocol 's key generation efficiency, and (c) the classic post-processing processing (for error correction and privacy amplification) protocol can also be built to help the ultimate key generation. A Real QKD system without any cryptographic evidence is incomplete because we will never learn how to build a valid key and how stable it is.

After a qubit and base reconciliation, sender and receiver each have a sifted key. Ideally, all keys are the same. But certain causes of error are still in actual life, so certain conventional information retrieval methods such as error correction so data filtering are introduced by the sender and receiver of their documents. To access the same keys, the first and second protocols are needed for a secret key. In essence, the problem with eavesdropping is finding protocols which can contain an authentically secured sender- and recipient key or stop the protocol as the sender and recipient can only measure the QBER and alert the users that it has failed in the key distribution. It is a complex issue at the crossroads between quantum mechanics and knowledge theory. It also entails several eavesdropping problems according to the exact procedure.

Many limited-generality eavesdrop strategies have been developed and evaluated in order to simplify the issue (Lütkenhaus 1996), (Biham, E & Mor, 1997). Especially important is Eve 's assumption to add individual samples to each song and test each sample one by one. We may be listed as:

Single attack: Eve independently launches an assault on a signal for a single attack. The intercept-resend assault is an illustration of a person's assault. Imagine a simple example of the intercept-resending attack by Eve, an eavesdropper who arbitrarily checks each photon and sends it back to Bob. Eve 's calculation will disrupt the photons Alice prepared on the diagonal bases and randomly respond, if for example Eve executes a clear measurement. E.g. When Eve sends straight images to Bob, when Bob makes a vertical calculation, he gets random replies. Since each group randomly selects such two bases, a bit error rate of 0.50.5 + 0.5 = 25 percent is provided by such an intercept resending attack, which Alice and Bob readily detect. Strong QKD assaults are occurring. Thankfully, the health of QKD has now proved itself.

Collective attacks: A more general type of attacks is a cumulative attack where Eve separately couples it with an ancillary quantum device, usually referred to as ancilla, with each signal, and the combination signal / ancilla grows as a entity. She's going to send Bob the next signals, however she can catch all of the ancillas herself. In response to individual attacks, Eve is postponing her calculation decision. It is only after having a public debate between Alice and Bob that Eve decides what check to take on her ancilla to gather the final key information.

Joint attacks: The most frequent form of intrusion is mutual attack. Eve treats both signals as a specific quantum network during a joint assault instead of treating each signal separately. Then she enters the ancilla in the signal network and generates an interconnected signal and ancil frame unitarily. Before deciding the measure of her simple to behave, she watches the public conversation between Alice and Bob.

Of joint and community attacks Eve is typically just researching until any of the meetings on counseling, error fixing and privacy enhancement have been completed by Alice and Bob. Another assumes that Eve still exists as the grounds of the healing mechanism for public discussion within the more moral people attacks. This would therefore be fair to assume for modern technologies that Eve should quantify her analysis of person attacks before consolidating the base. (Malaney & Robert,2010).

SECURE COMMUNICATIONS USING QUANTUM KEY DISTRIBUTION

QKD does not necessarily encrypt user data, but encourages users to pass keys freely to each other, which can then be used for the resulting encrypted contact.

By using a security system, any sort of private information have to be held hidden almost always. Knowledge is shared in symmetric key systems in the form of a key but in asymmetric systems, each node has its own key when it exchsts the public key. In every instance, the mail is enabled with bugs. Symmetric key schemes often focus on physical key exchange – some financial firms with mobile storage mail – to bootstrap. They can share an encryption key for the further use on a secure connection via an asymmetrical system. One explanation for this is that asymmetric structures like Public Key do not allow secrets to be exchanged through the medium (in this case, private keys), whereas symmetrical structures are more powerful and therefore more stable, despite the large data volume after exchanging keys.

Quantum Key Distribution (QKD) is the most well-known and sophisticated method of quantum cryptography which require the use of quantum communication to define a shared key between two parties without third party information, however all communications between two parties may be refused

Figure 1. Diagram of the stages of a protocol of the quantum key distribution. Classically authenticated stage with dual lines.

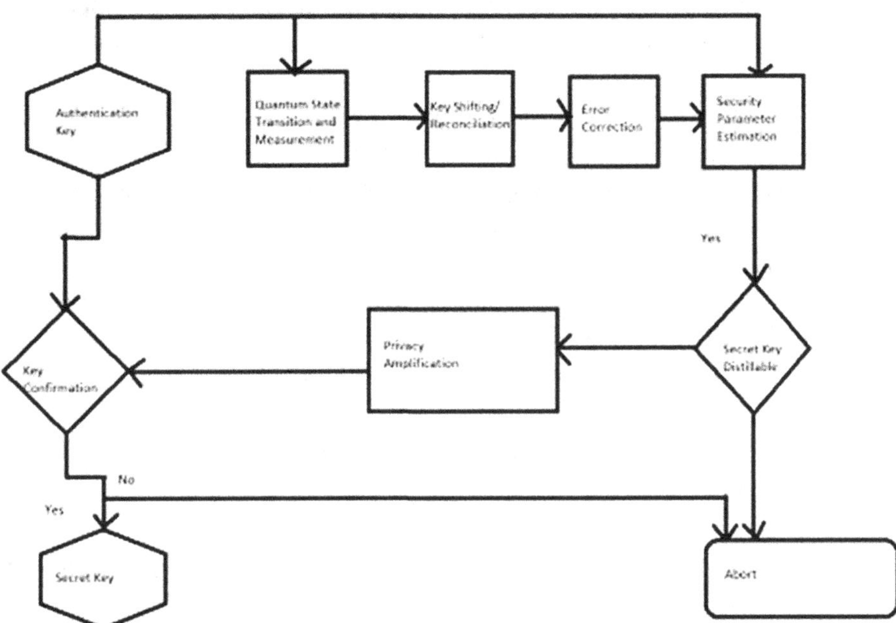

by third parties. If third parties try to find out about the key, discrepancies will occur that will notice two parties. Once the key has been defined, it is typically used with traditional techniques for encrypted communication. The shared key for symmetrical encryption may be used, for example.

Unlike the classical key distribution, the security of the quantum key distribution may be proved mathematically without adding any constraint on the eavesdropper 's capability. It is generally defined as "unconditional protection," but a minimum of suppositories is needed, including the implementation of the laws of quantum mechanics and the identification of two parties, i.e. third parties would not be able to impersonate any side, or a man-in-the-middle attack could be feasible.

QKD is a modern tool in a cryptographer toolbox: it makes secure key agreements on an untrustworthy path, in which the output key is entirely different from all input values, an unrelated job. QKD does not eliminate the need to develop systems with state-of - art security elements such as authentication, but does QKD.

A secret-key agreement has been drawnup on a public channel for overcoming the noise and wire-tapping errors in the quantum channel, information reconciliation and confidentiality enhanced can be used to distribute the quantic key, or the cleanup of the quantum congestion should be used. The first general but very complex evidence of unconditional safety (Mayers, 2001), followed by several other evidence. (Mayers, 2006) In Mayers' proofs the BB84 scheme proposed by Bennett and Brassard proved to be safe. Lo and Chau suggested a conceptually simplified protection proof focused on the principle of quantum privacy enhancement (Lo & Chau,1999).

Two parties have these quantum states in QKD and check them. The research discusses to decide which findings may relate to hidden main bits. Others are tossed out as a sifting technique because of the incompatibility of the measuring settings. They fix the mistakes and then follow a security parameter that indicates how much the eavesdropper learns about the most critical information. If that is beyond a certain threshold, they must abort as they can no longer ensure any confidentiality. When the level is greater, secrecy will be improved to delete all residual information that the eavesdropper may potentially have and to insert a secret key. Each classic communications must be checked in order to avoid man-in-the-middle attacks.

Quantum Key Distribution (QKD) is a way to transmit encryption keystrokes which involve some very rare, technologically at least unhackable, subatomic particle behavior. QKD's land based variant is a network where photons are transmitted through a fiber optic cable one at a time. If someone is eavesdropping, then the polarization of the photons is influenced according to the rules of quantum physics, and the receiver may complain the message is not secure. (QuantumXchange, 2020)

Cryptography is the practice of encrypting messages, or translating plain text to encrypted text so that it can be interpreted only by anyone who has the correct "key." By contrast, quantum cryptography actually utilizes the concepts of quantum mechanics to encode and transfer data in a way that cannot be hacked out.

Although the concept sounds straightforward, the difficulty lies behind quantum cryptography in the concepts of quantic mechanics, such as:

- Particles which make up the universe are inherently uncertain and may exist in more than one place or more than one state of being at the same time.
- The photons are spontaneously produced in one of two quantum states.
- A quantum property can't be calculated without modifying or disrupting it.
- We can clone some of the particle's quantum properties but not the entire particle.

All these principles play a role in how quantum cryptography works.

POST-QUANTUM CRYPTOGRAPHY

Post-quantum cryptography is used for encryption algorithms (usually public key) defined as quantum computer-safe algorithms. These complicated mathematical calculations require months and even years for modern computers to break down. Quantum computers running the Shor algorithm separate mathematical programs at times.

In comparison to logical encryption, quantum cryptography utilizes the concepts of quantum mechanics to generate secure correspondence. Quantum computers become a technical reality; therefore, it is important to analyze the cryptographing schemes of opponents who have access to a quantum computer. The study of these structures is often referred to as post-quantum cryptography. The criteria for post-quantity cryptography are intended to bypass some traditional encrypting and signature systems (ECC and RSA-centered systems) by utilizing Shor 's algorithm to factor and measure distinctive logarithms on a quantum machine. McEliece and lattice-based systems as well as other symmetric keys are now recognizing the meanings of systems that have been defending against quantum adversaries.(Bernstein, 2009) Post-quantum cryptography surveys can be conducted. (Bernstein, 2009)

There is still some emphasis on improving existing techniques of cryptography to cope with quantum adversaries. For instance, different methods must be used to build zero-knowledge evidence systems which are safe from quantum adversaries. In a classical environment, a study of the zero-Knowledge-

Bestoff method typically requires a rewinding, a procedure that allows the opponent's internal state to be replicated. Copying a state in a quantum setting is not always feasible (no-cloning theorem); the rewinding technique variant must be used (Watrous, 2009).

Post-quantum algorithms are often labeled "quantum resistant" because, unlike the spread of the quantum key, it is not understood or proven that any future quantum attacks against them do not occur. Though not susceptible to the Shor Algorithm, the NSA declares the decision to switch to quantum-resistant algorithms. The NINST appears to believe it is time for quantum-safe primitives. (CoinFabrik, 2017)

Post-quantum cryptography deals with cryptosystems that run on ordinary computers and that are free from attacks in quantum computation. This field was developed as most common public-key encryption schemes rely on the problem of integer factorization or a discrete logarithm which can be solved easily on large enough quantum computers using the Shor algorithm. While the latest publicly accessible computational theoretical computer program is about as effective as possible to target actual crypto schemes, other cryptographers are researching new techniques if quantum computation becomes a threat. Most symmetric encryptions (symmetric ciphers and hash functions) are by contrast secured against quantum computers. In this respect. The Quantum Grover algorithm speeds up attack on symmetrical ciphers, however, the key scale can be counteracted. Post-quantum cryptography also does not rely on symmetrical algorithms. Therefore, post-quantum encryption has no relation to quantum encryption and is connected to the usage of quantum effects of secretion. The cryptography post-quantum currently focuses mainly on four different methods:

Post-quantum cryptography is usually also another matter than quantum cryptography:

- As with most of the cryptography, post-quantum encryption covers a large range of protected mail functions, ranging from secret, public-key, and encryption to high-ranking activity like secure online voting. Quantum cryptography performs only one function: extending a brief common secret into a long shared secret.
- Like in other cryptographic approaches, post-quantum cryptography has some secure solutions but also has other, cost-effective methods. Quantum encryption prevents conjectural systems, initially asking how the key could be exchanged between Alice and Bob in a secure way.
- Post-quantum cryptography requires a range of techniques that can be used for a small fraction of today's Internet communication — the sender and receiver need to compute and relay certain data, but no additional hardware is required. The overwhelming majority of internet users at least currently do not need modern network devices for quantium cryptography.

Quantum encryption so far mainly deals with the development of quantum distribution protocols. Sadly symmetrical key-distributed cryptosystems for wide networks (many users) are unstable since many secret keys need to be configurated and exploited in pairings (the so-called "key-management problem."). Nevertheless, this task alone does not tackle a variety of other cryptographic operations and roles that are important in everyday life. Kak 's three stage protocol has been suggested as a secure communication mechanism that is totally quantum unlike the quantum key distribution, which utilizes classic algorithms for cryptographic transformation (Thapliya.& Pathak,, 2018)

ASYMMETRIC SYMMETRIC ENCRYPTION

Binary digits (0s and 1s) are transferred regularly from one position to another, and decryted by means of a symmetrical (private)/asymmetrical (public) key. Encrypt runs on "normal" devices. The Advanced Encryption Standard (AES) symmetric key cipher uses the same key to encrypt a letter or the file and asymmetrical ciphers, such as RSA, use both private and public linked keys. The secret key for decrypting information is kept secure, while the public key is shared. (Maria & Doug, 2019)

The first objective of quantity machinery encryption is the weakest link in the ecosystem of cryptography: asymmetric cryptography. This is the RSA encryption standard PKI. The asymmetric encryption of emails, blogs, financing transfers and much more protects them. The typical explanation is that everyone may encrypt a message with the intended Public Key of the recipient but only the recipient may decode it with the corresponding private Key. This two-key approach is focused on the premise that it is far easier to do some kinds of mathematical operation than to reverse it. One could break a shell, but it's much harder to get it back together.

Longer keys are the first line of quantum encryption protection, and almost everyone is on board. In addition, NIST no longer considers the 1024-bit version of the RSA encryption standard safe, with a minimum of 2048 bits. Longer keys make for sluggish and more costly decoding, though, so the length of the key will greatly increase so that the quantum computers stay ahead. uMany authorities tend to research how different forms of encryption algorithms are being built that also involve public and private keys which work against quantum computers. For instance, adding two prime numbers together is easy, but it's very hard to break a large number back into its prime factors.

There is, however, no known quantum method to crack grid-based encryption that uses lattic-based cryptographic algorithms. A mixture of postquantum algorithms such as grid-based encryption, which safely exchange keys for initial communications and use symmetric encryption for large messages, may be the best option.

FUNCTIONS QUANTUM CRYPTOGRAPHY

Quantum cryptography (QKD) utilizes a series of photons (light particles) to pass data over a fiber optic wire, from one location to another. The two end points will decide what the secret is and if the usage is secure by measuring the measures of the characteristics of a fraction of such photons. Breaking the process down further helps to explain it better.

1. Sending the photons via a filter (or polarizer), which alertly provides them with one of the four possible polarizations or bit marks: Vertical (one bit), Horizontal (zero bit), 45 degree (one bit) or 45 degree (zero bit) on the left.
2. Photons are sent to a receiver, where the polarisation of each photon is "heard," utilizing two beam dividers (horizontal / vertical and diagonal). The receiver doesn't realize which beam splitter each photon will use and will infer which one to use.
3. When the photon stream was transmitted, the receiver told the recipient the splitter of the beam was included in the sequence of the photons, and the sender correlated the detail with the series of polarizers that the key was transmitted to. The images read using the incorrect beam fraction are discarded and the resultant fragment series is the key.

The condition of the photon will alter whether the photon is interpreted or replicated in some form by an eavesdropper. The transition is sensed via the endpoints. In other words, without being detected it is impossible to read and forward the photon or make a copy of it.

THE QUANTUM SECURITY FOR REMOTE HEALTH CARE DATA

Quantum computation is now a most common and important technology with large-scale players purchasing or developing their own quantum systems. In an almost different field: digital health care, a big investment in technology is also taking place. The healthcare sector for the Internet of Things (IoT) is rapidly growing and over the coming years, more businesses are aiming to have the technical data they need for the doctors and patients. But there's a threat associated here, i.e. health care data among the most popular cybercriminal targets, IoT devices notoriously lacking in effective safeguards and quantum computers on the brink of an encryption/decryption breakthrough, health agencies need a security prognosis and treatment plan as soon as possible. Health care companies recently more worry about the quantum security threats. Most of the health data breaches are due to criminal attacks. And these data breaches are high in terms of volume and frequency. The biggest threat of health care data breaches has come in the form of identity theft.

Despite the troubling track record of health care databases and networks, the industry is under pressure to increase availability of internet-based services. Few modern health care hospitals adopted 100 percent electronic health record (EHR) rate but these hospitals facing various difficulties to share this digital information with the agencies like laboratories or other health care facilities. IoT can provide a solution to this problem: By supplying doctors and nurses, locally and those in remote locations with mobile devices capable of connecting to hospital networks, it's possible to streamline communication and enhance collaboration. Patients outfitted with wearable devices, carrying easily accessible smartphones and tablets, create a massive pool of usable information for medical practitioners and the promise of better treatments directly informed by data. The problem of data security tends to be second (or third, or fourth) priority when designing IoT devices. When the IoT devices related to health care are hacked they may be life threatens devices. For example drug infusion pumps, if hacked it may change the delivered dosage. Increased efforts to mobilize health care may have the unintended consequence of ramping up security threats; not only is patient data up for grabs, but limited IT security could actually put lives at stake.

There should be a strong mechanism to combat the security gaps in existing health care industry. The health care data which is available on the network, an attacker may try to modify, intercept or even view this data stream. With the use of quantum security the quantum state of these photons changes alert the security pros that someone is trying to breach the link. It is very useful for the devices located at distance. If they're supported by a strong connection, key transmission and breach detection become almost instantaneous. Even if attackers are using traditional methods rather than quantum computers, their interference causes an observable state change that can be addressed immediately.

IOT APPLICATION IN HEALTHCARE

This section introduces a number of applications designed to help people and in particular the health sector:

IoT Applications

- Healthcare: Due to the availability of new technological technologies the idea of connected health care is increasing. Every day, a health application can be created to enable blood glucose levels to be monitored using IoT and new technologies, as well as automatically collecting patient data. The IoT device helps doctors to quickly respond to incidents and to track a patient's health in international hospitals. This enables the use of IoT equipment in the household, particularly for older persons with special needs, such as diabetes, congestive heart disease. The Medical RFID tag internet enables a smart individual to be easily and correctly identified, allowing fast and secure access to personal health information on the internet of things. (Domingo, 2012).
- People with Disability: People with hearing loss can receive (impairments in the ear) external or internal hearing aids for improved hearing. Cheap wirelesss, on the other side, help enhance the connectivity of the inexperienced and the deaf. It identifies and transforms hand gestures with a Java-enabled control station (Mobile Phone). The handle has bending controls on the finger side (passive resistors to sense twisting and stretching). It may also be utilized. The blind navigation helps them in seeking a place on the market. The shop's RFID system can use apps to direct shopping that is visually impaired. The market is divided in cells with a shelf, and RFID Tags for a cell pass are distributed on the whole. The monitoring station for mobile devices enables a person with visual impairments to inform the food company he or she wants to go. It allows the person to provide stronger confidentiality security by automatic classification of controls and changes to match individual preferences (Domingo, 2012).
- Tracking and Monitoring of objects and persons: Monitoring is an effort to detect an entity or a individual traveling (Kim, Seo, & Jeongwook,, 2016). Patient behaviour in the health system is controlled and recorded to increase patient efficiency and control mobility across choke points, for example access to specified areas. Most likely or not, follow up is performed to avoid operational problems, rather than constant maintaining supplies (e.g. maintenance, supply in instances of need and usage control) or material monitoring.
- Identification and Authentication: Patient detection is directed at preventing harmful patient incidents (for example, harmful medication / dose / time / procedure) and the complete and revised medical report defining, defining, and authenticating employees is used more commonly for obtaining entry and enhancing the ethics of workers focused on patient safety. (Anwar, Abdullah, Qureshi, & Majid, 2017).
- Transport and Data Collection: The wireless Bluetooth, Near Field Communication (NFC), ZigBee and Bluetooth Low Energy (BLE) systems now allow Personal Health applications to communicate information. Data delivery or automated compilation will reduce the preparation period, electronic diagnostics and the auditing and recording of medical procedures. This function refers to RFID integration technology.
- Clinical Care: The sensors are able to support hospitalized patients moving freely within the institution by committing to certain rooms. These are attached to other devices which avoid trouble going from pavilion to pavilion for measurement which review. This helps all healthcare providers perform their duties because it allows them to remotely monitor the condition of their patients and to work together to diagnose the condition of a patient across the various disciplines. It also saves doctors time between patients and their health. It saves them time. It will enable them respond

to an incident faster and encourage them to work with local facilities and track the condition of a patient.

- Continuous Cardiac Monitoring: A continuous monitoring program is a healthcare device built for patients to be closely tracked. The growing security issue drives scientists and businesses to try the safest and fastest path to remote cardiac surveillance by leveraging global economic technologies to deliver in real time medical record alerts on the internet.
- A continuous monitoring system is a treatment device developed for patients to be treated safely and closely tracked. The emerging health crisis leads scientists and companies, using global economic solutions, to search for the best and quickest path to remote control, with on-line real-time medical record warning signs. (Santos, Macedo, Costa, & JoãoNicolau, 2014).

Figure 2. IoT Healthcare Monitoring System

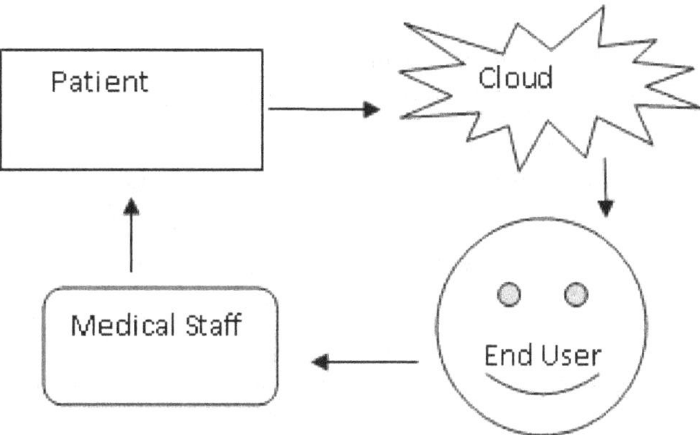

Examples of IoT in Healthcare

- Glucose-Level Monitoring: Most individuals have diabetes, so their glucose levels must be constantly tracked. The IoT device can continuously track glucose levels. Customizable sensors are used to evaluate health parameters and the captured data is distributed via an Internet Protocol (IPV6) network to major health care providers. The tracking device is fitted with a blood glucose monitor, a mobile phone and a diagnostic information screen based on IoT (Alqahtani, 2018). Monitoring of glucose levels involves specific trends of shifts in the glucose level which can be used to assess diet, physical activity, times etc.
- Electrocardiogram Monitoring: The device with the electrocardiogram (ECG) consists of a wireless transmitter and receiver. Automated use can detect a suspicious activity in the heart. The data is transmitted in real time via a network to remote and medical hospitals. The system manages HR and basic rhythm monitoring (Alqahtani, 2018).
- Blood Pressure Monitoring: The device consists of a BP unit with a network-based communication capability. Next, this machine records BP and then uploads the recorded data via the Wi-Fi network. It also has an LCD display of the recorded value of BP.
- Body Temperature Monitoring: The shifting temperature of the body is used to define homeostasis as a central aspect in healthcare. An embedded module for body temperature control is used in

TelosB mote in a clinical IoT device. The IoT Clinic gives the Jian and his partners (Jian, Zhanli and Zhuang, 2012) a body temperature regulation device with a home Server. For tracking the body's temperature, the home application uses infrared monitoring. The system mainly includes an RFID module which works with the body temperature monitoring unit.

- Wheelchair Management: Many studies to build electric wheelchairs for IoT users with disabilities have also been performed. For example (Yang, Ge, Li, Rao & Shen, 2014) an IoT health program supports disabled persons. The network uses wireless body area networks to monitor and coordinate various sensors through the WBAN technology. The machine monitors the movements of the wheelchair. This also monitors the individual with the wheelchair classification by tracking the person's sitting posture and gathering current environmental details.

COST AND FEATURES OF IOT SOLUTIONS FOR HEALTHCARE

IoT's currently happening all over the place. Companies have made significant investments in state-of - the-art technologies to streamline their business processes and cut costs. Consumers also buy smart home appliances and wearable devices to save time and change their own lifestyles. Everyone will need to know what it costs to build the IoT program if they are about to deploy their smart device or even imagine optimizing the company operation of their healthcare organization with any IoT solutions (Devtechnosys, 2018). Here's what the cost and features of IoT healthcare systems are. Components of Infrastructure of IoT and Additional Costs:

- Network: Despite low latency the IoT does not run without the provision of highly scalable or high-speed network infrastructure. Short-range wireless devices such as Wifi, Bluetooth and even cellular networks are often used to enable IoT connectivity. In this case, the IoT healthcare approach comprises of connected devices that communicate over a network, so it is appropriate to anticipate extra connectivity costs.
- Middleware: If someone is going to connect any third party device to their IoT ecosystem, then a software piece that is essentially used to interface between various IoT devices, known as middleware, will be required.
- Data Centre or Cloud-based infrastructure: There we find storage solutions as well as software that reduces to what is actually meaningful the enormous amount of raw data in gigabytes. IoT healthcare companies also make use of the application of small IoT healthcare devices and data analysis through various PaaS solutions.

Throughout the IoT-based healthcare system, as patient monitoring systems occur, there is a need for customer support staff along with electronic equipment and cellular network. This unit is helping people who have needed immediate assistance. In order to connect to the IoT healthcare solution, we must rely on cellular networks. There, there will be extra network expenses (Devtechnosys, 2018).

Cost of Healthcare IoT Application Development

Several factors that affect the development costs must be taken into account when developing IoT applications for health applications. They are (Devtechnosys, 2018):

- Total number of platforms endorsed.
- Full integration of different applications from third parties such as payment portals, healthcare APIs etc.
- Data source and requirements for data ingestion.
- Security standards.

If Bluetooth links the iOS and Android healthcare software to a variety of radiation monitoring devices, analyzes the readings of various sensors, produces medical reports, and also sends the results to any cloud-based server, then the total development hours will be around 2000. The estimated cost is around $70,000 for such a large-scale production of healthcare software. It takes nearly 6000 hours to build a multi-level IoT application with a web-based admin interface, with ERP / CRM applications and embedded software that operates on specialized medical devices and mobile applications. It could cost him approximately $200,000 to build an IoT framework (Devtechnosys, 2018).

Different factors decide the cost for IoT production of healthcare applications. The above cost of developing IoT applications in the medical industry is an estimation that offers an insight into the cost of developing IoT healthcare applications.

IoT Solutions to Health Providers

In delivering digital approaches to safety, we are heading into a whole new phase in medical treatment, clinical surveillance and management. Innovative healthcare innovations are now commonly implemented in medical institutions that enable healthcare facilities to hold costs down, optimize patients' safety and enhance workflows. Such strategies aim to alter the market significantly. Cell phones, mobile apps, bio-sensors, wearables, home virtual supports, blockchain-driven online surveillance networks, predictive analytics and automated data platforms represent a completely modern step of healthcare. In respect to the advantages of digital medicine, I would like, first of all, to mention the improved diagnosis procedure, the efficient handling of data and stronger customer support. In fact, organisations will benefit from automatic evaluations, continuous patient tracking and effective diagnosis through the use of advanced technological solutions. (Maltseva, 2018).

Sensors and Smart Devices

- Precise reading and evaluation of indicators for connecting sensors to mobile devices can help health centers substitute for large devices for smaller instruments. Sensor technology, such as smart monitors and apps, provides many benefits for health management.
- Intelligent devices such as sophisticated inhalers for bronchial asthma, syringe bolt monitoring diabetes mellitus, innovative smartphones and smart blisters have already been actively produced and introduced on the market. This intelligent technology render detection faster, treatment better and patient support more efficient, an significant move in the advancement of health care facilities. For example, the latest norm for medical care of bronchial asthma is smart inhalers. Many other significant smart technology uses, such as in real-time health services, sensors and automated health networks are available in the fields of healthcare (Maltseva, 2018).

Biosensors

- Biosensor is a key component of the physical safety movement. There are a number of biosensors that relay medical information through a wireless network to smartphones and web applications. Biosensors can support people throughout their lives, too, by gathering knowledge on both their daily life, sleep and general health care. Outside the hospital boundaries, the biosensors can monitor patient treatment. Biosensor systems, for example, can enable users to monitor insulin level, blood pressure, heart rhythm, oxygen content, pulse and blood alcohol levels. None of these methods are particularly sensitive and provide unique interventions that are especially valuable for managing the well-being of elderly patients with many chronic diseases.
- The capacity of biosensors to monitor patient medications in real time and provide physicians with all knowledge gathered, thus avoiding disease symptoms and improving diagnosis is essential. Because the data is read directly and is constantly monitored from the patient, the collected measurements are better than those submitted in patient visits and can give specialists a genuine clinical path in each individual case. (Maltseva, 2018).

Patient Health Portals

- Online information apps have already become a central feature of the healthcare industry. Improved client support and streamlined procedures, such as referrals for care and preparation, enhance physicians and patients' lives. Imagine, for example, a fitness network that helps patients to track tests and test information electronically with clinicians and experts, pay quickly and chat with patients to find nutritious food and suggestions and to have book meetings. IoT opportunities are not only restricted to medical professionals, but also patients and their relatives. The most impressive part of IoT is that global patient tracking is rendered better than ever because any medical clock from all around the planet is granted access to healthcare. Throughout the elderly region, IoT-enabled apps and tools are very useful (Maltseva, 2018).

Machine Learning Applications

- The healthcare sector, as with many other industries, gains from machine learning. Health organizations can enhance client satisfaction and derive value from a vast volume of knowledge, analyze health data correctly and optimize patients' care by machine learning technology. Health care and pharmaceutical firms utilize R&D analytics to develop their clinical trials and their decision-making processes for practical applications. When the judgments are drawn by specialists and other professionals, often it feels a bit confusing and complicated as a ton of knowledge can not be accessed quickly.
- There is also a high chance of human error. Intelligent data processing will make this possible by the integration of external data points from different outlets, the break down of information asymmetries and the implementation of sophisticated data mining algorithms. When types of evidence are increasingly diverse, innovative methods of knowledge gathering and interpretation may be found that enable researchers to assess increasingly easily and more comfortably.

- ML provides tremendous opportunities for innovation in clinical practice and enhancement in patient service, but the health industry currently lags behind software learner development deployments. (Maltseva, 2018).

Blockchain-Based Initiatives

- Blockchain technologies may be employed in numerous other areas, in addition to finance and funding. Although the system is identical, it has distinct uses and, in fact, healthcare professionals may profit tremendously from its use. The encrypted storing of data and protected processing are both benefits of Blockchain integrative Safe communication between healthcare institutions, unchanging data collection and open data transfer.
- Blockchain technology in the healthcare industry is becoming commonly used. For starters, the Estonian eHealth Fund and Guardtime cooperated in creating a Blockchain-based network that safeguards millions of medical documents. The healthcare industry is rapidly transforming by the development of revolutionary drugs and the implementation of emerging technology. They push into a whole new era of patient treatment and safety monitoring and automated diagnostic devices (Maltseva, 2018).

IMPACT OF QUANTUM COMPUTING IN HEALTHCARE

Quantum computers have profoundly groundbreaking consequences like medicine, pharms and health care – in many areas of our lives. (Shohini Gose, 2019)

Supersonic Drug Design

Pharmaceuticals are undoubtedly being produced through lengthy and expensive clinical trials: scientists and pharmaceutical firms began to experiment with alternative methods, for example through artificial intelligence, human chip organ or silicon trial, to speed up the process and improve the cost-effectiveness of the discovery and production of medicinal drugs.

Quantum computer searches may be carried out in the least time possible for any molecules at unprecedented pace, drug targeting experiments conducted on any cell model potential or in the human Silicon tissues and networks. This would open the doors to find the disease antidote we never thought of before.

Aging in Silicon Clinical Trials

For silicon clinical trials, there is no need for human or animal, or even a cell to test a new procedure, treatment choice or medication. It means a custom computer simulation used to create or control a medicinal drug, device or action.

The development of 'Virtual Human' and full simulations such as the HumMod which features more than 1,500 equations and 6,500 variables such as body fluid, breathing, electrolytes, hormones, metabolism and skin temperature will advance Quantum computing greatly. This also opened the door to "viving" clinical trials with the maximum number of simulated patients possible and tester loving components. The time needed for such trials, but also their quality and comprehensiveness, would be massively cut.

Sequencing and Evaluating the Maximum Pace of DNA

Quantum computation might provide an significant step into the area: it will require quicker sequencing and more detailed and quicker processing of the whole genome. For fact, forecasts would be more accurate because quantum computers will take far more knowledge into consideration than conventional computers, which may also apply a bit of genetic evidence to health records. Quantum computing could take the guesswork out of genomics and genetics to ensure better health for everyone.

Make Patients a Real Treatment Point

Quantum computation with measurements increases the prediction of lifestyle to a whole new level. While efforts are made to turn from preventive to predictive safety, these are intermittent and in their infancy. For instance, an ophthalmology app shows the patient how their vision would change with the cataract in five years. A detailed forecast of the potential wellbeing of a single entity can be achieved by the use of quantum computers supplied by a great deal of health parameters, genetic records, sensible details as well as other personal data. That is what we always should find safety predictive.

The Perfect Support System for Decision-Making

Quantum computing would make it entirely new and increase it even with special skills. They could skimp through all the studies, discover correlations and causes never found by the human eye, and stumble over diagnoses or treatment options the human physician would never find out. Quantums could develop an uplifted PubMed version in the endpoint of this development, with information not in the traditional written form, but in qubits of data, because nobody but the computer would 'read' the studies anymore.

Build the best Clinical Data Structures of all Time

The usage of quantum uncertainty as one of the most possible uses in quantum computation for encryption. It can be used to generate private keys to encrypt messages sent from one place to another – but hackers can't replicate the key exactly because of quantum uncertainty. To hack such keys, they must break the laws of quantum physics. Imagine that level of safety with respect to sensitive health information: electronic records of health, genetic and genomic data, or any personal information generated about our bodies by our health care system.

CONCLUSION

Worldwide academics have begun to uncover various technical approaches that strengthen healthcare through the application of IoT technology to expand current systems together. This chapter explores different aspects of the health system IoT and the structures of the numerous health networks that allow this IoT web integrated and enable patient data to be gathered and distributed. The chapter concluded with a study of the main problems that threaten consumer privacy in IoT's health care model.

Recent times have seen significant growth in the adoption of IoT. It is widely used in the healthcare industry for tracking progress and health status of patients. Hospitals and providers of health care can save the cost of operations, manage existing assets and spend more time enhancing overall performance of the system In the end, by increasing performance it saves their time. Overall efficiency of elderly care has improved in an IoT approach. This obviously has every benefit for the patients.

IoT is one of the world's most widely deployed development technologies in the health and medical industries. It is commonly used to build IoT healthcare applications with the help of sensors, biosensors and such other tools, to track patient processes, better management and advanced protection. The value of medical IoT is strengthened by the symbiosis of machine learning (ML) and artificial intelligence (AI). When large numbers of information are constantly being collected from sensor-aided systems, data analysis and ML, operational conclusions are drawn that help the therapeutic process much faster.

The potential of quantum computing in healthcare is to revolutionize patient care. Quantum computing can help to detect and detect diseases by identifying and forecasting malfunctions. Health researchers are currently working on how quantum computing-based cancer detection techniques can be used. Present technologies in cancer diagnosis require time, so it may be difficult to produce successful tests. More accurate, faster and more effective methods for optimizing the process are needed. In order to detect disease-specific clues and biomarkers, quantum data will look in greater depth at the data supplied for cancer testing. Quantum computing often theoretically enhances MRI technologies by incredibly accurate measurements that allow doctors to peer at tiny particles that could not be found in conventional computers any deeper (O'Dowd, 2017).

REFERENCES

Anwar, M., Abdullah, A. H., Altameem, A., Qureshi, K. N., Masud, F., Faheem, M., Cao, Y., & Kharel, R. (2018). Green communication for wireless body area networks: Energy aware link efficient routing approach. *Sensors (Basel), 18*(10), 3237. doi:10.339018103237 PMID:30261628

Bernstein, D. J. (2009). *Introduction to post-quantum cryptography*. Post-Quantum Cryptography. doi:10.1007/978-3-540-88702-7

Bernstein, D. J., Buchmann, J., & Dahmen, E. (Eds.). (2009). *Post-quantum cryptography*. Springer. doi:10.1007/978-3-540-88702-7

Bernstein. (2009). *Cost analysis of hash collisions: Will quantum computers make SHARCS obsolete?* (Report). Academic Press.

Biham, E., & Mor, T. (1997). Bounds on Information and the Security of Quantum Cryptography. *Physical Review Letters, 79*(20), 4034–4037. doi:10.1103/PhysRevLett.79.4034

Biham, E., & Mor, T. (1997). Security of Quantum Cryptography against Collective Attacks. *Physical Review Letters, 78*(11), 2256–2259. doi:10.1103/PhysRevLett.78.2256

Choi, J., In, Y., Park, C., Seok, S., Seo, H., & Kim, H. (2018). Secure IoT framework and 2D architecture for End-To-End security. *The Journal of Supercomputing, 74*(8), 3521–3535. doi:10.100711227-016-1684-0

Devtechnosys. (2018). *Cost and Features of IoT Solutions for Healthcare*. https://devtechnosys.com/cost-and-features-of-iot-solutions-for-healthcare

Domingo, M. C. (2012). An overview of the Internet of Things for people with disabilities. *Journal of Network and Computer Applications*, *35*(2), 584–596. doi:10.1016/j.jnca.2011.10.015

Gope, P., & Hwang, T. (2015). BSN-Care: A secure IoT-based modern healthcare system using body sensor network. *IEEE Sensors Journal*, *16*(5), 1368–1376. doi:10.1109/JSEN.2015.2502401

Gose. (2019). https://medicalfuturist.com/quantum-computing-in-healthcare/

Islam, S. R., Kwak, D., Kabir, M. H., Hossain, M., & Kwak, K. S. (2015). The internet of things for health care: A comprehensive survey. *IEEE Access: Practical Innovations, Open Solutions*, *3*, 678–708. doi:10.1109/ACCESS.2015.2437951

Johansson, M. (2019). *Synchronization of Acoustic Sensors in a Wireless Network*. Academic Press.

Ko, H., & Song, M. (2016). A study on the secure user profiling structure and procedure for home healthcare systems. *Journal of Medical Systems*, *40*(1), 1. doi:10.100710916-015-0365-5 PMID:26573639

Korolov & Drinkwater. (2019). https://www.csoonline.com/article/3235970/what-is-quantum-cryptography-it-s-no-silver-bullet-but-could-improve-security.html

Lloret, J., Canovas, A., Sendra, S., & Parra, L. (2015). A smart communication architecture for ambient assisted living. *IEEE Communications Magazine*, *53*(1), 26–33. doi:10.1109/MCOM.2015.7010512

Lo, B. P., Ip, H., & Yang, G. Z. (2016). *Transforming health care: body sensor networks, wearables, and the internet of things*. Academic Press.

Lo, H. -K, & Chau, H. F. (1999). Unconditional Security of Quantum Key Distribution over Arbitrarily Long Distances. *Science, 283*(5410), 2050-2056.

Lütkenhaus, N. (n.d.). *Security against eavesdropping in quantum cryptography*. Physical.

Malaney, R. (2010). Location-dependent communications using quantum entanglement. *Physical Review A.*, *81*(4). Advance online publication. doi:10.1103/PhysRevA.81.042319

Maltseva, D. (2018). *IoT Solutions for Healthcare Providers*. https://www.iotforall.com/topdigital-health-solutions/

Mathew, A., Sa, F. A., Pooja, H. R., & Verma, A. (2015). Smart disease surveillance based on Internet of Things (IoT). *International Journal of Advanced Research in Computer and Communication Engineering, 4*(5), 180-183.

Mayers, D. (2001). Unconditional security in quantum cryptography. *Journal of the Association for Computing Machinery*, *48*(3), 351–406. doi:10.1145/382780.382781

O'Dowd. (2017). https://hitinfrastructure.com/news/how-ibm-universal-quantum-computing-impacts-hit-infrastructure

Quantum Resistant Public Key Exchange: The Supersingular Isogenous Diffie-Hellman Protocol. (2016). CoinFabrik Blog.

Rao, S. (2019). *Evolution of IoT in Healthcare*. https://www.iotforall.com/evolution-iot-healthcare

Rghioui, A., & Oumnad, A. (2017). Internet of Things: Surveys for Measuring Human Activities from Everywhere. *International Journal of Electrical & Computer Engineering, 7*(5).

Rghioui, A., & Oumnad, A. (2018). Challenges and Opportunities of Internet of Things in Healthcare. *International Journal of Electrical & Computer Engineering, 8*.

Rghioui, A., Sendra, S., Lloret, J., & Oumnad, A. (2016). Internet of things for measuring human activities in ambient assisted living and e-health. *Network Protocols and Algorithms*, *8*(3), 15–28. doi:10.5296/npa.v8i3.10146

Sawand, A., Djahel, S., Zhang, Z., & Nait-Abdesselam, F. (2015). Toward energy-efficient and trustworthy eHealth monitoring system. *China Communications*, *12*(1), 46–65. doi:10.1109/CC.2015.7084383

SheaS. (2020). https://searchsecurity.techtarget.com/feature/Computer-Security-Fundamentals-Quantum-security-to-certifications

Singh, R. (2016). A proposal for mobile e-care health service system using IoT for Indian scenario. *Journal of Network Communications and Emerging Technologies*, *6*(1).

Sreekanth, K. U., & Nitha, K. P. (2016). A study on health care in Internet of Things. *International Journal on Recent and Innovation Trends in Computing and Communication*, *4*(2), 44–47.

Thapliyal, K., & Pathak, A. (2018). Kak's three-stage protocol of secure quantum communication revisited. *Quantum Information Processing*, *17*(9). Advance online publication. doi:10.100711128-018-2001-z

Watrous, J. (2009). Zero-Knowledge against Quantum Attacks. *SIAM Journal on Computing*, *39*(1), 25–58. doi:10.1137/060670997

Yu, L., Lu, Y., Tian, Y. M., & Zhu, X. L. (2012). Research on architecture and key technology of Internet of Things in hospital. *Transducer and Microsystem Technologies, 6*, 23.

This research was previously published in Limitations and Future Applications of Quantum Cryptography; pages 148-168, copyright year 2021 by Information Science Reference (an imprint of IGI Global).

Chapter 32
A HIPAA Security and Privacy Compliance Audit and Risk Assessment Mitigation Approach

Young B. Choi
Regent University, USA

Christopher E. Williams
Regent University, USA

ABSTRACT

Data breaches have a profound effect on businesses associated with industries like the US healthcare system. This task extends more pressure on healthcare providers as they continue to gain unprecedented access to patient data, as the US healthcare system integrates further into the digital realm. Pressure has also led to the creation of the Health Insurance Portability and Accountability Act, Omnibus Rule, and Health Information Technology for Economic and Clinical Health laws. The Defense Information Systems Agency also develops and maintains security technical implementation guides that are consistent with DoD cybersecurity policies, standards, architectures, security controls, and validation procedures. The objective is to design a network (physician's office) in order to meet the complexity standards and unpredictable measures posed by attackers. Additionally, the network must adhere to HIPAA security and privacy requirements required by law. Successful implantation of network design will articulate comprehension requirements of information assurance security and control.

INTRODUCTION

Cyberattacks are becoming more prevalent around the world and attackers are utilizing more adaptive and unpredictable processes for breaching various database networks and security systems. These data breaches have a profound effect on businesses associated with industries like the US healthcare system,

DOI: 10.4018/978-1-6684-6311-6.ch032

which have been tasked with safeguarding the medical data of millions of patients. This task extends more pressure on healthcare providers as they continue to gain unprecedented access to patient data, as the US healthcare system integrates further into the digital realm.

This paper shows how we can achieve a HIPAA security and privacy compliance audit and risk assessment mitigation by designing a network (physician's office) in order to meet the complexity standards and unpredictable measures posed by attackers especially compliant to HIPAA security and privacy requirements required by law. Successful implantation of network design will articulate comprehension requirements of information assurance security and control.

NETWORK DESIGN SECURITY REQUIREMENTS AND CONTROL

The evolution of the computer industry and consequent development of the Internet has brought about revolution, but what has remained consistent are the threats, vulnerabilities, and risks to information and information systems. According to Kovacich (2016), "What has changed is the level of sophistication of the threats—the attacks and the threat agents—as well as the exponentially growing number of them all over the world and from various sources" (p. 4).

Schoenfield (2015) states, "System architecture is the descriptive representation of the system's component functions and the communication flows between those components" (p. 58). In order to make informed network architecture decisions, one must immediately pose some important questions. What components make up the network architecture? Which network functions are relevant? What is a communication flow?

Network Purpose

The purpose of a physician's network is to safely and securely facilitate the duties and responsibilities of Confidentiality, Integrity, and Availability (CIA). According to Schoenfield (2015), network security architecture practices includes the following:

1. Sensitive data will be safeguarded in storage, transmission, and processing (consisting of patient medical data records, scheduling, and billing information).
2. Network access will be controlled (need-to-know, authentication, and authorization).
3. Protecting and safeguarding network equipment (systems are maintained in such a way that they remain available for use) (p.14).

Network Equipment

The physician's network (Figure 1) is based on a wireless architecture, consisting of two wireless access points in support of workstations (running Windows 10), printers, and IP phones for ten patient rooms, two doctor's offices, and Wi-Fi capable laptops and cell phones. The following six servers have been implemented with a switching component:

1. Domain Controller/Active Directory Server – Microsoft Windows
2. Scheduling Server – Running Snap Software

3. Billing Server – Running QuickBooks Software
4. Email Sever – Running Microsoft Exchange Software
5. Patient Database Server – Utilizing Oracle 12
6. Web Server – Internet (TCP/IP)
7. DMZ Server – Security added component

Figure 1. Physician's Network

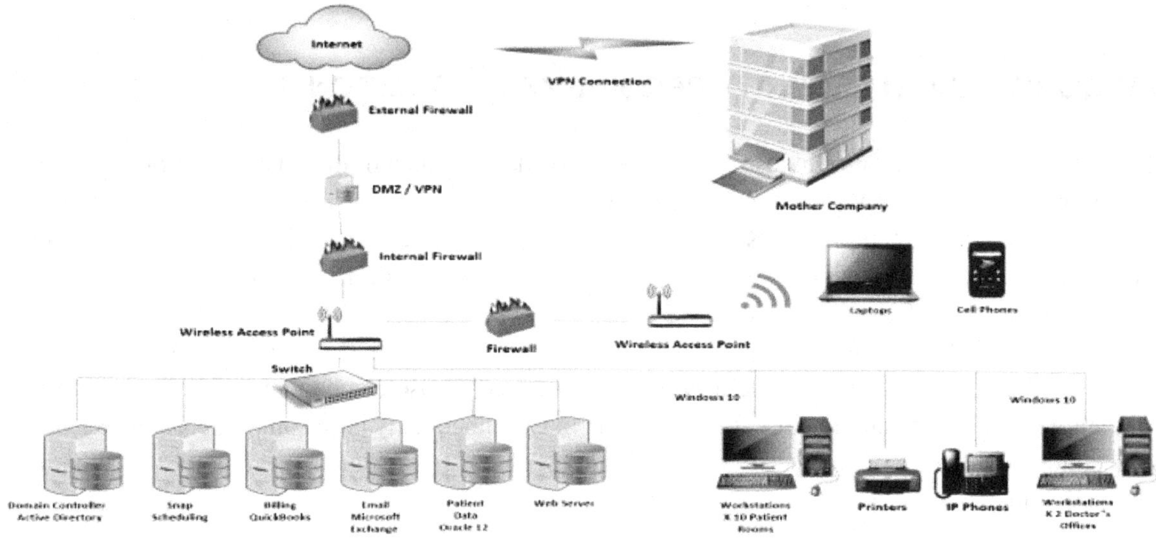

The network also consists of three Next Generation firewalls that add an additional level of security to the network architecture.

Security Management

According to Conklin & Shoemaker (2012), "The aim of the security management is to ensure continuous effectiveness and integrity of the system of security controls, processes, policies, and procedures that are established for day-to-day operation" (p. 110). In order to be regarded as properly structured, all technical controls for security should be consolidated into a coordinated and well-balanced functioning system. In order to assure continuous effectiveness, a security process must be established that can regularly verify the performance of all operational security technologies embedded in the organization's information processing function (Conklin & Shoemaker, 2012, p. 111).

The security controls of the physician's network begin with three defense layered Next Generation Firewalls (NGFW). According to Brook (2018), "A next generation firewall (NGFW) is a deep-packet inspection firewall that moves beyond port/protocol inspection and blocking to add application-level inspection, intrusion prevention, and bringing intelligence from outside the firewall" (NGFW Definition Section, para. 1).

The next portion of layered security is defined by the Demilitarized Zone (DMZ). According to Rouse (2018), "A (DMZ) is a physical or logical subnet that separates an internal local area network (LAN) from other untrusted networks, usually the Internet. This provides an additional layer of security to the (LAN) as it restricts the ability of hackers to directly access internal servers and data via the internet" (Definition Section, para. 1).

A Virtual Private Network (VPN), is the next level of layered security defense. Hoffman (2019) states, "A (VPN), or Virtual Private Network, allows you to create a secure connection to another network over the Internet. (VPNs) can be used to access region-restricted websites, shield your browsing activity from prying eyes on public Wi-Fi, and more" (para. 1). A (VPN) connection is also required for communicating with the mother company outside of the physician's network.

Security and control measures imbedded in Wireless Access Points (WAPs), switches, and servers are dependent on configuration and align with overall network architecture. Workstations will also utilize anti-virus and malware software for additional levels of security.

HIPAA SECURITY AND PRIVACY REQUIREMENTS

Protection of patient privacy and medical information are crucial aspects of the physician/client relationship. They protect patient sovereignty and confidence in physicians, without which patients would be much less likely to explore medical care. According to Yaraghi & Gopal (2018), "These values have been protected under the Health Insurance Portability and Accountability Act (HIPAA), which reduces administration inefficiencies by standardizing electronic transactions in the health care sector" (p.144). In recent years (HIPAA) has gained distinction after the implementation of the Health Information Technology for Economic and Clinical Health Act (HITECH), which resulted in widespread acquisition of heath information technologies. (HITECH) has created unprecedented opposition to patient privacy as more personal information is being collected, archived, transmitted, and accessed by authorized entities utilizing electronic resources (Yaraghi & Gopal, 2018, p. 144).

The U.S. Department of Health and Human Services (HHS) (2019) provides guidance on (HIPAA) compliance and delineates the following compliance guidelines:

1. **The Privacy Rule:** Establishes national standards to protect individuals' medical records and other personal health information and applies to health plans, health care clearinghouses, and those health care providers that conduct certain health care transactions electronically. The Rule requires appropriate safeguards to protect the privacy of personal health information and sets limits and conditions on the uses and disclosures that may be made of such information without patient authorization. The Rule also gives patients' rights over their health information, including rights to examine and obtain a copy of their health records, and to request corrections (Privacy Rule Section, para.1).
2. **The Security Rule:** Establishes national standards to protect individuals' electronic personal health information that is created, received, used, or maintained by a covered entity. The Security Rule requires appropriate administrative, physical and technical safeguards to ensure the confidentiality, integrity, and security of electronic protected health information (Security Rules Section, para. 1).
3. **Omnibus Rule:** Implements several provisions of the Health Information Technology for Economic and Clinical Health (HITECH) Act, enacted as part of the American Recovery and Reinvestment Act of 2009, to strengthen the privacy and security protections for health information established under (HIPAA) (Omnibus Rulemaking Section, para. 1).

Information security is the cornerstone of (HIPAA/HITECH) regulatory compliance. In this information age, privacy and security compliance standards must be in place to safeguard patient information. Network guidelines must therefore adhere to the technical safeguard section of the (HIPAA) Privacy & Security standards for addressing access control, audit control, integrity, person or entity authentication, and transmission security to ensure (HIPAA) compliance (Peterson & Watzlaf, 2015).

A successful information security system should have various layers of safeguards (Physical, Technical, and Administrative) by implementing the following procedures to preserve computer systems and the information contained within. According to Takyi (2018), "Physical security should be used to offer protection for physical items, objects, and sensitive areas from unauthorized access to misuse. This is normally accomplished by controlling access to sensitive rooms or areas in the organization, access to network cables and devices, and hardware and data disposal procedures" (p. 26).

Technical safeguards must be addressed through implementation of logical network security standards that offer protection for computer network components, connections, and data. According to Takyi (2018), "Standards must offer procedures that address access control, firewalls, intrusion detection and prevention systems, system redundancy, change management, and single point of failure. Servers and PCs must be protected through adoption of measures and procedures to manage software licenses, patches, and laptop security" (p. 26). Remaining current on software and computer updates reduces risk to privacy and security vulnerabilities.

Network Administrative safeguards are imperative to (HIPAA) compliance. The (HIPAA) security standards require medical facilities to have written security policies and procedures in place, including those that cover personnel training and sanctions for security policy violations. Office staff and employees must comprehend basic security logic and take their role in protecting patients' privacy seriously. According to Kibbe (2005), "Most security breaches occur when insiders – people working for the organization – exercise faulty judgment or fail to follow protocols in which they've been trained" (p. 46).

SECURITY CONTROL PURPOSE AND APPLICABILITY

The National Institute of Standards and Technology (NIST) is responsible for developing information security standards and guidelines. The purpose of this (NIST SP 800-53 rev 4) is to provide guidelines for organizations when designating and identifying security controls for information systems. The protection and privacy of patient data is imperative, as derived by (HIPAA) standards. These procedures provide the blueprint for organizations like healthcare professionals, when dealing with network boundary design. According to (NIST) (2013), "The guidelines apply to all components of an information system that process, store, or transmit federal information. These guidelines have been developed to achieve more secure information systems and effective risk management within the federal government" (p. 2). In addition, (NIST) states the following concerning security controls:

1. Provides a set of privacy controls based on international standards and best practices that help organizations enforce privacy requirements derived from federal legislation, directives, policies, regulations, and standards.
2. Establishes a linkage and relationship between privacy and security controls for purposes of enforcing respective privacy and security requirements, which may overlap in concept and in implementation within federal information systems, programs, and organizations (p. 2).

Incorporating concepts utilized for managing information security risk assists organizational efforts in implementing privacy controls in a manner that is more cost-effective and risked-based (NIST, 2013, p. 3).

(NIST SP 800-53 rev 4) publication was created with a centralized focus concerning various industries and community organizations of interest. In order to create a theoretically comprehensive set of security controls for information systems and organizations, (NIST) (2013) asserts, "A variety of sources were considered during the development of this special publication. The sources included security controls from the defense, audit, financial, healthcare, industrial/process control, and intelligence communities as well as controls defined by national and international standards organizations" (p. 3-4). (NIST) affords the prospects of building unanimity across various communities and cultivate security plans for organizational information systems that have wide-ranging support for any situation or circumstance that may arise (NIST, 2013, p. 40).

CONTROL FAMILIES

System and Information Integrity – SI

The System and Information Integrity control family includes requirements for responding to security alerts, advisories and directives, flaw remediation, including patching and malicious code protection (Odegard, 2017). Protection mechanisms for the physician's network boundary consists of firewalls, mail servers, web servers, workstations, mobile computing devices and various wireless access points. These information system entries and exit points are utilized to detect and eradicate malicious activity on the network (NIST, 2019).

System and Information integrity also requires information system monitoring and security function verification. According to (NIST) (2019), "Information system monitoring capability is achieved through a variety of tools and techniques (e.g., intrusion detection systems, intrusion prevention systems, malicious code protection software, audit record monitoring software, network monitoring software). Information system monitoring is an integral part of organizational continuous monitoring and incident response programs" (Information System Monitoring Section, para. 2).

Program Management – PM

Program Management requires an organizational Information Security Program Plan that describes how information security resources are implemented. It also defines and maintains a system inventory and enterprise architecture that measures Information Security performance (Odegard, 2017). According to (NIST) (2019), "The information security architecture (physician's network) is developed at a level representing an individual information system but at the same time, is consistent with the information security architecture defined for the organization" (Enterprise Architecture Section, para. 2). The organization must define how their business will operate (mission statement or business process), maintain and develop an information security workforce and allocate for training, monitoring and testing both personnel and system (Odegard, 2017).

SECURITY TECHNICAL IMPLEMENTATION GUIDES AND DATABASE

The Department of Defense (DoD) (2019), states the following concerning (DoD) instruction 8500.01:

Instruction 8500.01 requires that all IT that receives, processes, stores, displays, or transmits (DoD) information will be configured consistent with applicable (DoD) cybersecurity policies, standards, and architectures. Defense Information Systems Agency (DISA) develops and maintains Security Technical Implementation Guides (STIGs) that are consistent with (DoD) cybersecurity policies, standards, architectures, security controls, and validation procedures. (p. 1)

(STIGs) provide configurable operational security management for products being utilized by the (DoD). They also deliver foundational support for evaluating compliance with Cybersecurity controls/ control enhancements, which services system Assessment and Authorization (A&A) under the (DoD) Risk Management Framework (RMF) (DoD, 2019).

Oracle 12 (STIGs) are tools utilized to improve the security of (DoD) information systems. The following list of controls (20 total) have been identified for implementation into the network of the physician's office (hardening the Oracle server and preventing misuse or unauthorized access therein):

1. The Database Management System (DBMS) software installation account must be restricted to authorized users.

When dealing with change control issues, any changes to hardware, software, and/or firmware components of the physician's network and/or application can potentially have significant effects on the overall security of the system. Only qualified and authorized individuals shall be allowed to obtain access to network system components for purposes of initiating changes, including upgrades and modifications.

2. Oracle software must be evaluated and patched against newly found vulnerabilities.

Security faults with software applications and operating systems are discovered daily. Physician office administrators are required to promptly install security-relevant network software updates (e.g., patches, service packs, and hot fixes). Flaws also discovered during security assessments, continuous monitoring, incident response activities, or information system error handling, must also be addressed expeditiously.

3. The (DBMS) must employ cryptographic mechanisms preventing the unauthorized disclosure of information during transmission unless the transmitted data is otherwise protected by alternative physical measures.

Preventing the disclosure of transmitted information (patient/personnel data) requires that applications take measures to employ some form of cryptographic mechanism in order to protect personnel information during transmission.

4. The (DBMS), when using Public Key Infrastructure (PKI)-based authentication, must enforce authorized access to the corresponding private key.

The cornerstone of the (PKI) is the private key used to encrypt or digitally sign information. If the private key is stolen, this will lead to the compromise of the authentication and non-repudiation gained through (PKI) because the attacker can use the private key to digitally sign documents and can pretend to be the authorized user.

5. (DBMS) default accounts must be assigned custom passwords.

Any password, no matter how complex, can eventually be cracked. One method of minimizing this risk is to use complex passwords and periodically change them. If the application does not limit the lifetime of passwords and force users (physicians/personnel) to change their passwords, there is the risk that the system and/or application passwords could be compromised.

6. Database recovery procedures must be developed, documented, implemented, and periodically tested.

Information system backup is a critical step in maintaining data assurance and availability. User-level (patient/personnel) information is data generated by information system and/or application users. In order to assure availability of this data in the event of a system failure, DoD organizations are required to ensure user-generated data is backed up at a defined frequency.

7. The database must not be directly accessible from public or unauthorized networks.

Databases store critical and/or sensitive information (patient/personnel data) used by the physician's office. For this reason, databases are targeted for attacks by malicious users. Additional protections provided by network defenses that limit accessibility help protect the database and its data from unnecessary exposure and risk.

8. Use of the (DBMS) software installation account must be restricted.

This requirement is intended to limit exposure due to operating from within a privileged account or role. To limit exposure when operating from within a privileged account or role, the application must support organizational requirements that users of information system accounts, or roles, with access to organization-defined lists of security functions or security-relevant information, use non-privileged accounts, or roles, when accessing other (non-security) system functions.

9. The (DBMS) must enforce approved authorizations for logical access to the system in accordance with applicable policy.

Strong access controls are critical to securing application data. Access control policies (e.g., identity-based policies, role-based policies, attribute-based policies) and access enforcement mechanisms (e.g., access control lists, access control matrices, cryptography) must be employed by applications, when applicable, to control access between users (physicians/personnel) and objects (e.g., devices, files, records, processes, programs, domains) in the information system.

10. The (DBMS) must protect the integrity of publicly available information and applications.

The purpose of this control is to ensure the physician's office administrators explicitly address the protection needs for public information and applications with such protection likely being implemented as part of other security controls. Databases designed to contain publicly available information, though not concerned with confidentiality, must still maintain the integrity of the data they house. If data available to the public is not protected from unauthorized modification, then it cannot be trusted by those accessing it.

11. Database data files containing sensitive information must be encrypted.

Cryptography is only as strong as the encryption modules/algorithms employed to encrypt (patient/personnel) data. Use of weak or untested encryption algorithms undermines the purposes of utilizing encryption to protect data. Data files that are not encrypted are vulnerable to theft. When data files are not encrypted, they can be copied and opened on a separate system. The data can be compromised without the information owner's knowledge that the theft has even taken place.

12. Application owner accounts must have a dedicated application tablespace.

Separation of tablespaces by application helps to protect the application from resource contention and unauthorized access that could result from storage space reuses or host system access controls. Application data must be stored separately from system and custom user-defined objects to facilitate administration and management of its data storage. The system tablespace must never be used for application data storage in order to prevent resource contention and performance degradation.

13. (DBMS) processes or services must run under custom, dedicated Operating System (OS) accounts.

Separation of duties is a prevalent Information Technology control that is implemented at different layers of the information system, including the operating system and in applications. It serves to eliminate or reduce the possibility that a single user may carry out a prohibited action. Separation of duties requires that the person accountable for approving an action is not the same person who is tasked with implementing or carrying out that action. The (DBMS) must run under a custom dedicated (OS) account. When the (DBMS) is running under a shared account, users with access to that account could inadvertently or maliciously make changes to the (DBMS's) settings, files, or permissions.

14. The (DBMS) must take needed steps to protect data at rest and ensure confidentiality and integrity of application data.

This control is intended to address the confidentiality and integrity of information at rest in non-mobile devices and covers user information and system information. Information at rest refers to the state of information when it is located on a secondary storage device (e.g., disk drive, tape drive) within the network of the physician's office. If the confidentiality and integrity of application data is not protected, the data will be open to compromise and unauthorized modification.

15. System privileges must not be granted to public.

System privileges can be granted to users (physicians/personnel) and roles and to the user group public. All privileges granted to public are accessible to every user in the database. Many of these privileges convey considerable authority over the database and should be granted only to those persons responsible for administering the database. In general, these privileges should be granted to roles and then the appropriate roles should be granted to users. System privileges must never be granted to public as this could allow users to compromise the database.

16. A single database connection configuration file must not be used to configure all database clients.

Applications employ the concept of least privilege for specific duties and information systems (including specific functions, ports, protocols, and services). The concept of least privilege is also applied to information system processes, ensuring that the processes operate at privilege levels no higher than necessary to accomplish required physician office missions and/or functions.

17. The system must protect audit information from unauthorized deletion.

If audit data were to become compromised, then competent forensic analysis and discovery of the true source of potentially malicious system activity is impossible to achieve. To ensure the veracity of audit data the information system and/or the application must protect audit information from unauthorized deletion.

18. The (DBMS) must automatically audit account modification.

Once an attacker establishes initial access to a system, they often attempt to create a persistent method of re-establishing access. One way to accomplish this is for the attacker to simply modify an existing account. Auditing of account modification is one method and best practice for mitigating this risk. A comprehensive application account management process ensures an audit trail automatically documents the modification of application user accounts and, as required, notifies administrators, application owners, and/or appropriate individuals.

19. The (DBMS) must ensure users are authenticated with an individual authenticator prior to using a shared authenticator.

To assure individual accountability and prevent unauthorized access, application users (physicians/personnel) (and any processes acting on behalf of users) must be individually identified and authenticated.

20. The system must protect audit tools from unauthorized access.

Protecting audit data also includes identifying and protecting the tools used to view and manipulate log data. Depending upon the log format and application, system and application log tools may provide the only means to manipulate and manage application and system log data. It is, therefore, imperative that access to audit tools be controlled and protected from unauthorized access (DoD, 2019).

These specific (STIGs) comprise the technical guidance required to harden the physician's office network, which might otherwise be vulnerable to multiple level attacks. The overall goal is to continue developing (STIG) content as the number of applications used by various organizations continues to grow. The outcome: This implementation process will eventually become easier (Galliani, 2013).

HIPAA COMPLIANCE AUDIT

According to (HHS) (2019), "The (HIPAA) Audit Program reviews the policies and procedures adopted and employed by covered entities and business associates to meet selected standards and implementation specifications of the Privacy, Security, and Breach Notification Rules" (Audit Protocol Section, para. 1). The (HIPAA) Privacy Rule addresses the saving, accessing and sharing of medical and personal information of any individual, while the (HIPAA) Security Rule more specifically outlines national security standards to safeguard health data generated, received, preserved or transmitted electronically, also known as Electronic Protected Health Information (ePHI). (The HIPAA) Breach Notification Rule requires covered entities to notify patients when there is a breach of their (ePHI). The Breach Notification Rule also requires entities to notify the (HHS) of such a breach of (ePHI) and issue a notice to the media if the breach affects more than five hundred patients (HIPAA Journal, 2019). A covered entity (physician's office) must adopt and utilize practical policies and procedures to fulfill requirements set forth by program standards.

Program Audit Documentation

In preparation for (HIPAA) audits, organizations must obtain verifiable documentation proving certain administrative, physical and technical safeguards are in place. De Groot (2019) states the following documentation must be obtained concerning the physical and technical safeguards for (HIPAA) compliant organizations:

- **Physical Safeguards:** Including limited facility access and control, with authorized access in place. All covered entities, or companies that must be (HIPAA) compliant, must have policies about use and access to workstations and electronic media. This includes transferring, removing, disposing and re-using electronic media and (ePHI).
- **Technical Safeguards:** Require access control to allow only the authorized to access electronic protected health data. Access control includes using unique user IDs, an emergency access procedure, automatic log off, encryption, and decryption.
- **Audit Reports:** Tracking logs must be implemented to keep records of activity on hardware and software. This is especially useful to pinpoint the source or cause of any security violations.
- **Technical Policies:** Should cover integrity controls, or measures put in place to confirm that (ePHI) has not been altered or destroyed. IT disaster recovery and offsite backup are key to ensure that any electronic media errors or failures can be quickly remedied, and patient health information can be recovered accurately and intact.
- **Network, Transmission, and Security:** Technical safeguards required of (HIPAA) compliant hosts to protect against unauthorized public access of (ePHI). This concerns all methods of trans-

mitting data, whether it be email, internet, or even over a private network, such as a private cloud (Compliance Section, para. 5-9).

Vulnerability Assessment – Scanning

According to Schoenfield (2015), "Security architecture calls for its own unique set of skill requirements in the IT architect" (p. 353). This concept is predominantly guided around design, but also falls alongside the skillset of security vulnerability assessment. Vulnerability assessment is an integral component of a good security program. Along that aspect, vulnerability scanning is a crucial security technique utilized as part of an assessment, which identifies security weaknesses in an IT system.

According to Cannon (2019), "Vulnerabilities are flaws in software that can be exploited by hackers to gain access to your network or sensitive data including (ePHI)" (What is a Vulnerability Scan Section, para. 1). Vulnerabilities can be in computer operating systems such as Microsoft Windows 10 or Windows Server. They can be in commonly used software such as Microsoft Office, Adobe Acrobat, or any other software that may be installed on your servers, desktops, laptops and mobile devices. Vulnerabilities can also exist on hardware devices including network firewalls, switches, routers, printers, or any other device that is on the network. Identifying vulnerabilities or flaws in a network gives you the opportunity to apply patches to the network that will eliminate security weaknesses. Vulnerability scanning and associated remediation is an imperative process in keeping potential hackers out of networks, while increasing security concepts for preparation in conducting compliance audits (Cannon, 2019).

Physician's Network Vulnerability Assessment – Scanning

Vulnerability assessments are generally comprised of a network-based assessment and host-based assessment. The network-based vulnerability assessment tools allow a network administrator to identify and eliminate organizational network-based (entire network) security vulnerabilities. Host-based scanning tools allow network administrators to secure organizational internal systems (specific hosts) by providing an extra layer of security to confidential data (Shakeel, 2018).

The physician's network is based on a wireless architecture consisting of two wireless access points in support of workstations (running Windows 10), printers, and IP phones for ten patient rooms, two doctor's offices, and Wi-Fi capable laptops and cell phones. Wireless scanning of this specific architecture will be conducted while utilizing a combination of both network-based and host-based vulnerability scanning solutions. (NIST) (2013) states the following concerning wireless scanning:

Wireless scanning should be conducted using a mobile device with wireless analyzer software installed and configured. The scanning software or tool will allow the operator to configure the device for specific scans in both passive and active modes. The scanning software should also be configurable by the operator to identify deviations from the organization's wireless security configuration requirements. (p. 4-7)

The physician's office also includes the following six servers that have been implemented with a switching component:

1. Domain Controller/Active Directory Server – Microsoft Windows
2. Scheduling Server – Running Snap Software

3. Billing Server – Running QuickBooks Software
4. Email Sever – Running Microsoft Exchange Software
5. Patient Database Server – Utilizing Oracle 12
6. Web Server – Internet (TCP/IP)

Additionally, the network consists of three Next Generation firewalls that add an additional level of security to the network architecture.

When conducting a vulnerability assessment, network-based scanning is completed primarily, due to its ability to analyze network-based devices on an organization's network, discover unknown or unauthorized devices and systems on a network, and provide a comprehensive view of all operating systems and services running and available on a network (Internet Security Systems (ISS), n.d.). According to Shakeel (2015), "A network-based test provides the immediate results of highly severe vulnerabilities that needed a quick fix. A firewall not configured correctly or vulnerable web server, which is considered very severe vulnerabilities, can be detected easily by running a network vulnerability test" (p. 4). Network-based scanning performs quick, detailed analyses of an enterprise's critical network and system infrastructure from the perspective of an external or internal intruder trying to use the network to break into systems ((ISS), n.d.).

Based on the size of the physician's network (small number of hosts), host-based scanning can also be conducted. According to (ISS) (n.d.), "Host-based scanning's strengths lie in direct access to low-level details of a host's operating system, specific services, and configuration details. Host-based scanning can view a system from the security perspective of a user who has a local account on the system" (p. 4). Accessing user-driven security risks is imperative to the specific host affected, and to the security of the entire network. Host-based scanners are superb tools for assessing security risks associated with all types of user risks. Host-based scanners are also utilized as tools of resilience to network-based scanning. According to (ISS) (n.d.), "Host based scanners are also great tools for helping to lock down a critical system such as file, database, web and application servers, and firewalls. In addition to testing standard security features, they may also detect configuration errors that have left these devices open to intrusion" (p. 6).

PHYSICIAN'S OFFICE AUDIT/RISK ASSESSMENT MITIGATION

Risk mitigation is a strategy of deterrence that implements guidelines followed by organizations that offer steps to reduce the negative effects of threats and disasters on physical and logical boundaries of information systems. Mitigation includes reduction of the likelihood that a risk event will occur and/or reduction of the effect of a risk event if it does occur. According to Rouse (2018), "Rather than planning to avoid a risk, mitigation deals with the aftermath of a disaster and the steps that can be taken prior to the event occurring to reduce adverse, and potentially long-term, effects" (para. 2).

An audit of the physician's office was completed. The following vulnerabilities have been identified by auditors, matched by number to a control family, and offered the appropriate mitigation control guidance:

1. People can gain physical access to the physician's office without anyone checking ID:

   a. **Control Family and Control Number:** Physical Access Control (PE-3) - Enforces physical access authorizations at organization-defined entry/exit points to the facility where the information system resides.
   b. **Appropriate Mitigations:** Physician's office must verify individual access authorizations before granting access to the facility and maintain physical access audit logs (written or automated) for defined entry/exit points (NIST, 2013).
2. The server room does not have a lock on the door:
   a. **Control Family and Control Number:** Physical Access Control (PE-3) - Enforces physical access authorizations at organization-defined entry/exit points to the facility where the information system resides.
   b. **Appropriate Mitigations:** Physician's office must secure keys, combinations, and other physical access devices. They must also inventory physical access devices by organization-defined frequency (NIST, 2013).
3. There are default admin accounts with elevated privileges:
   a. **Control Family and Control Number:** Least Privilege (AC-6) - Organizations employ the principle of least privilege, allowing only authorized accesses for users which are necessary to accomplish assigned tasks in accordance with organizational missions and business functions.
   b. **Appropriate Mitigations:** Physician's office must review the privileges assigned to organization-defined roles or classes of users to validate the need for such privileges; and reassign or remove privileges, if necessary, to correctly reflect organizational mission/business needs (NIST, 2013).
4. The receptionist of the office provided the password to the server via an inbound phone call:
   a. **Control Family and Control Number:** Information Spillage Response (IR-9) - The organization responds to information spillage.
   b. **Appropriate Mitigations:** Physician's office must identify the specific information involved in the information system contamination. They must alert organization-defined personnel or roles of the information spill using a method of communication not associated with the spill. They must isolate the contaminated information system or system component and eradicate the information from the contaminated information system or component. They must identify other information systems or system components that may have been subsequently contaminated and conduct basic security awareness training with personnel as part of initial training for users; when required by information system changes and thereafter (NIST, 2013).
5. There are unused open ports on all the servers:
   a. **Control Family and Control Number:** Configuration Settings (CM-6) - Organizations establish and document configuration settings (Security-related parameters that include: (i) registry settings; (ii) account, file, directory permission settings; and (iii) settings for functions, ports, protocols, services, and remote connections) for information technology products employed within the information system using organization-defined security configuration checklists that reflect the most restrictive mode consistent with operational requirements.
   b. **Appropriate Mitigations:** Physician's office administrators must implement configuration settings. They must also identify, document, and approve any deviations from established configuration settings for information system components based on operational requirements. Lastly, administrators must monitor and control changes to the configuration settings in accordance with organizational policies and procedures (NIST, 2013).

6. The scheduling software shows verbose code:
   a. **Control Family and Control Number:** Flaw Remediation (SI-2) - The organization identifies, reports, and corrects information system flaws.
   b. **Appropriate Mitigations:** Physician's office administrators must test software and firmware updates related to flaw remediation for effectiveness and potential side effects before installation. The must install security-relevant software and firmware updates within organizational defined time period of the release of the updates and incorporate flaw remediation into the organizational configuration management process.
7. There is no encryption on the network. PHI/PII data is sent over the wireless network in clear text:
   a. **Control Family and Control Number:** Transmission Confidentiality and Integrity (SC-8) - The information system protects the confidentiality; integrity of transmitted information.
   b. **Appropriate Mitigations:** Physician's office must utilize information systems that implement cryptographic mechanisms to prevent unauthorized disclosure of information; detect changes to information during transmission unless otherwise protected by organization-defined alternative physical safeguards (NIST, 2013).
8. The PHI/PII data on the database server resides on unencrypted drives:
   a. **Control Family and Control Number:** Protection of Information at Rest (SC-28) - The information system protects the confidentiality and integrity of organization-defined information at rest.
   b. **Appropriate Mitigations:** Physician's office must employ different mechanisms to achieve confidentiality and integrity protections, including the use of cryptographic mechanisms and file share scanning. They must also employ other security controls including, for example, secure off-line storage in lieu of online storage when adequate protection of information at rest cannot otherwise be achieved and/or continuous monitoring to identify malicious code at rest (NIST, 2013).
9. In an interview with the nurse, she stated there is no training for HIPAA Security or Privacy provided:
   a. **Control Family and Control Number:** Role-Based Training (AT-3) - Organization provides role-based security training to personnel with assigned security roles and responsibilities.
   b. **Appropriate Mitigations:** Physician's office must conduct role-based training with personnel before authorizing access to the information system or performing assigned duties; when required by information system changes and thereafter (NIST, 2013).
10. On the desktops, there are Microsoft vulnerabilities in the Windows 10 OS which have not been patched:
    a. **Control Family and Control Number:** Flaw Remediation (SI-2) - Organization identifies, reports, and corrects information system flaws.
    b. **Appropriate Mitigations:** Physician's office administrators must test software and firmware updates related to flaw remediation for effectiveness and potential side effects before installation. They must install security-relevant software and firmware updates within organization defined time period of the release of the updates and incorporate flaw remediation into the organizational configuration management process (NIST, 2013).
11. The auditor watched an employee make changes to the Oracle server without following change management:

a. **Control Family and Control Number:** Configuration Change Control (CM-3) - Organization determines the type of changes to the information system that are configuration-controlled.

b. **Appropriate Mitigations:** Physician's office administrators must review proposed configuration-controlled changes to the information system and approve or disapprove such changes with explicit consideration for security impact analyses. They must document configuration change decisions associated with the information system, implement approved configuration-controlled changes to the information system, and retain records of configuration-controlled changes to the information system. Lastly, administrators must audit, and review activities associated with configuration-controlled changes to the information system and coordinate oversight for configuration change control activities through organization-defined configuration change control element (NIST, 2013).

TELEMEDICINE AND CHANGE MANAGEMENT

Telemedicine is a practice that has progressed to the forefront of the medical field by utilizing a combination of technology and telecommunications in the practice of medicine. According to Capitan, Choi, Chung, Hyewon & Krause (2006), telemedicine is defined as the "use of advanced telecommunication technologies to exchange health information and provide health care services across geographic, time, social, and cultural barriers" (para. 1). The expansion of technological resources in medicine have led to advances in the transfer of data and imagery; however, certain barriers still exist that prevent telemedicine from becoming the viable option in healthcare (Capitan et al., 2006).

Healthcare and telemedicine are both heavily reliant on technology. According to Robinson (2019), "Physicians rely on their hardware, technology-mediated communication, and digital retrieval and storage of data while conducting a telehealth consultation. Processing digital health data plays an increasingly important role in our healthcare industry, making the whole process more efficient – but also at risk of cyber threats" (para. 1). Additionally, there are several unresolved standardization issues that must be addressed before telemedicine can be utilized by the most efficient and effective means. According to Capitan et al. (2006), "Currently, inadequate standardization of procedures, terminology, equipment requirements, health provider identifiers, service identifiers, and data transfer are substantial barriers to the successful implementation of telemedicine. Poor standardization raises a number of important questions about the integrity and security of transfers and limits the interoperability and accessibility of information" (para. 2).

Several existing technical controls can protect against some standardization security risks. Tyson (2015) states the following are required to create lasting change in cybersecurity, where healthcare organizations should implement measures that include:

- End-to-end encryption
- Comprehensive identity and access management controls
- Distribution of telehealth applications in-person to patients
- Implementing intrusion detection systems
- Developing an incident response and remediation plan
- Conducting ongoing training and IT governance measures that empower all stakeholders to prevent phishing attacks and maintain good security hygiene practices (para. 5).

To develop more solutions to the standardization of telemedicine, there must be tangible rules established in place that permit interoperable collaboration amongst various network locations and types of hardware and software. Secondly, standards must be revised or generated specifically for telemedicine practice. Finally, the various personnel of the telemedicine community must be active contributors in deciding how services are rendered and employed under those specified guidelines. Ultimately, once those barriers are removed, telemedicine will become a viable option in health care (Capitan et al., 2006).

According to Pan-Canadian Change Management Network (PCCMN) (2013), change management is "a strategic and systematic approach that supports people and their organizations in the successful transition and adoption of electronic health solutions" (p. 8). Change, however, in the complexity of a telehealth services is often underestimated. Numerous factors have an impact on the success of teleservices. Some range from technical issues to infrastructure, regulation, change management and financial business models. Van Dyke (2014) states the following concerning telehealth services:

Telehealth services, by definition, are delivered over a distance and, thus, always span more than one organizational entity. These entities often exhibit conflicting organizational cultures and practices, as well as incompatible business models and governing processes. Furthermore, telehealth services involve multidisciplinary role players, ranging from a wide variety of healthcare workers and information and communication technologists, to economists, managers and policy makers. The way in which decisions are executed, problems solved and change managed is also often linked to a specific discipline, which adds to the complications emanating from the implementation of telehealth services. (Introduction Section, para. 2)

Sometimes implementing a new technology can create a certain culture within a healthcare organization rather than an organization creating its own change management culture that will support the technologies it needs. This aspect is why it is imperative that if healthcare organizations want to implement a new technology successfully, especially telehealth technologies, it needs to create a change management culture (Lee, 2017).

CONCLUSION

According to Appari & Johnson (2014), "Information security and privacy in the healthcare region is an aspect of emergent importance around the world. The implementation of digital patient records, improved regulation, provider alliances and increased requirements for safer information exchange between patients, providers and payers, all point towards the requirement for improved information security" (p. 279). In the healthcare sector, it is often necessary to share data across organizational boundaries to support the larger interests of multiple stakeholders as well as agencies involved with public health. However, the release of patient data could entail personally identifying information as well sensitive information that may violate privacy as well cause socio-economic repercussions for patients. Yet such data, when masked for identifying and sensitive information, must maintain the analytic properties to assure statistical inferences (Truta et al., 2004).

The prospect of storing health information in electronic form increases apprehension about patient privacy and data security. Any attempt to introduce computerized health-care information systems should therefore guarantee satisfactory safeguarding of the confidentiality and integrity of patient information.

Additionally, the patient information must also be readily available to all authorized health-care providers, in order to ensure the proper treatment of the patients (Lucente, 2018). Data privacy and security are important components of information systems in healthcare today. Privacy of data must be maintained and remain beneficial and accessible for both primary and secondary practices. Organizations must be aware of the laws and ensure that information platforms are secure and compliant to avoid unauthorized data access. There are various security risks, including illicit data access by insiders and hacking and phishing attacks from outside intruders. System security is a significant aspect of data protection in the healthcare field. Additionally, pinpointing data vulnerabilities is a vital and necessary part of preserving data privacy (Lucente, 2018).

Cyber-attacks are becoming more prevalent around the world. Attackers are utilizing more adaptive and unpredictable processes for breaching various database networks and security systems. These data breaches have a profound effect on businesses associated with industries like the US healthcare system, which have been tasked with safeguarding the medical data of millions of patients. Health Insurance Portability and Accountability Act (HIPAA), Omnibus Rulemaking, Security Technical Implementation Guides (STIGs) and Health Information Technology for Economic and Clinical Health (HITECH) laws and guidelines were enacted by the government to significantly increase the regulatory oversight and privacy protection requirements of medical business associates. The Defense Information Systems Agency (DISA) also develops and maintains Security Technical Implementation Guides (STIGs) that are consistent with (DOD) cybersecurity policies, standards, architectures, security controls, and validation procedures. These laws must be utilized in conjunction with network design in order to meet the complexity standards and unpredictable measures posed by attackers.

REFERENCES

Appari, A., & Johnson, M. E. (2014). *Information Security and Privacy in Healthcare: Current State of Research.* Retrieved from: https://clearwatercompliance.com/wp-content/uploads/Information-security-and-privacy-in-healthcare_Current-State-of-Research.pdf

Brook, C. (2018). *What is a Next Generation Firewall?* Retrieved from: https://digitalguardian.com/blog/what-next-generation-firewall-learn-about-differences-between-ngfw-and-traditional-firewalls

Cannon, J. (2019). *HIPAA Compliance and Vulnerability Scans.* Retrieved from: https://dentalcomplianceetn.com/2018/08/06/hipaa-compliance-and-vulnerability-scans/

Capitan, K. E., Choi, Y. B., Chung, K., Hyewon, S., & Krause, J. S. (2006). Telemedicine in the USA: Standardization through information management and technical applications. *IEEE Communications Magazine*, *44*(4), 41–48. doi:10.1109/MCOM.2006.1632648

Conklin, W. A., & Shoemaker, D. (2012). *Cybersecurity: The Essential Body of Knowledge*. Course Technology Cengage Learning.

De Groot, J. (2019). *What is HIPAA Compliance? 2019 HIPAA Requirements*. Retrieved from: https://www.otava.com/reference/what-is-hipaa-compliance/

Department of Defense (DoD). (2019). *Oracle Database 12c Security Technical Implementation Guide (STIG) Overview*. Retrieved from: https://public.cyber.mil/stigs/downloads/

Department of Health and Human Services (HHS). (2019a). *Omnibus HIPAA Rulemaking*. Retrieved from: https://www.hhs.gov/hipaa/for-professionals/privacy/laws-regulations/combined-regulation-text/omnibus-hipaa-rulemaking/index.html

Department of Health and Human Services (HHS). (2019b). *The Privacy Rule*. Retrieved from: https://www.hhs.gov/hipaa/for-professionals/privacy/index.html

Department of Health and Human Services (HHS). (2019c). *The Security Rule*. Retrieved from: https://www.hhs.gov/hipaa/for-professionals/security/index.html

Department of the Interior (DOI). (2011). *Security Control Standard System and Information Integrity*. Retrieved from: https://www.doi.gov/.../attachment_1_-_system_and_information_integrity_v1.1.docx

Galliani, J. (2013). *What Are STIGs and How Do They Impact Your Overall Security Program?* Retrieved from: https://www.seguetech.com/stigs-security-program/

HIPAA Journal. (2019). *HIPAA Compliance Checklist*. Retrieved from: https://www.hipaajournal.com/hipaa-compliance-checklist/

Hoffman, C. (2019). *What Is a VPN, and Why Would I Need One?* Retrieved from: https://www.howtogeek.com/133680/htg-explains-what-is-a-vpn/

Internet Security Systems (ISS). (n.d.). *Network and Host-based Vulnerability Assessment: A guide for information systems and network security professionals*. Retrieved from: https://pdfs.semanticscholar.org/502d/d80ec24419907b92379dc45be1d983365a5f.pdf

Kibbe, D. C. (2005). Ten Steps to HIPAA Security Compliance. *Family Practice Management*, *12*(4), 43–49. PMID:15889774

Kovacich, G. L. (2016). *The information systems security officer's guide: Establishing and managing a cyber security program* (3rd ed.). Butterworth-Heinemann.

Lee, K. (2017). *Change management culture to support telehealth technologies*. Retrieved from: https://searchhealthit.techtarget.com/tip/Change-management-culture-to-support-telehealth-technologies

Lucente, I. (2018). *Tackling Privacy and Security When Building AI in Healthcare*. Retrieved from: https://dzone.com/articles/tackling-privacy-and-security-when-building-ai-in

National Institute of Standards and Technology (NIST). (2008). *Technical Guide to Information Security Testing and Assessment* (NIST SP 800-115). Retrieved from: https://nvlpubs.nist.gov/nistpubs/Legacy/SP/nistspecialpublication800-115.pdf

National Institute of Standards and Technology (NIST). (2013). *Security and Privacy Controls for Federal Information Systems and Organizations* (NIST SP 800-53 R4). Retrieved from: doi:10.6028/NIST.SP.800-53r4

National Institute of Standards and Technology (NIST). (2019). *Security Controls and Assessment Procedures for Federal Information Systems and Organizations (Program Management Control Family)*. Retrieved from: https://nvd.nist.gov/800-53/Rev4/

Odegard, J. (2017). *RMF Control Family Descriptions.* Retrieved from: http://www.cyberperspectives.com/rmf-control-family-descriptions/

Pan-Canadian Change Management Network (PCCMN). (2013). *A Framework and Toolkit for Managing eHealth Change: People and Processes.* Retrieved from: https://www.infoway-inforoute.ca/en/component/edocman/1659-a-framework-and-toolkit-for-managing-ehealth-change-2/view-document?Itemid=0

Peterson, C., & Watzlaf, V. (2015). Telerehabilitation Store and Forward Applications: A Review of Applications and Privacy Considerations in Physical and Occupational Therapy Practice. *International Journal of Telerehabilitation, 6*(2), 75–84. doi:10.5195/IJT.2014.6161 PMID:25945231

Robinson, J. (2019). *Why You Must Consider Cyber-Security for Telehealth.* Retrieved from: https://cliniciantoday.com/why-you-must-consider-cyber-security-for-telehealth/

Rouse, M. (2018). *Demilitarized Zone (DMZ) Networking.* Retrieved from: https://searchsecurity.techtarget.com/definition/DMZ

Rouse, M. (2018). *Risk Mitigation.* Retrieved from: https://searchdisasterrecovery.techtarget.com/definition/risk-mitigation

Schoenfield, E. B. S. (2015). *Securing Systems: Applied Security Architecture and Threat Models.* CRC Press. doi:10.1201/b18465

Shakeel, I. (2015). *The Art of Network Vulnerability Assessment.* Retrieved from: https://resources.infosecinstitute.com/wp-content/uploads/The-Art-of-Network-Vulnerability-Assessment.pdf

Takyi, H. K. (2018). *Security, privacy, confidentiality and integrity of emerging healthcare technologies: A framework for quality of life technologies to be HIPAA/HITECH compliant, with emphasis on health kiosk design* (Order No. 13872157).

Truta, T. M., Fotouhi, F., & Barth-Jones, D. (2004). Assessing global disclosure risk in masked Microdata. *Proceedings of the 2004 Workshop on Privacy in Electronic Society*, 85–93. 10.1145/1029179.1029202

Tyson, K. (2015). *Incorporating cybersecurity into the DNA of telemedicine.* Retrieved from: https://www.healthcareitnews.com/blog/incorporating-cybersecurity-dna-telemedicine

Unified Compliance Framework (UCF). (2019). *Security Technical Implementation Guidelines (STIG) Viewer.* Retrieved from: https://www.stigviewer.com/stig/oracle_database_12c/

Van Dyke, L. (2014). *A Review of Telehealth Service Implementation Frameworks.* Retrieved from: https://www.ncbi.nlm.nih.gov/pmc/articles/PMC3945538/

Yaraghi, N., & Gopal, R. D. (2018). The role of HIPAA omnibus rules in reducing the frequency of medical data breaches: Insights from an empirical study. *The Milbank Quarterly, 96*(1), 144–166. doi:10.1111/1468-0009.12314 PMID:29504206

This research was previously published in the International Journal of Cyber Research and Education (IJCRE), 3(2); pages 28-45, copyright year 2021 by IGI Publishing (an imprint of IGI Global).

Chapter 33
A New Perspective on the Swiss Cheese Model Applied to Understanding the Anatomy of Healthcare Data Breaches

Faouzi Kamoun
https://orcid.org/0000-0002-3740-1452
ESPRIT School of Engineering, Tunisia

Mathew Nicho
Zayed University, UAE

ABSTRACT

The healthcare industry has been lagging behind other industries in protecting its vital data. Over the past few years, researchers and practitioners have been trying to gain a better understanding of the anatomy of healthcare data breaches. In this chapter, the authors show how Reason's swiss cheese model (SCM) provides a powerful analytic model to explain the human, technical, and organizational factors of healthcare data breaches. They also show how the SCM brings forwards the latent conditions of healthcare data breach incidents that have often been overlooked in previous studies. Based on an extensive literature review and an analysis of reported breaches from credible sources, the authors provide an explanation of the cheese layers and the associated holes. Since the SCM endorses the "defenses in depth" approach, it can assist healthcare organizations and business associates in developing a comprehensive and systematic approach to prevent and mitigate data breach incidents.

INTRODUCTION

Personal health records (PHR) and electronic medical records play an important role in managing health information and enhancing the quality of patients' healthcare through enhanced collection, compilation, storage, tracking and dissemination of health records and medical history among healthcare provid-

DOI: 10.4018/978-1-6684-6311-6.ch033

ers (Kierkegaard, 2012). Health information is considered among the most confidential of all types of personal information (Fernández-Alemán et al, 2013).The health sector is characterized by a wealth of ever growing information that is dispersed throughout the healthcare organization and its downstream chain of business associates (BA) which includes any person or entity that creates, receives, maintains, or transmits protected health information (PHI) in fulfilling certain functions or activities for the health organization (HHS, 2013a). At the same time, as the healthcare sector is shifting from paper-based to electronic records, electronic data archives are accumulating in healthcare facilities and administrative agencies (O'Keefe & Connolly, 2011). In this respect, modern technologies have amplified the number of potential medical records that can be exposed to theft, damage or loss (Agaku et al, 2014). The exchange of electronic protected health information (ePHI) and electronic health records (EHR) further accentuated the need to secure patients' health information against unauthorized access, while guaranteeing easy access and a smooth flow of this information among the authorized entities. Kotz et al (2015) argue that the acclaimed benefits of modern healthcare information systems will be diluted if the associated security concerns were not properly addressed.

According to Johnson (2009) healthcare data hemorrhages come from many different sources like ambulatory healthcare providers, acute-care hospitals, physician groups, medical laboratories, insurance carriers, back-offices of health maintenance organizations, and outsourced service providers such as billing, collection, and transcription firms. The effects of data breaches on these parties are manifold. The improper disclosure or misuse of health information can cause serious reputational harm such as discrimination, stigmatization, loss of insurance and/or employment (Kulynych & Korn, 2002). The financial costs of data breaches, which include both direct costs, such as "clean-up" costs, and indirect costs, such as loss of revenues from reputational harm, are perhaps the most damaging factors from an organizational perspective. Data breaches can also lead to privacy violations, medical identity fraud, financial identity theft (such as forged taxation, fake health insurance and drug prescription claims) and identity theft (Johnson, 2009). Thus healthcare information security and privacy is a major ethical and legal issue (Appari & Johnson, 2010). In particular, the ethical principle of personal autonomy suggests that individuals have the right to control all matters related to their own body, including their personal health information (Neame, 2012). This right translates into public expectations and legal requirements that healthcare providers shall secure the privacy and confidentiality of patients' health records.

Despite the ethical and legal obligations of healthcare providers to protect the confidentiality of patients' health records, the past few years have witnessed an increase in the number and scope of reported healthcare data breach incidents. This is due to many factors, including (1) the fact that breach reporting became mandatory in September 2009, (2) the ease at which the healthcare sector can be penetrated, (3) the wide adoption of IT for the storage, processing and transmission of electronic health records (Ben-Assuli, 2015), (4) the wealth of sensitive personal and financial information available and accessible to criminals in a patient's health record (Kruse et al, 2017) and (5) the lack of adoption of security technologies and solutions (Kwon & Johnson, 2014). For example, a PHR may reveal personal information (such as name, dates of birth, social security number, address, employer and phone numbers), financial and insurance information (such as bank account, credit card numbers, and insurance numbers) and health information (such as diagnosis results, medications, allergies, addiction problems and treatment types). Healthcare data breaches have evolved into four main themes, namely data loss, monetary theft, and attacks on medical devices and on infrastructures (Perakslis, 2014).

Despite all forms of legislation, data encryption, and security technologies made available during the past years, one fundamental question remains that is still not fully addressed: "why do data breaches[1] still occur in the healthcare sector?" While a thorough answer is not evident, this research aims to shed light on the anatomy of healthcare data breaches so that proper countermeasures can be put in place.

Few studies have been conducted to investigate the root cause of healthcare data breaches. For example, in its recent 2016 Cost of Data Breach Study, the Ponemon Institute revealed that among 874 reported data breach incidents, 568 were caused by employee or contractor negligence; 85 by outsiders using stolen credentials; and 191 by malicious employees and criminals (Ponemon, 2016a). Another study by the Ponemon Institute (Ponemon, 2016b) found that while external threats are predominant, internal problems, negligence, mistakes and unintentional employee actions are equally responsible for a significant percentage of the reported data breaches. More precisely, 36% of the surveyed healthcare organizations and 55% of business associates mentioned unintentional employee action as the source of data breach. Further 69% of the surveyed healthcare organizations mentioned the negligent or careless employee as the security threat that worries them most. In particular, careless employees losing laptops or other mobile devices, mishandling of data at rest and in motion and malicious employees or other insiders have been identified as the root causes of most of the reported data breaches. However, one might question whether these survey results were biased towards the "*careless worker*" myth that tends to put the blame on people and hence focuses on changing their behavior. One might also conjecture that other potential latent organizational factors may play an equally important role in healthcare data breaches.

This work is motivated by the fact that a good understanding of the root causes of data breach incidents is critical for instituting effective data breach risk management and security governance. The objective of this paper is to establish a better understanding of the anatomy of healthcare data breaches through the lens of a relevant analytical framework. This paper is organized as follows:

In section 2, we begin by surveying some recently reported healthcare data breach incidents. The relevant literature is reviewed and the research contribution is highlighted in section 3. Next, in sections 4 and 5, we provide a quick review of human error theory, with a special emphasis on the Swiss cheese model and its relevance to this research. In section 6, we describe our research methodology and outline the data collection approach. In section 7, we demonstrate how to apply the Swiss cheese model to better understand the anatomy of healthcare data breaches. Finally, in section 7, we summarize the usefulness of our proposed model and outline its practical implications.

HEALTHCARE DATA BREACHES: SOME ALARMING STATISTICS

Despite all mandates, regulations and security breach notification laws, there is ample evidence today that many health organizations and business associates are unprepared to prevent, cope with or respond to a data breach.

According to the Privacy Rights Clearing House (PRCH), three of the six most significant data breaches in 2016 were in the healthcare sector. In 2016, out of the 11,032,013 records in the PRCH database, 3,985,605 records were exposed, involving 567 public breaches fitting the criteria of Healthcare, Medical Providers & Medical Insurance Services. These breaches included (1) unintended disclosure of sensitive information posted publicly on a website, mishandled or sent to the wrong party via email, fax or mail; (2) hacking, spyware or malware; (3) payment card fraud; (4) insider threats; and (5) physical loss or stealing of non-electronic records, portable devices or stationary electronic devices (PRCH, 2016).

The Identity Theft Resource Center revealed that, as of January 18, 2017, 376 out of the all-time record high of 1,093 reported U.S. data breaches in 2016 were related to the health and medical industry, divulging 15,942,053 records out of the total of 36,601,939 exposed records (ITRC, 2017).

A 2016 study, conducted by the Ponemon Institute, revealed that 90% of the surveyed healthcare organizations reported that they had a data breach in the past two years, and 45% had more than five data breaches in the same time period. These data breaches cost the healthcare industry around $6.2 billion (Ponemon, 2016b). The study also revealed that criminal attacks and internal threats are the leading cause of data breaches, while concerns over evolving cyber-attack threats such as ransomware and malware have been escalating in 2016. Furthermore, 69% of healthcare organizations and 63% of business associates believe that they are exposed to a greater risk of data breach than other industries (Ponemon, 2016b).

The U.S. Department of Health and Human Services (HSS) reported in its 2013/2014 annual report to Congress that in 2013 and 2014 only 0.65% or the reported healthcare data breaches involved 500 or more individuals, yet they accounted for 98.44% of the individuals who were exposed to a breach in PHI. In other words, less than 1% of the reported breaches affected the majority of the exposed individual (HHS, 2014). The causes of these reported incidents are summarized in Table 1.

Table 1. Common causes of 2014 data breaches involving more than 500 individuals

Cause	Number of Reported Incidents	Number of Affected Individuals
Theft of electronic equipment/portable devices or paper containing PHI	105	6,615,929 31%
Unauthorized access or disclosure of records containing PHI	72	6,976,208 33%
Hacking/IT incident of electronic equipment or a network server	50	7,144,137 33%
Loss of electronic media or paper records containing PHI	21	174,074 1%
Improper disposal of PHI	13	116,596 1%
Other/unknown causes of breaches of PHI	16	318,296 1%

HHS, 2014.

The HHS reported that the largest breach in 2013 was the result of the theft of four unencrypted computers, containing PHI information, at the office of a covered entity that affected approximately 4 million individuals. The largest reported breach in 2014 was also the result of the theft of six desktop computers from the office of a business associate that affected 168,490 individuals (HHS, 2014). The HHS has also observed that in 2013 and 2014, theft of PHI continues to be the top threat that affects the greatest number of individuals.

In 2014, the HHS received approximately 53,970 reports of “smaller” breaches involving fewer than 500 individuals. These smaller breaches affected more than 269,296 individuals. Many of these reported breaches involved misdirected communications, including incidents where PHI records or test results were mistakenly sent to the wrong recipients, and files were attached to the wrong patient record (HHS, 2014).

In 2015, three major cyberattacks were reported by HIPAA-covered entities: Anthem Inc., Premera Blue Cross, and Excellus Health Plan that resulted in the theft of 78.8 million records, 11 million, and 10 million records respectively (HIPAA, 2016). Although insiders were not behind the largest healthcare data breaches in 2016, they continue to cause most harm to patients as stolen PHI is often used for the purpose of identity theft and fraud.

Recent studies have also shown that, besides employees' abuse of access privilege, negligence is still a major source of data breaches (Kobus, 2012), as evident from the following statistics:

- In a 2016 study conducted by the Ponemon Institute (Ponemon, 2016b), when asked why they believe that they might be targeted by a potential data breach, 54% of the business associates (compared to 35% for the surveyed healthcare organizations) mentioned the negligence of their employees in handling patient information.
- In the UK, figures released to the privacy campaign group Big Brother Watch revealed that for the years 2011 to 2014, at least 7,255 healthcare data breaches took place at 152 National Health Service (NHS) trusts. These breaches included at least 50 instances of data being posted on social media, at least 143 instances of data being accessed for "personal reasons", at least 124 instances of cases relating to vulnerabilities in IT systems, at least 103 instances of data loss or theft, at least 236 instances of data being shared inappropriately via Email, letter or Fax and at least 251 instances of data being inappropriately shared with a third party. There were also 115 cases of staff accessing their own records (BBW, 2014).
- In Europe, recent studies have shown that most of the healthcare data breaches were due to the lack of encryption and employee carelessness, as opposed to hackers. In particular, negligence and carelessness of hospital employees in handling sensitive medical records were identified as the leading cause of healthcare data breaches, accounting for 41 percent of all data breaches (Kierkegaard, 2012).
- According to a 2015 Mid-Year Cyber Risk Report published by SurfWatch Lab (SurfWatch, 2015), data breach incidents in healthcare are most often tied to employee negligence and insider activity (including unintentional errors and intentional criminal acts conducted by staff).
- Employee negligence has also been cited by Johnson & Willey (2011) who demonstrated with concrete examples how peer-to-peer (P2P) file-sharing networks contained leaked files that had significant PHI content.

While the majority of earlier studies have mostly focused on individual errors as the major cause of healthcare data breaches, we argue that other important organizational factors needs also to be taken into account In fact, a more thorough analysis of healthcare data breach incidents suggests that these breaches are not usually caused by a single failure and mistake, but can be traced back to a chain of errors. Hence, in order to mitigate the risks of data breaches, we must enhance our understanding of the anatomy of these breaches.

LITERATURE REVIEW AND RESEARCH CONTRIBUTION

We conducted a systematic review of the extant literature from the health informatics and Information Systems security research. Our review focused on identifying the anatomy, events, statistics, and taxonomies related to healthcare data breaches, with special focus on theoretical models that could help us better understand the nature and root causes of these breaches. This review enabled us to recognize that the lack of theoretical models that can explain the root causes of healthcare data breaches is a major gap in the existing literature. Accordingly, we looked at ways to integrate the various collected healthcare data breach literature contributions into a coherent model that would better explain the causes of data breach incidents.

To date, very limited research has been conducted to investigate the root causes of data breach incidents, as most of the earlier studies focused on outlining taxonomies of organizational data breaches, without delving deeper into the underlying causation factors. For example, based on the data breaches reported by the Privacy Rights Clearinghouse (PRCH, 2012) and the Data Loss DB (OSF, 2012), Neame (2012) classified data breaches into three main categories:

- **Losses:** Including accidental data loss and disclosure, improper data disclosure, re-identification of anonymized and pseudonymised data.
- **Abuses:** Including abuse of access privilege, abuse of privacy by IT staff and contractors and disclosure during routing data processing.
- **Hackers and Malware:** Unauthorized access from the outside.

Collins et al (2011) applied the Situational Crime Prevention (SCP) methodology to strengthen the security procedures and reduce the number of data breaches. They highlighted the fact that much of the available literature on data breaches had focused more on the technical perspectives, related to advanced computer-based defenses, and seemed to neglect the underlying human and organizational factors. In fact, previous research on healthcare data breaches has mainly focused on the technical aspects of security, including cyber-attacks. For instance, Kruse et al (2017) conducted an extensive literature review to identify cybersecurity trends (including ransomware) and to identify possible solutions. Their study revealed that the healthcare industry lags behind other industries in securing data. The authors suggested that healthcare organizations should invest more time and money to maintain their technology, train end-users and establish clear security policies. Among the very few contributions that focused on the organizational factors of healthcare data breaches, we can cite the work of Stevens et al (2017) where a case-study was conducted to further elucidate the role of maladministration (mainly in the form of poor information governance practices) as the number one cause for healthcare data breach incidents. The authors suggested that the prevention of data breaches requires good governance and a refocus of attention on insider behaviors.

To our knowledge, no prior study has been conducted to comprehensively understand the anatomy of healthcare data breaches in general and the underlying human and organizational factors in particular. Thus, the aim of this study is to address this gap and contribute to healthcare data breach literature by exploring the multifaceted roots of healthcare data breaches. More precisely, this contribution aims to add to the existing body of knowledge about healthcare data breaches by proposing an analytical theory, based on the SCM, to shed light on the human, organizational, and technical perspectives of healthcare data breach causation and prevention. In particular, this contribution provides a more holistic approach to uncover the root causes of human-induced healthcare data breaches that go beyond individual errors, omissions, or malicious acts to include potential latent organizational and technical deficiencies. This integrated approach to data breach causation and prevention can enhance the readiness of healthcare organizations to proactively manage future data breaches.

HUMAN ERROR THEORY

In this section, we provide a brief summary of the key concepts in the human error theory that are relevant to this research. Some of these concepts will be revisited in section 7.

In the context of healthcare security, human error is considered one of the most challenging issues that requires special attention (Ghazvini & Shukur, 2013). Various models and theories have been developed to explain human errors. For example, Reason (1990) distinguishes between:

- **Design vs. Human-Induced Errors:** For example, while fingers are often pointed at healthcare professionals, following a data breach, poor data management policies and processes (design errors) might be the root cause of the breach.
- **Variable Versus Constant Errors:** Variable errors are random in nature and difficult to predict, while constant errors follow some kind of consistent (yet risky) pattern that can be predicted and hence controlled. For example, among the top significant data breaches reported by the Privacy Rights Clearing House (ITRC, 2012) is the theft of laptop and desktop computers. In particular leaving laptops that contain unencrypted PHI unattended in employee vehicles has been a constant and recurring error that has led to numerous data breaches.

Based on the intention, errors can also be classified as slips, lapses, mistakes and violations (Reason, 1990).

- Slips are actions that were not performed as intended or planned.
- Lapses are missed actions or omissions caused by the lack of attention.
- Mistakes are errors emanating from faulty plans or intentions.
- Violations are errors that result from intentional or deliberate actions that are often against the established rules and regulations. These can be categorized as routine, situational and optimizing violations. Routine violations are errors that became the normal way of doing things, such as shortcuts to established procedures. Situational violations are the result of particular circumstances, such as time pressure or the difficulty to comply with the rules under the given circumstances. Optimizing violations involve breaking established rules for self-gratification (fun, curiosity, and thrill) or personal benefit.

Another key concept in human error theory is the "defenses in depth" approach towards error management (Reason, 1990). This concept is based on the principle that there are many stages where errors can occur, and hence various stages where defenses can be built to prevent them.

THE SWISS CHEESE MODEL (SCM)

The Swiss cheese model (Reason, 1990) of accident causation and response is a widely accepted model that brought major contribution to the discipline of organizational and human error management. This model reflects on contemporary attempts towards better understanding the complexity of the socio-technical systems. The SCM has been used in risk analysis and management of human systems, including aviation, emergency, engineering and medical safety. For instance, the International Civil Aviation Organization

Figure 1. Reason's Swiss cheese model
Reason, 1990.

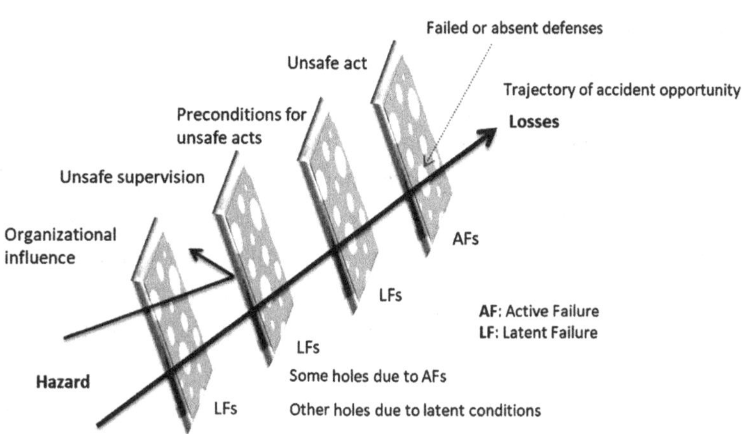

(ICAO) has formally adopted the SCM to better understand the human factors behind airplane crashes. As illustrated in Figure 1, the model depicts human systems as multiple slices of Swiss cheese that are stacked together. Each slice represents one layer of human system defense against failure.

Reason (1990) argues that most organizational errors can be traced to four or more levels, including organizational influences (such as lack of funding and training), unsafe supervision, preconditions for unsafe acts (such as mental fatigue and poor communication/coordination practices), and the unsafe acts themselves.

The holes in the cheese slices represent weaknesses in the individual parts of the system, and they continuously evolve by opening, shutting, and shifting their positions. When holes momentarily line up, a "trajectory of accident opportunity" is created, allowing the hazard to penetrate all the holes of the defense layers, leading to failure. The SCM endorses the concept of causation chain, which recognizes that most accidents happen when all windows of error opportunities, across all levels of the organization, align. The SCM also suggests that by putting more defensive layers (slices) and by keeping fewer/smaller holes, one can minimize the occurrence of potential errors. Reason (1990) noticed that investigators often focused their efforts on the unsafe act of the operators that led to the accident, while inadvertently neglecting other important factors. In fact, an important concept embedded in the SCM is the causal sequence of human failures which recognizes that holes in the defenses happen for two reasons, namely active (operational) failures and latent (organizational) failures.

Active failures are the unsafe acts committed by people who are in direct contact with the system and that can be directly related to the accident. They can take various forms such as slips, lapses, fumbles, mistakes, and procedural violations (Reason, 1990).

Latent failures are dormant weaknesses in the system (aka "resident pathogens") that, when manifested, combine with active failures to penetrate the layers of defenses and contribute to the accident. They often arise from strategic and top-level decisions, and occur because of poor regulations, unworkable procedures, poor documentation, inadequate tools, and bad decisions made by the top management. Latent failures can trigger two types of undesirable effects. First, they can develop towards error-provoking conditions such as time-pressure, inadequate training, fatigue, and inadequate equipment. Second, they can create ongoing holes in the defense lines (Reason, 1990). Compared to active failures, latent failures can be anticipated, identified and remedied much easier, thus promoting a proactive risk management approach.

Reason's SCM advocates that human error problems can be viewed from two perspectives: the person approach and the system approach (Reason, 2000). The person approach emphasizes the individuals' errors and procedural violation, blaming people for carelessness, inattention, poor motivation, negligence and recklessness. The counter-measures in this approach are mainly geared towards reducing unwanted variability in human behavior by raising safety awareness, refining existing procedures, and taking the necessary disciplinary actions (Reason, 2000). The system approach recognizes that human errors are unavoidable and can be expected even in high reliability organizations and that these mistakes are consequences rather than causes. Therefore, the approach turns its focus on the conditions under which the individuals work. It argues that errors are rooted deep in "upstream systematic factors". These include recurrent error traps and the underlying weaknesses that are often rooted in the organization's processes, culture, attitude towards risk-taking, and its aptitude to learn from past mistakes. The counter-measures in the system approach focuses on changing the conditions under which people work and on building safeguards and system defenses to mitigate errors (Reason, 2000). Reason (2000, p. 769) noted that

Two important features of human error tend to be overlooked. First, it is often the best people who make the worst mistakes – error is not the monopoly of an unfortunate few. Second, far from being random, mishaps tend to fall into recurrent patterns. The same set of circumstances can provoke similar errors, regardless of the people involved. The pursuit of greater safety is seriously impeded by an approach that does not seek out and remove the error-provoking properties within the system at large.

As a conceptual model, the SCM suggests that no one failure, human or technical, is sufficient to cause a mishap. Rather, accidents are the outcomes of a combination of several causal factors arising at different levels of the system (Reason et al, 2006).

RESEARCH METHODOLOGY AND DATA COLLECTION

To get deeper insights into the technical, human and organizational factors of healthcare data breaches we gathered and analyzed an extensive list of reported data breaches from various credible sources, as illustrated in Table 2.

In our case, we refined our queries to search for data breaches within the medical sector only. We also made use of the literature analysis methodology by conducting a systematic review of previous research on data privacy and security where healthcare data breach incidents were cited. In particular, we made use of the earlier work of Kobus (2012), Laja (2011), Johnson & Willey (2011), Walker (2011), Baker et al (2011), and Kierkegaard (2012). Further, as highlighted previously, earlier conceptual research, in the form of data breach taxonomies has also guided us in establishing our model for healthcare data breach causation and prevention.

Our preliminary analysis of the reported healthcare data breaches indicated that many data breach incidents were rooted in factors that go beyond the control of the individual healthcare worker. Based on our literature review and after an in-depth analysis of the reported healthcare data breach incidents, we were able to synthesize the fragmented body of knowledge on data breach causation and prevention and then apply Reason's Swiss cheese model to better understand how healthcare data breach incidents occur. This is discussed in the next section.

Table 2. Healthcare data breach sources

Organization	Description
Open Security Foundation (OSF, 2012)	Non-profit organization that specializes in searching for and archiving data loss incidents, including those that were not reported by the media
US Department of Health and Human Services (HHS, 2013b)	The Secretary of Health and Human Services provides a list of breaches of unsecured protected health information affecting 500 or more individuals, as required by section 13402(e)(4) of the HITECH Act. The list consists of brief descriptions of the breach cases that the office of civil rights has investigated and closed, as well as the names of private practice providers who have reported healthcare data breaches to the Secretary.
Privacy Right Clearinghouse (PRCH, 2012)	A nonprofit consumer advocacy and education center based in San Diego that maintains a comprehensive website with resources that include an online complaint submission form, numerous articles, and an online Chronology of Data Breaches since 2005.
Big Brother Watch (BBW, 2012)	British civil liberties and privacy pressure group whose research and online published reports uncovered hundreds of incidents whereby patient medical records were compromised

APPLICATION OF THE SCM TO HEALTHCARE DATA BREACHES

Based on the literature review and our analysis of healthcare data breach incidents, we propose in Figure 2 the Swiss cheese model for data breach causation and prevention. The model suggests that most healthcare data breaches can be traced to one or more of four levels of failures (slices). These levels consist of organizational influence factors, inadequate security defenses, precursors of unsafe data handling, and the unsafe act of data handling. This model advocates that the data breach incidents occur when holes in the four slices lineup, resulting in a trajectory of data breach opportunity.

In order to better understand and describe the holes in the cheese layers from a practical rather than a speculative perspective, we have re-examined the reported cases of healthcare data breaches to gain practical insights into the failed or absent defenses in each of the four layers.

SCM Layer Description

Organizational Influence

Many reported healthcare data breach incidents suggest that latent organizational weaknesses and failures have assisted data breach hazards to penetrate the layers of defenses:

1. The lack of training for healthcare employees on how to best handle and protect PHI is reflected in many reported data breach incidents. For example, in 2011, thousands of X-rays were stolen from St. Joseph Medical Center in Towson by a thief who successfully tricked hospital employees into believing that he was a contractor for a radiological film destruction company to gain access to the

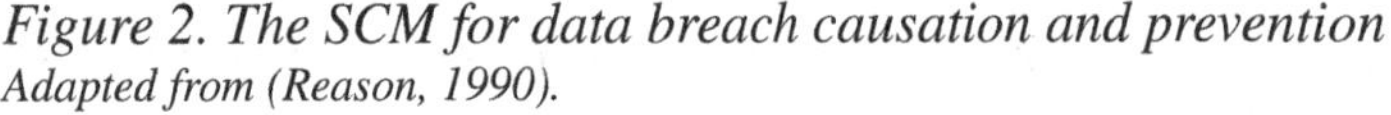

Figure 2. The SCM for data breach causation and prevention
Adapted from (Reason, 1990).

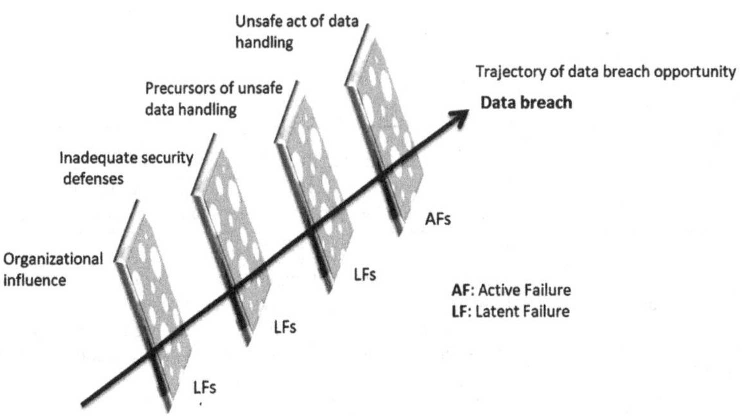

X-rays. It is believed that the X-ray films, which included private health information, were stolen for their silver content (Walker, 2011). In another incident, a "phishing" scam led a healthcare employee to share the login information for an email inbox, potentially jeopardizing the ePHI of 610 patients (HHS, 2011). On April 22, 2016, an employee of Symphony Health Solutions (SHS) Corporation sent PDF copies of W-2s forms for some personnel of SHS in response to a fraudulent email request, thus exposing the names, addresses, wages, and social security numbers of approximately 365 individuals (ITRC, 2016). One can argue that such incidents might have been mitigated if the hospital employees were trained to recognize and deal with social engineering tricks.

2. Poor or unforced data protection security policies and procedures can be inferred from many data breach incidents. For example, there is evidence that many healthcare organizations are lacking policies that dictate the separation of personal emails and data from organizational emails and PHI. For example, Kobus (2012) cited several incidents whereby healthcare employees posted on their Facebook and Twitter accounts information related to their patients' therapy. In another incident, one employee emailed unencrypted medical records to a personal email account, putting the PHI of more than 2,000 patients at risk (HHS, 2011). Johnson & Willey (2011) found medical settlement spreadsheets that contained names, addresses, dates of birth, social security numbers, phone numbers, diagnosis codes, and insurance information on peer-to-peer file-sharing networks. In its annual report to Congress on breaches of unsecured protected health information for calendar years 2013 and 2014, HHS (2014) cited some reported incidents that were related to improper disposal breaches including disposal of PHI records in recycling or trash bins rather than shred bins. In another reported incident, attackers were able to hack the Utah Department of Technology Services computer server on March 30, 2012 and access over 780,000 Medicaid claim records, because the servers were not configured according to normal policies and procedures (Gibson, 2012). A study conducted by the Ponemon Institute (Ponemon, 2012a) on the human factors of data protection, revealed that the bad practice of healthcare employees carrying unnecessary sensitive information on their laptops while traveling, was among the top ten data breach risky practices. The same study also found that the lack of physical access control policies led to situations where the healthcare employees left their computers, containing PHI, unattended after work. Another key finding of the Ponemon study (Ponemon, 2012a) is that 81 percent of the survey respondents allowed "Bring

Your Own Device" (BYOD) to access organizational data and that 54% said they were not sure if these devices were secure. Hence, the lack of in-depth understanding the security risks of a BYOD policy and the lack of employees' education on the usage of personal mobile devices such as smartphones and tablets to access organizational data can enable a trajectory for a data breach incident. According to HHS (2014), healthcare organizations and business associates must ensure proper training of their employees on their privacy and security policies and procedures, including the appropriate uses and disclosures of PHI, emerging malware and ransomware threats to ePHI, and the precautions that should be implemented to safeguard the information from improper uses and disclosures. In addition to this training, HHS (2014) recommends that employee should be aware of the sanction policies and the consequences for failure to enforce privacy and security policies and procedures.

3. Poor employment termination policy is another organizational flaw that was reflected in the case reported in (HHS, 2011) wherein one employee who was no longer employed had access to a password-protected website containing the PHI of more than 400,00 individuals. The largest breach in 2014 that is related to unauthorized access or disclosure of PHI involved a business associate who did not safeguard PHI upon the termination of contractual services. This breach affected two million individuals (HHS, 2014). In another incident, prior to leaving employment, a physical therapist copied the PHI of patients at Vail Valley on a USB drive and took the data to his new employer (ITRC, 2016)
4. According to the 2012 Redspin Breach Report (Redspin, 2012) more than half (57%) of all PHR breaches in the U.S involved a business associate. A particular major data breach incident was reported on September 14, 2011 in which the backup tapes containing ePHI of about 4.9 million patients were stolen out of the military contractor's car in San Antonio (PRCH, 2012). The largest breach in 2014 resulting from theft involved a business associate whose office was the subject of a theft of six desktop computers. This incident affected 168,490 individuals (HHS, 2014). These incidents are yet another indication that an organizational faux pas (poor selection, assessment and/or audit of business associate to ensure PHI protection and HIPAA-compliance) can be a latent facilitator of a data breach incident.

Inadequate Security Defenses

Many reported data breach incidents suggest that the damage of data exposure could have been mitigated if remedies against latent weaknesses in the security defenses were implemented in the first place.

1. Encryption is an effective method to protect PHI against unauthorized disclosure. However, the *de facto* lack of data encryption is perhaps the most noticeable flaw in the security defenses that, when combined with data theft or loss, amplifies the damages of a data breach. For instance, from the sample of data breach incidents listed in Table 3, the impact could have been lessened if the data was adequately encrypted or properly destructed upon disposal.

Table 3. Data breach incidents involving unencrypted ePHI

Data Breach Incident	Reference
In 2016, an employee at the Eastern Colorado Health Care System (ECHCS) emailed unencrypted documents to the personal email accounts of more than 2,100 Colorado veterans, thus exposing their names, last four digits of their Social Security numbers and their diagnoses.	(ITRC, 2016)
• Four unencrypted computers that contained individuals' PHI were stolen • An unencrypted flash drive went missing in 2013, affecting 49,000 individuals	(HHS, 2014)
Desktop computer with unencrypted data was stolen from Sutter Medical Foundations, Sacramento, CA.	(PRCH, 2012; Baker et al, 2011)
Unencrypted backup tapes were stolen from a car, exposing the health and personal information of more than 4.9 million patients.	(PRCH, 2012)
On August 25, 2009, a Blue Cross and Blue Shield laptop containing unencrypted ePHI of more than 800,000 physicians was stolen from an employee at the company's headquarter in Chicago	(OSF, 2012)
• In 2003, a psychiatric Hospital in Aarhus (Denmark) sent an unencrypted email to a doctor, containing PHI. A Virus on the doctor's computer caused the email to be forwarded to unauthorized recipients. • An employee at the secure mental health unit of the Scottish hospital lost USB stick containing unencrypted EPHI, including the criminal record of some violent patients being treated at the Tryst Park unit of Bellsdyke psychiatric hospital	(Kierkegaard, 2012)

2. The lack of proper physical security mechanisms is another sign of inadequate security defenses that has been cited in many reported healthcare data breach incidents. For example, in 2009, an intruder managed to steal 57 hard drives which contained ePHI of more than 1 million patients from BlueCross BlueShield of Tennessee (Johnson, & Willey, 2011). On April 11, 2016 thieves had broken the glass of a side window of the PruittHealth Hospice-Beaufort office and managed to break into patient file cabinets that contained paper medical records (ITRC, 2016). In another incident, an intruder managed to gain access to a locked office in Temple Community Hospital in Los Angeles and stole a computer that contained the names of 600 patients, their hospital account numbers and their individual CT scans (LA, 2012).
3. Recent ransomware attacks against healthcare organizations revealed how the lack of technical security safeguards can facilitate a trajectory of data breach opportunity. These attacks often target database servers containing PHI information and aim to encrypt the data and then ask the healthcare organization to pay a ransom to unlock the data. Recent examples of such attacks include the May 2017 WannaCry cyber-attack that affected the NHS, the February 2016 cyber ransom attack on the Hollywood Presbyterian Medical Center which forced the hospital to pay a $17,000 ransom in order to unlock its data, and the April 2016 ransomware attack that caused a temporary shutdown of MedStar Health's computer systems and locked up patient records (Gordon et al, 2017). In another 2012 security incident, the ePHI of patients from the Surgeons of Lake County in Libertyville, Ill., were kept hostage by hackers who penetrated the computer network, encrypted the data server and sent a ransom note, requesting payment in return for access to the ePHI (Robertson, 2012). In a study conducted by Healthcare IT News and HIMSS Analytics, as many as 75% of hospitals in the U.S. could have been victims of a ransomware attack in 2016 with a significant number unaware of the cyber intrusion (HIMSS, 2016). Several other incidents have shed light on the vulnerabilities of security defenses in thwarting data breaches. For instance, on February 2015, Anthem Inc., one of the U.S. largest health insurers was the subject of a sophisticated cyberattack whereby hackers were able to breach a database that contained as many as 78.8 million records of current and former

customers, as well as employees. The compromised data included names, birthdays, medical IDs, social security numbers, street addresses, e-mail addresses and employment information, including income data (Mathews & Yadron, 2015). The December 2012 security breach at the Carolinas Medical Center-Randolph is yet another example that illustrates how the lack of technical security safeguards can facilitate a trajectory of data breach opportunity. In this case, an unauthorized electronic intruder managed to access incoming and outgoing emails from a provider's account without the provider's or the hospital's knowledge, thus impacting approximately 5,600 patients (Walsh, 2012). On July 21, 2016, the Center for Neurosurgical and Spinal Disorders (CNSD) detected an unauthorized intrusion on one of their computers, which caused its immediate shutdown. In this case, a hacker gained remote access to the office manager's computer and installed one backdoor program which logged the user's keystrokes, and another program that periodically took screenshots of the computer's desktop display (ITRC, 2016).

In January 2011, hackers breached a server containing social security numbers and medical codes of around 230,000 Seacoast Radiology patients. The breach was initiated by gamers who were just looking for servers (space bandwidth) to play a best-selling video game (Goodin, 2011). In July 2009, the Alberta Health System was infected with the Coreflood virus which infiltrated the network via email. The virus relayed the ePHI of 11,582 patients back to the hacker (OSF, 2012). The lack of security safeguards was also reflected in the failure to properly clean hard disks and securely wipe the data before disposal. This was reflected for instance in the Affinity Health Plan Inc. data breach incident reported in (HHS, 2011) whereby hard drives, in more than twenty leased photocopiers, that might contain ePHI of up to 344,579 patients were returned intact to lessor.

Precursors of Unsafe Data Handling

Some reported healthcare data breach incidents can be traced down to some prior signs of poor communication and coordination, unclear instructions, or mental overload due to fatigue, distractions and stress.

1. In May 2012, the Aneurin Bevan Health Board in Wales received a £70,000 fine for breaching the Data Protection Act, following the release of sensitive personal data to the wrong person. The breach was attributed to poor communication between a doctor and his secretary who was not provided with enough details to correctly identify the patient to whom a letter should be sent. This resulted in PHI being mailed to a patient with a very similar name (NHS, 2012).
2. According to the U.S. Department of Health and Human Services (HHS, 2011), the most common human error that resulted in data breaches in 2010 was the misdirection of mailing involving paper records, where individuals received another patient's PHI because of the wrong mailing address. Misdirected emails and faxes were also cited as common data breach factors. For example, in June 2011, the Information Commissioner's Office has imposed a £120,000 fine on Surrey County Council as it repeatedly sent unencrypted ePHI to the wrong email recipients (ICO, 2011). While no study has been conducted to shed light on the root causes of PHI misdirection, the human factor theory seems to suggest that, besides the possibility of employee negligence, their lack of focus due to stress, fatigue and distractions might be contributing factors as well. In fact, a survey conducted by HealthLeaders Media for Kronos Inc. revealed that nurse fatigue is prevalent in the healthcare industry and is directly linked to on-the-job errors (Kronos, 2013). Further, according

to the Joint Commission review of research on healthcare workers, employee fatigue is directly linked to many adverse effects, like confusion, the inability to stay focused, and slower or faulty information processing and judgment; all of which can potentially be preconditions for unsafe handling and management of PHI (Joint, 2011). Lockley et al (2007) demonstrated how extended work hours lead to fatigue-related errors among healthcare workers. Sleep loss and impairments related to resultant fatigue are common among professionals working in healthcare settings. Long continuous duty hours, reduced opportunities for sleep with minimal recuperation time, and shift work all contribute significantly to impairments in physical, cognitive, and emotional functioning. Detrimental effects include those on personal health and well-being, patient health and safety, performance of job-related tasks, and professionalism.

Unsafe Act of Data Handling

The unsafe act of the individual who is in direct contact with the PHI and that led to the data breach constitutes an active failure that is directly related to the data breach. According to the human error theory, as discussed in section 4, these failures can take various forms such as slips, lapses, mistakes, and violations (routine, situational, or optimizing violations). Table 4 illustrates, via sample reported healthcare data breach incidents, each of these four error categories.

"Defenses in Depth" Approach to Healthcare Data Breaches

The "defenses in depth" concept is deeply rooted in Reason's approach towards human error management (Reason, 1990). This principle has also been adopted in physical security (see for example (Ward & Smithy, 2002)) where multiple rings (deter, detect, delay, respond and deny) act as safeguards within the physical asset's security perimeter.

As suggested by Reason (2000), we recognize that each hole in the SCM of Figure 2 represents an individual weakness in the healthcare system that can potentially lead to a data breach. At the same time, each slice can act as a defensive layer against potential breaches. Accordingly, to curtail the likelihood of potential data breaches, we outline herein some counter-measures that can potentially act as defensive layers and contribute towards minimizing or reducing the size of the individual holes.

Organizational Influence

A data safety culture, coupled with strong organizational policies, practices, leadership and oversight can act as a strong defensive layer against data breaches:

1. Building and maintaining an organizational culture of compliance to protect the patients' privacy rights is a key step towards data breach prevention. Such a culture should recognize that data breach incidents are often inevitable and accordingly should deeply internalize data safety within the healthcare organization and its BAs, based on all applicable data privacy regulations and mandates. An information security culture includes all the socio-technical measures that support technical security methods (Schlienger & Teufel, 2003). In fact, most of the processes needed to protect information assets are, to a large extent, dependent on human behavior (Van Niekerk & Von Solms, 2010). Hence an organizational approach to data breach prevention should put special

Table 4. Taxonomy of human errors that led to a healthcare data breaches

Error Category	Sample Cases
Slip	• On August, 2016, Madison-based University of Wisconsin Health Center mistakenly sent patient satisfaction surveys to some patients' parents instead of the patients themselves. The surveys contained the name of the health providers (ITRC, 2016) • On May 3, 2010, a business associate working for the Aramark Healthcare Support Services, Inc. sent an email to multiple patients where the names and email addresses were visible to all the 937 email recipients (HHS, 2011). • On October 2, 2012, a licensed clinical social worker at Town Council of Chapel Hill accidentally attached confidential patient information to an email that was forwarded to the town council colleagues (PRCH, 2012). • During the period 2007-2009, doctors' offices in Tennessee have been accidentally sending confidential patient information to an Indiana businessman's fax machine, instead of the Tennessee Department of Human Services (OSF, 2012). • On April 29, 2006, a programmer's error on the Valley Baptist Medical Center website exposed names, dates of birth, and SSNs of healthcare workers (OSF, 2012).
Lapse	• On March 9, 2009, an employee from the Massachusetts Physician Organization Inc. left PHI records of 192 patients of Mass General, including patients with HIV/AIDS, on a subway train while commuting to work (Kierkegaard, 2012). • In May 2010, an NHS worker at the secure mental health unit of the Scottish hospital lost USB stick containing unencrypted EPHI, including the criminal record of some violent patients at the Tryst Park unit of Bellsdyke psychiatric hospital (Kierkegaard, 2012). • On June 3, 2006, an insurance company employee at Humana downloaded a file containing customers' personal information into a hotel computer and then forgot to delete the files (OSF, 2012).
Mistake	• In February 2010, a healthcare employee uploaded records of 9,000 patients to an unsecured website (HHS, 2011). • In June 2010, a doctor from the California Center for Development and Rehabilitation left office cleaning to his sons, who dumped 1,000 patient files at the West Mecklenburg Recycling Center. The files contained names, addresses, dates of birth, SSNs, drivers' license numbers, insurance account numbers, and health information of 1,600 patients (Kierkegaard, 2012; PRCH, 2012). • In December 2010, an employee at Adventist Behavioral Health mistakenly sent sensitive patient documents to a recycling facility instead of a shredding facility (PRCH, 2012). • In February 2011, a member of staff at the University Hospital and Coventry & Warwickshire NHS Trust accidentally disposed of the medical records of 18 patients (along with other rubbish) in a his communal waste bin at a residential apartment block (PRCH, 2012)
Routine / Situational violation	• On December 2016, an Atmore Community Hospital employee accessed the electronic record of approximately 1,000 patients without a valid work-related reason (ITRC, 2016). • On April 23, 2012, a Naugatuck Valley Community College instructor used, without permission, patient X-rays from St. Mary's Hospital to teach radiology technology. The X-rays contained PHI. The instructor told students not to reveal the practice (PRCH, 2012). • On March 27, 2012, a physician at the Affordable Medical and Surgical Services dumped over 1,000 abortion records in a dumpster without attempting to properly destroy them (PRCH, 2012). • On January 10, 2013, an employee at Good Health Systems, a third-party contractor for Utah's Medicaid, saved beneficiary personal information of around 6,000 patients onto an unencrypted thumb drive that he subsequently lost while driving between Salt lake City, Denver, and Washington D.C (Gibson, 2013).
Optimizing violation	• On March 17, 2016, a former Ambucor employee downloaded certain Stony Brook Internists, UFPC patient information to thumb drives and retained those drives shortly before his employment at Ambucor ended (ITRC, 2016) • On October 18, 2016, and prior to leaving employment, a former employee at CalOptima #2 downloaded the ePHI of individuals who were enrolled in the county's health plan for low-income and disabled Californians (ITRC, 2016). • A curious medical staff was caught examining the health records of friends and family members (Baker et al, 2011). • On November 10, 2009, two employees at the Massachusetts Eye and Ear Infirmary, who had access to the PHI of 1,076 individuals, misused patient credit information for personal gain (HHS, 2011). • On March 1, 2013, a therapist at the South Miami Hospital, Baptist Health disclosed and sold Social Security numbers, dates of birth, patient names, and other data to another party later used them to file fraudulent tax returns (PRCH, 2012). • On March 11, 2010, an employee at the University of Pittsburgh Student Health Center stole and then destroyed documents containing PHI of approximately 8,000 individual (HHS, 2011). • On April 2009, a patient registration secretary at John Hopkins was suspected of identity theft that affected as many as 49 patients (Johnson & Willey, 2011).

emphasis on employee behavior, as the organization's success or failure is closely related to the things that its employees do or fail to do (Da Veiga & Eloff, 2010). Accordingly, and in congruence with Reason's safety culture model (Reason, 1997), there is a need for:

   a. An *informed culture*, where supervisors and healthcare employees have sound knowledge and awareness about the technical, human and organizational factors that have influence on the safety of personal health records.
   b. A *reporting culture*, where healthcare employees are willing to promptly report data breach incidents.
   c. A *Just culture*, where data breach incidents are seen as opportunities to learn from in order to enhance the organizational preparedness against potential future breaches.
2. Since institutional factors are key ingredients in the success of any IS security strategy (Angst et al, 2017), it is important that healthcare organizations and BAs adopt best IT governance practices. These include top management support, establishing a data protection team, securing adequate resources, conducting compliance auditing and monitoring, performing regular data inventories, establishing data classification schemes, conducting security clearance, adhering to well-established IT security frameworks, establishing formal incident response process, and appointing a security officer in charge of PHI protection, (Ponemon, 2012b).
3. It is compulsory for covered entities to develop, document, and maintain clear and effective policies and procedures governing the handling of personal and health records, both at rest and in motion, and from acquisition to disposal. These policies and procedures should be revised, strengthened and publicized to cover (1) the usage of social media and file-sharing sites (Kobus, 2012), (2) access authorization, (3) PHI disposal, (4) acceptable/ethical usage and sanctions, (5) mandatory training, (6) internal monitoring and auditing, (7) data breach response procedures, (8) separation of personal emails and data from organizational emails and data, and (9) effective password management.
4. It is important to educate, train and retrain the medical staff and all employees who are in direct contact with PHI on the importance of protecting this information and on how to safely and securely handle devices that contain ePHI. Training should cover common risky PHI handling practices, while highlighting best practices to respond to common security threats, including social engineering tricks.
5. There is a strong need for the covered entities to carefully select and assess their vendors and business associates to ensure the proper handling of PHI so that data privacy is protected. In fact earlier studies (see for example (Khalfan, 2004)) have shown that organizations need to exercise diligence when selecting a business or outsourcing partner. Accordingly, BA's contracts should be carefully drafted and revised if necessary to further emphasis the protection of PHI, including detailed provisions for the protection of PHI and the requirement for a third-party vulnerability assessment of the BA security measures.
6. Sound risk analysis and risk management programs play a central role in reducing data breach vulnerabilities to an adequate level. The presence of a robust risk management process is also a privacy mandate under the HIPPA. At the core of this process lies the risk assessment phase, where a structured and thorough assessment of potential threats to the confidentiality, availability and integrity of the PHI need to be conducted. Risk analysis should cover security risks and vulnerabilities for all electronic equipment and information systems that are either owned or leased and it should address and mitigate potential security risks and vulnerabilities. Data breach risk assessment should also make use of unstructured approaches such as considering specific scenarios of common data breach patterns to understand how these may occur, and outline what can be done to thwart them. As suggested by Straub & Welke (1998), effective risk management also requires

managers to be aware of the full array of security controls that are available and to implement those most ones.

Inadequate Security Defenses

Information security technologies and physical security controls can add an extra layer of defense against potential data breaches. This is particularly important in light of the emerging denial of service (DoS), ransomware and malware attacks. Hence healthcare organizations and BAs should invest in modern security and encryption technologies and solutions, hire and train enough skilled security professionals to operate, administer, manage and provision these technologies. While building their security defenses, healthcare organizations and their BAs should carefully consider and "scan" the entire attack surface which includes applications, physical servers, virtual machines, storage and network devices, medical devices, mobile devices, and digital media, among others.

The recent data healthcare data breach incidents involving the loss and inappropriate disposal of paper records and electronic devices containing PHI suggest that the damages could have been minimized if the following security safeguards were implemented:

- Shredding obsolete medical paper records and wiping hard drives before disposal.
- Adopting encryption technologies on hard drives and memory sticks.
- Improving physical security by installing new security systems or by moving PHI records to a more secure area
- Separating personal information data from medical records (Neame, 2012).
- Moving PHI from paper and legacy systems (such as spreadsheet, ad hoc databases, and word processing files) to secured enterprise-class health record systems (Johnson & Willey, 2011).
- Adopting password locking and remote data wiping security solutions.
- Changing passwords on a regular basis.

Physical safeguards and controls can also play an important role in protecting electronic storage media containing PHI. These safeguards include the appropriate usage of identity and access management solutions, including locked doors, badge access, alarm systems, physical locks for computer devices, biometric access controls, and CCTV security cameras.

An equally important consideration is related to the need for proper change management policies and procedures to handle operations and maintenance activities that have potential impact on the security of PHI. These include for instance software and hardware upgrades, new installations, network reconfigurations and office reallocation. These operations must have supporting documentation that must be tested and validated to ensure the security of PHI during and after the change procedures.

Other security technologies can contribute towards protecting ePHI from loss, unauthorized access or alteration. These solutions include Virtual Private Networks (VPNs), firewalls, encryption solutions, endpoint security management software, file integrity monitoring solutions and intrusion detection and prevention systems.

Precursors of Unsafe Data Handling

To mitigate the threat of unsafe data handling due to potential employee fatigue, healthcare organizations should strive to set and enforce policies that set limits on the number of working hours. Ensuring adequate staffing to reduce overload can facilitate in achieving such a goal. It is also helpful to educate employees who are in direct contact with PHI on fatigue management, limitations of human performance and short-term memory, and impact of pressure and stress on the safety of PHI.

CONCLUSION

This paper contributes to healthcare data breach prevention by proposing an analytical theory, based on the SCM that integrates the human, organizational and technical factors of healthcare data breach causation and prevention. The SCM is found to be a useful theoretical model to elucidate the anatomy of healthcare data breaches, as we seek a better understanding of the reasons behind healthcare data breaches. In particular, the model brings forwards the latent conditions of data breach incidents that have often being neglected in the literature.

Our research advocates that individual characters and behaviors such as carelessness, malice and unawareness are not the only contributing factors to data breaches. In other words, data breaches are sometimes the outcomes of circumstances that are beyond the control of those who were directly linked to the breach incident. Hence, because humans are fallible, organizational and technological systems must be designed to prevent data breaches, taking into account the imperfection of human performance.

What does this research imply for healthcare professionals and managers? This research suggests that instead of trying to simply pass the blame of data breaches on employees, healthcare providers should set up proper IT governance, policies, practices and information security technologies to account for data breach risks and minimize them. In fact, we argue that data breaches are the inevitable outcomes of not only human imperfection, but also poor organizational and technical systems design. At the same time, this research suggests that human and organizational aspects of data breach prevention need to be taken into account alongside the technical factors as well. Hence, this paper highlights the need to revisit the causal factors of healthcare data breaches from a broader socio-technical perspective.

Since the SCM endorses the "defenses in depth" security approach, it can assist healthcare organizations develop a more comprehensive and systematic approach to reduce data breach risks. In particular, the SCM suggests that inserting additional layers into the healthcare data handling system can prevent future data breach incidents.

REFERENCES

Agaku, I. T., Adisa, A. O., Ayo-Yusuf, O. A., & Connolly, G. N. (2014). Concern about security and privacy, and perceived control over collection and use of health information are related to withholding of health information from healthcare providers. *Journal of the American Medical Informatics Association*, *21*(2), 374–378. doi:10.1136/amiajnl-2013-002079 PMID:23975624

Angst, C. M., Block, E. S., D'Arcy, J., & Kelley, K. (2017). When Do IT Security Investments Matter? Accounting for the Influence of Institutional Factors in the Context of Healthcare Data Breaches. *Management Information Systems Quarterly*, *41*(3), 893–916. doi:10.25300/MISQ/2017/41.3.10

Appari, A., & Johnson, M. E. (2010). Information security and privacy in healthcare: Current state of research. *Int. J. Internet and Enterprise Management*, *6*(4), 279–314. doi:10.1504/IJIEM.2010.035624

Baker, A., Vega, L., DeHart, T., & Harrison, S. (2011). Healthcare and security: Understanding and evaluating risks. In M.M. Roberston (Ed.), Ergonomics and health aspects of work with computers. Berlin: Springer-Verlag.

BBW. (2012). *Big Brother Watch*. Retrieved December 3, 2012 from, http://www.bigbrotherwatch.org.uk/

BBW. (2014). *NHS Data Breaches: A Big Brother Watch Report, November 2014*. Retrieved August 10, 2017 from, https://www.bigbrotherwatch.org.uk/wp-content/uploads/2014/11/NHS-Data-Breaches-Report.pdf

Ben-Assuli, O. (2015). Electronic health records, adoption, quality of care, legal and privacy issues and their implementation in emergency departments. *Health Policy (Amsterdam)*, *119*(3), 287–297. doi:10.1016/j.healthpol.2014.11.014 PMID:25483873

Collins, J. D., Sainato, V. A., & Khey, D. N. (2011). Organizational data breaches 205-2010: Applying SCP to the healthcare and education sectors. *International Journal of Cyber Criminology*, *5*(1), 794–810.

Da Veiga, A., & Eloff, J. H. P. (2010). A framework and assessment instrument for information security culture. *Computers & Security*, *29*(2), 196–207. doi:10.1016/j.cose.2009.09.002

Fernández-Alemán, J. L., Señor, I. C., Lozoya, P. Á. O., & Toval, A. (2013). Security and privacy in electronic health records: A systematic literature review. *Journal of Biomedical Informatics*, *46*(3), 541–562. doi:10.1016/j.jbi.2012.12.003 PMID:23305810

Ghazvini, A., & Shukur, Z. (2013). Security challenges and success factors of electronic healthcare system. *Procedia Technology*, *11*, 212–219. doi:10.1016/j.protcy.2013.12.183

Gibson, S. (2012). 'Configuration error' leads to breach of nearly 780,000 records. *Healthcare Tech Review*. Retrieved September, 2012 from, http://healthcaretechreview.com/configuration-error-leads-to-breach-of-nearly-780000-records/

Gibson, S. (2013). Lost USB drive leads to breach of 6,000 patient records. *Healthcare Tech Review*. Retrieved March, 2013 from, http://healthcaretechreview.com/data-breach-lost-usb-drive/

Goodin, D. (2011). Gamers raid medical server to host Call of Duty: 230,000 patient records exposed. *The Register*. Retrieved November, 2012 from, http://www.theregister.co.uk/2011/01/14/seacoast_radiology_server_breach/

Gordon, W. J., Fairhall, A., & Landman, A. (2017). Threats to Information Security-Public Health Implications. *The New England Journal of Medicine*, *377*(8), 707–709. doi:10.1056/NEJMp1707212 PMID:28700269

HHS. (2011). *U.S. Department of Health & Human Services, Annual report to congress on breaches of unsecured protected health information for calendar year 2009 to 2010*. Retrieved December 20, 2012 from, http://www.hhs.gov/ocr/privacy/hipaa/administrative/breachnotificationrule/breachrept.pdf

HHS. (2013a). *U.S. Department of Health & Human Services, Standards for privacy of individually identifiable health information*. Retrieved September 16, 2013 from, http://aspe.hhs.gov/admnsimp/final/PvcPre02.htm

HHS. (2013b). *U.S. Department of Health & Human Services, Breaches affecting 500 or more individuals*. Retrieved December 3, 2012 from, http://www.hhs.gov/ocr/privacy/hipaa/administrative/breachnotificationrule/breachtool.html

HHS. (2014). *U.S. Department of Health & Human Services, Annual report to congress on breaches of unsecured protected health information for calendar years 2013 and 2014*. Retrieved may 20, 2017 from, https://www.hhs.gov/sites/default/files/rtc-breach-20132014.pdf

HIMSS. (2016). Ransomware Attacks Hit Three Quarters of Hospitals - Without Them Knowing. *Healthcare IT News*. Retrieved August 5, 2017 from, https://healthmanagement.org/c/it/news/ransomware-attacks-hit-three-quarters-of-hospitals-without-them-knowing

HIPAA. (2016). Largest healthcare data Breaches of 2016. *HIPAA Journal*. Retrieved May 7, 2017 from, https://www.hipaajournal.com/largest-healthcare-data-breaches-of-2016-8631/

ICO. (2011). ICO issues monetary penalty over misdirected emails. *Information Commissioner Office Council Release*. Retrieved September, 2012 from, http://www.ico.org.uk/~/media/documents/pressreleases/2011/monetary_penalty_surrey_council_release_20110609.ashx

ITRC. (2012). *Identity Theft Research Center: 2012 Data breach stats*. Retrieved November 11, 2012 from, http://www.idtheftcenter.org/ITRC%20Breach%20Stats%20Report%202012.pdf

ITRC. (2017). *Identity Theft Research Center, Data Breach Reports: 2016 End of Year Report*. Retrieved September 5, 2017 from, http://www.idtheftcenter.org/images/breach/2016/DataBreachReport_2016.pdf

Johnson, M. E. (2009). Data hemorrhages in the health-care sector. In Financial Cryptography and Data Security. Berlin: Springer-Verlag.

Johnson, M. E., & Willey, N. (2011). Will HITECH heal patient data hemorrhages? *Proceedings of the 44th Hawaii International Conference on Systems Sciences*, 1-10.

Joint. (2011). The Joint Commission, health care worker fatigue and patient safety. *The Joint Commission Sentinel Event Alert, 48*. Retrieved September, 2012 from, http://www.jointcommission.org/assets/1/18/sea_48.pdf

Khalfan, A. M. (2004). Information security considerations in IS/IT outsourcing projects: A descriptive case study of two sectors. *International Journal of Information Management, 24*(1), 29–42. doi:10.1016/j.ijinfomgt.2003.12.001

Kierkegaard, P. (2012). Medical data breaches: Notification delayed is notification denied. *Computer and Security Review, 28*, 168–183.

Kobus, T. J. III. (2012). The A to Z of health care data breaches. *Journal of Healthcare Risk Management*, *32*(1), 24–28. doi:10.1002/jhrm.21088 PMID:22833327

Kotz, D., Fu, K., Gunter, C., & Rubin, A. (2015). Security for mobile and cloud frontiers in healthcare. *Communications of the ACM*, *58*(8), 21–23. doi:10.1145/2790830

Kronos. (2013). *Kronos survey reveals nurse fatigue is pervasive in the healthcare industry and directly linked to on-the-job errors*. Kronos Inc. Press Release, March 2013. Retrieved April, 2013 from, http://www.kronos.com/pr/kronos-survey-reveals-nurse-fatigue-is-pervasive-in-the-healthcare-industry-and-directly-linked-to-on-the-job-errors.aspx

Kruse, C. S., Frederick, B., Jacobson, T., & Monticone, D. K. (2017). Cybersecurity in healthcare: A systematic review of modern threats and trends. *Technology and Health Care*, *25*(1), 1–10. doi:10.3233/THC-161263 PMID:27689562

Kulynych, J., & Korn, D. (2002). The effect of the new federal medical-privacy rule on research. *The New England Journal of Medicine*, *346*(3), 201–204. doi:10.1056/NEJM200201173460312 PMID:11796857

Kwon, J., & Johnson, M. E. (2014). Proactive Versus Reactive Security Investments in the Healthcare Sector. *Management Information Systems Quarterly*, *38*(2), 451–472. doi:10.25300/MISQ/2014/38.2.06

LA. (2012). Patient data stolen from Temple Community Hospital. *Los Angeles Times*. Retrieved November, 2013 from, http://latimesblogs.latimes.com/lanow/2012/08/patient-data-stolen-from-temple-community-hospital-.html

Laja, S. (2011). NHS Staff Breach Personal Data 806 Times in Three Years. *Guardian Professional*. Retrieved December 3, 2012 from, http://www.guardian.co.uk/healthcare-network/2011/oct/28/nhs-staff-breach-personal-data-806-times

Lockley, S. W., Barger, L. K., Ayas, N. T., Rothschild, J. M., Czeisler, C. A., & Landrigan, C. P. (2007). Effects of health care provider work hours and sleep deprivation on safety and performance. *Joint Commission Journal on Quality and Patient Safety*, *33*(11), 7–18. doi:10.1016/S1553-7250(07)33109-7 PMID:18173162

Mathews, A. W., & Yadron, D. (2015). Health Insurer Anthem Hit by Hackers. *The Wall Street Journal*. Retrieved August 3, 2017 from, https://www.wsj.com/articles/health-insurer-anthem-hit-by-hackers-1423103720

Neame, R. (2012). Practical measures for keeping health information private. *Electronic Journal of Health Informatics*, *7*(2).

NHS. (2012). £70,000 fine for Aneurin Bevan health board after data breach. *NHS News*. Retrieved January, 2013 from, http://www.nhis.info/news/nhs-news/%C2%A370000-fine-for-aneurin-bevan-health-board-after-data-breach/327/

O'Keefe, C. M., & Connolly, C. (2011). Regulation and Perception Concerning the Use of Health Data for Research in Australia. *Electronic Journal of Health Informatics*, *6*(2).

OSF. (2012). *Open Security Foundation, Data Loss DB*. Retrieved December 19, 2012 from, http://datalossdb.org/

Perakslis, E. D. (2014). Cybersecurity in health care. *The New England Journal of Medicine*, *371*(5), 395–397. doi:10.1056/NEJMp1404358 PMID:25075831

Ponemon. (2012a). *The Human Factor in Data Protection*. Ponemon Research Report. Retrieved October12, 2012, from http://www.trendmicro.com/cloud-content/us/pdfs/security-intelligence/reports/rpt_trend-micro_ponemon-survey-2012.pdf?ClickID=anpnsknps09tprya9k9ovzpzrnvrln99wrl

Ponemon. (2012b). *2011 Cost of Data Breach: United States*. Ponemon Research Report. Retrieved December 20, 2012 from, http://www.ponemon.org/local/upload/file/2011_US_CODB_FINAL_5.pdf

Ponemon. (2016a). *2016 Cost of Data Breach Study: Global Analysis, Benchmark research sponsored by IBM*. Ponemon Institute LLC. Retrieved July 20, 2017 from http://www-01.ibm.com/common/ssi/cgi-bin/ssialias?htmlfid=SEL03094WWEN

Ponemon. (2016b). *Sixth Annual Benchmark Study on Privacy & Security of Healthcare Data*. Ponemon Institute. Retrieved August 25, 2017 from, https://www.ponemon.org/local/upload/file/Sixth%20Annual%20Patient%20Privacy%20%26%20Data%20Security%20Report%20FINAL%206.pdf

PRCH. (2012). *Privacy Rights Clearing House, Chronology of Data Breaches 2005- Present*. Retrieved October 8, 2012, from, http://www.privacyrights.org/data-breach/new

PRCH. (2017). *Privacy Rights Clearing House, Chronology of Data Breaches 2005- Present*. Retrieved September 2017, from, https://www.privacyrights.org/data-breaches

Reason, J. (1990). *Human error*. Cambridge, MA: Cambridge University Press. doi:10.1017/CBO9781139062367

Reason, J. (1997). *Managing the risks of organizational accidents*. Aldershot, UK: Ashgate.

Reason, J. (2000). Human errors: Models and management. *British Medical Journal*, *320*(7237), 768–770. doi:10.1136/bmj.320.7237.768 PMID:10720363

Reason, J., Hollnagel, E., & Paries, E. J. (2006) Revisiting the "Swiss Cheese" model of accidents. *EUROCONTROL Experiment Center (EEC) Note No. 13/06*. Retrieved December 3, 2012 from, http://www.eurocontrol.int/eec/gallery/content/public/document/eec/report/2006/017_Swiss_Cheese_Model.pdf

Redspin. (2012). Protected Health Information. *Redspin Breach Report*. Retrieved November, 2013 from http://www.redspin.com/docs/Redspin_Breach_Report_2012.pdf

Robertson, J. (2012). Hackers steal, encrypt health records and hold data for ransom. *Bloomberg Report*. Retrieved November, 2012 from, http://go.bloomberg.com/tech-blog/2012-08-10-hackers-steal-encrypt-health-records-and-hold-data-for-ransom/

Schlienger, T., & Teufel, S. (2003). Information security culture: From analysis to change. *Proceedings of the Third Annual IS South Africa Conference*.

Stevens, L., Dobbs, C., Jones, K., & Laurie, G. (2017). Dangers from Within? Looking Inwards at the Role of Maladministration as the Leading Cause of Health Data Breaches in the UK. In R. Leenes, R. van Brakel, S. Gutwirth, & P. De Hert (Eds.), *Data Protection and Privacy: (In) Visibilities and Infrastructures. Law, Governance and Technology Series* (Vol. 36). Springer. doi:10.1007/978-3-319-50796-5_8

Straub, D. M., & Welke, R. J. (1998). Coping with systems risk: Security planning models for management decision making. *Management Information Systems Quarterly*, *22*(4), 441–469. doi:10.2307/249551

SurfWatch. (2015). *SurfWatch Labs 2015 Mid-year Cyber Risk Report*. Retrieved December 20, 2016 from, http://info.surfwatchlabs.com/2015-mid-year-cyber-risk-report

Van Niekerk, J. F., & Von Solms, R. (2010). Information security culture: A management perspective. *Computers & Security*, *29*(4), 476–486. doi:10.1016/j.cose.2009.10.005

Walker, A. K. (2011). Thousands of X-rays stolen from St. Joseph hospital: Police believe film was targeted for silver. *Baltimore Sun*. Retrieved from http://articles.baltimoresun.com/2011-11-04/health/bs-hs-stolen-xrays-20111104_1_x-rays-film-hospital

Walsh, B. (2012). Email intruder causes N.C. hospital data breach. *Clinical Innovation + Technology*. Retrieved January, 2013 from, <http://www.clinical-innovation.com/topics/privacy-security/email-intruder-causes-nc-hospital-data-breach>

Ward, P., & Smith, C. L. (2002). The development of access control policies for information technology systems. *Computers & Security*, *21*(4), 356–371. doi:10.1016/S0167-4048(02)00414-5

ENDNOTE

[1] For the purpose of this study, and consistent with the definition of breach in section 13400(1)(A) of the HITECH Act, we define "healthcare data breach" as the acquisition, access, use, or disclosure of protected health information which compromises the security or privacy of this information.

This research was previously published in the Handbook of Research on Emerging Perspectives on Healthcare Information Systems and Informatics; pages 58-81, copyright year 2018 by Medical Information Science Reference (an imprint of IGI Global).

Chapter 34
Exploring System Thinking Leadership Approaches to the Healthcare Cybersecurity Environment

Darrell Norman Burrell
https://orcid.org/0000-0002-4675-9544
The Florida Institute of Technology, USA & Capitol Technology University, USA

Amalisha Sabie Aridi
Capitol Technology University, USA

Quatavia McLester
https://orcid.org/0000-0003-1596-0517
The Chicago School of Professional Psychology, USA

Anton Shufutinsky
https://orcid.org/0000-0003-3819-0623
Cabrini University, USA

Calvin Nobles
https://orcid.org/0000-0003-4002-1108
University of Maryland Global Campus, USA

Maurice Dawson
https://orcid.org/0000-0003-4609-3444
Illinois Institute of Technology, USA

S. Raschid Muller
https://orcid.org/0000-0002-1742-7575
Capitol Technology University, USA

ABSTRACT

A Florida-based obstetrics and gynecology facility reported in February 2019 that they lost data because of a ransomware attack. In November 2017, 107,000 healthcare records were exposed from data breaches, and 340,000 records were exposed in December 2017. In 2019, 23,000 patient records at Critical Care, Pulmonary & Sleep Associates were compromised when a hacker gained access to an employee's email account and sent out phishing emails to the other employees, eventually exposing the patient data. On January 11, 2018, Adams Memorial Hospital and Hancock Regional Hospital, both in Indiana, experienced independent ransomware attacks, with Hancock Regional Hospital paying $50,000 in ransom. These incidents point to significant and complex cybersecurity risks for all healthcare organizations. Effectively managing these risks requires healthcare managers to develop system thinking and adap-

DOI: 10.4018/978-1-6684-6311-6.ch034

tive leadership skills. This paper explores the nuances and complexities around systems thinking in the healthcare cybersecurity environment.

INTRODUCTION

System thinking is a holistic approach intended to analyze how the parts of the system interact and how the emergence changes as a whole entity (Nobles, 2018). Unlike reductionist thinking, which treats the world from a static, simple, and one-sided perspective, this holistic thinking emphasizes the complexity, dynamism, and entirety of the system and the interconnected and multifaceted relationships between the system components (Nobles, 2018).

Healthcare systems in the United States have discovered the massive potential for digital technology to enhance clinical outcomes and change care delivery (Coventry & Branley, 2018). Technologies range from telemedicine technology providing care remotely, storing electronic health records (EHRs), and devices that deliver medication or monitor health (Coventry & Branley, 2018). Health care devices and their interconnectivity continue to evolve (Coventry & Branley, 2018). Many healthcare devices are now incorporated into the hospital network. There are approximately 10-15 connected devices per bed in United States hospitals (Coventry & Branley, 2018). The benefits of interconnection include automation, efficiency, error reduction, and remote monitoring (Coventry & Branley, 2018). EHRs make health information more generally accessible. With this evolving technology, health professionals can observe and modify implanted devices without patients ever needing to visit a hospital or have an invasive procedure (Coventry & Branley, 2018). The benefits of interconnectivity are altering the treatment of acute and chronic ailments.

Despite its improvements to clinical outcomes and patient care delivery, interconnection presents unique cybersecurity vulnerabilities. Healthcare faces more significant cyber risks than other sectors. Due to its fundamental weaknesses in its security posture, healthcare is one of the most targeted sectors globally (Martin, Martin, Hankin, Darzi, & Kinross, 2017). Common and emerging cyber threats in healthcare include: Data theft for financial gain; Data theft for impact; Ransomware; Data corruption; Denial of service attacks; Business email compromise, and the unwitting insider. In 2015 alone, 110 million patients in the United States had their data compromised (Martin et al., 2017). These numbers come from 81% of 223 organizations surveyed in 2015. About 50% of these providers believe they can defend themselves from cyberattack (Martin et al., 2017).

There has been a 300% increase in cyberattacks in the healthcare industry (Janofsky, 2019). Some healthcare centers shut down for good because they could not handle the post-attack disruption. COVID-19 has further intensified this developing issue. A typical cyberattack during the COVID-19 pandemic is hacking patients' medical devices (Morgan, 2020). Due to the pandemic, more patients are utilizing remote care (Morgan, 2020). The contrived facilities being utilized for individuals infected with the virus have generated more vulnerabilities for hackers to manipulate (Morgan, 2020). Phishing has exploded during the COVID-19 pandemic, with many scams coming from organizations like the Centers of Disease Control (CDC) and the World Health Organization (WHO). The healthcare industry is projected to spend $125 billion on cybersecurity from 2020 to 2025 (Morgan, 2020). The increasing cost and threat to cybersecurity, especially amid a global pandemic, highlights organizations' immediate need to utilize system thinking to prevent continuous loss.

Digital transformation in healthcare has offered exponential advances in capabilities and efficiencies, improving access, quality of care, chronic disease management, public health surveillance, and population

Figure 1. Deadly Khan, Brohi, & Zaman (2020)

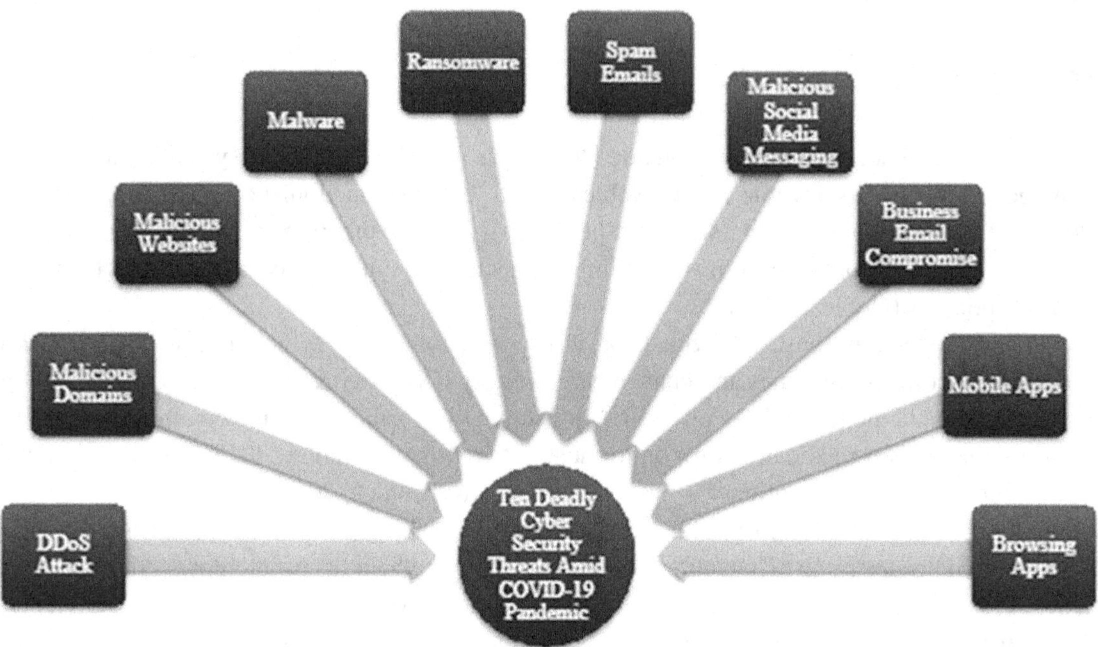

health (Burrell et al., 2020; Wickham, 2019). However, the speed of change left security lagging, exposing cyber vulnerabilities that cost the U.S. 6.2 billion dollars annually, at an average cost of 2.2 million dollars, and 3,128 records breached per incident (Burrell et al., 2020). Despite significant investments to close the gap on cyber vulnerabilities, cybersecurity remains a critical issue (Burrell et al., 2020). The forecast for the next few years suggests that the cost of cyberattacks will rise from $3 trillion (2015) to $6 trillion (2021), with cybersecurity spending expected to exceed $1 trillion (2017-2021). Similarly, cybercrime incidents will be three times greater than the number of unfilled cybersecurity positions, which is projected to reach 3.5 million cybersecurity job openings (2021), further exacerbating the cyber vulnerability associated with a shortage of cybersecurity workforce (Wickham, 2019).

Unlike compromised credit cards that can be canceled and changed once reported to the banks, patient Electronic Health Records (EHRs) are permanent (Wickham, 2019). These records contain personal, financial, and medical information that can be stolen for illegal activities. EHRs are lucrative commodities fetching $50 per record in the black market (Martin et al., 2017). For instance, the Anthem data breach of 80 million records brought 1 billion dollars into the darknet (Martin et al., 2017). In a survey conducted by Ponemon, close to 2 million Americans spent over $12 billion out of pocket to deal with the aftermath of compromised medical records or insurance files (Luna et al., 2016). As a result, the need to develop system thinking skills around project management skills, leadership skills, and cybersecurity expertise for health care professionals has become paramount (Burrell, 2019; Burrell et al., 2020).

Organizations use the concept of systems thinking to challenge traditional assumptions on how to plan and whom to involve in organizational planning (Leidtka, 1998). With systems thinking, top management influences the organization's success by formulating strategies for the future with the prescribed method of achieving success (Stacey, 2011). Skarzauskiene (2010) stated the need for organizational leaders to use systems thinking (rather than analytical thinking) as a health care management tool to address the complexity of project dynamics and systems and the ever-changing external environment impacting organizational performance. Senge (2006) described systems thinking as a framework for seeing connectivity (instead of seeing the individual parts of the whole) that gives systems their nature. Interactional relationship connects people and the workplace, with the workplace environment impacting workers' conduct either negatively or positively (Senge, 2006). The interaction between organizations and employees during operational performance results in enacting organizational behavior (Brief & Weiss, 2000).

The Aim of this Research

This research discussion aims to use the literature's contextual review to examine healthcare cybersecurity organizational behavior through systems thinking lens and how organizations employ systems for project risk management and healthcare leadership.

RESEARCH METHOD

This paper utilizes content analysis of existing literature that explores the complexities and challenges of cybersecurity risk management systems in healthcare. The value of a content analysis review of the literature is the ability to take dispersed concepts, theories, and practices on emerging research on a topic and articulately merge them for practitioner digestion or as a base-level foundation for future academic research. Databases used include ResearchGate, Academia.edu, Google Scholar, Medline, Business Source Corporate, ProQuest Business, CINAHL, Nature Journals On-line, ICPSRm ProQuest Health. Search words used included:

Information systems and systems thinking,
organizational behavior and healthcare cybersecurity,
information security management and healthcare.

Review of Literature

Complexity is the most prominent cybersecurity characteristic and has infiltrated each part of the cybersecurity landscape (Nobles, 2018; Dawson, 2018; Dawson, 2020). First, cybersecurity complexity embodies the diversity in security issues and the multiplicity in influence factors (Nobles, 2018; Dawson, 2018; Dawson, 2020). Cybersecurity is a complex intercross area, covering multiple fields, such as sociology, psychology, information technology, etc. The cybersecurity issues are stemmed from these fields and are affected by the combination of factors that can lead to errors, risks, and unprotected vulnerabilities (Nobles, 2018; Dawson, 2018; Dawson, 2020). Moreover, the interrelationships between components in cyberspace are incredibly complicated (Nobles, 2018; Dawson, 2018; Dawson, 2020). Each component could interact with others in each field. As the center of cyberspace, the human is the interface between people systems, organizational systems, and technology (Nobles, 2018; Dawson, 2018; Dawson, 2020).

Chaiken and Holmquest have concluded, "Errors occur because of defects in processes, not the unpredictability of human error. In fact, human error is quite predictable and should be expected in all processes." (Chaiken and Holmquest, 2003). Leape argues that "Errors result from defects in the design and conditions of medical work that lead careful, competent, caring physicians and nurses to make mistakes that are often no different from the simple mistakes people make every day, but which can have devastating consequences for patients" (Leape, 2000). According to Reason (2000), small errors, or failures, can cascade into the sentinel events. Reason (2000) outlines that understanding of errors in the division between two approaches: the person approach (where we blame the person) and the system approach (where we understand the system in which the error occurred).

Reason (2000) describes the system as slices of Swiss cheese with defensive layers that are continually opening, shutting, and shifting their location. In most situations, one hole's presence does not cause an error because of the catching of the error in the next layer of the Swiss cheese. However, the holes will tend to line up through coincidence, and the trajectory of an accident occurs when active failures and latent failures in the system occur (Reason, 2000). Active failures are the unsafe acts committed by people who are in direct contact with the patient or system. They take various forms: slips, lapses, fumbles, mistakes, and procedural violations (Reason, 2000). The complexity of redesigning the process is exponentially increased as the various managers are all being provided with different priorities and directions from their respective managers (Reason, 2000).

Systems thinking requires a shift in perception influenced by the organizational culture to ensure a fit between strategic choice and organizational performance (Reason, 2000). Stacey (2011) described an organization as a chaotic and overwhelming complex adaptive system that requires adaptive health care leadership to lead, think, and do things differently to develop the organizational behavior and culture, leading to value creation for sustainable advantage. Adaptive health care leadership unleashes interactive events to enact knowledge development, action preferences, and behavior change, provoking an organization to become more adaptive to establish the organization's behavior (Stacey, 2011). Effective interaction and relationships within the complex adaptive system aid in building confidence and responsibility to dissipate the helplessness complexity of systems that can pose to an organization's performance (Nobles, 2018). In these interactions, organizations define who they are and their focus for future sustainability in the ever-changing and dynamic environment (Nobles, 2018). These interactions can generate tensions that tend to stretch teams' imaginations to initiate innovative and adaptive behaviors, fostering diversity to develop organizational learning cultures (Nobles, 2018). Developing a culture of interrelationships out of chaotic systems leads to more profound and new insights and new ideas to solving issues relating to risk management performance through an effective feedback system (Stacey, 2011) as systems thinking helps organizations discover hidden talents and innovative ideas by breaking paradigms for business sustainability (Luntz, 2011). Senge (2006) further elaborate this fact by indicating that the fight for terrorism can give rise to discovering a deeper appreciation of the relevance of building a cycle of security.

Therefore, organizations need to study and analyze organizational behavior in the context of all the elements that link employee relationship to the organization. Brief and Weiss (2000) suggested that organizations must connect an employee's emotional, social, and educational status to organizational reward, value, and financial system (Brief & Weiss, 2000). Organizational behavior (OB) is a scientific discipline that relates to the study of people's conduct in a defined environment and culture (Brethower, 2010). The discipline identifies the organization as a complex system within which individuals interact and perform, influenced by reward, value, operational system, and culture (Brethower, 2010). Per the Brethower in the Cambridge Centre of Behavioral System (CCBS), the OB system concentrates on studying the factors that impact and increase the productivity and performance of the organization through the following factor; (a) identifying the factors that effects increase or decrease performance, (b) specify the internal and external changes that might affect the improvement of business productivity, and (c) identify the factors and changes that might support, redesign, and improve the organizational system to help improve productivity through enhanced organizational behavior (Brethower, 2010).

Systems theory

A trend towards generalized theories took place in many fields like the biological, behavioral, and social sciences. Lotka and Volterra developed a theory of the dynamics of biological populations. The theory delves into the struggle for existence and biological equilibria (von Bertalanffy, 1968). The theory functions with biological ideas, like species, competition, individuals, etc. (von Bertalanffy, 1968). A comparable method is applied in econometrics and quantitative economics. The equation models used in quantitative economics and econometrics are like those of Lotka and chemical kinetics, but "the model of interacting entities and forces is again at a different level" (von Bertalanffy, 1968).

Another example can be found when examining living organisms. Living organisms are open systems. Theory in conventional physics and physical chemistry has traditionally dealt with closed systems, but it has expanded to include permanent processes, open systems, and disequilibrium states (von Bertalanffy, 1968). If one applies the model of open systems to animal growth phenomena, one will come to a generalization of theory denoting biological elements and not physical elements (von Bertalanffy, 1968). These examples illustrate our dealing with generalized systems.

Laws, principles, and models exist that apply to generalized systems, regardless of their specific "kind, the nature of their component elements, and the relations of "forces" between them" (von Bertalanffy, 1968). Since it could be seen that certain principles apply to generalized systems, a theory needed to be created. The theory would explain universal principles applying to systems in general. General System Theory (GST) is the origin and creation of those ideologies which are true of "systems" in general (von Bertalanffy, 1968). GST would be used to find structural parallels or isomorphisms in different fields (von Bertalanffy, 1968).

According to Anderson (2016), the application of systems theory relies on the notion that most individuals strive to do well at work, but they are acted upon by various stimuli. Casual Analysis grounded in Systems Theory states that when mistakes happen, one should focus on individual failings and the environment that permitted such events to occur (Anderson, 2016; Shufutinsky, 2019).From this aspect, systems theory can help organizations to examine their environment and determine the cause of their success or failure from an organizational level (Shufutinsky, 2019).

What is a System?

According to Meadows (2015), a system is a set of interconnected elements that yield a graphic pattern of behavior over time. The system may be bound, buffeted, motivated by external forces, or triggered (Meadows, 2015; Burrell, 2020; Shufutinsky, 2019). Each element alone has a distinct and limited role. Nevertheless, when each element is gathered in a system, the elements can yield outcomes that are more than the sum of each part (Fachot, 2013).

Elements within the system may show dynamic, adaptive, and evolutionary behavior (Meadows, 2015). These outcomes could not be attained outside the system. When one takes a systems viewpoint, it helps one understand how several elements impact one another or the system in its entirety (Fachot, 2013).

With this perspective, one can figure out whether an advance or enhancement in one part of the system may negatively affect another part of the system through influencing leverage points (Shufutinsky, 2019).

At the core of the principle of leverage exists "leverage points." Leverage points are places within a complex organizational system where a tiny change in one thing can generate substantial shifts in everything (Meadows, 1999). Meadows (1999) proposes nine leverage points. The nine leverage points include:

- Numbers (subsidies, taxes, standards)
- Material stocks and flows
- Regulating negative feedback loops
- Driving positive feedback loops
- Information flows
- The rules of the system (incentives, punishments, constraints)
- The power of self-organization
- The goals of the system
- The mindset of paradigm out of which the goals, rules, feedback structure arise.

This relates to the concepts of Chaos and Complexity because systems can be both complex and chaotic. Complex systems are highly composite (Rickles, 2007). Complex systems are constructed from large numbers of interacting sub-units whose frequent exchanges result in collective behavior that feeds back into the individual parts' behavior (Rickles, 2007). Chaotic systems may have limited interacting sub-units, but they interact in such a way as to yield complicated dynamics (Rickles, 2007).

System Archetypes and their Negative Impact on Organizations

In systems thinking, archetypes refer to systemic structures found in various types of organizations, under many circumstances, at distinct levels, from global international relations to internal personal dynamics (Kim & Anderson, 1998). Senge (2006) identified two fundamental system archetypes that, when not effectively managed, can cause a demerit to an organization's performance. These two archetypes are (a) the limits to growth and (b) shifting the burden. According to Senge (2006), many efforts are intended to improve the system rather than retard growth. This limit to growth can be seen in an organization pushing the boundaries to meet deadlines and achieve the target, leading to subpar performance in risk management and risk reduction performance due to employees' added stress and frustration (Burrell, 2020; Shufutinsky, 2019). Health organizations need to apply systems thinking and build effective communication systems to the amplifying process they set in motion to produce a sustained desired result. This approach will assist in removing the factors that tend to limit growth. Senge (2006) described the second archetype as the process of shifting the burden to other solutions and 'quick fixes,' which worsens the situation in the long run and create symptomatic solutions (Senge, 2006). The second archetype resembles the archetype fixes that fail, or fixes that backfire, as it is used to describe a situation where a fix effective in the short-term creates side effects for the long-term behavior of the system and may result in the need for additional fixes or corrective actions that fail (Braun, 2002). Health organizations need to understand how shifting the burden of information security risks can impact the whole operational system. By not solving problems from a holistic system, perspective can understand how well-intended solutions can worsen in the long term (Nobles, 2018). Organizations will have to strengthen the response by developing solutions that address the fundamental causes and information security risks around patient electronic medical records and medical devices.

The Negative Impact of Measurement and Reward Systems on Organizational Performance

An organization's reward system is a significant factor that impacts the way employees perform their assigned roles and responsibilities, influencing employees' choice of an employer over another (Mathis & Jackson, 2000; Burrell, 2020). An organization's compensation system must be connected to its strategic objectives and operational goals to prevent the negative effect of free-riding associated with large group rewards (Wageman & Baker, 1997). Rewards and incentives are among the tools most organizations use to motivate employees to ensure performance aligns with organizational objectives (Rehman & Ali 2013;(Burrell, 2020; Shufutinsky, 2019). A compensation program in an organization is required to fulfill the following purposes:

- Legal Compliance with all compensation legal laws and regulations.
- Cost measurements and effectiveness for the financial system of the organization.
- Financial and Individual equity for employees; and
- Productivity and performance fostering and elevation for the organization (Mathis & Jackson, 2000).

Achieving performance excellence in an organization requires health care managers to design their compensation and reward system in connection with its strategic performance, vision, and goals (Thigpen, Beaucher, Carroll, 2012). Organizations nowadays are facing severe pressure to base compensation systems on strategic performance philosophy. Thus, bonuses and incentives are based on organizational performance outcomes and not necessarily on individual performance and contribution to organizational achievement (Thigpen et al., 2012). Organizations need to motivate employees for peak performance. Measurement and rewards can harm an organization's performance when there is a gap between rewards and operational/strategic goals around information and data security (Nobles, 2018). Appraisal systems are one useful tool to measure employee performance and institute rewards accordingly based on risk project management activity results. According to Rehman and Ali (2013), a manager's obligation to keep and retain employees may influence the manager to rate employees high unrelated to their actual performance. However, health care leadership is recently required to use the reward system as a motivational strategy to achieve organizational productivity and performance. Nevertheless, the organization must align its compensation and reward system with a motivational competency-based pay strategy (Mathis & Jackson, 2000). This strategy will enhance the organizational performance-oriented culture and motivate the employees' productivity daily around information security in healthcare.

Use of Project Health Care Leadership to Mitigate the Downside of Systems

Project health care leadership is one of the various elements organizations can use to alleviate organizational systems' drawbacks. Laufer (2012) enumerated nine project leadership practices that can unleash organizations' adaptive health care leadership skills to manage the chaotic and adaptive systems that constitute an organization. Organizational leaders who embrace the "living order" can tolerate and deal with chaos in the system to gain a competitive advantage (Burrell, 2020; Shufutinsky, 2019). The practice of adjusting project practices to a specific context adds to the organization's learning culture, where individual teams and departments can appreciate the need to strike a balance between the application of organizational knowledge and creating an innovative culture for peak performance (Burrell, 2020; Shufutinsky, 2019). Laufer (2011) encouraged project leaders to challenge the status quo to create the needed tension that leads to innovative ideas to enhance systems performance (Stacey 2011). Stacey (2011) stated that people and organizations are not separate entities but relational realities that develop from interactions. People are the make or break factor of the organization and choosing the right people (agents in the system) will determine the effectiveness of the organizational systems (Laufer 2012). As discussed above, culture defines an organization's behavior, which in effect showcases what the organization believes in. Project health care leadership practice of shaping the right culture will impact positively on organizational systems.

Planning is essential and impacts significantly on the organization's performance (Burrell, 2020). The project assists leaders in the organization to plan, monitor, and anticipate attaining the desired outcome (Laufer, 2012). According to Laufer (2012), organizations may not meet operational success when leaders are not action-oriented and fail to achieve the result. Leaders can positively influence the chaotic systems when they focus on results because they will be able to navigate through the changing environment to attain the result (Burrell, 2020; Shufutinsky, 2019). Effective organizational health care leadership is an antidote to chaotic and disordered systems (Senge, 2006). Effective leaders gain the mastery to unearth the potential for personal and organizational growth, giving leaders the tools and skills to manage chaotic systems effectively (Laufer, 2012; Senge, 2006; Burrell, 2020; Shufutinsky, 2019).

CONCLUSION

According to Barry and Perlroth (2020) on October 28, 2020, the University of Vermont Medical Center phone system stopped working, the Internet stopped working, and employees lost access to critical systems including work related databases, digital health records, scheduling systems, and other online tools they rely on for patient care. This outages were the result of a cyberattack, becoming one of the most recent and visible examples of a wave of digital assaults taking U.S. health care providers hostage as COVID-19 cases surge nationwide. The impact was devastating including medical treatment delays, communications problems, and lifesaving medical equipment failures during a time when the hospital was attempting to treat COVID-19 and other ill patents (Barry & Perlroth, 2020).

The COVID-19 pandemic has resulted in widespread disruption to the healthcare industry (Barry & Perlroth, 2020). Alongside complex issues relating to ensuring sufficient healthcare capacity and resourcing, healthcare organizations and universities face heightened cyber-security threats during the pandemic (Barry & Perlroth, 2020). Since the emergence of COVID-19, various medical centers worldwide have been targeted in various complex and coordinatized cyber-attacks (Barry & Perlroth, 2020). Unfortunately, healthcare companies and medical practices often lack system resources expertise to protect against cyber-attacks and can be badly affected by the cost and long-term impacts of security breaches (Barry & Perlroth, 2020).

Pressures to increase access, reduce costs, improve safety, and integrate emerging technologies and EHRs pose significant challenges for healthcare executives operating in a fiscally constrained environment (Burrell et al., 2020). Payment reforms, marketplace competition, financial risk, and uncertainties add to the complexity of balancing requirements for government mandates and priorities for sustainability (Burrell et al., 2020). The Ponemon Institute's 2018 Cost of Data Breach study representing 17 industry sectors provided critical insight into the magnitude of cost (Ponemon, 2018). According to the report, compared to other countries, the U.S. has the highest costs in a data breach ($7.91 million average total costs), a notification ($740,000), and post-data breach response ($1.76 million). Of the 17 sectors, healthcare ranked #1 in per capita data breach cost at $408, followed by the financial industry at $206 (Ponemon, 2018). Furthermore, U.S. and Canada spend the most to resolve malicious or criminal attacks at $258 and $213 per record, respectively (Ponemon, 2018).

World Wide Web can be deemed as the ultimate complex adaptive system of interlocked heterogeneous features, such as multiple types of networks, devices, and stakeholders, intermingled with human behavioral and technical elements (Yan, 2020; Nobles, 2018). Complexity is the most notorious attribute of the cybersecurity topography and universe (Yan, 2020; Nobles, 2018; Dawson, 2018; Dawson, 2020). Complexity in cybersecurity personifies the multiplicity in security concerns and often shifting influential dynamics (Yan, 2020; Dawson, 2018; Dawson, 2020).

As interfaces exist among components and dynamic effects of the numerous categories of factors, cyber and information security presents a challenging level of unpredictability and complexity (Yan, 2020; Dawson, 2018; Dawson, 2020). To further explain, the cyber attacker engages in exploitation activities as vulnerability testing, intelligence gathering, weaponization, and potentially data theft (Yan, 2020; Dawson, 2018). At the same time, the cybersecurity team must sure of vulnerabilities, respond to attacks, assess the impact of intrusions, and adapt to new (Yan, 2020). This process is not linear or predictable (Dawson, 2018; Dawson, 2020).

According to Senge (1990), "Systems thinking is a discipline for seeing wholes. It is a framework for seeing interrelationships rather than things, for seeing patterns of change rather than static 'snapshots.'' System thinking is important because Cybersecurity tends to have a technology focus and provides a defensive, static, security environment versus its adversaries' dynamic behavior (Yan, 2020; Dawson, 2020). The behavior of defensive-oriented cybersecurity is asymmetrical, which gives the adversaries the "first move" advantage that must then be detected, identified, and protected against (Yan, 2020; Dawson, 2018). The result is a patch, upon patch, in response to adversarial attacks (Yan, 2020; Dawson, 2018). Cybersecurity behaves as an evolutionary system, not a purpose-designed system (Yan, 2020; Dawson, 2018). Often traditional approaches to cybersecurity are often absent of approaches to proactively protect against human factor vulnerabilities and a critical understanding that cybersecurity is everyone's responsibility not just those that work in information technology (Nobles, 2018).

Kauffman (1980) defines the exploration of systems as an analysis of their properties, as well as complex system characteristics and problems. Several properties of a system that Kauffman identifies are highly relevant to cyber security:

- Systems cope with problems by reacting to warnings.
- The obvious solution often makes things worse.
- Solving one problem almost always creates others.

Systems thinking allows us to think about cybersecurity risks and vulnerabilities from a holistic and rational perspective (Wickham, 2019). On the one hand, systems thinking provides a conceptual blueprint or framework for cybersecurity, where the components, factors, and environments are integrated dynamically (Wickham, 2019). System thinking enjoins healthcare organizations to connect all the individual parts of the whole system and not operate the systems in their parts to achieve the best results and develop the culture of innovation and responsive behavior (Laufer, 2011). Effect healthcare organizations should eliminate the negative influence of systems archetypes to enhance performance around information security (Wickham, 2019). Organizations should strive to utilize systems thinking and appropriate rewards systems to manage risks and projects connected to managing these information security risks (Dawson, Burrell, Rahim, & Brewster, 2010). Adaptive cyber project health care managers must ensure the management of human behavior to allow a reasonable degree of consensus between individuals within the system, enforcing a learning culture through which the organization ensures effectiveness around healthcare cybersecurity risks (Wickham, 2019).

Cybersecurity activities of patching vulnerabilities as they are discovered leave the initiative to the adversaries and do not solve the underlying structural problems (Dawson, 2020). Systems thinking addresses the wholeness and interrelated, the dynamic behavior of this domain (Yan, 2020). Systems thinking is considered to offer a novel and comprehensive perspective to reveal the entire process of cybersecurity as a system (Yan, 2020; Dawson, 2018). By these systems thinking approaches, professionals can use conceptual framework for measuring and evaluating a cybersecurity system, and it constitutes, such as defensive measures, human factors, security policy (Yan, 2020; Dawson, 2018). Thus, the typical goals of the systems thinking for cybersecurity modeling are exemplified as follows: (1) discovering the multiple impact factors and their interacting effects; (2) investigating fundamental laws in cybersecurity; (3) exploring the theoretical and real solution to the specific security issue; (4) evaluating effective attack weapons and defense measures in the specific scenario in healthcare environments (Yan, 2020; Dawson, 2018). The emergence of COVID-19 has made the ability to understand and apply systems thinking approaches to healthcare cybersecurity a critical matter of patient safety and patient care.

RECOMMENDATIONS FOR FUTURE RESEARCH

Future research should investigate other aspects of enforcing a learning culture, like personal mastery and shared vision, and how they might play a part in healthcare cybersecurity risks. This future study should seek to determine if organizations that enforce a learning culture that encompasses all Senge's (2006) identified components of a learning organization are less susceptible to cybersecurity risks. The exploration could occur in the form of a multiple organization qualitative case study to find out the best practices being used by hospitals and medical centers to approaches to critical incident analysis, addressing human factor risks in cybersecurity, addressing business continuity planning, addressing crisis management, and cybersecurity penetration testing.

REFERENCES

Anderson, B. R. (2016). Improving Healthcare by Embracing Systems Theory. *The Journal of Thoracic and Cardiovascular Surgery*, *152*(2), 593–594. doi:10.1016/j.jtcvs.2016.03.029 PMID:27113625

Barry, E., & Perlroth, N. (2020, December 14). Patients of a Vermont Hospital Are Left 'in the Dark' After a Cyberattack. *The New York Times*.

Braun, W. (2002). *The System Archetypes*. Retrieved from: https://www.albany.edu/faculty/gpr/PAD724/724WebArticles/sys_archetypes.pdf

Brief, A. P., & Weiss, H. M. (2002). Organizational behavior: Affect in the workplace. *Annu Rev. Psychol, 53*, 279-307.

Brethower, D. (2010). Behavioral system analysis. *CCBS Journal*. Retrieved from http://www.behavior.org/resource.php?id=755

Burrell, D. N. (2018). An Exploration of the Cybersecurity Workforce Shortage. *International Journal of Hyperconnectivity and the Internet of Things*, *2*(1), 29–41. doi:10.4018/IJHIoT.2018010103

Burrell, D. N., Bhargava, N., Springs, D., Dawson, M., Burton, S. L., Anderson, D. P., & Wright, J. B. (2020). Adopting Organizational Cultural Changes Concerning Whistle-Blowing in Healthcare Around Information Security in the "Internet of Things" World. *International Journal of Hyperconnectivity and the Internet of Things*, *4*(1), 13–28. doi:10.4018/IJHIoT.2020010102

Burrell, D. N. (2019). Assessing the Value of Executive Leadership Coaches for Cybersecurity Project Managers. *International Journal of Human Capital and Information Technology Professionals*, *10*(2), 20–32. doi:10.4018/IJHCITP.2019040102

Burrell, D. N. (2020). Understanding the Talent Management Intricacies of Remote Cybersecurity Teams in Covid-19 Induced Telework Organizational Ecosystems. *Land Forces Academy Review*, *25*(3), 232–244. doi:10.2478/raft-2020-0028

Carmeli, A., & Sheaffer, Z. (2008). How leadership characteristics affect organizational decline and downsizing. *Journal of Business Ethics*, *86*(3), 363–378. doi:10.100710551-008-9852-7

Chaiken & Holmquest. (2003). Patient Safety: Modifying Processes to Eliminate Medical Errors. *Nursing Outlook, 51*(3), S21.

Coventry, L., & Branley, D. (2018). Cybersecurity in healthcare: A narrative review of trends, threats, and ways forward. *Maturitas*, *113*, 48–52. doi:10.1016/j.maturitas.2018.04.008 PMID:29903648

Dawson, M. (2018). Applying a holistic cybersecurity framework for global IT organizations. *Business Information Review*, *35*(2), 60–67. doi:10.1177/0266382118773624

Dawson, M. (2020). Cybercrime: Internet Driven Illicit Activities and Behavior. *Land Forces Academy Review*, *25*(4), 356–362. doi:10.2478/raft-2020-0043

Dawson, M., Burrell, D. N., Rahim, E., & Brewster, S. (2010). Examining the role of the chief information security officer (CISO) & security plan. *Journal of Information Systems Technology & Planning*, *3*(6).

Fachot, M. (2013). *System: more than the sum of its parts*. Retrieved from https://iecetech.org/issue/2013-01/System-more-than-the-sum-of-its-parts

Janofsky, A. (2019, October 6). Smaller medical providers get burned by ransomware. *Wall Street Journal*. https://www.wsj.com/articles/smaller-medical-providers-get-burned-by-ransomware-11570366801

Khan, N., Brohi, S., & Zaman, N. (2020). Ten Deadly Cyber Security Threats Amid COVID-19 Pandemic. doi:10.36227/techrxiv.12278792.v1

Leape, L. L. (2000). Institute of Medicine Medical Error Figures Are Not Exaggerated. *JAMA, 284*(1), 95.

Kauffman, D. (1980). Systems One: An Introduction to Systems Thinking. Future Systems, Inc. In *Originally the Human Environment: An Introduction to Environmental Systems. Developed under a grant to the Office of Environmental Education, Office of Education, Department of Health*, Education, and Welfare.

Liedtka, J. M. (1998). Linking strategic thinking with strategic planning. *Strategy and Leadership*, *26*(4), 30–35. https://search.proquest.com/docview/194364332?accountid=14872

Luna, R., Rhine, E., Myhra, M., Sullivan, R., & Kruse, C. S. (2016). Cyber threats to health information systems: A systematic review. *Technology and Health Care*, *24*(1), 1–9. doi:10.3233/THC-151102 PMID:26578272

Martin, G., Martin, P., Hankin, C., Darzi, A., & Kinross, J. (2017). Cybersecurity and healthcare: How safe are we? *BMJ (Clinical Research Ed.)*, *4*, j3179. Advance online publication. doi:10.1136/bmj.j3179 PMID:28684400

Mathis, R. L., & Jackson, J. H. (2000). Human resources management (9th ed.). South-Western College Publishing. Thomason Learning.

Meadows, D. (1999). Leverage points: places to intervene in a system. The Sustainability Institute.

Meadows, D. H., & Wright, D. (2015). *Thinking in systems: A primer*. Chelsea Green Publishing.

Morgan, S. (2020, September 8). Healthcare industry to spend $125 billion on cybersecurity from 2020 to 2025. *Cybercrime Magazine*. https://cybersecurityventures.com/healthcare-industry-to-spend-125-billion-on-cybersecurity-from-2020-to-2025/

Nobles, C. (2018). Botching Human Factors in Cybersecurity in Business Organizations. *HOLISTICA – Journal of Business and Public Administration, 9*(3), 71-88. doi:10.2478/hjbpa-2018-0024

Ponemon. (2018). *2018 Cost of a Data Breach Study: Global Overview*. Retrieved from https://securityintelligence.com/series/ponemon-institute-cost-of-a-data-breach2018/

Reason, J. (2000). Human error: Models and management. *BMJ (Clinical Research Ed.)*, *320*(7237), 768–770. doi:10.1136/bmj.320.7237.768 PMID:10720363

Rehman, R., & Ali, M. A. (2013). Is pay for performance the best incentive for employees? *Journal of Emerging Trends in Economics and Management Science*, *4*, 512–514. https://search.proquest.com/docview/1493991654?accountid=1487

Senge, P. M. (2006). *The fifth discipline: The art & practice of the learning organization*. Doubleday.

Rickles, D., Hawe, P., & Shiell, A. (2007). A simple guide to chaos and complexity. *Journal of Epidemiology and Community Health*, *61*(11), 933–937. doi:10.1136/jech.2006.054254 PMID:17933949

Senge, P. (1990). *The Fifth Discipline: The Art & Practice of The Learning Organization*. Currency Doubleday.

Shufutinsky, A. (2019). Tribalism and Clone Theory in New Leaders and the Resulting Degradation of Organizational Culture. *Psychol Behav Sci Int J.*, *10*(2), 555788. doi:10.19080/PBSIJ.2018.09.555788

Skarzauskiene, A. (2010). Managing complexity: Systems thinking as a catalyst of the organizations performance, Managing Business Excellence. *Emerald Group Publishing Ltd.*, *14*(4), 49–64. doi:10.5539/ijbm.v8n8p133

Stacey, R. (2011). *Strategic management and organizational dynamics: The challenge of complexity to ways of thinking about organizations* (6th ed.). Pearson Education Ltd.

Thigpen, M. L., Baeudair, T. J., & Carroll, S. (2012). *Achieving Performance Excellence: The influence of leadership on organizational performance*. National Institute of Correction. Retrieved from static.nicic.gov/Library/025338.pdf

von Bertalanffy, L. (1968). The Meaning of General Systems Theory. In *General Systems Theory: Foundations, Development, Applications* (pp. 30–53). George Braziller, Inc.

Wageman, R., & Baker, G. (1997). Incentives and cooperation: The joint effects of task and reward interdependence on group performance. *Journal of Organizational Behavior, 18*, 139-158. doi: 1099-1379(199703)18:2<139:: AID-JOB791>3.0.CO;2-R doi:10.1002/(SICI)

Waraich, S. B., & Bhardwaj, G. (2011). Coping strategies of executive survivors downsized organizations in India. *S.A.M. Advanced Management Journal*. Advance online publication. doi:10.1002/pmj.21327

Wickham, M. H. (2019). *Exploring data breaches and means to mitigate future occurrences in healthcare institutions: A content analysis* (Order No. 13861149). Available from ProQuest Dissertations & Theses Global. (2216485062)

Yan, D. (2020). *A Systems Thinking for Cybersecurity Modeling*. arXiv preprint arXiv:2001.05734.

This research was previously published in the International Journal of Extreme Automation and Connectivity in Healthcare (IJEACH), 3(2); pages 20-32, copyright year 2021 by IGI Publishing (an imprint of IGI Global).

Chapter 35
Adopting Organizational Cultural Changes Concerning Whistle-Blowing in Healthcare Around Information Security in the "Internet of Things" World

Darrell Norman Burrell
https://orcid.org/0000-0002-4675-9544
The Florida Institute of Technology, USA

Nimisha Bhargava
AUL Corporation, Napa, USA

Delores Springs
https://orcid.org/0000-0003-0940-1225
Regent University, USA

Maurice Dawson
https://orcid.org/0000-0003-4609-34444
Illinois Institute of Technology, USA

Sharon L. Burton
https://orcid.org/0000-0003-1653-9783
Grand Canyon University, USA

Damon P. Anderson
https://orcid.org/0000-0003-4161-1775
Capitol Technology University, USA

Jorja B. Wright
https://orcid.org/0000-0002-7028-995X
The University of Charleston, USA

ABSTRACT

Medical labs, hospitals, doctor's offices, and medical devices face significant cyber risks. The insecurity of medical devices, including imaging hardware, threatens patient safety. Health organizations are rich with valuable data as well as weak with information security expertise, protocols, and infrastructure. It is critical for more health organizations to focus creating organizational cultures with processes that offer all employees to fully understand the nature of information security risks and have the ability to be active participants in the minimization and reporting of observable risks. This article will lay a foundation to establish techniques and practices for open door policies.

DOI: 10.4018/978-1-6684-6311-6.ch035

INTRODUCTION OF SECURITY VULNERABILITIES

More than 29.1 million patient records have been breached or stolen in the United States between 2010 and 2013 (McCoy & Perlis, 2018), with 7 million breaches affecting 500 or extra sufferers stated in 2013 alone accounting for a 137% growth over the previous 12 months (Collier, 2014). The increase in offenses illustrates the fact that the progressed access to health care data and the consequent increase in clinic revel is an alternate-off with statistics security. Hospitals, medical labs, medical offices, and medical devices face significant cyber risks (Martin et al., 2017). A report by KPMG states that in 2015, 110 million patients in the U.S. had their data compromised (KPMG, 2015). Cyber-attacks have gone up 300% in the past three (3) years (Martin et al., 2017). The insecurity of medical devices, including imaging hardware, threatens patient safety. For cybercriminals, health organizations are rich with valuable data (2017). At the same time, these organizations are weak with cybersecurity expertise, protocols, and infrastructure to minimize the risks (2017). Whereas the cybersecurity risks in different industries can be severe, the same exposure within healthcare has more severe risks because the data they use is critical to making life-saving decisions (Coventry & Branley, 2018). The clinical statistics saved in EHRs consist of individually identifiable information (PII), which include highly sensitive information like a patient's medicines, ailments, biometric data, sexual records, hospitalization facts, and laboratory test results (Coventry & Branley, 2018). Information security breaches in healthcare consist of identification robbery, unauthorized personal information disclosures, Internet of Things (IoT) tool loss, system hacking, and, wrong disposal of Health care statistics (Coventry & Branley, 2018) There is a dire need to minimize the threats to electronic health records(Coventry & Branley, 2018 The introduction of processes that can protect health data could enhance safety, lessen medical errors, and improve affected person care and improve treatment.

Cybersecurity in health care has become so severe that the U.S. Food and Drug Administration (FDA) and the Department of Homeland Security (DHS) have introduced a memorandum of settlement to encourage collaboration and enlarge synchronization of their efforts around data security (Martin et. Al., 2017). The security of medical devices has long been a worry. Cybersecurity failings in scientific devices can expose patients to harm by allowing hackers to alter and falsify medical test results and medical diagnoses, as an increasing number of clinical gadgets connect to healthcare networks and the Internet (2017). Medical devices are a likely frail point for exploitation (2017). Susceptibilities can also be exploited to intentionally cause harm to patients due to a lack of adequate information security processes and protocols (2017).

Healthcare organizations often suffer from cultures and processes that create risks including deficiencies when updating their software due to asynchronous communication amid distributed system components, the void of a devoted staff, minimal on-site cybersecurity know-how, and unplanned time or the lack of resources to test patches before installing them into production systems (Iqbal et al., 2016; Packer-Tursman, 2015). The average time to prepare a patch depends upon the system, and its number of components (Rosen, 2011); and testing before implementation could cause a long delay. The various healthcare information technology leaders developed an increase in hacking concerns, as well as the void of hacking information-sharing unveiling existing and emerging risks. A salient point to remember is that adding software patches may initiate security susceptibilities. If new-users add equipment, applications, or components, this paves the way for more ethics concerns due to non-transparency (Bhargava, Madala, & Burrell, 2018). As a result, there is a dire need to understand further immeasurable threats concerning EHR to proffer a security strategy that would enhance security, reduce medical errors, and improve patient care.

HEALTHCARE, ETHICAL STRUCTURAL CULTURES, AND DECISION-MAKING PROCESSES

The culture of healthcare understandably focuses on caring for patients, even at the expense of security (Martin et al., 2017). One symptom of this 'patient-centered' culture is the widespread tension between ethics and transparency concerning the interests of the patient and the interests of the organization. Ethics becomes even more complicated when healthcare organizations place their emphasis on utilizing quicker paths to what is considered a cure and a practice for those who are sick and diseased; these cures and practices could be in opposition to the beliefs and practices of the patients (Sedig, 2016). A significant concern in health care is data security and privacy, with 25% of R.N.s and 40% of administrative staff naming data security and confidentiality and concern (Walker, 2018). When information security breaches occur, healthcare organizations must be open and honest with those impacted and at risk. Twenty seventeen data research reports show widespread hacking in the healthcare industry with just "one in five registered nurses (RNs) and health administrators, stating they have undergone patient data breaches (2018). The U.S. Security and Exchange Commission (2018) outlines that companies should have controls and procedures in place to properly evaluate cyber incidents and disclose material information to investors. For example, within the first six months of 2018, the healthcare institutions suffered more than six million data breaches (Cylance, 2018). Often organizations do not openly disclose the extent and nature of data thefts and breaches, and often it is whistleblowing that leads to the public finding out the severity of the attack (Bhargava, Madala, & Burrell, 2018). These data breaches and failures to disclose their severity require the need for cultures around the ethical and organizational importance of whistleblowing when there are cybersecurity breaches (2018).

THE WHISTLE-BLOWER

A whistle-blower is one who provides information on a person or organization participating in an unlawful activity (Bazzetta, 2015). Miceli and Near (1992) defined whistleblowing as the disclosure by current or former members of an organization of immoral, unethical, illegitimate, or illegal activities related to an organization or its employees. Other researchers have described whistleblowing as an ethical issue of great significance in protecting all stakeholders against activities that may adversely impact economic, environmental, financial, and public safety, whether locally or globally (Courtemanche, 1988; Hoffman & McNulty, 2010; Weiss, 2006). According to Lee (2005) and Stewart (1996), an individual who reveals necessary acts of fraud, errors, corruption, abuse, waste, or misuse of power or authority in breach laws, policy, safety, or regulations is known as a whistle-blower.

Whistle-Blowing and Whistle-Blower Traits

Whistleblowing is among the conceivable possibilities an employee can choose to relay illicit information. Bazzetta (2015) noted whistleblowing is a revelation by organizations' members, past or present, of illegal, immoral, or prohibited practices under the influence of their employers, to individuals/organizations that could have the ability to influence action. A primary instrument for encouraging individual, organizational accountability, whistleblowing, is a complex process involving personal and organizational cultural factors (Wilde, 2013). Research into whistleblowing is essential because unethical behavior is a continuing problem in a variety of organizations (Bhargava, Madala, & Burrell, 2018). Serious consequences can result from whistleblowing, both for an organization and for the whistle-blower, who may suffer bullying, termination, marginalization, and isolation in retaliation (Wilde, 2013). Both the positive and negative aspects of whistleblowing deserve critical attention (Bhargava, Madala, & Burrell, 2018).

Research exists that explains several distinct whistle-blower traits (Hermann et al., 2013). These traits point to the motivations, agendas, and objectives that can drive individuals to speak up with confronted with an issue around ethics, honesty, equity, justice, and fairness. These traits include:

- **The Altruist:** The moral voice or voice of justice and fairness in the organization;
- **The Avenger:** This individual craves vengeance and reckoning in the organization;
- **Organization Man:** Whistle-blows to protect the organization's financial interests, economic interests, and reputation;
- **The Alarmist:** This individual is a constant protester and complainer with a limited tolerance for error and seeks to perpetuate dreadful penalties and consequences if inaction proceeds and issues remain unaddressed for an extended time;
- **The Bounty Hunter:** A result of whistleblowing, recognition, reward, or gain motivates this individual.

An additional viewpoint recognizes the complexities around ethics, openness, and honesty when choosing to whistle-blow or not when issues arise (Bhargava, Madala, & Burrell, 2018). Employees often face quandaries amid steadfastness to maintain moral values towards righteousness and justice (Waytz, Dugan, & Young, 2013). The conflict results in an emotional reasoning struggle for employees firmly committed to organizational citizens unable to stay quiet when wrong, even while observing questionable incidents, or when speaking out about wrongs, the perception and reputation of that organization may become tarnished (Bhargava, Madala, & Burrell, 2018).

Research (Vadera et al., 2009) frames the elements that influence honesty and speaking up in an organization that includes:

- Leadership and organizational governance
- Perceived backing and support
- Organizational justice
- Organizational climate and culture
- Organizational type and structure
- Risk of reprisal

With the growth of cybercrime and identity theft, it is now more critical for healthcare organizations understand the risks around information security and the importance of embracing ethical cultures and open cultures that value and embrace openness, transparency, and honesty. If things related to a patient's medical records and identity are lost and stolen, it seems ethical and right to notify stakeholders of risks immediately so that they can engage in some form of countermeasure and protective actions. Just as critical is to create cultures where everyone in the organization can play a supportive role in information security (Bhargava, Madala, & Burrell, 2018). The use of healthcare technology has picked up the pace in the past few decades (Thakkar & Davis, 2006). The increasing use of EHR (Electronic Health Records) by most of the healthcare systems in the country has allowed for patients to have their medical information anytime, anywhere, but has also made the PHI (Protected Health Information) susceptible to breaches (Thakkar & Davis, 2006). Because healthcare organizations have the responsibility of adequately securing personal information like credit card numbers, health information, and social security numbers, ethical decision making, and transparent cultures is critical at all levels and creates avenues for employees to come forward when there are concerns around ethics, errors, and wrongdoing (Thakkar & Davis, 2006).

The Figure 1 represents a flowchart model proposed by D. Burrell and N. Bhargava (2018), which represents the six levels of ethical, moral, and legal decision making when emotions are involved.

Information Security Management is a set of policies, standards, and procedures by which an organization protects its vital information assets, especially the ones that hold sensitive information, and close the gap in their security systems and processes through risk management (Gardiyawasam-Pussewalage & Oleshchuk, 2016). An information security policy is the foundation of any information security management system as it defines the roles, responsibilities, and decision-making activities that tie information security in the daily business processes and procedures (Edwards, 2013). An organizational security policy typically defines the domain to be protected, access control to assets, and the number of resources that need to be committed based on the identified criticality of the protected assets (Table 1).

However, security policies are often at crossroads with costs and user experience, hence making it difficult for security professionals to maintain them. Management support is critical to the successful implementation and execution of security policies; thus, the commitment of the executive tier of management is a requirement for fair resource allocation essential for policy implementation (Soomro, Shah, & Ahmed, 2016). In the past, considerable efforts on information security focused on technical modalities and solutions to deal with security threats and attacks; however, these efforts have now shifted more towards the human factor and the need for the alignment of I.T. to business objectives. As a result, the need to have systems encourage employees at all levels to support the information security apparatus has never been more critical.

The Ponemon Institute (2016) recorded that 50% of data breaches in Health care organizations were a result of malicious or criminal attacks, 23% to negligent employees, and 27% to system glitches, including I.T. and process failures. Each of these causes is different and requires different security actions to prevent a successful attack. Data breaches are impactful to the affected patients as well as the health care institution. Researchers' opinions on the fundamental cause of security breaches are diverse. They include that most data breaches are a result of insufficient security of critical or sensitive data, malicious employee theft, and intrusion attempts (Holtfreter & Harrington, 2015).

The research analyzed substantial breaches and found inadvertent disclosure of information causes numerous data breaches. One such study analyzed 2633 data breaches that cost U.S. organizations over 500 million lost individual records between 2005 and 2011 (McLeod & Dolezel, 2018). The conclusion from the resultant investigations is that human factors and the institution of security policies were significantly related to an increase in data breaches, thereby fueling the call for organizations to invest more in security and tight integration of processes and workflow with security (2018). Results from McLeod and Dolezel's (2018) study on factors associated with data breaches show that human actions, behavior, organizational culture, and personal motivation are leading causes of security breaches. Health

Figure 1. Flowchart

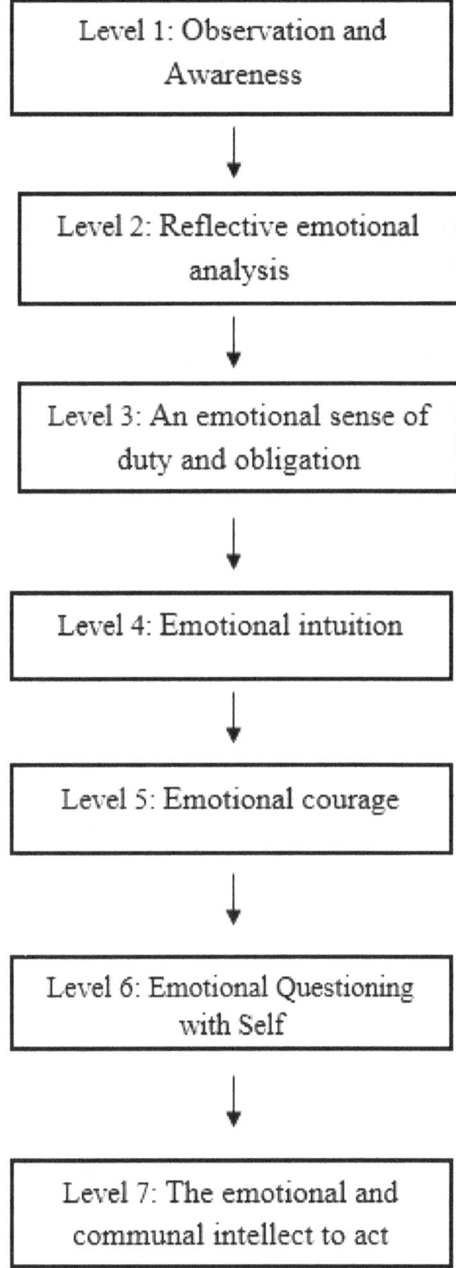

care workers are often given unmonitored access to confidential health information as a requirement of their jobs, ultimately posing information security governance concerns.

Management often finds it more comfortable to authorize the purchase of automated solutions instead of investing in the effort to change the corporate culture (McLeod & Dolezel, 2018). This attitude often results in an environment with detached, challenging solutions that produce inherent security holes (2018).

Table 1. D. Burrell and N. Bhargava's Emotional Acumen Model for Ethical, Moral, and Legal Decision Making (2018)

Model	D. Burrell and N. Bhargava's Emotional Acumen Model for Ethical, Moral, and Legal Decision Making (2018)
Level 1	Observation and Awareness – At this stage, there is a discovery, observation, and a witness of an ethical, moral, or legal issue of concern.
Level 2	Reflective emotional analysis – At this stage, there is a level of significant disquiet that leads to a profoundly reflective and critical emotional examination about the issue of concern and how serious it is or has the potential to be. At this stage, an individual must try his/her best to gather the facts and be as neutral as possible while describing or analyzing those facts. One should refrain from distorting the facts or information for personal benefits.
Level 3	An emotional sense of duty and obligation – At this stage, either an emotional inability to remain a bystander about the issue results in inaction, or there is personal emotional onus and responsibility to act.
Level 4	Emotional intuition – This stage is about intuitions or conscience. When cultivating emotions by compassion, then at times, the cognizant and coherent mind is overlooked. Our emotions are one mode to check or to see whether one is rationalizing.
Level 5	Emotional courage – At this stage, there is an in-depth exploration of the range of emotions that could include fear of retaliation and apprehension of the potential backlash. However, there are still compelling overriding reasons to take action and do something. Here, a prediction about the future is made, which is relevant to the situation(s) at hand. Though an individual can never predict the future, yet certain things are more likely than others.
Level 6	Emotional Questioning with Self – At this stage, an individual should always ask oneself before acting the following questions: a) Will I be able to live with myself if I made a particular choice? b) Will I feel better or worse about myself? c) Am I willing to let other people know about the situation or my decision to act? d) Will I feel guilty or ashamed of not taking any action sooner, or will I feel proud of my decision to act? e) Do I want everyone around me to act the way I did?
Level 7	The emotional and communal intellect to act – At this stage, there is an understanding of how to manage the emotional perceptions and emotional consequences that are required to act and navigate the social interactions, politics, and fallout.

What does an organization that supports the whistleblowing/open door process/policy around information security look like? Below is an information security framework that is critical to creating an organizational culture where all employees can assist in minimizing and addressing information security risks. This framework stems from the U.S. Department of Homeland Security that tells all stakeholders, "If you see something, say something" (Table 2).

CONCLUSION

Hospitals, medical labs, medical offices, and medical devices face significant cyber risks (Martin et al., 2017). A report by KPMG in 2015, 110 million patients in the U.S. had their data compromised (KPMG, 2015). Exposing highly sensitive healthcare information threatens the patient's privacy, information security, and poses a risk to critical life-saving decisions. Susceptibilities can intentionally cause harm to patients if inadequate information security processes with overlooked protocols (Martin et al., 2017). Organizations need to strengthen cybersecurity expertise, protocols, and infrastructure to minimize the risks (Martin et al., 2017). A dire need to understand further immeasurable threats require implementing a security strategy that enhance security, reduce medical errors, and improve patient care. To reduce threats, healthcare practitioners can improve ethical decision-making by adopting cultural norms and best practices to disclose the information breaches (Sedig, 2016). Whistleblowing is part of the complex decision-making process to encourage individuals to speak up when confronted with an issue around security breaches and disclosing the severity and impact to patients (Wilde, 2013).

Table 2. Burrell Whistle Blowing/Open Door Information Security Model Framework (2020)

Element 1	A clear definition of what constitutes a cybersecurity whistle-blower. An example could be: An information security "whistle-blower" is an individual who reports information he/she reasonably believes pieces of evidence: A violation of any law, rule, or regulation around information security. Gross mismanagement may include a substantial risk of significant adverse impact on a mission around the protection and security of personally identifiable information (PII). Abuse of authority: an arbitrary decision for personal gain and to injure others concerning information security. Compromised information security is a substantial and specific danger to public health or safety. A "reasonable belief" generally means that a disinterested observer with knowledge of the essential facts known to and readily ascertainable by the employee or applicant can reasonably conclude that the actions of the agency official evidenced such violation, mismanagement, waste, abuse, or danger. This standard excludes rumors, speculation, and nonspecific allegations.
Element 2	A transparent and formal process for information security whistle-blowers to disclose observable risks, errors, and possible wrongdoing including: • A managerial open door formal process that allows employees at all levels to discuss any cybersecurity or information security work-related issue or concern with any organizational supervisor or manager beyond informal discussions with his or her immediate supervisor. • An anonymous reporting hotline and an anonymous reporting process. • Strict prohibitions including employee protections against retaliation for protected disclosures remedies if there is evidence of retaliation against for making protected disclosures. If one disclosed wrongdoing, it would prohibit threats and adverse personnel actions against an employee. Adverse personnel actions include poor performance reviews, demotion, suspension, or other forms of retaliation for filing an appeal, complaint, or grievance.
Element 3	Employee engagement actions focused on creating an organizational culture that is respectful and encourages all employees to raise concerns and differing views promptly and without fear of reprisal. The free and open exchange of views or ideas, conducted in a non-threatening environment, provides a forum to consider concerns and addresses alternative views in an efficient and timely manner around information security management.
Element 4	Training and awareness programs for all employees.
Element 5	Staff ownership and employee resources that can manage the program and can fairly and adequately investigate submissions and complaints.

Healthcare organizations need to gain cybersecurity business acumen to understand how to embrace whistleblowing, ethical cultures, moral reasoning, and decision-making that lessen susceptibility to breaches (Waytz, Dugan, & Young, 2013). Information Security Management policies, standards, and procedures protect an organization's vital information assets and function to close system and process gaps (Gardiyawasam-Pussewalage & Oleshchuk, 2016I). The implementation of security policies limits malicious employee theft and intrusion attempts (Holtfreter & Harrington, 2015). Adopting an information security framework that creates a proactive and open-door policy about concerns, risks, and violations is critical to minimizing and addressing information security risks. This approach is not about creating a fearful tattle-tale culture. Adopting a culture that is open and transparent around whistleblowing is whistleblowing about creating a culture of vigilance where issues and mistakes are not deal with retribution but are deal with constructive and productive problem-solving approaches. Health organizations that are not aware of risks cannot create interventions that can effectively address risks. Organizations that can constructively develop a transparent and formal process for whistleblowing can be more responsive in addressing the risks around cybersecurity and data security. The key is around new policies and approaches that support a robust information security culture. Approaching data security risks requires training and awareness programs for all employees, to have staff ownership, and for organizational leadership to allocate employee resources that can better manage information security processes, policies, and programs (Bhargava, Madala, & Burrell, 2018).

REFERENCES

Bazzetta, D. J. (2015). Whistle-blowers and post-conventional moral development: Toward identifying ethical & moral leadership. Retrieved from https://proxy.cecybrary.com/login?url=https://search-proquest-com.proxy.cecybrary.com/docview/1673895415?accountid=144459

Bhargava, N., Madala, M. K., & Burrell, D. N. (2018). Emotional Acumen on the Propensity of Graduating Technology Students to Whistle-Blow About Organizational Cyber Security Breaches. *International Journal of Smart Education and Urban Society*, *9*(4), 1–14. doi:10.4018/IJSEUS.2018100101

Collier, R. (2014). U.S. health information breaches up 137%. *Canadian Medical Association Journal*, *186*(6), 412. doi:10.1503/cmaj.109-4731 PMID:24616131

Courtemanche, G. (1988, February). The ethics of whistleblowing. *Internal Auditor*, 36-41

Coventry L., Branley D. (2018). Cybersecurity in healthcare: A narrative review of trends, threats and ways forward. Maturitas: European Menopause Journal.

Cylance. (2018). *Leveraging to protect hospital Infrastructure*. Retrieved from https://pages.cylance.com/en-us-2018-12-HIMSS-Leveraging-AI-WP-PDFViewer.html?aliId=eyJpIjoiVHRRczFGRG5IT-k1XNkYzQiIsInQiOiJYXC9mSWV3alwvRnk4YnNaNm9vbVJHN2c9PSJ9

Edwards, C. K. (2013). A framework for the governance of information security [Doctoral dissertation].

Gardiyawasam-Pussewalage, H. S., & Oleshchuk, V. A. (2016). Privacy-preserving mechanisms for enforcing security and privacy requirements in E-health solutions. *International Journal of Information Management*, *36*(6), 1161–1173. doi:10.1016/j.ijinfomgt.2016.07.006

Heumann, M., Friedes, A., Cassak, L., Wright, W., & Joshi, E. (2013). The world of whistleblowing: From the altruist to the avenger. *Public Integrity*, *16*(1), 25–52.

Hoffman, W., & McNulty, R. E. (2010). A business ethics theory of whistleblowing: Responding to the $1 trillion question. In M. Arszulowicz & W. Gasparski (Eds.), *Defense of proper action: The whistle-blowing* (pp. 45–60). Piscataway, NJ: Transaction Publishers.

Holtfreter, R. E., & Harrington, A. (2015). Data breach trends in the United States. *Journal of Financial Crime*, *22*(2), 242–260. doi:10.1108/JFC-09-2013-0055

Internet of things: The industry connection (2017). London: Fitch Solutions Group Limited. Retrieved from https://proxy.cecybrary.com/login?url=https://search-proquest-com.proxy.cecybrary.com/docview/1913959024?accountid=144459

Iqbal, S., Altaf, W., Aslam, M., Mahmood, W., & Khan, M. U. G. (2016). Application of intelligent agents in healthcare [Review]. *Artificial Intelligence Review*, *46*(1), 83–112. doi:10.100710462-016-9457-y

KPMG. (2015). Health care and cybersecurity: increasing threats require increased capabilities. KPMG. Retrieved from https://assets.kpmg.com/content/dam/kpmg/pdf/2015/09/cyber-health-care-surveykp-mg-2015.pdf

Lee, E. (2005). Whistle-blowers: Heroes or villains? *Accountants Today*, 14-18.

Martin, G., Martin, P., Hankin, C., Darzi, A., & Kinross, J. (2017, July). Cybersecurity and healthcare: How safe are we*? British Medical Journal*. PMID:28684400

McCoy, T. H. Jr, & Perlis, R. H. (2018). Temporal Trends and Characteristics of Reportable Health Data Breaches, 2010-2017. *Journal of the American Medical Association*, *320*(12), 1282–1284. doi:10.1001/jama.2018.9222 PMID:30264106

McLeod, A., & Dolezel, D. (2018). Cyber-analytics: Modeling factors associated with Health care data breaches. *Decision Support Systems*, *108*, 57–68. doi:10.1016/j.dss.2018.02.007

Miceli, M., & Near, J. P. (1992). *Blowing the whistle*. New York, NY: Lexington Books.

Ponemon Institute. (2016). Fourth annual report: Is your company ready for a big data breach? Retrieved from http://www.experian.com/assets/data-breach/white-papers/2016-experian-data-breach-preparedness-study.pdf

Rosen, J. M. (2011). How long does it take to repair a computer? *Computer Sales and Service*. Retrieved from http://jonrosensystems.com/2011/03/faq-how-long-does-it-take-to-repair-a-computer/#.XNeQwHdFyUk

Sedig, L. (2016). What's the role of autonomy in patient- and family-centered care when patients and family members don't agree? *American Medical Association Journal of Ethics*. Retrieved from https://journalofethics.ama-assn.org/article/whats-role-autonomy-patient-and-family-centered-care-when-patients-and-family-members-dont-agree/2016-01

Soomro, Z. A., Shah, M. H., & Ahmed, J. (2016). Information security management needs a more holistic approach: A literature review. *International Journal of Information Management*, *36*(2), 215–225. doi:10.1016/j.ijinfomgt.2015.11.009

Stewart, D. (1996). *Organization ethics*. New York, NY: McGraw-Hill Companies, Inc.

Thakkar, M., & Davis, D. C. (2006). Risks, barriers, and benefits of EHR systems: A comparative study based on the size of hospital. *Perspectives in Health Information Management*, *3*(5), 34–44. PMID:18066363

U.S. Securities and Exchange Commission. (2018, February 21). SEC adopts statement and interpretive guidance on public company cybersecurity disclosures. Retrieved from https://www.sec.gov/news/press-release/2018-22

Vadera, A. K., Aguilera, R. V., & Caza, B. (2009). Making Sense of Whistle-Blowing's Antecedents: Learning from Research on Identity and Ethics Programs. *Business Ethics Quarterly*, *19*(4), 553–586. doi:10.5840/beq200919432

Walker, T. (2018). Healthcare data breaches: 4 tips for healthcare execs. *E-end*. Retrieved from https://www.eendusa.com/indusry-news/ healthcare-data-breaches-4-tips-for-healthcare-execs?_vsrefdom=adwords&gclid=CjwKCAjw5dnmBRACEiwAmMYGOdocwjl0Vw511P-b3e7xQXCdMWHahU-jqh_D933CvMCUKIKhziP7DBxoC228QAvD_BwE

Waytz, A., Dungan, J., & Young, L. (2013). The whistleblower's dilemma and the fairness–loyalty tradeoff. *Journal of Experimental Social Psychology*, *49*(6), 1027–1033.

Weiss, J. W. (2006). *Organization ethics* (4th ed.). Ontario, CA: Thompson/South West.

Wilde, J. H. (2013). Citizen watch in the accounting department? Tax and financial reporting responses to employee whistleblowing allegations. Retrieved from https://search-proquestcom.contentproxy.phoenix.edu/docview/1497226692?accountid=35812

This research was previously published in the International Journal of Hyperconnectivity and the Internet of Things (IJHIoT), 4(1); pages 13-28, copyright year 2020 by IGI Publishing (an imprint of IGI Global).

Chapter 36
Opinions on Cyber Security, Electronic Health Records, and Medical Confidentiality:
Emerging Issues on Internet of Medical Things From Nigeria

Ibrahim Taiwo Adeleke
Federal Medical Centre, Bida, Nigeria

Qudrotullaah Bolanle Suleiman Abdul
University of Ilorin Teaching Hospital, Nigeria

ABSTRACT

IoMT has helped to improve health safety and care of billions of people and at least, health-related parameters can now be monitored from home in real time. This chapter deployed a cross-sectional design to determine perceptions of Nigerian healthcare providers toward medical confidentiality and cyber security in the wake of electronic health records and IoMT. Participants' opinions on the workings of EHRs in Nigeria include: security of health records (79.4%); aiding effective healthcare data backup (88.2%); enhancement of medical confidentiality (89.2%); speeding up documentation process (93.1%); and that EHRs will generally bring about positive changes in the country healthcare system. Nearly a third (31.4%) of participants have heard about audit trail, which they admitted (43.1%) have the capabilities to facilitate effective medical confidentiality. Healthcare providers in Nigeria have some concerns over security of patient health information on the Cloud, but are hopeful of the workability of IoMT for its promises to improve healthcare quality.

INTRODUCTION

Internet of things (IoT) is a combination of various technologies that empower a diverse range of ap-

DOI: 10.4018/978-1-6684-6311-6.ch036

pliances, devices and objects to interact and communicate with each other using different networking technologies (Kodali, Swamy & Lakshmi, 2015). In the healthcare context, internet of things (IoT) or internet of medical things (IoMT) extends the Web through the deployment of ubiquitous devices with capabilities for embedded identification, sensing, and data exchange features (Miorandi et al., 2012). In IoT-based healthcare, diverse distributed devices aggregate, analyze and communicate real time medical information to the cloud, thus making it possible to collect, store and analyze the large amount of data in several new forms and activate context based alarms (Kodali, Swamy & Lakshmi, 2015). IoMT plays a key role in the growth of medical information systems. IoT has potentials to collect and integrate possibly more precise, relevant, and high-quality data in real time to monitor processes and outcomes (Gupta, Maharaj & Malekian, 2016). With IoMT, patient's health records and related data can be accessed from anywhere in the world using any Internet-enabled device like PC, tablet or smart phone (Kodali, Swamy & Lakshmi, 2015). A healthcare provider can automatically collect information about the patient, applies decision support rules and as such, speed up treatment process (Chacko & Hayajneh, 2018).

The need to cut cost, improve medical care and adopt electronic health record (EHR) is driving hospitals to implement IT solutions that streamlines procedures such as billing, medical imaging and electronic medical record (EMR) processing. EHR is being defined (NAHIT, 2011) as an electronic record of health-related information on an individual that conforms to nationally recognized interoperability standards and that can be created, managed, and consulted by authorized clinicians and staff across more than one healthcare organization. In other words, EHR is a repository of patient data in digital form, stored and exchanged securely, and accessible by multiple authorized users. It contains retrospective, concurrent, and prospective information and its primary purpose is to support continuing, efficient and quality integrated health (Hayrinen, Saranto & Nykanen, 2008). Electronic health record has evolved to play a major role in healthcare in modern society.

IoMT allows billions of smart devices to communicate and share data, and millions of new devices are connected to the Internet every day (Gartner, 2015). It enables healthcare providers to automatically collect information and apply decision support rules to allow for earlier intervention in the treatment process (Chacko & Hayajneh, 2018). Securing healthcare data requires enforceable security policies and implementing solutions that focus on vulnerabilities, configuration assessments, malware defenses, as well as activity and event monitoring (Chacko & Hayajneh, 2018). There are three main components of information security, which are captured in the CIA Triad of TechTarget (TechTarget, 2015); confidentiality, which limits access to the information in IoT devices; integrity, which ensures that information in IoT devices is trustworthy and accurate and lastly, availability, which guarantees reliable access to the information in IoT devices by authorized people. Traditionally, healthcare organizations have proven to be eminently capable of ensuring the integrity and availability of information within their connected devices.

Yet as cyber security threats intensify, ensuring confidentiality has become increasingly difficult. Storing sensitive information such as EHRs in the Cloud means that precautions must be taken to ensure the safety and confidentiality of the data. Medical confidentiality on the other hand, is the limiting of health information to only those for whom they are appropriate (Adeleke et al., 2011). With the emergence of IoT and Cloud computing, EHR management systems are facing an important platform shift, but such important changes must be approached carefully (Rodrigues, 2013). The adoption of EHRs with information exchange among patients, providers and payers, increased regulation and provider consolidation indicate the need for better information security (Appari, 2010). Although EHRs provide considerable benefits to patients and healthcare providers, there have been concerns (Adeleke et al., 2015; Hoffman, 2007; Taitsman, Grimm & Agrawal, 2013) over confidentiality, integrity, and availability of the data.

Similarly, the rate at which encrypted messages are being sent over the internet makes them susceptible to the dangers of hacking and other cyber threats (Alhassan et al., 2016). Evidence (Hoffman, 2007) has shown that confidentiality of patient's health records is being threatened and that such violations tend to increase in the wake of computerization, IoMT and centralization of health records. These necessitate the need for an efficient, secure, accurate, reliable way of securing user information such as data encryption as recommended in a recent study (Waziri et al., 2016).

In Nigeria, healthcare providers have shown a lack of adequate understanding of their respective responsibilities toward medical confidentiality (Adeleke, 2011; Adeleke et al., 2015b; Aliyu et al., 2015) and were reported to lack the right computing knowledge and skills (Bello et al., 2004; Adeleke et al., 2014; Adeleke et al., 2014b; Adeleke et al., 2015c; Adeleke et al., 2015d; Abodunrin & Akande, 2009). As such, it can be said that they may be short of major prerequisites to the successful adoption and implementations of EHRs and IoMT in the country. Likewise, providers of healthcare services in Nigeria though have the right skills for appropriate documentation (Adeleke et al., 2012), they lack the will to ensure quality healthcare documentation (Adeleke et al., 2012; Abdulkadir et al., 2011). In terms of policy making, the World Health Report in year 2000 ranked Nigeria 187 out of 191 countries in healthcare infrastructure and health services provision (Idowu, Adagunodo, & Adedoyin, 2016) and Nigerian healthcare policy makers as well, lack a clear understanding of the usefulness of hospital information systems (Idowu, Adagunodo, & Adedoyin, 2016).

The aim of this chapter is to present knowledge, attitude and opinion of Nigerian healthcare providers toward medical confidentiality and cyber security in the wake of electronic health records and Internet of medical things.

This chapter is structured as follow. In the first section, the authors introduce our work. The second section describes the background in Internet of medical things., electronic health records, cyber security and medical confidentiality. In the third section, the authors describe the methods and materials deployed in the course of the study. This includes the setting, design, population, sampling techniques, sample size and ethics. In the fourth section, findings from the study are narrated. The fifth section discusses the study's findings in relation to previous studies and prevailing realities. Finally, the authors offer our conclusion and look to the future as it relates to the work.

BACKGROUND

Since its emergence, internet of medical things has helped to improve health safety, and care of billions of people (Sun et al., 2018). Nowadays, health-related parameters can be monitored from home in real time and outcome transferred to cloud storage after processing (Sun et al., 2018). The most promising benefits of IoMT might be in increasing workforce productivity, cost savings, operation efficiencies, improved patient experience and care, and reduction in human error (Riggings & Wamba, 2015; Alsmirat et al., 2016 and Joyia et al., 2017). Studies in the last decade have tuned their focus on security, data privacy, and concerns on trust associated with IoMT (Gubbi et al., 2013, Atzori, Iera, & Morabito, 2010 and Perera, 2014). A more recent study reveals that 78% of the IoMT users were apprehensive of the technology owing to personal data hacking distress (Irdeto, 2017).

Solangi et al., (2018) alerted "Although currently data security and privacy may be insignificant, they could be amplified fully in future so policymakers should proactively address the issues and carefully weigh the cost associated with IoT against the enormous projected benefits. IoT privacy and security issues are much in excess of a thought of individualistic or individual damages. It is a fundamental component of a strong and independent society. Protecting it as innovation advances is both an individual and social concern". In spite of these, Chen et al., opined "future healthcare systems specifically ehealth, would be embedded with IoMT to provide advanced medical services with more secure and efficient authentication for users". Likewise, Kulkar & Sathe (2014) reasoned "The Internet of things will change our society, and will bring seamless 'anytime, anywhere' personalized healthcare and monitoring over fast reliable and secure networks. This implies that we are approaching the end of the divide present between digital, virtual and physical worlds".

MATERIALS AND METHODS

This study was carried out at the venue of the 19th Annual National Conference/Annual General Meeting of the Islamic Medical Association of Nigeria (IMAN) held between 2nd and 8th July 2018 in Birni Kebbi, Nigeria. The study design was cross-sectional survey of major key contributors and users of patients' health records, which include medical practitioners, health records professionals, nurses, medical laboratory scientists and pharmacists. The study participants were recruited from among the healthcare providers in attendance at the venue of the above mentioned conference with an average annual attendance of 500. A total sample size of 217 using the online sample size calculator, Survey System sample size calculator, was recruited. A 25-item questionnaire that elicit data on participants' socio-demographic characteristics, computer and internet use, knowledge on medical confidentiality, awareness on cyber threats, workability of electronic health records in the wake of IoMT was deployed. The statistical software SPSS version 16 was used to compute the data. Analysis carried out on the data include descriptive and the use of chi square to elicit relationships. Tables and charts were also deployed for illustrations. The ethics approval to conduct this study was obtained from the Health Research Ethics Committee of Federal Medical Centre, Bida. Informed consent was explicitly worded on the first page of the instrument. This was done in order to solicit participants' permission before the administration of questionnaire.

PERCEPTIONS OF NIGERIAN HEALTHCARE PROVIDERS ON THE SUBJECT

One hundred and two (45.3%) of the 225 questionnaires distributed were returned and analyzed. Most participants were males (81.4%), nearly a third (32.4%) were nurses and more than one-third were below ten years in professional practice. Two-third of participants possess personal laptop and more than half (54.9%) surf the internet daily. The majority of participants (91.2%) enjoy working with computer while a two-third of them preferred working with computer to manual. Overwhelmingly, the majority of participants acknowledged inherent benefits of information and communication technologies especially in healthcare delivery system.

Participants' opinions on the workings of EHRs in Nigeria include security of health records (79.4%); aiding effective healthcare data backup (88.2%); enhancement of medical confidentiality (89.2%); speeding up documentation process (93.1%) and that EHRs will generally bring about positive changes in the country healthcare system. Nonetheless, a notable portion of participants (59.8%) opined that technology freely opens health information to cyber threats, that patient health records can be hacked like Facebook account (50.0%), all which may negatively affect (20.6%) medical confidentiality.

Many (60.8%) participants have heard about cyber security mostly (41.2%) through social media and nearly a third (31.4%) has heard about audit trail, which they admitted (43.1%) have the capabilities to facilitate effective medical confidentiality. Overall, participants envisioned holistic paperless (54.9), feasibility (95.1%) and workability (62.7%) of full EHRs implementation in the country.

PERCEPTIONS OF NIGERIAN HEALTHCARE PROVIDERS ON THE SUBJECT IN THE LIGHT OF PREVIOUS STUDIES

Although the Nigerian healthcare system has not fully embraced ICT owing to some reported human and political challenges (Adeleke et al., 2014), most participants in this current study appreciate the gains of ICT and they prefer working with ICT than the proliferated paper-based system. Most of these participants have heard about cyber security in their course of accessing the social media platforms and nearly a third have heard about audit trial, for its capability to ensure confidentiality in an electronic environment. However, a recent study from Nigeria reveals that most of those who are supposed to promote the tenets of medical confidentiality in the country are mixed with unqualified personnel mostly at private medical offices in the country (Adeleke et al., 2018). Traditionally, it is upon the healthcare practitioners to promote the tenets of medical confidentiality. As the country's healthcare system is said to be flooded with unqualified practitioners, this may pose danger to medical confidentiality.

Although more than half of participants opined that emerging technologies open health information freely to cyber threats, the study shows healthcare providers who believe in the workings of electronic health records especially for its enhancement of medical confidentiality, assurances of data security and potentialities of stimulating positive changes in the country's healthcare delivery systems. The apprehensions held by participants in this study as regard concerns over security in the use of IoMT is in tandem with that of Solangi et al., (2018), who opined that security threats with IoMT could be amplified in future. Nevertheless, opinions on positive workability of IoMT agree with reports from Kulkar & Sathe (2014) and Solangi et al., (2018) futuristic opinion. Findings from this study show a group of healthcare providers with an improved attitude toward patient's health records and clinical documentation. It could be recalled that earlier studies found them to lack adequate understanding of their respective responsibilities toward medical confidentiality (Adeleke, 2011; Adeleke et al., 2015b; Aliyu et al., 2015); lack the right computing knowledge and skills (Bello et al., 2004; Adeleke et al., 2014; Adeleke et al., 2014b; Adeleke et al., 2015c; Adeleke et al., 2015d; Abodunrin & Akande, 2009); though have the right skills for appropriate documentation (Adeleke et al, 2012), but, lack the will to ensure quality healthcare documentation (Adeleke et al., 2012; Abdulkadir et al., 2011).

SOLUTION AND RECOMMENDATIONS

Healthcare providers require continuing professional education especially on Internet of things. Authorities and stakeholders in the Nigerian healthcare system should rise up to adopt and implement electronic health records to move the system forward for improved healthcare quality.

FUTURE RESEARCH DIRECTIONS

Studies in future should focus advancement of IoMT such that current concerns are addressed.

CONCLUSION

Healthcare providers in Nigeria though hold some concerns over security of patient's health information on the cloud, are hopeful of the workability of IoMT, for its promises to improve healthcare quality.

ACKNOWLEDGMENT

The thank Mr. A. A. Adebisi for his assistance during data collection; Mr. Usman Isah for his assistance during electricity power fluctuation; Drs. Yaqub Ibn Muhammad and Tajudeen Abiola both officials of IMAN, for the enabling environment during data collection.

The authors specially appreciate the 102 participants in this study.

REFERENCES

Abodunrin, A. L., & Akande, T. M. (2009). Knowledge and perception of e-health and telemedicine among health professionals in LAUTECH Teaching Hospital, Osogbo, Nigeria. *Int J Health Res.*, *2*(1), 51–58.

Adeleke, I. T., Adekanye, A. O., Jibril, A. D., Danmallam, F. F., Inyinbor, H. E., & Omokanye, S. A. (2014). Research knowledge and behaviour of health workers at Federal Medical Centre, Bida: A task before learned mentors. *El Med J.*, *2*(2), 105–109. doi:10.18035/emj.v2i2.71

Adeleke, I. T., Adekanye, A. O., Onawola, K. A., Okuku, A. G., Adefemi, S. A., Erinle, S. A., & ... & AbdulGhaney, O. O. (2012). Data quality assessment in healthcare: A 365-day chart review of inpatients' health records at a Nigerian tertiary hospital. *Journal of the American Medical Informatics Association*, *19*, 1039–1042. doi:10.1136/amiajnl-2012-000823

Adeleke, I. T., Asiru, M. A., Oweghoro, B. M., Jimoh, A. B., & Ndana, A. M. (2015). Computer and internet use among tertiary healthcare providers and trainees in a Nigerian public hospital. *American Journal of Health Research*, *3*(1), 1–10. doi:10.11648/j.ajhr.s.2015030101.11

Adeleke, I. T., Erinle, S. A., Ndana, A. M., Anaman, T. C., Ogundele, O. A., & Aliyu, D. (2015). Health information technology in Nigeria: Stakeholders' perspectives of nationwide implementations and meaningful use of the emerging technology in the most populous black nation. *American Journal of Health Research*, *3*(1), 17–24. doi:10.11648/j.ajhr.s.2015030101.13

Adeleke, I. T., Ezike, S. O., Ogundele, O. A., & Ibraheem, S. O. (2015). Freedom of information act and concerns over medical confidentiality among healthcare providers in Nigeria. *IMAN Medical Journal*, *1*(1), 21–28.

Adeleke, I. T., Lawal, A. H., Adio, R. A., & Adebisi, A. A. (2014). Information technology skills and training needs of health information management professionals in Nigeria: A nationwide study. *The HIM Journal*, *44*(1), 1–9. doi:10.12826/18333575 PMID:27092467

Adeleke, I. T., Salami, A. A., Achinbee, M., Anama, T. C., Zakari, I. B., & Wasagi, M. H. (2015). ICT knowledge, utilization and perception among healthcare providers at National Hospital Abuja, Nigeria. *American Journal of Health Research.*, *3*(1), 1–10. doi:10.11648/j.ajhr.s.2015030101.17

Adeleke, I. T., Suleiman-Abdul, Q. B., Aliyu, A., Ishaq, I. A., & Adio, R. A. (2018, Sept. 20). Deploying unqualified personnel in health records practice – role substitution or quackery? Implications for health services delivery in Nigeria. [Epub ahead of print]. *Health Information Management*. doi:10.1177/1833358318800459 PMID:30235948

Aliyu, D., Adeleke, I. T., Omoniyi, S. O., Samaila, B. A., Adamu, A., & Abubakar, A. Y. (2015). Knowledge, attitude and practice of nursing ethics and law among nurses at Federal Medical Centre, Bida. *American Journal of Health Research*, *3*(1), 32–37. doi:10.11648/j.ajhr.s.2015030101.15

Alsmirat, M. A., Jararweh, Y., Obaidat, I., & Gupta, B. B. (2016). Internet of surveillance: A cloud supported large-scale wireless surveillance system. J Supercomput. 1;73(3):973-992. doi:10.1007/s11227-016-1857-x

Appari, A., & Johnson, M. E. (2010). Information security and privacy in healthcare: Current state of research. *Int. J. Internet and Enterprise Management*, *6*(4), 279–314. doi:10.1504/IJIEM.2010.035624

Atzori, L., Iera, A., & Morabito, G. (2010). The internet of things: A survey. *Computer Networks*, *54*(15), 2787–2805. doi:10.1016/j.comnet.2010.05.010

Bello, I. S., Arogundade, F. A., Sanusi, A. A., Ezeoma, I. T., Abioye-Kuteyi, E. A., & Akinsola, A. (2004). Knowledge and utilization of information technology among health care professionals and students in Ile-Ife, Nigeria: A Case Study of a University Teaching Hospital. *Journal of Medical Internet Research*, *6*(4), e45. doi:10.2196/jmir.6.4.e45 PMID:15631969

Chacko, A., & Hayajneh, T. (2018). Security and privacy issues with IoT in healthcare. *EAI Endorsed Transactions on Pervasive Health and Technology.*, *4*(14), e2.

Chen, M., Gonzalez, S., Vasilakos, A., Cao, H., & Leung, V. C. M. (2011). Body area networks: A survey. *Mobile Networks and Applications*, *16*(2), 171–193. doi:10.100711036-010-0260-8

Gartner Says 6.4 Billion Connected "Things" Will Be in Use in 2016, Up 30 Percent From 2015. Available at www.gartner.com/newsroom/id/3165317

Gubbi, J., Buyya, R., Marusic, S., & Palaniswami, M. (2013). Internet of things (IoT): A vision, architectural elements, and future directions. *Future Generation Computer Systems*, *29*(7), 1645–1660. doi:10.1016/j.future.2013.01.010

Hayrinen, K., Saranto, K., & Nykanen, P. (2008). Definition, structure, content, use and impacts of electronic health records: A review of the research literature. *International Journal of Medical Informatics*, *77*(5), 291–304. doi:10.1016/j.ijmedinf.2007.09.001 PMID:17951106

Hoffman, S. (2007). In Sickness, Health, and Cyberspace: Protecting the security of electronic private health information. *Boston College Law Review. Boston College. Law School*, *48*(2), 331–386.

Idowu, B., Adagunodo, R., & Adedoyin, R. (2006). Information technology infusion model for health sector in developing country: Nigeria as a case. *Technology and Health Care*, *14*(2), 69–77. PMID:16720950

Irdeto organization. (2017). Irdeto Global Consumer Piracy Survey.

Joyia, G. J., Liaqat, R. M., Farooq, A., & Rehman, S. (2017). Internet of medical things (IoMT): Applications, benefits and future challenges in healthcare domain. *Journal of Communication*. doi:10.12720/jcm.12.4.240-247

Adeleke, I. T., Adekanye, A. O., Adefemi, S. A., Onawola, K. A., Okuku, A. G., Sheshi, E. U., ... & Tume, A. A. (2011). Knowledge, attitude and practice of confidentiality of patients' health records among healthcare professionals at Federal Medical Centre, Bida. *Nigerian Journal of Medicine*, *20*(2), 228–235. PMID:21970234

Kodali, R. K., Swamy, G., & Lakshmi, B. (2015). An implementation of IoT for healthcare. *IEEE Conference Paper*. 10.1109/RAICS.2015.7488451

Kulkar, A., & Sathe, S. (2014). Healthcare applications of the Internet of things: A review. *International Journal of Computer Science and Information Technologies*, *5*(5), 6229–6232.

Abdulkadir, A., Yunusa, G., Tabari, A., Anas, I., Ojo, J., Akinlade, B., ... & Uyobong, I. (2011). Medical record system in Nigeria: Observations from multicentre auditing of radiographic requests and patients' information documentation practices. *J. Med. Med. Sci.*, *2*(5), 854–858.

Miorandi, D., Sicari, S., De Pellegrini, F., & Chlamtac, I. (2012, September). Internet of things: Vision, applications and research challenges. *Ad Hoc Networks*, *10*(7), 1497–1516. doi:10.1016/j.adhoc.2012.02.016

National Alliance for Health Information Technology. NAHIT releases HIT definitions. Electronic health records. Available at https://www.healthcare-informatics.com/news-item/nahit-releases-hit-definitions

Perera, C., Zaslavsky, A., Christen, P., & Georgakopoulos, D. (2014). Context aware computing for the internet of things: A survey. *IEEE Communications Surveys and Tutorials*, *16*(1), 414–454. doi:10.1109/SURV.2013.042313.00197

Riggins, F. J. & Wamba, S. F. (2015, January). Research Directions on the Adoption, Usage, and Impact of the Internet of things through the Use of Big Data Analytics. (2015). Presented at *2015 48th Hawaii International Conference on System Sciences,* Kauai, HI, p. 40. doi:10.1109/HICSS.2015.186

Rodrigues, J. P. C., de la Torre, I., Fernández, G., & López-Coronado, M. (2013). Analysis of the Security and Privacy Requirements of Cloud-Based Electronic Health Records Systems. *Journal of Medical Internet Research*, *15*(8), e186. doi:10.2196/jmir.2494 PMID:23965254

Solangi, Z. A., Solangi, Y. A., Chandio, S., Abd-Aziz, M. S., Hamzah, M. S., & Shah, A. (2018, May). The future of data privacy and security concerns in Internet of things. *2018 IEEE International Conference on Innovative Research and Development (ICIRD)*. 10.1109/ICIRD.2018.8376320

Sun, W., Cai, Z., Li, Y., Liu, F., Fang, S., & Wang, G. (2018). Security and privacy in the Medical Internet of things: A review. *Hindawi Security and Communication Networks*, 1–9. doi:10.1155/2018/5978636

Taitsman, J. K., Grimm, C. M., & Agrawal, S. (2013). Protecting patient privacy and data security. *The New England Journal of Medicine*, *368*(11), 977–979. doi:10.1056/NEJMp1215258 PMID:23444980

TechTarget. Confidentiality, integrity, and availability (CIA triad). Available at https://whatis.techtarget.com/definition/Confidentiality-integrity-and-availability-CIA

Waziri, V. O., Alhassan, J. K., Ismaila, I., & Egigogo, R. A. (2016). Securing file on cloud computing system using encryption software: a comparative analysis. *International Conference on Information and Communication Technology and Its Applications (ICTA 2016)*. 97-104.

This research was previously published in Incorporating the Internet of Things in Healthcare Applications and Wearable Devices; pages 199-211, copyright year 2020 by Medical Information Science Reference (an imprint of IGI Global).

APPENDIX

Table 1. Percentage of those who prefer computer to manual documentation

Prefer computer to manual					
		Frequency	**Percent**	**Valid Percent**	**Cumulative Percent**
Valid	Yes	69	67.6	67.6	67.6
	No	21	20.6	20.6	88.2
	I don't know	5	4.9	4.9	93.1
	NR	7	6.9	6.9	100.0
	Total	102	100.0	100.0	

Table 2. Feasibility of EHRs in Nigeria

EHR implementation in Nigeria is feasible					
		Frequency	Percent	Valid Percent	Cumulative Percent
Valid	Yes	97	95.1	95.1	95.1
	No	3	2.9	2.9	98.0
	NR	2	2.0	2.0	100.0
	Total	102	100.0	100.0	

Table 3. Hospitals with full implementation of EHRs in Nigeria

Hospitals with full EHRs operation in Nigeria					
		Frequency	**Percent**	**Valid Percent**	**Cumulative Percent**
Valid	Yes	23	22.5	22.5	22.5
	No	44	43.1	43.1	65.7
	I don't know	31	30.4	30.4	96.1
	NR	4	3.9	3.9	100.0
	Total	102	100.0	100.0	

Table 4. Functionality of EHRs to enhance medical confidentiality

EHR will enhance confidentiality					
		Frequency	**Percent**	**Valid Percent**	**Cumulative Percent**
Valid	Yes	91	89.2	89.2	89.2
	No	5	4.9	4.9	94.1
	I don't know	4	3.9	3.9	98.0
	NR	2	2.0	2.0	100.0
	Total	102	100.0	100.0	

Figure 1. Electronic health records will bring about positive changes to Nigerian healthcare systems

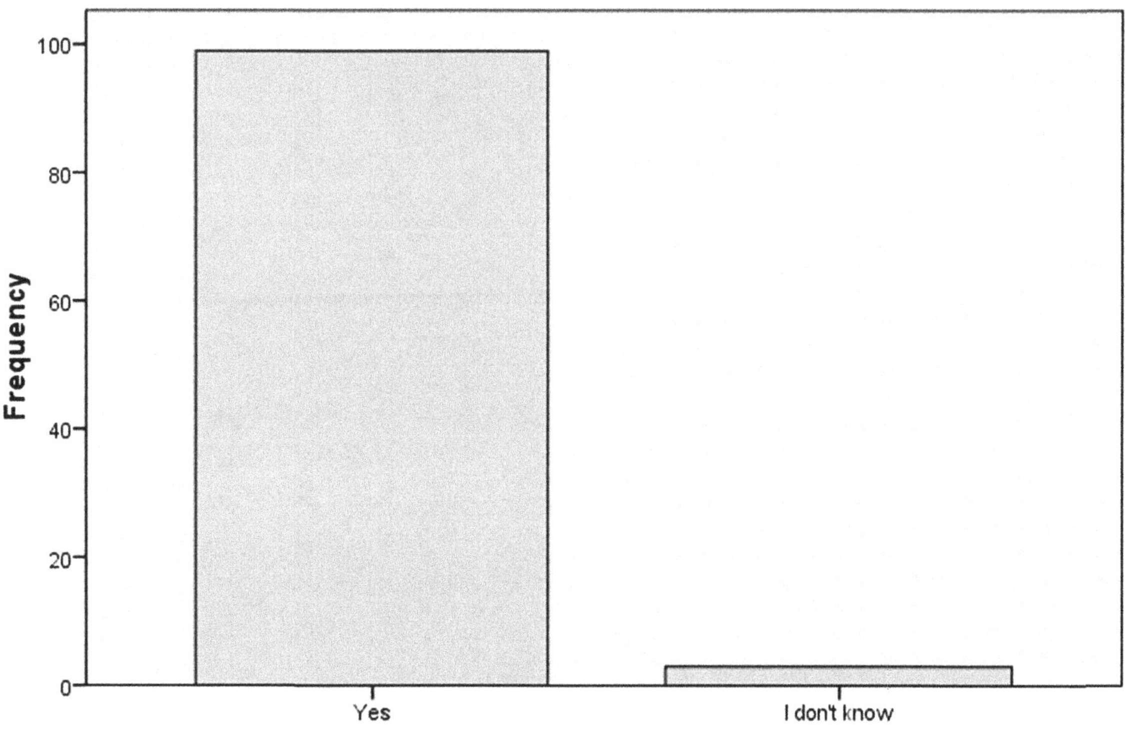

Figure 2. Electronic health records secure patients' health records

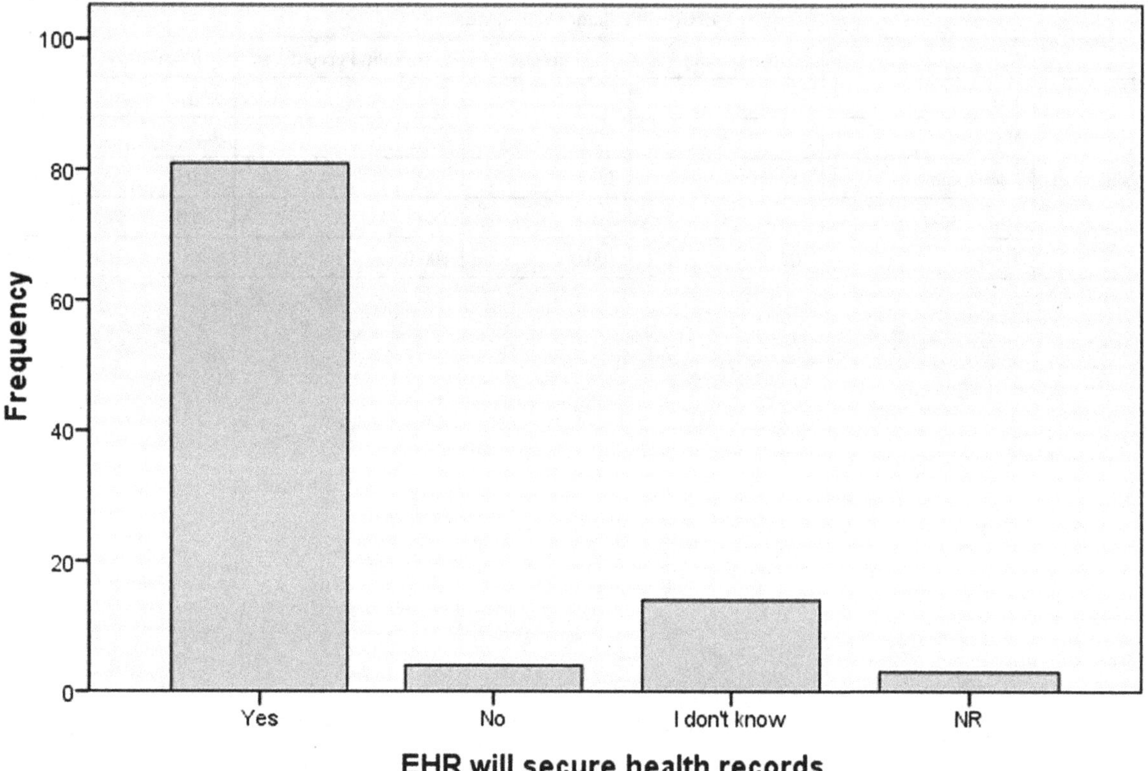

Figure 3. Sources of awareness on cyber security among participants

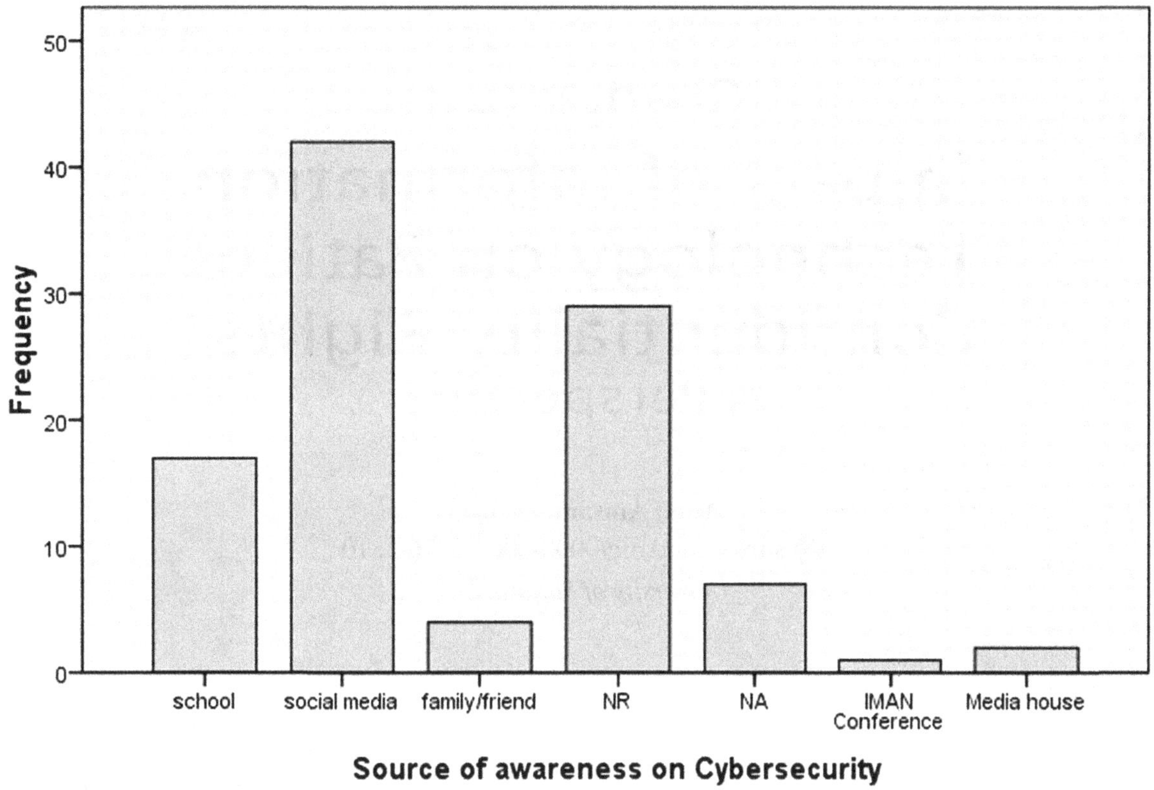

Chapter 37
Impact of Information Technology on Patient Confidentiality Rights:
A Perspective

Abba Amsami Elgujja
https://orcid.org/0000-0003-0476-8810
University of Salford, UK

ABSTRACT

Advances in information technology, be it by way of social media or use of the electronic medical information systems, has changed the way we deal with patient confidential information. The hitherto clear professional relationship with the patient has been blurred using social media, just like the unprecedented rate at which electronic health information is used to access and share patient's confidential information among healthcare professionals. However, given the special professional relationship of confidence which traditionally bonds the healthcare practitioner with the patient, use of these technologies by the healthcare professionals portends the risk of breach of that duty of confidentiality. Although the patient's right to demand confidentiality of his information is not absolute, an unlawful breach could result in a crime, actionable tort, or become a subject of disciplinary action. This chapter undertakes a general review of the benefits and dangers of embracing these new information technologies and their impact on the confidentiality of sensitive health data.

INTRODUCTION

Advances in information technology have led to diverse impact on patient experience in healthcare (Rauv, 2017). Information technology, be it by way of social media, use of the electronic medical information systems or web-based other smart applications/tools is, therefore, a welcome idea. Its use heralds numerous far-reaching benefits for health communication between and among the public, patients, and health professionals. However, it also has changed the way we deal with confidential patient informa-

DOI: 10.4018/978-1-6684-6311-6.ch037

tion. The impact of technology on non-financial outcomes such as patient satisfaction and quality is gaining interest (Wallwiener, Wallwiener, Kansy, Seeger, & Rajab, 2009). Information is the lifeblood of modern medicine, while the health information technology (HIT) infrastructure could be considered as its circulatory system. Without that system, neither individual physicians nor health care institutions can perform at their best or deliver the highest-quality care (Wallwiener et al., 2009).

Health information technology (IT) has the potential to improve the health of individuals and the performance of providers, yielding improved quality, cost savings, and greater engagement by patients in their own health care (Buntin, Burke, Hoaglin, & Blumenthal, 2011). As the transition of healthcare from paper to an increasingly electronic world ensues, a new debate over privacy of individually identifiable health information has emerged. The concept of privacy and confidentiality ensures a win-win situation for both the patient and the healthcare professional. Healthcare professionals need the confident patient to divulge all pertinent information necessary for diagnosing and treating the patient, while the patients need to feel confident that they can receive needed health care without the risk that their private information will be inappropriately disclosed. Any such concerns might result in withholding of information and lead to potentially negative clinical consequences (Kuhn, 2011).

Major sources of disagreement over privacy issues can sometimes be traced back to the use of different definitions for key terms. Therefore, it would be proper to define the terms with a view avoiding confusion during the discussion in the subsequent sections. Many at times, we feel tempted to use the terms "privacy" and "confidentiality" interchangeably as if they bear one and the same meaning or connotation. The terms privacy and confidentiality are sometimes distinguished on the basis that privacy refers to physical matters, while confidentiality refers to informational material (Goodman, Miller, & Informatics, 2006). In other words, the right to privacy is the limitation placed on the right of others to have access to information about, or the physical space, of an individual (James, 1975). It should be noted that the privacy limitation placed on information is regarding unlawful access rather than its unlawful sharing with (or disclosure to) third parties, which comes within the ambit of confidentiality.

Conversely, confidentiality is simply, the duty to maintain patient's private information revealed during a professional relationship (Folkman, 2000). The information sought to be protected must be unique to that particular patient (as opposed to information that could be attributable to any person qua person) (Everstine et al., 1980). The lawful access to patient's private data or other similar information of this kind, therefore, creates an obligation in, or a commitment by the healthcare professionals to keep that data in confidence (Parent, 1983).

Privacy is the right of patients for their personal information not to be accessed and divulged (disclosed) to others, while confidentiality is the obligation of all holders of Individually Identifiable Health Information (IIHI) to protect the information according to the privacy interests of the patients to whom the information relates (US Department of Health and Human Services, 2001). A patient expects (trusts) that data that have been shared with a provider will not be further shared inappropriately. On the other hand, individually identifiable health information is any health data or record that could be correlated with a particular individual (Kuhn, 2011).

Patient privacy must be a major consideration in the development of information systems. Systems have to be designed not only to meet current legal requirements, but to anticipate future requirements. The system has to put into consideration, the multiple conflicting interests, to wit, the patient's interest to ensure that no one has unnecessary access to his data, the hospital administrator's interest to ensure an unimpeded access to data needed for management, and the physicians' interest to avoid time-consuming limitation on medical practice. (Brannigan, 1992). In addition to the electronic health information systems, other information technologies that have impact on healthcare and the patient, is the advent of Internet communication, and especially the social media. These technologies have the potential of "inadvertently blurring the interface between work and personal time (Thompson et al., 2008) as well as their professional relationship (Nelson & Staggers, 2014). Patients, too, mostly unknowingly, do leave behind a trail of personal information during their online explorations for answers to their health issues. (Denecke et al., 2015a).

Many hospitals have introduced electronic health information systems (also called, E-health) to replace the traditional paper-based medical records (Bah et al., 2011) and implement electronic systems (Alsulame, Khalifa, & Househ, 2016 p. 204). The advantage of enhanced convenience of accessibility and distribution of health information attributable to electronic health information system also creates the dangers related to privacy and confidentiality of patients' data (Barrows, Jr. & Clayton, 1996). Because they contain large amounts of highly detailed clinical information about patients in an extremely compact form that can be easily stored and rapidly transmitted between healthcare professionals and institutions.(Sade, 2010) In Saudi Arabia, the use of electronic health record system is a new experience for many of the health care professionals that could create a new ethical-legal dilemma about their duty of confidentiality.

This risk is further compounded by the ubiquitous nature of those technologies all over the world. The world continues to embrace them even the more on every evolving day. For instance, in Saudi Arabia, as part of its popularly coined Vision 2030, the Kingdom has an ambitious technological growth plan in the healthcare sector to ensure a smooth integration of medical records among their health care institutions. The plan includes the integration of electronic health information records of the primary healthcare clinics with that of the specialist tertiary health institutions to enable healthcare professionals to, securely and seamlessly, share patient data as they deal with millions patients annually (Chikhaoui, Sarabdeen, & Parveen, 2017, p. 7). In view of the increasing and rapid demand for healthcare services, and a blossoming ICT community, this ambitious government's plan could help it achieve its vision of becoming a regional and global leader in IT healthcare systems development and adoption (Chikhaoui et al., 2017, p.7). Several indicators seem to suggest that the healthcare industry could maintain the momentum of its rapid growth, at least, in the near future. The most prominent indicator of this direction is the growing desire among the current population to improve their wellbeing (Chikhaoui et al., 2017, p.7). In addition to the immensely growing Saudi healthcare workforce (Health, 2013), the Kingdom of Saudi Arabia has been welcoming hundreds of thousands of healthcare practitioners from all over the globe (The Saudi Commission for Health Specialties, 2014). This could have a significant implication on the clinicians' perceptions related to patient confidentiality given the diversity of their training and practice backgrounds.

However, integration or interlace of electronic health records between entities or among clusters of hospitals could present a huge challenge and a serious concern related to unauthorized access, security violation, and difficulties in securing a safe and seamless transfer from one hospital to another (Chikhaoui et al., 2017, p.8). Consequently, the increasing electronic health information systems would require a suitable legal and ethical environment that safeguards data privacy, security and confidentiality. In particular, there must be respect, and taking responsibility, for fundamental human rights and, especially, the right to privacy and confidentiality of sensitive patient's data by the healthcare professionals and health institutions (Chikhaoui et al., 2017, p. 8).

In addition to the dangers attributable to the adoption of electronic health information systems by healthcare institutions in most of the countries all over the world, another factor that could affect the patient's confidentiality rights is the use of social media for healthcare communication. Therefore, given to the special professional relationship of confidence which traditionally bonds the healthcare practitioner with the patient, use of these technologies by the healthcare professionals portends a new risk of breach of that duty of confidentiality. Although the patient's right to demand confidentiality of his information is not absolute, an unlawful breach could result in a crime, actionable tort or become a subject of disciplinary action.

The focal point is the impact of these information technologies on the confidentiality of patients' personal data, and the possible gap, if any, between technology and the law, has been adequately bridged. It also explores the adequacy of the legal safeguard of patient confidentiality in view of the new challenges brought about by the use of information technologies. On the other hand, it also attempts to proffer practical ways of ensuring that, in spite of the technologies, practitioners maintain their solemn duty of securing and maintaining the confidentiality of the patients' sensitive health information.

Although the approach would be a holistic review of the prevailing challenges all over the world, the author's approach is heavily influenced by his experience in the Saudi Arabian healthcare system, and in many instances, the expositions might apply globally, but only to the Saudi Arabian jurisdictions. It would not be surprising, therefore, to find several references made to the Saudi Arabian jurisdictions in this chapter. Another point worthy of note is that, this review is made from the legal purview.

As much as technologies have brought about numerous benefits to humanity, patients and healthcare delivery, its limitations and dangers associated with its use cannot easily be discounted. In particular, the easy accessibility and the ease of distribution of information through the advances in information technologies have also made personal individually identifiable health information vulnerable to unjustifiable disclosure to third parties. It would seem necessary to examine the impact of information technology on patient confidentiality with a view to identifying ways to curtail possible unlawful breaches.

THE IMPACT OF INFORMATION TECHNOLOGY ON PATIENT CONFIDENTIALITY

E-Privacy remains a challenge, as highly advanced privacy invasive technologies continue to emerge and evolve, exposing more private data than previously envisaged (Alharbi & Zyngier, 2012). Increasingly, personal data ends up in a *bucket* of data that can be used and re-used for all kinds of known and unknown purposes. This poses critical questions on the requirements for gathering, storing, analyzing and ultimately erasing data. Little is known about these systems, how they impact privacy and civil liberties, and how they address accuracy problems (Cannataci, 2017).

In many countries, laws have lagged behind the advances in technology, leaving significant lacunae in the adequacy of data protections (Campaign, 2001). The recent advances in the information technologies and social media networking seem to be a new challenge to managing the patient's confidential information. Saudi Arabia has witnessed a spectacular progress in health care, arguably the best among its peers, and is investing heavily in electronic health information systems and aiming to build a single electronic health system by 2020 (MOH, 2017). Consequently, the use of electronic medical information systems is on the rise in Saudi Arabia, perhaps because, during the preceding decade, the implementation of an electronic health information system for hospitals has been among the top priorities of Saudi Arabia. On the other hand, Internet use is becoming ubiquitous among the Saudi public and health care professional. For instance, statistics show that, as of the first quarter of the year 2012, about half (47.5%) of the Saudi populations use the Internet of which 82% of these utilize Facebook, while the number of

Twitter users has risen exponentially. The trend is expected to steadily rise even higher recently (Al-Khalifa & Garcia, 2013).

However, recently, concerns related to patient confidentiality breaches have been increasing as healthcare information management is increasingly becoming more digitized, disseminated and portable without a commensurate knowledge of the root cause of breaches in confidentiality. This creates a new and complex challenge to the healthcare professionals and organizations in their bid to establish proper controls and security (Kamoun & Nicho, 2014).

To emphasize this further, stories surrounding the UK's experience with mass surveillance through bulk acquisition of patients' data could be quite disturbing. In mid-2015, a public hospital contracted with Google DeepMind Technologies Limited, an information technology company that had no prior experience in healthcare services, to develop software using patients' health information from the Trust's database (Powles & Hodson, 2017). The data package involved patient identifiable information including demographic details, the results of every blood tests recorded at the hospital in the previous five years before the transfer, and the electronic records of patients' diagnoses, procedures and treatment courses while at the hospital (Powles & Hodson, 2017). The dilemma was in the choice of the right approach to deploy data-driven innovations to improve patient care and at the same time maintaining public trust in the use and security of their sensitive health information (King et al., 2018).

The Special Rapporteur on Privacy Cannataci (2017) stressed this, when he stated thus:

There is also growing evidence that the information held by states, including that collected through bulk acquisition or "mass surveillance" is increasingly vulnerable to being hacked by hostile governments or organised crime. The risk created by the collection of such data has nowhere been demonstrated to be proportional to the reduction of risk achieved by bulk acquisition. (Cannataci, 2017)

It is evident that some of the data protection principles were not followed in the contract. The Data Protection Act (DPA), 1998 (and the recently created General Data Protection Regulation (GDPR), 2016 which became applicable in May, 2018) require that the purpose for which personal data is processed must be clearly stated by the data controller, at a time no later than when the information is collected (purpose specification principle). Under section 22 of the DPA (and Article 5 (1) (b) of the recently created GDPR), where an information is processed for an alternative purpose, there must be a corresponding legal basis since the data controller cannot rely on the initial legal basis. The Trust initially claimed that the identifiable patient data was being processed for the purpose of direct patient care, however, investigation had found out, the purpose was actually for the clinical safety testing of *Streams* app developed by Google. The Trust had already shared the patient's data long before a privacy impact assessment agreement formalized (Powles & Hodson, 2017).

Presently, under Clause 40 of the GDPR (2016), the data controllers that did not fulfil the data protection principle requiring that the data controllers must, unless exempted by some other legitimate basis (as laid down by law), obtain consent of the data subject before lawfully sharing their personal data with third parties. The change in the initial purpose of processing the patient records for patient care to another one for testing an app rules out the assumption of implicit consent. Where processing is based on the data subject's consent, the controller should be able to show evidence that the data subject has freely given an informed consent in writing to the processing operation (a separate consent for any subsequent processing under Clause 42, GDPR). The evidence should demonstrate that the data subject is aware of, among other particulars, the identity of the controller and the purposes of the processing for his data, and that he/she was given the option to refuse or withdraw consent without detriment. Therefore, because the patients have not been properly informed, they were unable to exercise their right to opt out from the program which would have effectively prevented the processing of their personal data (Powles & Hodson, 2017).

Furthermore, Clause 49 of the GDPR requires that the personal data should be processed to the extent strictly necessary and proportionate for the purposes of ensuring network and information security. The Trust was unable to justify that sharing such a huge bulk of patient health records was necessary and proportionate for testing of the application. The impression left in the mind of the data subject, would seem to be that although they did not expect that the Trust would share their data with a third party company for testing a mobile application, they were not informed of the fact that it would occur. The Information Commissioner's Office conclusion was that this sharing of patients' data was in violation of the 1998 Data Protection Act (Powles & Hodson, 2017).

From the foregoing, we could deduce that despite the great advantages of adopting the electronic health information technologies, that enhances convenience of accessibility and distribution of health information, it also creates the risk related to privacy and confidentiality of patients' data. As can be seen from the Google case, his risk is real, and the impact it could cause to patients could be huge. Unfortunately, other information technologies, including social media use, eHealth concepts etc., too, portend similar risks to patient confidentiality.

ELECTRONIC MEDICAL RECORDS/E-HEALTH INFORMATION RISKS

The increasing demand for advanced information technology in the health sector is seemingly outpacing the law and regulations governing confidentiality rights. The health care settings, too, are embracing the fluidity of the changes happening in the society where they operate as they strive to meet the challenges of increased demand for higher quality medical services for less money in an increasingly competitive business environment. Therefore, healthcare providers and research institutions are searching for solutions that would maximize efficiency at a reduced cost (Chikhaoui et al., 2017, p.6).

Developing countries face several challenges associated with maintaining the confidentiality of health-related information, which include the data subjects' "diminished autonomy, language barriers, limited health literacy, and cultural barriers resulting from paternalism and social diversity" (Nair & Ibrahim, 2015, p. 211). Unfortunately, one of the limitations of the Saudi Arabian policy considerations for privacy and confidentiality is that, the Arabic culture gives priority to family values over individual autonomy and encourages conformity to family norms. Although this may have helped in protecting physical and proprietary privacy, data privacy of the data subjects could face significant challenges in such environment (Edwards, 2016).

It is apparent that the modern health institutions of both the developed and developing countries have continued to embrace and adopt the electronic health information systems in an unprecedentedly massive rate. There has been a varying rate of growth in the use of electronic health information systems or electronic medical record system in Saudi Arabia. Despite the exponential growth of electronic medical record system in a particular region Saudi Arabia reported (Bah et al., 2011), it is still generally lagging behind as reported in others (Hasanain, Vallmuur, & Clark, 2015; Jabali & Jarrar, 2018). However, many hospitals are in varying stages of introducing electronic health information systems to replace the traditional paper-based medical records and implement electronic systems (Alsulame et al., 2016).

The use of electronic health record systems is a new experience for many of health care institutions and professionals that could create a new ethical-legal dilemma about their duty of confidentiality.

Recently, there has been a noticeable shift in our understanding of health information systems and technologies, which raises concerns about their safe use by health professionals (Fernandez-Luque, Elahi, Grajales, & Iii, 2009). It is understandable that the proliferative use of electronic health information systems for health care delivery presents significant benefits for the patients and the health care providers in terms of enhancing patient autonomy, improving patient treatment outcomes, advances in health research and public health surveillance, etc. However, it also presents new legal challenges including that of privacy and confidentiality of identifiable health information (Hodge, Gostin, & Jacobson, 1999). For instance, Alhammad's (2017, p. 3) assessment of "outpatients' attitudes and expectations towards electronic personal health records (ePHR) systems in secondary and tertiary hospitals in Riyadh, Saudi Arabia" buttresses just that. The study noted that three-quarters of respondents believed that the security and confidentiality of their private health information are important (75%). The author, however, lamented that more research is required to further explore the ePHR privacy concerns of patients and the key factors in improving the use of ePHRs among specific populations (Alhammad, 2017).

Despite the varying degrees of awareness to their right to privacy, most patients do understand that the issue of confidentiality is important but are, nevertheless, in favor of permitting their healthcare providers and some family members to have access to healthcare or research related data. For instance, Alahmad and others studied a cross-section of patients for their attitude towards medical and genetic confidentiality in the Saudi research bio bank. Most respondents agreed to some specifically justifiable disclosures, however, they emphasized the importance of maintaining patient/donor confidentiality (Alahmad, Hifnawy, Abbasi, & Dierickx, 2016).

Similarly, other studies have shown patients' qualified acceptance of medical students in their care for confidentiality breach concerns (Al Ghobain et al., 2016) or show a preference for a physical examination by a lone physician (Al-Harbi & Al-Harbi, 2010). Some patients, who were studied on their attitude towards shared medical appointments, have shown a preference for an individual appointment approach because of concerns about possible unwarranted disclosure of confidential information to strangers (Alhowimel, 2013). The author, therefore, argues that patient confidentiality could be a decisive factor to patients in their willingness to freely disclose pertinent information to their healthcare professionals (Alkabba, Hussein, Albar, Bahnassy, & Qadi, 2012). Confidentiality could be a decisive factor to patients in their willingness to freely disclose pertinent.

IMPACT OF SOCIAL MEDIA ON PATIENT CONFIDENTIALITY

Apart from the increasing use of electronic health information systems, the social media that is now becoming part of daily life experience for a majority of people with access to the Internet, too, pose similar risks of breaches of confidentiality (Ahmed et al., 2013; Farnan et al., 2013). Social media use has, apparently, become ubiquitous in all facets of society, including and especially, among healthcare professionals. This might relate to the availability and accessibility to the Internet and other information technologies across the globe. Unlike before the proliferation of Internet and social media when people interacted on face-to-face basis, by mail or telephones, individuals have suddenly found themselves interacting with strangers who might be far across the borders. This sudden emergence of blurred boundaries of relationships has the potential to affect the confidential professional relationship between the healthcare professionals and the patients (Casella, Mills, & Usher, 2014). This development could potentially raise the temptation for Internet users to, unknowingly, carelessly, or negligently, share even sensitive data with completely unknown, or partially known third parties on the Internet.

Social media are a user-created content and communications tool hosted on a web-based application which may be in a form of networking sites e.g. Facebook or Twitter; media sharing sites e.g., Instagram; or blogs. Their popularity is rapidly rising from 'obscurity to ubiquity' (Bosslet, 2011) over the recent years. Social media is now used in almost all sectors of human endeavours, be it social, professional, academic, business or even in the healthcare sector. Just like in the other sectors, its use is even accelerating more quickly than envisaged (George, Rovniak, & Kraschnewski, 2013 p. 4). Social media is now increasingly being used for, among others, disseminating information among patients and professional colleagues (George et al., 2013), and recently, as source of data for surveillance and research (McKee, 2013). In the same vein, the use of social media among healthcare professionals is on the rise reaching about 90% among doctors and much higher among medical students as of 2011 (Prasanna, Seagull, & Nagy, 2011).

The professional relationship between the patient and healthcare professionals may be under a threat with the advent of the Internet, and more specifically, the large-scale use of social media platforms by individuals in society, health care professionals inclusive. For, instance, in the U.S., the scale of Facebook's online network is immense, with an estimated number of 149 million Americans using it every month, with each one connected to an average of 214 people (Collingwood, 2013). The growth of the number of people with Internet access continues to rise and a consequence of this is that it is becoming the norm for people to conduct significant parts of their lives through online social networks. Similarly, just like elsewhere, the daily use of Internet among adults has increased tremendously in the UK from about 60% in 2010 (White & Selwyn, 2013) to nearly 90% in 2015 (Meeker, 2015), and this figure might continue to increase.

Social media platforms generally enable users to form an online profile, to share personal information, to learn and keep up to date with knowledge, to facilitate virtual attendance at medical conferences, and to measure impact within a field (Roupret et al., 2014, p. 629). In addition, in this respect, Facebook offers something unprecedented, i.e., a direct real time access to an individual's social network, and without the need for tedious network registration by participants (Cobb & Graham, 2012, p. 571). Facebook provides such tools as *pages* and *groups* that allow self-enrolment and sharing of information via groups, and *applications* that provide direct access to all the aforementioned tools (Cobb & Graham, 2012). These facilities offered by the social media seem to create a virtual communication environment that could potentially affect how and what we communicate to whom, more especially within the context of the professional relationship between the patient and the health professionals.

This is even more so social media use amongst health care professionals continue to increase. For instance, recent estimates of the use of social media by doctors has escalated dramatically from 41% in 2010 to 90% in 2011, whereas the rates of use have been found to be above 90% for medical students (George et al., 2013, p. 454). Among pharmacy students in the UK, for example, a study showed that most of the respondents (91.8%) reported using social networking web sites, with 98.6% using Facebook and 33.7% using Twitter (Hall, Hanna, & Huey, 2013 p. 9). A growing minority of physicians also uses social media to communicate directly with patients to augment clinical care (Ventola, 2014, p. 491).

Conversely, patients join and use social media for increasing their knowledge about their health conditions, for social support, for exchanging advice among themselves (Antheunis, Tates, & Nieboer, 2013) and for self-help (Hamm et al., 2000). A majority of modern patients, more especially those with chronic conditions, seek social media and other online sources to obtain information on health issues, to link up with others with similar conditions, and to participate more actively in decisions affecting their health care. This ubiquitous use of social media by both health care professionals and patients over the last several years shows that these technologies will soon be part of modern medicine (George et al., 2013, p. 454).

However, by their nature, medical practice and social media use are contradictory. Medicine, by its nature involves private communications, privacy, confidentiality, and formal conduct, whereas social media entails values sharing and openness, connection and transparency, and informality. Therefore, any attempt to converge the two could create some concern in the professional practice (George et al., 2013, p. 454). Hence, social media fora, like Facebook, Twitter, WhatsApp as well as the ubiquitous search engines like Google, are raising an unprecedented level of medical legal/ethical dilemmas as health care professionals around the world struggle to responsibly incorporate these new technologies into their professional lives (Devi, 2011, p. 1141).

Undoubtedly, these concerns might have stemmed from the issues of privacy/confidentiality, consent, and other ethical issues of consequence to health professionals (George et al., 2013, p. 454). In addition, emerging evidence abound showing that medical professionals have discovered a new means of safely and productively navigating through social media for use in health care. These moves could illustrate that social media has been accepted as a tool to complement modern medical practice as it could provide unprecedented opportunities for cost-effective 2-way communication between health professionals and patients (George et al., 2013, p. 454). In spite of the currently available privacy safeguards, and the ability of users to navigate safely, there still exists the potential risks of blurring the boundaries to professional confidential relationships.

The use of social media through smart phones or computer has become a common outlet where patient's confidential information could be leaked because practitioners are mostly likely to use it for exchanging information about patient care (including sensitive patient information). Although patient's privacy is among the top dilemmas for public and private healthcare practitioners in Saudi Arabia (Ebad, Jaha, & Al-Qadhi, 2014), it is instructive to note that Saudi literature on medical/clinical ethics remains limited in terms of volume and scope (Alkabba et al., 2012). A study by Al Qaryan et al. (2016) has noted that a significant proportion of medical interns used personal mobiles to keep in contact with team members regarding the patient, while some 16% of participants did not have any security features on their smart-phones. Although this study relates to medical interns and final year students, in the absence of similar Saudi study on qualified professionals, its findings could serve as a tip of an iceberg in this respect.

This discussion is undertaken within the context of the larger society in which social media is considered a useful tool for sharing personal information with friends and family members in their social circle, within which health providers may find themselves involved just like any other member of the society. The public, the patient as well as healthcare professionals use it frequently because of its distinctive features e.g., encouraging greater interactions with others, it is free, available, shared, and has personalized information; and it is readily accessible with wider coverage (Moorhead et al., 2013, p. 8). It can also be used to provide peer/social/emotional support or to support public health surveillance, and therefore, has the potential to influence health policy.

The main challenge that healthcare professionals face on social media is how to keep appropriate professional relationships boundaries safe when interacting with patients online and, how to ensure that patient privacy/confidentiality is maintained (Alsughayr, 2015, p. 108). Therefore, the health care professionals' online behaviour and content of their posts can adversely affect their professional reputation, which may ultimately have far-reaching consequences on their careers as well. Unsurprisingly, the UK's General Medical Council advises doctors to "make sure that (their) conduct at all times justifies their patients' trust in them and the public's trust in the profession" (General Medical Council, 2018).

Social media, whether used by individual healthcare professionals, by healthcare institutions or by the patients has a lot to offer in terms of creating new approach to networking, seeking and sharing information about health needs, or communicating with others. Social media has created opportunities for communications between healthcare professionals and institutions on the one hand, and the patients on the other, as well as communication among patient populations. However, the hitherto clear confidential relationship and boundary becomes blurred with individually identifiable health information.

Benefits of Social Media in Healthcare Communication

Without doubt, social media heralds numerous all-encompassing benefits for health communication between and among the public, patients, and health professionals. Social media users can control the dynamics of interaction and therefore, increase the frequency and number of interactions. So, social media provides readily available, shared, and customized health information to deal with health issues (Adams, 2010, p. e89), with a potential to improving health outcomes (Moorhead et al., 2013).

Social media has largely affected the practice of healthcare professions, perhaps most publicly by facilitating improved communication with and among patients (von Muhlen, Ohno-Machado, 2012, p.777). One of the main benefits of social media for health care communication is the availability and broadened access to health information for all, irrespective of gender, age, socio-economic status, race, or geographic locality, as compared to conventional communication approaches (Moorhead et al., 2013, p. 11/36). Social media also can provide for easier and wider access than the traditional methods where some people, such as youth and those in lower socioeconomic groups would not have easy access to health information (Moorhead et al., 2013). Interestingly, Facebook offers something unprecedented, i.e., a direct access to someone's social network, without the necessity of enrollment by participants (Cobb & Graham, 2012).

In addition, health related social media sites have changed traditional patient–physician relationships. They provide an accessible platform for discussing sensitive and complex issues / information with health professionals. In some social networking sites, patients form groups, share experiences and assist each other (Colineau & Paris, 2010). It is quite interesting to note that social media has, in many ways, broadly affected medical practice, perhaps, by enabling increased communication with and among patients. Instances include the use of social media, e.g., Twitter or Facebook, to conduct emergency broadcasts during natural disasters. (von Muhlen et al., 2012 p. 777).

Not only patients alone form communities on social media. Social media provide health care professionals with the wherewithal to share professional information, to debate health care issues related to policies and/or practices, and post beneficial comments for both patients and fellow colleagues (Nyongesa, Munguti, Omondi, & Mokua, 2014, p. 3). Health care professionals also can use social media to potentially improve patient's health outcomes, develop a professional network, keep up to date with news and discoveries, motivate patients on their illnesses and treatment options, as well as provide reliable health information to the community (Ventola, 2014 p. 491). For instance, the *Google Hangout* platform provides a forum where health care providers can communicate or interact with his or her patients, follow up on their conditions and proffer appropriate measures before complications set in (Nyongesa, Munguti, Omondi, & Mokua, 2014, p. 3).

The era of communicating disease information through leaflets and pamphlets is running toward extinction giving in to the easy, available and low-cost use of social media fora. Therefore, many health care professionals and institutions take advantage of these benefits that become available by merely joining the social media platform (Nyongesa et al., 2014, p. 2). An example of such experience is the one shared by the European Association of Urologists where the association used the social media to keep its members updated with urologic literature and news, followed live reportage of academic conferences, participated in discourse on a barrage of ideas, and networked with colleagues from around the world (Roupret et al., 2014, p. 628); and engaged with academic medical content (Roupret et al., 2014, p. 629). Conversely, health care institutions are increasingly involved in the social media both as a marketing avenue and a platform for providing information about their available services (Nyongesa et al., 2014, p. 3).

Social media not only supports healthcare processes through gathering and sharing information among communities and groups but, also supports patient empowerment, by getting patients into the position to take control of their healthcare needs (Denecke et al., 2015, p. 137). The communities of networking and data sharing platforms encourage and support sharing experiences about their sickness conditions, and treatment options/outcomes, as well as enabling members to track personal health and be actively involved in their own care (Denecke et al., 2015b).

Another health communication use of social media is in the field of public health surveillance. Social media are recently being seen as a source of data for surveillance and research by providing an opportunity for real time and, at relatively low cost, communication tool to track public concerns or capture discourses undertaken outside traditional media channels (McKee, 2013 p. 298). These may include monitoring public response to health issues, tracking and monitoring disease outbreak, identifying target areas for intervention efforts, and for disseminating pertinent health information to targeted communities (Moorhead et al., 2013, p. 8/36). Moreover, social media also is used to recruit patients for clinical trials based on social-media profiles or the mining of such data for epidemiological studies, or to crowdsource answers to individual clinical questions, e.g., use of posted tweets data to detect and monitor disease activity such cholera outbreaks (Denecke et al., 2015, p. 137).

While social media are primarily used for social interactions and keeping in touch with friends and family, we have realized from the foregoing that they are increasingly being used for health-related purposes (Ahmed et al., 2013, p. 328). Social media can also contribute to medicine by improving communication with patients, enhancing professional development, and contributing to public health research and service (Winkelstein, 2013, p. 454), thereby enhancing outcomes (Fisher & Clayton, 2012, p. 100). However, discourse on the limitations and dangers of social media use health care has overshadowed consideration of its potential benefits (Winkelstein, 2013).

Social media has obviously come to stay in our society. It has become ubiquitous in our lives, and it seems to transcend to every nook and crannies of our lives. Furthermore, social media offers society many benefits as individuals, professionals or healthcare organizations. It allows unhinged communications between and among individuals, groups, and between individuals and organizations. These communications include healthcare communications. However, the question remains: is there any limitation(s) or inherent to, or associated with, risks caused by social media used for healthcare communications? The next section attempts to answer this question.

Limitations and Dangers of Social Media for Healthcare Communication

There is no doubt that social media use in health care is a welcome idea. However, it has its own limitations and dangers. The quality of information derived from social media interactions is usually variable and inconsistent, as social media tools are largely an informal and unregulated tool used for data collection, sharing, and dissemination (Moorhead et al., 2013, p. 11/36). Both patients (and the public at large) as well as health care professionals may encounter certain barriers to social media use. For patients and other users of social media, their main concern is the risk of privacy infringement, and the unreliability of the information obtained therein. Whereas the professionals' main barriers were inefficiency and lack of skills (Antheunis et al., 2013).

Apart from the limitations alluded to previously and the enormous benefits already considered, all users of social media should be cautious of the inherent risks associated with the unaccredited nature of its informational content (Nyongesa et al., 2014, p. 3). Moreover, social media use also has the potential to create dual (professional versus private) relationships between health care professionals and patients, or blur the boundaries of the patient/professional relationship (Aylott, 2011; Casella et al., 2014). The potential risk associated with breaching patient confidentiality or posting unprofessional content (M. von Muhlen et al., 2012, p. 779) can be brought about by the "immediate and extensive visibility of online postings, and their permanence on the sites" (Marnocha et al., 2015, p. 119).

It is no wonder, therefore, that the press is awash with headlines of reports implicating health care professionals in unprofessional conduct on social media. ''Medical students' cadaver photos get scrutiny after images show up online'' (Heyboer, 2010), ''Nursing students expelled from university after posting pictures of themselves posing with a human placenta on "Facebook'' (Daily Mail, 2011), "Five nurses were fired for Facebook postings", etc., (Fink, 2011). Similarly, twenty-three incidents of patient information postings on social networking sites by NHS staff were reported to the Information Commissioner's Office in 2011 alone. These incidents involved 13 medical personnel from 11 trusts across the UK including a doctor who was dismissed for posting a picture of a patient on Facebook (Caldicott, 2013, p. 52).

In addition, in the year 2012, severe data losses in England were reported to the Department of Health mostly involving the loss or theft of data. Almost one-third were related to unauthorized disclosures (Caldicott, 2013, p. 49). Another report released to Guardian Healthcare showed that 16 trusts had brought 72 separate actions against their staff for inappropriately using social media at various times between 2008 and October 2011. The 'inappropriate use" included inappropriate conversations/comments on/about patient/patient-care or, posting pictures of the workplace on social media platforms (Laja, 2011). More often, social media users are unaware of the risks of wrongful disclosure of personal information online, (Adams, 2010) or of sharing harmful or incorrect advice on social media (Adams, 2010, p. 391-400). Just like other members of the public, it is clear that some clinicians use social media in their professional lives, but the respect for privacy remains a concern to everyone (Ventola, 2014). Therefore, discussion of the dangers of these technologies in medicine has overwhelmed consideration of positive applications (George et al., 2013).

As much as social media offers us benefits, there are attendant risks of the breach of confidentiality associated with its use in healthcare communications. It would, therefore, require all healthcare professionals and organizations to use it with caution, lest, professional boundaries become blurred, and individually identifiable health information becomes at risk of being unlawfully shared with third parties.

eHEALTH AND mHEALTH IMPACTS ON PATIENT'S CONFIDENTIALITY RIGHTS

Another evolving new technology that is used for collecting and managing patients' health information is the eHealth concept. E-health is a rather new healthcare practice supported by information technology that evolved within the preceding decade (Della Mea, 2001). This concept is referred to as *eHealth* for any kind online or offline computer-based application or electronic device, or *mHealth* for any (mobile) monitoring system that healthcare professionals use in healthcare practices to monitor or improve the patient's health status (Kampmeijer, Pavlova, Tambor, Golinowska, & Groot, 2016). Other similar concepts with like impact on patient confidentiality include *ePrescribing* (access to prescribing options, printing prescriptions to patients and sometimes electronic transmission of prescriptions from doctors to pharmacists), *telemedicine* (physical and psychological diagnosis and treatments at a distance, including telemonitoring patients' functions), wearables, fitness trackers, and others still evolving.

E-Health or similar applications offer healthcare professionals an access to medical knowledge and patient data at the point of care but studies have emphasized that they could be potentially dangerous (Lewis & Wyatt, 2014). These new applications potentially empower patients to get healthier or possibly enhance clinicians to become more effective and efficient (Musiat, Goldstone, & Tarrier, 2014). Physicians now have new ways to conduct professional communication, have easier access to decision support and expedited, efficient specialist consultation (Bromwich & Bromwich, 2016). However, these advantages of eHealth are not without some corresponding disadvantages. There are a number of concerns related to treatment credibility, user privacy and confidentiality. The potential risks to recording, storing and sharing patient information or images on such devices is further heightened if electronic mobile devices are hacked, lost or stolen (Bromwich & Bromwich, 2016). Basically, mobile security risks are high because *eHealth* tools give hackers an "easier direct access to more valuable organizational assets than any other intrusion point" (Gruessner, n.d.). Reports of data protection violations seem to even outweigh magnitude of real damage to health caused by health apps (Albrecht, 2016).

The key to successful data protection related to eHealth is the consistent implementation of existing laws along with obtaining valid informed consent, freely given, to enable data users to make their own decisions with regards to sharing their data (Albrecht, 2016, p. 26). The modern Internet-enabled smartphones with health technologies are easy to use and portable, but they are an easy prey for hackers. This is because a smartphone is like a micro-computer that has a microphone, a camera, a GPS and an antenna to connect from, and share all information including telephone numbers, address, emails, photos, contacts and, bank accounts and credit cards anywhere. Therefore, a smartphone could be a dangerous treasure of sensitive information that arguably is part of lives, but at a very high risk (Alvarez, McGlaughlin, & Wirth, 2017).

Apart from the e-Health tools discussed supra, there are several technologies in the hospitals, malls, public places and the street that collect, analyze and store our personal data on daily basis. Consequently, by merely walking out of one's home to work or school, multiple cameras track movement making it possible to reconstruct one's tracks with great precision, although the subject did not know about it nor give his consent. More often, signposts in public places alert people of the presence of CCTV cameras, whereupon, the only option open for non-consent is to avoid going to such places. However, that would mean that one could only avoid these cameras in modern cities by staying indoors, at home without going out to work. This would not only be impracticable but would have serious ramifications on society. Therefore, it could be argued that these serious privacy concerns create new challenges to the privacy laws. As a result, it is appropriate to assess whether adequate legal protections exist as safeguards for information privacy and confidentiality exist under current laws, or whether substantial gaps in the legal regime need to be filled with new laws or regulations.

E-Health technologies, no doubt, offer patients and doctors, the ability to remotely interact and communicate regarding diagnosing and managing patient ailments without the necessity for a face-to-face encounter. However, use of these tools, along with cloud services, allow for collection and processing of huge amount of health information which may, ultimately come to the possession of third parties without the knowledge and consent of the data subjects.

HAS THE LAW ADEQUATELY PROTECTED PATIENT CONFIDENTIALITY RIGHTS?

More often than not, laws lag behind modern developments which could include technological advancement (Dror, 1958). Novel technological innovation often raises gray areas in prevailing laws (Herz, 2009). It is not unexpected, therefore, that conventional law is unable to apply precisely on innovations and advancements in technology over time. It would have been sufficient that key principles are available to support adequate and extensive protection of human rights in a digital age (Electronic Frontier Foundation, 2014). Unfortunately, gaps exist between regulations provided by laws and the technological revolution, which grows even wider proportionately to the speed of technology advancement. Consequently, gaps in privacy laws, too, are widening rapidly (Wadhwa, 2014).

There is no doubt that novel technological advancements have potentially positively impacted humans' lives, although, using these technologies could portend potential security risks and challenges (Chikhaoui, Sarabdeen, & Parveen, 2016, p. 3): "[l]aw is always going to be playing catch up to technology," Bridget Treacy, leader of UK Privacy and Information Management practice at law firm Hunton & Williams in UK, had once asserted (Burn-Murdoch, 2013). It has been argued that the main problem with information security in health care is not technology, but a lack of cohesive security rules and policy. Relevant policy must shape technology and guide its use, and not the other way around. Security policy defines what is to be protected, to what reasonable degree protections will be afforded, and who is privileged to access protected items. (Randolph, 1996). Although, in every country, there are an array of privacy and data protection laws and regulations, they are not without a number of significant flaws. Often, in response to fast and often unforeseen dynamics in the technological landscape of privacy, surveillance, and data sharing, the law reactively and irregularly develops in a sporadic manner, thereby giving rise to gray areas in the protection of individuals' rights of privacy and confidentiality.

Major barriers to adopting cloud computing includes the lack of practical knowledge among users, and weak laws dealing with privacy. Privacy issues have almost always delayed the adoption of cloud computing (Chikhaoui et al., 2017, p. 10). Many countries do not yet have comprehensive data protection laws though they have devised strategic plans for privacy protection (Chikhaoui et al., 2017, p. 8). In countries, like Saudi Arabia and Nigeria, to mention two, have scattered pieces of legislation on patient confidentiality spread across several laws. They are lacking in both structure and substance. For instance, there is no available definition of "personal data", data processor, or safeguards against abuse in any of the existing Saudi Arabian legislation (Chikhaoui et al., 2017, p. 8).

Another explanation for lapses in the law is that, except for some recent regulations e.g., the European General Data Protection Regulation (GDPR) (European Union, 2016), most existing laws on information privacy and confidentiality are not based on standardized data protection principles. This means each piece of law, be it legislation, case law, or professional code must be contextualized to understand and interpret its impact. As a result, determining each case regarding data collection, processing and storage becomes burdensome. The ripple effect includes increased risks of privacy and confidentiality breaches and abuses by unlawful disclosure to unknown third parties. Modern data protection law should provide adequate safeguards from potential risks of arbitrary misuse of patients' personal data. In respect to Saudi Arabian settings, the assessment by triple test has shown that such safeguards are defective and inadequate.

CONCLUSION

There is no doubt that advances in information technology are fast-evolving, and transforming our lives in many ways. The transformation includes healthcare delivery. Health professionals can now use technology to easily and efficiently diagnose, treat and rapidly follow up on their patients. Patients can seek health information, tips and advice on the Internet or through social media. Social media can be used in crowdsourcing for research, contact tracing during disaster, epidemics and outbreaks. It is no longer in dispute that information benefits society in many ways.

However, technology, especially and particularly information technology, be it social media or electronic health information systems, or eHealth concepts, have made our social interaction easier, and improved the way patients and the healthcare professionals interact within the purview of confidential professional relationships. For these relationships to thrive, and nurture required mutual trust between patient and healthcare professionals, the latter commits to their duty to maintain the confidentiality of any personal information the patient divulges to enable them to identify and treat his ailment smoothly and successfully. However, advances in modern information technology have created a potential risk to this right of confidentiality which the patient has always enjoyed, as protected by the laws.

It has been argued that the laws are not able to keep up with the technology revolution. This ensuing gap potentially gives way to unresolved gray areas. Of course, some regional bodies are making efforts to reduce, if not eliminate such risks. A good example of such effort is the European Union's General Data Protection Regulation, 2016 which came into effect on May 26th, 2018. It not only laid down basic data protection principles, but also gave rights and powers to data subjects, in this case, the patients, to control how, who and for how long his/her personal data may be processed and shared. While the GDPR may be considered a wakeup call to all countries to optimize their laws to deal with the impact of technologies on the patient's confidentiality rights, professional bodies and regulators should also tailor their professional ethics and code to be contemporaneous with the advances in technology, as well as ensure compliance with same, and the law.

Technology is good for the patient, the healthcare professional and society at large, but it must be used with caution against the attendant risk to the closely guarded trust created by the professional relationships between them. Trust is difficult to gain and easy to lose (Pattinson, 2017).

ACKNOWLEDGMENT

I genuinely acknowledge and highly appreciate the review and contribution of my PhD research supervisor, Dr. Nicolas Kang-Riou of Salford Business School, University of Salford, Greater Manchester. My appreciation also goes for Dr. Augustine Edobor Arimoro, of University of Cape Town, for his review and invaluable input that immensely helped shaped the chapter.

REFERENCES

Adams, S. A. (2010). Blog-based applications and health information: Two case studies that illustrate important questions for Consumer Health Informatics (CHI) research. *International Journal of Medical Informatics*, *79*(6), e89–e96. doi:10.1016/j.ijmedinf.2008.06.009

Ahmed, O. H., Sullivan, S. J., Schneiders, A. G., Anderson, L., Paton, C., & McCrory, P. R. (2013). Ethical Considerations in Using Facebook for Health Care Support: A Case Study Using Concussion Management. *PM & R*, *5*(4), 328–334. doi:10.1016/j.pmrj.2013.03.007

Al Ghobain, M., Alghamdi, A., Arab, A., Alaem, N., Aldress, T., & Ruhyiem, M. (2016). Patients' perceptions towards the participation of medical students in their care. *Sultan Qaboos University Medical Journal*, *16*(2), 224–229. doi:10.18295qumj.2016.16.02.014

Al-Harbi, M., & Al-Harbi, K. (2010). Patient attitudes towards interns and medical students rotating in dermatology clinics in Almadinah Almunawwarah Region, Saudi Arabia. *Sultan Qaboos University Medical Journal*, *10*(3), 377–381.

Al-Khalifa, H. S., & Garcia, R. A. (2013). The state of social media in Saudi Arabia's higher education. *International Journal of Technology and Educational Marketing*, *3*(1), 65–76. doi:10.4018/ijtem.2013010105

Alahmad, G., Hifnawy, T., Abbasi, B., & Dierickx, K. (2016). Attitudes toward medical and genetic confidentiality in the Saudi research biobank: An exploratory survey. *International Journal of Medical Informatics*, *87*, 84–90. doi:10.1016/j.ijmedinf.2015.12.015

Albrecht, U.-V. (2016). Rationale. *Chances and Risks of Mobile Health Apps (CHARISMHA)*, 2–5.

Alhammad, O. S. (2017). Assessing Outpatients' Attitudes And Expectations Towards Electronic Personal Health Records (ePHR) Systems. In *Secondary and Tertiary Hospitals In Riyadh*. Saudi Arabia: McMaster University.

Alharbi, I. M., & Zyngier, S. (2012). A holistic view on the opportunities and risks faced by Saudi Arabia government in their adoption of the new law regulating electronic privacy. *WIAR 2012; National Workshop on Information Assurance Research*, 1–7.

Alhowimel, M. H. (2013). Attitudes of physicians toward implementing shared medical appointments at national guard family medicine centers in Riyadh. *Value in Health*, *16*(7), A538. doi:10.1016/j.jval.2013.08.1354

Alkabba, A. F., Hussein, G. M. A., Albar, A. A., Bahnassy, A. A., & Qadi, M. (2012). The major medical ethical challenges facing the public and healthcare providers in Saudi Arabia. *Journal of Family & Community Medicine*, *19*(1), 1–6. doi:10.4103/2230-8229.94003

Alqaryan, S., Alkhalifa, M., Alharbi, M., Alabaishi, S., & Aldrees, T. (2016). Smartphones and professionalism : A cross-sectional study on interns and final-year medical students. *International Journal of Medical Research & Health Sciences*, *5*(9), 198–202.

Alsughayr, A. (2015). Social media in healthcare: Uses, risks, and barriers. *Saudi Journal of Medicine and Medical Sciences*, *3*(2), 105. doi:10.4103/1658-631X.156405

Alsulame, K., Khalifa, M., & Househ, M. (2016). E-Health status in Saudi Arabia: A review of current literature. *Health Policy and Technology*, *5*(2), 204–210. doi:10.1016/j.hlpt.2016.02.005

Alvarez, B., McGlaughlin, C., & Wirth, A. (2017). The benefits and risks of health technology in the digital era – HIMSS Privacy and Security. Retrieved from https://staysafeonline.org/blog/health-technology-digital-era-benefits-risks/

Antheunis, M. L., Tates, K., & Nieboer, T. E. (2013). Patients' and health professionals' use of social media in health care: Motives, barriers and expectations. *Patient Education and Counseling*, *92*(3), 426–431. doi:10.1016/j.pec.2013.06.020

Aylott, M. (2011). Blurring the boundaries: Technology and the nurse-patient relationship. *British Journal of Nursing (Mark Allen Publishing)*, *20*(13), 810–812, 814–816. doi:10.12968/bjon.2011.20.13.810

Bah, S., Alharthi, H., El Mahalli, A. A., Jabali, A., Al-Qahtani, M., & Al-kahtani, N. (2011). Annual survey on the level and extent of usage of electronic health records in government-related hospitals in Eastern Province, Saudi Arabia. Perspectives in Health Information Management / AHIMA, American Health Information Management Association.

Barrows, R. C. Jr, & Clayton, P. D. (1996). Privacy, confidentiality : And electronic medical records. *Journal of the American Medical Informatics Association*, *3*(2), 139–148. doi:10.1136/jamia.1996.96236282

Bosslet, G. T. (2011). Commentary: The good, the bad, and the ugly of social media. *Academic Emergency Medicine*, *18*(11), 1221–1222. doi:10.1111/j.1553-2712.2011.01197.x

Brannigan, V. M. (1992). Protecting the privacy of patient information in clinical networks: Regulatory effectiveness analysis. *Annals of the New York Academy of Sciences*, *670*(1 Extended Clin), 190–201. doi:10.1111/j.1749-6632.1992.tb26090.x

Bromwich, M., & Bromwich, R. (2016). Privacy risks when using mobile devices in health care. CMAJ : Canadian Medical Association Journal = Journal de l'Association Medicale Canadienne, 188(12), 855–856. doi:10.1503/cmaj.160026

Buntin, M. B., Burke, M. F., Hoaglin, M. C., & Blumenthal, D. (2011). The benefits of health information technology: A review of the recent literature shows predominantly positive results. *Profiles of Innovation in Healthcare Delivery*, *30*(3). doi:10.1377/hlthaff.2011.0178

Burn-Murdoch, J. (2013, April 12). Data protection law is in danger of lagging behind technological change. *The Guardian*.

Caldicott, F. (2013). Information: To share or not to share. Information Governance Review. Information: To Share or Not to Share.

Campaign, G. I. L. (2001). *Privacy and Human Rights: An International Survey of Privacy Laws and Practice*. Global Internet Liberty Campaign.

Cannataci, J. A. (2017). Report of the Special Rapporteur on the right to privacy A/HRC/34/60.

Casella, E., Mills, J., & Usher, K. (2014). Social media and nursing practice: Changing the balance between the social and technical aspects of work. *Collegian (Royal College of Nursing, Australia)*, *21*(2), 121–126. doi:10.1016/j.colegn.2014.03.005

Chikhaoui, E., Sarabdeen, J., & Parveen, R. (2016). Privacy and security issues in the use of clouds in E-Health in the Kingdom Of Saudi Arabia. In Communications of the IBIMA (pp. 1–18). doi:10.5171/2017.369309

Chikhaoui, E., Sarabdeen, J., & Parveen, R. (2017). Privacy and security issues in the use of clouds in e-Health in the Kingdom of Saudi Arabia. Communications of the IBIMA, 1–18. doi:10.5171/2017.369309

Cobb, N. K., & Graham, A. L. (2012). Health behavior interventions in the age of facebook. *American Journal of Preventive Medicine*, *43*(5), 571–572. doi:10.1016/j.amepre.2012.08.001

Colineau, N., & Paris, C. (2010). Talking about your health to strangers: Understanding the use of online social networks by patients. *New Review of Hypermedia and Multimedia*, *16*(1-2), 141–160. doi:10.1080/13614568.2010.496131

Collingwood, L. H. (2013). Privacy protection under the English legal system: is it adequate given the challenges raised by online communicating between individuals? (Doctoral dissertation, Kingston University).

Della Mea, V. (2001). What is e-health?: The death of telemedicine? *Journal of Medical Internet Research*, *3*(2), E22. doi:10.2196/jmir.3.2.e22

Denecke, K., Bamidis, P., Bond, C., Gabarron, E., Househ, M., Lau, A. Y., ... Hansen, M. (2015a). Ethical issues of social media usage in healthcare. *Yearbook of Medical Informatics*, *10*(1), 137–147. doi:10.15265/IY-2015-001

Denecke, K., Bamidis, P., Bond, C., Gabarron, E., Househ, M., Lau, A. Y. S., ... Hansen, M. (2015b). Ethical issues of social media usage in healthcare. *Yearbook of Medical Informatics*, *10*(1), 137–147. doi:10.15265/IY-2015-001

Devi, S. (2011). Facebook friend request from a patient? *Lancet*, *377*(9772), 1141–1142. doi:10.1016/S0140-6736(11)60449-2

Dror, Y. (1958). Law and Social Change. *Tulane Law Review*, 33.

Ebad, S. A., Jaha, E. S., & Al-Qadhi, M. A. (2014). Analyzing privacy requirements: A case study of healthcare in Saudi Arabia. *Informatics for Health & Social Care*, *41*(1), 47–63. doi:10.3109/17538157.2014.965301

Edwards, L. (2016). Privacy, Security and data protection in smart cities: A critical EU law perspective. *European Data Protection Law Review*, *2*(1), 28–58. doi:10.21552/EDPL/2016/1/6

Electronic Frontier Foundation. (2014). *NECESSARY & PROPORTIONATE: International Principles on the Application of Human Rights Law to Communications Surveillance*. Retrieved from http://www.ohchr.org/Documents/Issues/Privacy/ElectronicFrontierFoundation.pdf

European Union. (2016). Regulation 2016/679 of the European Parliament and the Council of the European Union. *Official Journal of the European Communities, 2014*(April), 1–88.

Everstine, L., Everstine, D. S., Heymann, G. M., True, R. H., Frey, D. H., Johnson, H. G., & Seiden, R. H. (1980). Privacy and confidentiality in psychotherapy. *The American Psychologist*, *35*(9), 828–840. doi:10.1037/0003-066X.35.9.828

Farnan, J. M., Sulmasy, L. S., Worster, B. K., Chaudhry, H. J., Rhyne, J. A., & Arora, V. M. (2013). Online medical professionalism: Patient and public relationships: Policy Statement From the American College of Physicians and the Federation of State Medical Boards. *Annals of Internal Medicine*, *158*(8), 620. doi:10.7326/0003-4819-158-8-201304160-00100

Fernandez-Luque, L., Elahi, N., Grajales, F. J., & Iii, F. J. G. (2009). An analysis of personal medical information disclosed in youtube videos created by patients with multiple sclerosis. In Studies in Health Technology and Informatics (pp. 292–296). doi:10.3233/978-1-60750-044-5-292

Fink, J. (2011, Nov. 19). Five nurses fired for Facebook postings. Scrubs.

Fisher, J., & Clayton, M. (2012). Who gives a Tweet: Assessing patients' interest in the use of social media for health care. *Worldviews on Evidence-Based Nursing*, *9*(2), 100–108. doi:10.1111/j.1741-6787.2012.00243.x

Folkman, S. (2000). Privacy and Confidentiality. In B. D. Sales, & S. Folkman (Eds.), *Ethics in research with human participants* (1st ed., p. 215). American Psychological Association.

General Medical Council. (2018). Confidentiality - GMC good medical practice. Retrieved from https://www.gmc-uk.org/ethical-guidance/ethical-guidance-for-doctors/confidentiality

George, D. R., Rovniak, L. S., & Kraschnewski, J. L. (2013). Dangers and opportunities for social media in medicine. *Clinical Obstetrics and Gynecology*, *56*(3), 453–462. doi:10.1097/GRF.0b013e318297dc38

Goodman, K. W., Miller, R. A., & Informatics, H. (2006). Ethics and health informatics : Users, standards, and outcomes. In E. H. Shortliffe, & J. J. Cimino (Eds.), *Biomedical Informatics Computer Applications in Health Care and Biomedicine* (3rd ed., pp. 379–402). New York, NY: Springer. doi:10.1007/0-387-36278-9_10

Gruessner, V. (n.d.). Why mobile security risks are healthcare's biggest liability. Retrieved from https://mhealthintelligence.com/news/why-mobile-security-risks-are-healthcares-biggest-liability

Hall, M., Hanna, L.-A., & Huey, G. (2013). Use and views on social networking sites of pharmacy students in the United Kingdom. *American Journal of Pharmaceutical Education*, *77*(1), 9. doi:10.5688/ajpe7719

Hamm, M. P., Chisholm, A., Shulhan, J., Milne, A., Scott, S. D., Given, L. M., & Hartling, L. (2000). Social media use among patients and caregivers: a scoping review. doi:10.1136/bmjopen-2013

Hasanain, R. A., Vallmuur, K., & Clark, M. (2015). Electronic medical record systems in Saudi Arabia: Knowledge and preferences of healthcare professionals. *Journal of Health Informatics in Developing Countries*, *9*(1), 23–31.

Health, M. (2013). Saudi Arabia Ministry of Health Achievements 2013.

Herz, M. (2009). Law lags behind: FOIA and affirmative disclosure of information. *Cardozo Public Law, Policy, and Ethics Journal*, *7*(3).

Heyboer, K. (2010, March 26). Medical students' cadaver photos gets scrutiny after images show up online. New Jersey Real-Time News.

Hodge, J. G. Jr, Gostin, L. O., & Jacobson, P. D. (1999). Legal issues concerning electronic health information: Privacy, quality, and liability. *Journal of the American Medical Association*, *182*(15), 1466–1471. doi:10.1001/jama.282.15.1466

Jabali, A. K., & Jarrar, M. (2018). Electronic health records functionalities in Saudi Arabia: Obstacles and major challenges. *Global Journal of Health Science*, *10*(4), 50. doi:10.5539/gjhs.v10n4p50

James, R. (1975). Why privacy is important. *Philosophy & Public Affairs*, *4*(4), 323–333.

Kamoun, F., & Nicho, M. (2014). Human and organizational factors of healthcare data breaches: The Swiss cheese model of data breach causation and prevention. [IJHISI]. *International Journal of Healthcare Information Systems and Informatics*, *9*(1), 42–60. doi:10.4018/ijhisi.2014010103

Kampmeijer, R., Pavlova, M., Tambor, M., Golinowska, S., & Groot, W. (2016). The use of e-health and m-health tools in health promotion and primary prevention among older adults: A systematic literature review. *BMC Health Services Research*, *16*(S5), 290. doi:10.118612913-016-1522-3

King, D., Karthikesalingam, A., Hughes, C., Montgomery, H., Raine, R., Rees, G., & Team, O. (2018). Letter in response to Google DeepMind and healthcare in an age of algorithms. *Health and Technology*, *8*(1–2), 11–13. doi:10.100712553-018-0228-4

Kuhn, T. (2011). Health Information Technology and Privacy- American College of Physicians A Position Paper July 2011.

Laja, S. (2011, Nov. 9). Trusts reveal staff abuse of social media | Healthcare Professionals Network | The Guardian. *The Guardian*.

Lewis, T. L., & Wyatt, J. C. (2014). mHealth and mobile medical Apps: A framework to assess risk and promote safer use. *Journal of Medical Internet Research*, *16*(9), e210. doi:10.2196/jmir.3133

Mail, D. (2011, Jan. 3). Four nursing students expelled from university after posting pictures of themselves posing with a human placenta on Facebook. *Daily Mail*.

Marnocha, S., Marnocha, M. R., & Pilliow, T. (2015). Unprofessional content posted online among nursing students. *Nurse Educator*, *40*(3), 119–123. doi:10.1097/NNE.0000000000000123

McKee, R. (2013). Ethical issues in using social media for health and health care research. *Health Policy (Amsterdam)*, *110*(2–3), 298–301. doi:10.1016/j.healthpol.2013.02.006

Meeker, M. (2015). 2015 Internet Trends. Retrieved from https://www.kleinerperkins.com/perspectives/2015-Internet-trends

Moh, S. (2017). National E- Health Strategy - MOH Initiatives 2030. Retrieved from https://www.moh.gov.sa/en/Ministry/nehs/Pages/vision2030.aspx

Moorhead, S. A., Hazlett, D. E., Harrison, L., Carroll, J. K., Irwin, A., & Hoving, C. (2013). A new dimension of health care: Systematic review of the uses, benefits, and limitations of social media for health communication. *Journal of Medical Internet Research*, *15*(4), e85. doi:10.2196/jmir.1933

Musiat, P., Goldstone, P., & Tarrier, N. (2014). Understanding the acceptability of e-mental health-attitudes and expectations towards computerised self-help treatments for mental health problems. *BMC Psychiatry*, *14*(1), 109. doi:10.1186/1471-244X-14-109

Nair, S. C., & Ibrahim, H. (2015). Assessing subject privacy and data confidentiality in an emerging region for clinical trials: United Arab Emirates. *Accountability in Research*, *22*(4), 205–220. doi:10.1080/08989621.2014.942452

Nelson, R., & Staggers, N. (2014). *Health Informatics : An Interprofessional Approach*. Elsevier Health Sciences.

Nyongesa, H., Munguti, C., Omondi, C., & Mokua, W. (2014). Harnessing the power of social media in optimizing health outcomes. *The Pan African Medical Journal*, *18*, 1–5. doi:10.11604/pamj.2014.18.290.4634

Parent, W. A. (1983). A new definition of privacy for the law. *Law and Philosophy*, *2*(3), 305–338. doi:10.1007/BF00144949

Pattinson, S. D. (2017). Medical Law and Ethics (5th ed.). London, UK: Sweet and Maxwell.

Powles, J., & Hodson, H. (2017). Google DeepMind and healthcare in an age of algorithms. *Health and Technology*, *7*(4), 351–367. doi:10.100712553-017-0179-1

Prasanna, P. M., Seagull, F. J., & Nagy, P. (2011). Online social networking: A primer for radiology. *Journal of Digital Imaging*, *24*(5), 908–912. doi:10.100710278-011-9371-4

Rauv, S. (2017, June 14). The impact of technology in healthcare. Retrieved from https://www.elcomcms.com/resources/blog/the-impact-of-technology-in-healthcare-trends-benefits-examples

Roupret, M., Morgan, T. M., Bostrom, P. J., Cooperberg, M. R., Kutikov, A., Linton, K. D., ... Catto, J. W. F. F. (2014). European Association of Urology (@Uroweb) recommendations on the appropriate use of social media. *European Urology*, *66*(4), 628–632. doi:10.1016/j.eururo.2014.06.046

Sade, R. M. (2010). Breaches of health information: Are electronic records different from paper records? *The Journal of Clinical Ethics*, *21*(1), 39–41.

The Saudi Commission for Health Specialties. (2014). *Code of Ethics for Healthcare Practitioners*. Saudi Commission for Health Specialties.

Thompson, L. A., Dawson, K., Ferdig, R., Black, E. W., Boyer, J., Coutts, J., & Paradise Black, N. (2008). The intersection of online social networking with medical professionalism. *Journal of General Internal Medicine*, *23*(7), 954–961. doi:10.100711606-008-0538-8

US Department of Health and Human Services. (2001, Sept. 5). Protecting the privacy of patients health information. Retrieved from https://aspe.hhs.gov/basic-report/protecting-privacy-patients-health-information

Ventola, C. L. (2014). Social media and health care professionals: Benefits, risks, and best practices. *P&T, 39*(7), 491.

von Muhlen, M., & Ohno-Machado, L. (2012). Reviewing social media use by clinicians. *Journal of the American Medical Informatics Association, 19*(5), 777–781. doi:10.1136/amiajnl-2012-000990

Wadhwa, V. (2014). Laws and ethics can't keep pace with technology. Retrieved from https://www.technologyreview.com/s/526401/laws-and-ethics-cant-keep-pace-with-technology/

Wallwiener, M., Wallwiener, C. W., Kansy, J. K., Seeger, H., & Rajab, T. K. (2009). Impact of electronic messaging on the patient-physician interaction. *Journal of Telemedicine and Telecare, 15*(5), 243–250. doi:10.1258/jtt.2009.090111

White, P., & Selwyn, N. (2013). Moving on-line? An analysis of patterns of adult Internet use in the UK. *Information Communication and Society, 16*(1), 1–27. doi:10.1080/1369118X.2011.611816

Winkelstein, P. (2013). Medicine 2.0: Ethical challenges of social media for the health profession. In C. George, D. Whitehouse, & P. Duquenoy (Eds.), *eHealth: Legal, Ethical and Governance Challenges* (pp. 227–243). Berlin, Germany: Springer Berlin Heidelberg; doi:10.1007/978-3-642-22474-4_10

KEY TERMS AND DEFINITIONS

Confidentiality: Literally, it is the state of keeping or being kept secret or private. In medical practice, confidentiality is the duty to keep and/or maintain (not to unlawfully disclose to third person) the patient's private information (secrets) revealed during a professional relationship.

Data Controller: A person, or an organization that determines the purpose and means of collecting and processing a person's personal data. For example, in the case of health information systems, the person responsible for deciding what data are collected, the purpose for its use, and the way and manner it may be processed.

eHealth: A novel technological concept that enables an electronic delivery of healthcare services online via the Internet.

Electronic Health Information System: An electronic system used by healthcare facilities to collect, store, manage and share a patient's electronic health or medical records for the purpose of patient care, research and quality management.

Electronic Health Records: An electronic form of the patient's paper-based medical or health record that can be instantaneously made securely and promptly available to authorized persons.

General Data Protection Regulation (GDPR): A legal framework that sets guidelines for the collection and processing of personal information from individuals who live in the European Union.

Health Information Technology (IT): Information technology applied to health and health care.

Individually Identifiable Health Information (IIHI): Information, including demographic data, that relates to: the individual's physical or mental health or condition (past, present or future), the provision of health care (including the payment therefor) to the individual that identifies (or for which there is a reasonable basis to believe it can be used to identify) the individual (See 45 C.F.R. § 160.103 HIPAA).

mHealth (mobile health): The use of mobile phones or other wireless (mobile) technology in healthcare, medical practice or public health.

Personal Data: Any information or different pieces of information that relates to a particular identified or identifiable living individual.

Privacy: The right of individuals, in the exercise of their autonomy, to control access to their private personal information by others.

Social Media: Websites and applications that enable users to create and share content or to participate in social networking.

This research was previously published in Impacts of Information Technology on Patient Care and Empowerment; pages 365-387, copyright year 2020 by Medical Information Science Reference (an imprint of IGI Global).

Chapter 38
Blockchain for Healthcare and Medical Systems

Sanaa Kaddoura
https://orcid.org/0000-0002-4384-4364
Zayed University, UAE

Rima Grati
Zayed University, UAE

ABSTRACT

Blockchain is one of the trendy technologies in the current era. All industries are merging blockchain with their production line to benefit from its features such as security and decentralized data. One of the main problems in the healthcare system is the lack of interoperability (i.e., data should be patient-centered and not institution-centered). Healthcare information systems, in the current state, cannot communicate. Each organization works within its boundaries and owns its data. To make this shift, many challenges should be solved such as data privacy, standards, scalability, and others. Blockchain can solve these problems by giving the patients control over their data; therefore, they can share it with any institution for a time period. It is expected that blockchain will improve healthcare data management. In this chapter, the authors study the opportunity of blockchain to leverage biomedical and healthcare applications and research. Blockchain also contributes to the medication manufacturing area.

INTRODUCTION

Various countries are experiencing a rapid increase in the number of patients at hospitals and medical centers, making it hard to handle and manage through the existing infrastructure by available doctors and staff according to Tanwar et al. (2020). In fact, the recent technological breakthroughs bring up major updates and enhancements for healthcare centers to better capture the different challenges imposed with this increase. Healthcare systems are currently being directed with such vision in many aspects. It is expected that in 2030, healthcare systems will integrate different technologies to allow monitoring the health situation of each patient and allow accurate measurement of information that may help save the

DOI: 10.4018/978-1-6684-6311-6.ch038

lives of patients and increase their well-being. Internet of Things (IoT) and wearable devices are key enablers for this vision, leading to a higher quality of care for patients. Being tailored for individual's use, doctors are able to monitor each patient through his/her own IoT and wearable device, and thus treating more patients efficiently and accurately without the need to regularly visit clinics and hospitals, except in case of emergency. Patients are thus able to constantly update their doctors with their continuous changes to increase welfare and life-expectancy. This also reduces medical costs and helps in better utilization of resources in available healthcare.

This transformation towards a technological based healthcare system is expected to generate a massive amount of data that is created, stored, and accessed daily. However, this data is subject to multiple challenges imposed due to the nature of communication over the Internet. In fact, data security and privacy in healthcare systems are considered a top concern to be addressed when discussing healthcare data corresponding to patients. In 2018, over 13 million healthcare records were breached (Moro Visconti, 2020). Due to the sensitivity of healthcare data, healthcare data centers may be an attractive place to attackers who aim at financially benefiting from this information through selling it to a third-party provider. This raises the demand for a system that reserves healthcare data of the patients from any fraud. Saha el al. (2020) developed a new scheme that increases security and patients' data privacy against attackers. This approach showed efficiency in terms of computation cost with respect to other relevant approaches. Further, limitations on the patient's ownership of his/her medical data is a main concern as the patient is in need of a system that allows him/her to control access to this data.

Blockchain technology is one of the novel efforts that are being explored to solve this problem, which can offer an important solution that solves multiple challenges imposed by healthcare systems and hence provide better experience for users (De Aguiar et al., 2020). Blockchain can be defined as a decentralized and distributed digital ledger that allows recording transactions in a chain of immutable blocks linked together by cryptographic hashes. In a blockchain system, transactions are stored over multiple network participants whereby there is no need for a central authority to manage the transactions being done. The procedure starts by the user requesting a certain transaction which can be of any type of data including financial, health, or even a message. The user then provides a signature with his private key for this transaction, enabling other entities to verify the authenticity of this transaction using the public key of this user. The transaction is then sent to the entire network of peer-to-peer participants. Blockchain miners, a community of people responsible for ensuring the security of moving data over blocks in blockchain, select a batch of the available transactions to form a block. Each miner tries to find the correct hash output for the given batch of encoded transactions within this block. Whenever a blockchain miner is able to add a block of transaction to the blockchain, this block is considered complete, locking the ability to alter it. This necessitates recomputing the whole block and the blocks added after it. The complexity of this process protects the transactions from fraud and attacks as it involves high computational power to try different combinations of strings until the output string matches the stipulated requirements, hence, providing a highly secure aspect. Further, being a decentralized technology is also a key advantage, it hinders the action of malicious users through replicating data over multiple nodes and eventually malicious users should alter data across all nodes which are a hard task. For this reason, blockchain has been considered as a key solution to transform the current healthcare systems into a patient-centered systems through which the patient has his/her healthcare data records properly secured and shared everywhere at any time (Chen et al, 2019). A patient would then use mobile applications to record his/her data and send it to healthcare providers within seconds through the private blockchain network. This will enable patients to control and restrict the access over their data to only the concerned medical practitioners.

Figure 1 depicts a summary of the overall procedure. Blockchain aims to organize the process of healthcare while solving key issues in secure and privacy.

Figure 1. A Summary of Blockchain based Healthcare Systems

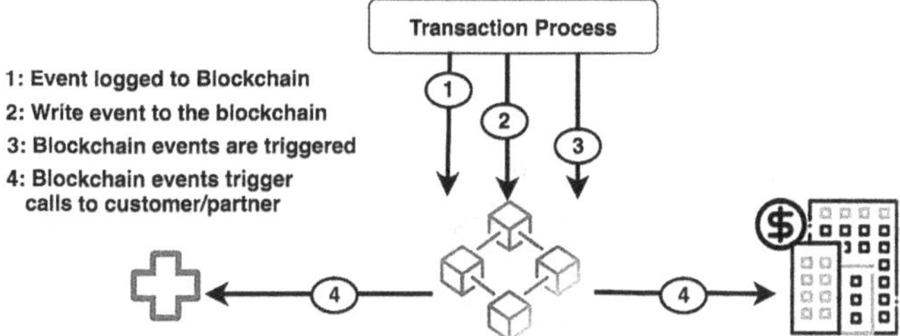

The main objective of this chapter is to gain a deeper understanding of blockchain technology and its potential improvements over healthcare systems. Section II discusses background information related to blockchain in terms of definition and types. It also presents the relation between blockchain with the healthcare systems and its limitations. Moreover, it describes how blockchain can support the current healthcare system. Section III discusses blockchain for medical health records privacy. Section IV presents ongoing research trends for blockchain in the healthcare system. In section V, the contributions of blockchain into the pharmaceutical and medications manufacturing is presented. Section VI shows how blockchain can help and contribute to biomedical and healthcare applications. Finally, section VII derives conclusions and Section VIII poses future research questions related to the contribution of blockchain in the healthcare domain.

BACKGROUND

In this section, some background information about blockchain technology in terms of its definition and types is discussed. In addition, the limitations of healthcare systems are presented to show how blockchain may help healthcare systems in tackling some of its challenges.

Blockchain: A Distributed Ledger Technology

According to Bashir (2018), blockchain is a peer-to-peer, distributed ledger technology (DLT) which is characterized with cryptographically secure, append-only, immutable and updateable-only mechanism done through consensus or agreement among peers. Blockchain uses a database which is consensually shared and synchronized between multiple independent computers available at different geographical areas. Each computer is known as a node or a peer, used to record certain transactions. While blockchain requires global consensus across all nodes to confirm a certain transaction, a DLT does not enforce global consensus because the latter allows achieving the consensus without having to validate the transaction' data across the entire blockchain.

Blockchain arranges data into blocks which can only be chained through appending them to each other without the ability to remove or modify any block. It allows transactions to have public entities that can check the authenticity of transactions. Any participant of the network is able to view the shared recordings across that network and can own a copy of it. Within seconds, the updates done on a certain ledger are directly apparent to all participants. A blockchain makes it possible for more than two entities to carry out transactions in a distributed environment with no need for a centralized trusted entity. This contributes to overcoming the single point of failure problem.

Blockchain Types

Due to the variety of objectives needed by each organization and entity at different scopes, blockchain has various types. This chapter focuses on three main types: Public blockchain, private blockchain and consortium blockchain (Sanka et al., 2021).

Public Blockchain

A public blockchain is a distributed and public ledger. It maintains the records of all the transactions by allowing anyone to join the blockchain network with read and write access permission. They are open to the public, and anyone can participate in the decision-making process as a node. Public blockchain allows any person to access information, submit transactions, and participate in the consensus procedure. Each entity that participates in contributing to the consensus procedure may or may not be rewarded for sharing its computational resources in the process of validating transactions and applying cryptographic hashes. All users of these permissionless ledgers maintain a copy of the ledger on their local nodes and use a distributed consensus mechanism to decide the eventual state of the ledger. Furthermore, the anonymity of the identity of each node is implemented to ensure a seamless protection. Key examples of public blockchain systems are Bitcoin, Ethereum, and Litecoin. Another popular example of public blockchain is cryptocurrency. Since anyone joins the network with read and write permission, all Bitcoin transactions are available to the public. You may see the sender' address, balance, and amount that has been transferred to the recipient' address. This brings up key advantages for public blockchains including:

- Open read and write: any person or entity can create transactions over the blockchain and anyone can access the transaction.
- Immutability: whenever the transaction is stored into blocks, it cannot be modified or deleted as there is no central entity that can control these actions.
- Security: the consensus mechanism or agreement ensures that all nodes in the network will approve on the same block that contains the created transactions.
- Scalability: The blockchain structure itself is replicated across the nodes. Thus, the network scalability is proportional to the miners who join or leave the network.

Private Blockchain

Private blockchain intersects with public blockchain through various similarities in terms of structure and mechanism. Both are the same in terms of technology, but with different roles. While public blockchain focus on transparency through providing access to everyone about each transaction, a private blockchain stipulates multiple rules to prevent misuse of information. A private blockchain is controlled by one organization which restricts access to this blockchain. This type of blockchain is mostly applied in database management and audit for certain organizations. Hence, this requires a trusted authority to work on the consensus. Private blockchain are considered permission-based blockchains allowing read and write access to be controlled by a certain entity or organization and access to blocks and transactions is usually restricted. The identity of users is needed to grant them access. This targets organizations that may not want all available users to access the details of each transaction. The owner of the private blockchain can then have a centralized access control on who can read or write to it. The owner needs to know the identity of involved users to define the permission rules about their type of access to data that can be committed to the ledger and what data can be retrieved from it.

The owner of a private blockchain should understand the responsibility of users so that the type of access should be granted for each user can be determined. In other words, users will be well known with their profiles shared with the owner of the private blockchain.

Private blockchain offers the following privileges:

- Permissioned access whereby a central entity controls access to the blockchain.
- Faster transactions: the lower number of miners available in a private blockchain makes a transaction faster to process.
- Scalability: the owner has the control over the number of miners added to the network on demand.

Examples on private blockchains include HydraChain and Quorum. Both of these blockchains have the option to run in a public mode if required, but they were developed with the purpose of providing a private blockchain.

Consortium Blockchain

Consortium blockchain, or semi-decentralized blockchain, is not granted to a single entity as a private blockchain; rather, it is granted to a group of approved individuals. It is a group of pre-defined nodes on the network. Therefore, it provides security inherited from public blockchains. Typically, consortium blockchains are associated with a group of collaborating organizations that aims to improve their businesses through leveraging blockchain technology. Nevertheless, this type of blockchain may allow certain participants to access or adopt a hybrid access method. It may allow everyone, or only participants, to access or adopt a hybrid access method. For instance, the root hash and its Application Program Interface (API) may be open to the public. Therefore, external entities can use this API to make a certain number of inquiries and obtain certain information related to blockchain status. Examples of consortium blockchains include: Hyperledger, and Corda.

Table 1 compares the three different types of blockchain in terms of participation, security, centralization, scalability, and efficiency (Sanka et al., 2021).

Limitations of Current Healthcare Systems

Most current healthcare systems maintain the records of patients on outdated systems, making the diagnosis a complex procedure and time-consuming for both doctors and patients. Thus, the implementation and maintenance of a patient-oriented healthcare system may incur high costs which the current healthcare system may not afford.

Table 1. Blockchain Types Comparison

Blockchain Type	Permission?	Security Level	Centralization
Public	Permission-less	High	Decentralized
Private	Permissioned	Fair	Centralized
Consortium	Permissioned	Good	Semi-centralized

Furthermore, current healthcare systems rely on centralized data storage as all records are stored in one central database (Khan & Hoque, 2016). This slows down the access to medical data and makes it prone to errors and lack of interoperability. Records that are available at various branches of the hospital can be lost and thus cannot be accessed by patients. Moreover, patients do not have a unified view of health data records that combines all their treatment history as well as healthcare centers may not have access to up-to-date patient's data if the records are located elsewhere. This makes data gathering and combining from multiple sources a very essential step before integrating any type of technology.

Systems impact patient care as doctors should be able to utilize available resources with an optimal vision to serve most patients while accommodating to the limitations of the systems which they operate on. This introduces clinical scenarios in which lab doctors cannot process patients' needs efficiently and thus increase the margin of error. This can be reflected in people's reaction towards healthcare and the high costs incurred by current health systems.

Blockchain Support for Current Healthcare Systems

Blockchain based healthcare systems have been in action worldwide. Blockchain has been enhancing the lives of patients and healthcare professionals. Further, the given blockchain implementations in healthcare domains are being enhanced to better use patients' data without compromising their privacy. Federated learning, homomorphic encryption and zero-knowledge proofs are examples on new components brought to existing blockchain technology. Popular use cases of blockchain in healthcare include the management of electronic medical records (EMRs), Drug/Pharmaceutical Supply Chain, Remote Patient Monitoring (RPM), Health Insurance Claims, Health Data Analytics (HDA), and clinical trials among others (Agbo et al., 2019). Blockchain can help healthcare systems in solving different challenges such as data privacy, redundancy decrease, transparency and trust, health data ownership and fewer errors due to decentralization. For this purpose, Albanese et al. (2020) developed an approach for trusted and decentralized management of dynamic consent in clinical trials based on blockchain technology.

Data Privacy

The property of immutability offered by blockchain technology helps in securing health stored on it, as the integrity of health data, once saved, cannot be modified or retrieved. Furthermore, the health data on the blockchain are encrypted and appended at a certain sequence that makes it harder to be attacked by malicious entities. Additionally, health data are saved on blockchain using cryptographic keys which help in protecting the identity of the patients. Yap et al. (2021) highlight privacy as a top priority due to the danger that may happen if the patient's data was breached. Any breach will affect the whole system, i.e. patients, stakeholders, and the miners who will lose their trust with it. The authors present the current state-of-the-art on blockchain-based medical healthcare system. Xia et al. (2017) proposed a lightweight blockchain-based framework with the aim of providing fast and secure transactions while preserving the autonomy of data over a cloud environment. The proposed framework controls access to the system, allowing only privileged users to have access to it. The system acts as a mediator between users and sensitive healthcare data.

Al Omar et al. (2019) proposed a blockchain-healthcare data management system to support accountability, anonymity and integrity. This is ensured by developing a protocol that encrypts data through different cryptographic mechanisms. The user will be able to log in through a secured channel to make any transaction. Guo et al. (2018) present an attribute-based signature (MA-ABS) scheme with multiple authorities with the aim of preserving the privacy of patients and maintaining the immutability of EHRs. The authors address collusion attacks through proposing a pseudorandom function seed is shared in every two authorities and preserved secretly. Moreover, in KeyGen, the private key of each authority is embedded into the private key of the patient. Given this strategy, the protocol resists N−1 corrupted authorities collusion attacks.

Redundancy Decrease

Blockchain ensures replicating transactions over multiple nodes, thus ensuring the availability of the health data stored on it. This contributes in building robust and resilient systems against data losses, data corruption and other data availability attacks (Abdu & Wang, 2021).

Transparency and Trust

Since blockchain ensures trust through allowing access to transactions by all minors, healthcare stakeholders may rely on it to develop their healthcare applications (Yaqoob et al., 2021).

Health Data Ownership

Using blockchain, patients will be able to control their data and its usage. Patients can monitor their health data which may be misused by other stakeholders and detect when such misuse occurs. Blockchain helps in achieving these requirements through cryptographic protocols and smart contracts (Ahmad et al., 2021).

Fewer Errors Due to Decentralization

According to Agbo et al. (2019), the decentralized nature of blockchain allows health practitioners and doctors to manage health data from different locations and by different entities, decreasing the errors that can be made on health systems and have controlled access over the same health records.

LITERATURE REVIEW FOR BLOCKCHAIN IN HEALTHCARE SYSTEMS

High research interests are being focused on enabling Blockchain in Healthcare systems. The first Subsection focuses on blockchain for patient-driven interoperability in healthcare (Bennet et al., 2017). The second subsection provides insights about the current emerging blockchain based solution for healthcare management systems.

Blockchain for Patient-Driven Interoperability

Blockchain technology aims at enabling peer-to-peer digital exchange of data and, hence, enabling patient-driven interoperability through allowing data to be in control of the patient (Gordon & Catalini, 2018). Health data thus can be available over multiple systems whenever the patient needs through sharing this data (Figure 2).

Figure 2. Blockchain for Patient-Driven Interoperability

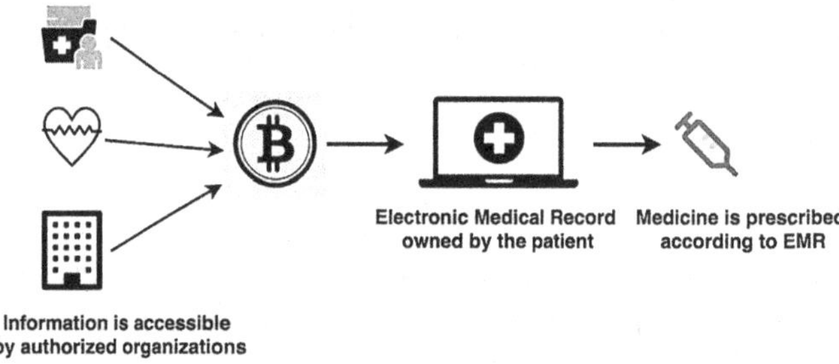

This gives patients a higher level of control over their data at any time. Several blockchain features can be exploited to enable a patient-centric interoperability including digital access rules, data aggregation, data liquidity, patient identity as well as data immutability (Chelladurai el al., 2021). Digital access rules associate all patients' data to his/her corresponding public key and thus allow the patient to assign access rules for each authority to the needed data. Data aggregation enables patients to connect to any institutional interface through his\her blockchain public key and thus reducing the overhead of sharing information again and again for every institution. Data liquidity allows patients to issue any time sensitive data that may help in better treating the patients. For example, a patient can announce on a public blockchain his/her allergy to some types of medicine. Whenever a certain emergency takes place, the healthcare staff will have this important information and will then be able to treat this patient with the type of medicine that fits him/her. Further, patients can use a multi-sig wallet or mobile device to manage their public key infrastructure along with their identity to protect their identity and ensure a trusted environment. As for data immutability, health data integrity is ensured through offering audit and append-only models by blockchain.

In fact, blockchain technology places patients at the center of the healthcare systems while enhancing system security, privacy and interoperability. For this purpose, many architecture and system designs based on blockchain for healthcare applications were proposed. Hussien et al. (2019) proposed a decentralized attribute-based signature (ABS) scheme for blockchain healthcare applications with the aim of preserving the privacy of the patient over the EHR system. The proposed approach relies on an on-chain and off-chain collaboration storage model which has been developed to ensure sharing data across multiple healthcare providers in a verifiable and immutable way. Guo et al. (2018) presents an ABS-based mechanism that allows different authorities in a decentralized EHR to maintain confidentiality of patient data.

Dagher et al. (2018) proposed a framework that uses smart contracts in an Ethereum blockchain to allow access control and artificial intelligence (AI) in EHR to provide a secure management system. Harshini et al. (2019) also consider using blockchain and AI in their work. The proposed framework is modelled with the constrained goal model (CGM) to meet multiple requirements. Uddin et al. (2018) proposed a tier that uses an end-to-end architecture with a patient center agent (PCA) using blockchain to maintain privacy of data streaming from body area sensors and stores them securely. The proposed architecture allows medical data to be shared in EHR among different health organizations while preserving privacy. Griggs et al. (2018) proposed a smart contract based IoT-RPM to manage medical devices and secure sensors. Ellouze et al. (2020) proposed a novel framework of modified blockchains for IoT devices that utilizes their distributed nature to provide secure management and analysis of big data in RPM. The additional security and privacy properties are based on big data analytics in RPM. Brogan et al. (2018) proposed an FHIR chain model to enhance the support for collaborative clinical decisions in the IoT-RPM through using blockchain technology and public-key cryptography. Pham et al. (2018) proposed a processing mechanism that aims to efficiently and moderately store medical device information in accordance with the health status of patients.

Zhou et al. (2018) proposed a MIStore blockchain to store medical insurance data with the aim of providing high-level credibility to individual patients. The data of patients' expenses are entered in the blockchain ledger to be protected by the tamper-resistant property. Wang et al. (2018) consider an artificial system based parallel healthcare system to improve accuracy and efficient. The proposed system utilizes consortium blockchain in order to link patients, healthcare providers and medical expert communities to comprehensive data sharing. Choudhury et al. (2019) proposed a permissioned blockchain based framework to reduce the administrative burden to ensure data integrity and privacy. Zhang et al. (2018) consider blockchain technology to develop a multi-level privacy preservation of location sharing of Telecare medicine information system (TMIS) in order to enable patients' access medical services or data from remote sites. Multi-level location sharing privacy is implemented on order-preserving symmetric encryption to be able to compare transactions to be applied directly to encrypted data without decryption.

Rathee et al. (2019) considers a healthcare blockchain based key management scheme for body sensor networks (BSNs). The proposed lightweight key management scheme for backup is based on BSNs and health blockchain. This development scheme contains storage keys entered into the ledger of blockchain to refuse statistical attacks. Agbo et al. (2019) design an architecture based on blockchain technology to meet the requirements of a healthcare system and address special needs to maintain storage of EHR with the goal of preserving patient's privacy. Zhang et al. (2017) provides a complete workflow for blockchain healthcare applications that considers multiple objectives including feasibility, capacity, user identification and authentication, interoperability and scalability. Zheng et al. (2018) proposes Byzantine fault tolerance (PBFT), a consensus mechanism for healthcare blockchain network, to simulate the response time for PBFT with continuous Markov chain (CTMC) model. Asamoah et al. (2017) proposed a blockchain system, MedShare, based on smart contracts, for data authenticity, auditing, and protection to support medical data exchange among multiple organizations with different backgrounds. The proposed model focused on determining data behavior and detecting cyberattacks of the entities offending behavior.

Rouhani et al. (2018) proposed a hyper ledger blockchain system with the aim of facilitating the efficient exchange of medical data between multiple entities, including patients and practitioners. Tian et al. (2019) introduce a blockchain based prototype system for medical data management through maintaining a shared key that can be rebuilt using legitimate parties prior to starting the diagnosis process. Rathore et al. (2020) develop a blockchain based system that focuses on implementing integrity of the patient's data, anonymity of patients, automation of workflows, audit and accountability. Drosatos et al. (2019) proposed a blockchain based data preservation system as a storage solution to ensure verifiability of data while maintaining user's privacy. McBee et al. (2020) proposed a framework for cross-domain image sharing in which blockchain functions are used to build a ledger of patient permissions for radiological studies.

Blockchain for Intelligent Healthcare Data Management

Sharing healthcare data managed by different organizations will help in deriving smart solutions that allow better understanding patterns and trends in public health and disease to ensure a higher quality of health care (Yaqoob et al., 2021). However, a big challenge for moving into intelligent healthcare solutions is the management of healthcare data available. In other words, gathering, storing, and analyzing personal healthcare while accounting for security and privacy concerns can be impossible without solutions that meet the patient and organizational concerns. Figure 3 shows how data should be synchronized from all types of organizations and entities such as hospitals, wearable device, and insurance companies among others to ensure a seamless workflow that achieves the highest levels of accuracy.

Figure 3. Intelligent Healthcare System combining multiple organizations close to the patient

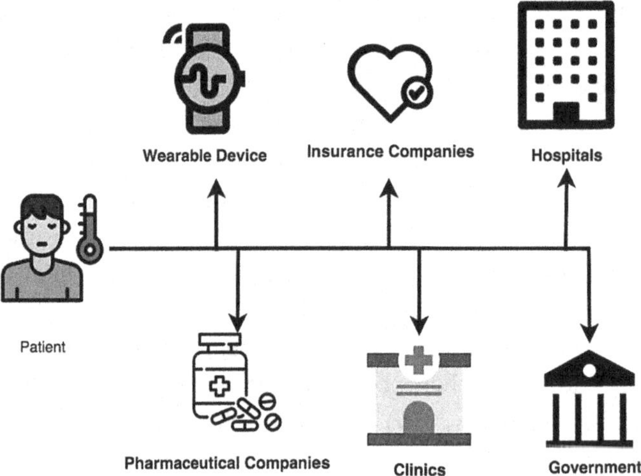

Introducing AI in various healthcare applications along with blockchain technologies introduces many powerful and resilient capabilities (Boulos et al., 2018). While deep learning and machine learning based solutions improve the advancement of automation, more data is needed to allow machine learning based solutions to predict patterns accurately (Mamoshina et al., 2018). Kuo et al. (2018) introduce Model-Chain, a framework that uses private blockchain to enable multiple institutions to contribute health data to train a machine-learning model to improve care while accounting for the privacy of health records. Wang et al. (2018) proposed a blockchain based parallel healthcare system (PHS), relying on artificial systems, and parallel execution (ACP) that captures multiple patients data attributes including patient's diagnosis, condition, and treatment process.

Table 2. Contributions and Limitations for EHR Systems illustrated in the literature

Research Paper	Main Technology	Contribution	Limitation
Al Omar el al. (2017)	PKE	Patients data protection and patients right of privacy	High computation due to the cryptography used
Zheng el al. (2018)	Cloud storage	Storage reduction for gigabytes dynamic data	Data is not protected due to a third party storage platform
Guo el al. (2018)	MA-ABS	Resistance to collusion attacks	High cost computation
Wang el al. (2018)	IPFS	Higher data throughput and lower prices in storage	Lack of strong privacy due to the cryptography used
Nguyen et al. (2019)	IPFS	High storage and data retrieval improvement	Leakage in personal information due to miners

Maddux et al. (2017) described the opportunity of blockchain technology in the healthcare big data sector. This study mentioned data portability and distribution can be more secure using this technology. Blockchain stores every detail of a data distribution so interparty (data owners and researchers) communication develops in context with information validation, time proof, and identity justification etc. Yue et al. (2016) proposed a blockchain based Healthcare Data Gateway (HGD) architecture to enable patients to own, control and share data easily and securely without violating privacy. The proposed purpose-centric model access model allows the patient to control his\her data. Azaria et al. (2016) proposed MedRec as a decentralized record management system to handle EMRs, using blockchain technology. The proposed model leverages the unique blockchain properties such as authentication, confidentiality, accountability and data sharing- crucial considerations when handling sensitive information. The proposed model integrates multiple data sources such as local data storage solutions and provider's data while accounting for supply big data research. Zhang et al. (2018) study applying blockchain technology to clinical data sharing in the context of technical requirements defined in the "Shared Nationwide Interoperability Roadmap'' from the Office of the National Coordinator for Health Information Technology (ONC). They analyze the ONC requirements and their implications for blockchain-based systems and then present FHIRChain, a blockchain-based architecture designed to meet ONC requirements. The authors demonstrate a FHIRChain-based decentralized app using digital health identities to authenticate participants in a case study of collaborative decision making for remote cancer care.

According to Gropper (2016) focus on the creation and use of blockchain-based identities to credential physicians and address the patient matching challenge facing health IT systems. The patients are supposed to have a digital wallet on their personal devices to create their blockchain-based IDs, which can then be used to communicate with the rest of the network. Instead of storing patient information, the proposed an approach that utilizes only blockchain-based ID and uses it to secure and manage access to patient data located in EHR systems.

BLOCKCHAIN FOR MEDICAL HEALTH RECORDS PRIVACY

One of the privacy concerns in healthcare systems is the electronic health records (EHR). Blockchain can be viewed as a solution for this problem. EHR is defined as a collection of electronic medical records for patients. EHR systems should ensure confidentiality, integrity, and availability (Shi et al., 2020). Many researches addressed the challenge of data privacy and security. Table 2 shows a comparison and analysis about some proposed systems in the literature. It is important to note that most of the mentioned systems use encryption techniques such as the cryptographic technology to increase both privacy and security. However, it is also well known that no security technique can ensure high level of privacy. Moreover, cryptography technology is also a computational cost. Table 2 shows some approaches in the literature that emphasized the problem of data security showing one contribution and one limitation for each.

It is important to note that all of these systems have guaranteed a certain level of security, privacy, anonymity, integration, and authentication requirements for a feasible and applicable system.

BLOCKCHAIN CONTRIBUTION TO PHARMACEUTICAL AND MEDICATIONS MANUFACTURING

The integration of blockchain into the healthcare system spans over a wide number of applications and offers significant contributions (Haq et al., 2018). However, blockchain enhancements to the pharmaceutical and medications manufacturing focus on digitizing the drug supply chain which brings up multiple benefits which are discussed in this subsection.

Drug Supply Chain Digitization

Multiple possibilities are being envisioned to implement blockchain in pharmaceutical and medication systems, but one core pharmaceutical landscape is particularly the drug supply chain. Drug supply chain is very important as counterfeit medicines are increasing the burden over governmental and medical systems in terms of the economic cost of this global illegitimate market and endangering human lives that are prone to death if counterfeit drugs did not have the same active pharmaceutical ingredients or dosage levels as the realistic drug. Further, counterfeit drugs trade is very difficult to trace, with the World Health Organization announcing $75bn in 2010 for fake drug sales globally despite major international investigations whose aim is to reduce this type of trade – several moves are being done to overcome this great challenge. Governments are imposing multiple requirements on their supply chains to hinder the effect of counterfeit drugs in terms of integrity. The US introduced the Drug Supply Chain Security Act in 2013, giving the industry until 2023 to institute full, unit-level track-and-trace systems for products as they move through the supply chain. The U.S. Food and Drug Administration issued a series of guidance and policy documents concerning DSCSA to allow tracing all pharmaceutical products in the U.S. All trading partners in the drug supply chain should share an authorized “transaction information” regarding the exchange of pharmaceutical products. The trading partners should directly produce transaction information and collect and produce all transaction information data produced by the drug manufacturer via an interoperable electronic system.

However, as the challenge remains, pharmaceutical companies and distributors are keen to find other options for improving supply chain security, integrity and traceability. Being an evolving technology with various benefits, blockchain technology has been considered one a significant option to be considered by companies in that conversation. Yet the question on how to implement blockchain into the drug supply chain is a main question due to the complexities and solutions that can be considered in this regard.

The digitization of supply chains is attracting high research interests from multiple angles. In fact, supply chains are being generalized into various disciplines such as businesses, healthcare, environmental and farming among others. Hence, the identification of supply chain examples using blockchain exemplifies the breadth of blockchain technology application. Blockchain technology can support data collection, storage, and management, supporting significant product and supply chain information bringing up openness, transparency and security for all supply chain agents. Blockchain is offering various contributions at the level of drug supply chain digitization. First, it allows product identification as each product will be associated with a product identifier which is required to validate the needed information on the side chain. Second, it allows product tracing through requiring manufacturers and distributors to provide information in a shared ledger that allows automatic verification for important information. Moreover, it allows product verification by creating public solutions that entails verification of different combinations of information related to this drug. This helps better capture any illegitimate drug and notify the corresponding agencies about it.

Tseng et al. (2018) considered Gcoin blockchain as a base of the data flow of drugs to create transparent drug transaction data. The suggested regulation model of the drug supply chain can be changed to include a surveillance net model, and every unit that is involved in the drug supply chain would be able to participate simultaneously to prevent counterfeit drugs and to protect public health. Jamil et al. (2019) proposed a novel drug supply chain management using Hyperledger Fabric based on blockchain technology to handle secure drug supply chain records. The proposed system conducts drug record transactions on a blockchain to create a smart healthcare ecosystem with a drug supply chain with a support to launching a time-limited access to electronic drug records and patient electronic health records. We also carried out a number of experiments in order to demonstrate the usability and efficiency of the designed platform. Schöner et al. (2017) proposed LifeCrypter, a blockchain-based prototype system for tracking medical products through the supply chain with the aim of showing the benefit of the blockchain technology and illustrating how this prototype can guard patient lives with a patient-empowering blockchain solution.

Increasing the Safety and Transparency of the Pharmaceutical Supply Chain

With an estimation of 10-30% of medicine being fake in some countries, counterfeit drugs present a major and serious problem in the field of pharmacology producing different side effects to human health. According to WHO (World Health Organization), 30% of the total medicine sold in Africa, Asia, and Latin America is counterfeit. Being distributed through different complex networks represents one of the key challenges for governments and agencies that hinder capturing the increasing number of counterfeit drugs. An authentic supply chain is thus needed to ensure the safety of the pharmaceutical supply chain which can be enabled through blockchain technology.

With the help of smart contracts, blockchain allows real-time transactions to occur automatically in a secure manner. Blockchain can help connect stakeholders, eliminating some unwanted middlemen that may sell a non-authorized version of the medicine. Blockchain technology also helps to operate across borders so that users can operate everywhere, reaching underserved markets and hence enhancing the health of the communities.

Blockchain can help in producing precision medicine as genomic data components can be stored and shared over it which offers a higher level of security and trust than other traditional methods. Data cannot be altered over blockchain and this is a very important need in the medical field. Further, blockchain enables privacy and thus ensures that people's identities are accessed only by authorized users (Frost and Sullivan, 2019). Nørfeldt et al. (2019) proposed the concept of crypto-pharmaceuticals through which pharmaceutical products are connected in a patient-specific blockchain of individual dosage units. The proposed approach is based on the concept where each produced dosage unit has a unique information-rich pattern. A proof-of-concept application that can be used for integration of a pharmaceutical product into an IoT-based health-care system is introduced and a technical platform for integrating machine learning-based diagnosis with the patient's own data and leading to a safe manufacturing chain of fully serialized personalized products is produced. Blockchain's advanced features make it capable of providing a basis for complete traceability of drugs, from manufacturer to end consumer, and the ability to identify exactly where the supply chain breaks down during an issue. Blockchain covers different holes in pharmaceutical supply chains globally through providing a strong foundation of trustworthiness and safe practices for all patients and the community. Blockchain integrates these values by generating informative, real-time responses to events potentially impacting patient health, such as life-saving prescription medication debuts and product recalls.

Managing pharmaceutical production is another issue that blockchain can solve allowing public access to data announcements and thus offering higher safety for patients. Up to one million people are killed each year worldwide as a result of these types of errors, and better tracking through the supply chain would have a significant effect on the current pharmaceutical supply chain model (Bhardwaj, 2018).

Creating a greater sense of trust through blockchain and ensuring patients are safer will go far in creating a better relationship between pharmaceutical companies and the public. Additionally, product recalls will allow medicines to be returned much more efficiently through the supply chain than ever before. Patients want accurate results, and they want to know what they have done is helpful for future research. Using blockchain can make up-to-the-minute data available at any moment for all stakeholders.

BLOCKCHAIN CONTRIBUTION IN BIODMEDICAL AND HEALTHCARE APPLICATIONS

Blockchain has been also contributing for biomedical and healthcare applications (Kuo et al., 2017). This subsection goes over key contributions and improvements in Clinical Trials, medical record management and Internet of Medical Things (IoMT).

Improvements in Clinical Trials

Clinical trials play a key role in healthcare systems. However, clinical trials are coupled with different challenges including missing data, data dredging and endpoint switching hindering the full utilization of findings in this domain. Several efforts are being focused on clinical trials. Nugent et al. (2016) extend the idea of proving the existence of documents describing pre-specified endpoints over blockchain using smart contracts that resides at a specific address in a blockchain, and show that blockchain smart contracts provide a novel technological solution to the data manipulation problem, by acting as trusted administrators and providing an immutable record of trial history. Benchoufi et al. (2017) to implement a process allowing for collection of patients' informed consent, storing and tracking the consent in a secure, unfalsifiable and publicly verifiable way, and enabling the sharing of this information in real time. They design a proof-of-concept protocol consisting of a time-stamping sequence of steps using blockchain and then archive the consent through cryptographic validation in a transparent way. The proposed procedure ensures that the document cannot be corrupted on a dedicated public website.

Angeletti et al. (2017) present a secure way to control the flow of personal data for the case of recruitment of participants for clinical trials while ensuring the privacy of data of participating patients and providing useful and authentic data to the Clinical Research Institute. They provide a proof-of-concept implementation and study its performance based on a real-world evaluation. Wong et al. (2019) proposed a blockchain-based system to ensure immutability, traceability and trustworthiness of data collected in the clinical trial process. The authors use raw data from a real completed clinical trial, simulate the trial onto a proof of concept web portal service, and test its resilience to data tampering. Shae and Tsai (2017) proposed blockchain platform architecture for clinical trial and precision medicine and provide insights about the requirements needed to launch this platform. The objective of the proposed approach is to ensure data integrity and sharing which are two main challenges faced by clinical trials. Choudhury et al. (2017) proposed a novel data management framework based on permission blockchain technology using smart contracts with the aim of reducing the management burden, time, and enhancing data integrity and privacy in multi-site Clinical trials. They demonstrate how smart contracts and private channels can enable confidential data communication, protocol enforcement, and an automated audit trail and then evaluate the effectiveness of their in comparison with other approaches.

Improved Medical Record Management

The lack of interoperability in medical records systems prevents the realization of its benefits. The evolving concerns with respect to the security of medical data breaches, and the debates concerning data ownership, requires high research and development of efficient methods to administer medical records. With the increase of data generated by wearable devices, medical systems are expected to face a main challenge that corresponds to managing this increasing number of health data. Blockchain for medical record management will come to enable data integrity and transparency, automate data collection and other routine processes, and eventually improve data management. In addition to that, blockchain might also indirectly help solve another problem of medical record management system: access control granted by administrator. System administrators will control access of patient's data allowing authorized users only to view, edit or delete their information. Adopting blockchain will enforce data interoperability for easier patient identification (and many other purposes). Furthermore, updates in the medical record management are significantly changing in comparison with previous years and blockchain technology is the main driver of this change.The concept of Blockchain-based medical record management deployed by multiple companies (Moss et al., 2017). Estonia has secured more than one million citizens' records in a ledger in collaboration with Guardtime. According to Bau (2017), the system has proven that interoperability can be achieved and allowed easier tracking for health epidemics. Harshini et al. (2019) proposed a patient-driven model of record maintenance using Blockchain technology where smart contracts are incorporated to help in data exchange. He also considers using blockchain and AI in their work. The proposed framework is modelled with the constrained goal model (CGM) to meet multiple requirements. Vazirani et al. (2020) focus on showing how Electronic Medical Records can be managed by Blockchain, and how the introduction of this novel technology can create an interoperable infrastructure to manage records that leads to improved healthcare outcomes, while maintaining patient data ownership.

Internet of Medical Things (IoMT)

The internet of medical things (IoMT) is developed with the aim of improving healthcare services through providing customized medical solutions to people all over the world. The IoMT spans on different types of smart devices,including on-body and in-home segments among others. On-body segments are composed of health wearables and medical and clinical-grade wearables. Most of these devices are not regulated by health authorities but may be endorsed by experts for specific health applications based on informal clinical validation and consumer studie. In-home segment includes personal emergency response systems (PERS), remote patient monitoring (RPM) and telehealth virtual visits. Instead of consulting doctors and going to the hospital each time, doctors can remotely observe the data of the patient and process it in real time. The capabilities of IoMT allow more accurate diagnoses, less mistakes and lower costs of care. Paired with smartphone applications, this technology enables patients to send their health information to doctors in order to better surveil diseases and track and prevent chronic illnesses (Perez & Domingo-Palaoag, 2021). Further, this data can be shared with research organizations for intelligent decision making. While it is expected that IoMT devices will be between 20 and 30 billion by 2020, medical devices are moving away from restricted healthcare networks into public and thus posing increased security risks.

As IoMT can be considered as an important source of data, security and privacy are considered major concerns as this increasing growth of sensitive data should not be tampered or altered by malicious entities. One of the core technologies that offer such privileges for IoMT is blockchain which allows a peer-to-peer secure communication. According to Pilkington (2017), IoMT can help in tracking critical elements such as vital signs, electrocardiogram (ECG) and skin temperature through which blockchain can maintain and ensure collaborative patient health information sharing, and high quality of data reporting. Multiple works have considered blockchain within the scope of IoMT with various objectives. Dilawar et al. (2019) proposed a blockchain based IoMT security architecture to ensure the security of data transmission between connected nodes. With IoMT technology integrated to the patient-driven systems, Khezr et al. (2019) suggests that IoMT devices can be stored on blocks or to cloud storage and AI will help in dynamically creating those blocks in a way help in protecting sensitive data as blockchain and decentralized AI systems can cooperate to ensure a high level of security. Further, only authorized owners can seek access for this data and have it safely.

CONCLUSION

Blockchain is an advanced and recommended technology, which can be integrated into healthcare systems. This technology has massive profits such as data security, cost-saving in data access and storage, high privacy, speed, and central authorities. Hence, this chapter addressed the different types of blockchain, its limitations in the healthcare systems. Moreover, this chapter highlighted the main research topics that characterize the common issues of ongoing health-related systems and how real-world blockchain applications can help enhancing this domain.

OPEN RESEARCH DIRECTIONS IN BLOCKCHAIN AND HEALTHCARE

The studied domains could provide a basis for research directions to identify what enhancements can be done for blockchain-based healthcare systems. As blockchain technology has started to be used in a wider range of health applications, the volume of data generated in this era of the IoMT is growing significantly, limiting the functionality of blockchain systems to transactions' throughput and storage capacity. Hence, it is important for the blockchain system to be able to understand the transaction before adding it to the block in order to better utilize the given resources. Hence, one research direction can be transforming blockchain based healthcare systems to self-learners through utilizing intelligent and machine learning based solutions that can help in reducing redundant data storage and computation at later stages.

REFERENCES

Abdu, N. A. A., & Wang, Z. (2021, March). Blockchain for Healthcare Sector-Analytical Review. *IOP Conference Series. Materials Science and Engineering*, *1110*(1), 012001.

Agbo, C. C., Mahmoud, Q. H., & Eklund, J. M. (2019, June). Blockchain technology in healthcare: a systematic review. In Healthcare (Vol. 7, No. 2, p. 56). Multidisciplinary Digital Publishing Institute.

Ahmad, R. W., Salah, K., Jayaraman, R., Yaqoob, I., Ellahham, S., & Omar, M. (2021). The role of blockchain technology in telehealth and telemedicine. *International Journal of Medical Informatics*, 104399.

Al Omar, A., Rahman, M. S., Basu, A., & Kiyomoto, S. (2017, December). Medibchain: A blockchain based privacy preserving platform for healthcare data. In *International conference on security, privacy and anonymity in computation, communication and storage* (pp. 534-543). Springer.

Albanese, G., Calbimonte, J. P., Schumacher, M., & Calvaresi, D. (2020). Dynamic consent management for clinical trials via private blockchain technology. *Journal of Ambient Intelligence and Humanized Computing*, 1–18.

Angeletti, F., Chatzigiannakis, I., & Vitaletti, A. (2017, September). The role of blockchain and IoT in recruiting participants for digital clinical trials. In *2017 25th International Conference on Software, Telecommunications and Computer Networks (SoftCOM)* (pp. 1-5). IEEE.

Asamoah, F., Kakourou, A., Dhami, S., Lau, S., Agache, I., Muraro, A., ... Sheikh, A. (2017). Allergen immunotherapy for allergic asthma: A systematic overview of systematic reviews. *Clinical and Translational Allergy*, *7*(1), 1–12.

Azaria, A., Ekblaw, A., Vieira, T., & Lippman, A. (2016, August). Medrec: Using blockchain for medical data access and permission management. In *2016 2nd International Conference on Open and Big Data (OBD)* (pp. 25-30). IEEE.

Bashir, I. (2018). *Mastering Blockchain: Distributed ledger technology, decentralization, and smart contracts explained*. Packt Publishing Ltd.

Bau, T. (2017). *Why Estonia is a good place for eHealth (and why you should attend eHealth Tallinn).* https://www.himss.eu/himss-blog/why-estonia-good-place-ehealth-and-why-you-should-attend-ehealth-tallinn

Benchoufi, M., Porcher, R., & Ravaud, P. (2017). Blockchain protocols in clinical trials: Transparency and traceability of consent. *F1000 Research*, 6.

Bennett, B. (2017). Blockchain HIE overview: A framework for healthcare interoperability. *Telehealth Med. Today*, *2*(3), 1–6.

Bhardwaj, G. (2018, April 25). Five use cases for blockchain in pharma. *Pharmaphorum.* https://pharmaphorum.com/views-and-analysis/five-use-cases-for-blockchain-in-pharma/

Boulos, M. N. K., Wilson, J. T., & Clauson, K. A. (2018). *Geospatial blockchain: promises, challenges, and scenarios in health and healthcare*. Academic Press.

Brogan, J., Baskaran, I., & Ramachandran, N. (2018). Authenticating health activity data using distributed ledger technologies. *Computational and Structural Biotechnology Journal, 16*, 257–266.

Chelladurai, U., & Pandian, S. (2021). A novel blockchain based electronic health record automation system for healthcare. *Journal of Ambient Intelligence and Humanized Computing*, 1–11.

Chen, H. S., Jarrell, J. T., Carpenter, K. A., Cohen, D. S., & Huang, X. (2019). Blockchain in healthcare: a patient-centered model. *Biomedical Journal of Scientific & Technical Research, 20*(3), 15017.

Choudhury, O., Fairoza, N., Sylla, I., & Das, A. (2019). *A blockchain framework for managing and monitoring data in multi-site clinical trials.* arXiv preprint arXiv:1902.03975.

Dagher, G. G., Mohler, J., Milojkovic, M., & Marella, P. B. (2018). Ancile: Privacy-preserving framework for access control and interoperability of electronic health records using blockchain technology. *Sustainable Cities and Society*, *39*, 283–297.

De Aguiar, E. J., Faiçal, B. S., Krishnamachari, B., & Ueyama, J. (2020). A survey of blockchain-based strategies for healthcare. *ACM Computing Surveys*, *53*(2), 1–27.

Dilawar, N., Rizwan, M., Ahmad, F., & Akram, S. (2019). Blockchain: Securing internet of medical things (IoMT). *Int. J. Adv. Comput. Sci. Appl*, *10*(1), 82–89.

Drosatos, G., & Kaldoudi, E. (2019). Blockchain applications in the biomedical domain: A scoping review. *Computational and Structural Biotechnology Journal*, *17*, 229–240.

Ellouze, F., Fersi, G., & Jmaiel, M. (2020, June). Blockchain for Internet of Medical Things: A Technical Review. In *International Conference on Smart Homes and Health Telematics* (pp. 259-267). Springer.

Frost & Sullivan. (2018). *The role of blockchain in precision medicine: Challenges, Opportunities, and Solutions*. https://ww2.frost.com/wp-content/uploads

Gordon, W. J., & Catalini, C. (2018). Blockchain technology for healthcare: Facilitating the transition to patient-driven interoperability. *Computational and Structural Biotechnology Journal*, *16*, 224–230.

Griggs, K. N., Ossipova, O., Kohlios, C. P., Baccarini, A. N., Howson, E. A., & Hayajneh, T. (2018). Healthcare blockchain system using smart contracts for secure automated remote patient monitoring. *Journal of Medical Systems*, *42*(7), 1–7.

Gropper, A. (2016, August). Powering the physician-patient relationship with HIE of one blockchain health IT. In *ONC/NIST use of Blockchain for healthcare and research workshop*. ONC/NIST.

Guo, R., Shi, H., Zhao, Q., & Zheng, D. (2018). Secure attribute-based signature scheme with multiple authorities for blockchain in electronic health records systems. *IEEE Access: Practical Innovations, Open Solutions*, *6*, 11676–11686.

Haq, I., & Esuka, O. M. (2018). Blockchain technology in pharmaceutical industry to prevent counterfeit drugs. *International Journal of Computers and Applications*, *180*(25), 8–12.

Harshini, V. M., Danai, S., Usha, H. R., & Kounte, M. R. (2019, April). Health record management through blockchain technology. In *2019 3rd International Conference on Trends in Electronics and Informatics (ICOEI)* (pp. 1411-1415). IEEE.

Hussien, H. M., Yasin, S. M., Udzir, S. N. I., Zaidan, A. A., & Zaidan, B. B. (2019). A systematic review for enabling of develop a blockchain technology in healthcare application: Taxonomy, substantially analysis, motivations, challenges, recommendations and future direction. *Journal of Medical Systems*, *43*(10), 1–35.

Jamil, F., Hang, L., Kim, K., & Kim, D. (2019). A novel medical blockchain model for drug supply chain integrity management in a smart hospital. *Electronics (Basel)*, *8*(5), 505.

Khan, S., & Hoque, A. (2016). Digital health data: A comprehensive review of privacy and security risks and some recommendations. *Computer Science Journal of Moldova*, *71*(2), 273–292.

Khezr, S., Moniruzzaman, M., Yassine, A., & Benlamri, R. (2019). Blockchain technology in healthcare: A comprehensive review and directions for future research. *Applied Sciences (Basel, Switzerland)*, *9*(9), 1736.

Kuo, T. T., Kim, H. E., & Ohno-Machado, L. (2017). Blockchain distributed ledger technologies for biomedical and health care applications. *Journal of the American Medical Informatics Association*, *24*(6), 1211–1220.

Kuo, T. T., & Ohno-Machado, L. (2018). *Modelchain: Decentralized privacy-preserving healthcare predictive modeling framework on private blockchain networks.* arXiv preprint arXiv:1802.01746.

Maddux, D. (2017). *Cybersecurity and Blockchain in Healthcare*. Acumen Physical Solutions.

Mamoshina, P., Ojomoko, L., Yanovich, Y., Ostrovski, A., Botezatu, A., Prikhodko, P., ... Zhavoronkov, A. (2018). Converging blockchain and next-generation artificial intelligence technologies to decentralize and accelerate biomedical research and healthcare. *Oncotarget*, *9*(5), 5665.

McBee, M. P., & Wilcox, C. (2020). Blockchain technology: Principles and applications in medical imaging. *Journal of Digital Imaging*, *33*(3), 726–734.

Moss, J., Smith, C. & Davies, J. (2017). *Blockchain shows promise in healthcare.* Medical Industry Week, BMI Country Industry Reports.

Nguyen, D. C., Pathirana, P. N., Ding, M., & Seneviratne, A. (2019). Blockchain for secure ehrs sharing of mobile cloud based e-health systems. *IEEE Access: Practical Innovations, Open Solutions*, *7*, 66792–66806.

Nørfeldt, L., Bøtker, J., Edinger, M., Genina, N., & Rantanen, J. (2019). Cryptopharmaceuticals: Increasing the safety of medication by a blockchain of pharmaceutical products. *Journal of Pharmaceutical Sciences*, *108*(9), 2838–2841.

Nugent, T., Upton, D., & Cimpoesu, M. (2016). Improving data transparency in clinical trials using blockchain smart contracts. *F1000 Research*, 5.

Perez, A. O., & Domingo-Palaoag, T. (2021, February). Blockchain-based Model for Health Information Exchange: A Case for Simulated Patient Referrals Using an Electronic Medical Record. *IOP Conference Series. Materials Science and Engineering*, *1077*(1), 012059.

Pham, H. L., Tran, T. H., & Nakashima, Y. (2018, December). A secure remote healthcare system for hospital using blockchain smart contract. In *2018 IEEE Globecom Workshops (GC Wkshps)* (pp. 1-6). IEEE.

Pilkington, M. (2017). Can blockchain improve healthcare management? *Consumer Medical Electronics and the IoMT.* https://ssrn.com/abstract=3025393

Rathee, G., Sharma, A., Saini, H., Kumar, R., & Iqbal, R. (2019). A hybrid framework for multimedia data processing in IoT-healthcare using blockchain technology. *Multimedia Tools and Applications*, 1–23.

Rathore, H., Mohamed, A., & Guizani, M. (2020). A survey of blockchain enabled cyber-physical systems. *Sensors (Basel)*, *20*(1), 282.

Rouhani, S., Butterworth, L., Simmons, A. D., Humphery, D. G., & Deters, R. (2018, July). MediChain TM: a secure decentralized medical data asset management system. In *2018 IEEE International Conference on Internet of Things (iThings)* and *IEEE Green Computing* and *Communications (GreenCom)* and *IEEE Cyber, Physical and Social Computing (CPSCom)* and *IEEE Smart Data (SmartData)* (pp. 1533-1538). IEEE.

Saha, S., Sutrala, A. K., Das, A. K., Kumar, N., & Rodrigues, J. J. (2020, June). On the design of blockchain-based access control protocol for IoT-enabled healthcare applications. In *ICC 2020-2020 IEEE International Conference on Communications (ICC)* (pp. 1-6). IEEE.

Sanka, A. I., Irfan, M., Huang, I., & Cheung, R. C. (2021). A survey of breakthrough in blockchain technology: Adoptions, applications, challenges and future research. *Computer Communications.*

Schöner, M. M., Kourouklis, D., Sandner, P., Gonzalez, E., & Förster, J. (2017). *Blockchain technology in the pharmaceutical industry.* Frankfurt School Blockchain Center.

Shae, Z., & Tsai, J. J. (2017, June). On the design of a blockchain platform for clinical trial and precision medicine. In *2017 IEEE 37th international conference on distributed computing systems (ICDCS)* (pp. 1972-1980). IEEE.

Shi, S., He, D., Li, L., Kumar, N., Khan, M. K., & Choo, K. R. (2020). Applications of blockchain in ensuring the security and privacy of electronic health record systems: A survey. *Computers & Security*, *97*, 101966.

Tanwar, S., Parekh, K., & Evans, R. (2020). Blockchain-based electronic healthcare record system for healthcare 4.0 applications. *Journal of Information Security and Applications*, *50*, 102407. doi:10.1016/j.jisa.2019.102407

Tian, H., He, J., & Ding, Y. (2019). Medical data management on blockchain with privacy. *Journal of Medical Systems*, *43*(2), 26.

Tseng, J. H., Liao, Y. C., Chong, B., & Liao, S. W. (2018). Governance on the drug supply chain via gcoin blockchain. *International Journal of Environmental Research and Public Health*, *15*(6), 1055.

Uddin, M. A., Stranieri, A., Gondal, I., & Balasubramanian, V. (2018). Continuous patient monitoring with a patient centric agent: A block architecture. *IEEE Access: Practical Innovations, Open Solutions*, *6*, 32700–32726.

Vazirani, A. A., O'Donoghue, O., Brindley, D., & Meinert, E. (2020). Blockchain vehicles for efficient medical record management. *NPJ Digital Medicine*, *3*(1), 1–5.

Visconti, R. M. (2020). Portfolio of Intangibles, Smart Infrastructural Investments, and Royalty Companies. In *The Valuation of Digital Intangibles* (pp. 449–490). Palgrave Macmillan. doi:10.1007/978-3-030-36918-7_18

Wang, S., Wang, J., Wang, X., Qiu, T., Yuan, Y., Ouyang, L., ... Wang, F. Y. (2018). Blockchain-powered parallel healthcare systems based on the ACP approach. *IEEE Transactions on Computational Social Systems*, *5*(4), 942–950.

Wong, D. R., Bhattacharya, S., & Butte, A. J. (2019). Prototype of running clinical trials in an untrustworthy environment using blockchain. *Nature Communications*, *10*(1), 1–8.

Xia, Q. I., Sifah, E. B., Smahi, A., Amofa, S., & Zhang, X. (2017). BBDS: Blockchain-based data sharing for electronic medical records in cloud environments. *Information*, *8*(2), 44.

Yap, K., Ali, E. E., & Chew, L. (2021). *The Need for Quality Assessment of mHealth Interventions*. Design and Quality Considerations for Developing Mobile Apps for Medication Management. doi:10.4018/978-1-7998-3832-6.ch004

Yaqoob, I., Salah, K., Jayaraman, R., & Al-Hammadi, Y. (2021). Blockchain for healthcare data management: Opportunities, challenges, and future recommendations. *Neural Computing & Applications*, 1–16.

Yue, X., Wang, H., Jin, D., Li, M., & Jiang, W. (2016). Healthcare data gateways: Found healthcare intelligence on blockchain with novel privacy risk control. *Journal of Medical Systems*, *40*(10), 1–8.

Zhang, P., Walker, M. A., White, J., Schmidt, D. C., & Lenz, G. (2017, October). Metrics for assessing blockchain-based healthcare decentralized apps. In *2017 IEEE 19th International Conference on e-Health Networking, Applications and Services (Healthcom)* (pp. 1-4). IEEE.

Zhang, P., White, J., Schmidt, D. C., Lenz, G., & Rosenbloom, S. T. (2018). FHIRChain: Applying blockchain to securely and scalably share clinical data. *Computational and Structural Biotechnology Journal, 16*, 267–278.

Zheng, K., Liu, Y., Dai, C., Duan, Y., & Huang, X. (2018, October). Model checking PBFT consensus mechanism in healthcare blockchain network. In *2018 9th International Conference on Information Technology in Medicine and Education (ITME)* (pp. 877-881). IEEE.

Zhou, L., Wang, L., & Sun, Y. (2018). MIStore: A blockchain-based medical insurance storage system. *Journal of Medical Systems, 42*(8), 1–17.

KEY TERMS AND DEFINITIONS

Biomedical: Biomedical sciences are a group of disciplines that use elements of natural science, structured science, or both to establish information, interventions, and technology for use in healthcare and public health.

Blockchain: Blockchain is a system used for storing data so that it is difficult or impossible to alter, hack, or trick it. A blockchain is a decentralized ledger of transactions distributed through the blockchain's entire network of computer systems.

Clinical Trials: Clinical trials are human clinical experiments that are used to assess the effectiveness of medical, surgical, or behavioral intervention.

Healthcare System: Is a group of individuals, organizations, and resources that provide health-care services to meet the needs of specific populations.

Internet of Medical Things: Clinical trials are human clinical experiments that are used to assess the effectiveness of medical, surgical, or behavioral intervention.

Interoperability: The ability of various information technology systems and software applications to communicate and share data correctly, efficiently, and reliably

Pharmaceutical Manufacturing: Pharmaceutical production refers to synthesizing pharmaceutical drugs on a large scale in the pharmaceutical industry. The production of drugs can be broken down into a sequence of unit operations.

This research was previously published in Enabling Blockchain Technology for Secure Networking and Communications; pages 249-270, copyright year 2021 by Information Science Reference (an imprint of IGI Global).

Chapter 39
Security and Privacy for Electronic Healthcare Records Using AI in Blockchain

Ramani Selvanambi
Vellore Institute of Technology, Vellore, India

Samarth Bhutani
Vellore Institute of Technology, Vellore, India

Komal Veauli
Vellore Institute of Technology, Vellore, India

ABSTRACT

In yesteryears, the healthcare data related to each patient was limited. It was stored and controlled by the hospital authorities and was seldom regulated. With the increase in awareness and technology, the amount of medical data per person has increased exponentially. All this data is essential for the correct diagnosis of the patient. The patients also want access to their data to seek medical advice from different doctors. This raises several challenges like security, privacy, data regulation, etc. As health-related data are privacy-sensitive, the increase in data stored increases the risk of data exposure. Data availability and privacy are essential in healthcare. The availability of correct information is critical for the treatment of the patient. Information not easily accessed by the patients also complicates seeking medical advice from different hospitals. However, if data is easily accessible to everyone, it makes privacy and security difficult. Blockchains to store and secure data will not only ensure data privacy but will also provide a common method of data regulation.

INTRODUCTION

Blockchain technology began from Bitcoin, giving stability against failure and cyber assaults. It utilizes technologies, for example, hash chains, digital signatures, and consensus mechanism to record bitcoin

DOI: 10.4018/978-1-6684-6311-6.ch039

exchanges by building dispersed, shared database in decentralized way. Such technologies make interactions secure by providing services like distributed storage, non-repudiation, time-based traceability for exchange substance, which frame a vital framework. Albeit, at first developed for bitcoin, it was later understood that this innovation could also profit in different fields. It was then implemented in different fields, for example, healthcare, fintech, computational law, review, notarization, et cetera by outlining different keen contracts in view of blockchain. This paper includes the way in which blockchain can be used to solve the above-mentioned problem and make electronic healthcare data storage easier and more secure.

As to Bitcoin, (Nakamoto, 2008) Pierro depicts each Bitcoin as a number, and that these numbers are the response for a condition. Each new response for the condition makes another bitcoin and the exhibition of creating an answer is assigned "mining." Once mined, a bitcoin can be traded or exchanged, and each trade produces a segment into the blockchain's activity log. This is regularly suggested as a "record." What makes the blockchain champion is that the record isn't guaranteed or taken care of by one association, yet rather every trade drove has a copy of the focal points of that trade set aside on every PC that was a piece of the trade.

(Ekblaw et. al., 2016) study shows that clinical data is not, at this point restricted to compose news, study of images, and testing blood sample. Genomic information and to facilitate gathered by wearable gadgets, for example, arm bands and watches installed with sensors, are progressively aggregated. Whenever abused viably, the accessibility of the new types of information may prompt superior healing choices and results and might likewise be analyzed by medical coverage organizations offer limits designed for "solid" conduct. Further advantages emerge in the domain of computerized reasoning. (Zhang et. al., 2017) at the point when given the suitable information, this can gather patterns from the information that are then used to produce populace level knowledge, thus accomplish populace wellbeing overall. These new information designs, nonetheless, will require cautious combination to permit suitable examination while keeping up quiet protection and protection from programmers.

(Crosby, 2016) identifies that despite the fact that digitization of wellbeing records has been set up in the overall specialist (GP) area for more than 30 years (though inadequate with regards to fundamental information sharing and trading capacities), optional consideration has not yet effectively accomplished this true norm. Appropriated record innovation, started and exemplified by the bitcoin blockchain, is growingly affecting IT conditions in which compliance to authoritative guidelines and support of open trust is progressively foremost, and it might be utilized in acknowledging digital objective. The point of this survey be to sum up the proof identifying with the execution of blockchain to oversee electronic wellbeing records (EHRs) in addition to examine whether this might get better productivity of record the executives.

(Danbar, 2012) said it is additionally significant that the target of this survey isn't simply to distinguish the utilization or the instances of blockchain based application in medical services, yet in addition to comprehend the constraints and difficulties for the blockchain-based medical care applications just as the momentum patterns regarding the specialized methodologies, strategies, and ideas utilized in building up these applications (defeating the restrictions) in a vision to unwind the territories for prospect examination. Also, this audit covers numerous new equipment that has not been distributed by the hour of the past surveys. As eminent before, the utilization of blockchain in medical care is a generally new worldview which is developing quickly.

The remainder of the paper discusses the vulnerabilities in present healthcare data storage system and how these can be overcome using blockchain. Each vulnerability is discussed along with how it affects the security and access of data in section 3. Centralized data has been a popular data storing approach in healthcare; however, alternative approaches have not been explored. Further, section 4 explains the basic working of blockchain. Terminologies such as "distributed ledger technology" and "SSL certificate" are explained. It also explains the decentralized storage and traceability of blockchain. Section 5, the final section, discusses the integration of blockchain in healthcare and how its use can transition the healthcare storage for the better.

Inspiration and Contribution

As opposed to the referenced documents, this proposed work depicts an orderly audit plus investigation of the cutting edge blockchain investigation in the ground of medical care. The aim of this work is likewise to show the expected use of block chain in medical care and to give you an idea about the difficulties and likely bearings of research in blockchain. This orderly audit just incorporates research that presents another arrangement, calculation, strategy, philosophy, or design in the ground of medical services. Audit form research, conversations of potential use as well as utilizations of blockchain, and various not significant distributions are avoided.

LITERATURE REVIEW

Few education institutes, organizations have linked blockchain technologies into teaching, and largely universities and organizations use it to help managers learn and learn the summative assessment of outcomes. This technology is able to calculate the entire transcription. In official learning environment, these include learning content and results, as well as academic performance and academic statements. In these areas, in the leisure learning environment, data on research engagement, competence, web-based learning, and additional single premiums are included. This information can be securely placed and arranged in a blockchain in a fitting manner.

Decentralization points to procedures for the identification, storage, support and dissemination of information on blockchains, which depend on the framework of the dissemination. In this arrangement, the faith flanked by the communicating hubs is achieved through science and technology to a certain extent than the gathering of associations.

Traceability includes that every exchanges on the blockchain are planned in sequential requests, while squares identify two consecutive squares by cryptographic hashing. In this way, each exchange can be identified by looking at the square data connected by the hash key. Blockchain technology is permanent for two reasons. From one point of view, all exchanges are placed in a square where one hash key joins the past square and a hash key indicates the square behind. Chaos of any exchange produces various hashes and is therefore recognized by the various centres that run similar approval calculations. Then, the blockchain is a shareable open record, placed on many hubs, and all records are constantly being adjusted. Effective changes require changes to more than 51% of system records.

(Mettler M, 2016) Blockchain technology and encryption funds cannot distinguish any blockchain organization with digital currency attributes. The essence of blockchain technology is peer-to-peer exchange, which does not include outsiders, which means that all exchanges do not require the cooperation of outsiders. The dissemination of advanced funds that rely on blockchain technology has been resolved. In the Bitcoin the age of advanced cash is achieved through the use of explicit mining calculations and is limited by pre-characterized formulations. Therefore, problems such as swelling or falling do not occur. In the Blockchain version 2.0 and version 3.0 applications, a mix of different exercises, like management exercises, teaching exercises, plus money-related exercises, can make these non-currency practice cash assets.

VULNERABILITIES IN HEALTH CARE DATA STORAGE

Current Infrastructure

Currently, there are a number of different health data frameworks that store individual patient information in a large health data warehouse. These data systems are ordered in a variety of ways. In order to solve the problem of connecting a unique health information storage system, various standards have emerged. In the current agreement, to hand is no extensively recognized agreement, the issue of information trading is again a real problem.

Centralized Data Storage

A centralized framework can provide the information you need in a fairly smooth way, with a focus on centralization itself. Excessive authorization in the hands of the central government has led to a complex licensing system that includes the possibility of data breaches and information disclosure.

Multiple Devices

Medical institutions are equipped with a variety of gadgets. As healthcare workers use their gadgets for expert purposes, it becomes more and more complex. Customers, IT increases the risk of security, which is now diverse and difficult to explain.

Embedded Devices

Even if the problem is solved, the connection is prone to problems. The same seamless connection enables tracking and logging to easily open healthcare IT networks to various forms of cyber threats, including viruses.

Patient data availability

Information is one of the most significant resources in the creation of medical care frameworks. Getting to this advantage makes a great deal of issues. Members inspired by this information are basically patients, care suppliers and outsiders who can utilize this information for various interests. Locale ought to give clear rules with regards to which outsiders, under what conditions and for what reason. Currently, the regulations are unclear and inconsistent, so if the healthcare system even contains any solutions, it usually contains inconsistent solutions.

Interoperability

Wellbeing information is dynamic and broad, and consistent trade of wellbeing information across wellbeing data frameworks would be invaluable. As it would not be reasonable regarding speed, stockpiling limit, or supportability to repeat all wellbeing records on each PC in the blockchain organize, rather activist blockchain as a strategy in the direction of oversee right of entry control (savvy indenture the board) by efficiently putting away a list of all clients' wellbeing accounts and connected metadata. Every occasion information is put to the EHR by a specialist (portable application), a metadata pointer to this be further added to the blockchain, whilst the information are put away safely resting on cloud. A complete file of a specific patient's accounts is put away in a solitary area alongside related metadata, paying little heed to the whereabouts of the clinical information. The blockchain, with this made sure about file of records, at that point guides approved people to the cloud-based information, along these lines permitting the prompt trade of data between endorsed experts, while likewise keeping an unchanging record of those pursuers.

(Ivan D, 2016) described the method that blockchain relies upon open source programming moreover has potential focal points, as prosperity trust can use the open application programming border to fuse data, give them ideal induction to correct information in a setup which can be used by them. Trying interoperability is moreover a key part of the Health Information Technology for Economic and Clinical Health Act, inferred 2011; American clinical consideration providers have been known cash related spurring powers to display critical usage of EHRs.

Health

Quick admittance to a far reaching group of patient information permit specialists to get patients devoid of the necessitate hang tight for the appearance of past outcomes. The accessibility of brief as well as more continuous information would permit doctors to make specific treatment plans based on results and treatment adequacy. Day by day wellbeing information would likewise draw in a patient added in their medical services, and get better quiet consistence a notable test in the domain. The capacity of customized medication, consequently, is better with this interoperability, as a solitary passageway for every one constant wellbeing information is made for every patient. Information accumulated from handheld sensors and portable applications would add data on the dangers and advantages of medicines, in addition to persistent announced result process.

Reliability

The unchanging nature of a blockchain that comes as of connecting the hash of resulting squares conveys by means of characteristic trustworthiness because squares can't be revised devoid of the coordinated effort of a larger part of hubs. This is critical to keeping up a genuine documentation of patient supplier communications just as information starting from gadgets, the two of which could impact clinical choices as well as those including protection. A framework that permits patients to maintain ownership of their clinical pictures, alongside a permanent chain of guardianship. Impermanent tokens are able to be made by blockchain clients and voted for onto those, for example, medical concern suppliers, life insurance provider agencies, giving brief access to patients.

The voucher is free of the information, contain just approval orders, and is checked and approved previous to the necessary information are sent. Respectability may likewise be kept up by the utilization of outside evaluators, who may confirm framework exactness continuously and reflectively. Expected approaches to improve the respectability are to utilize daze marks, which fortify assurance from altering just as affirming the sender's and watcher's characters, or to utilize marks from different specialists.

Security

(Guo, 2018) explained touchy information must be remained careful from spies and interlopers. Penetrates negatively affect the open view of the medical services field and take steps to obstruct future exploration through more tough administrative limitations. The WannaCry assault of May 2017 contaminated a large number of PCs around the world. One prior assault in US States focused on electronic health records specifically, requesting a huge number of dollars in recover. A blockchain is safer than heritage techniques, which give patients with qualifications. It accomplishes these belongings by the utilization of open key cryptography. This includes creating an open and private key for every client utilizing a single direction encryption work, known as a hash. It's absolutely impossible for anybody yet the beneficiary to observe data conveyed over the blockchain, as it is made sure about by their secret key.

WORKING OF BLOCKCHAIN

The blockchain is essentially a decentralized, digitized, open record that includes all the cryptocurrency exchanges and uses known to distributed ledger technology. (Underwood, 2016) mentioned the use of a centralized architecture and simple login is an important part of a regular system. There is not much money available for investment security, and all of these efforts can be made if employees and customers can use it to modify or destroy it. Blockchain offers powerful opportunities and solves a single point at a certain time. With the help of blocking, the security system used in the organization can provide users with useful devices and distributed public key information structures. This security system provides a specific SSL certificate for each device. The production of the certificate was carried out on the blockade, which made it impossible for the manufacturer to use the fake certificate.

Decentralized Storage

Blockchains prevent users from placing their computers on their computers in their network. Still, they can be sure that this product will not collide. In the real world, if someone who is not the owner of a component (such as a component) tries to block the component, the entire system excludes a block that can prevent it from being distinguished from other components. If this type of block is located by the system, it simply excludes the block from the block and identifies it as valid.

Traceability

Every task performed on a private or public block is done in a time and digitally signed manner. This way you can complete each task in a public place and then find the corresponding features on the block. This situation relies on non-repudiation: some people have not proved that their signal is the authenticity of the document. This blocking feature increases the reliability of the system and encrypts the user with each check.

BLOCKCHAIN IN HEALTHCARE

The constantly updated distributed database brings much reward to healthcare industry. The reward is more than ever exciting as multiple parties want to access the same data. For example, medical treatment in areas of aged care or chronic disease is a predetermined field of application in which blockchain technology can create added value. (Broderson et. al., 2016) the number of media disruptions involved in the treatment of patients involved in various mediators, media changes, numerous clinical health facts and incompatible IT interfaces may result in prolonged with supply wide correlations Certification and information flow for medicinal stakeholders.

(Yue et. al., 2016) the implementation of blockchain in healthcare will work similarly to how a bitcoin transaction takes place. The patient and the doctor will be the two parties involved in the transaction and all the medical data of the patient will be stored in the form of chains with hash functions for extraction of data. This will enable the patient or the doctor to extract data whenever necessary. Blockchain will also provide data security as the medical information is only accessible by the parties involved and does not require authorization by a third party. Since it is decentralized, it also prevents access of data by any third party. All the information is traceable and is time-stamped for ease of availability of healthcare information.

A US company is effectively engaged with this region and, accordingly, delivered the Gem Health network dependent on the Ethereum technology. This mutual organization foundation; diverse medical services specialists can get to similar records. These likewise allow the making of another polish of Blockchain based applications in medical care that would open squandered assets and healing issues. (Peterson et. al., 2016) Consequently, the Gem wellness network speaks to medical services environmental factors that consolidate the two organizations, people and specialists and which, simultaneously, upgrade understanding focused on care while tending to operational execution issues. This organization is a case of a Blockchain approach that offers all pertinent clinical partners straightforward and clear admittance to bleeding edge treatment data. Additionally, the Swiss computerized wellbeing, fire up, adopts a drastically new strategy with regards to the treatment of information exchanges and the sharing of individual wellbeing information. This start company offers its clients a stage on which they can store and deal with their wellbeing data in a safe situation.

(Banerjee et. al., 2018), the Blockchain library model sponsorships the ability to create and change essentially all through the blockchain lifetime by including new individuals with varying legitimate connections. Its advancement is particularly useful for recording the steady and predictable improvement of trades. EHR structure, there is an upper bound on the quantity of records, which is the quantity of occupants it serves. People improvement is by and large more slow than the advancement of the quantity of monetary trades, for the model, in the Bitcoin technology. Chain structure in blockchain also maintains the ever-creating clinical files by keeping up a reliably creating associated summary of clinical records; in which each square contain a details of timestamp and an association with a past square.

(Mannaro et. al., 2018) an elective arrangement would be a Blockchain containing pointers to off-chain information; the metadata which are related with the pointers be able to incorporate data requisite for following interoperability. With this methodology, paper information, counting imaging test outcome, might be put away off-chain. With regards to the sharing of imaging test result, a couple of creators proposed putting away encoded wellbeing data legitimately on the Blockchain; in any case, putting away the scrambled imaging investigations of all patients would bring about a tremendous Block chain, that is excessively huge for a hub which is running on a cell phone or an advanced computer unit to extract, store up, approve.

(Kleinaki et. al., 2016) the size of the blockchain is difficult which is under dynamic investigation and it is demonstrated to be a restricting element in any event, for chains that store basic conditional information, considerably less the monstrous hinders that might be required to put away clinical studies. When blockchain keeps on developing, the versatility of the framework might be undermined in light of the fact that just clients who have enormous extra rooms and high computational force will have the option to participate in Blockchain as diggers or complete hubs. To defeat this subject, this technology commonly bolsters 3 kinds of hubs: Complete hubs, light hubs, and document hubs:

Complete Hubs: It is the measure of each exchange and stores each square in the Blockchain.

Light Hubs: It is possible to ensure trades instead of running a full framework centre. Customers should simply maintain a copy of the square headers of the best confirmation of work chain, which can be acquired by addressing framework centre points till they obtain the best lengthy chain. By taking care of the square header, a light centre can watch that a trade is not adjusted devoid of submitting colossal fragments of blockchain memory. Light centres can in like manner contact the data they want.

Document Hubs: It stores each exchange with square on the technology blockchain. Likewise, they store up exchange receipts and the whole position tree.

CONCLUSION

This paper has shown how the use of blockchain in the healthcare industry for the use of storing data can help solve the various problems. Although this technology has been around for a few years, it has still not been utilized to its full potential. Integrating blockchain with healthcare information storage will not only provide the much-needed security but will also enable patients to access their data without the presence of a middle man. This omission of a middle party prevents many errors and security faults which are otherwise common. Migrating the existing network to blockchain could initially be expensive. However, as shown above, the overall advantages of this outweigh the limitations by a large degree. This technology opens new doors to the working and management of the healthcare industry.

Today, some of the people own belongings but can't establish possession or rights, like intellectual property disputes. It might cause clashes with others. Some business information, for example, auxiliary outlines, corporate plans, perhaps taken. The innovation of blockchain can be utilized to secure these asset benefits by putting away information in a block chain network. Blockchain innovation shields instructors' encouraging plans from being usurped, along these lines improving the security of protected innovation insurance. Security implies that every center keeps the whole record, including all information aside from the genuine element. So as to secure protection, the client's particular distinguishing proof is totally demonstrated by the ID number. This implies blockchain innovation can ensure the protection of brokers as just they will have the private key.

REFERENCES

Banerjee, M., Lee, J., & Choo, K. K. R. (2018). A blockchain future for internet of things security: A position paper. *Digital Communications and Networks*, *4*(3), 149–160. doi:10.1016/j.dcan.2017.10.006

Brodersen, C., Kalis, B., Leong, C., Mitchell, E., Pupo, E., Truscott, A., & Accenture, L. (2016). *Blockchain: Securing a new health interoperability experience.* Accenture LLP.

Crosby, M., Pattanayak, P., Verma, S., & Kalyanaraman, V. (2016). Blockchain technology: Beyond bitcoin. *Applied Innovation*, *2*(6-10), 71.

Dankar, F. K., & El Emam, K. (2012, March). The application of differential privacy to health data. In *Proceedings of the 2012 Joint EDBT/ICDT Workshops* (pp. 158-166). 10.1145/2320765.2320816

Ekblaw, A., Azaria, A., Halamka, J. D., & Lippman, A. (2016). A Case Study for Blockchain in Healthcare:"MedRec" prototype for electronic health records and medical research data. Proceedings of IEEE open & big data conference, 13.

Fan, K., Ren, Y., Wang, Y., Li, H., & Yang, Y. (2017). Blockchain-based efficient privacy preserving and data sharing scheme of content-centric network in 5G. *IET Communications*, *12*(5), 527–532. doi:10.1049/iet-com.2017.0619

Gordon, W. J., & Catalini, C. (2018). Blockchain technology for healthcare: Facilitating the transition to patient-driven interoperability. *Computational and Structural Biotechnology Journal*, *16*, 224–230. doi:10.1016/j.csbj.2018.06.003 PMID:30069284

Guo, R., Shi, H., Zhao, Q., & Zheng, D. (2018). Secure attribute-based signature scheme with multiple authorities for blockchain in electronic health records systems. *IEEE Access: Practical Innovations, Open Solutions*, *6*, 11676–11686. doi:10.1109/ACCESS.2018.2801266

Ivan, D. (2016, August). Moving toward a blockchain-based method for the secure storage of patient records. In *ONC/NIST Use of Blockchain for Healthcare and Research Workshop. Gaithersburg, Maryland, United States: ONC/NIST* (pp. 1-11). Academic Press.

Kleinaki, A. S., Mytis-Gkometh, P., Drosatos, G., Efraimidis, P. S., & Kaldoudi, E. (2018). A blockchain-based notarization service for biomedical knowledge retrieval. *Computational and Structural Biotechnology Journal*, *16*, 288–297. doi:10.1016/j.csbj.2018.08.002 PMID:30181840

Kuo, T. T., Kim, H. E., & Ohno-Machado, L. (2017). Blockchain distributed ledger technologies for biomedical and health care applications. *Journal of the American Medical Informatics Association*, *24*(6), 1211–1220. doi:10.1093/jamia/ocx068 PMID:29016974

Lohr, K. N., & Donaldson, M. S. (Eds.). (1994). *Health data in the information age: use, disclosure, and privacy*. National Academies Press.

Mannaro, K., Baralla, G., Pinna, A., & Ibba, S. (2018). A blockchain approach applied to a teledermatology platform in the Sardinian region (Italy). *Information*, *9*(2), 44. doi:10.3390/info9020044 .

Mettler, M. (2016, September). Blockchain technology in healthcare: The revolution starts here. In *2016 IEEE 18th international conference on e-health networking, applications and services (Healthcom)* (pp. 1-3). IEEE.

Nakamoto, S. (2008). *Bitcoin: A peer-to-peer electronic cash system.* Retrieved from https://bitcoin.org/ bitcoin.pdf

Peterson, K., Deeduvanu, R., Kanjamala, P., & Boles, K. (2016, September). A blockchain-based approach to health information exchange networks. In *Proc. NIST Workshop Blockchain Healthcare* (*Vol. 1*, No. 1, pp. 1-10). Academic Press.

Pilkington, M. (2016). Blockchain technology: principles and applications. In *Research handbook on digital transformations*. Edward Elgar Publishing. doi:10.4337/9781784717766.00019

Wang, H., & Song, Y. (2018). Secure cloud-based EHR system using attribute-based cryptosystem and blockchain. *Journal of Medical Systems*, *42*(8), 152. doi:10.100710916-018-0994-6 PMID:29974270

Yue, X., Wang, H., Jin, D., Li, M., & Jiang, W. (2016). Healthcare data gateways: Found healthcare intelligence on blockchain with novel privacy risk control. *Journal of Medical Systems*, *40*(10), 218. doi:10.100710916-016-0574-6 PMID:27565509

Zhang, P., White, J., Schmidt, D. C., & Lenz, G. (2017). *Applying software patterns to address interoperability in blockchain-based healthcare apps.* arXiv preprint arXiv:1706.03700

Zyskind, G., & Nathan, O. (2015). Decentralizing privacy: Using blockchain to protect personal data. In 2015 IEEE Security and Privacy Workshops (pp. 180-184). IEEE.

This research was previously published in Applications of Artificial Intelligence for Smart Technology; pages 90-102, copyright year 2021 by Engineering Science Reference (an imprint of IGI Global).

Chapter 40
Geo-Location-Based File Security System for Healthcare Data

Govinda K.
VIT University, India

ABSTRACT

Nowadays, a person's medical information is just as important as their financial records as they may include not only names and addresses but also various sensitive data such as their employee details, bank account/credit card information, insurance details, etc. However, this fact is often overlooked when designing a file storage system for storing healthcare data. Storage systems are increasingly subject to attacks, so the security system is quickly becoming a mandatory feature of the data storage systems. For the purpose of security, we are dependent on various methods such as cryptographic techniques, two-step verification, and even biometric scanners. This chapter provides a mechanism to create a secure file storage system that provides two-layer security. The first layer is in the form of a password, through which the file is encrypted at the time of storage, and second is the locations at which the user wants the files to be accessed. Thus, this system would allow a user to access a file only at the locations specified by him/her. Therefore, the objective is to create a system that provides secure file storage based on geo-location information.

INTRODUCTION

The ways of the healthcare industry have changed significantly over the previous decade, as those who give health related administrations have started moving from paper-based procedures to electronic strategies. Today, it is not unusual to have a specialist enter an exam room with a portable workstation close by rather than use paper based charts. The medicinal services business produces enormous amount of information and those in the field perceive the advantages of consolidating more computerized procedures into their day to day operations such as cost investment funds, expanded effectiveness, and enhanced interchanges, to name a few.

DOI: 10.4018/978-1-6684-6311-6.ch040

The class of people who work towards obtaining people's sensitive information and misuse it have now become more interested in their healthcare records as it provides them not only with their personal details such as name, address etc., but also other valuable information such as employer details, bank accounts/credit card information. By taking a patient's personal information and medical data, they can illicitly get medical goods and services. The victims are then left to manage the specialists, hospitals, insurance agencies etc. to determine the resulting monetary aftermath. Now and again, the victim can even lose their insurance, bringing about unreasonable out-of-pocket instalments to have their insurance re-established. There is additionally the threat of the true patient's medical records being changed or inaccurate data being inserted as a consequence of abuse or carelessness, which may keep them from getting legitimate treatment.

However, this sensitive nature of healthcare information is often overlooked when designing a file storage system for storing healthcare data. Therefore there is a need to implement secure file storage systems for healthcare data. This security can be authorized by utilizing various cryptographic procedures. Along with the assistance of these procedures the imperative documents can be encrypted and the clients can be given their suitable cryptographic keys.

Two-factor authentication systems have usually joined something you know, for example, a secret key or passphrase, with a second component to expand verification quality: either something you have, (for example, an entrance card or token), or something you are, (for example, biometrics). A supplementary component has recently been added to this to improve validation abilities: "somewhere you are", also called geolocation. Using this feature in a multi-element verification system, we can limit remote access of documents to specific trusted areas.

Geolocation is a term used in information systems security circles to extrapolate the geographical location of a subject (a system or a person), based on available information. This location capability is commonly performed by isolating a host system's IP address from a packet header, identifying the owner of the IP address range associated with the target system, discovering the owner's mailing address, and drilling down further -- with the objective of pinpointing the physical location of the target IP address (*What is Geolocation and How Does it Apply to Network Detection?*).

The suggested file security system encrypts the files using Rijndael Algorithm (AES), In order for the file to be stored in a more secured manner, the system uses two more security mechanisms (*AES: The Advanced Encryption Standard*). First, each file has a password associated with it, without which the file cannot be accessed. This password is defined by the user and stored in the database after being hashed using SHA-512 algorithm. Secondly, at the time the user uploads the file, the system records the user's current location and defines a trusted area, such that the file is accessible only within it. Therefore, when the user tries to access the file the system again captures the user's location and checks whether it is in the confinement of the trusted area. To provide additional security the location for describing the trusted area is also encrypted using the Rijndael Algorithm (AES).

Various existing techniques used for cloud storage have been discussed.

Identity Based Authentication

In Cloud Computing, resources and services are distributed across numerous consumers. So there is a chance of various security risks. Therefore authentication of users as well as services is an important requirement for cloud security and trust. When SSL Authentication Protocol (SAP) was employed to cloud, it becomes very complex. As an alternative to SAP, proposed a new authentication protocol based on identity which is based on hierarchical model with corresponding signature and encryption schemes (Kahanwal, Dua & Singh, 2012).

Efficient Third Party Auditing

A novel and homogeneous structure is introduced to provide security to different cloud types. To achieve data storage security, BLS (Boneh–Lynn–Shacham) algorithm is used to signing the data blocks before outsourcing data into cloud. BLS (Boneh–Lynn–Shacham) algorithm is efficient and safer than the former algorithms.

Effective and Secure Storage Protocol

Current trend is users outsourcing data into service provider who have enough area for storage with lower storage cost. A secure and efficient storage protocol is proposed that guarantees the data storage confidentiality and integrity. This protocol is invented by using the construction of Elliptic curve cryptography and Sobol Sequence is used to confirm the data integrity arbitrarily. Cloud Server challenges a random set of blocks that generates probabilistic proof of integrity (Rajathi, & Saravanan, 2013).

PROPOSED APPROACH

User Login

1. Every user is assigned an ID and password at the time of registration.
2. This password is stored in the database after hashing using the hashing algorithm.
3. At the time of login, the users are prompted to enter their valid ID and password.
4. The entered password is hashed using the same algorithm and then matched with the password associated with the user in the database,
5. Once the user logs in, a session is established which allows the user to access the features of the system. i.e. unless one enters the valid credentials, one cannot access the system.

File Upload and Storage Procedure

1. Once the user enters the system, he gets the option to upload a file.
2. The user can browse the system and select a text file to upload.
3. If the users tries to upload a file other than a text file, an error message is displayed prompting the user to select a text file.
4. Every file is associated with a password which is defined by the user at the time of uploading.
5. This password is hashed and stored in the database along with the path of the associated file.
6. The user also specifies a radius which is used while accessing the file to define a trusted area.
7. At the time of uploading the file, the user is given an option to specify the locations where the file can be accessed. The user can provide multiple access locations.
8. These locations are specified by giving the name of the locations on the map shown on the screen.

9. The system then obtains the co-ordinates of these locations specified by the user which are then encrypted and stored in the database.

File Encryption Procedure

1. At the time of uploading, the text file is encrypted and stored at the server.

File Download Procedure

1. Once the user logs in to the system, the user gets an option to download an already uploaded file.
2. The system displays the list of files uploaded by the user.
3. When the user selects a file for download, the system accesses the user's current coordinates.
4. The system decrypts the co-ordinates associated with the file and checks whether the current co-ordinates fall within the trusted area of the file using the radius given by the user at the time of file upload.
5. If the current co-ordinates fall within the trusted area, then the user is prompted for the password associated with the file, else the user is denied access to the file.
6. Only when both the co-ordinates as well the password are validated the user is granted access to the file.

Hash Salt Algorithm

The basic hashing algorithm used is SHA-512.The message digest obtained from the algorithm is appended with the hash of a salt. The salt used is the user's login id for the user's login password and the id of the file for the file's password.

Overview of SHA-512 (Data Protection for the Healthcare)

SHA-512 is a variant of SHA-256 which operates on eight 64-bit words. The message to be hashed is first:

1. Padded with its length in such a way that the result is a multiple of 1024 bits long, and then;
2. Parsed into 1024-bit message blocks M(1) ; M(2), …..,M(N). The message blocks are processed one at a time: Beginning with a fixed initial hash value H(0), sequentially compute:

$$H(i) = H(i-1) + CM(i)\,(H(i-1));$$

where C is the SHA-512 compression function and + means word-wise mod 2^{64} addition. H(N) is the hash of M.

Encryption Algorithm

The algorithm used for encrypting the file and the coordinate values is the Rijndael Algorithm (AES). The key used in the algorithm is the message digest obtained after hashing the password entered by the user while accessing the file. The message digest is obtained using the ripemd128 algorithm.

Overview of AES (Kahanwal, Dua & Singh, 2012)

AES is a block cipher with a block length of 128 bits. AES allows for three different key lengths: 128, 192, or 256 bits. With regard to using a key length other than 128 bits, the main thing that changes in AES is how you generate the key schedule from the key. Encryption consists of 10 rounds of processing for 128-bit keys, 12 rounds for 192-bit keys, and 14 rounds for 256-bit keys. Except for the last round in each case, all other rounds are identical. Each round of processing includes one single-byte based substitution step, a row-wise permutation step, a column-wise mixing step, and the addition of the round key. The order in which these four steps are executed is different for encryption and decryption.

RESULTS

The basic UI design for the various functionalities mentioned above is given in Figures 1-8.

CONCLUSION

The proposed system ensures the security of the file stored on the server by using a two factor verification method one of which is the password which is used to encrypt as well as access the file and the other utilizes the concept of a trusted area therefore ensuring that the file cannot be accessed by anyone unless they are at the right place and have the right credentials. Such kind of authentication process can be used to improve the file storage systems in hospitals and other services which record a user's personal and healthcare information and who want to store sensitive data and allow access to it only at certain specific locations.

Figure 1. Client Login Page: user has to enter valid user name and password to open account (http://php.net/docs.php)

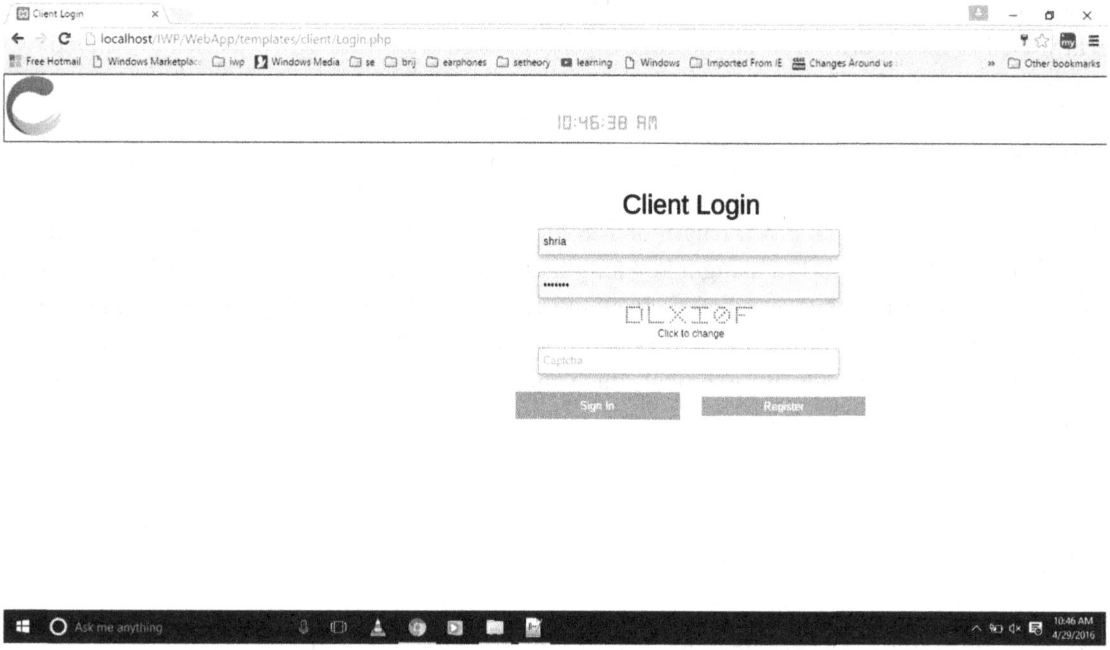

Figure 2. Home Page

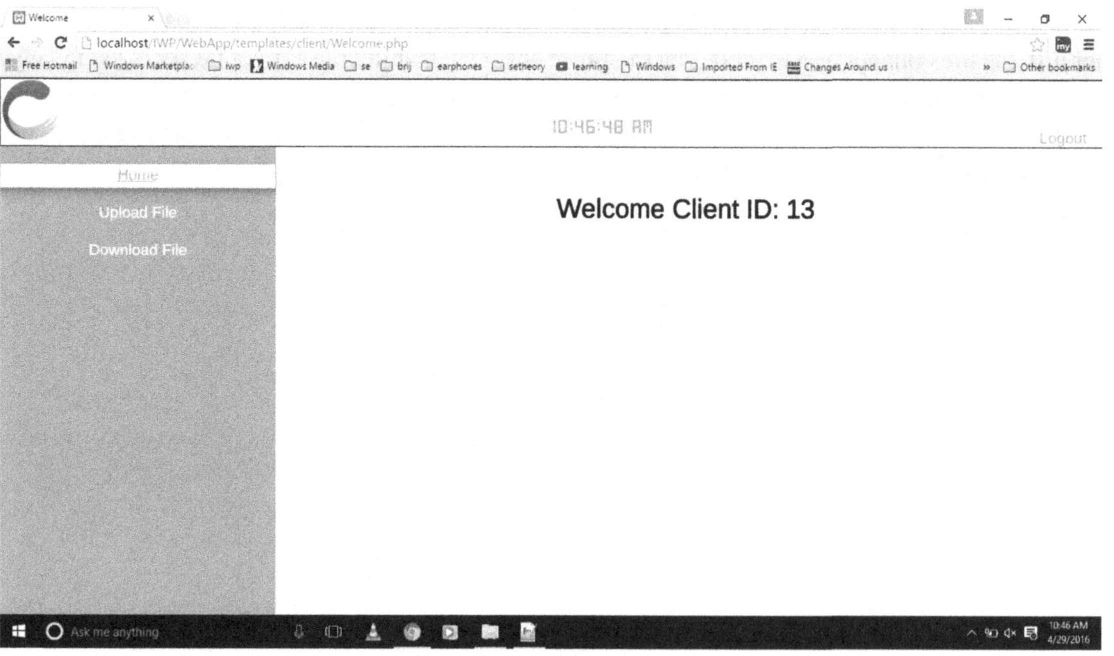

Figure 3. File Upload Page: after successful login use has to upload file

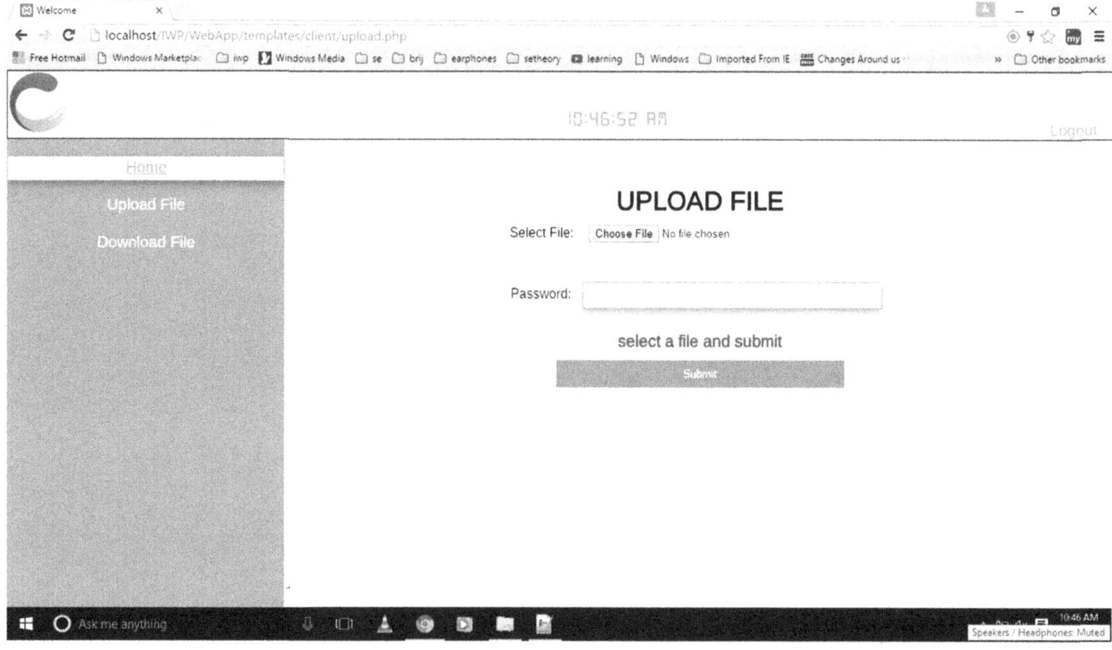

Figure 4. File Upload: No File Selected. (http://www.iwar.org.uk/comsec/resources/cipher/sha256-384-512.pdf)

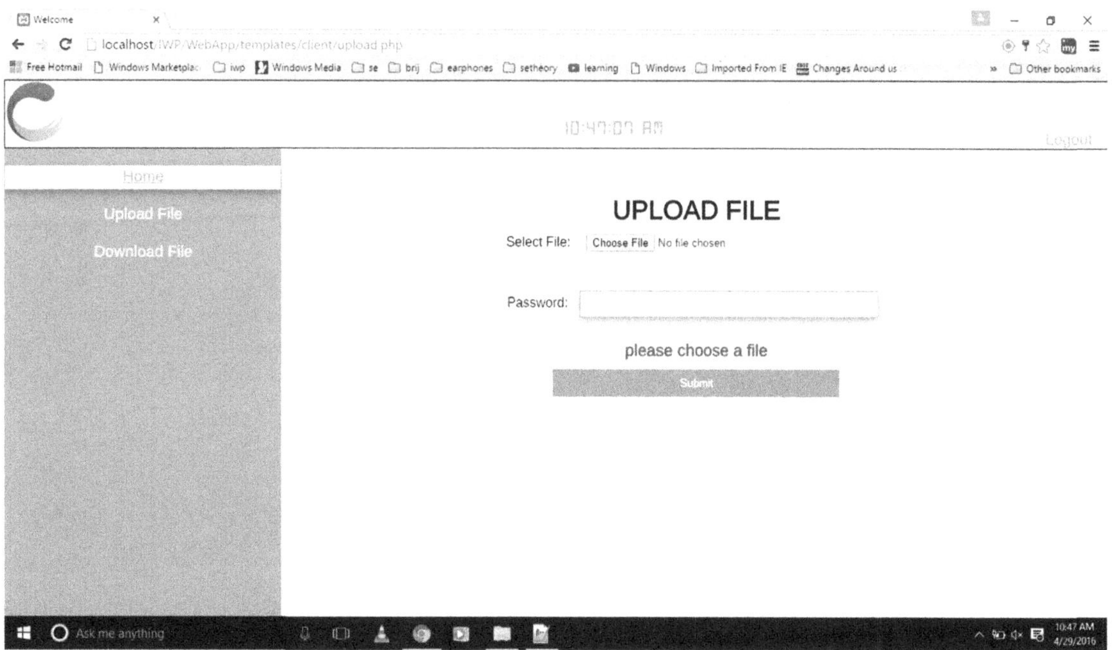

Figure 5. File Upload: No Password Specified

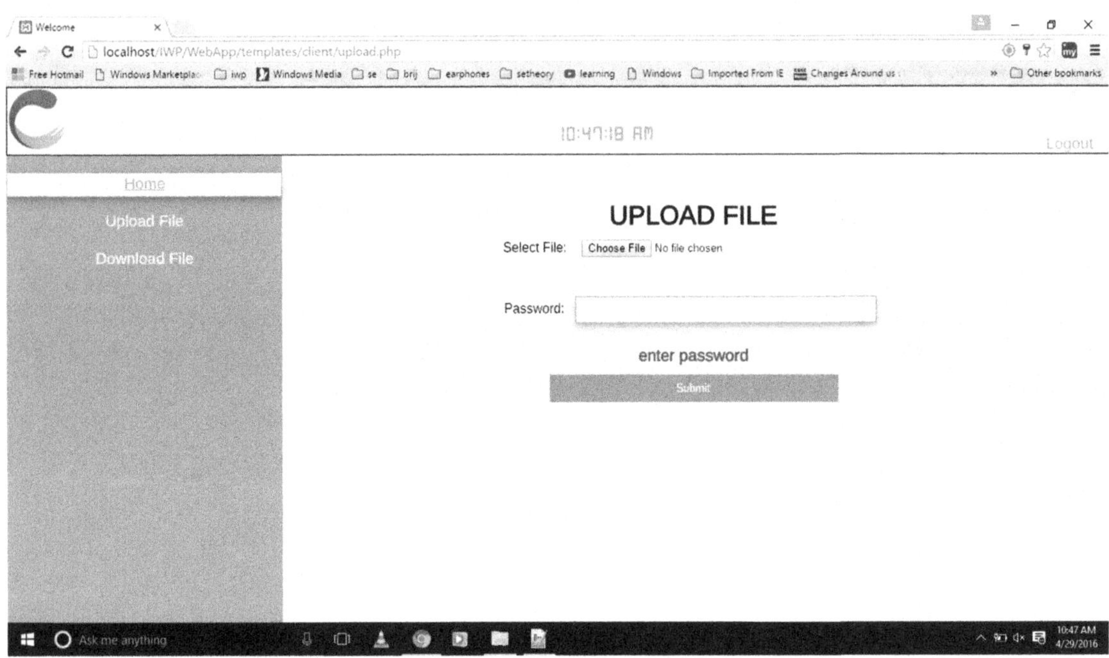

Figure 6. File Upload: Internet Connectivity Error. (http://www.iwar.org.uk/comsec/resources/cipher/sha256-384-512.pdf)

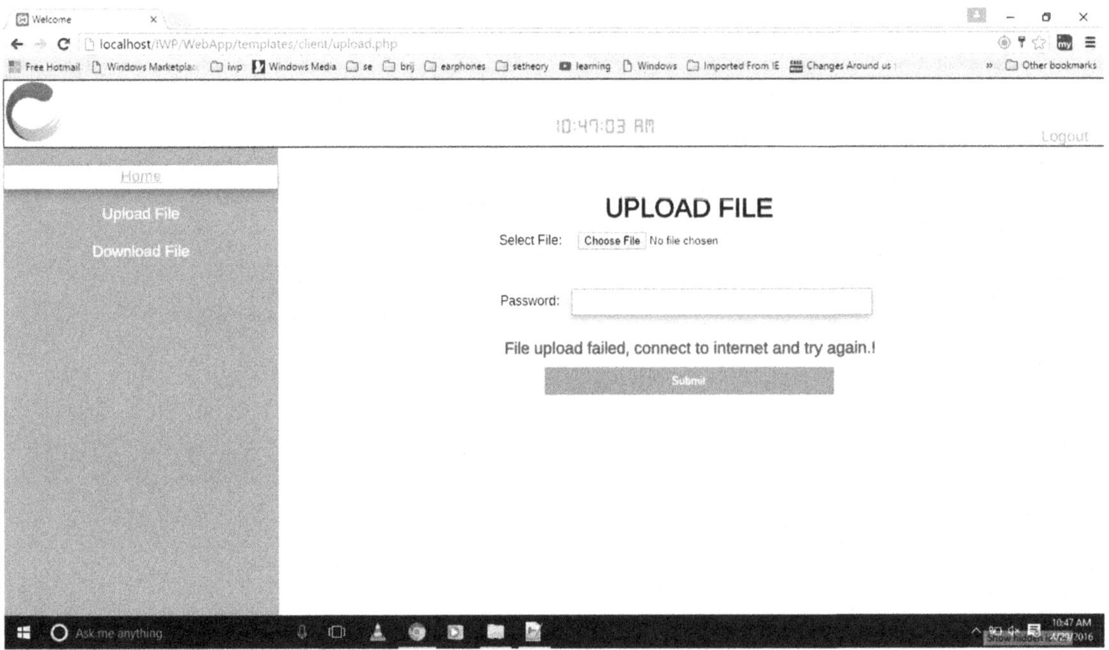

Figure 7. File Upload Successful Message

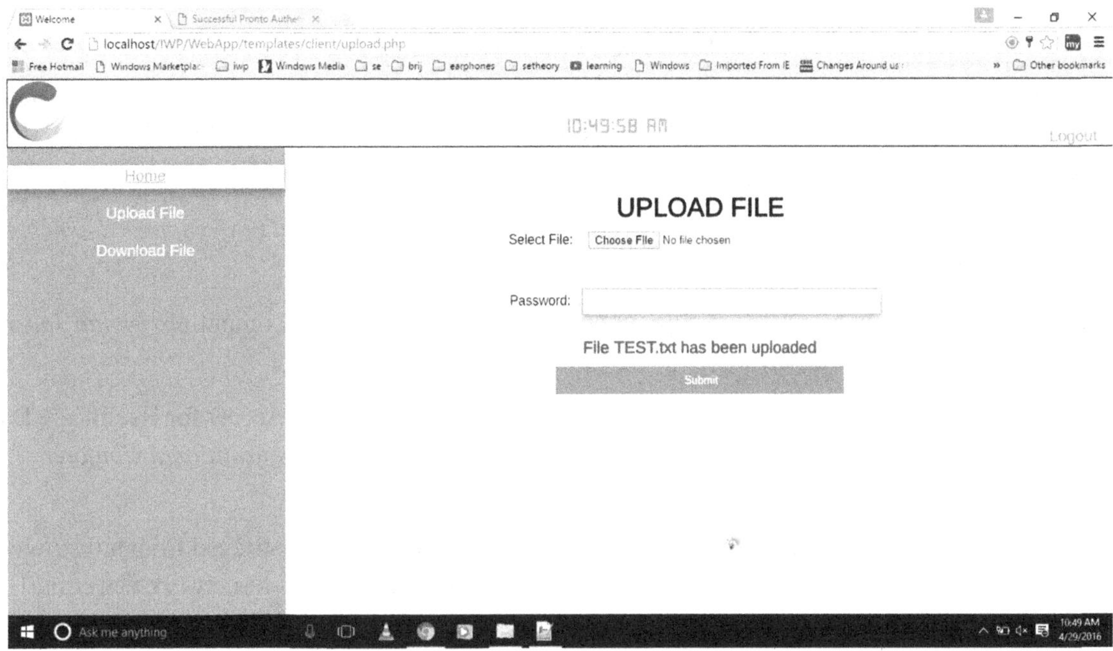

Figure 8. File Download: Uploaded File List

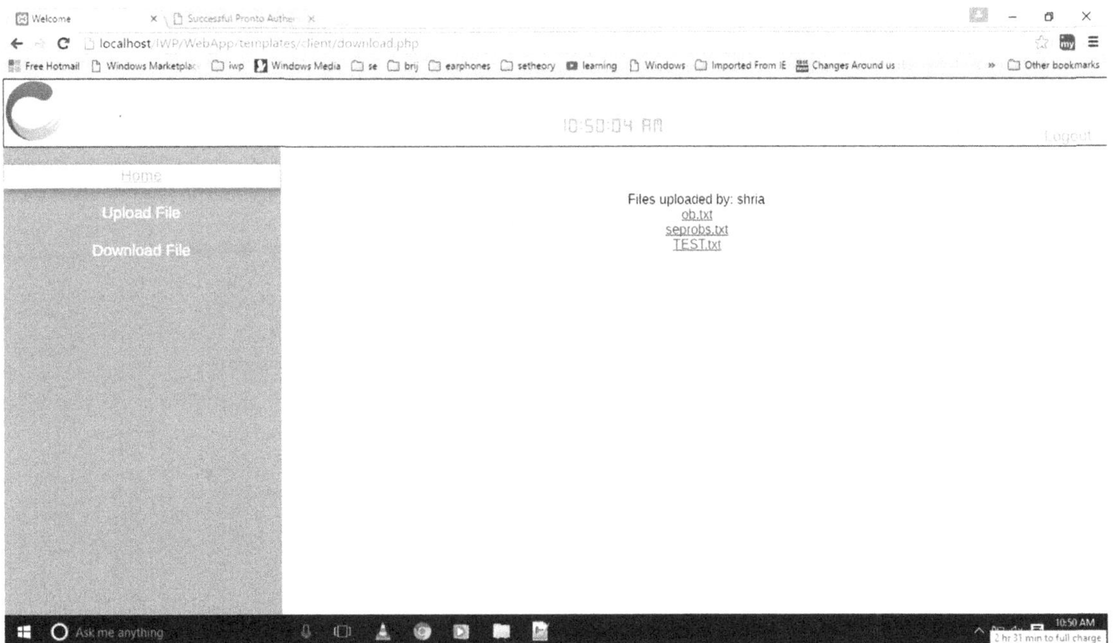

REFERENCES

AES. (n.d.). Retrieved from https://engineering.purdue.edu/kak/compsec /NewLectures/Lecture8.pdf

Data Protection for the Healthcare Industry. (n.d.). Retrieved from http://www.safenet-inc.com/uploadedF iles/About_SafeNet/Resource_Library/Resource_Items/White_PapersSFDC_Protected_EDP/SafeNet%20Data%20Protection%20Healthcare%20White%20Paper.pdf

Kahanwal, Dua, & Singh. (2012). Java File Security System. *Global Journal of Computer Science and Technology Network and Web Security, 12*(10).

Rajathi, A., & Saravanan, N. (2013). A Survey on Secure Storage in Cloud Computing. *Indian Journal of Science and Technology*, *6*(4).

Suhair, A. B., Golisano, T., Radziszowski, S. P., & Raj, R. K. (2012). Secure Access for Healthcare Data in the Cloud Using cipher text-Policy Attribute-Based Encryption. *Proc of International Conference on Data Engineering Workshop*.

What is Geolocation and How Does it Apply to Network Detection? (n.d.). Retrieved from https://www.sans.org/security-resources/idfaq/what-is-geolocation-and-how-does-it-apply-to-network-detection/1/28

This research was previously published in Contemporary Applications of Mobile Computing in Healthcare Settings; pages 125-135, copyright year 2018 by Medical Information Science Reference (an imprint of IGI Global).

Chapter 41
Electronic Health Record Security in Cloud:
Medical Data Protection Using Homomorphic Encryption Schemes

Desam Vamsi
VIT-AP, India

Pradeep Reddy
VIT-AP, India

ABSTRACT

Security is the primary issue nowadays because cybercrimes are increasing. The organizations can store and maintain their data on their own, but it is not cost effective, so for convenience they are choosing cloud. Due to its popularity, the healthcare organizations are storing their sensitive data to cloud-based storage systems, that is, electronic health records (EHR). One of the most feasible methods for maintaining privacy is homomorphism encryption (HE). HE can combine different services without losing security or displaying sensitive data. HE is nothing but computations performed on encrypted data. According to the type of operations and limited number of operations performed on encrypted data, it is categorized into three types: partially homomorphic encryption (PHE), somewhat homomorphic encryption (SWHE), fully homomorphic encryption (FHE). HE method is very suitable for the EHR, which requires data privacy and security.

INTRODUCTION

The "Internet of things" (IoT) is becoming an increasing subject of discussion in the latest technology advancements. It means the interconnection of physical devices, applications, sensors and objects that communicate and share information among them. The distinguishing feature of the IOT in the medical system is the patient's continuous monitoring of different parameters, and the history of such continuous surveillance also yields excellent results. In past times, despite 24 hours of monitoring, the doctor can-

DOI: 10.4018/978-1-6684-6311-6.ch041

not be notified about an emergency on time and also sharing of patient's real time data with specialists, family members, and friends was difficult. Currently, all the instruments in the hospital's ICU are fitted with medical sensors to avoid hurdles faced in the past. The technology that enhances such hurdles is available, but most of them are expensive and not accessible. IoT plays an important role in providing improved medical facilities to patients and also facilitates physicians & hospitals with better monitoring methods. A health surveillance system is composed of a wearable device which monitors patients' health continuously. This wearable unit comprises of various sensors like a sensor for temperature, heart rate, blood pressure etc. This device not only collects the data in bio-signals from sensors and transfers it to the hospital cloud server, which is used for further storage and processing accordingly. This information is accessible from anywhere on the IOT to physicians on the Cloud. Wireless and wearable sensors have become standard instruments for monitoring patients at risk for certain chronic diseases.

Researchers have found many applications using IOT technology over the time. For example, BSN (Body Sensor Network) is a network for particular purposes designed to connect with several medical sensors and implants inside and outside the human body autonomously (Vippalapalli & Ananthula, 2016). Using this, we can monitor human's physiological social information, to monitor hospital patients, to administer drugs at clinics, etc. The progress of bio instructors (Kale & Khandelwal, 2013) and telecommunications techniques make it easier for a home-based monitoring system to collect, display, record and communicate physiological information from a human body to any place. (Chakraborty, Gupta, & Ghosh, 2016) using a smartphone explains telemedicine system for a chronic wound (CW) monitoring. The primary purpose of this study is to design and create a Tele-wound technology network (TWTN) system to capture process and track issues associated with CW using a low-cost smartphone and improve general system efficiency. (Chakraborty, & Kumari, 2016) identified that iris recognition is one of the essential biometric technique to identify a person based on iris. In (Chakraborty, Gupta, & Ghosh, 2014), a low-cost integrated smartphone and an efficient quality-based metadata creation process for acquiring chronic wound image and provide a smooth interaction between doctor and patient.

This paper covers healthcare data aggregation approaches using IOT systems and its applications in medical field. The main focus of this chapter is to identify the methods that provide security storage systems to healthcare records using several cryptographic frameworks. The rest of the paper is covered as follows. Section 1 gives an idea of cloud computing importance and its characteristics, cloud service models, deployment models. Section 2 covers a quick review of cloud computing architecture and its components. Section 3 deals with security concerns of the cloud and controls methods to ensure data protection. Section 4 explains importance of cryptography and several encryption methods. HE schemes along with related work are covered in detail in this section. Section 5 ends the paper with a conclusion

APPROACHES OF DATA AGGREGATION IN SENSOR NETWORKS

The data aggregation is described as the method by which data from various sensors are aggregated to remove redundancy and provide the base station with complete information. Data aggregation usually includes the fusion of data at medium nodes from multiple sensors and the transfer of such aggregated data to the base station (sink). In this section, the data aggregation in Sensor Networks and the methodologies used are discussed. The data aggregation is performed in four ways, namely centralized, tree-based approach, cluster-based approach, and in-network aggregation.

1. **Centralized Approach**: In this strategy, each node transmits its sensed information to the primary node, generally the mote node (e.g., power, bandwidth, etc.). Central address routing along with multi-hop algorithms is used in every intermediate node by considering the cost. The primary node task is to add the data received from other nodes to the base station and to report that data. Traffic is the main issue in this data gathering methodology. In the paper (Fouchal, Herbin, & Blanchard, 2015) a centralized approach that monitors energy usage of all nodes (about their principal activities: communication) is discussed. The authors present a network-based model that assesses how the residual energy of every node is handled. The primary aim is to estimate the energy consumption of all nodes (after a learning phase). Many methods could be used to discover a cure for such disorders (wake up sleeping neighboring nodes, increasing radio ranges of some neighboring nodes).
2. **In-Network Aggregation:** Data is processed at intermediate nodes in this methodology in order to reduce the consumption of critical resources such as energy, computation time, etc. This strategy also improves the network lifetime of each node by decreasing its energy consumption. There are two more ways of aggregation within the network: Loss aggregation with a reduction in packet size or lossless data aggregation without a reduction in packet size. Data is collected from different sources and certain group functions, for example, sum, count, maximum, and minimum, are then applied over the collected information in loss aggregation. In Networked sensors, if they have worn on the body or embedded in our living environments, provide ample data of the physical and mental health (Hassanalieragh et al., 2015). Such data is continuously collected, aggregated, and efficiently mined, which can bring a significant variation in the health environment. In particular, the accessibility of information on unimaginable scales and time lengths combined with a present generation of smart processing algorithms likely to promote the development of medical practice, from its current post-facto reactive paradigm to the proactive prevention, cure, and illness diagnosis framework.
3. **Tree-Based Approach:** In this approach, a composite tree is usually a minimum threaded tree is built first. The root node acts as a base station, leaf nodes act as a source node, and middle nodes act as parent nodes within this tree. Leaf node sends your sensed node in a path found between the leaf node and the base station. In (Habib et al., 2016), the authors discussed various approaches of tree-based data aggregation techniques right from data management framework for biosensors to decision making. Initially, the authors suggested a biosensor-level adaptive information collection method. Secondly, they present a coordinator-level information fusion model with a choice matrix and fuzzy set theory. The findings demonstrate that this strategy decreases the number of redundancy of information gathered and preserves data integrity.
4. **Cluster-based Approach:** This approach divides the nodes into several groups called clusters. A cluster head is chosen within each group and the primary task of the cluster head is to aggregate the data. Each node senses and reports the required information to the cluster head of the same cluster instead of sending the information to the base station because of which it saves a lot of energy. Authors (Nie & L, 2011), addressed the application of Structured Health Monitoring [SHM] using Cluster based Data Aggregation approach and shown the results that this Cluster based technique of data aggregation reduces computing tasks and saves energy of sensors while monitoring patients data.

CLOUD COMPUTING

An increasing number of businesses have already adapted and started working on the cloud atmosphere due to its inherent benefits of flexibility, accessibility, security, and cost-effectiveness. Resources like services, infrastructure, software are shared among all stakeholders in Cloud computing. Hence, cryptography plays an important role in cloud computing because the data is to be secured from all kinds of threats or misuse when it is placed over the cloud. There are various cryptographic techniques evolved for this reason which ensures the security of data on the cloud environment. Security strategy no longer uses a single encryption method rather it makes utilization of multiple encryption methods. These security measures involve encryption of the information, converting the information to unreadable format and decoding at the end with the key which is unique. Currently, various encryption methods are in usage for ensuring the safety of data in different applications. Hence utilizing the cryptographic strategies inside the cloud will guarantee the integrity and information security to users which form essential characteristics of the cloud.

Cloud computing is portable in nature where end users have the flexibility to handle the data from anywhere when connected to the cloud. It uses a network of a large group of servers connected both publicly and privately, thereby providing massive infrastructure for data storage and application. Cloud Computing permit platform independence to users so as to rely on shared computing services like hardware and software rather than having a local infrastructure set-up. During pre-cloud computing days, companies used to manufacture their own servers for meeting various demands, which were highly capital intensive and time taking. With the advent of cloud computing, companies can offer their virtual machines and distribute information to anyone on the cloud with ease. This way, many firms drifted towards the variable priced model from a capital intensive model.

Cloud computing is a broadly utilized strategy for storing information on-demand but it also faces several risk factors including but not limited to data confidentiality, security, access-controls, privacy protection, etc. In the current study, several encryption methods that are used to protect sensitive data on the cloud are examined in detail. Various encryption strategies are analyzed and studied to distinguish enhancement highlights for cloud security. The research in cryptography has become widely and popularly known in the advent of computers. A lot of scopes is there for the researchers and academicians in this area.

CLOUD CHARACTERISTICS

The five important characteristics of cloud computing defined by the National Institute of Standards and Technology's (NIST) (Mell & Grance, 2011) are:

1. **On-demand Self-Service:** A consumer can unilaterally access computing resources, such as server time and network storage, as needed automatically without requiring any human interaction with each service provider. Services such as email, social networking applications are provided without any intervention with service providers. Salesforce.com, Gmail, Facebook, Amazon Web Services are some examples falls under this characteristic.

2. **Broad Network Access**: Cloud computing resources are accessible through multiple devices. User can access by not only using common devices like laptops and personal computers, but they can also be accessed via mobiles, tablets and so on.
3. **Resource Pooling:** Consumers are served by pooling of the service provider's computing resources using a multi-tenant model. It involves allocation and reallocation of different physical and virtual resources as per users demand. The user may not be able to identify the exact coordinates of resources thereby having a sense of location independence. However, the user may be able to specify the location at a broad level of abstraction (e.g. country, state, core data center). Storage-space, memory, e-mail services, and network bandwidth form some examples of cloud computing resources.
4. **Rapid Elasticity:** Resources can be elastically provisioned when needed, and removed when not required. Resources can be scaled up/down basis the requirements (or) in some cases automatically, to commensurate with demand. To the consumer, the services available for usage often appear unlimited and can be appropriated in any quantity at any time.
5. **Measured Service:** The usage of resources (e.g. storage, applications, and hardware) is monitored, controlled and sent to the users. This usage is metered and companies pay as per it, for what they have used. It maintains transparency in terms of utilization rates and costs.

CLOUD SERVICE MODELS

Depending on the business objectives, work requirements and storage needs, companies decide on a specific service model or a combination of models. There are 3 types of service models discussed (Kavis & M. J, 2014), and those are represented in Figure 1:

1. **Infrastructure as a Service (IaaS):** A service provider gives customers pay-as-you-go access to systems administration, storage, servers, and other assets in the cloud. IaaS rapidly scales all over with interest, giving a chance to customer, to pay just for what they use. It helps the client to evade the cost and multifaceted nature of purchasing and dealing with their own physical servers and other data center infra. Every asset is offered as a different segment, and they just need to lease a specific one for whatever duration of time that they need it.
   a. Key Features:
      i. Instead of purchasing hardware completely, users pay for IaaS on demand.
      ii. Infrastructure is scalable depending on processing and storage needs.
      iii. Saves enterprises the costs of buying and maintaining their own hardware.
      iv. Because data is on the cloud, there can be no single point of failure.
      v. Enables the virtualization of administrative tasks, freeing up time for other work.
   b. IaaS Business Scenarios:
      i. Test and advancement: Companies can rapidly set up test conditions, put up new applications for sale to the public user with ease. Also, IaaS makes it brisk and efficient to scale up device-test situations.
      ii. Site facilitating: Running sites utilizing IaaS can be more affordable than customary web facilitating.

iii. Web applications: IaaS gives all the resources to help web applications, including storage-space, web & application servers, and systems administration resources. Companies can customize the web applications on IaaS and scale up the framework as and when required.

2. **Platform as a Service (PaaS):** It empowers the cloud consumer to convey everything from straightforward cloud-based applications to complex cloud-empowered advance applications. The consumer buys the assets they need from a cloud specialist on a pay per use model and accesses them over a protected internet association. PaaS is intended to help the total web application lifecycle like building, testing, sending, managing, and restoring. PaaS enables the consumer to evade the cost and multifaceted nature of purchasing and managing programming licenses, the hidden application framework, and hardware or advanced machines. The consumer deal with the applications and administrations they create and the cloud provider usually manages everything else.
   a. Key Highlights:
      i. PaaS gives resources to test, create applications in a similar situation.
      ii. Empowers companies to concentrate on advancement without agonizing over hidden framework.
      iii. Suppliers oversee security, working frameworks, server programming and reinforcements.
      iv. Encourages community-oriented work regardless of whether groups work remotely.
   b. PaaS Business Scenarios:
      i. Improvement system: PaaS gives a system that designers can expand upon to create or alter cloud-based applications. Like the manner in which the client make an Excel spreadsheet, PaaS gives designers a chance to make applications utilizing programming segments decrease the measure of coding that designers must do.
      ii. Examination or business knowledge: PaaS enable companies to break down and extract their information, discovering bits of knowledge, designs and see results to improve company returns, and different business choices.
      iii. Extra administrations: PaaS suppliers may offer different administrations that upgrade applications, for example, work process and security.
3. **Software as a Service (SaaS):** It is a distributed computing offering where clients access to a provider's cloud-based programming. Clients don't develop applications on their gadgets rather the applications dwell on a remote cloud which can be accessed through the web or an API. Through the application, clients can store and investigate information and team up on activities. SaaS gives a total programming arrangement that the customer buys on a pay per use model from the cloud service providers. Customer leases the utilization of an application for their companies and to their clients interface with it over the Internet, more often than not with an internet browser. The majority of the basic hardware, application programming, and application information are situated with the cloud service provider's server. The service provider company deals with equipment and programming. With the proper administration, they will guarantee the accessibility and the security of the application.
   a. Key Highlights:
      i. SaaS sellers give programming and applications to clients by means of a membership display.
      ii. Clients don't need to manage, develop or update programming; SaaS suppliers deal with this.

iii. Utilization of software can be scaled relying upon company needs.
iv. Applications are accessible from practically any web associated gadget, from any place on the planet.

b. Regular SaaS Situations:

i. If the cloud consumer utilizes an electronic email administration such as Outlook, Hotmail, or Yahoo! Mail, at that point they are using a type of SaaS. With these applications, they can sign into their record over the internet, regularly from an internet browser.
ii. Email programming is situated on the cloud providers system. Users can get to their email and place messages through an internet browser on any PC or Internet-associated gadget.
iii. For organizational use SaaS provides profitability applications, for example, email, and calendaring; and advanced business applications, like, customer relationship management (CRM), Enterprise Resource Planning (ERP) which helps in organizational growth. Companies pay for the utilization of these applications by membership or as per the utilization.

Figure 1. Cloud service models

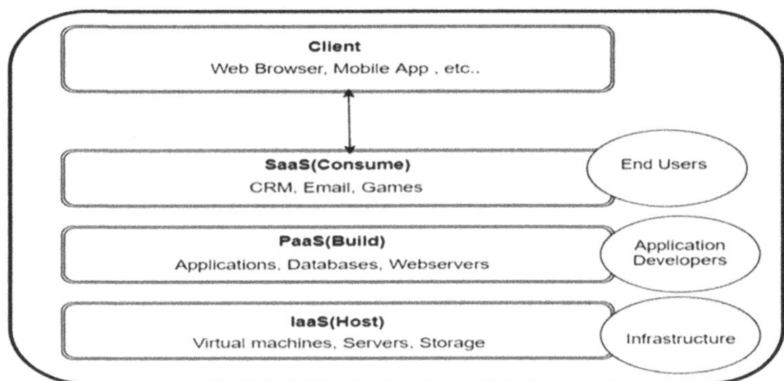

CLOUD DEPLOYMENT MODELS

Basis the configuration of cloud factors like accessibility, storage space, and ownership certain cloud deployment models are available. Depending on the business objectives, work requirements, storage needs companies to decide on specific cloud deployment model (Furht & Escalante, 2010). There are 4 common cloud deployment models shown in Figure 2:

1. **Public Cloud:** As the name indicates, the clouds infrastructure is available for open use to everyone. The responsibility of the creation and routine maintenance of the cloud and its IT infrastructure lies with the cloud owner/the third party. Users can't be guaranteed for information security & integrity because of dependence on an external party for monitoring the cloud. This model is preferred by industries with low-security concerns.
2. **Private Cloud:** The design of a private cloud is similar to public cloud technically. The only difference is that the cloud resources are provisioned for selective use by a company having many

users (e.g., business divisions). The cloud can be managed by a third party though it is being used by an organization on a private basis. Only selective persons will be able to access the information, thereby avoiding common public accessing it. This model is preferred by companies with high-security concerns.

3. **Community Cloud:** This cloud resembles a private cloud to a major extent. Unlike only single company owns resources in a private cloud, in community cloud, companies with common backgrounds share the resources on the cloud. This model is preferred by companies that involve joint projects.
4. **Hybrid Cloud:** The hybrid cloud model is a combination of at least two above-mentioned deployment models (private, public and community) as per the requirements. For instance, a company can manage its workload by placing critical ones on private cloud and locating less sensitive ones on the public cloud.

Figure 2. Cloud Deployment Models

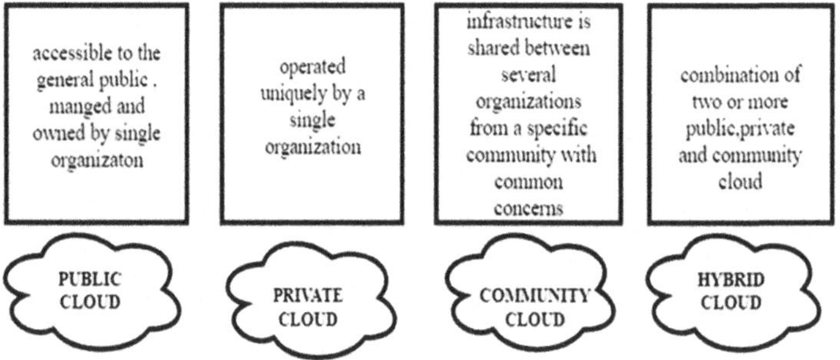

CLOUD COMPUTING ARCHITECTURE

The cloud computing architecture is broadly divided into two parts: front end and back end which are connected through the internet or virtual network. Both Front end and Back end connects by means of the internet.

a) **Front-End:** The interface that is visible to the computer users or clients defines the front end. User interface and user's network which is used for connecting the cloud system form the components of Front End. Various user interfaces are available for various cloud computing systems. For instance, users have a category of web browsers (chrome, internet explorer, firefox) to choose from, but the salesforce interface is not quite the same as that of Google Docs.
b) **Back-End**: On the other side, where the service provider operates the back end. Comprising all the resources including computers, virtual machines, data storage systems, servers and programs required for cloud-computing services forms components of Back end. It is the obligation of back end to provide an inherent security & management mechanisms, protocols and traffic control to all users.

Figure 3. Cloud Architecture

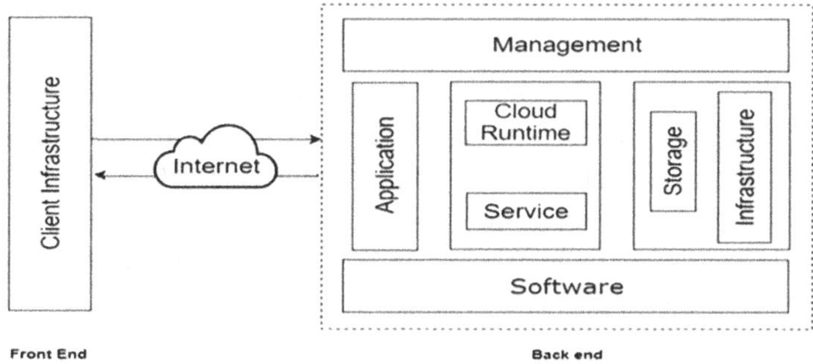

Components of Cloud Computing Architecture

The relationship of components in cloud Architecture is shown in Figure 3, and the components are discussed in this section.

1. **Management Software:** The performance of the cloud can be enhanced by using different plans and methodologies of Management software. Some features of this software include timely delivery of data, security and anytime access. Critical characteristics of Management Software include backup plans, compliance auditing, and disaster management.
2. **Deployment Software:** Deployment software helps in initiating the task (SaaS, PaaS, and IaaS) that can be accessed by users. It involves mandatory installations and configurations of the cloud
3. **Route of Connectivity:** It is an essential part of the design through which the entire cloud gets linked. The speed of exchange relies upon the internet connection. With the assistance of this virtual route, all the cloud servers get connected. Also, users can customize the flow and protocol using this.
4. **A Server of the Cloud:** It is a virtual server which is hosted using a cloud computing platform via the internet. These servers are stable, fast and safe which can be accessed from everywhere. Businesses prefer cloud servers over physical servers to escape from hardware issues and increase options of scalability to optimize cost.
5. **Storage of Cloud:** This is the place where all the data is placed, monitored and protected from outsiders. The data can be accessed from any place and they act as offsite storage for organizations with options for automatic scalability.

SECURITY ISSUES RELATED WITH THE CLOUD

Both the traditional data center environment and cloud environment experience similar threats at a higher level. Cloud computing depends on software which is vulnerable to several attacks. These attackers attempt to misuse those vulnerabilities. In cloud computing, unlike IT systems in the traditional data center, the onus of controlling risks is shared between cloud user and cloud service provider. Hence, users must perceive the responsibilities and work in coordination with cloud service providers. With most of the companies migrated to cloud, the security threat is a major concern for everyone. The following are some of the major risks identified by (Cameron Coles, 2019) are explained.

1. **Theft or Misuse of Company's Intellectual Property:** Many researchers found that around 20% of the files transferred to cloud-based storage services have sensitive and patented information such as licenses, blueprints, strategies, etc. Cybercriminals attack the cloud servers for obtaining such critical information of the companies and try to misuse them. In certain cases, some cloud services are prone to risk which claim ownership of the information on the cloud through terms and agreements signed during the early contractual stage.
2. **Less Control on Insiders:** Organizations have trust in their employees who are given access to cloud on a daily routine. However, there is a risk of privacy from some workers who give importance to personal benefits over organizational values. For example, a sales representative who is going to leave from the organization could download a report of all client contacts, transfer the information to personal storage, and share that information to the competitor. This way insiders misuse their authorized access.
3. **Incomplete Data Deletion:** Consumers are not aware of the physical location of own data and also not sure of the complete deletion of their data without any traces. This risk is concerning because the information is spread over various storage devices inside the cloud service provider's infrastructure. Companies are not in a position to confirm that their information was safely erased and that leftovers of the information are not available to attackers.
4. **Loss of Client's Trust in Cloud**: Users trust is being diminished due to data breaches in large volumes over the world. In one of the largest breakages of credit card information, cyber lawbreakers stole more than 40 million customer card information from cloud servers. This made clients to maintain distance from the cloud, thereby reducing the company's revenue
5. **Stolen Credentials:** If the credentials fall in the hand of attackers, then they could use cloud resources to target the company's administrative users and also other companies using services of the same providers. If the attacker gets the credentials of the cloud service provider administrator, they will be able to exploit the agency's data & systems. The role of administrator varies between a company and a cloud service provider. The cloud administrator has access to network, applications and other resources on the cloud, however, the company's administrator access is limited to the company's cloud usage.
6. **Authoritative Ruptures with Clients or Colleagues:** Contracts among business parties define the usage of data and authorized persons who can access it. At the point when worker moves some confidential information into the cloud without approval, then it is a violation of the contract and has legal implications. If in case cloud service provider sells data on the cloud to outsiders as per the terms and conditions, this will further complicate the situation and result in breach of confidentiality under business contract.
7. **Breach Intimation to Victims and Disclosures:** Certain regulations in an industry require disclosure of any information breach related to stakeholders. Such companies are required to publish and send notifications to exploited people. Regulators can impose fines against an organization after mandated disclosures. Also, it's rightful for customers whose information was breached to file legal suits.

8. **Reduced Client Base:** Clients may take their business to another company in the event they presume that their information isn't completely secure by security controls. It is suggested to maintain distance from cloud providers who don't ensure client security.
9. **Incomplete Due Diligence:** Before migrating to the cloud, companies should perform detailed due diligence. Incomplete due diligence results in moving information to the cloud without understanding the full scope, the safety methods used by the cloud service provider, and their own obligation to give safety mechanisms. This way some companies choose lower secured cloud services without giving detailed attention to them.

CLOUD SECURITY CONTROLS

It is often believed by many that cloud service provider (CSP) is solely responsible for the security of the cloud. Though cloud providers, deal with security for their server hardware and data centers, they rely on individuals for ensuring the security of virtual machines and applications. CSP's provide various security tools to ensure the safety mechanisms in place, but the users have to really execute the essential defenses. Hence it is non-beneficial if the users do not ensure safety for their own networks and applications, there is no use of having numerous security defenses from cloud service providers.

Irrespective of who is using it such as security team, administrator and service provider, many people do not have a comprehensive understanding of how to configure the cloud. Organizations shall implement the following security control measures by (Rashid, 2017) to ensure the safety of applications, data and cloud form hackers.

1. **Data Protection:** Data transiting channels should be safeguarded against any kind of altering or stealing through encryption methods. It is considered as highly insecure to keep data unencrypted on cloud. Cloud security intelligence discovered that around 82 percent of databases in the open the cloud is not encoded. Voter data and government confidential documents were stolen on the grounds that the information was not encoded and the servers were open to unauthorized groups. Hence, storing confidential information on a cloud without proper security encryptions is dangerous.
2. **Security Mechanisms:** Deploying best security mechanisms at every stage helps in securing cloud environment. If one security feature fails, there is always another control which protects the network, data, and applications in cloud architecture. For example, Multiple factor authentication (MFA) is always more secure than single or double factor authentication making it difficult for hackers to break in. Many researchers suggest that around 60 percent of users do not have MFA enabled to their accounts makes them vulnerable to attacks.
3. **Infrastructure Protection:** All physical components in cloud system which store and process the information should be secured from any seizure, theft, fire, damage and physical altering. The locations of the storage servers, data center buildings should be monitored with physical protection including video surveillance. The hardware should be disposed of in a way that does not compromise the security of the user stored, once its life is over.
4. **Continuous Monitoring:** The responsibility of monitoring the services and infrastructure lies with cloud service providers and the monitoring of applications and virtual machines are with end users. CSPs play a major role in identifying any unauthorized access of applications and systems using security tools. Consumers also should take responsibility to escalate the issue of any unexpected

behavior observed while using cloud services without any delay. Both CSP and consumer should coordinate with each other to ensure the security of data systems.

5. **Supply Chain Security Control:** As most of the cloud services are provided by third parties, they can affect the general security of the services. Companies should generate a list of approved vendors after a review process and they are to be complied with security policies before granting them access to information systems and facilities. If this control is not followed, it might compromise the security of service and effects the implementation of other security controls.

For implementing cloud security controls, cloud users should develop a comprehensive understanding of the services they are using. Threats or unauthorized access shall be avoided by using tools supplied by cloud service providers like multi-factor authentication, configured access control. Small & medium companies can avoid risks associated with moving data to the cloud by approaching renowned and established cloud service providers. These cloud service providers should not just provide services, but they should come along with best security practices, encrypting methods and good governance.

FUNDAMENTALS OF CRYPTOGRAPHY

Fundamentals of Cryptography

Cryptography plays an important role in many organizations all around the world because the data is to be secured from threats or misuse when it is placed over the cloud. Initially, from Caesar cipher to Enigma machines and AES to RSA, where the confidentiality is needed so, the cryptography has occurred. To maintain the confidentiality of the information shared, encryption techniques are designed. The secrecy of the key used in the encryption process helps the security of encryption techniques. Encryption methods are categorized into two types: symmetric and asymmetric encryption method.

Symmetric Encryption Method

In this approach, both sender and receiver of data share a single key. This is a secret key which will be used by both for encryption as well as decryption of the messages. Only one secret key is used in Symmetric encryption as shown in Figure 4. Hence, every time different keys are needed for communicating with different persons. This method becomes more complex for generating and managing a huge number of keys. This technique is used in applications, where high efficiency of execution is required. The popular symmetric encryptions are Snow (Ekdahl & Johansson, 2002) and AES (Daemen & Rijmen, 2000; Daemen & Rijmen, 2002).

Asymmetric Encryption Schemes

Unlike symmetric encryption where a single key is used, Asymmetric encryption uses two keys as shown in Figure 5. One key for the encryption and is publically available while the other is for the decryption and is secret. The private key is assigned for the person itself and the public key is meant for every person of the group. Thus this application provides the establishment of secure communication among

Figure 4. Symmetric encryption technique

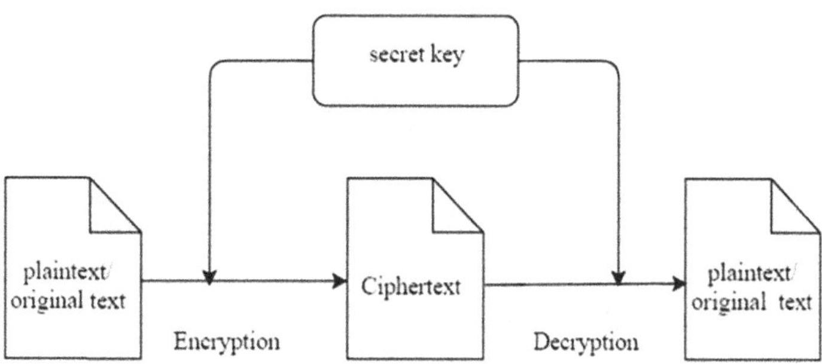

the groups, which does not require the prior acceptance before communication. The two well-known asymmetric encryption schemes are ElGamal (ElGamal, 1985) and RSA (Rivest et al., 1978b).

Figure 5. Asymmetric encryption technique

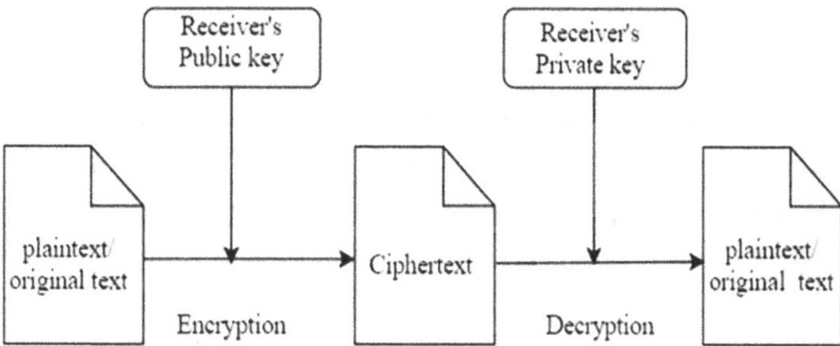

HOMOMORPHIC ENCRYPTION SCHEMES

In ancient Greece, the word *homo* refers to as "same", *morphe* refers as "shape". The word homomorphism is originated in many areas such as cryptography, medical science, and abstract algebra by Malik et.al in (Malik et al., 2007). In cryptography, a homomorphism is one of the encryption type used to secure the data. Homomorphic Encryption (HE) gives the output data in encrypted form. When a third party performs computations on ciphertext, results in the encrypted data. When decryption is performed the output matches the operations as if they had performed on plaintext to maintain the privacy of the data. The multiplicative HE schema example is performed on two messages t_1 and t_2, the result is $E(t_1 * t_2)$ by using $E(t_1)$ and $E(t_2)$ without knowing t_1 and t_2 explicitly. Where E refers to Encryption function.

The security is provided for electronic health record that is stored in the cloud by using homomorphic encryption techniques. The patient's medical and personal data is stored in EHR. The healthcare organizations are storing these records in the cloud. There are many privacy issues as EHR information is exposed to unauthorized parties and third-party servers. So, the best method is to encrypt the Electronic Health Record before storing it to cloud to provide confidentiality, security, and efficiency. Based on attributes and roles the patient's data can be accessed.

Figure 6. Client-server HE scheme, where U is user and C is cloud

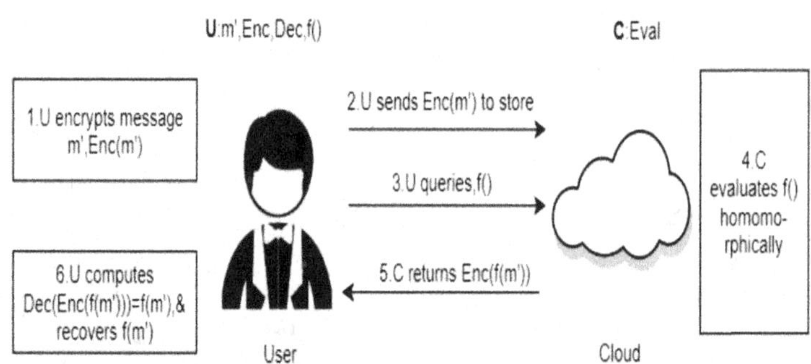

In cryptology, the word homomorphism is coined by Rivest, Adleman, and Dertouzos in 1978, which allows encrypted data to be computed on, without initial decryption of the operands they named it as "***privacy homomorphism***". They give some simple and modest examples of homomorphism scheme to explain the validity of the idea. After (Rivest et al., 1978a) there is plenty of work done by many researchers around the globe represented with a huge set of operations called homomorphic scheme. The main motive of this HE surveys is that there are many further enhancements in the HE schemes like Partially, Somewhat, Fully HE schemes. Figure 6 gives a clear example of HE for a cloud application.

The early attempt of Yao's 'garbled circuit' proposed a two-party communication which solved the millionaire's problem. It compares a wealth of 2 rich people without showing the exact amount to each other. In Yao's proposal, the size of ciphertext grows linearly with the computations and hence it results in too much complexity in communication protocol and very poor computational efficiency (Yao, 1982). For the next three decades, there is no secure homomorphism scheme is obtained.

Until Gentry's innovation (Gentry & Boneh, 2009), all the researchers performed either one type of operations or a very limited number of operations on the ciphertext. All these attempts are categorized into three types based on type and number of operations that are performed. 1. Partially Homomorphic Encryption (PHE), 2. Somewhat Homomorphic Encryption (SWHE). 3. Fully Homomorphic Encryption (FHE).

Definition: An encryption scheme has to satisfy the following equation in order to call it as homomorphic.

$$E\left(t_1\right)+E\left(t_2\right)=E\left(t_1+t_2\right),\ \forall t_1,t_2 \in M. \tag{1}$$

where E - encryption algorithm and M - set of all messages

In Homomorphic Encryption schemes, the same key can be used for encryption and decryption (secret key encryption) or different keys to encrypt and decrypt (public key encryption). H is a set of four functions in Homomorphic Encryption. H = {KeyGen_H, Enc_H, Dec_H, Eval_H}, where KeyGen_H is the function which generates a single key for secret key encryption and secret, public key pair for public key encryption. Enc_H (Encryption) and Dec_H (Decryption) are as same as they performed in Conventional encryption schemes. However, Eval_H is the function where it takes the ciphertext as input and generates a ciphertext according to a functioned plaintext as output. The ciphertext obtained as output after the evaluation is preserved in order to decrypt it correctly. To support the unlimited number of operations, the size of the ciphertext has to be constant. Otherwise, it restricts the number of operations as it requires additional resources. Either additive or multiplicative operations are supported by $Eval_H$ function in PHE schemes, and the only limited number of operations are supported by SWHE schemes, while FHE schemes support the evaluation of arbitrary functions with the unlimited number of times over ciphertext. After Gentry's work, the significance of the HE has gained momentum to a great extent. Figure 7 displays the overall view of the HE schemes until Gentry's first FHE scheme. These homomorphic encryption algorithms can apply on electronic health records to secure the data which is to be stored in a cloud.

Figure 7. A graphical representation of time-period of HE Schemes.

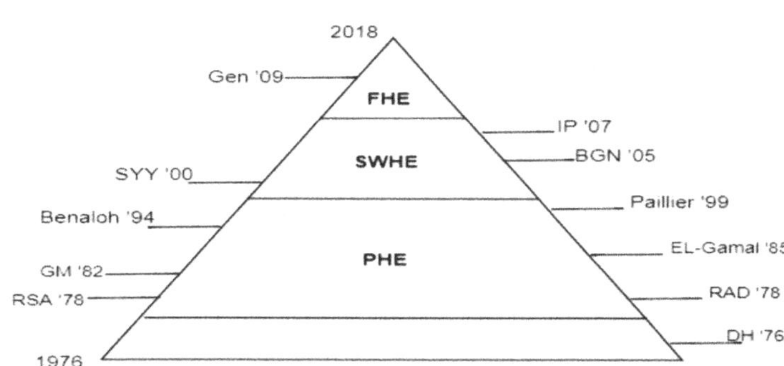

Steps for Homomorphic Encryption Scheme

The encryption needs four functions, key Generation algorithm, Encryption algorithm, Decryption algorithm, Evaluation function (Homomorphic additive and multiplicative).

Step 1: The key generation algorithm $KeyGen_H$, generates the public and secret key pair (pu_k, pr_k);
Step 2: The algorithm of encryption Enc_H (pu_k, x) which encrypts the plaintext x with the public key pu_k;
Step 3: The algorithm of decryption Dec_H (pr_k, c) which decrypts the ciphertext c using private key pr_k;
Step 4: The homomorphic additive function Add (c_1, c_2) where, the inputs c_1, c_2 are the ciphertexts of message x_1 and x_2, it gives the output as ciphertext by encrypting the addition of two plaintexts x_1 and x_2 ;
Step 5: The homomorphic multiplicative function Mul (c_1, c_2) where, the inputs c_1, c_2 are the ciphertexts of message x_1 and x_2, it gives the output as ciphertext by encrypting the product of two plaintexts x_1 and x_2;

Partially Homomorphic Encryption

Various popular and useful instances of PHE schemes will be elaborated in this section, which are the foundations for other PHE schemes. The notation *E(t)* is used to encrypt the message '*t* '.

a. RSA: The RSA Cryptosystem is the initial paradigm of PHE presented by Rivest, Shamir, and Adleman (Rivest et al., 1978b) after the invention of asymmetric cryptography by Diffie and Hellman

(Diffie and Hellman, 1976). The RSA Homomorphic property was done by Rivest, Adleman, and Dertouzos (Rivest et al., 1978a), shortly after the invention of the RSA (Rivest et al., 1978b). The decryption key which is kept secret (private) is different from the encryption key that is public. The RSA cryptosystem is based on the difficulty of factorization problem of the product of two large prime numbers. In RSA, the Homomorphic property $E(t_1 * t_2)$ is directly calculated from $E(t_1)$ and $E(t_2)$ without decrypting them. The homomorphic addition is not performed on ciphertexts and only homomorphic multiplication is performed in RSA.

To encrypt the message t in RSA, $E(t) = t^e \mathrm{mod} n$, where e is exponent and the public key is modulus n. The *Homomorphic property* of RSA Cryptosystem is:

$$\begin{aligned} E(t_1) * E(t_2) &= t_1^e t_2^e \bmod n, \\ &= (t_1 t_2)^e \bmod n, \\ &= E(t_1 * t_2). \end{aligned} \quad (2)$$

b. Goldwasser-Micali: The GM Cryptosystem is a two-pair key encryption algorithm developed by (Goldwasser and Micali, 1982). It is the first probabilistic asymmetric key encryption scheme based on the hardness of the quadratic residuosity problem. In GM there is only homomorphic over addition and homomorphic multiplication on ciphertexts is not possible.

To encrypt the bit b in GM Cryptosystem, $E(b) = p^b r^2 \bmod n$ for some random variable $r \in \{0,\ldots,n-1\}$, where p is quadratic non-residue, and the public key is modulus n, $\oplus$ indicates addition modulo 2.

The *Homomorphic property* of GM Cryptosystem is:

$$\begin{aligned} E(b_1) * E(b_2) &= p^{b_1} r_1^2 p^{b_2} r_2^2 \, mod\, n, \\ &= p^{b_1 + b_2} (r_1 r_2)^2 \, mod\, n, \\ &= E(b_1 \oplus b_2) \end{aligned} \quad (3)$$

c. El-Gamal: The Taher Elgamal developed a new asymmetric key encryption algorithm in (Elgamal, 1985). It is an upgraded version of the authentic Diffie-Hellman Key Exchange [7] based on the discrete logarithm. The Digital signature algorithm is a slightly different form of the Elgamal signature scheme that should not be confused with Elgamal encryption. The Homomorphic property of El-Gamal supports over multiplication and homomorphic addition operation over ciphertext is not supported here.

To encrypt the message x in El-Gamal Cryptosystem, $E(x)=(g^r, x, p^r)$, for some random variable $r \in \{0,\ldots,p-1\}$, where a cyclic group G of order p with generator g, the public key is (G, p,g,q), and $q=g^c$ where, c is a secret key.

The *Homomorphic property* of El-Gamal Cryptosystem is:

$$
\begin{aligned}
E\left(x_1\right) * E\left(x_2\right) &= \left(g^{r_1}, x_1 . q^{r_1}\right)\left(g^{r_2}, x_2 . q^{r_2}\right), \\
&= \left(g^{r_1+r_2}, \left(x_1 * x_2\right) q^{r_1+r_2}\right), \\
&= E\left(x_1 * x_2\right)
\end{aligned} \tag{4}
$$

d. Benaloh: In 1994, Benaloh proposed a scheme which is an addition of GM cryptosystem. Instead of encrypting bit by bit it encrypts long blocks of the message (Benaloh, 1994). Mainly this algorithm is based on higher residuosity problem, where it is a generalization of quadratic residuosity problems used in GM cryptosystem. The additive homomorphic property of Benaloh is calculated directly from the encrypted messages $E(t_1)$ and $E(t_2)$ so, it is additively homomorphic.

To encrypt a message *m*in Benaloh Cryptosystem, $E(m) = g^m r^b \mathrm{mod} n$, for some random variable $r \in \{0,\ldots,n-1\}$, where the public key is modulus *n*, base *g* with block size *b*.

The *Homomorphic property* of Benaloh Cryptosystem is:

$$
\begin{aligned}
E(m_{1)} * E\left(m_2\right) mod\, n &= \left(g^{m_1} r_1^{\ b}\right)\left(g^{m_2} r_2^{\ b}\right) mod\, n, \\
&= g^{m_1+m_2}\left(r_1 r_2\right)^b, \\
&= E\left(m_1 + m_2\right)
\end{aligned} \tag{5}
$$

e. Paillier: The Pascal Paillier in 1999, introduced a probabilistic asymmetric algorithm based on composite residuosity problem for public key cryptosystem (Paillier, 1999). Quadratic and higher residuosity problem that is used in GM & Benaloh is very identical to composite residuosity problem. The homomorphic property in Paillier Cryptosystem is homomorphic over addition.

To encrypt the message *m* in Paillier Cryptosystem, $E(m) = g^m r^n \mathrm{mod} n^2$, for some random variables $r \in \{0,\ldots,n-1\}$, where the public key is modulus *n*, the base *g*.

The *Homomorphic property* of Paillier Cryptosystem is:

$$
\begin{aligned}
E\left(m_1\right) * E\left(m_2\right) &= \left(g^{m_1} r_1^{\ n}\right)\left(g^{m_2} r_2^{\ n}\right) mod\ n^2, \\
&= g^{m_1+m_2}\left(r_1 r_2\right)^n mod\, n^2, \\
&= E\left(m_1 + m_2\right)
\end{aligned} \tag{6}
$$

f. Others: Later there are few PHE algorithms proposed based on the previous algorithms. By changing the set of functions, they introduced a new PHE scheme and improved the computational efficiency explained in (Okamoto and Uchiyama, 1998). Later, Naccache-Stern (Naccache & Stern, 1998) introduced another PHE, where the security rests on higher residuosity problem and this algorithm is generalization of Benaloh Cryptosystem to enhance computational performance. Damgard and

Jurik (DJ), proposed a PHE algorithm that is the generalization of Paillier is explained in (Damgard & Jurik, 2001). The security of DJ that has been shown to be true by decisional composite residuosity assumption. Galbraith (Galbraith, 2002), introduced a Cryptosystem by performing elliptic curves even though the homomorphic property is still preserving. It is a more real generalization of Paillier Cryptosystem. All these PHE algorithms are additively homomorphic.

Somewhat Homomorphic Encryption

In SWHE only a limited number of operations are performed. SWHE can only be operated to assess lower degree polynomial over ciphertext data. It is constrained mainly due to noisy nature of ciphertext. Further, this noise gets augmented on performing addition and multiplication operations on ciphertext. This complex nature makes the deciphering of ciphertext cumbersome. The main pillar behind the FHE scheme is SWHE scheme and can be applied to real time applications like medical, electronic voting, financial etc. SWHE is much faster than FHE and are replacing FHE schemes, to increase the performance.

Before Gentry's work, there were some well-known SWHE schemes that were developed. Yao's (Yao, 1982), the evaluating size is arbitrary over 'garbled circuit' where the ciphertext size grows linearly. The (Sander et al. 1999) SWHE scheme on the semi-group is supported by only one OR/NOT gate and many polynomially many ANDing of encrypted data. The size of ciphertext grows exponentially with each OR/NOT gate evaluation. In (Boneh et al., 2005), the 2-DNF (Disjunctive Normal Form) formulas on ciphertext are evaluated and performed operations on encrypted data with one multiplication and unlimited additions keeping the ciphertext constant. In (Yuval Ishai and Paskin, 2007) they presented a public key encryption and evaluated branching program on the ciphertext. The size of ciphertext size doesn't depend on the size of the function. The unique characteristic of this protocol is that in a server-client relationship, the client cannot see the size of server's input. In BGN (Boneh et al., 2005), the size of the ciphertext stays constant whereas, with each homomorphic operation in (Sander et al., 1999; Yuval Ishai & Paskin, 2007; Yao, 1982), the ciphertext size grows. However, in homomorphic addition the ciphertext size is constant while the ciphertext grows exponentially in homomorphic multiplication. Because of constant size of the ciphertext in BGN (Boneh et al., 2005) cryptosystem, it is further used to obtain FHE schemes.

Fully Homomorphic Encryption

Almost 30 years from the institution of privacy homomorphism idea by (Rivest et al., 1978a), Gentry (Gentry, 2009) proposed the first viable scheme in his PhD thesis to a longstanding open issue, which acquires a scheme called FHE. The Fully Homomorphic Encryption (FHE) performs unlimited number of operations on the ciphertext and gives the resultant output within the ciphertext space. In Figure 8 there are mainly four FHE families after Gentry's innovation are represented.

Gentry's scheme acts as a framework to obtain an FHE scheme. After his work, many researchers have tried to design a secure FHE scheme. Gentry (Gentry, 2009) introduced Ideal lattice-based FHE scheme showing signs of future success and had a lot of hindrances like the cost to implement in real life and executing advanced mathematical functions. Later many of them work on Gentry's proposal addressing the hindrances. All the work done till now is to achieve a new secure FHE scheme which solves the hardships on lattices. Later the work done on lattices becomes popular for the cryptographic researchers, after gentry scheme. Firstly, a small work is done by the researchers (Smart and Vercauteren, 2010) to

Figure 8. Fully Homomorphic Encryption (FHE) categories

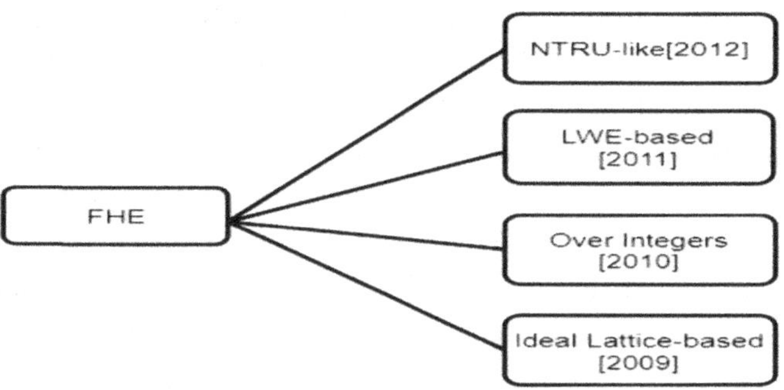

enhance the Gentry's ideal lattice-based FHE scheme and later they introduced the FHE scheme over integers. The main motive behind this scheme is to make it more conceptually understandable based on Approximate-GCD problems by (Van Dijk et al., 2010). Then, (Brakerski and Vaikuntanathan, 2011) suggested another FHE scheme based on the hardness of Ring Learning with Error problems which assure some efficiency characteristics. At last, NTRU-like FHE is presented by (Lopez-Alt et al., 2012), is an old systematic lattice-based-encryption scheme with good efficiency and standardized homomorphic properties.

RELATED WORK DONE ON HE SCHEMES

The homomorphic encryption scheme has its application in many areas and has already given the best results. In ideal lattice-based FHE, bootstrapping and squashing techniques are included. The latest work that has been done in (Zhou et al., 2018), where they accelerated the bootstrapping by three improvements which gave the better performance in data protection. In (Chatterjee & Sengupta, 2018), by using FHE, encrypting the sensitive data and storing on the cloud for confidentiality, they obtained a way to translate algorithms and handling the termination between client and server by passing the message. In bioinformatics for providing privacy (Dowlin et al., 2017) proposed a Homomorphic Encryption for sensitive health and genomic data using a Simple Encrypted Arithmetic Library (SEAL) which made it publicly accessible. Secret sharing of data is one of the important components in cryptography, a novel HE scheme is proposed (Zhang et al., 2017) for outsourcing secret sharing data. By applying ring-LWE and ideal-lattice homomorphic encryption (Yasuda, 2017) developed secure maintenance of the biometric system in (Yasuda, 2017). The first multi-hop homomorphic identity-based proxy re-encryption scheme is discussed in (Li et al., 2017a), it can be useful for many applications like securing e-mail forwarding, data sharing, and access control systems. In (Cheon & Kim, 2015) constructed a hybrid scheme by concatenating Goldwasser-Micali and ElGamal schemes. In (Wu et al., 2018) the server builds an inverted encryption index structure to reduce the single keyword search time complexity without query trapdoor mechanism. Not only the confidentiality but also the integrity protections are proposed in (Tsoutsos & Maniatakos, 2018), which gives encrypted computations efficiently using additive HE. Based on Homomorphic Encryption (Yang et al., 2018), proposed a secure verifiable e-voting system in which they used ElGamal cryptosystem.

HElib, which is termed as 'assembly language for HE, without using commands and functions of programming language deals with the hardware constraints of the computer. Microsoft has released other HE library named Simple Encrypted Arithmetic Library -SEAL (Laine et al. 2017) with an aim to provide a well-documented HE library. It can be accessed by both crypto and non-crypto experts including practitioners in bioinformatics. It acts independently using automatic parameter selection and noise eliminator tools. Fastest Homomorphic Encryption in the West - FHEW, a major application is developed by Ducas and Micciancio documented in (Ducas and Micciancio 2015). The time required to bootstrap the ciphertext is reduced to "in less than a second" claiming homomorphic evaluation of a NAND gate. There are some publicly accessible FHE implementations which can be used by the researchers. A few implementations that are publicly accessible are displayed in the Table 1.

Table 1. Publicly accessible FHE applications

Name	Language	Authors
SEAL	C++	Laine et al .,2017
TFHE	C++	Chillotti et al .,2017
HElib	C++	Halevi and Shoup, 2015
FHEW	C++	Ducas and Micciancio, 2014

FURTHER RESEARCH DIRECTIONS

FHE can be still explored to different applications like multi-party FHE, multikey FHE and also in designing Attribute Based Encryption (ABE) and Identity Based Encryption (IBE) with FHE. These ABE and IBE are suitable for access control to data that is stored in the cloud. Some works are done on these applications, but their performance doesn't match with traditional approaches so, these problems can lead to promising research applications. FHE also solves Functional Encryption (i.e., ABE, IBE). FE restricts the access of data but allows operations on it based on their attribute or identity characteristics. Later a standard model, an efficient identity based FHE scheme is designed in two-levels in (Hu et al., 2018) i.e. first-level is multi-bit IBE and the second level is batch identity-based fully homomorphic encryption (IBFHE). In FHE, one of the processes that increases the computational cost is bootstrapping, which is helpful in decreasing the noise in evaluated ciphertext, and these are still an open issue. Another important application of FHE is multi-party computation which takes multiple inputs from different users and makes the computation function by keeping the inputs hidden. In (Clear & McGoldrick, 2015) the multi-identity and key based FHE from learning with errors are reported. This multi-key FHE with the unlimited number of users is one of the new promising approaches in the future. These attribute and identity based encryptions are used to secure the sensitive data of the patient health records. Using attribute based encryption the personal health records are securely shared in the cloud (Li et al., 2013b).

Challenges

1. IoT systems capture and communicate real-time information. Data Security and privacy is one of the most important threat for IoT System Design in Healthcare.

2. Multiple device integration and protocols also creates hindrance in the healthcare industry IoT applications.
3. IoT devices keep recording a ton of information. The information gathered by IoT devices is used to obtain vital signs. However, the quantity of information is so huge that it becoming highly hard for physicians to give treatment from it, which eventually impacts decision-making quality.
4. IoT has not yet made healthcare affordable to the ordinary man. The boom in healthcare expenses is a worrying sign for the developed countries in particular.

CONCLUSION

IoT technologies are evolving around the world than ever before. So, protecting the data plays a key role. Many applications based on IOT technology found its usage in medical field and all the patient's information is gathered and stored in cloud. The significance increases for sensitive industries like healthcare, where the documents stored in the cloud must be protected from both malign and benign third parties. Security is one of the most important tasks nowadays. In a smart healthcare system, the Electronic Health Records are the major modules which share the medical data between healthcare providers and patients. Encryption is the main means to protect the privacy of the data. Its performance is evaluated by security, speed, and understandability. Homomorphic Encryption is the special kind of encryption scheme where the computations are done on ciphertext without deciphering it. Applying this encryption algorithm for EHR data will provide better security when it is stored in the cloud.

REFERENCES

Benaloh, J. (1994, May). Dense probabilistic encryption. In *Proceedings of the workshop on selected areas of cryptography* (pp. 120-128). Academic Press.

Boneh, D., Goh, E. J., & Nissim, K. (2005, February). Evaluating 2-DNF formulas on ciphertexts. In *Theory of Cryptography Conference* (pp. 325-341). Springer.

Brakerski, Z., & Vaikuntanathan, V. (2011, August). Fully homomorphic encryption from ring-LWE and security for key dependent messages. In *Annual cryptology conference* (pp. 505-524). Springer. 10.1007/978-3-642-22792-9_29

Cameron, C. (2019). *Cloud computing security risks every company faces.* Retrieved from https://www.skyhighnetworks.com/cloud-security-blog/9-cloud-computing-security-risks-every-company-faces/

Chakraborty, C., & Kumari, S. (2016). Bio-metric Identification using Automated Iris Detection Technique. *IEEE: 3rd International Conference on Microelectronics, Circuits, and Systems*, 113-17.

Chakraborty, C., Gupta, B., & Ghosh, S. K. (2014). Mobile metadata assisted community database of chronic wound images. *Wound Medicine*, *6*, 34–42. doi:10.1016/j.wndm.2014.09.002

Chakraborty, C., Gupta, B., & Ghosh, S. K. (2016). Mobile telemedicine systems for remote patient's chronic wound monitoring. In *M-Health innovations for patient-centered care* (pp. 213–239). IGI Global. doi:10.4018/978-1-4666-9861-1.ch011

Chatterjee, A., & Sengupta, I. (2018). Translating algorithms to handle fully homomorphic encrypted data on the cloud. *IEEE Transactions on Cloud Computing*, *6*(1), 287–300. doi:10.1109/TCC.2015.2481416

Cheon, J. H., & Kim, J. (2015). A hybrid scheme of public-key encryption and somewhat homomorphic encryption. *IEEE Transactions on Information Forensics and Security*, *10*(5), 1052–1063. doi:10.1109/TIFS.2015.2398359

Chillotti, I., Gama, N., Georgieva, M., & Izabachène, M. (2017). *TFHE: Fast FullyHomomorphicEncryptionLibraryovertheTorus*. Retrieved from https://github.com/tfhe/tfhe

Clear, M., & McGoldrick, C. (2015, August). Multi-identity and multi-key leveled FHE from learning with errors. In *Annual Cryptology Conference* (pp. 630-656). Springer. 10.1007/978-3-662-48000-7_31

Daemen, J., & Rijmen, V. (2000). The Block Cipher Rijndael. In *Proceedings of International Conference on Smart Cards Research and Applications (CARDS'98), Lecture Notes in Computer Science* (Vol 1820, pp. 247-256). Springer-Verlag. 10.1007/10721064_26

Daemen, J. & Rijmen, V. (2002). *The Design of Rijndael*. AES- The Advanced Encryption.

Damgård, I., & Jurik, M. (2001, February). A generalisation, a simpli. cation and some applications of paillier's probabilistic public-key system. In *International Workshop on Public Key Cryptography* (pp. 119-136). Springer. 10.1007/3-540-44586-2_9

Diffie, W., & Hellman, M. (1976). New directions in cryptography. *IEEE Transactions on Information Theory*, *22*(6), 644–654. doi:10.1109/TIT.1976.1055638

Dowlin, N., Gilad-Bachrach, R., Laine, K., Lauter, K., Naehrig, M., & Wernsing, J. (2017). Manual for homomorphic encryption for bioinformatics. *Proceedings of the IEEE*, *105*(3), 552–567.

Ducas, L., & Micciancio, D. (2015, April). FHEW: bootstrapping homomorphic encryption in less than a second. In *Annual International Conference on the Theory and Applications of Cryptographic Techniques* (pp. 617-640). Springer. 10.1007/978-3-662-46800-5_24

Ducas & Micciancio. (2014). *A Fully Homomorphic Encryption library*. Retrieved from https://github.com/ lducas/FHEW

Ekdahl, P., & Johansson, T. (2002, August). A new version of the stream cipher SNOW. In *International Workshop on Selected Areas in Cryptography* (pp. 47-61). Springer.

ElGamal, T. (1985). A public key cryptosystem and a signature scheme based on discrete logarithms. *IEEE Transactions on Information Theory*, *31*(4), 469–472. doi:10.1109/TIT.1985.1057074

Fouchal, H., Herbin, M., & Blanchard, F. (2015, August). Centralized energy monitoring over wireless sensor networks. In *2015 International Wireless Communications and Mobile Computing Conference (IWCMC)* (pp. 788-792). IEEE. 10.1109/IWCMC.2015.7289183

Furht, B., & Escalante, A. (2010). *Handbook of cloud computing* (Vol. 3). New York: Springer. doi:10.1007/978-1-4419-6524-0

Galbraith, S. D. (2002). Elliptic curve Paillier schemes. *Journal of Cryptology*, *15*(2), 129–138. doi:10.100700145-001-0015-6

Gentry, C., & Boneh, D. (2009). A fully homomorphic encryption scheme: Vol. 20. *No. 09*. Stanford, CA: Stanford University.

Goldwasser, S., & Micali, S. (1982, May). Probabilistic encryption & how to play mental poker keeping secret all partial information. In *Proceedings of the fourteenth annual ACM symposium on Theory of computing* (pp. 365-377). ACM. 10.1145/800070.802212

Habib, C., Makhoul, A., Darazi, R., & Salim, C. (2016). Self-adaptive data collection and fusion for health monitoring based on body sensor networks. *IEEE Transactions on Industrial Informatics, 12*(6), 2342–2352. doi:10.1109/TII.2016.2575800

Halevi & Shoup. (2013). *An Implementation of homomorphic encryption*. Retrieved from https://github.com/ shaih/HElib

Hassanalieragh, M., Page, A., Soyata, T., Sharma, G., Aktas, M., Mateos, G., & Andreescu, S. (2015, June). Health monitoring and management using Internet-of-Things (IoT) sensing with cloud-based processing: Opportunities and challenges. In *2015 IEEE International Conference on Services Computing* (pp. 285-292). IEEE. 10.1109/SCC.2015.47

Hu, M., Ye, Q., & Tang, Y. (2018). Efficient batch identity-based fully homomorphic encryption scheme in the standard model. *IET Information Security, 12*(6), 475–483. doi:10.1049/iet-ifs.2017.0567

Ishai, Y., & Paskin, A. (2007, February). Evaluating branching programs on encrypted data. In *Theory of Cryptography Conference* (pp. 575-594). Springer. 10.1007/978-3-540-70936-7_31

Kale, S., & Khandelwal, C. S. (2013, March). Design and implementation of real time embedded telehealth monitoring system. In *2013 International Conference on Circuits, Power and Computing Technologies (ICCPCT)* (pp. 771-774). IEEE. 10.1109/ICCPCT.2013.6528842

Kavis, M. J. (2014). *Architecting the cloud: design decisions for cloud computing service models (SaaS, PaaS, and IaaS)*. John Wiley & Sons. doi:10.1002/9781118691779

Laine, K., Chen, H., & Player, R. (2017). *Simple Encrypted Arithmetic Library*. Retrieved from https:// sealcrypto. codeplex.com/

Li, M., Yu, S., Zheng, Y., Ren, K., & Lou, W. (2013b). Scalable and secure sharing of personal health records in cloud computing using attribute-based encryption. *IEEE Transactions on Parallel and Distributed Systems, 24*(1), 131–143. doi:10.1109/TPDS.2012.97

Li, Z., Ma, C., & Wang, D. (2017a). Towards multi-hop homomorphic identity-based proxy re-encryption via branching program. *IEEE Access: Practical Innovations, Open Solutions, 5*, 16214–16228. doi:10.1109/ACCESS.2017.2740720

López-Alt, A., Tromer, E., & Vaikuntanathan, V. (2012, May). On-the-fly multiparty computation on the cloud via multikey fully homomorphic encryption. In *Proceedings of the forty-fourth annual ACM symposium on Theory of computing* (pp. 1219-1234). ACM. 10.1145/2213977.2214086

Malik, D. S., Mordeson, J. N., & Sen, M. K. (2007). *MTH 581-582 Introduction to Abstract Algebra*. Academic Press.

Mell, P., & Grance, T. (2011). *The NIST definition of cloud computing*. Academic Press.

Naccache, D., & Stern, J. (1998, November). A new public key cryptosystem based on higher residues. In *Proceedings of the 5th ACM conference on Computer and communications security* (pp. 59-66). ACM. 10.1145/288090.288106

Nie, P., & Li, B. (2011, July). A cluster-based data aggregation architecture in WSN for structural health monitoring. In *2011 7th International Wireless Communications and Mobile Computing Conference* (pp. 546-552). IEEE. 10.1109/IWCMC.2011.5982592

Okamoto, T., & Uchiyama, S. (1998, May). A new public-key cryptosystem as secure as factoring. In *International conference on the theory and applications of cryptographic techniques* (pp. 308-318). Springer. 10.1007/BFb0054135

Paillier, P. (1999, May). Public-key cryptosystems based on composite degree residuosity classes. In *International Conference on the Theory and Applications of Cryptographic Techniques* (pp. 223-238). Springer. 10.1007/3-540-48910-X_16

Rashid, F. Y. (2017). Top cloud security controls you should be using. *InfoWorld*. Retrieved from https://www.csoonline.com/article/3208905/top-cloud-security-controls-you-should-be-using.html

Rivest, R. L., Adleman, L., & Dertouzos, M. L. (1978a). On data banks and privacy homomorphisms. *Foundations of Secure Computation, 4*(11), 169-180.

Rivest, R. L., Shamir, A., & Adleman, L. (1978b). A method for obtaining digital signatures and public-key cryptosystems. *Communications of the ACM, 21*(2), 120–126. doi:10.1145/359340.359342

Sander, T., Young, A., & Yung, M. (1999). Non-interactive cryptocomputing for NC/SUP 1. In *Foundations of Computer Science, 1999. 40th Annual Symposium on* (pp. 554-566). IEEE.

Standard. Information Security and Cryptography. (2002). New York, NY: Springer.

Tsoutsos, N. G., & Maniatakos, M. (2018). Efficient Detection for Malicious and Random Errors in Additive Encrypted Computation. *IEEE Transactions on Computers, 67*(1), 16–31. doi:10.1109/TC.2017.2722440

Van Dijk, M., Gentry, C., Halevi, S., & Vaikuntanathan, V. (2010, May). Fully homomorphic encryption over the integers. In *Annual International Conference on the Theory and Applications of Cryptographic Techniques* (pp. 24-43). Springer.

Vippalapalli, V., & Ananthula, S. (2016, October). Internet of things (IoT) based smart health care system. In *2016 International Conference on Signal Processing, Communication, Power and Embedded System (SCOPES)* (pp. 1229-1233). IEEE. 10.1109/SCOPES.2016.7955637

Wu, D. N., Gan, Q. Q., & Wang, X. M. (2018). Verifiable Public Key Encryption With Keyword Search Based on Homomorphic Encryption in Multi-User Setting. *IEEE Access: Practical Innovations, Open Solutions, 6*, 42445–42453. doi:10.1109/ACCESS.2018.2861424

Yang, X., Yi, X., Nepal, S., Kelarev, A., & Han, F. (2018). A Secure Verifiable Ranked Choice Online Voting System Based on Homomorphic Encryption. *IEEE Access: Practical Innovations, Open Solutions, 6*, 20506–20519. doi:10.1109/ACCESS.2018.2817518

Yao, A. C. (1982, November). Protocols for secure computations. In *Foundations of Computer Science, 1982. SFCS'08. 23rd Annual Symposium on* (pp. 160-164). IEEE. 10.1109/SFCS.1982.38

Yasuda, M. (2017). Secure Hamming distance computation for biometrics using ideal-lattice and ring-LWE homomorphic encryption. *Information Security Journal: A Global Perspective, 26*(2), 85-103.

Zhang, E., Peng, J., & Li, M. (2017). Outsourcing secret sharing scheme based on homomorphism encryption. *IET Information Security, 12*(1), 94–99. doi:10.1049/iet-ifs.2017.0026

Zhou, T., Yang, X., Liu, L., Zhang, W., & Li, N. (2018). Faster bootstrapping with multiple addends. *IEEE Access: Practical Innovations, Open Solutions, 6*, 49868–49876. doi:10.1109/ACCESS.2018.2867655

This research was previously published in Smart Medical Data Sensing and IoT Systems Design in Healthcare; pages 22-47, copyright year 2020 by Medical Information Science Reference (an imprint of IGI Global).

Chapter 42
Provably Secure Data Sharing Approach for Personal Health Records in Cloud Storage Using Session Password, Data Access Key, and Circular Interpolation

Naveen John
Nesamony Memorial Christian College, Marthandam, India

Shatheesh Sam
Manonmaniam Sundaranar University, India

ABSTRACT

Personal health record (PHR) system has become the most important platform to exchange health information, in which the patients can share and manage personal health information more effectively in cloud storage. However, the cloud server is unreliable, and the secure data of users may be disclosed. Therefore, a secure data sharing mechanism is developed in this research using the proposed session password, data access key, and circular interpolation (SKC)-based data-sharing approach for the secure sharing of PHR in the cloud. The proposed SKC-based data sharing approach provides high efficiency and high-security guarantee. It effectively satisfies various security properties, such as tamper resistance, openness, and decentralization. The proposed SKC-based data sharing approach is the reliable mechanism created for the doctors to share the PHR and to access the patient historical data while meeting the privacy preservation.

1. INTRODUCTION

Cloud computing emerges as the major computing framework, which provides on-demand and pervasive accessibility of various resources, such as infrastructure, storage, software, and hardware. Commercial

DOI: 10.4018/978-1-6684-6311-6.ch042

cloud-based platforms like Amazon web services (AWS), Google cloud platforms (GCP) were used to manage the data in various aspects. The AWS has 33% of the cloud, and GCP has 9% of all clouds (Amazon AWS). The cloud computing framework facilitates organizations to trust third-party Information Technology (IT) services by quitting them from the protracted development of job infrastructure (Ge, *et al.,* 2020 ; Florence, *et al.*, 2019 ; Abbas, *et al.,* 2015). The cloud computing paradigm has gained more potential among various healthcare stakeholders to increase coordination among them and ensure scalability and health information availability. Accordingly, cloud computing incorporates various limitations in healthcare domains, like nursing staff, service providers, clinical laboratory personnel, hospital staff, including doctors, insurance providers, pharmacies, and patients (Athena and Sumathy, 2019 ; Abbas and Khan, 2014). These factors were integrated with the cloud results in the growth of a collaborative and cost-effective health ecosystem. Here, the patients can create and maintain their personal health records (PHRs) (Au *et al.,* 2017). In general, the PHR consists of various information, such as private notes, past surgeries, diagnosis, treatments, laboratory reports, data regarding health insurance claims, demographic information, patients' medical history, and allergies observed from the patient health conditions (Doshi, *et al.,* 2019 ; Zhang, *et al.,* 2019 ; Ali, *et al.,* 2018).(Visalatchi *et al.*, 2017) The resource required for this is allocated based on payment.

The PHR is managed using internet-based tools that allow the user to create and modify the health-based information (Kaelber, *et al.,* 2008). However, health information is considered a lifelong record accessible to the person who has access rights (Chiang, *et al.,* 2020 ; Kaelber, *et al.,* 2008). However, the PHR enables the patient to communicate with the care providers and doctors more effectively to keep the updated health records, seek and inform about the symptoms for making the treatment and diagnosis (Ali, *et al.,* 2018). For the patients, the disease may be caused by another pathogen. In this case, the accuracy of diagnosis gets affected due to the precision of patient health information reported by doctors. The doctors will provide some information to the patient regarding the health issues by querying the patient. It is not effective to assist the diagnosis due to the following reasons: i) The patient may forget the things that happened before, like medical examination or medicine that he or she has taken, and the precision of treatment or diagnosis that he or she had got. ii) The patient cannot describe the treatment or diagnosis due to their limited knowledge that degrades the judgment of the current doctor. Hence, the current doctor cannot produce accurate information regarding the diagnosis. The promising solution used to solve the above issue is to share the patient record to access the doctor's record for improving the diagnosis. When the patient visits some other doctor in the medical institution or the same hospital and the health records related to the patients are recorded in the institution. The doctors can access the health records directly from the area network for the consent of the patient. In practice, the patient can visit different doctors at different medical institutions in terms of varying symptoms. In such a case, the medical institution rejects the doctor to agree with the PHR. Zaghloul, *et al.,* 2019 ; Hema and Kesavan, 2019 *;* Zhang and Lin, 2018).

Cloud-assisted health record sharing is a promising paradigm developed in the e-health system to store and manage health care information. These works offer a promising solution to the PHI sharing between the medical institutions in the e-health system. However, privacy preservation and security are the major critical concerns in the e-health system, agronomy (L Leso, *et al.*, 2018) ; (Freitas, *et al.,* 2017), and so on. The above works are highlighted to achieve security functions in the cloud-assisted environment. However, the cloud is considered the trusted center used to store and manage the information exposed to loss, theft, abuse, and leakage if the cloud is under supervision or attacks. However, the countermeasures are developed using different cryptographic primitives and other methods (Shen, *et al.,* 2014 *;* Yang and Ma, 2016 *;* Zhou, *et al.,* 2015). However, security becomes a major issue in the cloud (Zhang and Lin, 2018).

This research is focused on designing a new Session password, Data access key, and Circular interpolation (SDC)-based data sharing approach to enable secure data sharing of PHR in cloud storage. The proposed SDC-based data sharing approach consists of four different entities: user, Data Owner (DO), cloud server, and Trusted Authority (TA). The proposed data sharing approach is enabled using seven different phases. They are the server registration phase, Data Owner registration phase, user registration phase, encryption phase, control setup phase, verification phase, decryption, and data download phase. In the server registration phase, the cloud server creates its credentials and verifies them with the Trusted Authority using the session password of the server.

Similarly, the Data Owner and the user create their credentials and verify them with the cloud server using the private key of the Data Owner and the user's private key. Once the credentials are registered with the server and Trusted Authority, the encryption process is carried out by the Data Owner at the encryption phase. Here, the data is encrypted using the encryption function based on the Data Owner's private key. The user generates the authentication messages at the control setup phase using the session password of the user. Finally, the user performs the verification procedure and decrypts the data using the decryption function.

The major contribution of this research is elaborated as below:

- The proposed SDC-based data sharing approach has the facility to share and manage the PHR in the cloud by seven different phases and four different entities. Thus, secure information sharing is achieved, and the proposed method's efficiency is also improved compared to the existing techniques.
- The credentials like server registration, Data owner registration, and user registration are verified with the trusted Authority. Hence, the information in the cloud is shared securely.
- The proposed SDC-based data sharing approach has the facility to share and manage the PHR in the cloud. The user, server, and Data owner credentials are verified with the trusted Authority to enhance the secure sharing of data. The data is encrypted using the private key by the Data owner and is decrypted using the data access key. Moreover, by using the Chebyshev polynomial, the data authentication is obtained.

The rest of the paper is organized as follows: section 2 elaborates the review of the existing secure data sharing methods. Section 3 describes the proposed SDC-based data sharing approach to enable secure data sharing in the cloud. Section 4 elaborates on the results and discussion of the proposed data sharing model, and finally, section 5 concludes the paper.

2. MOTIVATION

In this section, some of the existing data sharing methods in the cloud are discussed along with their merits and demerits, which motivate the researchers to develop a new data-sharing model named the SDC-based data sharing approach.

2.1 Literature Survey

Various existing data-sharing techniques are reviewed in this section. (Ali, *et al.,* 2018) developed a Secure Sharing of Personal Health Record (SeSPHR) model for sharing the PHR in the cloud. This method ensures patient-centric control and preserves the confidentiality of PHR. The encrypted PHR is placed in the un-trusted server, and the access right is granted to the user. This method was highly secure against insider attacks and enforced backward and forward access control. However, the computational complexity of this method was too high. (Xiong, *et al.,* 2018) developed an attribute-based privacy-preserving model to reveal the hidden access policy and enable the data owner to share the data under multiple participants. Here, each PHR shares its features with the group identity and the group of attributes such that the shared are encrypted with the access policy and group identity. Here, the user who belongs to the specified group can decipher the data. (Yuan, *et al.,* 2018) developed an oblivious random access memory (ORAM) to access the pattern hiding in cloud storage. This method guarantees high efficiency and high data security and prevents the information blocks against arbitrary modification using shuffle correctness proof. However, the computational complexity of this method was low, but it failed to concentrate on the involvement of the data owner. (Zhang and Lin, 2018) developed a blockchain-based secure and privacy-preserving PHI sharing (BSPP) model for improving the diagnosis in the e-health system. Here, two types of blockchain, like consortium and the private blockchain, are designed by devising the consensus and data structure. It effectively performs access control, secure search, privacy preservation, and data security in the cloud. However, it failed to consider the keyword search and verifier election algorithm in the e-health blockchain. Liang, *et al., (*2019) developed multi-source order-preserving encryption (MSOPE) approach to enable queries over health records in the cloud-based e-health system. It effectively identifies the threat in the health care systems, like frequency analysis, exact data inference, and privacy leakage. However, it failed to protect the order of data in Electronic Health Record (EHR) against the cloud server. (Liang, *et al.,* 2019) developed an attribute-based encryption (ABE) mechanism to provide secure sharing of health records between two parties. It makes the Authority generate the decryption key to the user and hide the attributes through an anonymous key agreement. It effectively realized the privacy preservation to hide the access policy, but it failed to maintain the efficiency and security of the health care system. (Zhang, *et al.,* 2016) modeled an ABE approach to offer fine-grained access control to the PHR files. It not only provided security but also enable the privacy preservation of health data. However, the public and the private keys generated using this model were very short, making the model more effective and efficient. It achieved tight security, but it failed to provide strong security. (Liu, *et al.,* 2019) developed a blockchain-based medical data sharing and protection approach for increasing the e-health system in the hospital. This model satisfies various security factors, like openness, tamper resistance, and decentralization. It created a reliable mechanism for storing and accessing historical data in the cloud. However, the computational complexity and the communication cost of this method were low, but it failed to consider the security. (Sabitha, *et al.*, 2020) developed ABE for the secure transmission of data. It reduces communication costs and improves the performance of the system by constant key size and prevents the security issues like forward and backward secrecy issues. It is not applicable for real time applications because it controls the access of the user. (Anirban Chakraborty, 2020) devised ABE for the secure transmission of data. This method is stable and provides security to PHR against maltreatment in the cloud. PHR owner gives absolute control to validate patient-centered PHR. So, a third-party cloud platform is used. It is difficult for fine entry. The privacy preservation methods make sure integrity, accountability, audit trial, authenticity, and confidentiality. Confidentiality states that the health data is completely concealed by the unsanctioned parties, while integrity is used to maintain the originality of information in the cloud storage (Xiao and Xiao, 2012). Authenticity states that the health data is accessed only by authorized entities, while accountability defines the data access policy complying with the agreed-upon procedure. However, monitoring the usage of health care data and providing the access right for accessing the data is called an audit trial (Abbas and Khan, 2014)(Ali, M *et al.* 2020).

The exiting data-sharing techniques are summarized in Table 1.

2.2 Challenges

Some of the challenges associated with the existing data sharing methods are discussed as follows:

- Designed the anonymous attribute-based encryption scheme with the constant ciphertext and the secret key size poses a great challenge. It is very difficult to trace or identify the malicious user, as the malicious user discloses the decryption privilege to the group identity to gain financial benefits.
- The ORAM approach had more computational complexity issues such that minimizing the data owner involvement in the data-sharing mechanism poses a great challenge.
- The multi-source order-preserving encryption (MSOPE) mechanism failed to secure the order of information in the EHR content concerning the cloud server. It enables the adversary to retrieve the data about EHR, which results in a challenging issue in cloud storage.
- The encryption mechanism provides weak security, and it is very difficult to model the privacy preservation and the security scheme in terms of strong security.
- To balance the efficiency and the security in the cloud data storage for constructing the prime order to health data poses a challenging task.

Thus, the challenges faced by the existing techniques are the size of the security key, computational complexity, secure information sharing, and the efficiency of the system. These are overcome by the proposed system using seven phases and four entities: encryption and decryption with public and private keys of server and data owner and user. Thus the security in the data sharing is improved, and the efficiency of the system is also improved. By using this, the time complexity is reduced.

3. PROPOSED SDC-BASED DATA SHARING APPROACH FOR SECURE SHARING OF PHR IN CLOUD

Due to the complexity and the openness of the internet, data security, secure data sharing, and data privacy have become major concerns in the cloud framework. Therefore, a robust data sharing approach named SDC-data sharing is proposed in this research to provide security to the PHR in the cloud. For secure data sharing in the cloud, the proposed SDC-based data sharing approach involves seven phases: server registration phase, Data Owner registration phase, user registration phase, encryption phase, control setup phase, verification phase, and decryption and data download phase, respectively. The proposed SDC-based data sharing approach consists of four different entities: user, Data Owner, cloud server, and Trusted Authority. Each entity in the data-sharing model performs its operations to share the PHR can be effectively achieved securely. Initially, the cloud server registered itself with the Trusted Authority by

Table 1. An existing methods review

Authors	Methods	Advantages	Disadvantages
Ali, M.*et al.*	Setup and Reencryption Server-Personal Health Records (SRS-PHR)	This methodology was secured against insider threats and also enforced a forward and backward access control	High computational complexity
Xiong, H.*et al.*(Florence and Suresh 2019)	anonymous attribute-based broadcast encryption (AABBE)	The access policy with the ciphertext will not be disclosed by anyone, not even the legitimate PHR data receivers	It failed to design the scheme with the constant-size secret key and ciphertext size
Yuan, D.*et al.* (Abbas, 2015)	oblivious random access memory (ORAM)	Low computational complexity	This method failed to reduce data owner involvement and a new data sharing scheme based on ORAM in a malicious adversarial model.
Zhang, A., and Lin, X.(Athena and Sumathy 2019)	blockchain-based secure and privacy-preserving PHI sharing (BSPP) scheme	Improved performance from the aspects of storage overhead, communication overhead, and time overhead	It failed to include the conjunctive keyword search and specific miner and verifier election algorithm for the e-Health blockchains.
Liang, J. *et al.* (Abbas and Khan, 2014)	multi-source order-preserving encryption (MSOPE) scheme	MSOPE scheme enabled the doctors to perform privacy-preserving range queries over outsourced EHRs from multiple patients in cloud-based e-Health systems	It failed to protect the order information of EHR contents against cloud servers
Liang, P. *et al.*(Au, 2017)	Attribute-based encryption (ABE)	This method not only realizes the user's identity privacy preservation but also hides the attribute in the access policy	This method failed to maintain the security and the efficiency of the system
Zhang, L.*et al.* (Doshi, 2019)	Attribute-Based Encryption (ABE)	The proposed schemes have many advantages over the available, such as short private keys and public keys. Also, the proposed schemes achieve compact security in the standard model and prime order group	This method failed to construct secure and privacy-preserving schemes based on the AABE, especially the HAABE scheme with strong security.
Liu, X.*et al.*(Zhang, 2019)	hospital's private blockchain	Low computational and communication cost	This method failed to enhance the security
Sabitha, *et al.*(Sabitha and Rajasree, 2020)	Attribute-based Encryption (ABE)	It reduces communication costs and improves the performance of the system by constant key size. It prevents the security issues like forwarding and backward secrecy issues.	It does not apply to real time applications because it controls the access of the user.
Anirban Chakraborty (Chakraborty, 2020)	Attribute-based Encryption (ABE)	This method is stable and provides security to PHR against maltreatment in the cloud.	PHR owner gives absolute control to validate patient-centered PHR. So third-party cloud platform is used. It is difficult for fine entry.
(Abbas and Khan, 2014)	Review of cloud-based approaches	Classifies the review in terms of cryptographic and non-cryptographic approaches	-
(Xiao and Xiao, 2012)	Studied attribute-driven methodologies	Spotted the different attributes for security in the cloud network, and the several attacks were also discussed.	-

sending the request using the password and ID of the cloud server. The Trusted Authority accepts and the request and performs the hashing function using the ID and password of the server to register the server with the Trusted Authority. Similarly, the Data Owner sends the registration request to the cloud server to register with the server in the cloud environment. In the user registration phase, the user registered themselves with the cloud server using the ID and the device number of the user. The Data Owner

Figure 1. Schematic diagram of the proposed SDC-based data sharing in the cloud

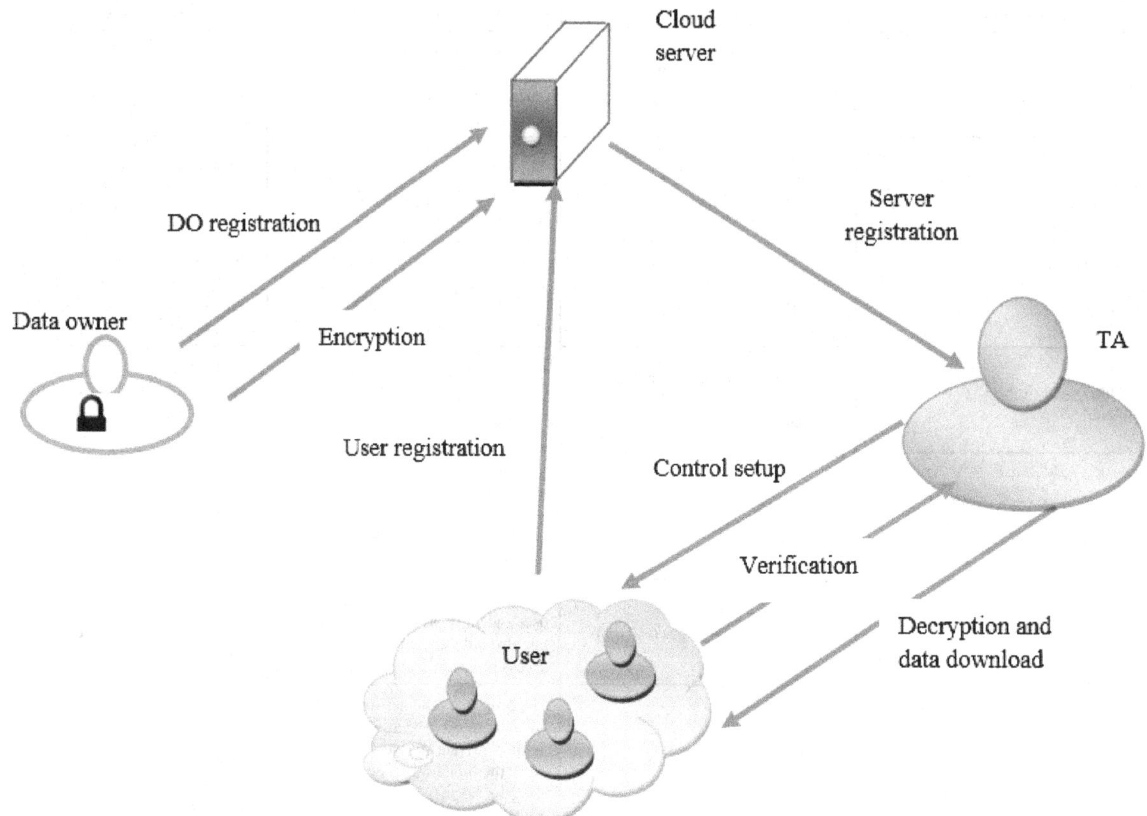

encrypts the data at the encryption phase using the encryption function. In the control setup phase, the cloud server accepts the user's request and generates its session password using the hashing function. The user generates the authentication messages at the verification phase and records the messages in the Trusted Authority. Finally, the uscr receives the Trusted Authority data and decrypts the data using the decryption function at the decrypt and data download phase. Figure 1 portrays the schematic diagram of the proposed SDC-based data sharing approach in the cloud.

3.1 Server Registration Phase

Server registration is the initial phase of the proposed SDC-based data sharing approach in the cloud environment used to share the PHR effectively. The cloud server runs the server registration phase. In contrast, the cloud user runs the user registration process, and the Data Owner runs the Data Owner registration process. However, the user can share the PHR in the cloud with high security. The registration phase includes user registration, server registration, and the Data Owner registration phase. The server registration process is carried out between the cloud server and the Trusted Authority. In contrast, the Data Owner registration process is carried out between the Data Owner and cloud server, and the cloud server accepts the user registration request. In the server registration phase, the server registered itself with

Table 2. Symbol description of the proposed SDC-based data sharing approach in cloud

Symbol	Description
B_{id}	SERVER ID
B_{pwd}	SERVER PASSWORD
B_{sespwd}	SESSION PASSWORD OF SERVER
Z_{id}	DATA OWNER ID
Z_{pwd}	PASSWORD OF DATA OWNER
Z_{pk}	PRIVATE KEY OF DATA OWNER
X_{id}	ID OF USER
X_{pwd}	PASSWORD OF USER
X_{dno}	DEVICE NUMBER OF USER
X_{pk}	PRIVATE KEY OF USER
T^c	CIPHER TEXT
R	DATA REQUEST MESSAGE
X_{sespwd}	SESSION PASSWORD OF USER
a	SECURITY PARAMETER
r	RANDOM NUMBER
k	PUBLIC KEY OF USER
M_1, M_2	AUTHENTICATION MESSAGES
Y_d	DATA ACCESS KEY
$E(.)$	ENCRYPTION
$D(.)$	DECRYPTION
$H(.)$	HASHING
$\otimes$	CIRCULAR INTERPOLATION
$*$	STORED VALUES
W	TIMESTAMP
//	CONCATENATION OPERATOR
$\oplus$	EX-OR OPERATION

the Trusted Authority by sending the registration request using the ID and the server's password. Table 2 represents the symbol and its description of the proposed SDC-based data sharing model in the cloud.

Initially, the cloud server creates the ID and password of the server and sends the cloud server ID B_{id} and the password of the server B_{pwd} to the Trusted Authority. The Trusted Authority receives the server ID B_{id} and the password B_{pwd} and recorded them in the Trusted Authority as B^*_{id} and B^*_{pwd}. After receiving and storing the ID and password of the server, the Trusted Authority generates the session password of the server using the B^*_{id} and B^*_{pwd} by applying the hashing function. However, the session password of the user that the Trusted Authority creates is represented as:

Figure 2. Server registration phase of the proposed SDC-based data sharing approach in cloud

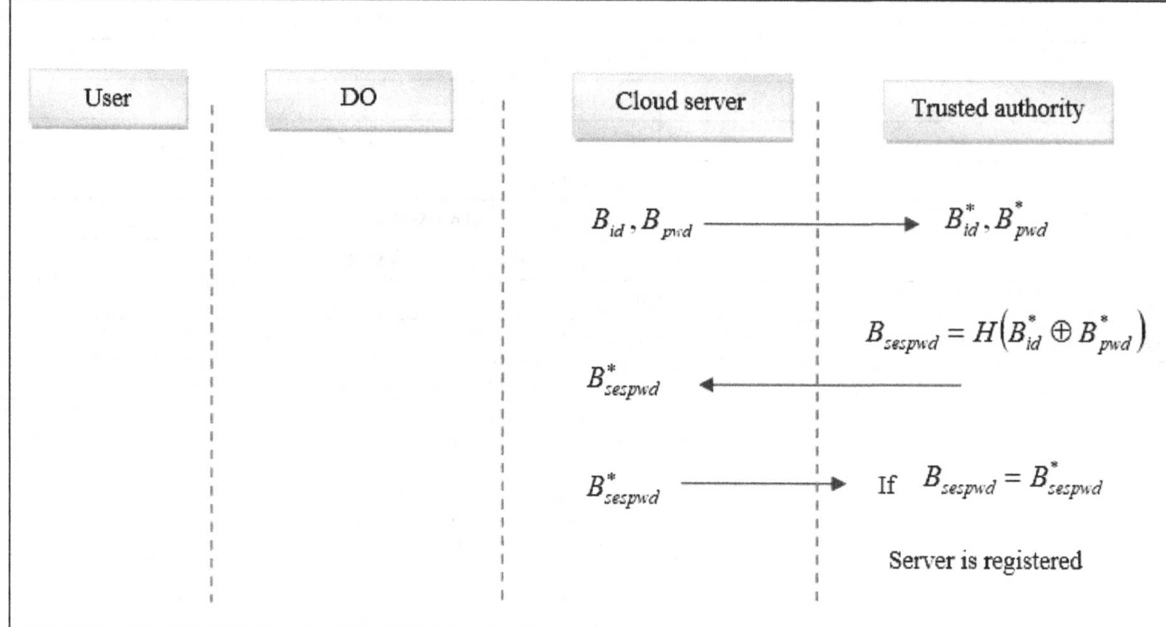

$$B_{sespwd} = H\left(B^*_{id} \oplus B^*_{pwd}\right) \quad (1)$$

The ID of the server B^*_{id} that is stored in the Trusted Authority and the server password B^*_{pwd} is allowed to perform the EX-OR operation, which is then applied to the hashing function to generate the server's session password. The Trusted Authority generates the session password of the server and sends it to the cloud server, which receives the session password and is stored in the cloud server as B^*_{sespwd}. The Trusted Authority receives the session password B^*_{sespwd} and verifies the session password B_{sespwd} with B^*_{sespwd}. If $B_{sespwd} = B^*_{sespwd}$, then, the server's registration request to the Trusted Authority is accepted so that the server gets registered with the Trusted Authority. Once the server registration process is completed, the Data Owner begins to send the registration request to the cloud server. Figure 2 portrays the server registration phase of the proposed SDC-based data sharing approach in the cloud.

3.2 Data Owner Registration Phase

The second phase to be performed in the proposed SDC-based data sharing approach is the Data Owner registration phase. The Data Owner runs the Data Owner registration phase with the cloud server. In the Data Owner registration phase, the Data Owner generates the ID Z_{id} and the password Z_{pwd} of the Data Owner and sends them to the cloud server to register the Data Owner with the server. The cloud server receives the ID and password of the Data Owner and stores them in the server as Z^*_{id} and Z^*_{pwd}, respectively. The cloud server generates the private key of the Data Owner using the ID Z^*_{id} and the

Figure 3. DO registration phase of the proposed SDC-based data sharing approach in cloud

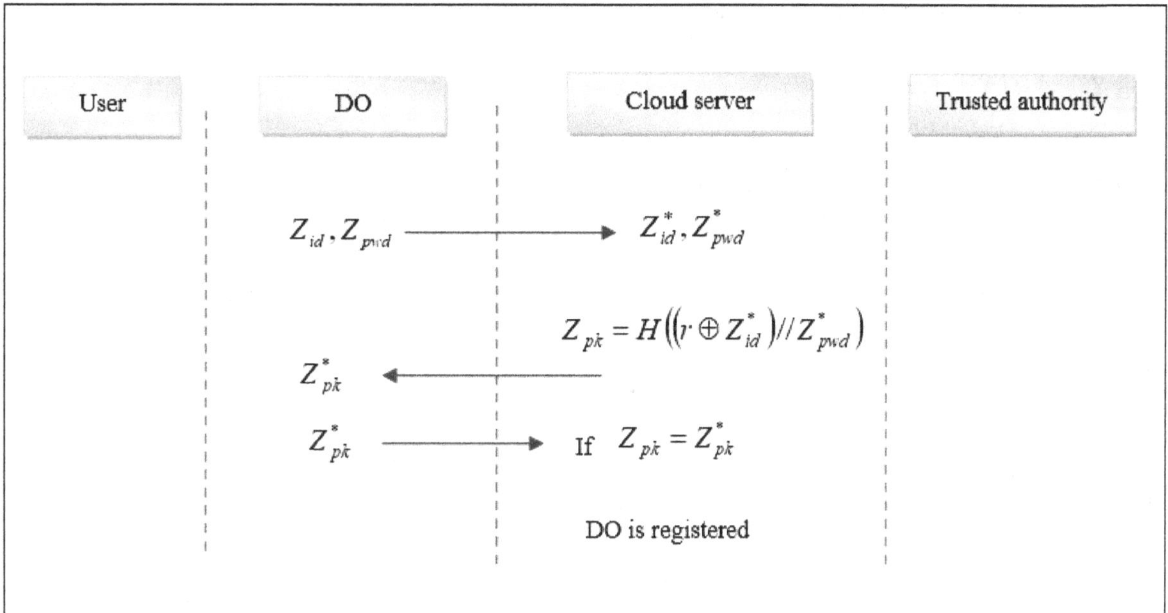

password Z^*_{pwd} of the server. However, the private key of Data Owner generated by the cloud server is represented as:

$$Z_{pk} = H\left(\left(r \oplus Z^*_{id}\right) / / Z^*_{pwd}\right) \tag{2}$$

The ID of the Data Owner stored in the cloud server is allowed to perform the EX-OR operation with the random number r, which is then concatenated with the password of DO stored in the server. The resultant factor is then applied to the hashing function to generate the Data Owner's private key Z_{pk}. The server sends the private key of the Data Owner to the Data Owner, which receives the private key and records it in the Data Owner as Z^*_{pk}. The private key of the Data Owner stored in the server is verified with the Data Owner's private key recorded in the Data Owner. If $Z_{pk} = Z^*_{pk}$ the server accepts the Data Owner's registration request, the Data Owner gets registered with the cloud server. After performing the Data Owner registration process, the next step is the user registration phase. Figure 3 portrays the Data Owner registration phase of the proposed SDC-based data sharing approach in the cloud.

3.3 User Registration Phase

The user registration process is carried out only after the Data Owner registration process is completed. In the user registration phase, the user sends the server's registration request by creating the ID X_{id} and the password as X_{pwd}. The user sends the ID X_{id} and the user's password to the cloud server, which receives the ID and password from the user and records them in the server as X^*_{id} and X^*_{pwd}, respectively. The cloud server generates the message x using the device number of users and the random number. However, the message generated by the cloud server is expressed as:

$$x = X^*_{dno} \oplus H\left(X^*_{dno} / / r\right) \tag{3}$$

The device number of users stored in the server is concatenated with the random number and applied to the hashing function. The resultant hashed factor is then allowed to perform the EX-OR operation with the device number of users stored in the cloud server. The server then sends the message x to the user, which receives the messages and stored it in the user as $\tilde{x}$, which is represented as:

$$\tilde{x} = X_{dno} \oplus H\left(X_{dno} / / r\right) \tag{4}$$

The device number of users and the random number r are concatenated together, and the hashing function is applied to the concatenated factor. The resultant hashed factor is allowed to perform the EX-OR operation with the device number of users. The message generated by the server is verified with the message stored in the user. If $x = \tilde{x}$, the user gets registered with the server. Once the user is registered with the server, the cloud server generates the private key of the user using the security parameter a and the ID X^*_{id} and password X^*_{pwd} that is stored in the server. The private key of user-generated by the cloud server is represented as:

$$X_{pk} = X^*_{id} * H\left(a \oplus X^*_{pwd}\right) \tag{5}$$

The security parameter is allowed to perform the EX-OR operation with the user password, and the resultant expression is applied to the hashing function. The hashed factor is then combined with the ID of the user that is stored in the server. The server generates the user's private key and sends it to the user, which receives the private key and records it in the user entity. Once the user registration process is completed, the Data Owner begins to execute the encryption phase. Figure 4 represents the user registration phase of the proposed SDC-based data sharing approach in the cloud.

3.4 Encryption Phase

The Data Owner entity runs the encryption phase. The input data is considered as T, which is encrypted in the encryption phase by Data Owner. The data T encrypted by the Data Owner is specified as T^{en} and represented using the below equation as:

$$T^{en} = E\left(T / / Z_{id}\right) \oplus \left(a / / Z^*_{pk}\right) \tag{6}$$

The input data T is concatenated with the Data Owner's ID and applied to the encryption function. The security parameter is concatenated with the private key of the Data Owner. The concatenated security parameter and the resulted encrypted data are allowed to perform the EX-OR operation to encrypt

Figure 4. User registration phase of the proposed SDC-based data sharing approach in cloud

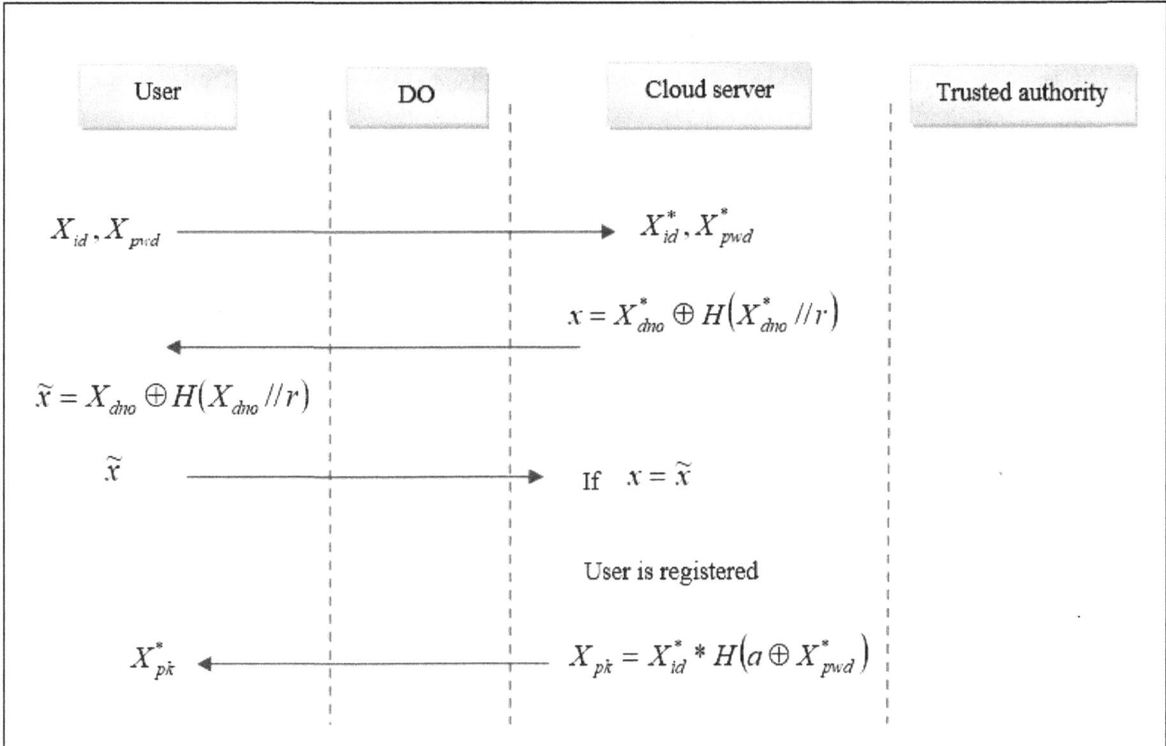

the data. Furthermore, the Data Owner generates the ciphertext T^c using the encrypted data and the data owner's ID. However, the ciphertext generated by the Data Owner is represented as:

$$T^c = E\left(T^{en} \otimes Z_{id}\right) * r \tag{7}$$

The encrypted data is interpolated with the ID of the Data Owner and is then applied to the encryption function. The resulted encryption factor is then combined with the random number to generate the ciphertext T^c. Accordingly, the ciphertext generated by the Data Owner is sent to the cloud server, which receives the ciphertext and stores it in the server entity T^{c^*}. Once the data is encrypted in the encryption phase, the user begins to execute the control setup phase. Figure 5 represents the encryption phase of the proposed SDC-based data sharing approach in the cloud.

3.5 Control Setup Phase

The next phase to be processed in the proposed SDC-based data sharing approach is the control setup phase. A new user registration process is carried out using the server and the user entity in the control setup phase. The user generates the data request message *R* and sends the message to the cloud server. The data request message generated by the user is represented as:

Figure 5. Encryption phase of the proposed SDC-based data sharing approach in cloud

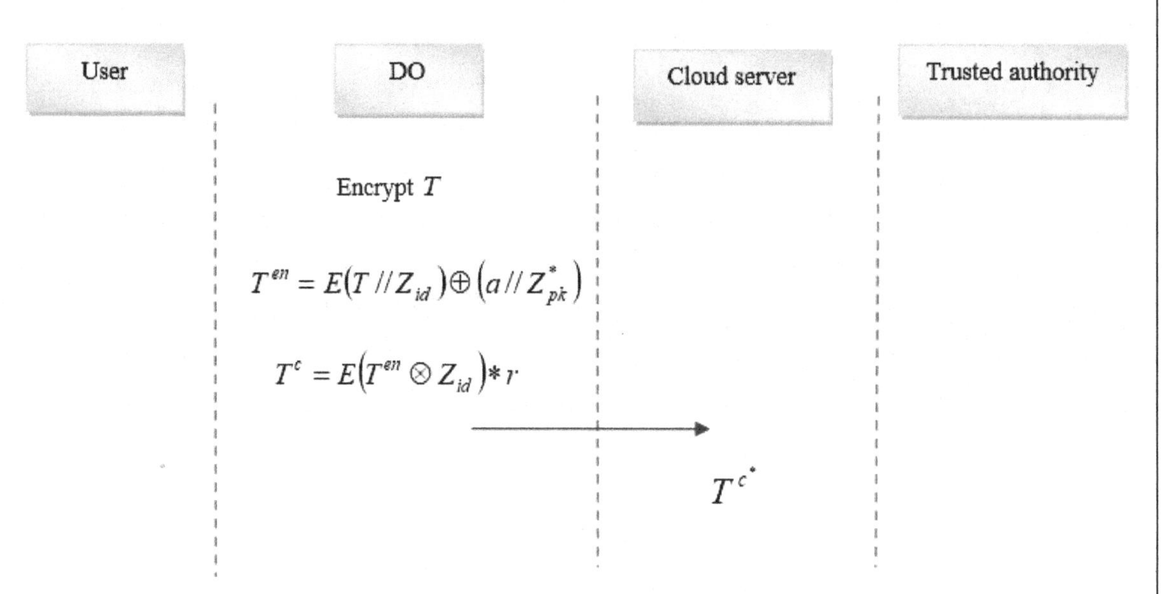

$$R = E\left(X_{pwd} \otimes H\left(X_{id} / / X_{dno}\right)\right) \tag{8}$$

The user ID is concatenated with the device number of the user, and the resultant factor is applied to the hashing function. The hashed factor is allowed to perform the circular interpolation operation with the user password. Finally, the resulted hashed factor is applied to the encryption function to generate the data request message. The data request message generated by the user is sent to the server, which receives the message and stores it in server entity as $\tilde{R}$, which is represented as:

$$\tilde{R} = E\left(X^{*}_{pwd} \otimes H\left(X^{*}_{id} / / X_{dno}\right)\right) \tag{9}$$

The data request message generated by the user is verified with the message stored in the server. If $R = \tilde{R}$, then the server accepts the request of the new user. Once the server accepts the new user request, the cloud server sends the data request message to Trusted Authority. The Trusted Authority generates the session password of the user using the user public key, random number, and the security parameter. However, the session password generated by the Trusted Authority is represented as:

$$X_{sespwd} = H\left(r / / a / / X^{*}_{id} \otimes k\right) \tag{10}$$

The random number, security parameter, and the user ID are concatenated together and are then circular interpolated with the user public key. The resultant concatenated factor is applied to the hashing function to generate the user session password. The Trusted Authority generates the user session password. It sends it to the server, which receives the session password of the user and stores it in the

Figure 6. Control setup phase of the proposed SDC-based data sharing approach in cloud

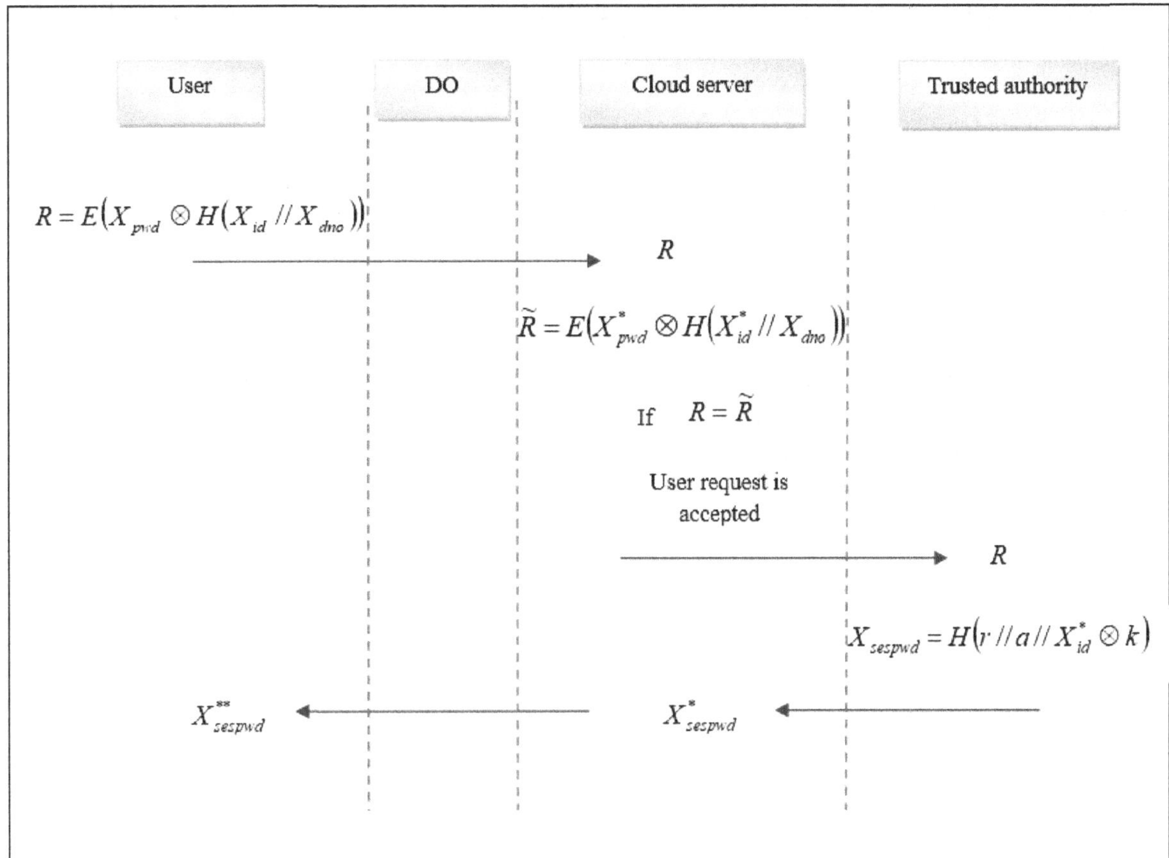

server entity as X^*_{sespwd}, which is further sent to the user and stored in the user entity as X^{**}_{sespwd}. After performing the control setup phase, the next step to be performed is the verification phase. Figure 6 portrays the control setup phase in the cloud.

3.6 Verification Phase

In the verification phase, the user generates the authentication messages M_1 and M_2 which are sent to Trusted Authority. The authentication messages generated by the user is represented as:

$$M_1 = E\left(X^{**}_{sespwd} \otimes H\left(r // X_{id}\right)\right) \tag{11}$$

The user ID is concatenated with the random number and is then applied to the hashing function. The resulted in hashed factor is circular interpolated with the session password of the user to generate the authentication message M_1. The authentication message M_2 is represented as:

$$M_2 = M_1 \oplus S \tag{12}$$

The authentication message M_1 is allowed to perform the EX-OR operation with the Chebyshev polynomial to compute the authentication message M_2. However, the Chebyshev polynomial factor is calculated as:

$$S = 8s^4 - 8s^2 + 1 \tag{13}$$

Here, the parameter s is specified as:

$$s = E\left(X_{dno} \, / \, / X^*_{pk}\right) \bmod r \tag{14}$$

The user device number and private key of the user are concatenated together and applied to the encryption function, then modulated with the random number. The user sends the authentication messages to the Trusted Authority, which receives the messages M_1 and M_2, then stored in the Trusted Authority entity as $\tilde{M}_1$ and $\tilde{M}_2$, which are represented as:

$$\tilde{M}_1 = E\left(X_{sespwd} \otimes H\left(r \, / \, / X^*_{id}\right)\right) \tag{15}$$

$$\tilde{M}_2 = \tilde{M}_1 \oplus S \tag{16}$$

The authentication message generated by the user is verified with the authentication messages stored in the Trusted Authority. If $M_1 = \tilde{M}_1 \,\&\, \tilde{M}_2 = \tilde{M}_2$, the user gets authenticated with the Trusted Authority. After performing the verification process, the user begins to execute the decryption and download phase. Figure 7 portrays the verification phase in the cloud.

3.7 Decryption and Data Download Phase

In the decryption and data download phase, the Trusted Authority generates the data access key using the user ID, user public key, and timestamp. However, the data access key generated by the Trusted Authority is represented as:

$$J_M = r * E\left(X^{**}_{id} \, / \, / k \, / \, / W\right) \tag{17}$$

The user ID is concatenated with the user public key and is further concatenated with the time stamp W. The encryption function is applied to the concatenated factor, and the resultant encrypted factor is combined with the random number. The Trusted Authority generates the data access key and sends it to the user, which receives the data access key and stores it in the user entity as J^*_M. Accordingly, the data accessed key that is stored in the user is sent to the cloud server. The server receives the data access key and stores it in the cloud server entity as expressed below:

Figure 7. Verification phase of the proposed SDC-based data sharing approach in cloud

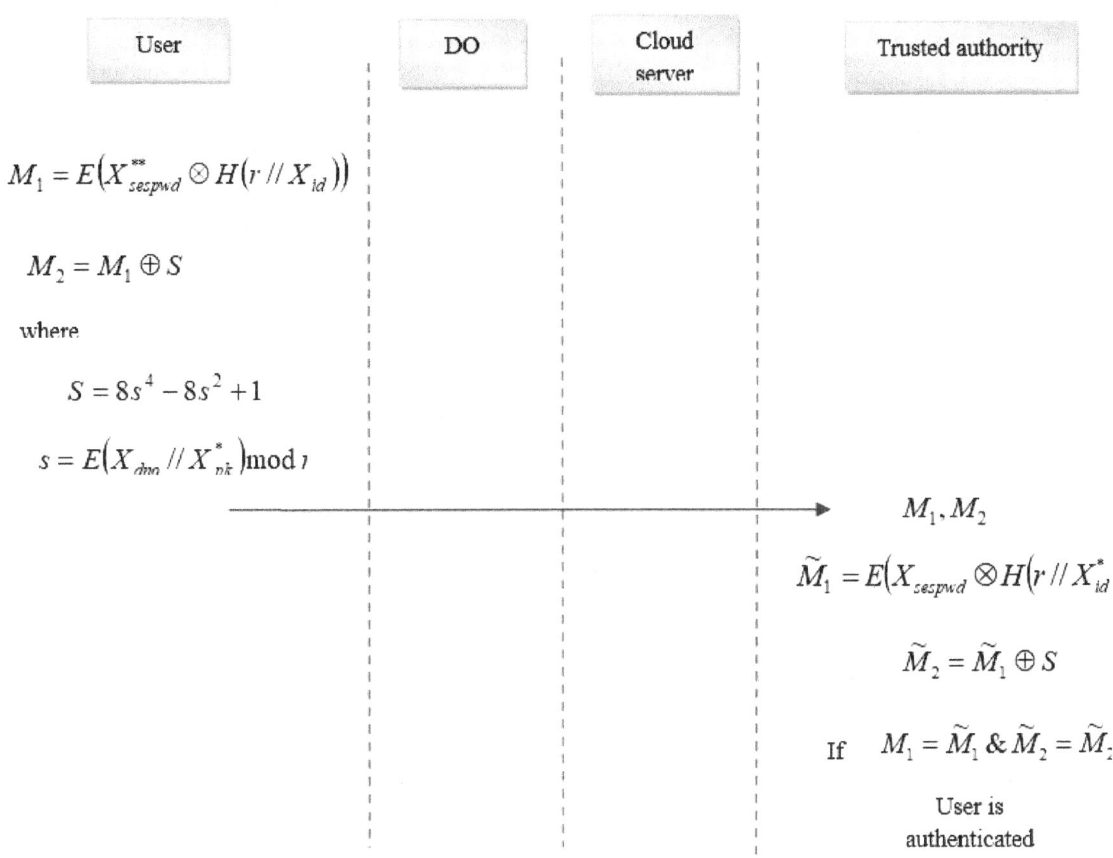

$$\tilde{J}_M = r * E\left(X^*_{id} / /k / /W\right) \tag{18}$$

The cloud server verifies the data access key such that if $J^*_M = \tilde{J}_M$, the server sends the ciphertext to the user. The user receives the ciphertext and decrypts the data using the below expression as:

$$T = D(T^c) \tag{19}$$

The user applies the decryption function to the ciphertext and retrieves the original data back in the decryption and data download phase. Figure 8 represents the decryption and data download phase of the proposed SDC-based data sharing approach in the cloud.

With the server registration phase, the cloud server makes the registration request to the Trusted Authority. In contrast, the Data Owner makes the registration request to the cloud server at the Data Owner registration phase. The Data Owner executes the encryption phase and generates the ciphertext through the encryption function. The user generates the authentication messages at the verification phase

Figure 8. Decryption and data download phase of the proposed SDC-based data sharing approach in cloud

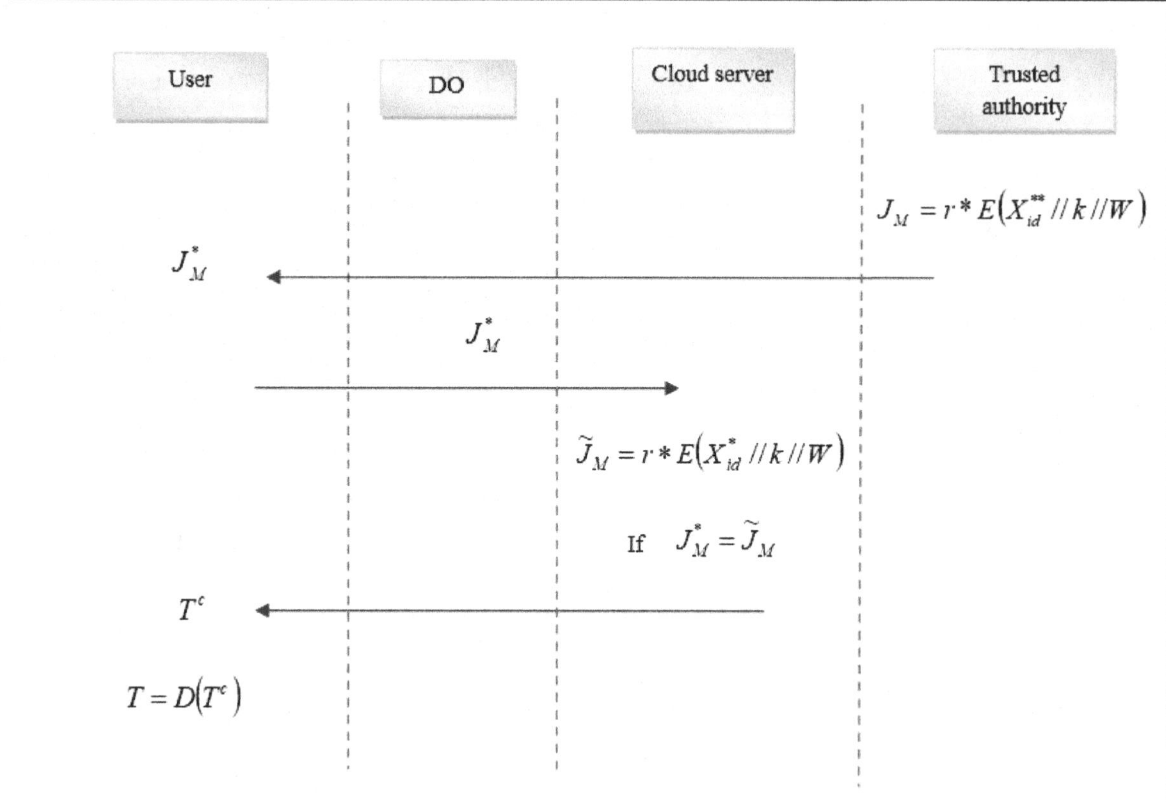

to register the request of new users with Trusted Authority. The user executes the decryption and the data download phase and decrypts the Trusted Authority's data using the decryption function.

4. RESULTS AND DISCUSSION

The results and discussion using the proposed SDC-based data sharing approach are discussed in this section regarding communication cost, time, and memory.

4.1 Experimental Setup

Implementing the proposed SDC-based data sharing approach is carried out in the JAVA tool using the dataset specified in (UCI machine learning repository). This dataset consists of 76 attributes, out of which the researchers commonly use 14 attributes. The presence of the disease is specified with the integer values ranging from one to four, while the absence of disease is specified as zero. The link for the dataset is: "https://archive.ics.uci.edu/ml/datasets/Heart+Disease"

4.2 Evaluation Metrics

The performance obtained by the proposed approach is evaluated by considering the metrics, such as communication cost, time, and memory:

- **Communication cost (bits):** The message transferred between the entities is calculated in decimal values. The communication cost is defined as the number of bits present in the decimal values of transmitted messages.
- **Time (ms):** It is otherwise called running time, which is the length of the time taken to complete the computational process.
- **Memory (bytes):** The system memory is used to record and process PHR data to achieve secure data sharing.

4.3 Comparative Methods

The performance enhancement of the proposed approach is evaluated by comparing the proposed with the existing methods, like Anonymous Attribute-based broadcast encryption (AABBE *;* Xiong, *et al.*, 2018), Oblivious random access memory (ORAM)-based data sharing (Yuan, *et al.,* 2018), Privacy-preserving decentralized Attribute-based encryption (PPD-ABE *;* Liang, *et al.,* 2019), Attribute-based encryption (ABE) Liang, P. *et al.*(Au, 2017), block chain-based secure and privacy-preserving PHI sharing (BSPP) Zhang, A., and Lin, X.(Athena and Sumathy 2019), and multi-source order-preserving encryption (MSOPE) Liang, J. *et al.* (Abbas and Khan, 2014) respectively.

4.4 Comparative Analysis

The comparative analysis of the proposed SDC-based data sharing approach is elaborated in this section.

4.4.1 Comparative Analysis With File Size=10Kb

Figure 9 represents the comparative analysis of the proposed SDC-based data sharing with the file size is 10Kb. Figure 9 a) portrays the analysis of communication cost by varying the key length. When key length=64, the cost utilized by the existing AABBE, ABE, ORAM-based data sharing, PPD-ABE, BSPP, and MSOPE, is 97790 bits, 97701 bits, 97618 bits, 97493 bits, 97401 bits, 97322 bits, and 97243 bits, while the proposed SDC-based data sharing utilizes less cost of 97171bits, respectively.

Figure 9 b) represents the analysis of time to the key length. When key length=64, the time measured by the existing AABBE, ABE, ORAM-based data sharing, PPD-ABE, BSPP, and MSOPE, 534 ms, 493 ms, 422 ms, 111 ms, 94 ms, 88 ms, and 79ms, while the proposed SDC-based data sharing acquires less time of 73ms, respectively.

Figure 9 c) represents the analysis of memory concerning the key length. When key length=64, the memory utilized by the existing AABBE, ABE, ORAM-based data sharing, PPD-ABE, BSPP, and MSOPE, is 15705504 bytes, 10256632 bytes, 6197784 bytes, 3211792 bytes, 3012365 bytes, 2752631 bytes, and 2335418 bytes, the proposed SDC-based data sharing utilize less memory of 1875064bytes, respectively.

Figure 9. Comparative analysis with file size=10Kb, a) communication cost, b) time, c) memory

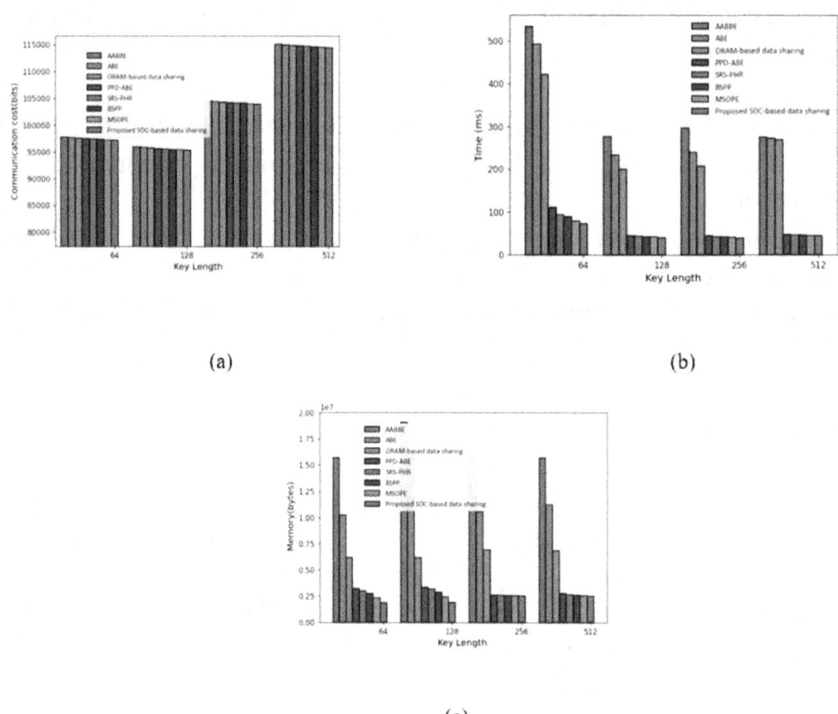

4.4.2 Comparative Analysis With File Size=100Kb

Figure 10 represents the comparative analysis of the proposed SDC-based data sharing with the file size as 10Kb. Figure 10 a) portrays the analysis of communication cost by varying the key length. When key length=64, the cost utilized by the existing AABBE, ABE, ORAM-based data sharing, PPD-ABE, BSPP, and MSOPE is 291156 bits, 291085 bits, 290827 bits, 290702 bits, 290641 bits, 290536 bits, and 290452 bits, while the proposed SDC-based data sharing utilizes less cost of 290380 bits, respectively.

Figure 10 b) represents the analysis of time to the key length. When key length=64, the time measured by the existing AABBE, ABE, ORAM-based data sharing, PPD-ABE, BSPP, and MSOPE is 359ms, 243ms, 195ms, 47ms, 42ms, 36ms, and 30ms, while the proposed SDC-based data sharing acquires less time of 26ms, respectively.

Figure 10 c) represents the analysis of memory with respect to the key length. When key length=64, the memory utilized by the existing AABBE, ABE, ORAM-based data sharing, PPD-ABE, BSPP, and MSOPE is 2868192 bytes, 2732154 bytes, 2603216 bytes, 2603056 bytes, 2585233 bytes, 2407892 bytes, and 2200524 bytes, while the proposed SDC-based data sharing acquires less memory of 1972088 bytes, respectively.

Figure 10. Comparative analysis with file size=100Kb, a) communication cost, b) time, c) memory

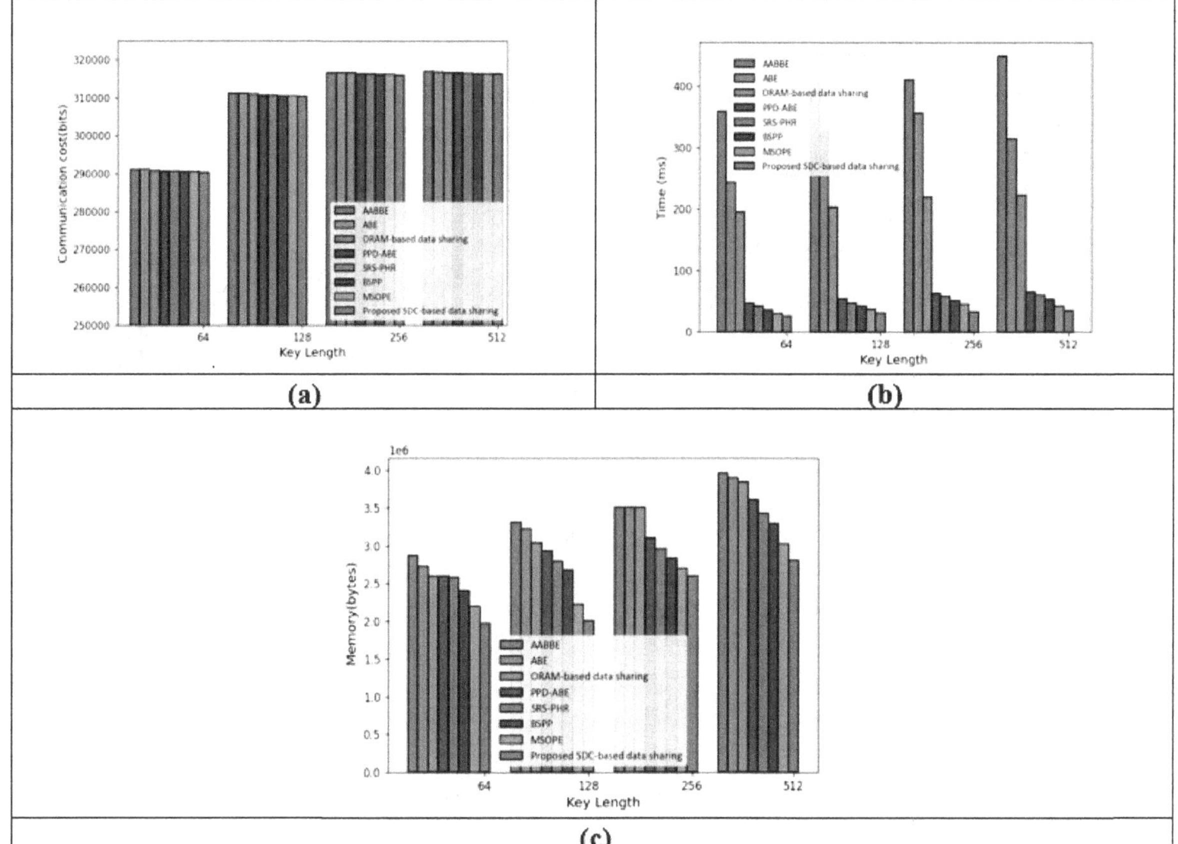

4.4.3 Comparative Analysis With File Size=1000Kb

Figure 11 represents the comparative analysis of the proposed SDC-based data sharing with the file size as 300Kb. Figure 11 a) portrays the analysis of communication cost by varying the key length. When key length=64, the cost utilized by the existing AABBE, ABE, ORAM-based data sharing, PPD-ABE, BSPP, and MSOPE is 3359114 bits, 3356231 bits, 3353953 bits, 3349798 bits, 3348123 bits, 3347321 bits, and 3346853 bits, while the proposed SDC-based data sharing utilizes less cost of 3345476bits, respectively.

Figure 11 b) represents the analysis of time with respect to the key length. When key length=64, the time measured by the existing AABBE, ABE, ORAM-based data sharing, PPD-ABE, BSPP, and MSOPE is 3416 ms, 3222 ms, 3152 ms, 1917 ms, 1632 ms, 1008 ms, and 984 ms, while the proposed SDC-based data sharing acquire less time of 698ms, respectively.

Figure 11 c) represents the analysis of memory with respect to the key length. When key length=64, the memory utilized by the existing AABBE, ABE, ORAM-based data sharing, PPD-ABE, BSPP, and MSOPE is 2.9E+08 bytes, 1.90E+08 bytes, 1.18E+08 bytes, 33046136bytes, 31025455 bytes, 29784123 bytes, and 27128741 bytes, while the proposed SDC-based data sharing utilize less memory of 2572889 6bytes, respectively.

Figure 11. Comparative analysis with file size=1000Kb, a) communication cost, b) time, c) memory

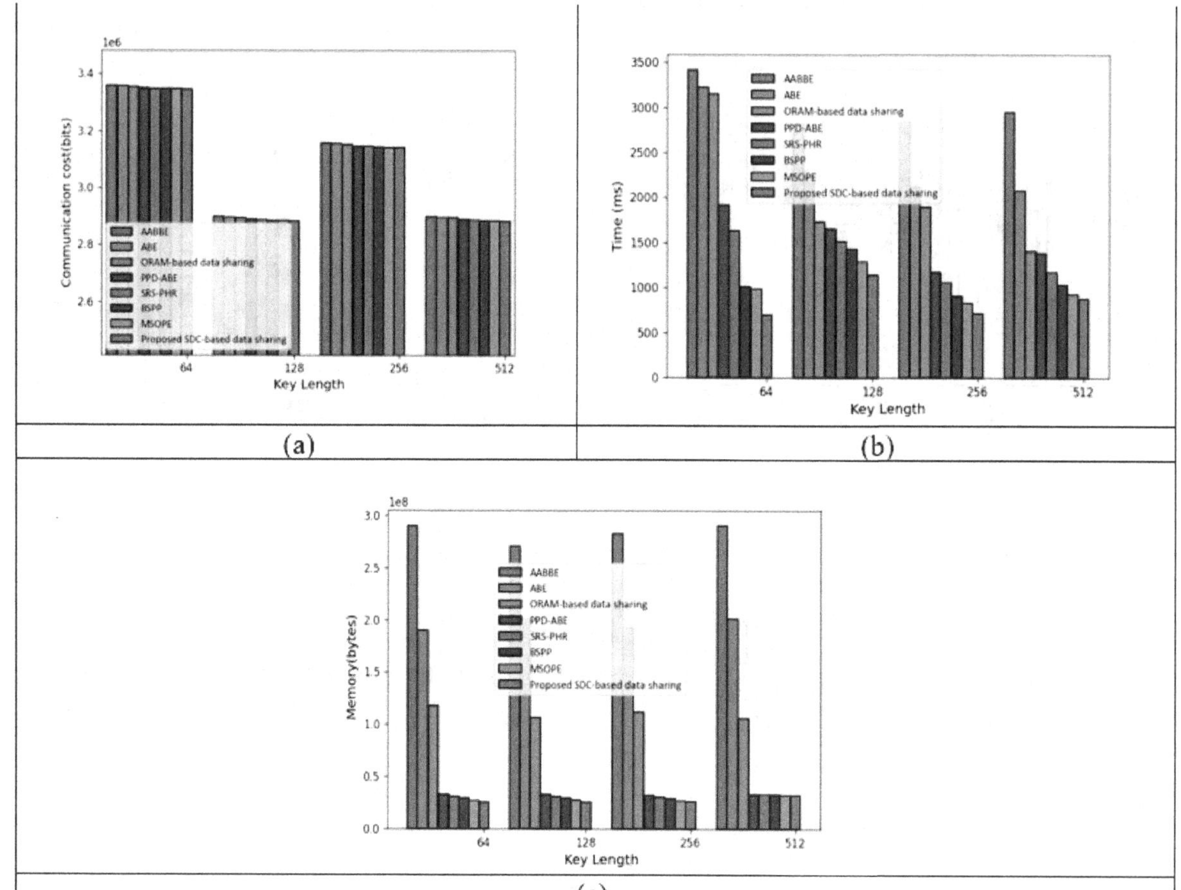

4.5 Comparative Discussion

Table 3 represents the comparative discussion of the proposed SDC-based data sharing approach in cloud storage. For file size=10Kb, the communication cost utilizes by the existing AABBE, ABE, ORAM-based data sharing, PPD-ABE, BSPP, and MSOPE is 97790bits, 97701bits, 97618bits, 97493bits, 97401bits, 97322bits, and 97243bits, whereas the proposed SDC-based data sharing approach utilizes less communication cost of 97171bits, respectively. Similarly, for 10Kb file size, the memory utilized by the existing AABBE, ABE, ORAM-based data sharing, PPD-ABE, BSPP, and MSOPE is 15705504 bytes, 10256632 bytes, 6197784 bytes, 3211792 bytes, 3012365 bytes, 2752631 bytes, and 2335418 bytes, whereas the proposed SDC-based data sharing approach utilized less memory of 1875064bytes, respectively. Similarly, for 100Kb file size, the time utilized by the existing AABBE, ABE, ORAM-based data sharing, PPD-ABE, BSPP, and MSOPE is 359ms, 243ms, 195ms, 47ms, 42ms, 36ms, and 30ms, whereas the proposed SDC-based data sharing approach utilized less memory of 26ms, respectively. Similarly, When the file size is increased to 100Kb, and 1000Kb the communication cost, memory utilized and time utilized by the proposed SDC-based data sharing approach having minimal values compared to the existing techniques. Thus, it is very clear that the proposed SDC-based data sharing

Table 3. Comparative discussion

Metrics/Methods		AABBE	ABE	ORAM-based data sharing	PPD-ABE	SRS-PHR	BSPP	MSOPE	Proposed SKC-based data sharing
File size=10Kb	*Communication cost (bits)*	97790	97701	97618	97493	97401	97322	97243	97171
	Time (ms)	534	493	422	111	94	88	79	73
	Memory (bytes)	15705504	10256632	6197784	3211792	3012365	2752631	2335418	1875064
File size=100Kb	*Communication cost (bits)*	291156	291085	290827	290702	290641	290536	290452	290380
	Time (ms)	359	243	195	47	42	36	30	26
	Memory (bytes)	2868192	2732154	2603216	2603056	2585233	2407892	2200524	1972088
File size=1000Kb	*Communication cost (bits)*	3359114	3356231	3353953	3349798	3348123	3347321	3346853	3345476
	Time (ms)	3416	3222	3152	1917	1632	1008	984	698
	Memory (bytes)	290238384	1.90E+08	117968592	33046136	31025455	29784123	27128741	25728896

approach obtained lower communication cost, time, and utilizes less memory of 97171bits, 26ms, and 1875064 bytes, respectively.

The proposed SDC-based data sharing approach is enabled using seven different phases: server registration phase, Data Owner registration phase, user registration phase, encryption phase, control setup phase, verification phase, decryption, and data download phase. In the registration phase, the server creates the credentials and checks them with the Trusted Authority using the session password of the server. Similarly, the Data Owner and the user create their credentials and verify them with the server using the private key of the Data Owner and the user's private key. Once the credentials are registered with the server and Trusted Authority, the encryption process is carried out by the Data Owner at the encryption phase. Here, the encryption is done based on the Data Owners private key. The user generates the authentication messages at the control setup phase using the session password of the user. Finally, the user performs the verification procedure and decrypts the data using the decryption function. Hence, by using the above seven phases, highly secure communication is possible with less cost, time, and memory.

5. CONCLUSION

In this research, an effective and robust data sharing approach named the SDC-based data sharing model is proposed for secure data sharing of PHR on cloud storage. The proposed SDC-based data sharing approach involves seven different phases: server registration phase, Data Owner registration phase, user registration phase, encryption phase, control setup phase, verification phase, decryption, and data download phase, respectively. The proposed SDC-based data sharing approach consists of four different entities: user, Data Owner, cloud server, and Trusted Authority. Each entity in the data-sharing model performs its operations to share the PHR can be effectively achieved securely. Each entity in the data-sharing model performs its operations to share the PHR in the cloud. The user registered themselves with the cloud server using the ID and the device number of the user at the user registration phase. The cloud server accepts the new user's request and generates the user's session password through the hashing function at the control setup phase. The Data Owner encrypts the data, whereas the Trusted Authority generates the data access key and delivers it to the user. It is proved that the proposed SDC-based data sharing approach requires less communication cost, time, and utilizes less memory of 97171bits, 26ms, and 1875064 bytes, respectively. In the future, the performance of data sharing in cloud storage will be enhanced using different entities.

REFERENCES

Abbas, A., Bilal, K., Zhang, L., & Khan, S. U. (2015). A cloud based health insurance plan recommendation system: A user centered approach,'. *Future Generation Computer Systems Systems*, *43*, 99–109. doi:10.1016/j.future.2014.08.010

Abbas, A., & Khan, S. U. (2014). A Review on the State State-of -thethe-Art Privacy Preserving Approaches in E E-Health Clouds'. *IEEE Journal of Biomedical and Health Informatics*, *18*(4), 14311431–14311441. doi:10.1109/JBHI.2014.2300846 PMID:25014943

Ali, M., Abbas, A., Khan, U., & Khan, S. U. (2018). SeSPHR: A Methodology for Secure Sharing of Personal Health Records in the Cloud. IEEE Transactions on Cloud Computing.

Athena, J., & Sumathy, V. (2019). TBAC: Tree-based access control approach for secure access of PHR in cloud'. *International Journal of Biomedical Engineering and Technology*, *29*(3), 246–272. doi:10.1504/IJBET.2019.097624

Au, M.H., Yuen, T.H., Liu, J.K., Susilo, W., Huang, X., Xiang, Y., & Jiang, Z.L. (2017). A general framework for secure sharing of personal health records in cloud system. *Journal of Computer and System Sciences*, *90*, 46-62.

Chakraborty, A. (2020). Class Access Control of Personal Health Information Using Cloud Computing. *International Research Journal of Engineering and Technology, 7*(6).

Chiang, D. L., Huang, Y. T., Chen, T. S., & Lai, F. P. (2020). Applying time-constraint access control of personal health record in cloud computing'. *Enterprise Information Systems*, *14*(2), 266–281. doi:10.1080/17517575.2018.1522452

Dataset: UCI machine learning repository: heart disease. (n.d.). https://archive.ics.uci.edu/ml/datasets/Heart+Disease

Doshi, N., Oza, M., & Gorasia, N. (2019). An Enhanced Scheme for PHR on Cloud Servers Using CP-ABE. In *Information and Communication Technology for Competitive Strategies* (pp. 439–446). Springer. doi:10.1007/978-981-13-0586-3_44

Florence, M. L., & Suresh, D. (2019). Enhanced secure sharing of PHR's in cloud using user usage based attribute based encryption and signature with keyword search'. *Cluster Computing*, *22*(6), 13119–13130. doi:10.100710586-017-1276-7

Freitas, Tinôco, Baêta, Barbari, Conti, & Júnior, & Sousa. (2017). Correlation between egg quality parameters, housing thermal conditions and age of laying hens. *Agronomy Research, 15* (3).

Ge, C., Susilo, W., Liu, Z., Xia, J., Szalachowski, P., & Liming, F. (2020). Secure Keyword Search and Data Sharing Mechanism for Cloud Computing. *IEEE Transactions on Dependable and Secure Computing*.

Gomathi, N., & Karlekar, N. P. (2019). Ontology and Hybrid Optimization Based SVNN for Privacy Preserved Medical Data Classification in Cloud. *International Journal of Artificial Intelligence Tools, 23*(3).

Hema, V. S. V., & Kesavan, R. (2019). ECC Based Secure Sharing of Healthcare Data in the Health Cloud Environment. *Wireless Personal Communications, 108*(2), 1021–1035. doi:10.100711277-019-06450-7

Kaelber, D.C., Jha, A.K., Johnston, D., Middleton, B., & Bates, D.W. (2008). A research agenda for personal health records (PHRs). *Journal of the American Medical Informatics Association Association, 15*(6), 729-736.

Leso, L., Conti, L., Rossi, G., & Barbari, M. (2018). Criteria of design for deconstruction applied to dairy cows housing: A case study in Italy. *Agronomy Research (Tartu), 16*(3).

Liang, J., Qin, Z., Xiao, S., Zhang, J., Yin, H., & Li, K. (2019). Privacy-preserving range query over multi-source electronic health records in public clouds. *Journal of Parallel and Distributed Computing*.

Liang, P., Zhang, L., Kang, L., & Ren, J. (2019). Privacy-preserving decentralized ABE for secure sharing of personal health records in cloud storage. *Journal of Information Security and Applications, 47*, 258–266. doi:10.1016/j.jisa.2019.05.012

Liu, X., Wang, Z., Jin, C., Li, F., & Li, G. (2019). A Blockchain-Based Medical Data Sharing and Protection Scheme. *IEEE Access: Practical Innovations, Open Solutions, 7*, 118943–118953. doi:10.1109/ACCESS.2019.2937685

Sabitha, S., & Rajasree, M. S. (2020). Multi-level on-demand access control for flexible data sharing in cloud. *Cluster Computing*. Advance online publication. doi:10.100710586-020-03195-y

Shen, Q., Liang, X., Shen, X., Lin, X., & Luo, H. (2014). Exploiting geo-distributed clouds for a e-Health monitoring system with minimum service delay and privacy preservation,'. *IEEE Journal of Biomedical and Health Informatics, 18*(2), 430–439. doi:10.1109/JBHI.2013.2292829 PMID:24608048

Vishalatchi, M., Krishnamoorthy, N., & Sangeetha, S. (2017). Optimised scheduling in cloud computing. *IEEE, 2017 International Conference on Algorithms, Methodology, Models and Applications in Emerging Technologies (ICAMMAET).*

Xiao, Z., & Xiao, Y. (2012). Security and privacy in cloud computing. *IEEE Communications Surveys and Tutorials, 15*(2), 1–17.

Xiong, H., Zhang, H., & Sun, J. (2018). Attribute-based privacy-preserving data sharing for dynamic groups in cloud computing. *IEEE Systems Journal.*

Yang, Y., & Ma, M. (2016). Conjunctive keyword search with designated tester and timing enabled proxy re-encryption function for e-Health clouds. *IEEE Transactions on Information Forensics and Security*, *11*(4), 746–759.

Yuan, D., Song, X., Xu, Q., Zhao, M., Wei, X., Wang, H., & Jiang, H. (2018). An ORAM-based privacy preserving data sharing scheme for cloud storage. *Journal of Information Security and Applications*, *39*, 1–9. doi:10.1016/j.jisa.2018.01.002

Zaghloul, E., Zhou, K., & Ren, J. (2019). P-mod: Secure privilege-based multilevel organizational data-sharing in cloud computing. *IEEE Transactions on Big Data*. Advance online publication. doi:10.1109/TBDATA.2019.2907133

Zhang, A., & Lin, X. (2018). Towards Secure and Privacy-Preserving Data Sharing in e-Health Systems via Consortium Blockchain. *Journal of Medical Systems*, *42*(8), 140. doi:10.100710916-018-0995-5 PMID:29956061

Zhang, L., Cui, Y., & Mu, Y. (2019). Improving Security and Privacy Attribute Based Data Sharing in Cloud Computing. *IEEE Systems Journal*.

Zhang, L., Wu, Q., Mu, Y., & Zhang, J. (2016). Privacy-Preserving and Secure Sharing of PHR in the cloud. *Journal of Medical Systems*, *40*(12), 267. doi:10.100710916-016-0595-1 PMID:27730393

Zhou, J., Cao, Z., Dong, X., & Lin, X. (2015). PPDM: A Privacypreserving protocol for cloud-assisted e-Healthcare systems. *IEEE Journal of Selected Topics in Signal Processing*, *9*(7), 1332–1344. doi:10.1109/JSTSP.2015.2427113

This research was previously published in the International Journal on Semantic Web and Information Systems (IJSWIS), 17(4); pages 76-98, copyright year 2021 by IGI Publishing (an imprint of IGI Global).

Chapter 43
TBHM:
A Secure Threshold-Based Encryption Combined With Homomorphic Properties for Communicating Health Records

Lalit Mohan Gupta
APJ Abdul Kalam Technical University, Lucknow, India

Abdus Samad
University Women's Polytechnic, Aligarh Muslim University, Aligarh, India

Hitendra Garg
GLA University, Mathura, India

ABSTRACT

Healthcare today is one of the most promising, prevailing, and sensitive sectors where patient information like prescriptions, health records, etc., are kept on the cloud to provide high quality on-demand services for enhancing e-health services by reducing the burden of data storage and maintenance to providing information independent of location and time. The major issue with healthcare organization is to provide protected sharing of healthcare data from the cloud to the decision makers, medical practitioners, data analysts, and insurance firms by maintaining confidentiality and integrity. This article proposes a novel and secure threshold based encryption scheme combined with homomorphic properties (TBHM) for accessing cloud based health information. Homomorphic encryption completely eliminates the possibility of any kind of attack as data cannot be accessed using any type of key. The experimental results report superiority of TBHM scheme over state of art in terms throughput, file encryption/decryption time, key generation time, error rate, latency time, and security overheads.

INTRODUCTION

The prompt and accurate e-health services in medical science completely change the era of medical di-

DOI: 10.4018/978-1-6684-6311-6.ch043

agnosis. In recent scenarios, the e-health system (Wang, Ma, Xhafa, Zhang, & Luo, 2017), telemedicine (Jin, & Chen, 2015 and Hsieh, & Hsu, 2012), healthcare diagnosis & monitoring (Miranda, Memon, Cabral, Ravelo, Wagner, Pedersen, et al., 2017; Abo-Zahhad, Ahmed, & Elnahas, 2014) and m-health systems (Ruiz-Zafra, Benghazi, Noguera, & Garrido, 2013; Bourouis, Feham, & Bouchachia, 2012), etc., drastically influence the e-health system when emerged with cloud computing. The cloud-based e-health services attract the e-health service providers to move their database over health cloud to reduce the burden of data storage and maintenance by providing healthcare information independent of location and time. Electronic health records (EHRs) is a centralized system for storing, processing, analyzing, accessing, sharing, maintaining and backing up e-health record efficiently and effectively manner but at the same time security of data is an challenging issue. EHRs consist of medical prescriptions, DNA reports, x-rays, MRI results, patient's medical private data that need to be protected. Global access to EHR is possible through the implementation of services over the cloud. In today's time, security of publically available data is not satisfactory and privatization in the Healthcare system is a critical issue, especially when persons access personal healthcare data of patients for their commercial use. Therefore, these EHR data need to be protected for unauthorized access over the cloud maintaining integrity, consistency, and security. EHR data over the cloud is usually stored in encrypted form as this essential data is a soft target for cybercriminals. A hospital usually contains a variety and volume of medical data like prescriptions, X-rays, CT reports, blood reports and other sensitive data of patients stored over the cloud that require additional affords for security and confidentiality of these data. Only authorized users can access these sensitive data but the leakage of these data violates patient privacy. Hence, nameless authentication is enviable in a cloud environment that equips patient individuality privacy (Daglish, & Archer, 2009 and Win, Susilo, & Mu, 2006). Nameless authentication itself is a challenging issue as it is difficult to track the valid patient if EHRs are modified by someone. Hence, such a situation can be managed by implementing additional security over ownership of records and procedures rather than expansive contract to the public.

Still, secure data storage (health care records) over cloud computing is a challenging issue. Considering these facts, the proposed work aims to recommend a better scheme based on a homomorphic method for trusted evidence for healthcare records available over clouds. Concretely, this paper will make pursuing contributions:

- To guarantee the confidentiality of health care records over the cloud using a stronger encryption method.
- To develop a shared secure layer over the health cloud using TBHM based on homomorphism mechanism as it is vastly scalable with limited resources and faster uploading time.
- To achieve better performance than existing schemes (Rachmawati, Tarigan, & Ginting, 2018) even at the same computation complexity.
- To provide a provable security technique to validate its security in the standard model.

The proposed paper is organized as: in next section, the general idea of related works in security of healthcare records over the cloud and provide the summary of solutions presented for providing security, Section III describes the TBHM model and idea behind it, design of TBHM is described in section IV, Section-V presents experimental work and result analysis. Section VI includes the conclusion and future direction of the proposed work.

RELATED WORK

Several data securing techniques for cloud computing are designed by various researchers with the intent of unauthorized access to publicly available e-health care data. Some data securing techniques for cloud computing and different architecture for the same purpose has been proposed in recent years based on RSA (Liu, Chen, & Huai-Ping, 2010), modified RSA digital signature scheme (Gola, Kamal, Gupta, & Iqbal, 2014), secure encryption methods (Arora, Rachna, & Parashar, 2013) that have been effectively applied in various applications. Moreover, these schemes are not commonly applicable to portable devices due to high computation efforts in keys generations. Garg, and Sharma, (2014) designed an efficient technique based on both RSA and Hashing methods to securely store data over the cloud. The major limitation of the scheme is that Cloud service providers (CSPs) store data in unencrypted form.

Rewadkar and Ghatage (2014) proposed a third-party auditor (TPA) responsible for the integrity checking of cloud data. Data has been encrypted before sharing with TPA using homomorphic encryption techniques. TPA has the complete right and knows everything about data during auditing process. The data is stored over the cloud server in the form of unencrypted blocks. So, data integrity and confidentiality are major concerns for Cloud Service Provider (CSP) as it is considered trustworthy.

Various methods use a combination of encryption methods to securely store data over the cloud. In the same way, Khanezaei and Hanapi (2014) suggested a scheme using a combination of RSA and AES encryption schemes. These schemes cause overhead on the system due to multiple encryption and decryption process.

Another method for the security of the e-healthcare system has suggested by Thiranant, Sain, and Lee, (2014) that provides the security of stored data over the cloud using web services. The data is stored in encrypted form over the cloud but the security of data is guaranteed by trusty service providers. Therefore stealing data is a major issue for data available in the public domain.

A "three-way mechanism" to enhance security over the cloud by using AES, Diffie-Hellman key exchange method and the digital signature has suggested by Mahalle and Shahade (2014). This mechanism is secure as it uses the Diffie-Hellman key exchange scheme; if a key has been hacked during the transmission then it is useless for the hacker due to the unavailability of legitimate user's private key.

An enhance health care service is claimed in which ECC implementation is carried out to incorporate data confidentiality security and integrity (Hema, Vigna, & Kesavan, 2019). The proposed mechanism is highly scalable, consumes a lesser number of resources with improved uploading time. The proposed ECC method is effective for the implementation of secure wireless communication such as electronic mail, web browsing, etc. However, the ECC algorithm has relatively short encryption key larger size of the encrypted message and more difficult to implement.

Although most of the existing work on health cloud security is based on conventional encryption methods that use a maximum of 256 bits key for encryption that can be easily decrypted. To overcome this limitation, this paper proposed a threshold base homomorphic technique for secure health record system. In the homomorphic technique, there is no need for the cloud users to decrypt the ciphertext from the cloud but it applies some computation on the existing data. It permits computation on encrypted texts, producing an encrypted outcome which when decrypted matches the outcome of the operations as they had been done on the plaintext. The homomorphic technique is used for privacy-preserving outsourced computation and storage. This allows data to be encrypted and out-sourced to commercial cloud environments for processing, all while encrypted. In the proposed technique the concepts of distributive data storage are applied against a single storage system which sometimes becomes the bottleneck for the overall performance of the system. Two kinds of the server are mainly storage server which stores encrypted plaintext block and key server which store user secret key. This arrangement prevents different types of attacks such as collusions, stealing of partially decrypted cipher text attacks on the storage server and stealing of communication commands.

In the proposed work, a dynamic system with a variable key size can be easily increased to 4096 bits and even more in the presence of a decent server (in terms of speed, storage, etc.). This can be achieved with the help of Big integer for big data infrastructures that help in mitigating both performance and scalability issues.

There are some applications in which the concept of threshold-based homomorphic encryption schemes has been widely used such as the multiparty computation schemes and secret sharing schemes. In the multiparty computation schemes, several parties are involved to perform a computation based on common public function with their inputs, while keeping their inputs private. In secret sharing schemes, parties share a secret so that no individual party can reconstruct the secret form the information available to it.

Boneh (2018) introduced a general method to adding a threshold functionality to a large class of (non-threshold) cryptographic schemes which enables a secret key to be split into several shares, such that only a threshold of parties can use the key, without reconstructing the key. Karabat, Kiraz, and Erdogan, (2015) develops new template protection and biometric verification system named THRIVE i.e "Threshold Homomorphic Encryption-based Secure and Privacy-Preserving Biometric Verification" system. This system incorporates novel enrolment and authentication protocols based on threshold homomorphic encryption where a private key is shared between a user and a verifier.

THRESHOLD BASED HOMOMORPHIC CHECKING FOR HEALTH RECORDS (TBHM)

In the planned TBHM cryptosystem, homomorphic encryption is applied to e-health data over the cloud-based on multiplicative and additive properties (Figure 1). These data in the future are decrypted depending upon the multiplicative or additive group it belongs to. The following points are worth observing before implementing the said method.

For an effective encrypted process, the size of ciphertexts remains polynomial restricted in the given security parameter during iterated reckonings. The security features, explanations, and replicas of homomorphic cryptosystems are similar to those for former cryptosystems Tibouch (2014).

Key Agreement for Health Care Records

The agreement on key sharing is not only restricted between two participants but involve any number of participants by performing iterations of the agreement procedure and sharing intermediate data (which is not kept as secret). Consider a scenario of hospital service providers (HSP) A, B, and C involves sharing in a key agreement as follows, with all computation procedures taken to modulo T:

1. The participants should approve of the procedure of public parameters T and E that are freely exchanged over the network.
2. The participants create their private keys, named a, b, and c.

Figure 1. Architecture for TBHM homomorphic encryption model

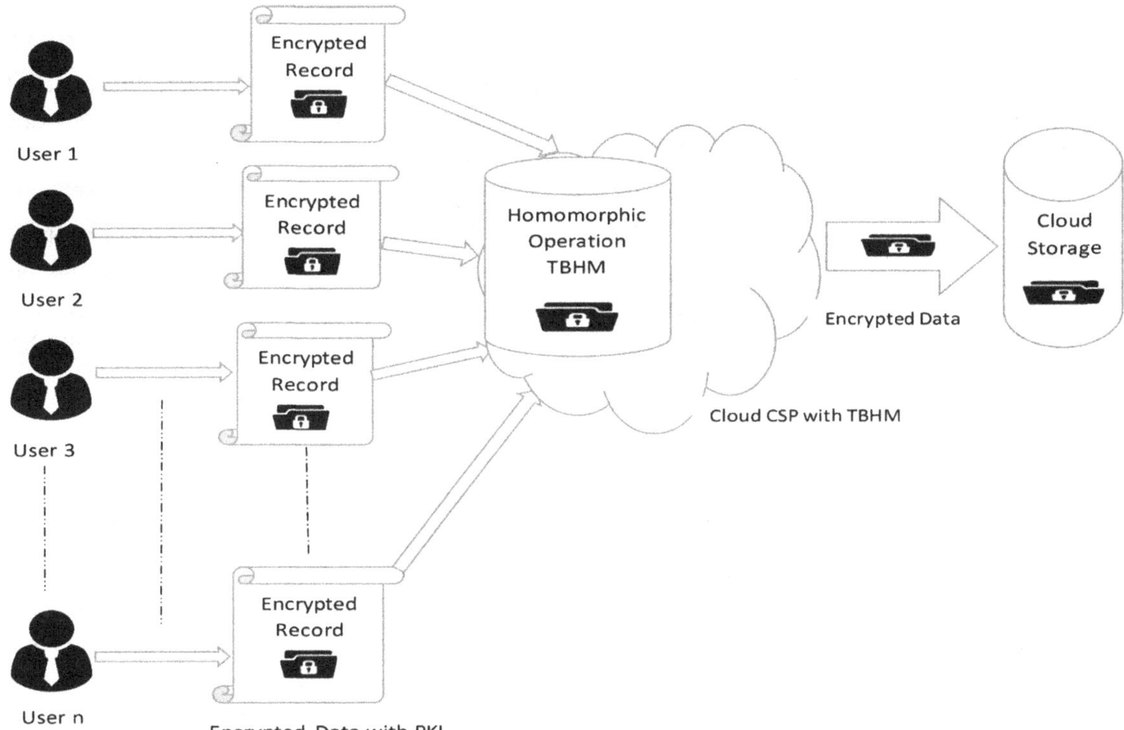

3. Participant A computes exponential on E using its private key a and transfer $(E)^a$ to participant B.
4. Participant B computes exponential on $(E)^a$ using his private key b, $(E^a)^b = E^{ab}$ and transfer E^{ab} to participant C.
5. Participant C computes exponential on (E^{ab}) using own private key c, $(E^{ab})^c = E^{abc}$ and uses E^{abc} as his secret key.
6. Similarly, Participant B computes exponential on E with own private key b and transfer $(E)^b$ to Participant C.
7. Participant C computes exponential on (E^b) using own private key c, $(E^b)^c = E^{bc}$ and transfer it to Participant A.
8. Participant A computes exponential on (E^{bc}) using own private key a, $(E^{bc})^a = E^{bca} = E^{abc}$ and uses E^{abc} as his secret.
9. Participant C computes exponential on E using own private key c and transfer $(E)^c$ to Participant A.
10. Participant A computes exponential on $(E)^c$ using own private key a, $(E^c)^a = E^{ca}$ and transfer E^{ca} to Participant B.
11. Participant B computes exponential on E^{ca} using own private key b, $(E^{ca})^b = E^{cab} = E^{abc}$ and uses E^{abc} as his secret.

Intruders can get only E^a, E^b, E^c, E^{ab}, E^{ac} and E^{bc} but can't be able to see any combination of these parameters to efficiently reproduce exponential using their own private key E^{abc}. To enhance the power of the proposed scheme is to share to t number of participants (i.e. in larger groups) following fundamental is to be ensured:

- Start with public parameter E, the privacy is obtained by computing exponential power of the existing value to each participant's private key only one time and it can be performed in any order (the first such exponentiation return the participant's public key).
- Obtained intermediate result (perform up to t-1 exponents, where t denote the number of participants in the group) may be disclosed publicly, but the last value (after performing all t exponents) produced the shared secret and hence not be disclosed publicly. Thus, each participant must find their secret copy by applying their private key at the end (otherwise there would be no way for the last contributor to communicate the final key to its recipient, as that last contributor would have turned the key into the very secret the group wished to protect).

These ideologies leave various alternatives for selecting the order of members to contribute to forming keys. The easiest and most understandable solution is to arrange the t members in around and have t keys to rotate around the circle until finally every key has been passed by all t members (lasting with its owner) and each member has contributed to t keys (ending with their own). However, this needs that each member computes t modular exponentiations.

By selecting a more ideal order, and trusting on the statement that keys can be duplicated, it is probable to lessen the number of modular exponentiations computation performed by each member to $\log_2(N) + 1$ using a divide and conquer approach. Consider a scenario for eight members:

1. Members P, Q, R, and S individually perform exponentiation, producing E^{pqrs}; E^{pqrs} is transferred to U, V, W, and X. In return, members P, Q, R, and S get E^{uvwx}.
2. Members P and Q, each compute single exponentiation, producing E^{uvwxpq}, this value is passed to R and S, while R and S do the same thing, producing E^{uvwxrs} and passed to P and Q.
3. Member P computes exponentiation, producing $E^{uvwxrsp}$ and passed to Q; Similarly, Q passed $E^{uvwxrsq}$ to P. R and S do the same.
4. Member P computes one final exponentiation, producing the secret $E^{uvwxrsqp} = E^{pqrsuvwx}$, while Q does the same to get $E^{uvwxrspq} = E^{pqrsuvwx}$; again, R and S do the same.
5. Members U through X concurrently computes the identical operations using E^{pqrs} as their starting point.

After, all the above operation has been completed. All participants will get the secret key $E^{pqrsuvwx}$, but every member will have to compute only four modular exponentiations, rather than the eight implied by a simple circular arrangement.

TBHM RECORD STORAGE

The proposed model introduces a secure e-healthcare storage system that consists of two kinds of servers: one used to store only patient's encrypted records, and the other is used to store a segment of a part of patient's secret key named as key servers k out of patient records, which are encrypted using patient's public key and secret parameter q are stored in storage servers. Then health storage servers encrypt these records using decentralized erasure code. Remember it, the user's key is partitioned into two parts, one part performs as a secret parameters q which is kept by the user, the other part is known as secret key s = p which is stored in the n key servers. Therefore, computing any partial decryption, we must have the user's secret parameter q. This approach will avoid the following kinds of conditions attacks:

- Possibilities of collusion attack among key servers and health storage servers.
- To stealing partially decrypted ciphertext to recover the actual records.
- To alter/modify the data by health storage servers.
- To takes the communication command between the used key servers and the storage servers: hid, then makes the key help do partial decryption to get actual records. The proposed model is designed to deliver security against these types of attacks.

In the traditional approach, the data storage system was done in a centralized way to systematize the data in a single or a lesser number of health storage servers. Such health storage conveniently makes data processing management. However, present commercial computation on data and the growing number of users becoming a big scale, use of the unit health storage system degrades the performance of the entire system. Therefore, distributed storage has become a novel research subject for researchers.

The computation on distributed storage manages as follows:

The original record R is partition into the equal length of r blocks. These blocks form a vector R= $(R_1, R_2, \ldots R_r)$. The proposed scheme uses encryption technique to form R redundant to obtain the secret code word in form of C= $(C_1, C_2, \ldots, C_n)$ by using erasure encode procedure (n, r). N of C_i is stored in n^{th} health storage servers. To recover the record R, select randomly k of C_i from n^{th} health storage servers by applying erasure code (n, r). Before the encoding to form C_i, all of the R_i must be collected hence, erasure code (n, r) works as a center of this health storage.

HOMOMORPHIC PROPERTIES OF THE ALGORITHM

When the healthcare records outsource to the cloud, the proposed model uses regular encryption techniques to protect the methods and the storage of the healthcare records. The planned model is believed to encrypt the healthcare records before handover it to the health cloud service provider. At last cloud providers require to decrypt healthcare records to perform every single operation. The client will request to deliver the private key to the health server (Cloud provider) to decrypt healthcare records beforehand to present the computation required, which could alter or modify the privacy and confidentiality of healthcare records stored in the cloud.

Homomorphic Encryption methods are used to existing processes on encrypted healthcare records by knowing the dependable key (without performing decryption); the user is the only owner of the secret key. After decrypting the result of each method, it is alike as if we able to grasp out the computation on the raw records. An encryption process is known homomorphic, if encryption $Enc_k(n)$ and $Enc_k(m)$are possible to calculate $Enc_k(f(n,m))$, where f can be one of the operations $(+, \times, \otimes)$ and without knowing the secret key. Among the Homomorphic encryption, we differentiate matching to the methods that permit to evaluate raw records, if perform only multiplication of the raw records then multiplicative homomorphic encryption cryptosystems are used, otherwise apply the additive homomorphic encryption that permits only addition on raw records that is ElGamal cryptosystems and RSA.

Enc_k is an encryption algorithm with key k.

Dec_k is a decryption algorithm.

$Enc_k(n) \times Enc_k(m) = Enc_k(n \times m)$ or $Dec_k(Enc_k(n \times m)) = Dec_k(Enc_k(n)) \times Dec_k(Enc_k(m)) = n \times m$

$Enc_k(n) \times Enc_k(m) = Enc_k(n+m)$ or $Dec_k(Enc_k(n+m)) = Dec_k(Enc_k(n)) + Dec_k(Enc_k(m)) = n+m$

The first property is known asmultiplicative homomorphic encryption and the second is known as additive homomorphic encryption. A methodthat implement both properties simultaneously are fully homomorphic.

Consider a situation, a user has to be processed a tiny sensitive record but require suitable computational power or the desirable proficiency; as a result, they need to charge a cloud ability to hold out the processing, but incomplete revealing these sensitive records in original form. The advised encryption proposals an easy determination to that problem; the user simply sends the records to the health cloud server in encoded form, and the health server process the records lacking decrypting it employing the property of the recommended encryption (this computation on encrypted records is called homomorphic evaluation of the corresponding function). At last, the user gets the encoded result from the server and decrypts it together with own key, finding the result of the processing lacking possessing exposed each record concerning the sensitive records.

TBHM Algorithm

1. Data Owner encrypts the health records using TBHM and outsource it to a cloud.
2. The cloud perform additive and multiplicative operations on outsources encrypted records and generate the decryption key for the sake of cloud user without decrypting the actual records.
3. Upon a data request from a cloud user (can be an authorized or unauthorized user), the service provider checks whether the cloud user is an authorized user if authorized then return the corresponding records to cloud user.
4. Service provider decrypts cloud user records only record by record, not all records at once. As a cloud service provider does not possess any decryption key, the privacy of the records remains to preserve.
5. The cloud health server performs computation and encodes the requested outcome, if there exists, and then revert to cloud user.
6. Moreover, Cloud user needs that cloud server clear all the remaining portion of records, computed key and the operation performs on the records from storage (primary and secondary disk), once the search has completed.
7. Cloud server doesn't get the benefit of cloud users because it is performing decrypting procedure on user records for their requests, to spy in other searches simultaneously, whether for any individual benefit or any one of the clouds user rivals.

IMPROVEMENTS OF TBHM METHOD

To solve the problems encountered with previous works our proposed model (TBHM) employs an object-based big integer which automatically adjusted the key size based on the requirement. One another advantage of the proposed scheme is that the encrypted message remains the same as a big integer number is taken as object which compromises prompt and strong security of data against insider threats.

As existing works have not complexly removed the probability of security on data against the insider threats which was removed using Homomorphic Encryption which completely eradicates the possibility of any kind of attack on data as, data is never opened using any key, all operations are done on data itself. Correspondingly, TBHM provides data integrity and verification by employing the MD5 hash function. we have selected MD5 as it was found using extensive research that MD5 has better performance than SHA256 even at same computation complexity as the complexity of the MD5 algorithm and SHA256 is equal and the value is $\Theta(N)$, but the running time of MD5 is faster than SHA256 (Ali et al., 2015, Atwood, 2012, and Newman et al., 2019).

EXPERIMENTAL WORK AND RESULTS ANALYSIS

Experimental Analysis

The proposed experiments are performed on Windows-7 (64-bits) Operating System, Intel i3 Processor 2.4 GHz and 8 GB RAM as system configuration. Three major entities are discussed in the system model: The patients, the EHR systems and the CSP. The TBHM simulator is designed in C# 4.5 and its associated libraries that communicate between entities. The Data layer is also implemented to generate HER records of patients that deliver data generation operations. MD5 algorithm ensures the integrity of e-health record in the proposed scheme. The system performance is analyzed in terms of throughput, error rate, key generation time, latency, file encryption time, file decryption time.

Error Rate

Error Rate (ER) is used to test the performance of an access EHR by the receiver. ER is the ratio of the number of records not successfully received by the node to the number of total records sent to the receiver by the CSP. Table 1 demonstrates the error rate in percentage with the number of requests. The curve is drawn to indicate the rate of change in error and is shown in Figure 2.

$$\text{Error Rate}\left(\text{ER}\right) = \frac{\text{Failed Records}}{\text{Total Records}}$$

It is clear from Figure 2 that the TBHM has the lowest error rate when requests keep on increasing and the efficiency can reach up to 98.19% as shown in Figure 3. Thus for modern infrastructures, TBHM can be considered as scalable architecture.

$$\text{Success rate} = \left(1 - \text{ Error Rate}\left(\text{ER}\right)\right)*100$$

Table 1. Error rate vs number of requests

No. of Request	Error Rate(%)
1000	0.030
5000	0.020
10000	0.018
20000	0.015
50000	0.011
100000	0.009
500000	0.007

Figure 2. Number of requests and the error rate of the TBHM scheme

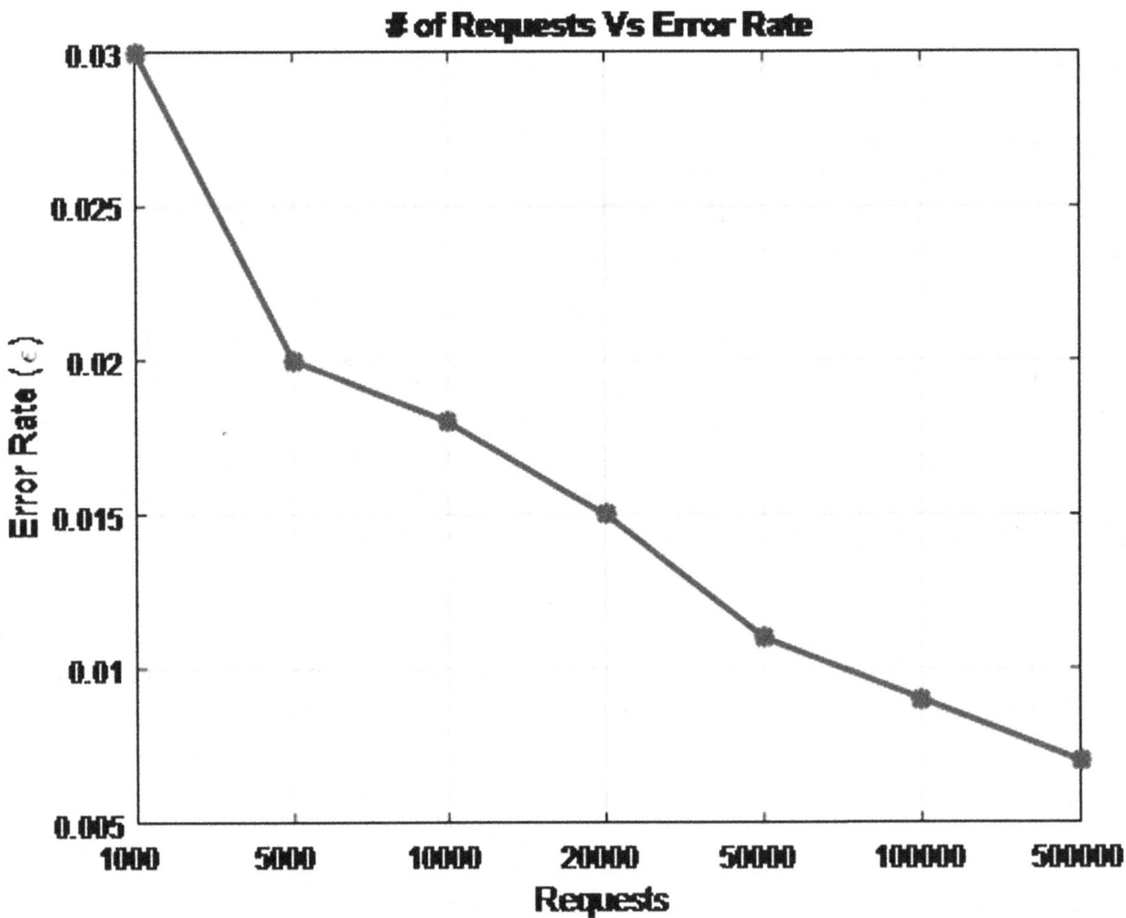

Figure 3. Success and failure rate of the TBHM scheme

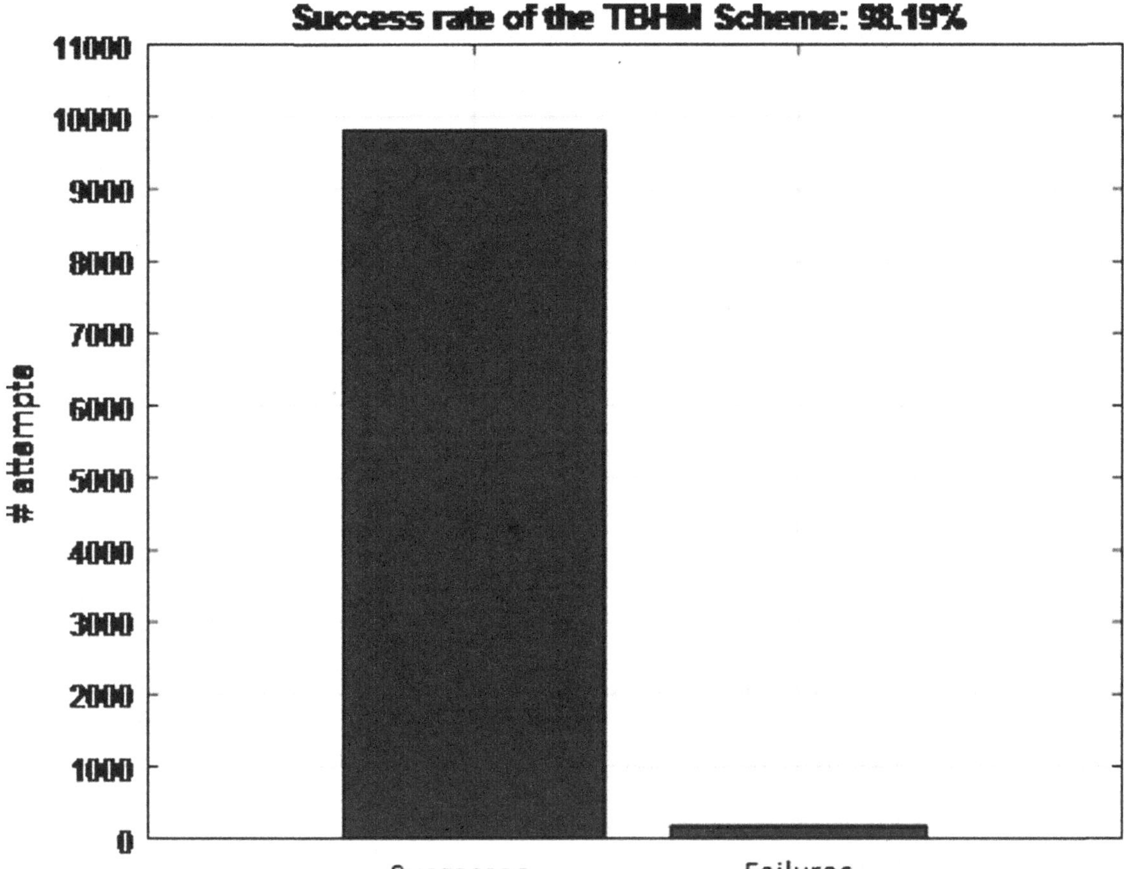

Throughput

Throughput is the number of EHR records that were received over some time (e.g. seconds, milliseconds) for a given key size. The path with the high packet receiving rate is preferred. The equation below was used to calculate throughput:

$$Throughput = \frac{recvd\_num}{sim\_time}$$

We represent the total simulation time by sim_time for all records, while recvd_num is the total number of EHR records received successfully. The behavior of throughput with the increasing key size is illustrated in Figure 4. The results shown in Figure 4 indicate that the TBHM scheme performs well as compared to ECC scheme for all cases of key sizes from 64-4096 bits. For modern key sizes, the TBHM can work on 5 records/sec, which is the highest security possible. Although 300% more efficiency can be achieved for a key size of 384 bits.

Figure 4. Throughput of TBHM compared with ECC scheme with increasing key size

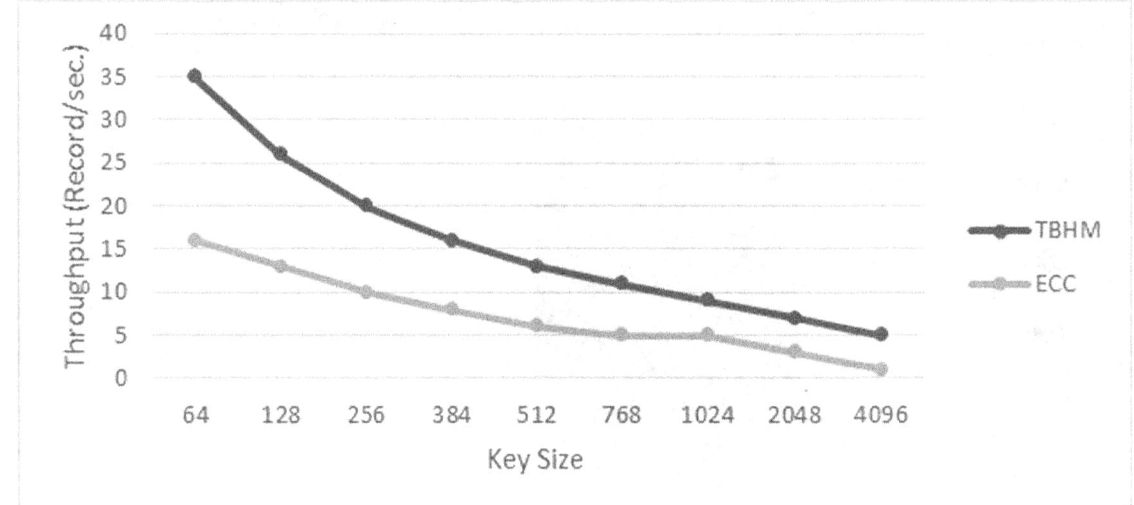

Latency

Latency is the delay in milliseconds taken by a health record (HER) to travel from CSP to the receiving end. Latency depends on several hops and congestion on the network. Lesser latency is desirable as excessive latency can also affect the throughput which is shown in Figure 5.

Key Generation Time

The time required for key generation is known as key generation time that includes both encryption/decryption processes. The key generation time in the proposed work is evaluated for 10-100 Cloud Users (CUs) at the time interval of 10 units as shown in Table 2.

In Table 2, key generation time for comparison of CL-PRE scheme (Xu, Wu, & Zhang, 2012), certificate less encryption (Seo, Nabeel, Ding, & Bertino et al., 2014), PRE scheme (Khan, Kiah, Madani, Ali, & Shamshirband et al., 2014), AES method (Ali et al., 2017), and ECC (Hema, V. et al., 2019) with respect to number of users is represented. The comparative analysis reports that ECC is more prominent and significant technique among these said techniques.

However, if we make a comparative analysis it is observed that the increase in time consumption is not directly proportional to the increase of cloud users. This trend is shown in Figure 6. With the rise of users from 10 users to 100 users, the time consumption for key generation in AES, ECC, and TBHM is almost the same. It differs approximately by 3 milliseconds for the ECC scheme but this figure is even lower for the TBHM algorithm as for all the users from 10 users to 100 users. The key generation time remains lower than 1ms that is 3 times better than the ECC scheme (Hema, V. et al., 2019) and more than 7 times the AES scheme (Ali et al. 2017). Therefore, key generation time does not affect the performance when cloud users increase

Figure 5. Latency of the TBHM at increasing record requests at CSP

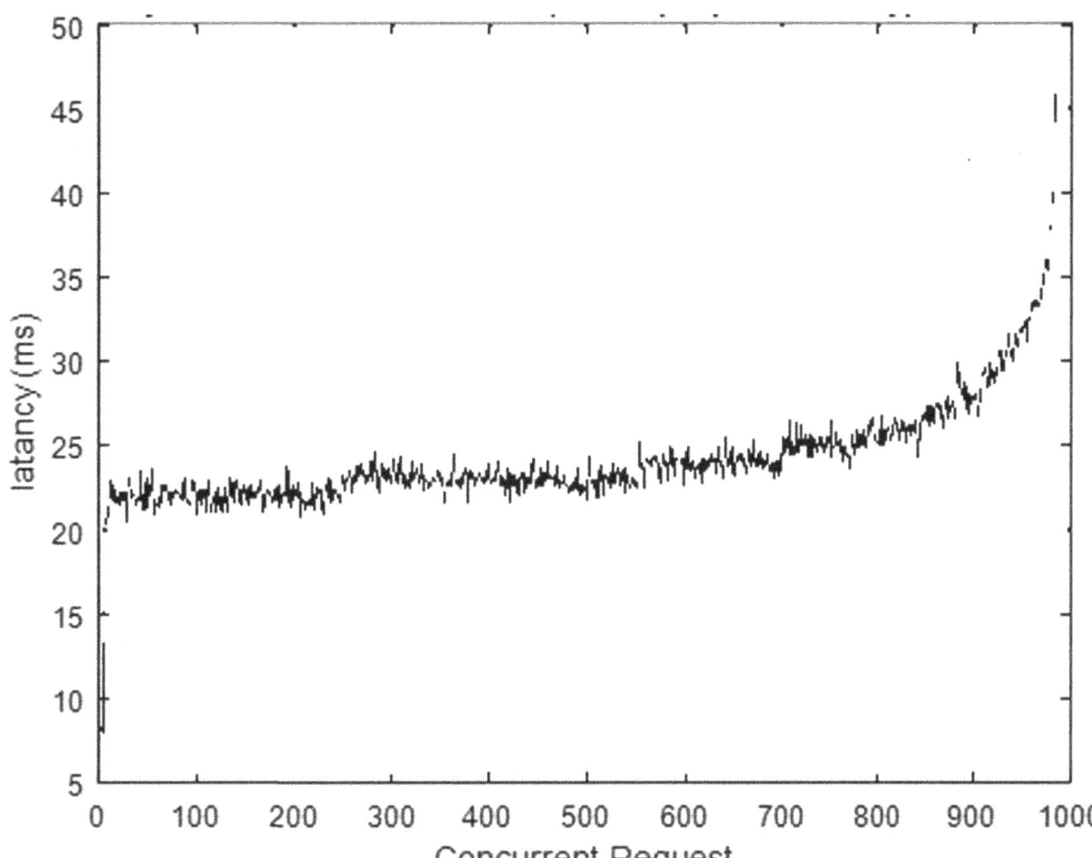

Table 2. Observations of time (in milliseconds) consumption for key generation

No. of users	CL-PRE	Certificateless Encryption	PRE	AES	ECC	TBHM
10	1494	1594	1534	0004	0021	0011
20	1598	1741	1606	0042	0023	0013
30	1673	2321	1684	0047	0028	0015
40	1791	1888	1799	0005	0003	0016
50	1907	1952	1866	0051	0032	0018
60	1954	2193	1923	0055	0035	0019
70	1994	2286	2034	0059	0039	0022
80	2092	2694	2129	0063	0042	0023
90	2401	2827	2388	0066	0046	0025
100	2495	2887	2545	0069	0049	0027

Figure 6. Increases in key generation time vs increases of cloud users

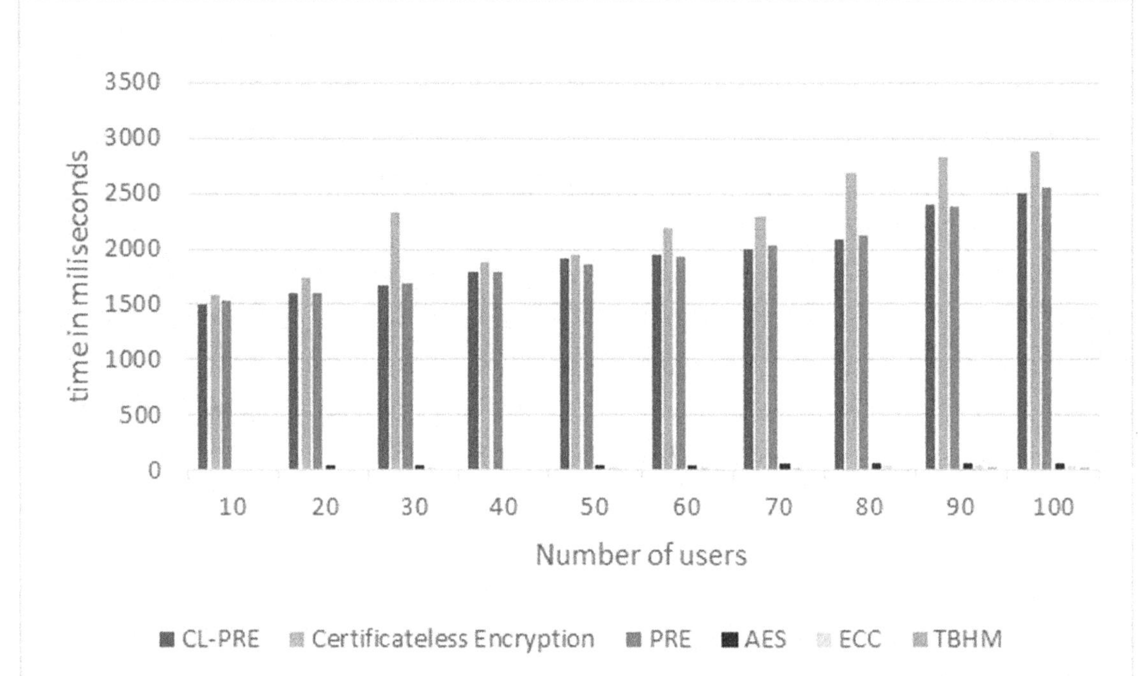

Figure 7 shows the results for key generation time on various file size (MB) in which TBHM take lesser time to generate the key as compared to AES and ECC algorithm.

Security Overhead

The ratio of time taken in security operation and file transmission is known as security overheads.

$$\text{Security overhead}\left(\%\right) = \frac{\text{Security Operation time}}{File\,Transmission\,time}$$

In the THBM-based system, there is less delay in the system over the CSP side due to the decreased security overhead which originates due to the lower complexity of the TBHM scheme. Table 3 displays the security overhead, which revealed that the percentage decreases for larger files, however, it is not more than 15.4% for ECC. With the proposed TBHM scheme the average security overhead is about 6.7% which is shown in Table 3.It is clear from Figure 2 that the TBHM has the lowest error when requests keep on increasing and the efficiency can reach up to 98.19% as shown in Figure 3. Thus for modern infrastructures, TBHM can be considered scalable architecture.

Success rate=1- Error Rate ER* 100

Figure 7. Key generation time vs file size

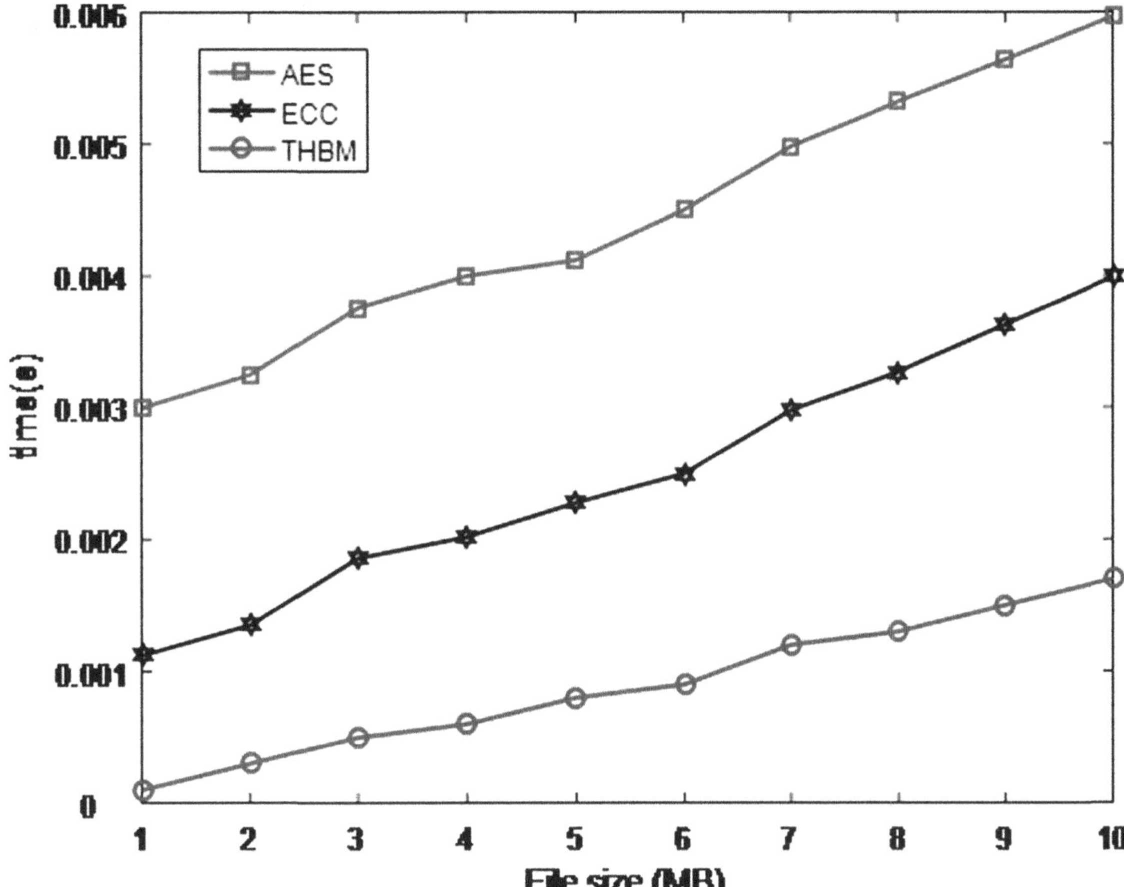

The graph shown in Figure 8 demonstrates that TBHM scheme is approximately 55% more efficient than ECC algorithm. It is therefore concluded that the security overhead of TBHM algorithm is reduced

Table 3. Security overhead the ECC and TBHM algorithm comparison with file size

File size (MB)	ECC	TBHM
0.1	19.0	7.3
0.5	18.8	7.3
1.0	18.0	7.0
10.0	15.0	8.0
50.0	14.0	5.7
100.0	13.0	5.3
250.0	13.0	7.3
500.0	13.0	5.3
Average Overhead (%)	15.4	6.7

Figure 8. Security overhead the ECC and TBHM algorithm compared

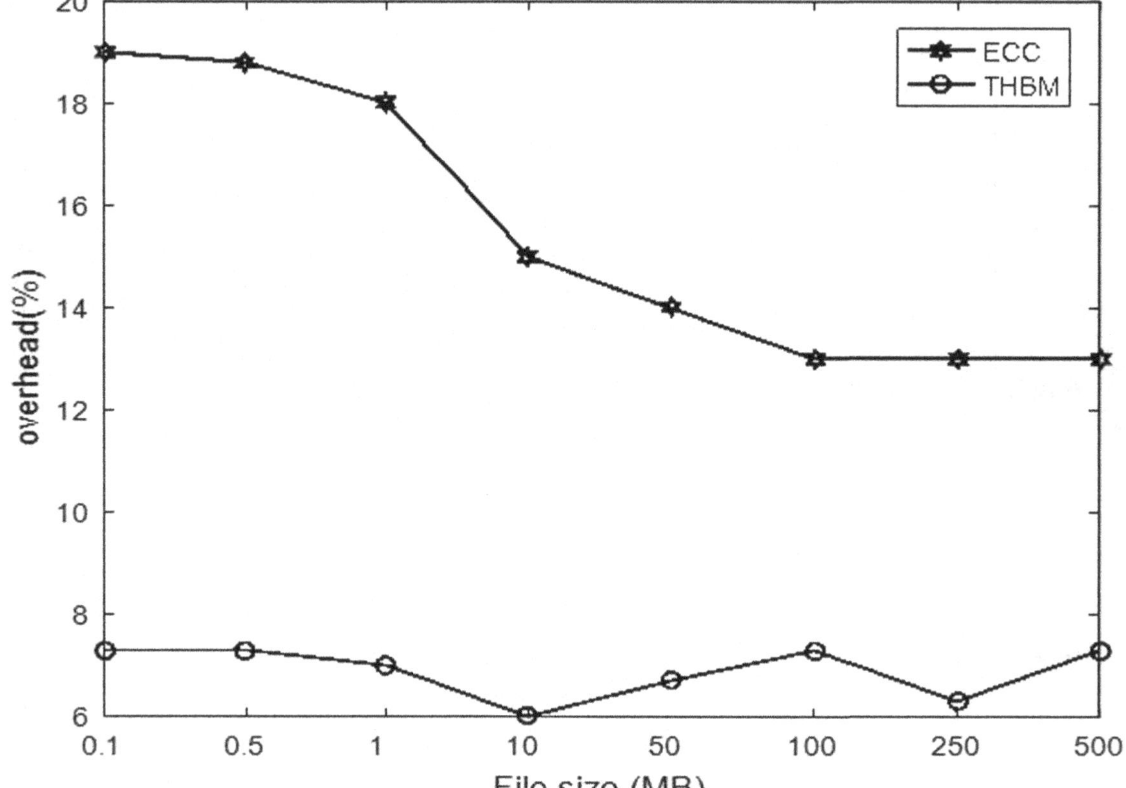

significantly.

CONCLUSION

Privacy and security of patient records are serious issues in all kinds of healthcare system particularly when information is stored over the cloud. This paper presents a novel scheme to maintain integrity, confidentiality, privacy, and security of the patient records. The proposed method named TBHM is based on a secure threshold-based encryption technique combined with homomorphic properties for communicating health records. Homomorphic encryption is implemented to completely eradicate the possibility of any kind of attack on e-health data. The proposed algorithm is implemented and the performance is evaluated with different parameters namely throughput, error rate, key generation time, latency, file encryption and decryption time. A comparative study is carried out by implementing state of the art techniques available for such systems. The results obtained show that the proposed TBHM scheme has the lowest error rate, minimum latency with lesser overhead. With the increase in the number of users, it produces better throughput with lesser time. The high population of users has no much impact on the key generation time and hence improves the performance. Therefore, it can be concluded that the TBHM is performing better as compared to existing techniques on several factors while maintaining secure e-health data over the cloud. The performance of compute-intensive tasks at Cloud Service Providers (CSP) motivates the implementation of TBHM based scheme over the mobile cloud computing environment. The TBHM frame can also be implemented and tested for video and audio data set over the cloud as a plan to achieving better security and reliability.

REFERENCES

Abo-Zahhad, M., Ahmed, S. M., & Elnahas, O. (2014). A wireless emergency telemedicine system for patients monitoring and diagnosis. *International Journal of Telemedicine and Applications*, *2014*, 4. doi:10.1155/2014/380787 PMID:24883059

Ali, M., Dhamotharan, R., Khan, E., Khan, S. U., Vasilakos, A. V., Li, K., & Zomaya, A. Y. (2015). SeDaSC: Secure data sharing in clouds. *IEEE Systems Journal*, *11*(2), 395–404. doi:10.1109/JSYST.2014.2379646

Arora, R. & Parashar, A. (2013). Secure user data in cloud computing using encryption algorithms. *International journal of engineering research and applications 3*(4), 1922-1926.

Atwood, J. (2012). Speed Hashing. Blog.codinghorror.com. Retrieved from https://blog.codinghorror.com/speed-hashing/Speed

Bourouis, A., Feham, M., & Bouchachia, A. (2012). A new architecture of a ubiquitous health monitoring system: A prototype of cloud mobile health monitoring system. *arXiv:1205.6910.*

Crypto++ 5.6.0 Benchmarks, Comparison of Popular Crypto Algorithms (2019). Cryptopp.com. Retrieved from https://www.cryptopp.com/benchmarks.html

Daglish, D., & Archer, N. (2009). Electronic personal health record systems: a brief review of privacy, security, and architectural issues. In *Proceedings of the 2009 World Congress on Privacy, Security, Trust and the Management of e-Business* (pp. 110-120). IEEE. 10.1109/CONGRESS.2009.14

Garg, P., & Sharma, V. (2014). An efficient and secure data storage in Mobile Cloud Computing through RSA and Hash function. *In Issues and Challenges in Intelligent Computing Techniques (ICICT) International Conference on IEEE.*

Gola, K. K., Gupta, B., & Iqbal, Z. (2014). Modified RSA digital signature scheme for data confidentiality. *International Journal of Computers and Applications*, *106*(13).

Hema, V. S. V., & Kesavan, R. (2019). ECC Based Secure Sharing of Healthcare Data in the Health Cloud Environment. *Wireless Personal Communications*, *108*(2), 1021–1035.

Hsieh, J. C., & Hsu, M. W. (2012). A cloud computing based 12-lead ECG telemedicine service. *BMC Medical Informatics and Decision Making*, *12*(1), 77. doi:10.1186/1472-6947-12-77 PMID:22838382

Jin, Z., & Chen, Y. (2015). Telemedicine in the cloud era: Prospects and challenges. *IEEE Pervasive Computing*, *14*(1), 54–61. doi:10.1109/MPRV.2015.19

Karabat, C., Kiraz, M. S., Erdogan, H., & Savas, E. (2015). THRIVE: Threshold homomorphic encryption based secure and privacy preserving biometric verification system. *EURASIP Journal on Advances in Signal Processing*, *2015*(1), 71. doi:10.118613634-015-0255-5

Khan, A. N., Kiah, M. M., Madani, S. A., Ali, M., & Shamshirband, S. (2014). Incremental proxy re-encryption scheme for mobile cloud computing environment. *The Journal of Supercomputing*, *68*(2), 624–651. doi:10.100711227-013-1055-z

Khanezaei, N. & Hanapi, Z. M. (2014). A framework based on RSA and AES encryption algorithms for cloud computing services. In *Proceedings of the 2014 IEEE Conference on IEEE Systems, Process and Control (ICSPC)*. IEEE Press.

Liu, D. L., Chen, Y. P., & Huai-Ping, Z. (2010, October). Secure applications of RSA system in the electronic commerce. In *Proceedings of the 2010 International Conference on Future Information Technology and Management Engineering* (Vol. 1, pp. 86-89). IEEE.

Mahalle, V. S., & Shahade, A. K. (2014). Enhancing the data security in Cloud by implementing hybrid (RSA& AES) encryption algorithm. In *Proceedings of the 2014 IEEE International Conference on Power, Automation and Communication (INPAC)*. IEEE Press.

Miranda, J., Memon, M., Cabral, J., Ravelo, B., Wagner, S. R., Pedersen, C. F., ... Nielsen, C. (2017). Eye on patient care: Continuous health monitoring: Design and implementation of a wireless platform for healthcare applications. *IEEE Microwave Magazine*, *18*(2), 83–94. doi:10.1109/MMM.2016.2635898

Newman, L., Nield, D., Barrett, B., Matsakis, L., & Baker-Whitcomb, A. (2019). A Super-Common Crypto Tool Turns Out to Be Super-Insecure. WIRED. Retrieved from https://www.wired.com/2017/02/common-cryptographic-tool-turns-majorly-insecure/

Rachmawati, D., Tarigan, J. T., & Ginting, A. B. C. (2018). A comparative study of Message Digest 5 (MD5) and SHA256 algorithm. *Journal of Physics: Conference Series*, *978*(1), 012116. doi:10.1088/1742-6596/978/1/012116

Rewadkar, D.N. & Ghatage, S.Y. (2014). Cloud storage system enabling secure privacy preserving third party audit. In *Proceedings of the International Conference on IEEE Control, Instrumentation, Communication and Computational Technologies (ICCICCT)*. IEEE Press.

Ruiz-Zafra, Á., Benghazi, K., Noguera, M., & Garrido, J. L. (2013). Zappa: An open mobile platform to build cloud-based m-health systems. In Ambient intelligence-software and applications (pp. 87–94). Springer.

Seo, S.-H., Nabeel, M., Ding, X., & Bertino, E. (2014). An efficient certificateless encryption for secure data sharing in public clouds. *IEEE Transactions on Knowledge and Data Engineering*, *26*(9), 2107–2119. doi:10.1109/TKDE.2013.138

Thiranant, N., Sain, M., & Lee, H. J. (2014). A design of security framework for data privacy in e-health system using web service. In *Proceedings of the 2014 16th International Conference on IEEE Advanced Communication Technology (ICACT)*. IEEE Press.

Boneh, D., Gennaro, R., Goldfeder, S., Jain, A., Kim, S., Rasmussen, P. M., & Sahai, A. (2018). Threshold Cryptosystems from Threshold Fully Homomorphic Encryption. In H. Shacham & A. Boldyreva (Eds.), Advances in Cryptology – CRYPTO 2018. Cham: Springer. doi:10.1007/978-3-319-96884-1_19

Tibouch, M. (2014). Fully Homomorphic Encryption over the Integers: From Theory to Practice. *NTT Technical Review*, *12*(7).

Wang, X. A., Ma, J., Xhafa, F., Zhang, M., & Luo, X. (2017). Cost-effective secure E-health cloud system using identity based cryptographic techniques. *Future Generation Computer Systems*, *67*, 242–254. doi:10.1016/j.future.2016.08.008

Win, K. T., Susilo, W., & Mu, Y. (2006). Personal health record systems and their security protection. *Journal of Medical Systems*, *30*(4), 309–315. doi:10.100710916-006-9019-y PMID:16978011

Xu, L., Wu, X., & Zhang, X. (2012). CL-PRE: A certificateless proxy re-encryption scheme for secure data sharing with public cloud. In *Proceedings of the 7th ACM symposium on information, computer and communications security* (pp 87–88). ACM. 10.1145/2414456.2414507

This research was previously published in the International Journal of Information Technology and Web Engineering (IJITWE), 15(3); pages 1-17, copyright year 2020 by IGI Publishing (an imprint of IGI Global).

Chapter 44
Secure Healthcare Monitoring Sensor Cloud With Attribute-Based Elliptical Curve Cryptography

Rajendra Kumar Dwivedi
https://orcid.org/0000-0001-6682-1942
Madan Mohan Malaviya University of Technology, Gorakhpur, India

Rakesh Kumar
Madan Mohan Malaviya University of Technology, Gorakhpur, India

Rajkumar Buyya
The University of Melbourne, Melbourne, Australia

ABSTRACT

Sensor networks are integrated with cloud in many internet of things (IoT) applications for various benefits. Healthcare monitoring sensor cloud is one of the application that allows storing the patients' health data generated by their wearable sensors at cloud and facilitates the authorized doctors to monitor and advise them remotely. Patients' data at cloud must be secure. Existing security schemes (e.g., key policy attribute-based encryption [KP-ABE] and ciphertext policy attribute-based encryption [CP-ABE]) have higher computational overheads. In this paper, a security mechanism called attribute-based elliptical curve cryptography (ABECC) is proposed that guarantees data integrity, data confidentiality, and fine-grained access control. It also reduces the computational overheads. ABECC is implemented in .NET framework. Use of elliptical curve cryptography (ECC) in ABECC reduces the key length, thereby improving the encryption, decryption, and key generation time. It is observed that ABECC is 1.7 and 1.4 times faster than the existing approaches of KP-ABE and CP-ABE, respectively.

DOI: 10.4018/978-1-6684-6311-6.ch044

Figure 1. Healthcare monitoring sensor cloud

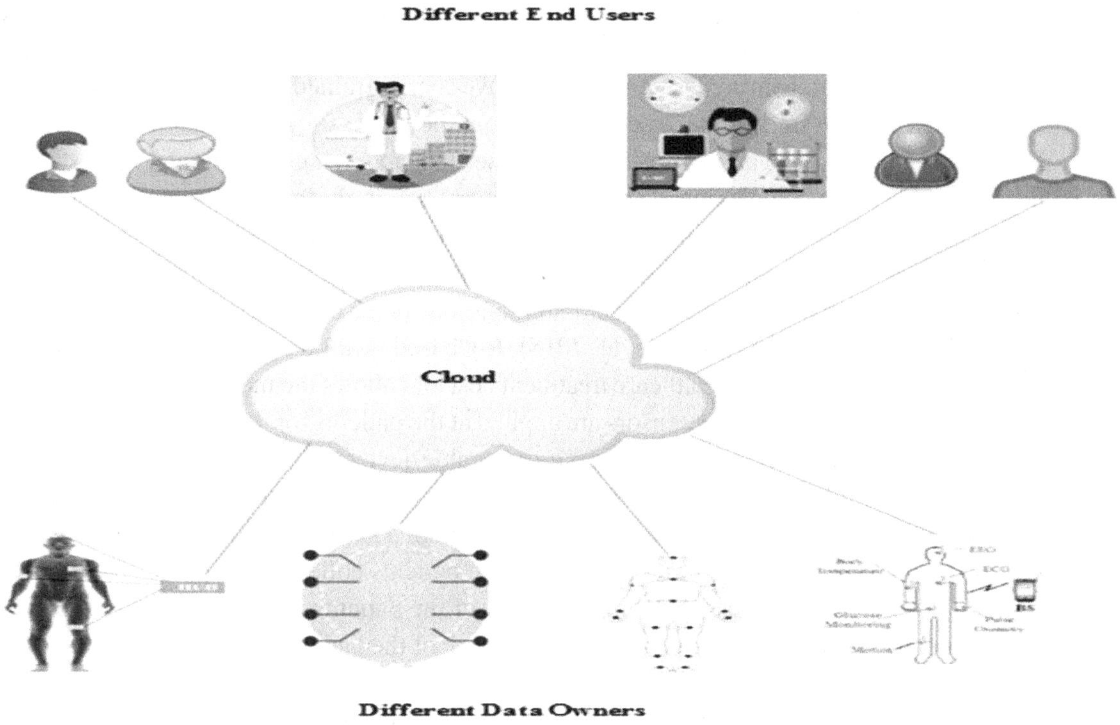

Different End Users

Cloud

Different Data Owners

1. INTRODUCTION

Sensor based Internet of Things (IoT) have various applications such as healthcare applications, battlefield monitoring, street monitoring, disaster management, military, forest fire detection, unmanned vehicles and manufacturing industries (Ahuja et al. 2020; Rashid et al. 2016). Such IoT applications generate a huge amount of data that is usually stored at cloud to increase the usefulness of resources (Lin et al. 2019; Zhou et al. 2018). Sensor networks are integrated with cloud to improve the effectiveness of the application. This integration is termed as sensor cloud which is beneficial for both sensor networks and cloud. Various sensor networks store their sensed data at the cloud and cloud provides sensor as a service with help of virtualization to the multiple users according to their choice and demand. Any genuine end user can access the data of one or all authorized sensor networks just in one click with help of this integration (Dwivedi et al. 2018). Figure 1 presents a healthcare monitoring system where each human body behaves as a sensor network. Here, data from various wearable body sensors of many patients have been stored at cloud through base station such as mobile phone. Different types of authorized users viz., doctors, medical students, researchers can access the health records of the patients using their credentials. Doctors can provide medical support to the patients anytime and from anywhere. They can help the patients instantly if the emergency case is monitored. Cloud can provide sensor as a service to the authorized students and researchers too by providing them various types of data. Thus, legitimate end users can get data of one or more patients easily and quickly. Doctors, students, researchers and patients may belong to either same or different hospitals. In this way, everyone is benefitted with this sensor cloud integration.

There are several challenges to sensor cloud and security is one of them (Altaf et al. 2019; Díaz et al. 2016). Various security mechanisms have been devised to provide data security at the cloud (Park et al. 2011; Fernández-Alemán et al. 2013; Sangeetha et al.2017; Masood et al. 2018; Sun et al. 2018; Dwivedi et al. 2019). Some of them are less complex but have coarse grained access control. On the other hand, some schemes provide fine grained access control but they have some computational overheads. Hence, there is a need to provide an improved security mechanism having fine grained access control with reduced computational complexities. This paper focuses its work on sensor cloud of healthcare monitoring system. There are many medical cases in which the continuous monitoring of health conditions is required which allow doctors to know the health status of the patients regularly or when required (Ghoneim et al. 2018; Liu et al. 2019). Several computations may be involved before fetching the desired information (Goléa et al. 2019; Al-Ayyoub et al. 2018). IoT based healthcare system is very helpful in such situations which minimizes the healthcare treatment cost and allows the mobility of patients (Ko et al. 2010). In such systems, various body sensors are applied at the patients for the purpose of continuous monitoring of their health status. These body sensors are wearable devices worn by patients that can collect various body data such as blood pressure, body temperature and heart beat rate. Data collected by these sensors are sent to gateways via wireless communication medium and from gateways finally transferred to the cloud for storage and processing. Medical data of the patients collected by various body sensors are very crucial. Any alteration or loss in the medical data of the patients may result in negative health conditions or sometimes lead to very serious stages even death of the patient. Hence, it must be secured.

Therefore, a novel design is proposed in this paper to secure the sensor cloud data for healthcare applications. Proposed approach uses attribute based elliptic curve encryption technique that provides fine grained access control and allows only authentic users to have access on the healthcare records of the patients. This approach improves the encryption, decryption and key generation time as compared to the existing schemes namely Key Policy Attribute Based Encryption (KP-ABE) and Ciphertext Policy Attribute Based Encryption (CP-ABE). Thus, it enhances security with reduced computational complexities. It also ensures confidentiality, integrity, reliability, availability, scalability, authenticity and collusion resistance. The major contributions of the paper are given below:

- Design of a security mechanism called Attribute Based Elliptical Curve Cryptography (ABECC) for sensor cloud of health monitoring system
- Security analysis to justify the novelty of the proposed work
- Complexity analysis to justify the improvements in the proposed scheme

The rest of the paper is organized as follows. Section 2 focuses on preliminaries and background. Survey of the related work is done in section 3. Section 4 describes the proposed scheme ABECC. Section 5 presents performance evaluation where proposed approach is compared with the existing schemes on certain parameters. This section also presents various characteristics of ABECC. Finally, section 6 concludes the paper with a proposal for future work.

2. BACKGROUND

Before moving further, we present some preliminaries of the related work as follows:

2.1 Attribute Based Encryption (ABE)

In ABE, the cryptographic process is improved. It states that the identity of the recipient is not atomic but comprises of multiple attributes. Here, size of ciphertexts increases with the increase of number of attributes (Li et al. 2012; Muller et al. 2008). Attribute based encryption allows decryption of the ciphertext only if the receiver has the key of corresponding attributes. The security policies are defined on the set of given attributes using conjunctions, disjunctions etc. The complete set attributes is known as universal attributes set and the policy describing the authorization such as "who can access what", using conjunctions, disjunctions etc. is called access structure. Let us say that {M, N, O, P} is the set of attributes. User ABC has attributes {M, N} while user XYZ has attribute {P}. Now suppose if the file is encrypted with the policy $(M \wedge O) \vee P$. The file will be accessible only to user XYZ because his attribute satisfies the access policy and thus further can decrypt it. On the other hand, user ABC cannot either access or decrypt the file because its attributes does not satisfy the access policy. ABE provides the fine grained access control and can be of two types:

2.1.1. Key Policy ABE (KP-ABE)

In this approach, sender labels the ciphertexts with attributes and trusted authority issues private key of the user. Private keys are accompanied with the policies known as access structures which tell about the key holder and ciphertexts i.e. who could decrypt which ciphertexts (Wang 2013; Goyal et al. 2006).

2.1.2. Ciphertext Policy ABE (CP-ABE)

In this method, the user's private key is combined via group of attributes. Here, ciphertext specifies security policies on the attributes (Premkamal et al. 2020; Bethencourt et al. 2007).

2.2 Elliptical Curve Cryptography (ECC)

Both the sender and receiver must agree on the common elliptic curve equation in this cryptography. ECC is used in many applications viz., smart cards, wireless communication devices, web servers that handle several encryption sessions etc. ECC is a form of asymmetric cryptography like RSA, AES and ElGamal in which every user has public-private key pair. But, ECC uses shorter key lengths for the purpose of encryption and decryption than other cryptosystems (Saran et al. 2019; Athena et al. 2017; Bansal et al. 2017).

2.3 Coarse and Fine Grained Access Control

Sometimes user is imposed with low level authorization like he is authorized to a particular page or a service on basis of only his role (Carvalho et al. 2018). This type of authorization is called role based access control or coarse grained access control. If authorization level is high then it is known as fine grained access control. Above scenario with further authorization to the page and service results in fine grained access control. For example, user has constraints on role, gender and age etc to access the page. Similarly, he may have constraints on role, location, service timings, IP address etc to access the service. Thus, it can be observed that security is increased in fine grained access control (Sambrekar et al. 2019).

3. RELATED WORK

Tembhare et al. (2019) presented a scheme for maintaining privacy of patient's records in healthcare application of cloud. This scheme is the integration of ABE and role based access control policy. It is a novel approach with lower computational complexity but may suffer from role explosion because of growing number of various roles.

Sun et al. (2018) have designed a framework for searchable personal health records. This scheme is a combination of ABE and search encryption technology. It provides secure and efficient solution in cloud-fog environment. This method provides keyword search function with fine-grained access control but has lack of expressive search.

Perez et al. (2017) have devised a CP-ABE and symmetric key encryption based scheme for securing data in Internet of Things (IoT) contexts. It is focusing on healthcare application of IoT. Method is good because privacy is preserved and data sharing is secure. But it has some computational overheads in real contexts which can be further optimized.

Lounis et al. (2016) proposed a secure framework for data collection from body sensor networks which is based on CP-ABE. It provides an easy data sharing among healthcare professionals in normal and emergency situations. This scheme provides fine grained access control and ensures confidentiality, integrity, scalability.

Thilakanathan et al. (2014) had given a secure scheme to monitor as well as share health related data in cloud environment. They used ElGamal-based proxy re-encryption method for implementing the security. It handles large datasets and efficient user revocation in healthcare monitoring cloud. Limitation of this scheme is that it assumes that data sharing party is fully trusted.

Li et al. (2013) provided a security mechanism for securing the health records while sharing by using ABE. The framework described in this approach consists of pre-defined list of legitimate users. The list includes medical professionals as well as family members. Attributes based on roles are assigned to each user. The corresponding secret keys are retrieved from the authority and distributed to the users. Role based policy provide better key management facility to the users. Also, this framework is much more effective than the existing schemes because data owners need not to be online always in this approach.

Hung et al. (2012) have given a multi user data encryption scheme through multiple proxies instead of just single proxy. Separate storage and query keys are provided to every user. This makes the queries of a user to remain unrevealed to the other user. Storage and query keys can be changed by the user even without decrypting the complete database.

Tu et al. (2012) proposed revocation mechanism using CP-ABE which provides fine-grained access control. This paper addresses major problems of sharing the data in cloud as well as removing the access rights from the same user when he is not the part of the system concerned. This approach is very efficient in revoking the access rights from the users but not suitable for very large datasets.

Tran et al. (2011) gave a framework which states that same group users can access the data of each other. This helps in data sharing among the group members. There is a group administrator who is responsible for the revocation of group members. This framework uses proxy re-encryption where private key of data owner is divided into two halves. The first part is stored on the proxy through which the complete data is encrypted. The second part is kept in machine of data owner by which he encrypts the data. In this scheme, proxy may suffer excessive encryption and decryption operations.

Yang et al. (2011) introduced a generic scheme using attribute based encryption with proxy re-encryption to secure the sharing of data in cloud environment. This scheme provides fine grained access

Table 1. Summary of security techniques used in sensor cloud

Authors (Year)	Technique Used	Findings	Limitations
Tembhare et al. (2019)	ABE with role based access control	Maintains privacy of patient's data in cloud with lower computational complexity	May suffer from role explosion because of growing number of various roles
Sun et al. (2018)	ABE with search encryption technology	Provides keyword search function with fine-grained access control	Lack of expressive search
Perez et al. (2017)	CP-ABE and symmetric key encryption	Privacy is preserved and data sharing is secure in healthcare application of IoT	Higher computational complexities in real contexts
Lounis et al. (2016)	CP-ABE based scheme	Provides fine grained access control and ensures confidentiality, integrity, scalability	Works for only single healthcare authority
Thilakanathan et al. (2014)	Proxy re-encryption with ElGamal encryption	Handles large data sizes and efficient user revocation in healthcare monitoring cloud	Assumes that data sharing party is fully trusted
Li et al. (2013)	ABE with role based access control	Supports dynamic modification of file attributes and security policy	Suffers from complex computational overheads in ABE
Hung et al. (2012)	Proxy re-encryption	Allows multiple users to access the shared database securely	More numbers of proxies are used
Tu et al. (2012)	CP-ABE based dual encryption system	Very efficient in revoking the access rights from the users	Not suitable for very large datasets
Tran et al. (2011)	Proxy re-encryption	Provides security and allows users to access another user's data who are in the same group	Proxy may suffer excessive encryption and decryption operations
Yang et al. (2011)	ABE with proxy re-encryption	Efficient scheme in case of simple user revocation	Fails when a revoked user joins again
Bethencourt et al. (2007)	CP-ABE	Secure against collusion attacks	Secure under generic group heuristic
Goyal et al. (2006)	KP-ABE	Fine grained access control	Does not hide the attributes

control. It is an efficient scheme in case of simple user revocation but fails when a revoked user joins again. Revocation of user does not cause key redistribution or data re-encryption.

Bethencourt et al. (2007) provided CP-ABE scheme. In this technique, several attributes specify user's private key and access policies are defined over the attributes which specifies that who can decrypt the data. If receiver satisfies these security policies then data will be available to the user. This design is secure against collusions but is proved secure.

Goyal et al. (2006) presented KP-ABE scheme in which ciphertexts are labeled with a number of attributes and private key is accompanied with access policies which control that a user can decrypt which ciphertexts. A user can decrypt the data if he satisfies the security policy. This technique provides fine grained access control but does not hide the set of attributes.

A summary of various existing security techniques used in sensor cloud is presented in Table 1. This table also describes the findings and limitations of the existing approaches. Earlier, many existing schemes use access control lists which provide coarse grained access to data. Later, ABE (KP-ABE / CP-ABE) has been used which provides fine grained access control, but it has some complex computations too which results in computational delay and other overheads. In order to reduce these complexities, there

Figure 2. Architecture of healthcare sensor cloud with proposed security scheme

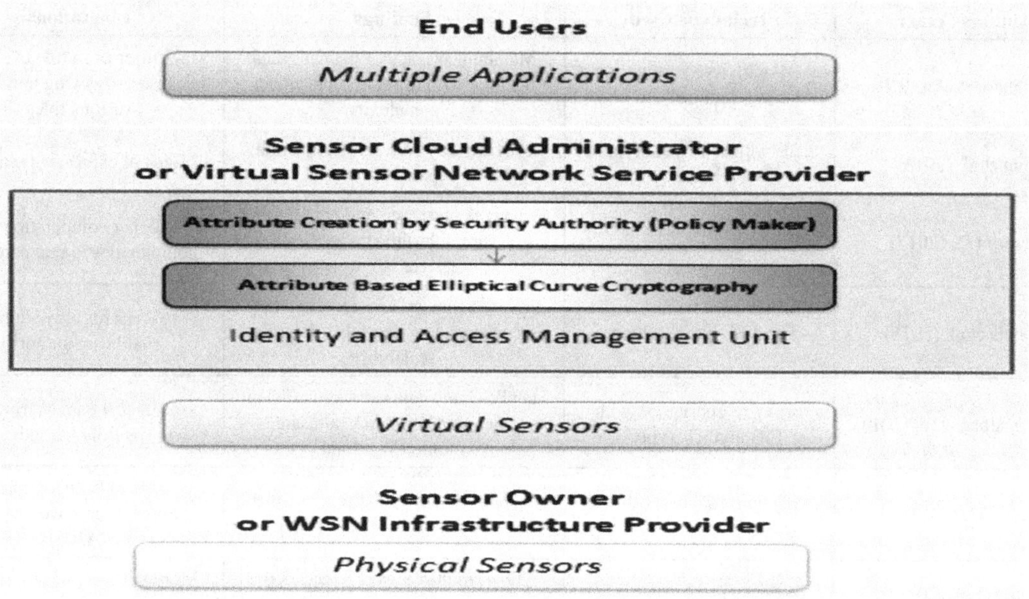

is a need to devise a security model to ensure the overall security of sensor data that guarantees the confidentiality and integrity and at the same time reducing the overall computational overheads with fine grained access control. This in turns makes the system more efficient.

4. PROPOSED APPROACH

This paper proposes a security mechanism termed as Attribute Based Elliptical Curve Cryptography (ABECC) which provides security with less computational overheads and fine grained access control.

Figure 2 describes sensor cloud architecture which incorporates the proposed security mechanism. There are four essential entities involved in this proposed approach viz., data consumer, security authority, cloud database and data owner. Healthcare monitoring system has various actors such as patient (P1, P2…Pz), relatives of patient (R1, R2…Rm), doctors (D1, D2…Dn), junior doctors (JD1, JD2…JDo), medical students (MS1, MS2...MSp), nurses (N1, N2...Nq), insurance company (IC1, IC2…ICr)) etc. These actors have various attributes like name, age, location, purpose etc. Here, patients are the data owners who are denoted at lower layer and other actors are the end users who are located at the upper layer of the system model. Middle layer of the model represents virtualization and security implementation at cloud. Security authority has information about the necessary attributes of data consumers which are obtained after their registration. The role for data owner is to collect the sensor data through various body sensors and also create role based policy on attributes provided by the security authority. Policies are created using conjunction or disjunction for the authentic data access which clearly states that who can access what. After this step, the data is encrypted through key provided by security authority and stored on the cloud. Only authentic data consumers whose attributes satisfies the security policy for selected file can decrypt the file with decryption key provided from security authority. This security model can serve various types of end users by providing them patients' data which can be obtained from multiple healthcare centers. This is possible because of virtualization at middle layer of sensor cloud integration. Proposed approach ABECC is described in Algorithm I. This algorithm is divided into two parts. First part explains "Attribute based policy creation for access control using ECC" and the second part describes "Authentication validation of end user to access the data".

```
Algorithm I.  Attribute Based Elliptical Curve Cryptography (ABECC)
A.  Attribute based policy creation for access control using ECC
Begin
Step 1:  Data collection from various body sensors
Step 2:  Attribute are decided by security authority
Step 3:  Role based policy creation on attributes by data owner
Step 4:  Data encryption using Elliptical Curve Cryptography (ECC)
Step 5:  Encrypted data is now ready for data processing at cloud
End;
B.  Authentication validation of end user to access the data
Begin
Step 1:  If (registered user) then
Step 2:          If (authenticated user: access policy is true) then
Step 3:                 Decrypt data and allow user to view or download the
data
Step 4:          Else
Step 5:                       Data access is not allowed
Step 6:  Else
Step 7:          Register to access the services
End;
```

5. PERFORMANCE EVALUATION

The work is implemented as a web application on x86_64 architecture based Intel core i7 processor with Windows 10 platform. We describe experimental setup as well as encryption, decryption and key generation time analysis in this section. Then we discuss some salient features of the proposed scheme.

5.1 Experimental Setup

ABECC is developed as a web application which consists of patients' health data. This application is deployed in cloud using virtualization. The proposed system has four modules namely Security Authority, Data Owner, Data Consumer and Cloud Database which are implemented through a web application in .NET framework. For cloud storage, the model uses Microsoft Azure SQL database. Encryption, Decryption and Key Generation Time are used as performance metrics. Table 2 presents the summary of the implementation setup.

Table 2. Implementation environment

Category	Implementation
IDE used	Visual Studio
Framework	Microsoft .NET
Front end	C#, ASP.NET
Back end	SQL Server
File size	100KB to 500KB
Number of attributes	2 to 10
Modules involved Performance Metrics	Security Authority, Data Owner, Data Consumer, Cloud Database
	Encryption, Decryption and Key Generation Time

5.2 Security Analysis

Proposed approach ABECC provides security with fine grained access control. The various security services of ABECC scheme such as data confidentiality, integrity, authenticity, availability, scalability, collusion resistance and reliability are discussed as follows:

5.2.1. Fine Grained Access Control

ABECC guarantees fine grained access control of records stored at the cloud. This access control is achieved due to use of ABE in the proposed scheme.

5.2.2. Data Confidentiality

Users who don't have the required attributes are not allowed to access the data. In this way, the proposed framework of ABECC guarantees the data confidentiality.

5.2.3. Integrity and Authenticity

A user authenticates any information obtained by the other user and then access is granted. Thus, proposed methodology ensures integrity of healthcare information during message communication.

5.2.4. Collusion Resistance

The approach ensures that users do not collude with each other to have any illegal access. ABECC provides collusion resistance to prevent from any unauthorized access.

5.2.5. Reliability

Probability of data loss or leak is very less in the proposed scheme because the data owner controls the process of sharing and storing data. Thus, we can say that proposed scheme is highly reliable.

Figure 3. Effect of file size on encryption time analysis

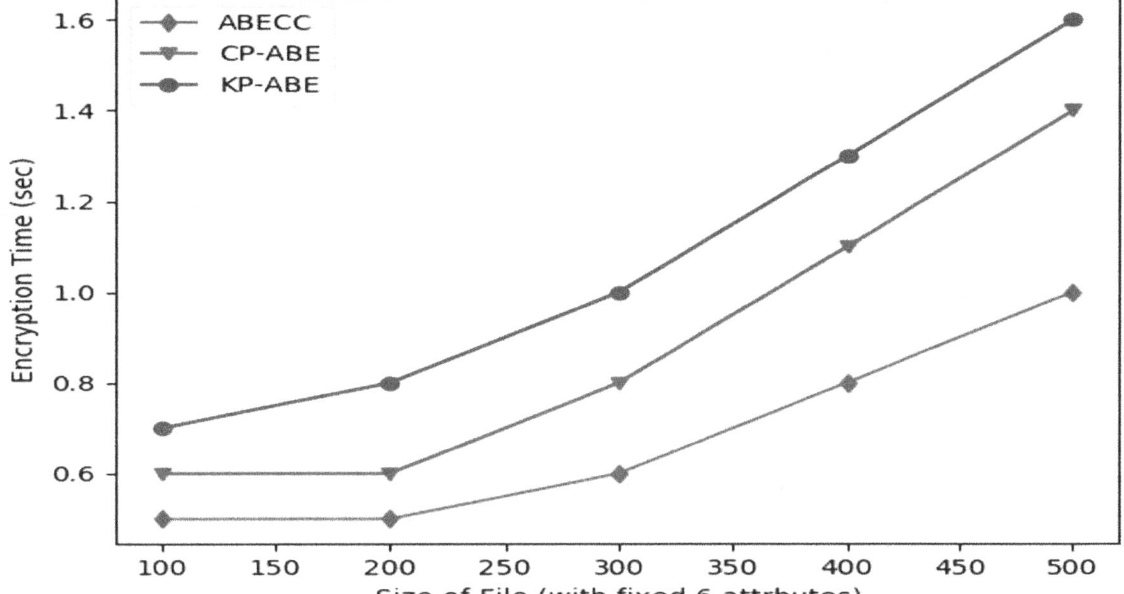

5.2.6. Scalability and Availability

Proposed model confirms availability of the service to authentic users as per the requirements. It is also robust to the access of large number of users concurrently.

5.3 Encryption, Decryption and Key Generation Time Analysis

Different files of size 100 KB to 500 KB which contain data from various medical sensors were used for evaluating the time needed for encryption, decryption and key generation by the proposed scheme (ABECC). Security policies were made for 2 to 10 number of attributes. First of all, numbers of attributes were fixed to 6 and results are obtained for various file sizes. Then file size is fixed to 300 KB and results are obtained on varying number of attributes. When comparison of ABECC is done with existing KP-ABE and CP-ABE schemes, it is found that ABECC produces better results at these three performance evaluation metrics.

5.3.1. Effect of File Size on Encryption, Decryption and Key Generation Time

Figure 3 presents the encryption time analysis for various file sizes with fixed number of attributes that is 6. It shows that encryption time taken by the proposed scheme (ABECC) is lower than the encryption time of existing security schemes (KP-ABE, CP-ABE). It is noticed that encryption time increases in all the three approaches when file size is increased but it is lowest in case of the proposed scheme. It is due to use of ECC which reduces the key length that in turns reduces the encryption time.

Figure 4 describes the decryption time analysis for different file sizes with fixed number of attributes that is 6. It can be found from the results that decryption time of ABECC is lesser than decryption time

Figure 4. Effect of File Size on decryption time analysis

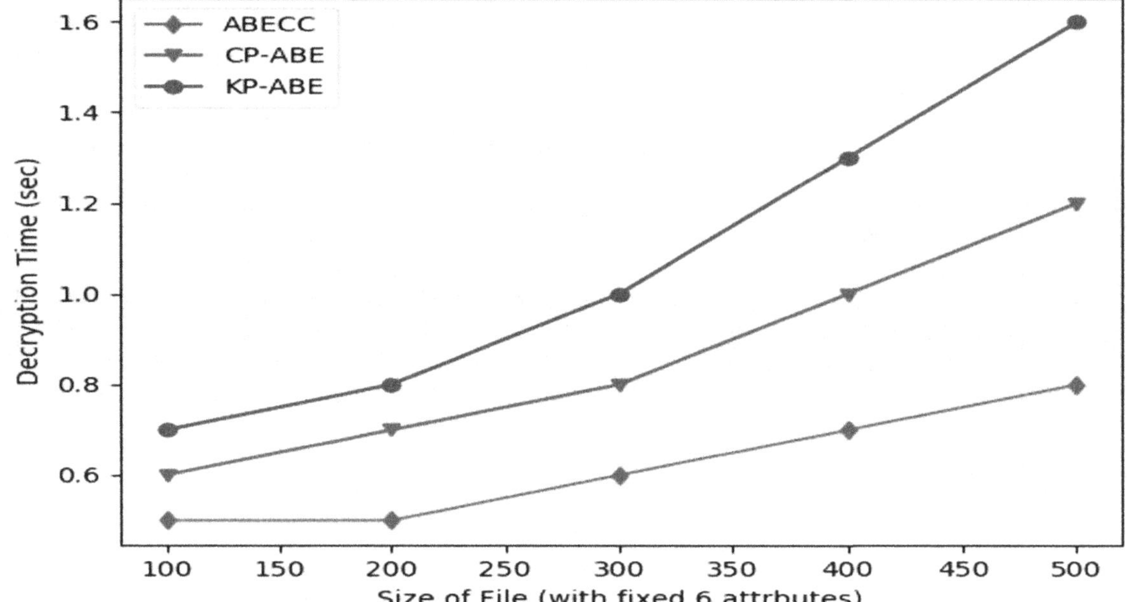

of existing security schemes (KP-ABE, CP-ABE). It is also observed that decryption time increases in all three mechanisms when size of file is increased but it is lowest in case of the proposed scheme. It is due to use of ECC which reduces the key length that in turns reduces the decryption time.

Figure 5 depicts the key generation time analysis for several file sizes with fixed number of attributes that is 6. Results show that key generation time of ABECC is also lower than key generation time of existing security mechanisms. It is also noticed that key generation time increases in all schemes presented here when file size is increased but it is lowest in case of the proposed scheme. It is due to use of ECC which reduces the key length that in turns reduces the key generation time.

5.3.2. Effect of Attributes on Encryption, Decryption and Key Generation Time

Figure 6 presents the encryption time analysis for numerous numbers of attributes with fixed file size of 300 KB. It shows that encryption time of ABECC is lower than that of existing KP-ABE and CP-ABE schemes. It can be seen that encryption time increases in all the three approaches when number of attributes is increased but it is lowest in case of the proposed scheme. It is due to use of ECC which reduces the key length that in turns reduces the encryption time.

Figure 7 describes the decryption time analysis for many numbers of attributes with fixed file size of 300 KB. It can be observed from the results that decryption time of the ABECC is lesser than that of KP-ABE and CP-ABE. It is also found that decryption time increases in all the three mechanisms when number of attributes is increased but it is lowest in case of the proposed scheme. It is due to use of ECC which reduces the key length that in turns reduces the decryption time.

Figure 8 explains the key generation time analysis for a number of attributes with fixed file size of 300 KB. Results show that key generation time of ABECC is also lower than that of security mechanisms KP-ABE and CP-ABE. It is also noticed that key generation time increases in all the three schemes when number of attributes is increased but it is lowest in case of the proposed scheme. It is due to use of ECC which reduces the key length that in turns reduces the key generation time.

Figure 5. Effect of File Size on key generation time analysis

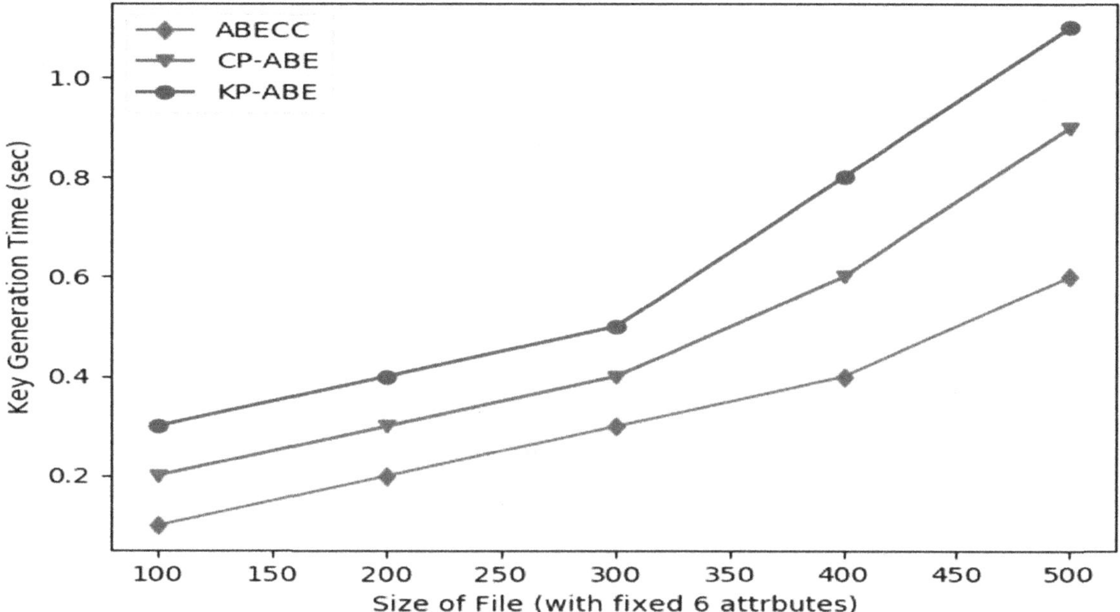

Figure 6. Effect of number of attributes on encryption time analysis

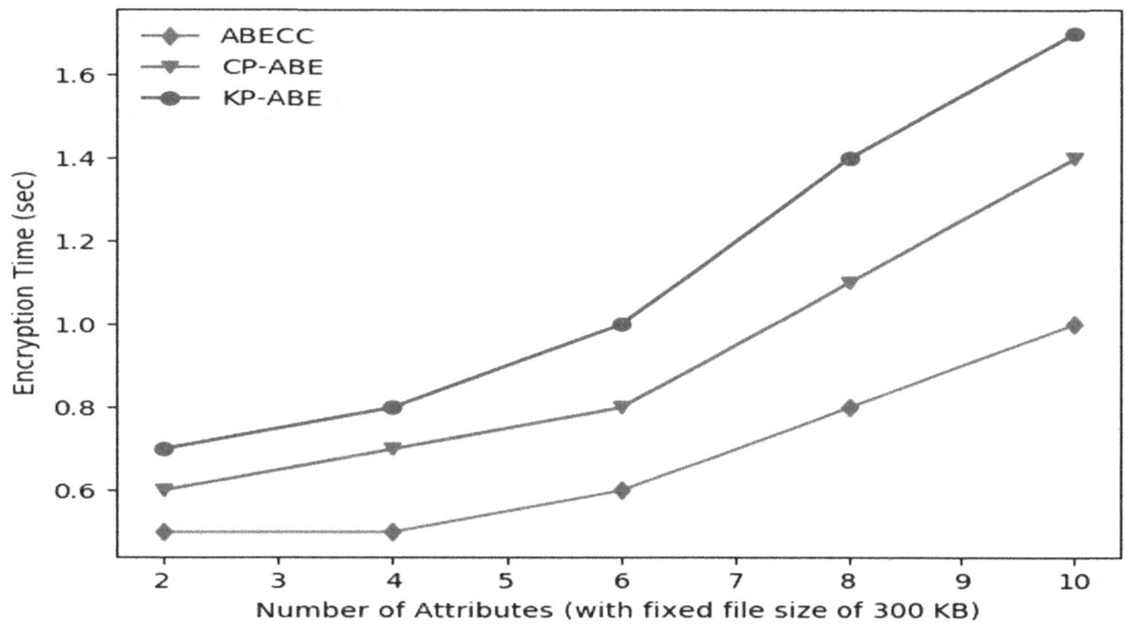

Figure 7. Effect of number of attributes on decryption time analysis

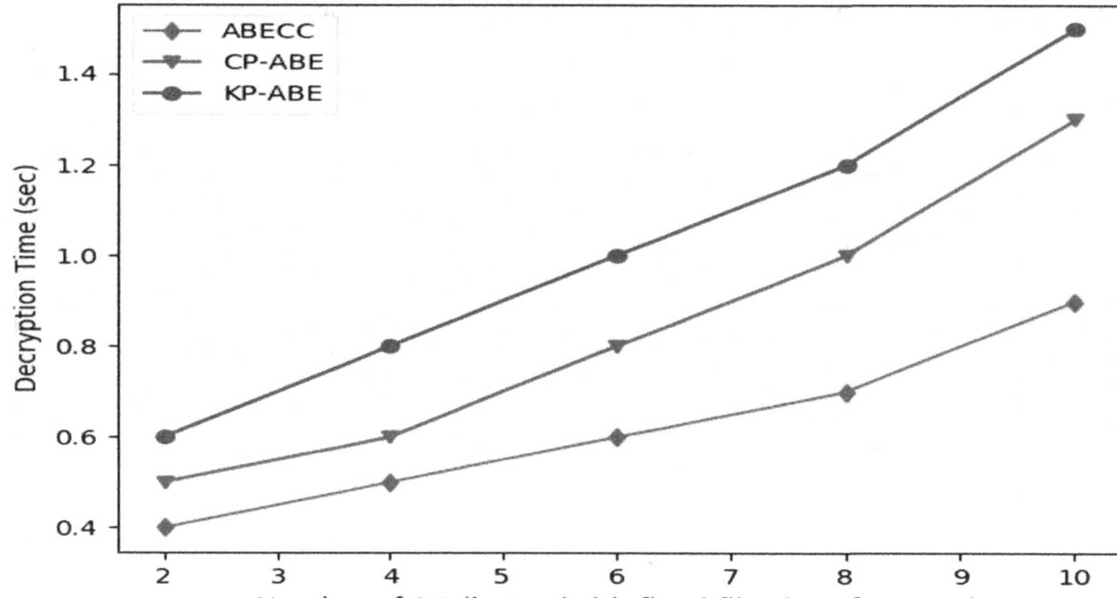

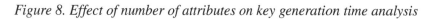

Figure 8. Effect of number of attributes on key generation time analysis

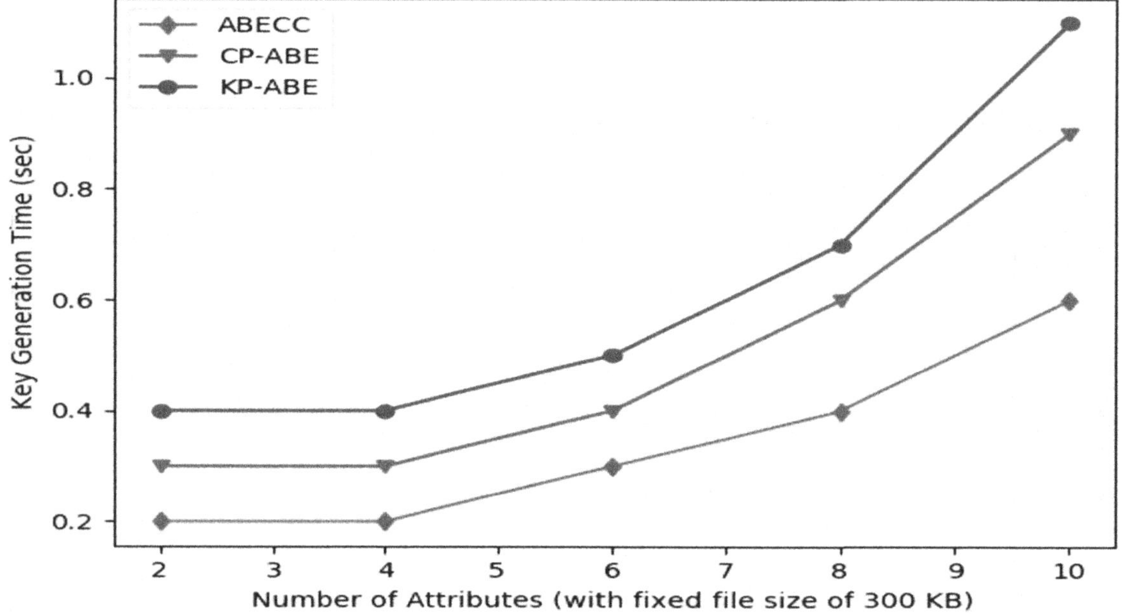

Table 3. Comparative analysis to know effect of file size

Number of attributes with fixed size file (300KB)	Encryption Time (sec)			Decryption Time (sec)			Key Generation Time (sec)		
	KP-ABE	*CP-ABE*	*AB-ECC*	*KP-ABE*	*CP-ABE*	*AB-ECC*	*KP-ABE*	*CP-ABE*	*AB-ECC*
2	0.7	0.6	**0.5**	0.6	0.5	**0.4**	0.4	0.3	**0.2**
4	0.8	0.7	**0.5**	0.8	0.6	**0.5**	0.4	0.3	**0.2**
6	1.0	0.8	**0.6**	1.0	0.8	**0.6**	0.5	0.4	**0.3**
8	1.4	1.1	**0.8**	1.2	1.0	**0.7**	0.7	0.6	**0.4**
10	1.7	1.4	**1.0**	1.5	1.3	**0.9**	1.1	0.9	**0.6**

5.3.3. Discussion

Table 3 presents a comparative analysis which describes the effect of file size on encryption, decryption and key generation time. Here, attribute count is same and is equal to 6 for all cases. This analysis shows that proposed ABECC scheme performs better than existing security schemes.

Table 4 presents the comparative complexity analysis which describes the effect of number of attributes on encryption, decryption and key generation time with fixed file size of 300 KB. Here, it can be observed that proposed ABECC scheme outperforms the existing schemes.

Table 4. Comparative analysis to know effect of number of attributes

Size of file (KB) with fixed attributes (6)	Encryption Time (sec)			Decryption Time (sec)			Key Generation Time (sec)		
	KP-ABE	*CP-ABE*	*AB-ECC*	*KP-ABE*	*CP-ABE*	*AB-ECC*	*KP-ABE*	*CP-ABE*	*AB-ECC*
100	0.7	0.6	**0.5**	0.7	0.6	**0.5**	0.3	0.2	**0.1**
200	0.8	0.6	**0.5**	0.8	0.7	**0.5**	0.4	0.3	**0.2**
300	1.0	0.8	**0.6**	1.0	0.8	**0.6**	0.5	0.4	**0.3**
400	1.3	1.1	**0.8**	1.3	1.0	**0.7**	0.8	0.6	**0.4**
500	1.6	1.4	**1.0**	1.6	1.2	**0.8**	1.1	0.9	**0.6**

5.4 Computational Overhead Analysis

Proposed approach ABECC ensures security with lower computational complexities as compared to the existing schemes (KP-ABE, CP-ABE). This is due to use of ECC which uses shorter key length. When we compute average encryption time of these schemes then we find that ABECC is 1.6 times and 1.3 times faster than the existing approaches of KP-ABE and CP-ABE respectively. Average decryption time computation shows that ABECC is 1.7 times and 1.4 times faster than these existing approaches respectively. Similarly, computation of average key generation time indicates that ABECC is 1.9 times and 1.5 times faster than the same existing approaches respectively. Finally, on computing the average of total computational time for these approaches, we observe that proposed scheme ABECC is 1.7 times

Figure 9. Effect of file size on computational overhead

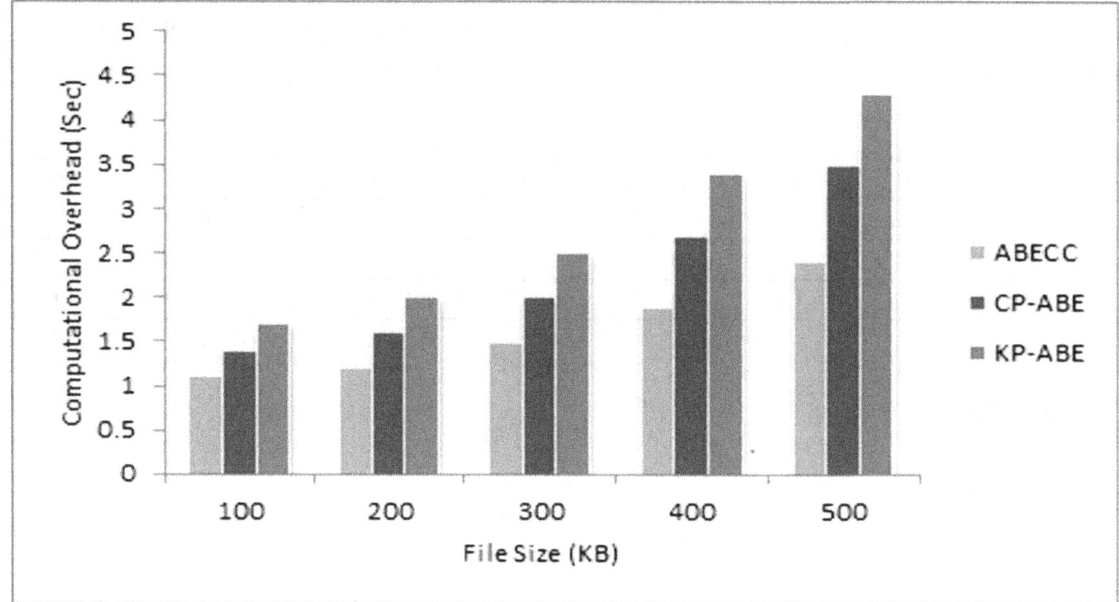

and 1.4 times faster than the existing approaches of KP-ABE and CP-ABE respectively. Thus, we can say that ABECC outperforms over the existing schemes.

5.4.1. Effect of File Size on Computational Complexity

Figure 9 presents the computational overhead analysis for various file sizes with fixed number of attributes that is 6. It shows that ABECC is on average 1.7 times and 1.4 times faster than the existing approaches of KP-ABE and CP-ABE respectively. This indicates that proposed scheme ABECC provides security with lesser computational overheads than the existing security schemes viz., KP-ABE and CP-ABE.

5.4.2. Effect of Number of Attributes on Computational Complexity

Figure 10 presents the effect of number of attributes on computational overheads with fixed file size of 300 KB. It shows that ABECC is on average 1.7 times and 1.4 times faster than the existing approaches of KP-ABE and CP-ABE respectively. Thus, it can be observed that that ABECC offers security with lesser computational overheads than the existing security schemes viz., KP-ABE and CP-ABE.

5.5 Novelty and Merits of ABECC

This manuscript proposes a novel security model viz., ABECC for providing security in the healthcare sensor cloud with lower computational overheads than the existing security schemes. ABECC uses attribute based elliptic curve encryption technique to design its security model. This approach offers fine grained access control that means a better security than the coarse grained access control. This approach improves the encryption, decryption and key generation time as compared to the existing schemes (KP-

Figure 10. Effect of number of attributes on computational overhead

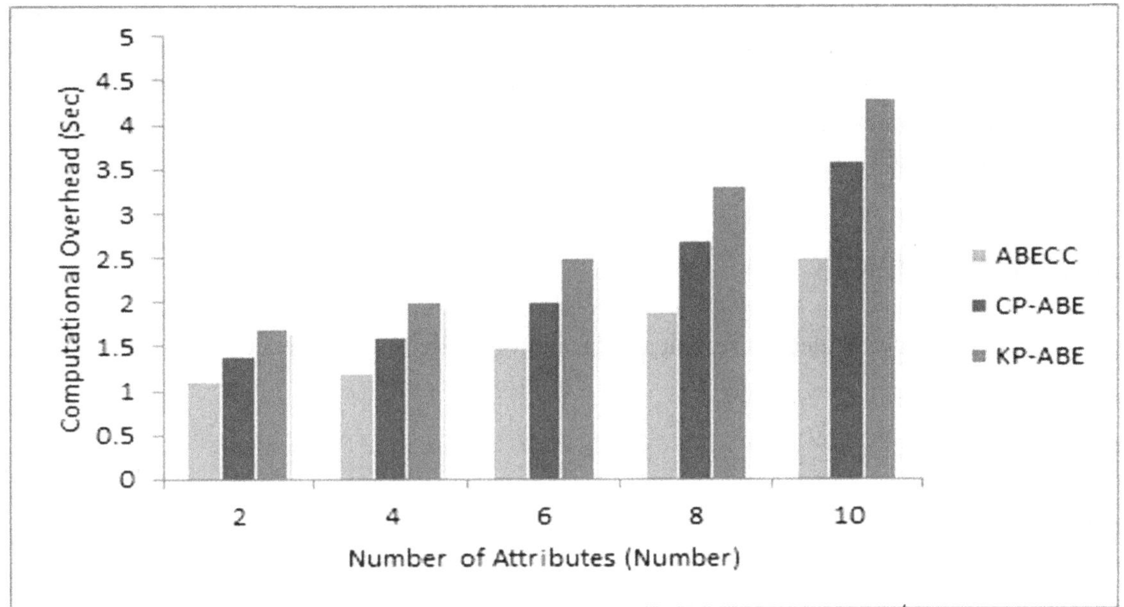

ABE and CP-ABE). Thus, it enhances security and reduces the computational overheads. It also ensures confidentiality, integrity, reliability, availability, scalability, authenticity and collusion resistance of the system. ABECC is a security scheme proposed for the healthcare information system. However, the core engine of this security model is also useful to various other industrial as well as non-industrial IoT and sensor cloud applications such as smart building, smart city, smart automotive manufacturing, smart agriculture, forest fire information system and military applications. Thus, we can say that ABECC is a novel security scheme and it has several advantages over the existing security schemes.

6 CONCLUSION AND FUTURE WORK

To implement dynamic and advanced security policies on patient's health records in any medical application, a novel design ABECC is devised in this paper which secures the healthcare data of patients in sensor cloud environment. The proposed security model encrypts sensor data on the basis of some access policies and users having the specified policies can decrypt that data. Here, an attribute based scheme is developed with elliptic curve cryptography (ECC) to maintain privacy of patient's data. Use of ECC reduces the key length that causes better performance. Results prove that ABECC outperforms the existing schemes KP-ABE and CP-ABE. ABECC provides security with improved efficiency and lower computational overheads. It makes the process 1.7 times and 1.4 times faster than the existing approaches of KP-ABE and CP-ABE respectively. It also ensures fine grained access control and offers confidentiality, integrity, authenticity, reliability, availability, scalability and collusion-resistance. This approach can cater the needs of multiple kinds of users and researchers by providing data that is obtained from several wearable sensors of patients from same or different healthcare centers. This is possible due to sensor cloud integration and virtualization.

In future, this work can be extended with more advanced constraints on access policies. This model can be made more secure and robust for very large datasets. Further, this technique could also be used in various other IoT and sensor cloud applications viz., agricultural IoT, industrial IoT, smart city, smart building, smart farming system, underground applications, underwater monitoring system, forest fire detection system and military applications. We can impose some application specific constraints too in the security schemes of such applications.

ACKNOWLEDGMENT

This research is partially funded by Technical Education Quality Improvement Program (TEQIP III).

REFERENCES

Ahuja, S. P., & Wheeler, N. (2020). Architecture of Fog-Enabled and Cloud-Enhanced Internet of Things Applications. *International Journal of Cloud Applications and Computing, 10*(1), 1-10.

Al-Ayyoub, M., AlZu'bi, S., Jararweh, Y., Shehab, M. A., & Gupta, B. B. (2018). Accelerating 3D medical volume segmentation using GPUs. *Multimed Tools Appl, Springer, 77*(4), 4939–4958. doi:10.100711042-016-4218-0

Altaf, A., Abbas, H., Iqbal, F., & Derhab, A. (2019). Trust models of internet of smart things: A survey, open issues, and future directions. *Journal of Network and Computer Applications, Elsevier, 137*, 93–111. doi:10.1016/j.jnca.2019.02.024

Athena, J., Sumathy, V., & Kumar, K. (2017). An identity attribute–based encryption using elliptic curve digital signature for patient health record maintenance. *International Journal of Communication Systems, Wiley, 31*(2), 1–22.

Bansal, A., & Agrawal, A. (2017). Providing security, integrity and authentication using ECC algorithm in cloud storage. *IEEE International Conference on Computer Communication and Informatics - ICCCI 2017*, 1-5. 10.1109/ICCCI.2017.8117749

Bethencourt, J., Sahai, A., & Waters, B. (2007). Ciphertext-Policy Attribute-Based Encryption. *Proceedings of the 2007 IEEE Symposium on Security and Privacy*, 321-334. 10.1109/SP.2007.11

Carvalho, M. A. Jr, & Bandiera-Paiva, P. (2018). Health Information System Role-Based Access Control Current Security Trends and Challenges. *Journal of Healthcare Engineering*, 1–8.

Díaz, M., Martín, C., & Rubio, B. (2016). State-of-the-art, challenges, and open issues in the integration of Internet of things and cloud computing. *Journal of Network and Computer Applications, Elsevier, 67*, 99–117. doi:10.1016/j.jnca.2016.01.010

Dwivedi, R. K., & Kumar, R. (2018). Sensor Cloud: Integrating Wireless Sensor Networks with Cloud Computing. *5th IEEE Uttar Pradesh Section International Conference on Electrical, Electronics and Computer Engineering – UPCON 2018*, 820-825. 10.1109/UPCON.2018.8597008

Dwivedi, R. K., Saran, M., & Kumar, R. (2019). A Survey on Security over Sensor-Cloud. *9th IEEE International Conference on Cloud Computing, Data Science & Engineering – Confluence 2019*, 31-37. 10.1109/CONFLUENCE.2019.8776897

Fernández-Alemán, J. L., Señor, I. C., Lozoya, P. A. O., & Toval, A. (2013). Security and privacy in electronic health records: A systematic literature review. *Journal of Biomedical Informatics, 46*(3), 541–562.

Ghoneim, A., Muhammad, G., Amin, S. U., & Gupta, B. (2018). Medical Image Forgery Detection for Smart Healthcare. *IEEE Communications Magazine*, *56*(4), 33–37. doi:10.1109/MCOM.2018.1700817

Goléa, N. E., & Melkemi, K. E. (2019). ROI-based fragile watermarking for medical image tamper detection. *International Journal of High Performance Computing and Networking, 13*(2), 199–210. doi:10.1504/IJHPCN.2019.097508

Goyal, V., Pandey, O., Sahai, A., & Waters, B. (2006). Attribute-based encryption for fine-grained access control of encrypted data. *Proceedings of CCS'06*, 89-98. 10.1145/1180405.1180418

Hung, N. T., Giang, D. H., Keong, N. W., & Zhu, H. (2012). Cloud-enabled data sharing model. *IEEE International Conference on Intelligence and Security Informatics*, 1-6.

Ko, J. G., Lu, C., Srivastava, M. B., Stankovic, J. A., Terzis, A., & Welsh, M. (2010). Wireless Sensor Networks for Healthcare. *Proceedings of the IEEE*, *98*(11), 1947–1960. doi:10.1109/JPROC.2010.2065210

Li, M., Yu, S., Zheng, Y., Ren, K., & Lou, W. (2013). Scalable and secure sharing of personal health records in cloud computing using attribute-based encryption. *IEEE Transactions on Parallel and Distributed Systems*, *24*(1), 131–143. doi:10.1109/TPDS.2012.97

Lin, H., Yan, Z., & Fu, Y. (2019). Adaptive security-related data collection with context awareness. *Journal of Network and Computer Applications, Elsevier*, *126*, 88–103. doi:10.1016/j.jnca.2018.11.002

Liu, H., Guo, Q., Wang, G., Gupta, B. B., & Zhang, C. (2019). Medical image resolution enhancement for healthcare using nonlocal self-similarity and low-rank prior. *Multimed Tools Appl, Springer*, *78*(7), 9033–9050. doi:10.100711042-017-5277-6

Lounis, A., Hadjidj, A., Bouabdallah, A., & Challal, Y. (2016). Healing on the cloud: Secure cloud architecture for medical wireless sensor networks. *Future Generation Computer Systems, Elsevier*, *55*, 266–277. doi:10.1016/j.future.2015.01.009

Masood, I., Wang, Y., Daud, A., Aljohani, N. R., & Dawood, H. (2018). Towards Smart Healthcare: Patient Data Privacy and Security in Sensor-Cloud Infrastructure. *Wireless Communications and Mobile Computing*, 1–23.

Muller, S., Katzenbeisser, S., & Eckert, C. (2008). Distributed Attribute-Based Encryption. *Proceedings of Springer International Conference on Information Security and Cryptology ICISC 2008*, 20-36.

Park, N. (2011). Secure Data Access Control Scheme Using Type-Based Re-encryption in Cloud Environment. In Semantic Methods for Knowledge Management and Communication. Springer. doi:10.1007/978-3-642-23418-7_28

Pérez, S., Rotondi, D., Pedone, D., Straniero, L., Núñez, M. J., & Gigante, F. (2017). Towards the CP-ABE Application for Privacy-Preserving Secure Data Sharing in IoT Contexts. In *International Conference on Innovative Mobile and Internet Services in Ubiquitous Computing*. Springer.

Premkamal, P. K., Pasupuleti, S. K., & Alphonse, P.J.A. (2020). Efficient Escrow-free CP-ABE with Constant Size Ciphertext and Secret Key for Big Data Storage in Cloud. *International Journal of Cloud Applications and Computing, 10*(1), 28-45.

Rashid, B., & Rehmani, M. H. (2016). Applications of wireless sensor networks for urban areas: A survey. *Journal of Network and Computer Applications, Elsevier*, *60*, 192–219. doi:10.1016/j.jnca.2015.09.008

Sambrekar, K., & Rajpurohit, V. S. (2019). Fast and Efficient Multiview Access Control Mechanism for Cloud Based Agriculture Storage Management System. *International Journal of Cloud Applications and Computing, 9*(1), 33-49.

Sangeetha, D., & Vaidehi, V. (2017). A secure cloud based personal health record framework for a multi owner environment. *Annals of Telecommunications, 72*(1-2), 95–104. doi:10.100712243-016-0529-4

Saran, M., Dwivedi, R. K., & Kumar, R. (2019). Attribute Based Elliptic Curve Encryption for Security in Sensor-Cloud. *2nd Springer International Conference on Data & Information Sciences – ICDIS 2019*, 1-11.

Sun, J., Wang, X., Wang, S., & Ren, L. (2018). A searchable personal health records framework with fine-grained access control in cloud-fog computing. *PLoS One*, *13*(11), 1–23. doi:10.1371/journal.pone.0207543 PMID:30496194

Sun, W., Cai, Z., Li, Y., Liu, F., Fang, S., & Wang, G. (2018). Security and Privacy in the Medical Internet of Things: A Review. *Security and Communication Networks*, 1–9.

Tembhare, A., Sibi Chakkaravarthy, S., Sangeetha, D., Vaidehi, V., & Venkata Rathnam, M. (2019). Role-based policy to maintain privacy of patient health records in cloud. *The Journal of Supercomputing, 11227*, 1-16.

Thilakanathan, D., Chen, S., Nepal, S., Calvo, R., & Alem, L. (2014). A platform for secure monitoring and sharing of generic health data in the Cloud. *Future Generation Computer Systems, Elsevier*, *35*, 102–113. doi:10.1016/j.future.2013.09.011

Tran, D. H., Nguyen, H. L., & Zha, W. (2011). Towards security in sharing data on cloud based social networks. *8th IEEE International conference on information, communications and signal processing*, 1–5. 10.1109/ICICS.2011.6173582

Tu, S., Niu, S., Li, H., Xiao-ming, Y., & Li, M. (2012). Fine-grained access control and revocation for sharing data on clouds. *26th international parallel and distributed processing symposium workshops and PhD forum,* 2146–2155. 10.1109/IPDPSW.2012.265

Wang, C., & Luo, J. (2013). An Efficient Key-Policy Attribute-Based Encryption Scheme with Constant Ciphertext Length. *Mathematical Problems in Engineering*, 1–7.

Yang, Y., & Zhang, Y. (2011). A Generic Scheme for Secure Data Sharing in Cloud. *40th IEEE International Conference on Parallel Processing Workshops*, 145-153. 10.1109/ICPPW.2011.51

Zhou, D., Yan, Z., Fu, Y., & Yao, Z. (2018). A survey on network data collection. *Journal of Network and Computer Applications, Elsevier, 116*, 9–23. doi:10.1016/j.jnca.2018.05.004

This research was previously published in the International Journal of Cloud Applications and Computing (IJCAC), 11(3); pages 1-18, copyright year 2021 by IGI Publishing (an imprint of IGI Global).

Chapter 45
Risk Reduction Privacy Preserving Approach for Accessing Electronic Health Records

V. K. Saxena
Vikram University, Ujjain, India

Shashank Pushkar
Birla Institute of Technology, Mesra, India

ABSTRACT

In the healthcare field, preserving privacy of the patient's electronic health records has been an elementary issue. Numerous techniques have been emerged to maintain privacy of the susceptible information. Acting as a first line of defence against illegal access, traditional access control schemes fall short of defending against misbehaviour of the already genuine and authoritative users: a risk that can harbour overwhelming consequences upon probable data release or leak. This paper introduces a novel risk reduction strategy for the healthcare domain so that the risk related with an access request is evaluated against the privacy preferences of the patient who is undergoing for the medical procedure. The proposed strategy decides the set of data objects that can be safely uncovered to the healthcare service provider such that unreasonably repeated tests and measures can be avoided and the privacy preferences of the patient are preserved.

1. INTRODUCTION

The electronic health records (EHR) (Ambinder, E. P., 2005) of the patients include detailed information concerning their health issues and medical history in the healthcare field. The records comprise susceptible data, such as previously diagnosed health diseases and drug maltreatment, of which the patient would

DOI: 10.4018/978-1-6684-6311-6.ch045

prefer to keep confidential. Distribution of such data, whether persistently or unintentionally, could invite grave harmful implications for the corresponding patient. Adverse consequences could range from social disgrace, complications in getting employment or health insurance policies and so forth (Rindfleisch, T. C., 1997). In attempts to bring patients more restraint over their EHRs, legislations such as the Health Insurance Probability and Accountability Act (HIPAA) has been developed. Therefore, the privacy of such records must be protected and, hence, has been under intensive research analysis (Yang et al., 2015; Gong et al., 2015, Salih et al., 2015; Zhou et al., 2015).

When the privacy of the medical records is being preserved, numerous techniques can be utilized. Normally, as shown in Figure 1, privacy can be managed by using cryptography, anonymization, or policy methods (Yang et al., 2015). Anonymization techniques contain, utilizing statistical measures to conceal the identity of the patient amongst other patients before the data is uncovered to the data requestors and is generally used for discharging huge quantities of medical data for analytical purposes (Sweeney, 2002; Agrawal et al., 2007). Cryptography techniques exertion by utilizing security measures such as encryption mechanisms to protect the susceptible records (Stallings et al. 2014; Gasarch et al., 2004). Finally, policy methods preserve the patient's privacy by employing rules and constraints for authenticating and authorizing access to the private data (Ferraiolo et al., 2001; Sandhu et al., 1996). As a result, preserving privacy of a scrupulous patient, who is currently undergoing a medical diagnosis or procedure, cannot be realized through means of anonymization methods because identity is lost among multiple datasets. Therefore, the feasible solution, in such circumstances, requires utilizing cryptography or policy methods or even a combination of the two (Yang et al., 2015).

Figure 1. Different privacy preserving approaches

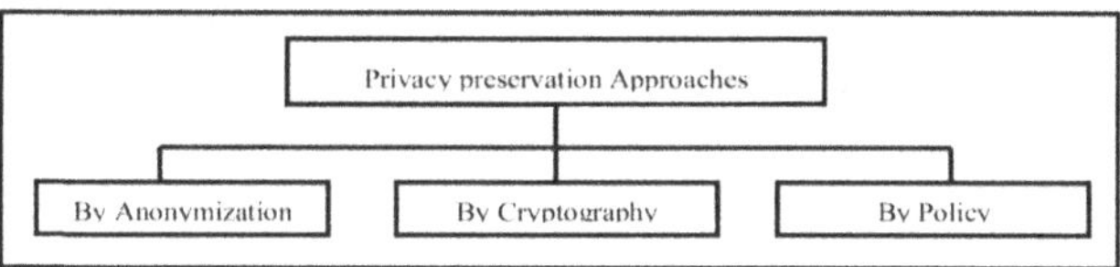

Access control technique is one of the major processes for preserving privacy of the medical records. This technique is elementary security mechanism that works by assessing an access request against a set of constraints and rules before finally granting or denying such access to system resources (Stallings et al., (2014). Several types of access control exist in the literature with different features: Mandatory Access Control (MAC) (Stallings et al., (2014), Role Based Access Control (RBAC) (Sandhu et al., 1996; Reid et al., 2003; Lampson, 1974; Graham et al., 1972, Sandhu et al., 2000), Attribute Based Access Control (ABAC) (Hu et al., 2013) and so on.

While access control can act as a first line of defence against illegal access by denying such access request, it is unable to defend against misuse of system resources by users who have been granted access (Wang et al., 2011). In the medical scenario, healthcare professionals can abuse their access rights with regards to patients' private health records; which could increase the risk of potential leakage of the sensitive information. In the United States, the Department of Health and Human Services has conducted an investigation with regards to patients' electronic health records in UCLA (University of California,

Los Angeles) hospital and found that they have been excessively viewed by medical staff without a valid reason (Hennessy, 2016).

In order to overcome the potential misuse of already authorized users, access control schemes can be amplified with risk assessment measures. One important measure is calculating the reliability of an access appellant. Reliability can be determined by several means. One way of calculating trust is by analyzing the user's past behaviour towards a system resource in order to grant or deny future access demand (Josang et al., 2007). In effect, the access control scheme becomes more adaptable and dynamic in responding to access requests due to the variability of the trust level of the access requestor, as opposed to traditional access control schemes (Wang et al., 2011; Hennessy, 2016; Josang et al., 2007; Kandala et al., 2011).

When Risk assessment measures are incorporated with access control techniques, a risky access demand can be allowed, rather than be denied, if it is within the tolerable thresholds. However, risk reduction strategies must be applied to lower the risk associated with such an access (Stoneburner et al., 2002; Guide, 2012). Risk reduction techniques are obligatory actions (Irwin et al., 2006; Pontual et al., 2011) that are performed to minimize the risk of access request such as increasing the security measures, performing anonymization to the datasets or employing system alerts and notifications (Diaz-Lopez et al., 2016).

This research tackles the issue of preserving privacy of the patient's EHR by incorporating a risk assessment element. More specifically, a risk reduction technique is proposed to lower the risk associated with an access request initiated by a healthcare professional to a particular patient's health record. That is, when a risky access request is made, the proposed technique will expose the patient's relevant and less sensitive data. Therefore, the risk reduction strategy is risk-aware and privacy preserving in addition to being HIPAA compliant.

This paper is intended as follows: section two shows the background information that act as the foundation of the research. Section three presents the related work. The proposed risk reduction strategy is analysed and described in section IV. The paper concludes with the discussions of related work in section V.

2. PRELIMINARIES

2.1. The Health Insurance Probability and Accountability Act (USA)

The HIPAA (1996) is a United States legislation, which provides rules and regulations for securing the electronic medical records for the ultimate goal of preserving the patient's privacy. The legislation consists of multiple titles. However, title II of the act is concerned with regulations for safeguarding the health records' transactions and distribution. Under title II, the Privacy Rule of the HIPAA describes national standards in order to preserve privacy of the patients. In effect, the rule prohibits healthcare professionals from releasing the patient's medical data, to third parties, without an explicitly written permission from the corresponding patient. Furthermore, access to the patients' medical records without a legitimate reason should not be allowed since it violates the privacy of the patient. However, in situations where the access of the patient's stored medical data is deemed necessary in order to further advance the current medical treatment, the HIPAA allows the medical professionals access to such records. Finally, the legislation describes penalties and fines upon violating the privacy rules stated therein.

2.2. Risk Assessment in Information Security

In their detailed risk assessment guide, the National Institute for Standards and Technology (NIST) (2012) describe the method by which risk assessment is conducted. According to the definitions stated in the guide, should an entity be vulnerable to a certain threatening event, the risk is defined as a function of the likelihood of the threat and its potential impact. That is:

$$\text{Risk} = \text{Likelihood} * \text{Impact} \quad (1)$$

3. RELATED WORK

3.1. Risk-Aware Access Control Models

Risk Aware Access Control schemes (RAAC) (Office, 2004) are considered as a dynamic and adaptable new type of access control models due to their inherent features of incorporating methods of risk assessment. In such models, the access is permitted or denied based on the outcome of a risk assessment function. When an access request is considered as risky but within acceptable intervals, risk reduction methods can be exploited such that the risk incurred of such access is minimized.

The National Institute of Standards and Technology has developed a general risk-based access control model according to the models proposed by (McGraw, 2009). Several elements are incorporated to assess the risk; namely; operational need, situational factor and risk measures. A conceptual model for risk-aware attribute based access control (Kandala et al., 2011) has been proposed based on these earlier works. Generally, risk-aware access control models proposed in the literature utilize the NIST definition of risk assessment and calculation where a risk is evaluated as the function of a threat likelihood multiplied by the associated impact (Dimmock et al., 2004; Zhang et al., 2006; Cheng et al., 2007, Ni et al., 2010, Burnett et al., 2014, Kamwan et al., 2016; Khambhammettu et al., 2013). The subject requesting access to particular object are both associated with security clearances or weights of which are then incorporated with the calculation of risk. Access control models that use trust evaluations can be generally divided into two categories: static trust evaluations (Cheng et al., 2007) and dynamic trust evaluations (Burnett et al., 2014; Kamwan et al., 2016; Khambhammettu et al., 2013; Zhou et al., 2015). Nonetheless, once a risky access request is allowed, risk should be lowered down to acceptable level using risk reduction techniques; an option that is employed by a subset of models.

3.2. Risk Reduction Techniques

Risk reduction in access control models are obligations that are usually required to be performed in order to lower the potential impact of a risky access request (Irwin et al., 2006; Pontual et al., 2011). Risk can be reduced by several means such as utilizing anonymization techniques (Armando et al., 2015; Taneja et al., 2015; Shaden et al., 2017) for protection against potential vulnerabilities, increasing security measures of the system by increasing the length of encryption keys or imposing a set of rules and required actions. Such obligations, of which all are supervised by the system, need to be satisfied by the user *before* or *after* access is granted (Díaz-López et al., 2016). Figure 2 illustrates risk reduction approaches that can be employed.

Figure 2. Risk reduction strategies for minimize the riskiness of an access request

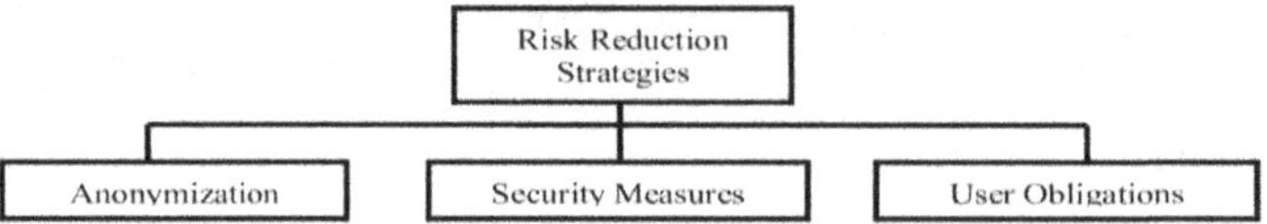

4. THE PROPOSED RISK REDUCTION STRATEGY

4.1. System Components

4.1.1. Trust Calculation

In order to assess the risk incurred of an access request, trust level of the requesting entity must be calculated and later it is evaluated in the other components. Trust is generally defined as forecasting an entity's future access, based on its historical behaviour (Josang et al., 2007). Trust can be evaluated in several ways, such as mining past behaviour, using recommender systems to associate a subject with a recommended trust level or, more statically, assign security clearances for each entity by the system administrator (Josang et al., 2006).

Since, trust calculation is application specific and the system administrator can choose the appropriate trust model based on the requirement of the system, the proposed system in this work assumes that trust values have already been computed and ready for evaluation by the risk reduction system. Nevertheless, one of the widely known trust calculation and evaluation methods that analyze the user's past behaviour in order to assist in making decisions regarding future access requests is the Subjective Logic model (Josang et al., 2006). In the model, the trust level of a user is computed using probabilistic methods that utilize Bayesian principles. An entity, *u*, requesting access to system resource, *i*, is given a trust or opinion representation that has been formed by entity *w*. that is, the opinion formed by *w* about access requestor *u* with regards to *i* is represented by the following tuple:

$$w^{w}_{u:i} = (b^{w}_{u:i}, d^{w}_{u:i}, u^{w}_{u:i}, a^{w}_{u:i}) \quad (1)$$

where:

$$b^{w}_{u:i} + d^{w}_{u:i} + u^{w}_{u:i} = 1, and\, a^{w}_{u:i} \in [0,1]. \quad (2)$$

In the above formula, $b^{w}_{u:i}, d^{w}_{u:i}, u^{w}_{u:i}$, represent the degree of *belief*, *disbelief* and *uncertainty* of entity *w* with regards to trusting system resource *i* to *u*. Furthermore, $a^{w}_{u:i}$ represents the a priori or base knowledge of entity *w* regarding *u* when no previous history is currently available; a typical situation when new users come into the system.

In order to allow for dynamicity, the trust levels need to be updated according to the perceived behavioural evidence. To update the trust values, two parameters are introduced: $r^{w}_{u:i}$ and $s^{w}_{u:i}$. The former parameter calculates the number of positive actions, while the later calculates the negative ones. Based on these parameters, the ultimate trust level of an entity requesting access can be updated using the following equations:

$$b^{w}_{u:i} = \frac{r^{w}_{u:i}}{r^{w}_{u:i} + s^{w}_{u:i} + 2}$$

$$d^{w}_{u:i} = \frac{s^{w}_{u:i}}{r^{w}_{u:i} + s^{w}_{u:i} + 2}$$

$$u^{w}_{u:i} = \frac{2}{r^{w}_{u:i} + s^{w}_{u:i} + 2} \tag{3}$$

Based on the above equations, the initial situation where there exists no behavioural history for the user, the values are:

$$b^{w}_{u:i} = 0, d^{w}_{u:i} = 0, u^{w}_{u:i} = 1 \ \ and \ \ a^{w}_{u:i} = 0.5$$

4.1.2. Disease Relevance Matrix

The purpose of the disease relevance matrix (DRM) is to provide relevance information for the different diseases. That is, for the set of *n* diseases, D_1, D_2, D_3,..., D_n, two diseases are relevant to one another if they have a positive relevance value. As illustrated in Figure 3, diseases D_1 and D_3 are correlated and relevant to each other because they have a positive relevance value. Relevance between the different diseases can be obtained using several approaches. One effective approach, as proposed in (Wang et al., 2012), is to mine for correlation information inside the database of the hospital. In their approach, the system maintains a log for all access requests that have been made on the patients' medical records for serving medical purposes, such as disease diagnosis purposes and so forth. Therefore, the access request information between the different patient records and the medical purposes to which they have been requested for access are available and used as observation instances. The relevance function, $f_n(r,p,t)$, calculates the total number of access requests that have been made by a healthcare professional *r* to the patients' health records of type *t* in order to serve a medical purpose *p* . Similarly, the function $f_n(r,p,t)$ yields the total number of access requests made by all healthcare professionals classified under the same group, G_r, and who have made access requests to medical records of type *t* in order to serve purpose *p*.

maintaining such information is crucial in order to assist in calculating and inferring correlation information between the different diseases. That is, if a medical record, of which is classified under type *t*, is being frequently accessed to serve some purpose *p*, and then it can be inferred that there exists a degree of correlation and relevance between the two and vice versa. Such relevance information is realized by means of utilizing Bayesian principal of independence as follows:

$$P(i / X) = P(i / r, p, t) = \frac{P(i)P(r / i)P(p / r, i)P(t / p, r, i)}{P(r, p, t)} \tag{4}$$

where *P*(1l*X*) denotes that the access request is relevant.

While *P*(0l*X*) denotes that the access request is not relevant.

The parameter *P*(i) yields the percentage of access requests that have been made in the past. The estimation of *P*(rli) can be found by calculating the total number of access requests made by entity *r*. However, to solve the issue when the entity requesting access is new in the system, smoothing methods can be applied by incorporating the total number of access requests made by the entire entities belonging to the same group. Therefore:

$$P(r / i) = \frac{\alpha f_n(r, i) + (1 - \alpha) f_n(G_r, i)}{f_n(i)} \tag{5}$$

where $\alpha \in [0,1]$.

Similarly, the estimation of P(p/r,i) and P(t/p,r,i) is:

$$P(p / r, i) = \frac{\beta f_n(p, r, i) + (1 - \beta) f_n(p, G_r, i)}{\beta f_n(r, i) + (1 - \beta) f_n(G_r, i)} \tag{6}$$

and:

$$P(t / p, r, i) = \frac{\gamma f_n(t, p, r, i) + (1 - \gamma) f_n(t, p, G_r, i)}{\gamma f_n(p, r, i) + (1 - \gamma) f_n(p, G_r, i)} \tag{7}$$

where $f_n(p, r, i)$ computes the total number of access requests that have been made by entity *r* to serve medical purpose *p*, and $f_n(t, p, r, i)$computes the total number of access requests for patients' records of type *t* of which have been made by entity *r* in order to serve purpose *p*.

In effect, the proposed analytical approach can decide whether an access request, made on a certain patient record, is relevant to the healthcare provider's own profession, as in Equation (6). Moreover, the approach can decide whether an access request made on the patient's record is relevant to the medical purpose associated, such as the purpose of diagnosing some disease as in Equation (7), which, effectively, can establish the relevance between the different types of diseases. Such correlation information can be stored in the Disease Relevance Matrix and updated frequently.

Figure 3. Disease Relevance Matrix: Two data objects are correlated if they have a positive intersecting value

	D_1	D_2	D_3	...	D_n
D_1	1	0	1	...	...
D_2	0	0	1	...	...
D_3	1	1	1	...	...
...	...	...	...	...	...
D_n	...	...	...	...	...

4.1.3. Patient Privacy Preferences

The privacy preferences for disease disclosure are obtained by the corresponding patient when they fill out their medical forms and, afterwards, entered into the system by healthcare staff. Therefore, each previously diagnosed, and stored, disease is associated with a privacy preference consulting how sensitive this data is with regards to the patient. In effect, for two disease objects *oi* and *oj*, having the corresponding sensitivity weights *wi* and *wj*, scaled between [0, 1], if $wi > wj$ then disease object *oi* is considered as more sensitive than disease *oj*, and vice versa.

4.1.4. The Risk Measure Formula

The risk measure formula is a mathematical equation, which will be developed in the future, of which assesses the riskiness of an access request to the patient's relevant data according to the trust level, t, of the doctor, and the privacy preferences, $\{w_1, w_2, \ldots, w_n\} \in W$, of the patient.

4.2. The Risk Reduction Strategy

In the proposed risk reduction strategy, every access request by healthcare professionals, to the patients' private data, need to be evaluated for potential risks. As illustrated in Figure 4, a doctor is treating a particular patient for a health issue. To avoid potential repeated tests and medical procedures as well as help assist in making better diagnostic decisions, the doctor issues an access request to the patient's stored health records. Upon receiving the access request, and to be consistent with HIPAA privacy rule, the risk reduction strategy operates by retrieving the patient's set of diseases that have a positive relevance to the current diagnostic effort alongside the corresponding sensitivity weights. Once such data is obtained, the Data Combination Risk Calculator, which applies the Risk Measure Formula, searches for the appropriate patient data combinations, those are, later, evaluated against the trust level of the doctor for potential data disclosure. Evidently, for two patients, who are being treated by the same doctor, and who also have the same set of already diagnosed and stored diseases, but with different privacy preferences, the output of the proposed risk reduction strategy will be different and tailored to each situation such that quality healthcare service is delivered without undermining the privacy preferences of each patient.

Figure 4. System components of high-level architecture for proposed risk reduction strategy

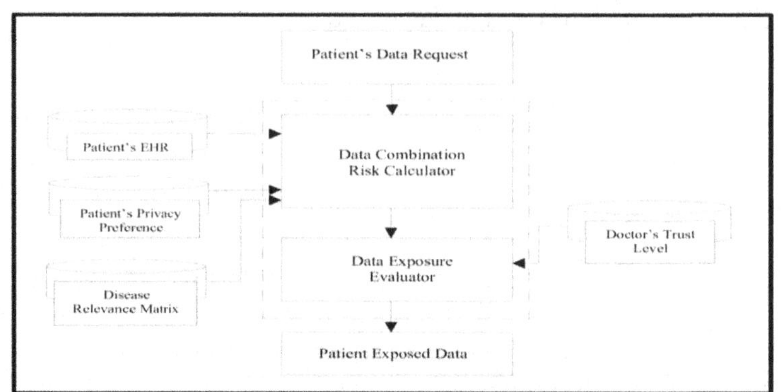

Figure 5 illustrates, in more detail, the activities and actions performed by the proposed Risk Reduction Strategy. When the system finds a set of relevant diseases from the patient's data to which a doctor requests access, the system computes the possible data combinations in a reverse manner. That is, the system begins by generating and computing the Risk Measure values for the combination that includes the total number of diseases, n. If the resulting Risk Measure value exceeds the trust level of the doctor, the system reiterates and generates data combinations of fewer numbers of diseases, by excluding one disease at a time and computing the Risk Measure value incurred, and so forth. The goal is to find the maximum possible number of diseases with maximum Risk Measure value. If such data combination is found and the risk incurred is below the trust level of the doctor, the data is then exposed and disclosed to the doctor. However, if the system fails to find a suitable relevant data combination for the doctor's trust level, then the data is regarded as highly private and an explicit consent must be obtained from the patient.

5. CONCLUSION

In the field of healthcare, preserving privacy of the EHR of the patients has been a most important issue. Numerous approaches have been suggested and implemented to undertake the issue of preserving privacy by means of risk assessment and estimation. In addition, risky access request can be allowed by performing a suitable reduction technique.

In electronic health record, there is a significant need to design privacy-preserving systems, following usable and well-organized data search strategies. In the midst of others, reliability and privacy are the two important requirements that may impact the likability of medical records in different HSPs. The reason is, Health Service Program (HSP) may not satisfy the patient safety needs and collecting data from such HSP, while aggregating data from all HSPs to create patient medical history will impact its reliability. In e-health, trust can be established based on the quality and reliability of HSP, health professionals and data standard. Researchers have been pursuing the goal of achieving semantic interoperability of EHRs to allow sharing of medical data across healthcare organizations, but it has not been realized yet. There is a need for improvement of standardization frameworks that hold data integrity and incorporate integrated EHR schema and common semantics, to allow data sharing across health information exchanges. Digital devices from mobile phones to smart cards and RFID tags are becoming more and more everywhere.

Figure 5. Main actions performed by the proposed risk reduction strategy where n denotes the total number of the patient's relevant diseases obtained by the DRM

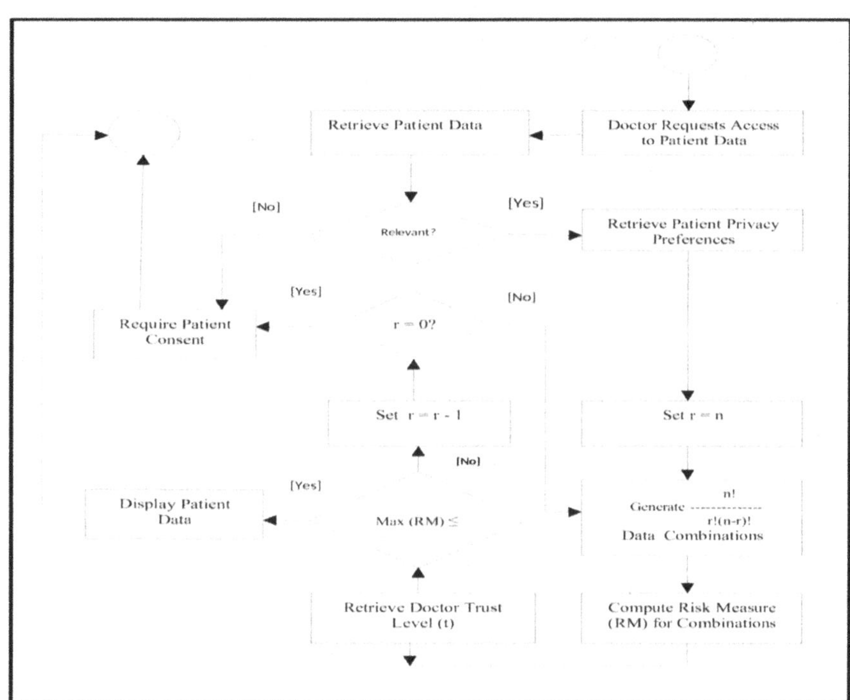

Rapid advancements in mobile technologies and applications resulted in new opportunities for the incorporation of mobile health into existing e-health services. This emphasizes on the need of designing insubstantial privacy-preserving e-health protocols which is suitable for resource-constrained devices. There are a number of open research issues in the field of privacy enabled e-health systems supporting varied environment including: (i) supporting heterogeneous environment, (ii) supporting different stakeholders by allowing different types of access and usage control, (iii) support for crisis conditions, (iv) trust and reputation modelling, (v) interoperability, (vi) data integrity, (vii) traceability of illegitimate distribution, and malicious users.

In this regard, the paper introduced a risk reduction strategy, which controls the access to the patient's susceptible data. These data is based on the dependability of the requesting healthcare contributor, which is according to the privacy preferences and represented as sensitivity weights, of the patient.

REFERENCES

Agrawal, R., & Johnson, C. (2007). Securing electronic health records without impeding the flow of information. *International Journal of Medical Informatics*, *76*(5-6), 471–479. doi:10.1016/j.ijmedinf.2006.09.015 PMID:17204451

Ambinder, E. P. (2005). Electronic health records. *Journal of Oncology Practice / American Society of Clinical Oncology*, *1*(2), 57–63. doi:10.1200/jop.2005.1.2.57 PMID:20871681

Armando, A., Bezzi, M., Metoui, N. & Sabetta, (2015). Risk-aware information disclosure. In *Data Privacy Management, Autonomous Spontaneous Security, and Security Assurance*. Springer.

Burnett, C., Chen, L., Edwards, P., & Norman, T. J. (2014). TRAAC: trust and risk aware access control. *Privacy, Security and Trust (PST), Twelfth Annual International Conference on*, 371-378.

Cheng, P. C., Rohatgi, P., Keser, C., Karger, P. A., Wagner, G. M., & Reninger, A. S. (2007). Fuzzy multi-level security: An experiment on quantified risk-adaptive access control. *Security and Privacy, SP'07. IEEE Symposium on*, 222-230.

Díaz-López, D., Dólera-Tormo, G., Gómez-Mármol, F., & Martínez-Pérez, G. (2016). Dynamic countermeasures for risk-based access control systems: An evaluative approach. *Future Generation Computer Systems*, *55*, 321–335. doi:10.1016/j.future.2014.10.012

Dimmock, N., Belokosztolszki, A., Eyers, D., Bacon, J., & Moody, K. (2004). Using trust and risk in role-based access control policies. *Proceedings of the ninth ACM symposium on Access control models and technologies*, 156-162. 10.1145/990036.990062

Ferraiolo, D. F., Sandhu, R., Gavrila, S., Kuhn, D. R., & Chandramouli, R. (2001). Proposed NIST standard for role-based access control. *ACM Transactions on Information and System Security*, *4*(3), 224–274. doi:10.1145/501978.501980

Gasarch, W. (2004). A survey on private information retrieval. Bulletin of the EATCS.

Gong, T., Huang, H., Li, P., Zhang, V., & Jiang, H. (2015). A Medical Healthcare System for Privacy Protection Based on IoT. *Parallel Architectures, Algorithms and Programming (PAAP), Seventh International Symposium on*, 217-222.

Graham, G. S., & Denning, P. J. (1972). Protection: principles and practice. *Proceedings of the May 16-18, spring joint computer conference,* 417-429.

Guide for Conducting Risk Assessments. (2012). National Institute of Standards and Technology, NIST Special Publication 800-30, Revision 1.

Health Insurance Portability and Accountability Act of 1996. (1996). *Pub. L. No.* 104-191.

Hennessy-Fiske, M. (2016). UCLA hospitals to pay $865,500 for breaches of celebrities' privacy. *Los Angeles Times*. Available: http://articles.latimes.com/2011/jul/08/local/la-me-celebrity-snooping-20110708

Hu, V. C., Ferraiolo, D., Kuhn, R., Friedman, A. R., Lang, A. J., Cogdell, M. M., Schnitzer, A., Sandlin, K., Miller, R., & Scarfone, K. (2013). Guide to attribute based access control (ABAC) definition and considerations (draft). *NIST Special Publication*, *800*, 162.

Irwin, K. Y. T. & Winsborough, W.H. (2006). On the modelling and analysis of obligations. *Proceedings of the 13th ACM conference on Computer and communications security*, 134-143.

Jøsang, A., Ismail, R., & Boyd, C. (2007). A survey of trust and reputation systems for online service provision. *Decision Support Systems*, *43*(2), 618–644. doi:10.1016/j.dss.2005.05.019

Jøsang, A., Hayward, R., & Pope, S. (2006). Trust network analysis with subjective logic. *Proceedings of the 29th Australasian Computer Science Conference, 48*, 85-94.

Kamwan, C., & Senivongse, T. (2016). Risk of privacy loss assessment of cloud storage services. *18th International Conference on Advanced Communication Technology (ICACT)*, 105-111.

Kandala, S., Sandhu, R., & Bhamidipati, V. (2011). An attribute based framework for risk-adaptive access control models. *Availability, Reliability and Security (ARES), Sixth International Conference on*, 236-241.

Khambhammettu, H., Boulares, S., Adi, K. & Logrippo, L. (2013). A framework for risk assessment in access control systems. *Computers & Security, 39*, 86-103.

Lampson, B. W. (1974). Protection. *Operating Systems Review*, *8*(1), 18–24. doi:10.1145/775265.775268

McGraw, R. (2009). Risk-adaptable access control (radac). In Privilege (Access) Management Workshop. NIST–National Institute of Standards and Technology–Information Technology Laboratory.

Ni, Q., Bertino, E., & Lobo, J. (2010). Risk-based access control systems built on fuzzy inferences. *Proceedings of the 5th ACM Symposium on Information, Computer and Communications Security*, 250-260. 10.1145/1755688.1755719

Office, J. P. (2004). *Horizontal integration: Broader access models for realizing information dominance.* MITRE Corporation Technical Report JSR-04-132.

Pontual, M., Chowdhury, O., Winsborough, W. H., Yu, T., & Irwin, K. (2011). On the management of user obligations. *Proceedings of the 16th ACM symposium on Access control models and technologies*, 175-184.

Reid, J., Cheong, I., Henricksen, M., & Smit, J. (2003). A novel use of RBAC to protect privacy in distributed health care information systems. Information Security and Privacy, 403-415.

Rindfleisch, T. C. (1997). Privacy, information technology, and health care. *Communications of the ACM*, *40*(8), 92–100. doi:10.1145/257874.257896

Salih, R. M., & Lilien, L. T. (2015). Protecting users' privacy in healthcare cloud computing with APB-TTP. *Pervasive Computing and Communication Workshops (PerCom Workshops),IEEE International Conference on*, 236-238.

Sandhu, R., Ferraiolo, D., & Kuhn, R. (2000). The NIST model for role-based access control: towards a unified standard. ACM workshop on Role-based access control.

Sandhu, R. S., Coyne, E. J., Feinstein, H. L., & Youman, C. E. (1996). Role-based access control models. *Computer*, *29*(2), 38–47. doi:10.1109/2.485845

Al-Aqeeli, Al-Rodhaan, & Tian. (2017). Privacy Preserving Risk Mitigation Strategy for Access Control in E-Healthcare Systems. In *International Conference on Informatics, Health & Technology (ICIHT)*. IEEE Xplore.

Stallings, W., & Brown, L. (2014). *Computer Security: Principles and Practice*. Pearson Education.

Stoneburner, G., Goguen, A.Y. & Feringa, A. (2002). *Sp 800-30. Risk management guide for information technology systems*. Academic Press.

Sweeney, L. (2002). k-anonymity: A model for protecting privacy. *International Journal of Uncertainty, Fuzziness and Knowledge-based Systems*, *10*(05), 557–570. doi:10.1142/S0218488502001648

Taneja, H., & Singh, A. K. (2015). Preserving Privacy of Patients Based on Re-identification Risk. *Procedia Computer Science*, *70*, 448–454. doi:10.1016/j.procs.2015.10.073

Wang, Q., & Jin, H. (2011). Quantified risk-adaptive access control for patient privacy protection in health information systems. *Proceedings of the 6th ACM Symposium on Information, Computer and Communications Security*, 406-410. 10.1145/1966913.1966969

Wang, Q., & Jin, H. (2012). An analytical solution for consent management in patient privacy preservation. *Proceedings of the 2nd ACM SIGHIT International Health Informatics Symposium*, 573-582. 10.1145/2110363.2110427

Yang, C. Y., Liu, C. T., & Tseng, T. W. (2015). Design and Implementation of a Privacy Aware Framework for Sharing Electronic Health Records. *Healthcare Informatics (ICHI), International Conference on*, 504-508.

Yang, J. J., Li, J. Q., & Niu, Y. (2015). A hybrid solution for privacy preserving medical data sharing in the cloud environment. *Future Generation Computer Systems*, *43*, 74–86. doi:10.1016/j.future.2014.06.004

Zhang, L., Brodsky, A., & Jajodia, S. (2006). Toward information sharing: Benefit and risk access control (BARAC). *Policies for Distributed Systems and Networks, 2006. Policy 2006. Seventh IEEE International Workshop on*, 9-53.

Zhou, J., Lin, X., Dong, X., & Cao, Z. (2015). PSMPA: Patient Self-Controllable and Multi-Level Privacy-Preserving Cooperative Authentication in Distributedm-Healthcare Cloud Computing System. *IEEE Transactions on Parallel and Distributed Systems*, *26*(6), 1693–1703. doi:10.1109/TPDS.2014.2314119

Zhou, L., Varadharajan, V., & Hitchens, M. (2015). Trust Enhanced Cryptographic Role-Based Access Control for Secure Cloud Data Storage. *IEEE Transactions on Information Forensics and Security*, *10*(11), 2381–2395. doi:10.1109/TIFS.2015.2455952

This research was previously published in the International Journal of Healthcare Information Systems and Informatics (IJHISI), 16(3); pages 46-57, copyright year 2021 by IGI Publishing (an imprint of IGI Global).

Chapter 46
An Extended Attribute-Based Access Control (ABAC) Model for Distributed Collaborative Healthcare System

Rabie Barhoun
Hassan II University, Faculty of science Ben M'sik, Casablanca, Morocco

Maryam Ed-daibouni
Hassan II University, Faculty of Science Ben M'sik, Casablanca, Morocco

Abdelwahed Namir
Hassan II University, Faculty of Science Ben M'sik, Casablanca, Morocco

ABSTRACT

The healthcare system is a real example of a distributed collaborative system, which aims to improve the patient's healthcare. The most important requirements of the healthcare system are the sensitivity of the medical data processed, large numbers of medical and para-medical interveners, as well as the medical treatment activity is a non-static process. Protecting data from unauthorized access and data sharing security in the healthcare environment is a critical process that influences system credibility. To achieve this goal and to meet the requirements of the healthcare system, the authors propose an extended Attribute-Based Access Control (ABAC) model by introducing the medical activity concept. This article defines the medical activity concept as an abstraction of collaboration in a care unit, defined by a medical activity purpose, in which the collaborators (or actors) realize their tasks in order to achieve the treatment purpose. The current access control model ABAC and these variants do not take into account the (business process) activity concept in the decision mechanism. In this paper, the authors propose a new access control model, called Medical-Activity-Attribute-Based Access Control (MA-ABAC), which can effectively enhance the security for healthcare system and produce more perfect and flexible mechanism of access control; order to strongly respond to the requirements of the distributed healthcare environment.

DOI: 10.4018/978-1-6684-6311-6.ch046

1. INTRODUCTION

Distributed collaborative environments are emerging technologies for future years that will significantly change how business is conducted in different sectors such as defense, commerce/trade and healthcare (McQuay, 2004). There are several motivations for using a distributed collaborative environment, for examples better information sharing, more efficient decision-making, coordination, and enhanced business cooperation, among others. Besides it's obvious that trends are clearly indicating that collaboration, in the future, will become a fundamental way of conducting many types of business activities. These environments provide efficient and scalable access to distributed computing capacity that also enable coherent information sharing between different distributed users. In a distributed collaborative system, subjects and shared objects of different sensitivity level are inherently large-scale distributed, and all groups of users from virtual organizations or administrative domains need to communicate and cooperate for achieving a common task (Araujo & Silva, 2013).

Distributed collaborative security is a recent area of research in security that supports different elements in order to execute a suitable security mechanism to improve the security of the entire environment. In recent years, collaborative security has been presented as an effective and sustainable approach to detecting fraud, preventing attacks, and protecting sensitive data. Collaborative security research is attracting more and more attention. Some recent studies show the importance of this subject and show that it is a hot topic in the field of security for the foreseeable future. The exactitude and efficient of security analysis are the mains success of distributed collaborative environment security. The implementation of such security must be aware of the disadvantages of different security approaches. For instance, communication inter-partners in a collaborative environment could be vulnerable to attacks, privacy may be divulged during collaboration, and furthermore the environment may be susceptible to internal attack. The security of a distributed collaborative system is often poorly treated. The different existing techniques lack an advanced and precise study. It is therefore necessary to conduct a comprehensive and in-depth study of distributed collaborative security in order to enrich this area of security more and more. This paper will address the main concern of distributed collaborative security, including the core components, mechanisms used, and critical issues related to the domain of activity when designing a collaborative security system.

Healthcare system is a real example of distributed collaborative environment in which the interveners as physicians, administrators and nurses collaborate to provide care to patients in a more efficient way (Moonian et al., 2008). However, using this system has resulted in new challenges concerning who can access, who can collaborate, who can share data, and based on which conditions. Issues, such as confidentiality, unauthorized access to medical data and collaborative process are among the main concerns that need adequate attention during all stages of system development (Araujo & Silva, 2013). In fact, the issue of security in the healthcare system is much more complicated than expected. Firstly, patient information is very sensitive and must be protected and confidential (Gajanayake et al., 2014). Secondly, different healthcare actors may need to collaborate and access patient data (Ray & Newell, 2008). A primary characteristic of healthcare system is the collaborative process between healthcare partners, that is also primordial for patients, (Araujo & Silva, 2013), who are transferred from one healthcare unit to another for specialized treatment where current situation of a patient medical activity could evolve over time, if the situation changes, the collaboration way of the actors should be changed.

There are several areas of security existing for distributed collaborative systems, in such system the collaborators need a convenient security mechanism, after strong authentication processes, so the system allows a better collaborative session management of files, applications, etc. Authorization or access control is especially important, because it can provide access to the various resources in the environment; especially, sensitive information. The access control policy defines the high-level rules such as who is authorized to access, to what and on which conditions the access is given or denied (Vasiliadis & Georgiadis, 2017; Samarati & di Vimercati, 2001). The access control models are developed based on the properties of the environments to strongly meet the security requirements of these systems. The access control for the different applications must enforce fine-grained access control at both the function and object level to ensure that users with permission to call a function also have appropriate access to target objects required to successfully perform a particular task. The healthcare system requires particular attention to the security models developed that support access control policies (Araujo & Silva, 2013). The access control management on a distributed collaborative system has been the subject of a large body of literature work that involves security relationships between all of the different actors, so as to protect the resources against unauthorized access within distributed units care and at the same time to ensure their availability through access control mechanisms (Paci et al., 2018). In this paper, we have focused on access control in a healthcare system that is part of security approaches that take into account the requirements of the collaborative environment and sensitive patient data, particularly when these environments can provide access to local or networked protected resources shared.

The rest of this paper is organized as follows. Section 2 presents related work of access control in a distributed collaborative environment. Section 3 proposes an improvement of ABAC model for a healthcare environment by integrating some medical concepts into the basic ABAC model. Section 4 presents a formal specification study of our proposed model. The design and implementation of our MA-ABAC model in healthcare environment finding is in section 5. Finally, conclusions and future work are given in section 6.

2. RELATED WORKS

The first versions of access control models have been a major issue, mainly in operating systems and information management in collaborative environments. Examples are discretionary access control (DAC) and mandatory access control (MAC) (TCSEC, 1985). In DAC the object access decision is according to an object's owner group and/or subjects. In MAC the access objects decision according to the ability of a subject or initiator to access or generally perform some sort of operation on an object or target. Several studies have been focused on the adapted of MAC and DAC models in a distributed collaborative environment, among these studies we refer to works; the Editing model (Shen & Dewan, 1992) and the SPACE model (Bullock & Benford, 1999). These two models provide an intuitive way to make access control decisions in a distributed collaborative environment. However, they suffer from flexibility, scalability and are not adaptable to a healthcare environment.

The next generation of access control models focuses on solving the two problems that correspond to separation of duty and least privilege. The most familiar is the role-based access control (RBAC) (Ferraiolo et al., 2003; Mitra et al., 2015) where roles are used as an intermediate between subjects and permissions, where roles are created for various job functions within an organization, and the permissions to perform certain operations that are assigned to a specific role. The standard RBAC model is not proper for distributed collaborative environments, because it does not include many data elements that are fundamental to these environments. Traditional RBAC model is very useful, but it has known disadvantages. Current researchers propose enhancements of the RBAC traditional.

A stable model is the basis of the new enhancements that can further extend the RBAC model to improve the access control of environments. Byun et al. (2007) suggest the extended RBAC model by showing the limitations of the initial state of the ANSI RBAC standard as well as the understanding of RBAC model. Liu et al. (2017) present an improved RBAC model to respond to all the requirements for access control and for resource sharing in multi-domain Manufacturing Internet of Things (MIoT). These improvements relate to advanced access control requirements assigning the request for permission for a certain role from a certain user, an authority action sequence named the authorization route are used to determine an adequate authorization state, but still the problem concerns the enterprises that use RBAC are now experiencing role explosion. The role explosion produces that the least-privilege principle is not supported.

To extend the RBAC model to a user group, the work Georgiadis et al., (2001) present the Team-based Access Control (TMAC) model grants more permission based on the team as compared to the standard RBAC approach. The team is the key element in TMAC model. A subject in a team can have all permissions granted to that team. The major default of TMAC model is too coarse, and then difficulty to manage within distributed collaborative environment.

The Task-Role-based Access Control (T-RBAC) model (Thomas & Sandhu, 1997; Oh & Park, 2000) introduces a task concept, that validates access permissions for users based on the assigned roles and the task the user has to perform with the assigned role. The T-RBAC has been considered a suitable model for collaborative environments, and it improves the management of access rights. Wang & Jiang (2015), propose an application of T-RBAC in a medical health-care environment. However, this model cannot manage a large number of protection states. Kim et al., (2006) try to combine three models cited below to compensate for shortcomings of each other, but this combining model produces a specification and management complicated. Zhang et al. (2006) as well as the work by Zhang et al. (2008), the authors present an access control model based on UCON model with dynamic authorization requirements in collaborative system. However, the proposed approach and implementations expose that the UCON framework uses centralized policy management, environment and attributes control that may have a major problem in a distributed environment. On the other hand, proposed usage session does not allow full functionality required for the generic authorization session management in a multi-domain environment.

The models-based attribute have appeared when the existing models are not enough to meet the security requirements in distributed collaborative environment, especially in healthcare system. This established particular attention to another model, the attribute-based access control (ABAC) model.

Bhatt et al., (2017) propose an implementation of the restricted HGABAC model that has introduced attribute hierarchies. The implementation of rHGABAC model is based on NIST Policy Machine (PM). The PM allows to define attribute-based access control policies and the attributes in PM are different in nature than attributes in traditional ABAC models. Ed-daibouni et al. (2015) present a comparative study of various access control models such as MAC, DAC, IBAC, RBAC and ABAC, based on different criteria, which will affirm that ABAC model is suitable for cloud computing environment. The Attribute-Based Access Control (ABAC) is regarded as the candidate to achieve flexible and dynamic access control. Attributes are associated with users (e.g. organization, department, role), objects (i.e., resources) (e.g. owner, size) and environment (e.g. time, location). Access requests are evaluated based on the attributes of involved entities. With ABAC, the IT administrator only needs to insert one policy,

Figure 1. Overview of attribute based-access control (ABAC) model

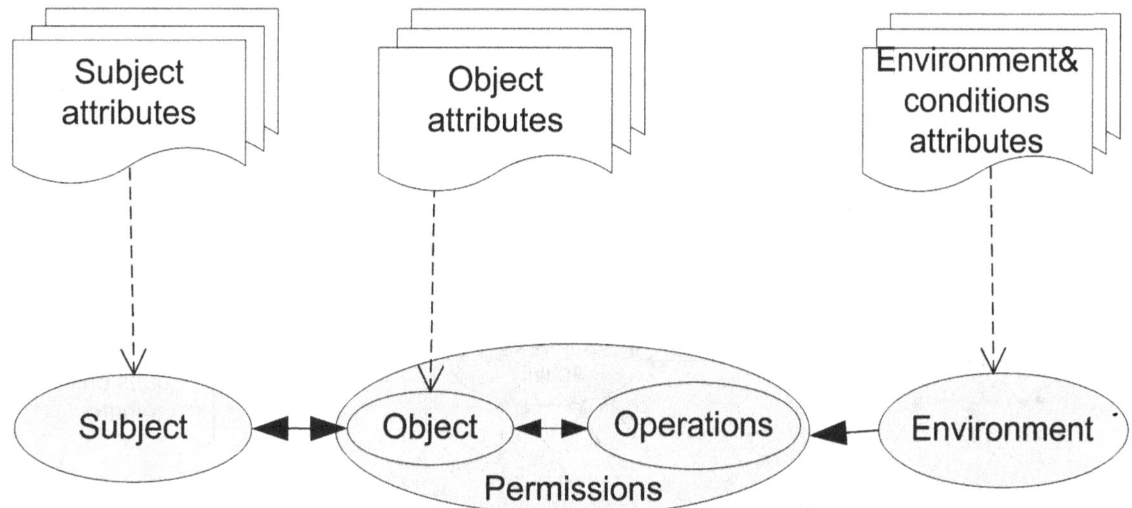

compared with the work of creating role, assigning permissions to role, and assigning users to roles explicitly in RBAC model (Ed-daibouni et al., 2015; Bhatt et al., 2016).

The ABAC policy provides more flexibility and dynamic in a distributed collaborative environment where the numbers of users are very high. Compared to the RBAC, Brossard et al. (2017) discusses ABAC model and proposes a systematic implementation of ABAC across an enterprise.

3. MEDICAL-ACTIVITY-ATTRIBUTE-BASED ACCESS CONTROL (MA-ABAC) MODEL

In traditional policies, the users can obtain their privileges through roles or directly, but it is possible that users can give certain privileges that they do not really need. This is contradictory to the least privilege principle which requires a subject that must be able to access only the information and resources that are necessary for its purpose. Currently, how to assign privileges to subjects so as to achieve this principle is still not solved. The policy ABAC (Brossard et al., 2017; Hu et al., 2014) is a recent policy that has drawn a particular attention, its principle of decision is based on taking into account the attributes of different actors (Subject, Object, and Environment Conditions) before giving access to resources.

The Overview of ABAC model is shown in Figure 1 permissions contain the combination of an object and operations, where the subject access to the object according to certain conditions. The operation describes the instructions to execute on the objects. Access rights can be defined in a subject attribute and permission. We can dynamically assign permissions to subjects and objects. ABAC uses subject, object, and their environment attributes (Hu et al., 2014). Before using these attributes for making access control decision the attribute resource is checked for the integrity and validation (Biswas et al., 2016; Mukherjee et al., 2017).

According to security constraint, the principle of least privilege, as an access control policy allows the assignment of least rights to different actors. This principle is important to protect information and sensitive resources in the design of an access control policy in a distributed collaborative environment.

Figure 2. Overview of MA-ABAC model

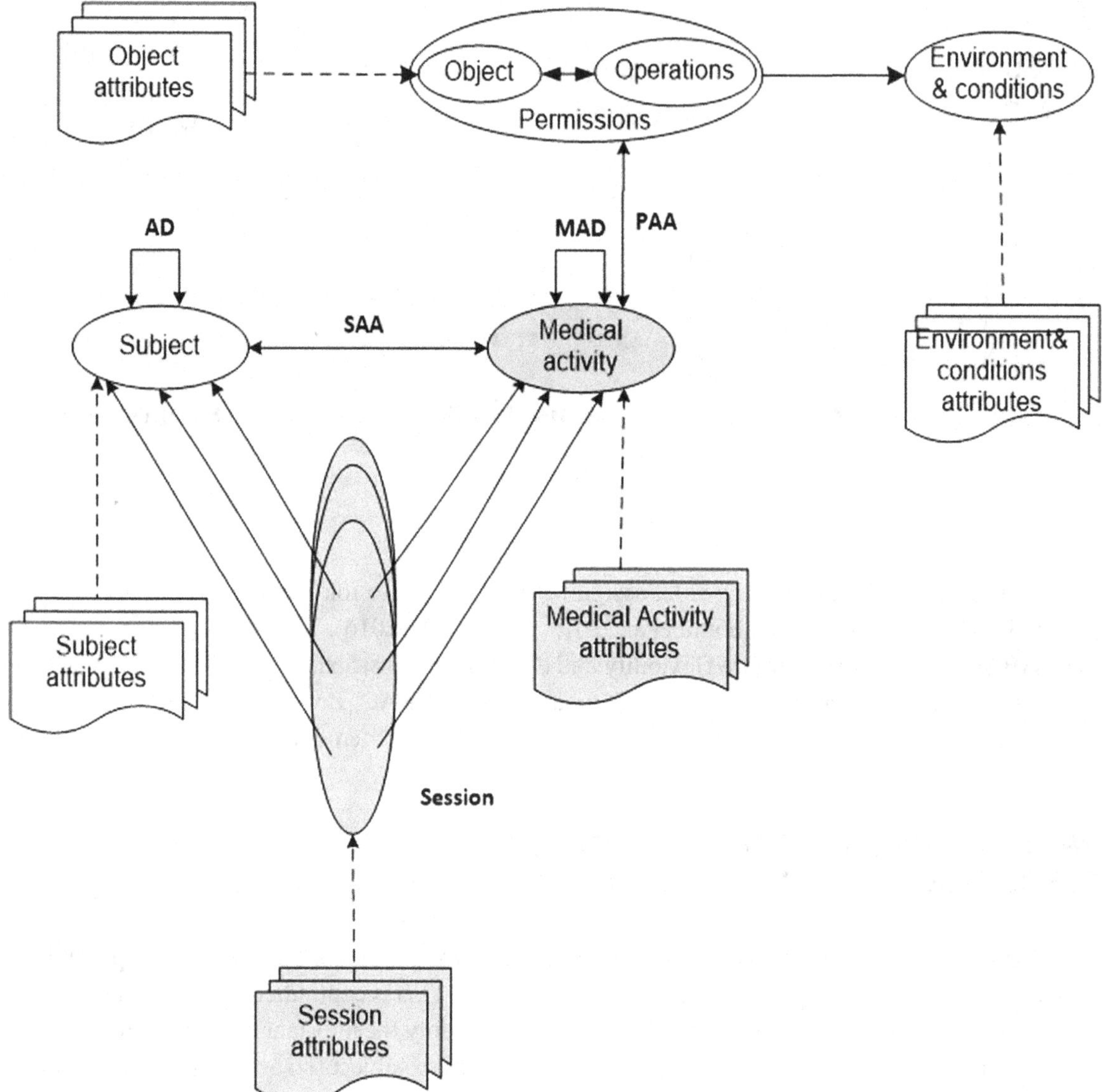

In this paper, we try to solve this problem as we propose a Medical-Activity-Attribute Based Access Control model (MA-ABAC) that extends the functionality of ABAC by introducing the medical activity concept, defined by treatment purpose, to respond to the requirements of distributed collaborative healthcare environment. Figure 2 shows the proposed MA-ABAC model.

Medical activity (MA) is an abstraction of the collaborative works, which provides a scope for resources, privileges, and roles defined by a medical activity purpose (MP) in a medical unit, in which the participants (collaborators) realize their tasks in order to achieve the medical activity purposes. In a distributed collaborative healthcare system that allows a group of medical actors to collaborate in order to treat a patient admitted in a hospital. In this example, we have the medical activity is consultation that corresponds to the following tasks:

Figure 3. Medical activity

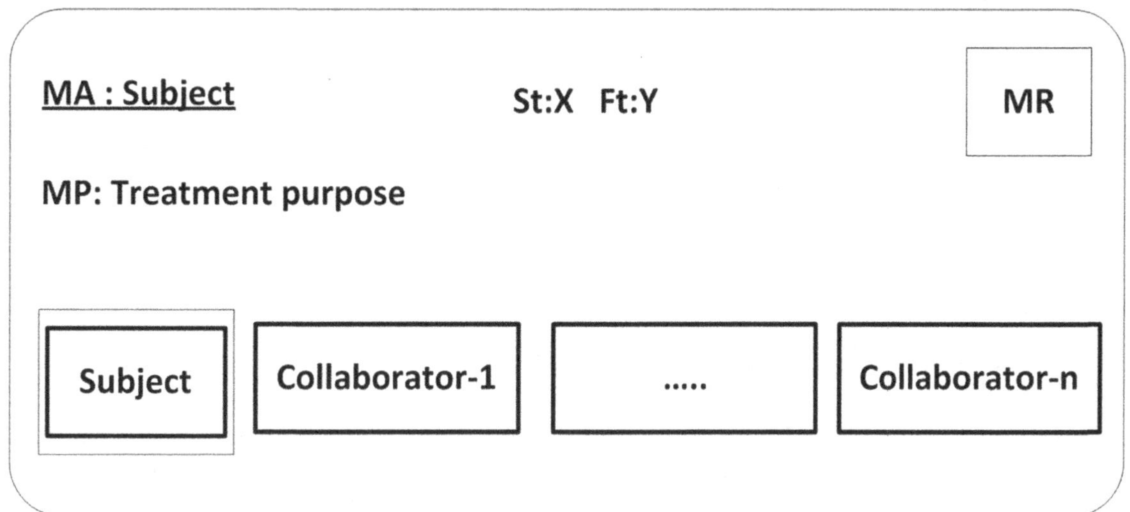

- read the medical record
- prepare the patient
- diagnosis
- print, etc.

The medical activity purpose (MP) is medical consultation patient in order to find a treatment for the patient. If a medical actor tries to access the resources or information outside of the medical activity purpose it will be considered a violation of the principle of least privilege. Hence, unauthorized access to the resource.

Formally, each medical activity (MA) is created by a special medical subject named creator, in which the collaborators (actors) realize their tasks in order to achieve the medical activity purposes (MP). A medical activity is defined by 6-tuples: see Figure 3.

MA=<Creator, Medical activity purpose, Start time, Finish time, Collaborator-1, …, Collaborators-n>

In a distributed collaborative healthcare environment, many medical activities exist, and new activities are created. An activity can also span across multiple environments. In most cases, the distributed collaborative environments need to be structured hierarchically. A medical collaboration specification needs to support decomposition of tasks into activities/sub-activities and planning how such activities can perform. Medical activity concept, planning, and its decomposition are widely used in collaboration systems, specifically in workflow environments (Riechert et al., 2016).

In our study, the medical activities/sub-activities can be classified or nested in the same way that human work activities are created. These medical activities can be mainly structured by different manners: Hierarchical, linear or hybrid as illustrated in Figures 4a, 4b and 4c.

Figure 4. (a) Hierarchical structure of medical activities (b) Linear structure of medical activities (c) Hybrid structure of medical activities

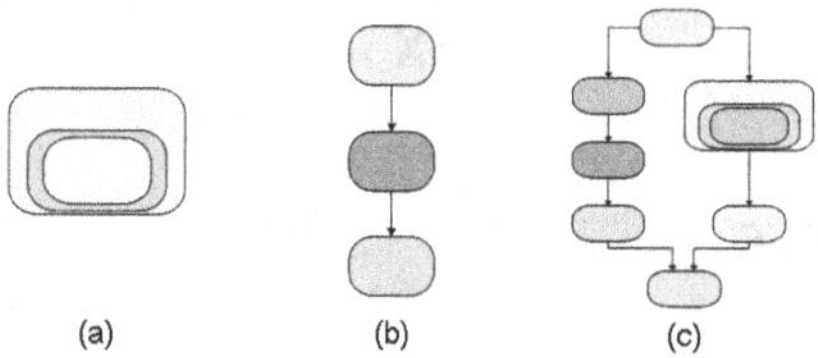

4. Formal specification of MA-ABAC model

As illustrated in Figure 2, the MA-ABAC model has defined some notations and explains characteristics by certain properties, set of elements and relations among those elements. These elements are of the following types: medical-activity, medical-activity-attributes, subject, subject-attributes, session, session-attributes, object, object-attributes, environment conditions, environment-attributes, operation, permissions and constraints. The corresponding sets are medical-activities, medical-activities-attributes, subjects, subject-attributes, sessions, session-attributes, objects, object-attributes, operations, permissions and constraints. The definition of these elements is as follows:

- **Medical-activity**: a medical activity is an abstraction of collaboration sessions. Formally: MEDICAL – ACTIVITIES = $2^{SESSIONS}$.
- **Medical-activity-attributes**: Each medical activity is characterized by certain attributes such medical activity purpose. ∀medical–activity ∈ MEDICAL–ACTIVITIES →∃ a finite set of medical–activity–attributes i.e. medical–activity–attributes ⊑ MEDICAL–ACTIVITIES– ATTRIBUTES.
- **Subject**: a subject ∈ SUBJECTS is defined as a medical or para-medical actor. The concept of the subject can be including system, intelligent agent or a human entity.
- **Subject-attributes**: Each subject has a certain set of attributes (such role). ∀subject ∈ SUBJECTS →∃ a finite set of subject–attributes i.e. subject–attributes ⊑ SUBJECTS–ATTRIBUTES.
- **Session:** a session ∈ SESSIONS is identified by session attributes. Formally SESSIONS=$2^{SUBJECTS}$.
- **Session-attributes**: ∀session ∈ SESSIONS →∃ a finite set of session–attributes i.e. session– attributes ⊑ SESSIONS–ATTRIBUTES.
- **Object**: An object ∈ OBJECTS is a system resource, such device, file, record, table, processes, network or as a container that contains information.
- **Object-attributes**: ∀object ∈ OBJECTS →∃ a finite set of object–attributes i.e object–attributes ⊑ OBJECTS–ATTRIBUTES. Formally, OBJECTS–ATTRIBUTES = $2^{object\text{–}attributes}$
- **Operation**: an operation ∈ OPERATION is an executable action such 'read', 'write' and 'execute'.
- **Permission:** permission ∈ PERMISSIONS is an authorization to perform the certain task in the activity. It defined as a subset of OBJECTS×OPERATIONS i.e. PERMISSIONS= $2^{(OBJECTS\times OPERATIONS)}$. Therefore, a permission p= {(o, op)| o∈OBJECTS, op∈OPERATIONS}. Permissions are assigned to the subject through the role or directly to the subject.
- **Environment-Conditions**: is situation context in which access process occur.

- **Environment-attributes**: ∀environment ∈ ENVIRONMENTS →∃ a finite set of environment–attributes i.e. environment–attributes ⊑ ENVIRONMENTS–ATTRIBUTES.
- **Constraint**: we define the concept of constraint as in RBAC model. Therefore, a constraint∈ CONSTRAINTS is defined as a predicate which applied to a relation between two elements of MA-ABAC model.

The associations between any two elements of the MA-ABAC model are specified by the following relations:

1. SAA ⊆ SUBJECTS×MEDICAL–ACTIVITIES. Defines the subject assignment relation. It is also a many-to-one relationship where a medical activity can be associated with many subjects but the same subject can be performed in one medical activity.
2. PAA ⊆ PERMISSIONS×MEDICAL–ACTIVITIES is a many-to-many permission to medical activity assignment relation. As the element in PAA is of type (p,a) where p ∈ PERMISSIONS and a ∈ MEDICAL–ACTIVITIES.
3. The function subject_activity_assignment is defined as- saa: SUBJECTS×SESSIONS → MEDICAL–ACTIVITIES defines the subject-activity assignment relation, saa(s, ss, a) for s∈ SUBJECTS, ss∈ SESSIONS and a∈ MEDICAL–ACTIVITIES shows that a single medical activity a is associated with the single subject S through the session ss. A subject S can invoke multiple sessions in one (single) medical activity.
4. The function permission_activity_assignment is defined as- paa: MEDICAL–ACTIVITIES $\rightarrow 2^{PERMISSIONS}$ the mapping of set permissions a onto a single medical activity. Formally: Permissions_activity_assignment(a)= {p∈ PERMISSIONS| (p,a)∈ PAA}.

The constraints are applied on the above assignment functions depending on the access control policies of the system. Our constraints are similar to the constraints on in classical RBAC model. We prefer not to specify any particular constraint on these functions.

We also introduce in our model a concept of a dominance of medical activity. The concept of Medical Activity Dominance is defined as role dominance in RBAC model. A role dominance relation denoted by RD and defined as follows:

Definition 1: "Role dominance noted by RD ⊑ ROLES×ROLES RD is a partial order on ROLESS also called the role hierarchy or role dominance relation written as ≤. For any two roles (r1,r2)∈ RD, we say r2 'dominates' (or senior) r1 only if all permissions assigned to r1 are also permissions of r2. This definition implies that any user having a role r2 have all the privileges corresponded to role r1".

By similarity, the Medical Activity Dominance relation, denoted by MAD is defined as follows:

Definition 2: Medical Activity Dominance noted by MAD ⊑ MEDICAL–ACTIVITIES × MEDICAL–ACTIVITIES is a partial order relation on and is denoted by ≤. For any two activities (MA1, MA2)∈ MAD, we say MA2 'dominates' MA1 and noted MA1≤MA2 if only if all medical tasks of MA1 are included in MA2.

Figure 5. Hybrid medical activities of general diagnosis

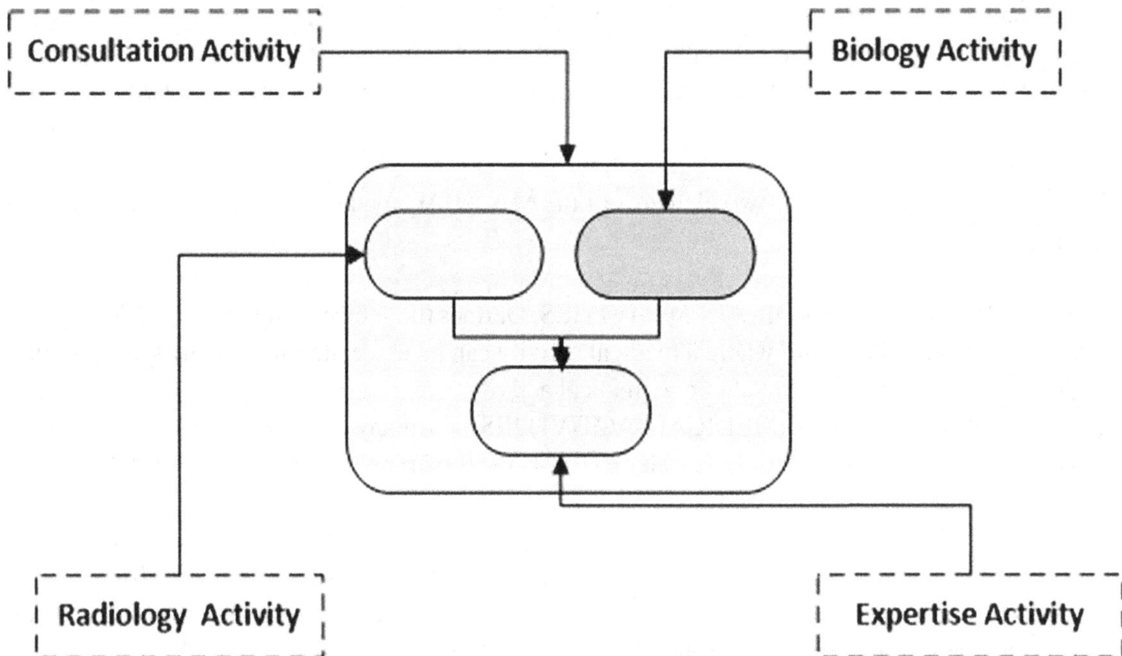

5. DESIGN AND IMPLEMENTATION OF THE MA-ABAC IN A DISTRIBUTED COLLABORATIVE HEALTHCARE ENVIRONMENT

As an illustration, consider a general physician trying to find a diagnosis (treatment) for a patient. This process is typically lengthy and goes through several medical activities, see Figure 5, which updates the patient's medical record in each medical activity.

The physician enters notes in the electronic medical record (EMR). During the radiology activity (or biology analysis activity) the general physician studies x-ray images (or biology analysis) with a radiologist (or with Biologist). At the expertise activity, the general physician discusses proper medication with colleagues while browsing medicine catalogs. Otherwise it is necessary to start another medical activity, as shown in Figure 6.

The proposed architecture of our policy to protected resources is shown in Figure 7.

When initiating an activity, the Activity Decision Module (ADM) retrieves the attributes of the triggered activity from Policy Information Point (PIP) entity. The Policy Activity server will generate an XML file containing all the permissions for the activity created. The ADM Manager will decide whether an action (executed in the medical activity) is allowed or not by consulting the XML file relating to the active medical activity on the one hand and on the other hand based on other attributes relating to: Subject, Environments and Object retrieved from PIP entity respectively by the managers: Subject Manager Module (SMM), Environment Manager Module (EMM) and Object Manager Module (OMM). The Administration Activity Policy (AAP) is used to define medical activities and its policies, see figure 8.

Figure 9 shows the architecture of our healthcare system. The secured healthcare system implementation has been based on JAVA language and API Framework over Linux Ubuntu 16.04 (32 bits). The choice of JAVA language is based on the fact that it is independent of the platform used; consequently, it does operate on a heterogeneous platform.

Figure 6. The activities of general diagnosis process of a patient

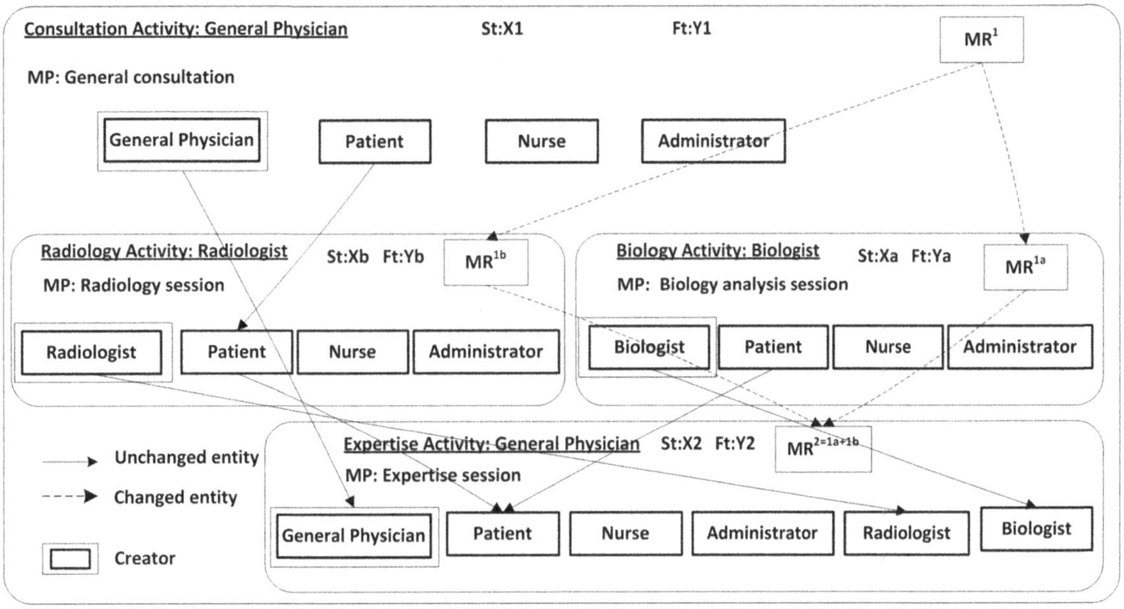

Figure 7. Architecture of MA-ABAC policy

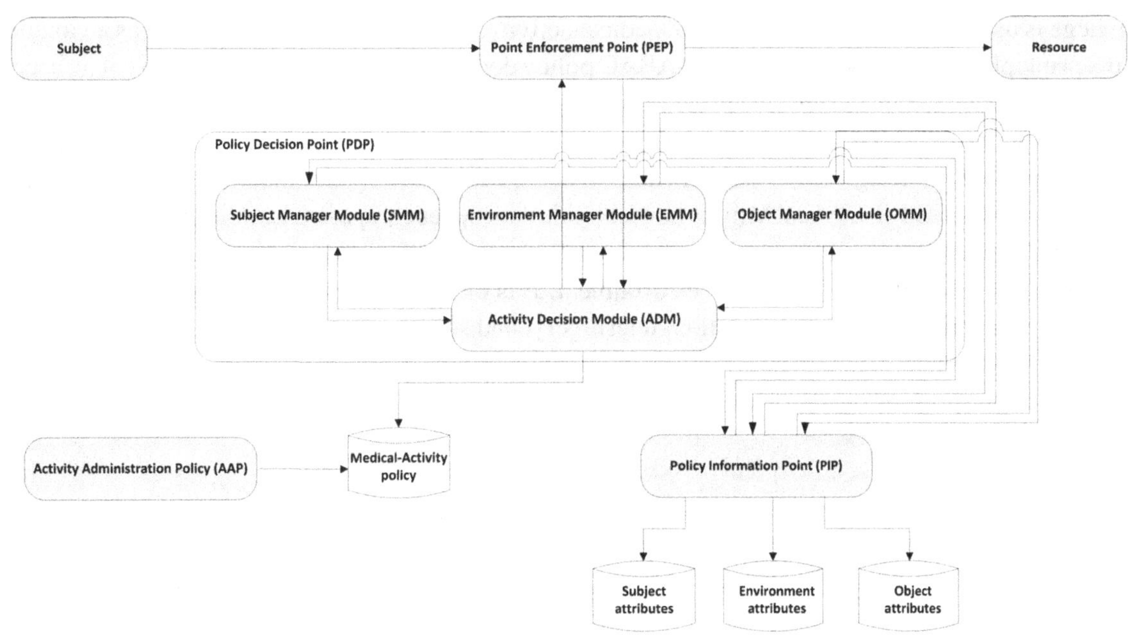

Figure 8. MA-ABAC prototype in authorization process - diagram sequence

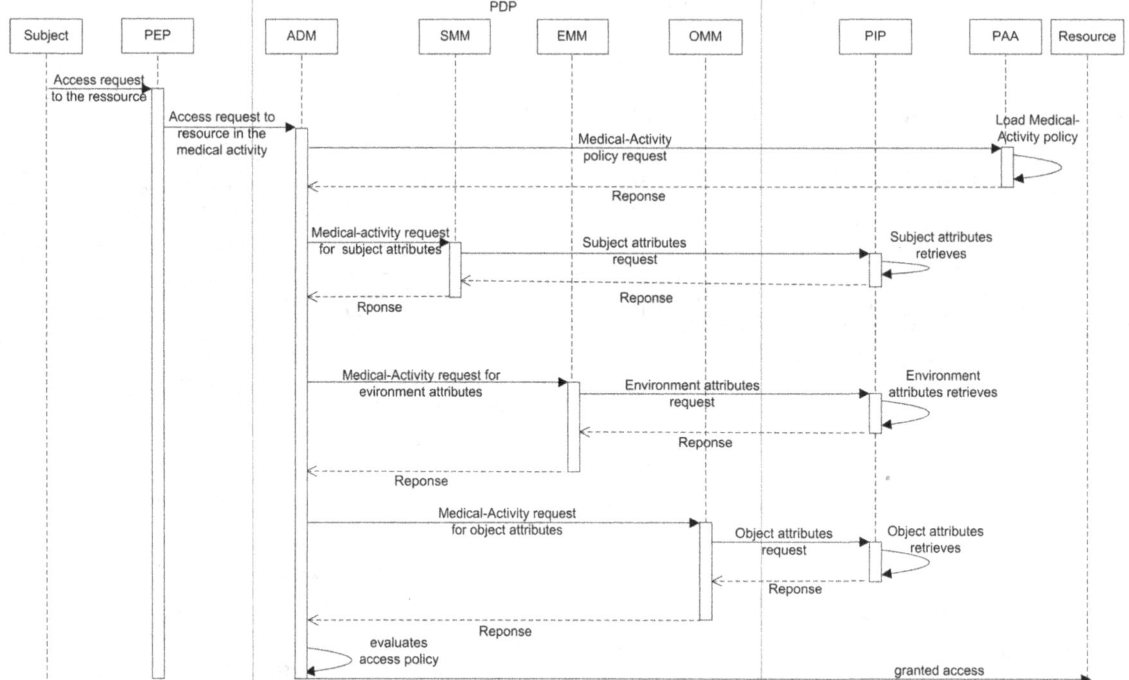

6. CONCLUSION AND FUTURE WORK

In this paper, we have proposed an extended of Attributed-Based Access Control (ABAC) model for distributed collaborative healthcare environment, called Medical-Activity-Attribute Based Access Control (MA-ABAC), that strongly includes healthcare requirements and the principle of least privilege. If a privilege is used outside the purpose of the medical activity, then this access is considered as a violation of the principle of least privilege. Our MA-ABAC policy does not only ensure the properties of an access control, but also strongly ensures the principles of least privilege. We opted for the extension of ABAC model, because it allows taking into consideration the dynamic parameters of policy through its attributes.

We presented the design of our implementation in the healthcare environment. In the current implementation, we focused on medical activity concept; this concept encompasses healthcare requirements as well as the implementation the principle of least privileges. We believe that our approach can be adapted to support any distributed collaborative environment. It is our future work to extend our framework in other environments, such as tele-education, telesurgery, and so on.

Figure 9. Architecture of our healthcare system

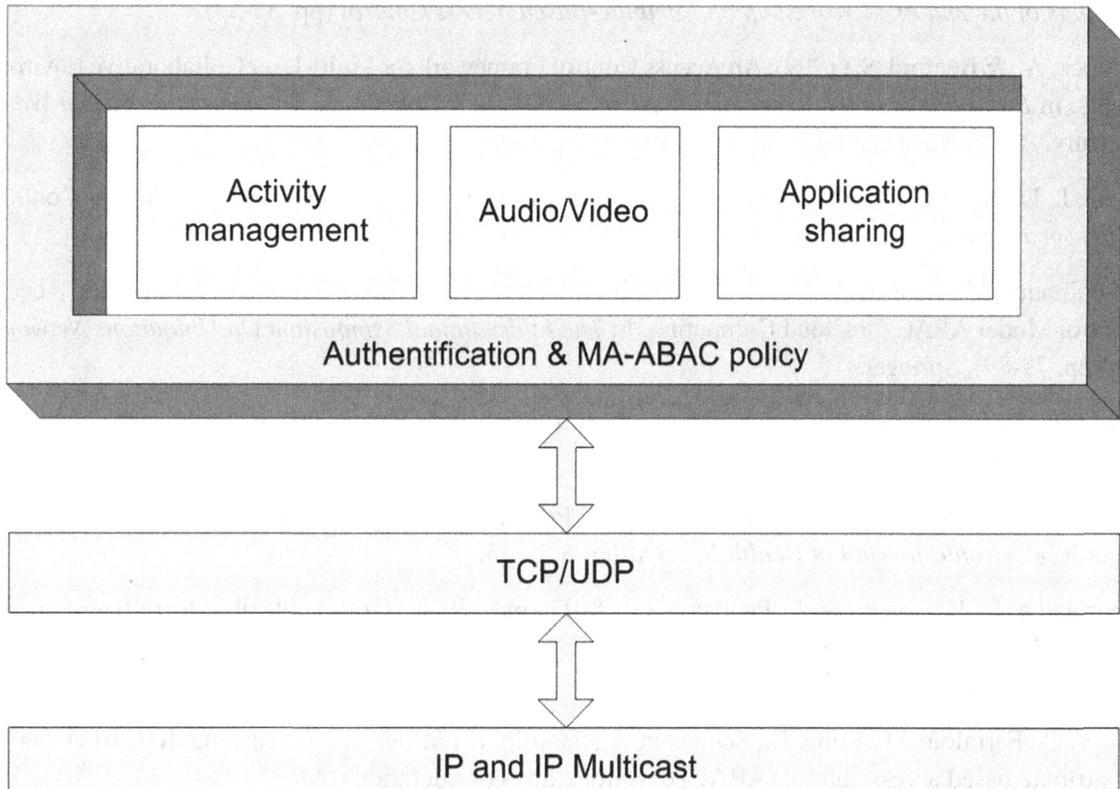

REFERENCES

Alshehri, S., & Raj, R. K. (2013). Secure access control for health information sharing systems. In *2013 IEEE International Conference on Healthcare Informatics (ICHI)* (pp. 277–286).

Araujo, R. V. L., & Silva, F. J. S. E. (2013). A Security Model for Distributed Collaborative Environments in the Healthcare. In *13th International Conference on Computational Science and Its Applications (ICCSA)*, Ho Chi Minh City, Vietnam (pp. 7-12). 10.1109/ICCSA.2013.12

Bhatt, S., Patwa, F., & Sandhu, R. (2016). An attribute-based access control extension for openstack and its enforcement utilizing the policy machine. In *IEEE 2nd International Conference on Collaboration and Internet Computing* (pp. 37-45). IEEE.

Bhatt, S., Patwa, F., & Sandhu, R. (2017). ABAC with Group Attributes and Attribute Hierarchies Utilizing the Policy Machine. In *Proceeding ABAC'17 Proceedings of the 2nd ACM Workshop on Attribute-Based Access Control* (pp. 17-28). 10.1145/3041048.3041053

Biswas, P., Sandhu, R., & Krishnan, R. (2016). Label-based access control, An ABAC model with enumerated authorization policy. In *ABAC '16 Proceedings of the 2016 ACM International Workshop on Attribute Based Access Control* (pp 1-12).

Brossard, D., Gebel, G., & Berg, M. (2017). A Systematic Approach to Implementing ABAC. In *Proceedings of the 2nd ACM Workshop on Attribute-Based Access Control* (pp. 53-59).

Bullock, A., & Benford, S. (1999). An Access Control Framework for Multi-User Collaborative Environments. In *Proceedings of the International ACM SIGGROUP Conference on Supporting Group Work*, Phoenix, AZ, November 14-17 (pp. 140-149). ACM. 10.1145/320297.320313

Byun, J., Li, N., & Bertino, E., (2007). A Critique of the ANSI Standard on Role-Based Access Control. *IEEE Security & Privacy*, *5*, 41-49. doi:10.1109/MSP.2007.158

Ed-daibouni, M., Lebbat, A., Tallal, S., & Medromi, H. (2015). Toward a new extension of the Access Control Model ABAC for Cloud Computing. In *The International Symposium On Ubiquitous Networking* (pp. 79-89). Springer.

Ferraiolo, D. F., Kuhn, D. R., & Chandramouli, R. (2003). *Role-Based Access Controls*. Boston, MA: Artech House.

Gajanayake, R., Iannella, R. & Sahama, T. (2014). Privacy oriented access control for electronic health records. *electronic Journal of Health Informatics*, *8*(2), 15.

Georgiadis, C. K., Mavridis, I., Pangalos, G., & Thomas, R. K. (2001). Flexible team-based access control using contexts., In *Proceedings of the sixth ACM symposium on Access control models and technologies* (pp. 21–27).

Hu, V. C., Ferraiolo, D., Kuhn, R., Schnitzer, A., Sandlin, K., Miller, R., & Scarfone, K. (2014). Guide to attribute based access control (ABAC) definition and considerations. *NIST*.

Kim, S., Zhu, J., Smari, W. W., & McQuay, W. K. (2006). Security and Access Control for a Human-centric Collaborative Commerce System. In *Proceedings of the 2006 International Symposium on Collaborative Technologies and Systems (CTS06)*, Las Vegas, NV, May 14-17 (pp. 429-439).

Liu, Q., Zhang, H., Wan, J., & Chen, X. (2017). An access control model for resource sharing based on the role-based access control intended for multi-domain manufacturing Internet of Things. *IEEE Access : Practical Innovations, Open Solutions*, *5*, 7001–7011. doi:10.1109/ACCESS.2017.2693380

Mcquay, W. K. (2004). Distributed collaborative environments for systems engineering. In Digital Avionics Systems Conference (DASC 04). doi:10.1109/DASC.2004.1390791

Mitra, B., Sural, S. & Atluri, V. (2015). The generalized temporal role mining problem. *Journal of Computer Security*, *23*, 31–58.

Moonian, O., Cheerkoot-Jalim, S., Nagowah, S. D., Khedo, K. K., Doomun, R., & Cadersaib, Z. (2008). Hcrbac–an access control system for collaborative context-aware healthcare services in mauritius. *Journal of Health Informatics in Developing Countries*, 2(2), 10–21.

Mukherjee, S., Ray, I., Ray, I., Shirazi, H., Ong, T., & Kahn, M. G. (2017, March). Attribute Based Access Control for Healthcare Resources. In *Proceedings of the 2nd ACM Workshop on Attribute-Based Access Control* (pp. 29-40). ACM.

Oh, S., & Park, S. (2000). Task-role-based access control model for enterprise environment. *J Korea Inst Information Security Cryptology*, *11*(1), 2000.

Paci, F., Squicciarini, A., & Zannone, N. (2018). Survey on Access Control for Community-Centered Collaborative Systems. *Journal ACM Computing Surveys*, *51*(1).

Ray, A., & Newell, S. (2008). Exploring information security risks in healthcare systems. In N. Wickramasinghe & E. Geisler (Eds.), *Encyclopedia of healthcare information systems* (pp. 573–577). Hershey, PA: IGI Global; doi:10.4018/978-1-59904-889-5.ch072

Riechert, J., Durst, C., & Wickramasinghe, N. (2016). The application of activity theory to explain collaborative technology use in healthcare: The case of a chemotherapy ordering system. In *Proceeding of the 49th Hawaii International Conference on System Sciences (HICSS)*. doi:10.1109/HICSS.2016.126

Samarati, P., & di Vimercati, S. D. C. (2001). Access Control: Policies, Models, and Mechanisms. In *Foundations of Security Analysis and Design, LNCS* (Vol. 2946, pp. 137–196). Springer. doi:10.1007/3-540-45608-2_3

Shen, H. H., & Dewan, P. (1992). Access control for collaborative environments. In CSCW '92, ACM conference on Computer-supported cooperative work (pp. 51-58). November 01 - 04.

TCSEC. (1985). *DoD National Computer Security Center*. Department of Defense Trusted Computer System Evaluation Criteria.

Thomas, R. K., & Sandhu, R. (1997). Task-based authorization controls (TBAC): a family of models for active and enterprise-oriented authorization management. In *Proceedings of the IFIP WG 11.3Workshop on Database Security*, Vancouver, Canada.

Vasiliadis, C. G., & Georgiadis, C. K. (2017). A Survey on Access Control Mechanisms in E-commerce Environments. In *Proceedings of BCI '17*, Skopje, Macedonia, September 20–23.

Wang, P., & Jiang, L. (2015). Task-role-based Access Control Model in Smart Health-care System, MATEC Web of Conferences 22, 01011. 2015.

Zhang, X., Nakae, M., Covington, M. J., & Sandhu, R. (2006). A usage-based authorization framework for collaborative computing systems. *In Proc. 11th ACM Symposium on Access Control Models and Technologies (SACMAT'06)*. ACM Press. 10.1145/1133058.1133084

Zhang, X., Nakae, M., Covington, M.J. & Sandhu, R. (2008). Toward a usage-based security framework for collaborative computing systems. *ACM Trans. Information and System Security*, *11*(1), 1–36.

This research was previously published in the International Journal of Service Science, Management, Engineering, and Technology (IJSSMET), 10(4); pages 81-94, copyright year 2019 by IGI Publishing (an imprint of IGI Global).

Chapter 47
Cybercrime and Private Health Data:
Review, Current Developments, and Future Trends

Stavros Pitoglou
https://orcid.org/0000-0002-5309-4683
National Technical University of Athens, Greece & Computer Solutions SA, Greece

Dimitra Giannouli
Computer Solutions SA, Greece & University of Leeds, UK

Vassilia Costarides
Institute of Communication and Computer Systems (ICCS), Greece

Thelma Androutsou
National Technical University of Athens, Greece

Athanasios Anastasiou
AiM Research Team, Biomedical Engineering Laboratory, National Technical University of Athens, Greece

ABSTRACT

As the adoption of electronic health records has reached unprecedented levels and continues to rise rapidly, the issue of criminal activity related with unauthorized patient data acquisition, black market distribution, and illegal exploitation/use becomes increasingly important. This article will provide a historical review of recorded data breaches that resulted in extensive patient data leaks as well as subsequent efforts of monetization via black market structures that utilize the anonymity and counter-tracking environment that the dark/deep web and cryptocurrency provide. It will also focus on the methods and tools used by the villains, the types of vulnerabilities that can result in a successful attack, as well as latest developments and future trends in the field of scientific, technical, and legal/regulatory countermeasures that can be employed in order to prevent sensitive health data from falling into the wrong hands.

DOI: 10.4018/978-1-6684-6311-6.ch047

INTRODUCTION

One significant benefit of the development of information technology is its positive impact on the health sector. Over the last years, the use of electronic patient records has illustrated rapid expansion. The advancements in health information technology, the limited potential of the traditional processes and the need for flexible access to health information, have promoted new paradigms and as a result, personal health record (PHR) systems, empowering both patients and healthcare providers, present a constantly evolving area for research, development, and implementation (Genitsaridi, Kondylakis, Koumakis, Marias, & Tsiknakis, 2015). The technological challenges intertwined with the increasing adoption of such tools and platforms are optimally addressed with the rise of Cloud Computing (Martens & Teuteberg, 2012) which is formally defined as *"a model for enabling ubiquitous, convenient, on-demand network access to a shared pool of configurable computing resources that can be rapidly provisioned and released with minimal management effort or service provider interaction"* (Mell & Grance, 2011). Promising coherence and economies of scale through the ability of robust sharing of computational resources, Cloud Computing has been a continuously evolving sector over the last decades (Guzek, Bouvry, & Talbi, 2015).

Furthermore, the availability of large medical datasets for secondary purposes such as research has become a powerful tool for producing knowledge and information, leading the medical and health care sector to a new, more personalized level. Large-scale biomedical databases are created and continuously enriched for research purposes while providing the right tools for handling and analyzing their content (Dankar & Al Ali, 2015). Researchers using personalized patient medical data have the ability to present valid and reliable data, to reuse existing data, and to compare the results of their study with similar ones based on the same database (Emam, 2013).

As the type of data shifts toward electronic records and large datasets are made accessible via distributed networks and the world wide web, hospitals, and other health providers increasingly suffer from data breaches whose nature likewise shifts toward electronic means, such as hacking (Spitzer, 2018). A data breach is *"an impermissible use or disclosure that compromises the security or privacy of the protected health information and is commonly caused by a malicious or criminal attack, system glitch, or human error"* (Bai, Jiang, & Flasher, 2017). Breaches can be conducted by a variety of ways, including credential-stealing malware, an insider who either purposefully or accidentally discloses patient data, or lost laptops and smart devices (Center for Internet Security, 2018).

Healthcare industry is highly targeted by cybercriminal organizations and individual hackers, as, according to research, an individual's medical data, are 20 to 50 times more valuable to cybercriminals and black market than other types of targeted information, e.g., personal financial data, credit card details, social security numbers, etc. (Center for Internet Security, 2018). Therefore, cybercriminals have higher incentives to target databases with medical content in order to sell or exploit the sensitive information for their own personal gain (Center for Internet Security, 2018). In this context, it is not a coincidence that the biggest recent data breaches have seized health care records as the prize.

Access to highly sensitive medical information which is exposed through data breaches, gives cybercriminals the opportunity to commit identity theft, medical fraud, extortion, and the ability to illegally obtain controlled substances (Kruse, Frederick, Jacobson, & Kyle, 2017). More specifically, patient records can be used for various types of financial gain, including (Boden, 2018):

- sale on the Dark Web
- fraud commitment (tax, insurance frauds)

- extortion of people whose disclosure of illness could provoke public relationships problems and difficulties in their working environment
- targeted phishing campaigns against individuals whose records were leaked

In the recent years there is an uptick in attacks against health care systems due to a variety of factors, including low organizational vigilance, inadequate and poorly trained staffing, insufficient technology investment and funding for information technology security, all these combined with the potential value of healthcare data as compared with other industries (Gordon, Fairhall, & Landman, 2017).

CURRENT TRENDS

In the past years, the growth of healthcare data breaches in both size and frequency was remarkable, with the largest breaches having an impact on millions of people (Chideya, 2015). In the years 2016-2017, approximately 90 percent of healthcare providers were faced with data breaches and cyber-attacks were up 125 percent since 2010 (Kruse et al., 2017). Currently, in the U.S., the number of individuals affected is estimated to be more than half of the total population.

A data breach outside of the USA that is worth mentioning is the Singapore Health cyberattack. The personal particulars of almost 1.5 million patients, including that of the country's Prime Minister, were stolen from the database. The data include both demographic and medication records (Singhealth et al., 2019). On the other hand, National Health Service (NHS) was on the top of the list for serious data breaches in 2014. The percent of severe data breaches that were reported to the Information Commissioner's Office was highly increased, while most of the incidents were related with human error and deficient data handling and not with technical reasons (Gilbert, Goldstein, & Hemingway, 2015).

Following the development of a market for stolen data and related hacking skills, hospitals and other healthcare providers have become popular targets for hackers and cybercriminals. As an example, in June 2016 a hacker offered for sale in "Real Deal" dark web marketplace more than 60.000 medical records from three different systems, one of which was an entire electronic health record, including screenshots. In the same month, cyber-attacks disclosed more than 11 million healthcare records (Chideya, 2015; Koczkodaj, Mazurek, Strzałka, Wolny-Dominiak, & Woodbury-Smith, 2018).

Table 1 presents the top 10 biggest healthcare data breaches, according to the U.S. Department of Health and Human Services Office for Civil Rights. The breaches are illustrated in descending order, regarding the number of individuals affected.

VULNERABILITIES - ATTACK METHODS

Social Engineering

Regardless of how strongly the security is maintained on the systems' level, human intervention always should be considered as the weakest link in the security chain. Social engineering is a set of techniques used by cybercriminals, that allows the access to buildings, systems or data by exploiting human psychology, or, defined from a different angle, "*the science of using social interaction as a means to persuade an individual or an organization to comply with a specific request from an attacker where either the*

Table 1. Top Healthcare Data Breaches in the U.S. [(a)] Lower rank number denotes larger impact [(b)] Estimated number of affected individuals (in millions) [(c)] After unusual activity was detected in Banner's servers a cybersecurity firm conducted further investigation that revealed two attacks. [(d)] The protocols that were supposedly enacted after a previous breach in 2009 were not activated at the affected offices by 2013. [(e)]The breach affected anyone who had received treatment at one of CHS's network-owned hospitals in the past five years or had been referred to CHS by an outside doctor during that period. [(f)] The data were not encrypted. [(g)] The breach involved active and retired military personnel as well as their families. [(h)] After a rash of cyber-attacks targeting healthcare data in early 2015, ordered a forensic investigation of Excellus systems took place after a peak of attacks in 2015. The discovered breach extended to December 2013. [(i)] The biggest recorded data breach to date. Source: (Lord, 2018a)

Rank[(a)]	Data Breach	Affected Individuals[(b)]	Month(s)/ Year	Data Compromised
10	NewKirk Products	3.47	August 2016	• Primary Care Provider Information, • Medicaid ID Numbers, • Names (including those of dependents), • Dates of Birth, • Premium Invoice Information, • Group ID Numbers.
9	Banner Health[(c)]	3.62	August 2016	• Names, • Passwords, • Credit Card Numbers and Expiration Dates, • Addresses, • Birth Dates, • Social Security Numbers, • Patient Records
8	Medical Informatics Engineering	3.9	July 2015	• Names, • Social Security Numbers, • Phone Numbers, • Mailing Addresses, • Dates of Birth, • Diagnoses
7	Advocate Health Care[(d)]	4.03	August 2013	• Medical and Claim Data
6	Community Health Systems[(e)]	4.5	April-June 2014	• Social Security Numbers, • Dates of Birth, • Phone Numbers • Physical Addresses.
5	University of California, Los Angeles Health[(f)]	4.5	July 2015	• Patient Records
4	TRICARE[(g)]	4.9	September 2011	• Social Security Numbers, • Phone Numbers • Home Addresses
3	Excellus BlueCross BlueShield[(h)]	10+	September 2015	• Medical Data, • Social Security Numbers • Financial Information.
2	Premera Blue Cross	11+	January 2015	• Bank Account Numbers, • Social Security Numbers, • Dates of Birth, • Claims Information.
1	Anthem Blue Cross[(i)]	78.8	January 2015	• Names, • Social Security Numbers, • Home Addresses • Dates of Birth. • Sensitive Medical Information

social interaction, the persuasion or the request involves a computer-related entity" (Junger, Montoya, & Overink, 2017).

Used as a technique to penetrate any type of system, exploiting humans related to it rather than vulnerabilities in the system itself, Social Engineering Attacks are rather powerful because they operate on a level such that there is no hardware or software that can prevent or even help defend against them (Koyun & Al Janabi, 2017). Although the nature of this attack is not considered as technical, social engineering methods are widely used by cybercriminals. These tactics, which are based on the manipulation of people's psychology by exploiting their possible lack of awareness and the tendency to trust easily are often far more effective and faster than software hacking. (Criddle, 2017). So, social engineers may use a combination of collected data regarding their victims in order to make them believe that they are authorized users, for example, IT employees, and reveal to them confidential information such as passwords. It is a fact that most people want to be kind and courteous and are trained to be compliant, especially in a work environment. If a potential intruder calls up as an angry executive and claims that he wants to know, for example, why nobody has taken care of a specific routing number and account number which were supposed to be changed, with a sense of urgency to it, employees tend to obey immediately.

A social engineering attack can be accomplished by a variety of ways; phone, web, email, USB drives to name such a few. Most common social engineering categories include:

- **Phishing** is the most widely known social engineering attack and is normally executed via emails and social media. Victims of such an attack usually receive emails or text messages from an entity that either they trust or seems to be legitimate, for example, a friend, their bank or university. These messages often contain malicious links that redirect recipients to websites which can either trick them into revealing sensitive information or automatically download malware which can encrypt useful files of the system (ransomware attack). The targeted phishing attacks are usually the most successful because criminals collect personal information from customers and use it in order to create more convincing emails. For example, criminals can imitate effectively emails from online shops just by mentioning the customer's name and the products they purchased. The more information an attacker has collected about the target, the better he can imitate emails from trusted entities. According to an experiment about phishing attacks, using data from social media, individuals are 4.5 times more likely to get deceived from a message sent from a contact they trust than from standard phishing attacks. It is important to be mentioned, that at the Corps of Cadets at West Point 512 students received a phishing email which concerned a problem with their grades. The vast percentage of 80% opened the link embedded in the email. (Junger et al., 2017).

The majority of criminals who perform phishing attacks aim to gain access to personal information, such as age, names, addresses, credit card details, social security numbers, and health records. Phishing methods exploit fear in order to deceive users and make them react thoughtlessly. For instance, criminals can send victims via email that the password for a service will be expired and they should update it within 24 hours, otherwise they will lose their account.

- **Pretexting** is another social engineering category, where attackers try to divulge victim into trusting them and give them access to either sensitive or non-sensitive personal information, by generating an effective pretext, a scenario that seems plausible or a story that cannot be doubted. Pretexting attacks aim to build a notional trust relationship with the target, in contrast to phishing tactics, which take advantage of emotions such as fear in order to manipulate individuals. (Bisson, 2015).

- **Baiting attack** is one of the simplest social engineering methods since, usually, all that it involves is an external storage device. This kind of attack exploits people's natural curiosity and its main difference from the other social engineering methods is that hackers use to tempt their victims by offering them an item or a service. For example, targets may be offered services like free movies or music, if they submit their login credentials to a given website in return. (Bisson, 2015).

Concerning baiting attacks through physical media, criminals often leave intentionally a device that contains malicious software in a public place, where potential victims can easily find and use it. This place could be a parking lot, a park, the corridors of a company, or even a pavement. If a number of individuals find such a device and plug it into their computers, curious to discover what will happen, baiting attack will achieve its purpose. In 2006, the founder of Secure Network Technologies Inc conducted an experiment in order to evaluate the security level of a client. His team scattered a significant number of malware-infected USB devices around the company's parking lot. Many of the company's employees plugged the devices into their computers and, as a result, they unintentionally activated a keylogger which exposed their login information.

- **Quid pro Quo attacks** are similar to baiting attacks, as they deceive people into believing that they will receive a service or a good if they provide information. In contrast to baiting, which usually relates to an item, quid pro quo attacks frequently use provision of services in order to attract victims. One typical instance of quid pro quo attack includes criminals who call targets and pretend to be IT experts who will help victims fix their software problems if, for example, they disable their antivirus program and install some updates on their computer, which is, in fact, malicious software. (Bisson, 2015).
- In **tailgating attacks,** fraudsters try to gain access to a restricted area, for example, a company, by exploiting an authorized person such as an employee. Frequently, criminals pretend to be delivery drivers or couriers and ask from the employees to hold the door for them. Tailgating is not effective in work environments such as large companies where all individuals who require to enter the building are obliged to use their personal card. (Bisson, 2015)

Web Application Security Risks

As an increasing number of patient data are made available to both patients and health professionals through web application interfaces, the "innate" security, which depends on careful and responsible application development processes, becomes of crucial importance. Vulnerabilities that derive from developers' sloppiness or lack of knowledge present a favorite hacking target, and they are, more often than not, easier targets to exploit compared to system level processes, which are typically hardened by default. There are numerous known vulnerabilities on that level. One of the most comprehensive lists, compiled by Common Weakness Enumeration (CWE), a *"community-developed list of common software security weaknesses,"* contains no less than 716 items ("CWE - CWE List Version 3.1," 2017).

Open Web Application Security Project (OWASP) is an international organization *"dedicated to enabling organizations to conceive, develop, acquire, operate, and maintain applications that can be trusted."* As part of their foundation statement they *"advocate approaching application security as a*

Table 2. Top Web Application Vulnerabilities. Selected from ("Top 10-2017 Details About Risk Factors - OWASP," 2017)

Risk	Exploitability	Prevalence	Detectability	Impact
Injection	Easy	Common	Easy	Severe
Broken Authentication	Easy	Common	Average	Severe
Sensitive Data Exposure	Average	Widespread	Average	Severe
Broken Access Control	Average	Common	Average	Severe
Security Misconfiguration	Easy	Widespread	Easy	Moderate
Cross-Site Scripting (XSS)	Easy	Widespread	Easy	Moderate
Vulnerable Components	Average	Widespread	Average	Moderate
Insufficient Logging Monitoring	Average	Widespread	Difficult	Moderate

people, process, and technology problem because the most effective approaches to application security include improvements in all of these areas" ("About The Open Web Application Security Project - OWASP," 2018). Among other activities, OWASP conducts worldwide research about the most prevalent web application vulnerabilities that allow successful attacks to internet users' privacy and security. Table 2 presents a selection of OWASP's top 10 vulnerability list, adapted to the specific nature of HealthCare systems, along with threat assessment classifications.

More specifically:

- **Injection:** Injection flaws occur when, under any circumstance, the user provided command or query data is allowed to be executed on the interpreter level, thus giving an attacker the opportunity to perform unintended commands without proper authorization. Given that this type of vulnerability is very common, particularly in legacy code, injection attacks are on the rise and can sometimes lead to complete host takeover. In the most typical scenario, a hacker executes a SQL query from the Internet to perform an operation on the recipient's database and transfer data back to themselves (Harries & Yellowlees, 2013).
- **Sensitive Data Exposure:** Data Attackers can steal or modify weakly protected data when there is no extra protection such as adequate encryption both when stored (at rest) and during the communication of the server with the user's client, e.g., internet browser (in transit). Often there is no encryption used whatsoever. However, even when crypto is employed, vulnerabilities could emerge from the use of weak and/or obsolete algorithms, as well as wrongly implemented key generation, exchange, and cipher usage.
- **Broken Authentication:** If application procedures related to authentication and session management are not implemented correctly, which is often the case, this allows attackers to assume other users' identities temporarily or permanently, making use of compromised passwords, keys, or session tokens. Common attack methods used are credential stuffing (as there are publicly available databases with millions of valid credential combinations as well as default administration account lists), dictionary/rainbow attacks, and automated brute force. Also, poorly implemented session management is a favorite target, as it lies in the center of authentication and access control mechanisms and exists in all stateful applications.

- **Broken Access Control:** Such flaws occur when an attacker can gain unauthorized access to functionality and/or data, due to poorly enforced restrictions on what authenticated users can do. Failure to implement effective access control, that is to enforce policies to prevent users from acting outside of their assigned permissions, can allow perpetrators to access administrative/privileged functions or to act on behalf of other users, increasing the probability of data disclosure, modification or destruction.
- **Security Misconfiguration:** This is one of the most commonly seen issues and can be observed at all levels of the application stack (network, platform, web/application/database server, virtual machines, containers, and storage). Lack of diligence and/or knowledge can result to a number of insecure configurations (default accounts with unchanged credentials, administrative or development access routes –e.g., ports, services- forgotten active and unprotected, etc.), allowing the attackers to relatively easily access sensitive functionality and data.
- **Cross-Site Scripting (XSS):** XSS flaws occur whenever malicious HTML and/or Javascript code included in user input is not properly handled (validated and/or escaped) and is allowed to be part of the web page output or to be executed in the victim's internet browser. This can happen during the same session (Reflected XSS), at a later time by another user (Stored CSS) or by exploiting dynamically structured web applications (DOM XSS). Executing hostile code via XSS in the user's browser can result in user session hijacking, defacing, or redirection the user to attacker-controlled sites.
- **Using Components with Known Vulnerabilities:** More often than not, development teams working with component-rich applications fail to keep track of which components they use, as well as keeping them updated and properly patched. Many of the large recorded breaches have relied on exploiting known vulnerabilities in third-party components, as, in most of the cases, they share the same execution privileges with the main application.
- **Insufficient Logging/Monitoring:** This flaw is the foundation of nearly every recorded major incident as it provides attackers with valuable time to achieve their goals before being detected. Data from 2016 suggest that the detection and identification of a breach took, on average, more than 190 days. Given the privilege of time, attackers can dig deeper, pivot to adjacent systems, and introduce new vulnerabilities. On the contrary, timely response to a security incident can, most of the times, reduce dramatically the final impact.

Database Anonymity Issues

Patient privacy must be one of the main considerations when attempting to distribute and share medical data for secondary purposes. Research has shown that datasets that may seem completely anonymized are prone to specific types of attacks that can result in one or more physical persons' identification. The identifiers through which an individual's identity may be revealed can be divided into two categories (El Emam, Rodgers, & Malin, 2015):

- **Direct Identifiers**: they include data allowing the immediate identification of the holder, such as the name, the identity card number, the social security number, etc.
- **Indirect Identifiers or Quasi-Identifiers**: They include characteristics such as age, gender, occupation, residence, etc., which do not directly identify an individual, but their combination may lead to revealing identity and violating personal privacy. Indirect identifiers may also include the

sub-category of sensitive attributes, which are not public data and can be harmful or lead to stigmatization when associated with a particular person. Such features include drug and intervention codes, as well as certain diseases (Eze & Peyton, 2015). The attack may involve either the identification or attribute disclosure. During the identification disclosure, the attacker uses the indirect identifiers of an anonymous record to associate them with a particular person. During the attribute disclosure, on the other hand, the perpetrator of the attack can infer some sensitive information about a person even if he/she cannot identify and find which unique record corresponds to him/her. A third and less frequent form of attack is membership disclosure, which is a probabilistic measure of the presence or absence of a person in a data set (Eze & Peyton, 2015).

Improper handling of these identifiers or their combinations can give attackers the opportunity to re-identify parts of the respective datasets, which, most of the times, given their medical research purpose, contain extremely sensitive data.

Attacks That Do Not Disclose Sensitive Data

Although the attacks that aim to the disclosure of personal health information are far more worrisome, cyber-attacks that do not necessarily result in data breaches, can potentially have a significant impact in terms of cost, loss of trust, etc. (Gordon et al., 2017) The most common types of these attacks are:

- **DoS (Denial of Service) Attacks**: Criminals can use a variety of methods in order to harm health care providers. A widely known category of attacks that are used against health care systems is Denial of Service (DoS) attacks which flood systems with a vast amount of network traffic in order to disable them. This kind of attacks in the healthcare sector may be dangerous or even fatal as they may affect operations such as surgical procedures or reporting of lab results by rendering hospital care systems unusable. (Gordon et al., 2017)
- **Ransomware:** Ransomware attacks have as main characteristic the encryption of selected files in an information system, for example, a patient database, and the request of a fee, usually in cryptocurrencies such as Bitcoin, in order to give victims, the key to regaining access to their files. (Gordon et al., 2017) Restricted files are usually highly significant for the smooth operation of hospital procedures, and as a result, hospitals are forced to pay the criminals. Otherwise, there is the possibility of losing vital data. Even if organizations keep daily backups of their files, there is always the risk of losing information if they restore from a backup after a ransomware attack.

The creation of ransomware dates back to 1989 when Dr. Joseph Popp used malware-infected floppy discs which distributed to attendees of the WHO (World Health Organization) conference that focused on AIDS research. Although Dr. Popp ended up in prison, his creation inspired many aspiring cyber attackers. A recent example of a ransomware attack is the WannaCry attack in 2017, which had an impact on NHS. Concerning the ransom fee, most of the times, it seems inferior to the consequences that will provoke a potential data loss to an organization, which may include profit lose and damaged security reputation. However, even payment does not ensure access to encrypted files, as ransomware victims are totally dependent on the attacker's reliability. (Gordon et al., 2017) *'Ransomware exposes and exploits the vulnerabilities of 21st-century information technology (IT) infrastructure'* (Kruse et al., 2017)

Monetization Routes

The main motivation for conducting a major attack to gain access to large datasets of private sensitive information is profit, thus, once the data acquisition is achieved, the next perpetrators' move, predictably, is the effort of monetization. Most of the times, the preferred method includes black market structures that utilize the anonymity and counter-tracking environment provided by dark/deep web and cryptocurrency, which are briefly presented in the subsequent sections.

Deep/Dark Web

What is known as Deep Web, Deep Net, Invisible Web, or Dark Web (Weimann, 2016), is the non-indexed by standard search engines content of the World Wide Web. If the Internet is considered as a multi-tiered structure, only the top tier, i.e., the surface web, can be accessed with the regular search engines that are commonly used (such as Google). The rest, the deepest tiers, which are the essential content of the Deep Web, is a wealth of information. Searching the internet has been compared to *"dragging a net across the surface of the ocean: a great deal may be caught in the net, but there is a wealth of information that is deeper and therefore missed"* (Bergman, 2001). In the early days of the Internet, as the size of information was not immense, it was indexed and accessed in an easier way. However, as its use inflated, conventional search engines are proving insufficient for searching and indexing dynamic pages, whereas they are adequate for static web pages. Dynamic pages can be accessed through specific and targeted queries and programs, while static pages are linked to other pages on the internet, therefore the name "Invisible" web.

The Deep Web is inaccessible by conventional means, with its contents hidden or often blocked. Although its size can't be measured, it has been estimated (Bergman, 2001) that public information on the Deep Web is currently 400 to 550 times larger than the commonly defined web, although there have been since more moderate estimations (Cox, 2015).

A segment of the Deep Web is the Dark Web that contains information that is considered generally illegal, antisocial and it is possible to access it only through specialized browsers, created for this specific task. Examples of such pages may include illegal paraphilia, leaks on unauthorized information, financial trails on money laundering, frauds, identity thefts, illegal transactions, trafficking, etc. Associated with the Dark Web is the rise of relevant sub-cultures (Bartlett, 2015) such as social media rapists, crypto-anarchists, transhumanists, traffickers, etc. The Dark Web can be visited by all Web users, by software such as Tor, free software for enabling anonymous communication. The name is derived from an acronym for the original software project name "The Onion Router." Tor directs Internet traffic through a free, worldwide, volunteer overlay network consisting of more than seven thousand relays to conceal a user's location and usage from anyone conducting network surveillance or traffic analysis. Another relevant software is the Invisible Internet Project (I2P), which is an anonymous network layer that allows for censorship-resistant, peer to peer communication (Ali et al., 2016; Astolfi, Kroese, & Van Oorschot, 2015). These anonymous connections are implemented by encryption (end-to-end) of the user's traffic and delivery of the information through a volunteer-run network of roughly 55,000 computers distributed around the world. Given the high number of possible paths the traffic can transit, a third party watching a full connection is unlikely to successfully gather information about the communication. The software that implements this layer is called an "I2P router", and a computer running I2P is called an "I2P node". I2P is free and open source and is published under multiple licenses. The overall principle is that whatever tool a visitor uses, one must know where exactly to find the website, by its Uniform Resource Locator. Once inside the Dark Web, communication means include secure email, Web Chatting, or Tor-hosted Personal Messaging (PM).

Cryptocurrency

Cryptocurrencies use decentralized control versus centralized digital currency and the traditional banking system. They are transferred between peers, and they are confirmed in a public ledger with a process that is called mining (Dziembowski, 2015).

More specifically, these public ledgers are storing all confirmed transactions, from the beginning of each cryptocurrency's creation. Information regarding the cryptocurrency's owners is encrypted, as well as the legitimacy of record keeping. When there is a transaction, meaning a transfer of funds between digital wallets, this is submitted to the abovementioned public ledger, while confirmation is pending. In order to provide mathematical proof and a legitimate link between the owner of the wallet and the relevant transaction, an electronic signature is used, which is an encrypted piece of data. Then 'mining' confirms the transactions, and they are added to the ledger. The mining process is what essentially gives value to the cryptocurrency and is its proof-of-work system. Cryptocurrency mining, or crypto mining as is otherwise known, is the process of transactions verification, by cryptocurrency miners, who are responsible for ensuring the authenticity of information and updating the blockchain. Cryptominers, compete with each other, in solving complex mathematical problems and the first one to find the solution, authorizes the transaction, while being rewarded for the service provided by earning small amounts of cryptocurrency.

Bitcoin, described as the currency of the Dark Web, was proposed in 2008 as an alternative and independent currency by S. Nakamoto (Nakamoto, 2008). Currently (Hurlburt, 2017), it is being rapidly replaced by Monero, a private, digital currency that is offering mechanisms that prevent the indirect tracing of those that are conducting transactions (Amsterdam, 2018; Noether, 2016).

COUNTERMEASURES

A countermeasure is a procedure that reduces vulnerability by eliminating or preventing it, by minimizing the harm it can cause, or by discovering and reporting it so that corrective action can be taken. A set of policies concerned with information security management has been developed to manage, according to risk management principles, the countermeasures in order to accomplish to a security strategy set up following rules and regulations applicable in the world. Below the various existing protocols of preventing any misuse of healthcare data are described.

Government Regulations

HIPAA (Health Insurance Portability and Accountability Act)

HIPAA (Health Insurance Portability and Accountability Act) is a United States legislation which provides guidelines regarding the security of sensitive medical information and enacted in 1996 by Bill Clinton (HIPAA, 2018)

Before the activation of HIPAA, there were no healthcare security guidelines or requirements with a focus on the protection of personal health data. The existence of such legislation has become vital during the last few years when the number of cyber-attacks targeting healthcare providers, which resulted in health data breaches illustrated a rapid increase.

HIPAA is organized into five (5) separate sections or "Titles" ("HIPAA (Health Insurance Portability and Accountability Act) | whatis.com," 2017):

- **Title I, "HIPAA Health Insurance Reform."** This section refers to new employees' medical insurance coverage. According to this title, employers should allow new employees' coverage to be uninterrupted regardless of any pre-existing conditions or health problems.
- **Title II, "HIPAA Administrative Simplification."** When mentioning HIPAA compliance, most people mean adhering to HIPAA Title II. This part of the legislation sets the national standards for processing electronic healthcare transactions. It also requires the implementation of secure electronic access to personal health information, and all healthcare organizations' activities must be in accordance with privacy rules.
- **Title III, "HIPAA Tax-Related Health Provisions."** In the presented title, tax-related provisions are concerned.
- **Title IV, "Application and Enforcement of Group Health Plan Requirements."** This section additionally provides information concerning insurance reform and provisions for individuals who request subjection to continuous insurance coverage.
- **Title V, "Revenue Offsets."** The presented title provides regulations concerning company-owned life insurance and the behaviour towards individuals who lose their U.S. citizenship for income tax purposes.

All HIPAA-covered entities, including healthcare clearinghouses and providers, are affected by HIPAA privacy rule. When a HIPAA-covered entity uses a contractor or a non-workforce member to accomplish "business associate" activities, the Rule requires that the covered entity include certain protections for the information in a business associate agreement. This contract imposes specific safeguards on the PHI (Protected Health Information) that the business associate uses or discloses. ("Summary of the HIPAA Security Rule | HHS.gov," 2013)

One of the most important aims of the Security Rule is to protect the privacy of individuals' sensitive medical information while allowing covered entities to improve the quality and efficiency of patient care by adopting new technologies. Due to the extended diversity of the health care marketplace, it should be ensured that the flexibility and scalability of the design of Security Rule would allow covered entities to *"implement policies, procedures, and technologies that are appropriate for the entities particular size, organizational structure, and risks to consumers' e-PHI (Electronic Protected Health Information)"*. ("Summary of the HIPAA Security Rule | HHS.gov," 2013) Protected Health Information is the definition used by HIPAA to define the type of patient information that falls under the jurisdiction of the law. Billing information from doctors, blood test results, phone records, and emails to doctors which concern a health problem or a medication the patient needs are only a few examples of PHI ("Protected Health Information (PHI) - TrueVault," n.d.). However, there are cases, such as employment records, that are not considered as PHI, and Privacy Rule does not support cover entities' individually identifiable health information. ("HIPAA Privacy Rule and Its Impacts on Research," 2005)

Data that have undergone the process of de-identification, *"a process that is applied to a dataset with the goal of preventing or limiting informational risks to individuals, protected groups, and establishments, while still allowing the production of aggregate statistics."* (Garfinkel, 2016) are no longer subject to the provisions of the HIPAA Rule.

The fine for a potential HIPPA violation can reach $50,000 per violation, while the annual maximum for repeat violations reaches the $1.5 million. Covered entities and individuals who are accused of intentional obtainment or disclosure of PHI in violation of the HIPAA Privacy Rule, can be fined up to $50,000 and receive up to one year in prison. If the HIPAA Privacy Rule is violated under false claims, the penalties can reach the amount of $100,000 and the number of 10 years in prison. ("HIPAA (Health Insurance Portability and Accountability Act) | whatis.com," 2017)

HITECH Act (Health Information Technology for Economic and Clinical Health)

On February 17, 2009, the Office for Civil Rights enacted the Health Information Technology for Economic and Clinical Health (HITECH) in order to "strengthen the privacy and security" portions of HIPAA regulations. The HITECH program authorized the Office of the National Coordinator (ONC) to "manage and set standards for the stimulus program''. (Hazard, 2017). It was created in order to prompt the implementation of electronic health records (EHR) and promote the application and the meaningful use of information technology in the area of the United States. *"HITECH Act was an ambitious effort to modernize the Health IT infrastructure to keep up with the demands of the 21st century."* (Washington, DeSalvo, Mostashari, & Blumenthal, 2017)

The HITECH Act expanded the privacy and security protections introduced by HIPAA by increasing the potential legal liability for non-compliance and providing more rigorous enforcement. ("What is the HITECH ACT? | What HITECH Compliance Means," 2009)

One of the issues that HITECH had to confront at the beginning was the generation of the interoperability in such an environment which characterizes from a mixed public and private economy and a sharing federal and state governing system. This kind of problems remained unsolved until today. Short-term priorities and experimentation with various models for engaging private providers, states, and health systems, constituted the main focus of the HITECH Act during the initial years of its enactment. (Gold & McLAUGHLIN, 2016)

HITECH extended the HIPAA security provisions and penalties beyond covered entities to include business associates. In the original HIPAA rule, it was stated that cover entities should get assurance from business associates they share information with, that they will protect individuals' personal information. However, most of the covered entities neglected this rule.

HIPAA violation penalties can extend up to $250,000, with repeat violations which remain uncorrected reaching $1.5 million. ("What is the HITECH ACT? | What HITECH Compliance Means," 2009; Withrow, 2010)

GDPR (General Data Protection Regulation)

The minimum guidelines concerning data processing in the EU were set by Data Protection Directive 95/46/EC until spring 2018 when it was replaced by General Data Protection Regulation (GDPR) as the primary law regulating how companies protect EU citizens' personal data. GDPR, which was voted by the European Parliament and Council in April 2016, reinforces and clarifies natural persons' rights in regards to the processing and free movement of natural persons' personal data, especially in IoT healthcare applications. ("Data protection in the EU | European Commission," 2016; Pulkkis, Karlsson, Westerlund, & Tana, 2017). GDPR regulation refers to every European Union member state and has as main purpose to protect effectively the personal information of European citizens. Through GDPR, a uniform data security law is imposed on all members of EU, so that each member state no longer needs to write its own data protection laws and laws are consistent across the entire EU. Except for EU members, GDPR regulation also concerns any company in the world that operates in the EU by marketing goods or services to EU residents. (Lord, 2018b)

Some of the GDPR guidelines are referred below:

- Subjects must allow the processing of their personal information
- Collected data should be subjected to an anonymization process in order to protect the data owner's privacy
- Natural persons should receive information about who owns the data if a data breach takes place
- The transfer of data across borders should be secure
- Companies should add to their human resources a data protection officer (DPO) to supervise GDPR compliance

GDPR provides individuals with a notable number of rights, as they have the ability to require the revelation or deletion of their personal data from the companies that hold them. Moreover, with GDPR, there is no need to launch separate actions in each jurisdiction, as regulators, for the first time, will be able to work in concert across the EU. (Hern, 2018)

A company found in violation of the Regulation may confront significant fines and compensation fees to data subjects, which may be up to 2% or 4% of total global annual turnover or €10m or €20m, whichever is greater. ("GDPR Article 83 – General conditions for imposing administrative fines," 2016)

Act on the Protection of Personal Information

The Act on the Protection of Personal Information is the key legislation governing the collection, storage, and use of personal information in Japan. It applies to business operators that handle personal information and has a comparable level of data protection to that of the European Union (Orito & Murata, 2005). Among others, the Act specifies the circumstances under which personal data can be collected, stored, and processed:

Processing: A business operator governed by the Act on the Protection of Personal Information must specify the purpose of use for personal information it handles (to the extent possible) and comply with the following rules:

- it must not change the purpose of use beyond a scope which has a reasonably substantial relationship with the original purpose of use; and
- it must not use the personal information beyond the scope necessary to achieve the purpose of use, without obtaining the individual's prior consent.

Collection: The following restrictions apply to the collection of personal information by business operators governed by the Act on the Protection of Personal Information:

- proper acquisition – a business operator must not acquire personal information by deception or other wrongful means;
- notice of purpose of use at the time of acquisition – once a business operator has acquired personal information, it must notify the individual of or publicly announce the purpose of use, unless it has already been publicly announced or one of the following applies:
- such notification or public announcement would likely cause harm to the life, body, property, rights or interests of an individual or third party;
- such notification would likely harm the business operator's rights or legitimate interests;
- cooperation with a state agency, local government or third party commissioned by a state or local agency is necessary to conduct certain affairs specified by laws and regulations and the notification, or public announcement of the purpose of use would likely impede the execution of such affairs; or
- the purpose of use is evident from the circumstances around the collection of personal information.

The guidelines issued by the Personal Information Protection Commission (PPC) include examples of how business operators can make such public announcement – namely, by posting it on their websites or displaying it in an easily viewable location within their places of business.

Business operators must not obtain sensitive information without the individual's prior consent. Sensitive information means personal information comprising a principal's race, creed, social status, medical history, criminal record, the fact of having suffered damage as a result of a crime, or other descriptions described by the cabinet order as those of which the handling requires special care so as not to cause unfair discrimination, prejudice or other disadvantages to the principal.

Storage: Business operators governed by the Act on the Protection of Personal Information must take security control measures in regards to personal data. The act imposes a broadly stated obligation on business operators to "take necessary and proper measures for the prevention of leakage, loss, or damage, and for other security control of the Personal Data." The act provides no concrete measures to satisfy this requirement. However, it is generally understood that such security control measures include:

- organisational measures;
- employee-related measures (e.g., personnel training);
- physical measures; and
- technical measures.

Specific actions to be taken for each type of measure are stipulated in the various guidelines issued by the PPC.

Preventing Social Engineering

Despite the variety of technical vulnerabilities and attack methods, the weakest link in security infrastructure is people, as unintentional negligence remains the biggest risk. Healthcare Organizations should raise awareness and regularly educate their employees: Security through education is the first, main, and most effective mitigation policy. If people aren't educated about the types of attacks being used, they have a very low possibility to defend against them. To this end, a security policy must be written and backed up by adequate awareness training. The policy must encompass clear sets of guidelines of response to any given situation. *"Absent such guidelines, employees will default to actions they perceive as helpful, which often means giving away information they shouldn't"* (Olavsrud, 2010).

Securing Web Applications

Mitigating the risks of a perpetrator exploiting flaws in one's web application stack is not to be considered a trivial task, as it requires vigilance and deep up-to-date knowledge through all levels and phases of the application development process. To this end, there exist well documented and continuously updated bodies of guidelines, like the one maintained by OWASP. Their recommended courses of action, regarding the vulnerabilities mentioned in a previous section, are presented in Table 3.

Preserving Anonymity

Taking into consideration the difficulties described above regarding the high cost that a possible online attack and interception of personalized medical data may entail, the imperative need for anonymization of medical information (El Emam & Arbuckle, 2013) arises. Data anonymization is the process of encrypting or removing information from a data set so that the identification of the persons is not anymore feasible. Thus privacy protection is achieved. From a legal point of view, anonymized data cease to be personal data, and as a result, their disposal does not require approval and consent (Emam, 2013). However, the process of anonymization should be done in a strict and methodical form in order to minimize the risk of disclosure. As mentioned above, the General Data Protection Regulation (GDPR) in Europe, along with the United States of America's Health Insurance Portability and Accountability Act (HIPAA) and the International Safe Harbor Privacy Principles in Europe and America, both give formal definitions regarding the security and confidentiality of personal data as well as their anonymization processes.

In a previous section, definitions were given for the direct and indirect identifiers that are included in medical datasets and can be exploited in order to reveal persons' identities. The main techniques used to handle the direct identifiers include either their removal from the database or their replacement with appropriate pseudonyms, depending on the purpose of the dataset (El Emam & Arbuckle, 2013). It is worth noting that, according to the General Data Protection Regulation: "Personal data which have undergone pseudonymization, which could be attributed to a natural person by the use of additional information should be considered to be information on an identifiable natural person.", that is, the pseudonymized data should not be regarded as anonymized, but rather as still personal potentially identifiable information.

Indirect identifiers or quasi-identifiers contain useful information for research and statistical purposes and as a result, are the characteristics to which data anonymization techniques aim. As the security of the data and the usefulness of the information they contain are inversely proportional, the anonymization process should follow a methodical form in order to achieve the best balance between them. The purpose of anonymization is to protect indirect identifiers and sensitive attributes from a reverse attempt to reveal the identity of the data. The techniques and anonymization algorithms are based on some basic models (Eze & Peyton, 2015). The most well-known model is k-anonymity (Samarati & Sweeney, 1998). k-anonymity ensures that every record of a dataset can't be distinguished from at least k-1 other records based on the available indirect identifiers. Therefore, any combination of indirect identifiers should either not appear at all or appear more than once in the dataset. k-anonymity protects from identity recognition, but not from field identifying and sensitive features. Another similar model that has been proposed, mainly to protect demographic components of a database, is k-map (Sweeney,

Table 3. Recommended preventive actions for the mitigation of Web Application vulnerability risks

OWASP recommendations to developer teams	Related Vulnerability
Use a safe API, which avoids the use of the interpreter entirely or provides a parameterized interface, or migrate to use Object Relational Mapping Tools (ORMs). Note that even when parameterized, stored procedures can still introduce SQL injection if PL/SQL or T-SQL concatenates queries and data, or executes hostile data with EXECUTE IMMEDIATE or exec().	Injection
Use positive or "whitelist" server-side input validation.	
For any residual dynamic queries, escape special characters using the specific escape syntax for that interpreter.	
Use LIMIT and other SQL controls within queries to prevent mass disclosure of records in case of SQL injection.	
Where possible, implement multi-factor authentication to prevent automated, credential stuffing, brute force, and stolen credential re-use attacks.	Broken Authentication
Do not ship or deploy with any default credentials, particularly for admin users. Implement weak-password checks, such as testing new or changed passwords against a list of the top 10000 worst passwords.	
Align password length, complexity, and rotation policies with NIST 800-63 B's (Grassi et al., 2017) guidelines in section 5.1.1 for Memorized Secrets or other modern, evidence-based password policies.	
Ensure registration, credential recovery, and API pathways are hardened against account enumeration attacks by using the same messages for all outcomes.	
Limit or increasingly delay failed login attempts. Log all failures and alert administrators when credential stuffing, brute force, or other attacks are detected.	
Use a server-side, secure, built-in session manager that generates a new random session ID with high entropy after login. Session IDs should not be in the URL, be securely stored and invalidated after logout, idle, and absolute timeouts.	
Classify data processed, stored, or transmitted by an application. Identify which data is sensitive according to privacy laws, regulatory requirements, or business needs.	Sensitive Data Exposure
Apply controls as per the classification.	
Don't store sensitive data unnecessarily. Discard it as soon as possible or use PCI DSS compliant tokenization or even truncation. Data that is not retained cannot be stolen.	
Make sure to encrypt all sensitive data at rest.	
Ensure up-to-date and strong standard algorithms, protocols, and keys are in place; use proper key management.	
Encrypt all data in transit with secure protocols such as TLS with perfect forward secrecy (PFS) ciphers, cipher prioritization by the server, and security parameters. Enforce encryption using directives like HTTP Strict Transport Security (HSTS).	
Disable caching for a response that contains sensitive data.	
Store passwords using strong adaptive and salted hashing functions with a work factor (delay factor), such as Argon2, scrypt, bcrypt, or PBKDF2.	
Verify independently the effectiveness of configuration and settings.	
Access control is only effective if enforced in trusted server-side code or server-less API, where the attacker cannot modify the access control check or metadata.	Broken Access Control
With the exception of public resources, deny by default.	
Implement access control mechanisms once and re-use them throughout the application, including minimizing CORS usage.	
Model access controls should enforce record ownership, rather than accepting that the user can create, read, update, or delete any record.	
Unique application business limit requirements should be enforced by domain models.	
Disable web server directory listing and ensure file metadata (e.g., .git) and backup files are not present within web roots.	
Log access control failures, alert admins when appropriate (e.g., repeated failures).	
Rate limit API and controller access to minimize the harm from automated attack tooling.	
JWT tokens should be invalidated on the server after logout. Developers and QA staff should include functional access control unit and integration tests.	
A repeatable hardening process that makes it fast and easy to deploy another environment that is properly locked down. Development, QA, and production environments should all be configured identically, with different credentials used in each environment. This process should be automated to minimize the effort required to set up a new secure environment.	Security Misconfiguration
A minimal platform without any unnecessary features, components, documentation, and samples. Remove or do not install unused features and frameworks.	
A task to review and update the configurations appropriate to all security notes, updates and patches as part of the patch management process (see A9:2017-Using Components with Known Vulnerabilities). In particular, review cloud storage permissions (e.g., S3 bucket permissions).	
A segmented application architecture that provides effective and secure separation between components or tenants, with segmentation, containerization, or cloud security groups (ACLs).	
Sending security directives to clients, e.g., Security Headers.	
An automated process to verify the effectiveness of the configurations and settings in all environments.	
Preventing XSS requires the separation of untrusted data from active browser content. This can be achieved by:	Cross-Site Scripting (XSS)
Using frameworks that automatically escape XSS by design, such as the latest Ruby on Rails, React JS. Learn the limitations of each framework's XSS protection and appropriately handle the use cases which are not covered.	
Escaping untrusted HTTP request data based on the context in the HTML output (body, attribute, JavaScript, CSS, or URL) will resolve Reflected and Stored XSS vulnerabilities.	
The OWASP Cheat Sheet 'XSS Prevention' has details on the required data escaping techniques.	
Applying context-sensitive encoding when modifying the browser document on the client-side acts against DOM XSS. When this cannot be avoided, similar context-sensitive escaping techniques can be applied to browser APIs as described in the OWASP Cheat Sheet 'DOM based XSS Prevention'.	
Enabling a <u>Content Security Policy (CSP) as a defense-in-depth mitigating control against XSS. It is effective if no other vulnerabilities exist that would allow placing malicious code via local file includes (e.g., path traversal overwrites or vulnerable libraries from permitted content delivery networks).	
Remove unused dependencies, unnecessary features, components, files, and documentation.	Using Components with Known Vulnerabilities
Continuously inventory the versions of both client-side and server-side components (e.g., frameworks, libraries) and their dependencies. Continuously monitor for known vulnerabilities in the components. Use software composition analysis tools to automate the process. Subscribe to email alerts for security vulnerabilities related to components you use.	
Only obtain components from official sources over secure links. Prefer signed packages to reduce the chance of including a modified, malicious component.	
Monitor for libraries and components that are unmaintained or do not create security patches for older versions. If patching is not possible, consider deploying a virtual patch to monitor, detect, or protect against the discovered issue.	
Ensure all login, access control failures, and server-side input validation failures can be logged with sufficient user context to identify suspicious or malicious accounts, and held for sufficient time to allow delayed forensic analysis.	Insufficient Logging / Monitoring
Ensure that logs are generated in a format that can be easily consumed by a centralized log management solution.	
Ensure high-value transactions have an audit trail with integrity controls to prevent tampering or deletion, such as append-only database tables or similar.	
Establish effective monitoring and alerting such that suspicious activities are detected and responded to in a timely fashion.	
Establish or adopt an incident response and recovery plan, such as NIST 800-61 rev 2 (Cichonski, Millar, Grance, & Scarfone, 2012) or later.	

2001) It considers larger information repositories, which are called population tables and is less restrictive than the k-anonymity model but weaker in terms of security. Three new models (Gionis, Mazza, & Tassa, 2008) have been proposed, called (1, k) -anonymity, (k, 1) -anonymity and (k, k) -anonymity (k, 1) - anonymity, (k, k) -anonymity) that approximate the logic of the k-map model. They provide greater information usefulness but less security than k-anonymity and differ in assumptions about the abilities of the attackers. For the protection of field and sensitive values, the l-diversity model (Machanavajjhala, Kifer, Gehrke, & Venkitasubramaniam, 2007) is used to ensure that there are at least l well-represented values for each sensitive feature, where the term well represented is usually defined by a probability threshold: an attacker can't combine his previous knowledge with any sensitive value with a probability of more than 1 / l. There are several versions of this model in the literature, such as distinct l-diversity and recursive (c, l) –diversity (Loukides, Gkoulalas-Divanis, & Malin, 2010). Other models that limit the number of distinct values of sensitive features in an anonymized dataset are (a, k) -anonymity (a, k) -anonymity (Wong, Li, Fu, & Wang, 2006) and k-anonymous p- k-anonymity) (Truta & Vinay, 2006). The t-closeness model (Li, Li, & Venkatasubramania, 2007) is also used to protect against field recognition and sensitive attributes. Accordingly, the distance of the distribution of the values of the sensitive attribute within each equivalence class from the distribution of its values to the total of data must not exceed the upper limit t.

Models have also been created for identity protection while anonymizing diagnostic codes that exist in electronic patient records. The strictest, security-wise, amongst these models, is full k-anonymity (He & Naughton, 2009) that requires at least k records in a publicized database to have the same diagnostic codes, can also be used to anonymize other codes and attributes. Other similar but more flexible models are km-anonymity (Terrovitis, Mamoulis, & Kalnis, 2008) and privacy-constrained anonymity (Loukides et al., 2010). In order to protect the field when the data set contains diagnostic codes, the p-uncertainty model has been proposed, which ensures that the probability that a person is associated with a diagnosis is less than π. Moreover, (h, k, p) -coherence (Cao, Karras, Raïssi, & Tan, 2010) and the PS-rule based anonymity (Loukides, Gkoulalas-Divanis, & Shao, 2013) models have been proposed, which prevent identification and recognition of sensitive features. The d-presence model is the one most commonly used to protect against participation recognition and specifically to ensure that the attacker can't surely know that a person is in the data repository with a probability greater than d. A similar model that does not require data holders to access all of a population's information has also been suggested (Loukides et al., 2010) and is called c-confident d-presence.

All algorithms developed for data anonymization have been based on the models described above. The way in which they process and change the indirect attributes, which is the main stage of anonymization, as well as other elements such as the heuristic strategies they use, is the information on which these algorithms can be compared and classified and finally, emerge as the most appropriate for the anonymization of a health database. (Gkoulalas-Divanis, Loukides, & Sun, 2014) present an analytical summary and classification of algorithms based on the aforementioned models. The most widespread technique used to transform the indirect characteristics of an information repository is generalization (Sweeney, 2002). In generalization, attribute values are replaced by more general ones, without altering their semantics and information they contain. When the attribute has a numerical value, it can be replaced by a range of values that contains the initial value, and if it has a categorical value, a hierarchy of generalization with a tree structure can be followed (for example, the municipality where a person is a resident can become a city or a geographical area when that is not enough, etc.). Applying generalization to all feature appearances is called global recording, while application only to specific occurrences is called local recording

(Nergiz & Clifton, 2007). One form of generalization is the micro-aggregation technique (Domingo-Ferrer & Mateo-Sanz, 2002), where the values of a set are replaced with a statistical value (e.g., mean, median). Finally, the technique of suppression is essentially the abstraction of attributes or even of whole records from a set of data. It is the technique used in the direct traits, as mentioned above, but also in the indirect traits that are so rare that they can reveal the identity of certain individuals.

DISCUSSION

Taking advantage of digital health records has the potential to improve drastically clinical care, as well as facilitate data-driven research in many medical fields. However, there is always the risk to rather harm than benefit patients if data security fails to prevent successful attacks, especially given the fact that the prolific integration of technology into medical environments is continuously generating new attack vectors (Seale, McDonald, Glisson, Pardue, & Jacobs, 2018).

Security companies and regulatory authorities are making progress in the effort to tackle the prevalence of cyber-crime, but, at the same time, many healthcare organizations, often simply by delaying to invest in upgrading their systems, thus remaining constantly susceptible to new hacking technologies, are left behind in effectively securing their data, compared to other target industries. For example, (Martin, Martin, Hankin, Darzi, & Kinross, 2017) report that *"many NHS organizations spend as little as 1-2% of their annual budget on IT, compared with 4-10% in other sectors and use many run-on legacy systems that are no longer supported. Indicative of this low level of investment many NHS trusts are still using Windows XP, an operating system that Microsoft stopped supporting in 2014"*. Implementing proper security policies and procedures, is inherently difficult for the healthcare industry, given that it consists of a large number of public and private institutions and lacks the homogeneity and the coordination potential of other sectors (e.g., financial services).

In 2009 Healthcare Information and Management Systems Society (HIMSS) conducted a survey and found that, at the time of the study, despite HIPAA and other initiatives, many of the surveyed healthcare organizations *"do not perform security risk analyses and therefore do not understand their vulnerability to cyber-attack"*, their *"budgets dedicated to security remain low"*, *"still do not have a formally designated Chief Information Security Officer or Chief Security Officer to provide the needed organizational leadership to focus on cybersecurity"*, *"are not using available technologies to secure data, such as encryption of computer hard drives"*, and *"do not have a plan for responding to threats or incidents relating to a security breach"* (Harries & Yellowlees, 2013).

Both Private and Public healthcare organizations should increase their efforts to protect themselves, as attacks targeting medical data will continue to increase, mindful of the potential harm to their customers/patients, to their reputation and their financial survivability (a successful breach is estimated to cost, on average, around 3.7 million dollars to clean up (Kruse et al., 2017)). It is therefore imperative that the necessary time and money are invested towards ensuring that healthcare organizations' software systems are adequately protected, developed, implemented and maintained for the ability to keep sensitive data private and prevent them from falling into the wrong hands.

In order for the new healthcare paradigms to thrive, the public's trust is imperative. Almost all of the modern medical tools employing personalized care principles and informed evidence-based clinical decisions are based on systems' interoperability and flexible data access which, in turn, need acceptance, trust, and consent on both personal and social level. Depriving medical practice of these tools due to distrust and fear can render it obsolete. Thus, one could argue that unsuccessful attempts to protect health data have an indirect but significant impact on the quality of the provided healthcare.

REFERENCES

About The Open Web Application Security Project - OWASP. (2018). Retrieved December 7, 2018, from https://www.owasp.org/index.php/About_The_Open_Web_Application_Security_Project

Ali, A., Khan, M., Saddique, M., Pirzada, U., Zohaib, M., Ahmad, I., & Debnath, N. (2016). TOR vs I2P: A comparative study. In *2016 IEEE International Conference on Industrial Technology (ICIT)* (pp. 1748–1751). IEEE. 10.1109/ICIT.2016.7475027

Amsterdam, J. von. (2018). *Monero versus Bitcoin: The battle of the cryptocurrencies* (vol. 4). Academic Press.

GDPR Article 83 – General conditions for imposing administrative fines. (2016).

Astolfi, F., Kroese, J., & Van Oorschot, J. (2015). *I2P - The Invisible Internet Project*. Academic Press.

Bai, G., Jiang, J., & Flasher, R. (2017). Hospital Risk of Data Breaches. *JAMA Internal Medicine*, *177*(6), 878. doi:10.1001/jamainternmed.2017.0336 PMID:28384777

Bartlett, J. (2015). *The dark net : Inside the digital underworld*. Academic Press.

Bergman, M. K. (2001). White Paper: The Deep Web: Surfacing Hidden Value. *The Journal of Electronic Publishing: JEP*, *7*(1). doi:10.3998/3336451.0007.104

Bisson, D. (2015). *5 Social Engineering Attacks to Watch Out For*. Retrieved December 6, 2018, from https://www.tripwire.com/state-of-security/security-awareness/5-social-engineering-attacks-to-watch-out-for/

Boden, E. (2018). *How hackers infiltrate healthcare organizations | eSentire*. Retrieved from https://www.esentire.com/blog/healthcare-cyber-attack-types/

Cao, J., Karras, P., Raïssi, C., & Tan, K.-L. (2010). ρ-uncertainty: Inference-proof transaction anonymization. *Proceedings of the VLDB Endowment International Conference on Very Large Data Bases*, *3*(1–2), 1033–1044. doi:10.14778/1920841.1920971

Center for Internet Security. (2018). *Data Breaches: In the Healthcare Sector*. Retrieved from https://www.cisecurity.org/blog/data-breaches-in-the-healthcare-sector/

Chideya, F. (2015). *Medical Privacy Under Threat in the Age of Big Data*. Retrieved from https://theintercept.com/2015/08/06/how-medical-privacy-laws-leave-patient-data-exposed/

Cichonski, P., Millar, T., Grance, T., & Scarfone, K. (2012). *Computer Security Incident Handling Guide : Recommendations of the National Institute of Standards and Technology*. doi:10.6028/NIST.SP.800-61r2

Cox, J. (2015). *The Dark Web as You Know It Is a Myth | WIRED*. Retrieved May 31, 2019, from https://www.wired.com/2015/06/dark-web-know-myth/

Criddle, L. (2017). *What is Social Engineering? Examples and Prevention Tips*. Retrieved from https://www.webroot.com/us/en/home/resources/tips/online-shopping-banking/secure-what-is-social-engineering

CWE List Version 3.1. (2017). Retrieved December 7, 2018, from https://cwe.mitre.org/data/index.html

Dankar, F. K., & Al Ali, R. (2015). A theoretical multi-level privacy protection framework for biomedical data warehouses. *Procedia Computer Science, 63*, 569–574. doi:10.1016/j.procs.2015.08.386

Data protection in the EU. (2016). European Commission.

Domingo-Ferrer, J., & Mateo-Sanz, J. M. (2002). Practical data-oriented microaggregation for statistical disclosure control. *IEEE Transactions on Knowledge and Data Engineering, 14*(1), 189–201. doi:10.1109/69.979982

Dziembowski, S. (2015). Introduction to Cryptocurrencies. In *Proceedings of the 22nd ACM SIGSAC Conference on Computer and Communications Security - CCS '15* (pp. 1700–1701). New York: ACM Press. 10.1145/2810103.2812704

El Emam, K., & Arbuckle, L. (2013). *Anonymizing health data: case studies and methods to get you started*. O'Reilly Media, Inc.

El Emam, K., Rodgers, S., & Malin, B. (2015). Anonymising and sharing individual patient data. *BMJ (Clinical Research Ed.), 350*(1), h1139. doi:10.1136/bmj.h1139 PMID:25794882

Emam, K. El. (2013). *Guide to the De-Identification of Personal Health Information*. doi:10.1201/b14764

Eze, B., & Peyton, L. (2015). Systematic Literature Review on the Anonymization of High Dimensional Streaming Datasets for Health Data Sharing. *Procedia Computer Science, 63*, 348–355. doi:10.1016/j.procs.2015.08.353

Garfinkel, S. L. (2016). *Draft (2nd) NIST SP 800-188, De-Identification of Government Datasets*. Academic Press.

Genitsaridi, I., Kondylakis, H., Koumakis, L., Marias, K., & Tsiknakis, M. (2015). Evaluation of personal health record systems through the lenses of EC research projects. *Computers in Biology and Medicine, 59*, 175–185. doi:10.1016/j.compbiomed.2013.11.004 PMID:24315661

Gilbert, R., Goldstein, H., & Hemingway, H. (2015). The market in healthcare data. *BMJ : British Medical Journal, 351*, h5897. doi:10.1136/bmj.h5897 PMID:26537618

Gionis, A., Mazza, A., & Tassa, T. (2008). k-Anonymization revisited. In *Data Engineering, 2008. ICDE 2008. IEEE 24th International Conference on* (pp. 744–753). IEEE.

Gkoulalas-Divanis, A., Loukides, G., & Sun, J. (2014). Publishing data from electronic health records while preserving privacy: A survey of algorithms. *Journal of Biomedical Informatics, 50*, 4–19. doi:10.1016/j.jbi.2014.06.002 PMID:24936746

Gold, M., & McLaughlin, C. (2016). Assessing HITECH Implementation and Lessons: 5 Years Later. *The Milbank Quarterly, 94*(3), 654–687. doi:10.1111/1468-0009.12214 PMID:27620687

Gordon, W. J., Fairhall, A., & Landman, A. (2017). Threats to Information Security— Public Health Implications. *The New England Journal of Medicine*, *377*(8), 707–709. doi:10.1056/NEJMp1707212 PMID:28700269

Grassi, P. A., Fenton, J. L., Newton, E. M., Perlner, R. A., Regenscheid, A. R., Burr, W. E., … Theofanos, M. F. (2017). *Digital identity guidelines: authentication and lifecycle management*. doi:10.6028/NIST.SP.800-63b

Guzek, M., Bouvry, P., & Talbi, E.-G. (2015). A Survey of Evolutionary Computation for Resource Management of Processing in Cloud Computing [Review Article]. *IEEE Computational Intelligence Magazine*, *10*(2), 53–67. doi:10.1109/MCI.2015.2405351

Harries, D., & Yellowlees, P. M. (2013). Cyberterrorism: Is the U.S. Healthcare System Safe? *Telemedicine Journal and e-Health*, *19*(1), 61–66. doi:10.1089/tmj.2012.0022 PMID:23113795

He, Y., & Naughton, J. F. (2009). Anonymization of set-valued data via top-down, local generalization. *Proceedings of the VLDB Endowment International Conference on Very Large Data Bases*, *2*(1), 934–945. doi:10.14778/1687627.1687733

Hern, A. (2018). *What is GDPR and how will it affect you? | Technology | The Guardian*. Retrieved from https://www.theguardian.com/technology/2018/may/21/what-is-gdpr-and-how-will-it-affect-you

HIPAA. (2018). *When Was HIPAA Enacted? HIPAA (Health Insurance Portability and Accountability Act) | whatis.com. (2017)*. Retrieved from https://searchhealthit.techtarget.com/definition/HIPAA

HIPAA Privacy Rule and Its Impacts on Research. (2005). Retrieved from https://privacyruleandresearch.nih.gov/healthservicesprivacy.asp

Hurlburt, G. (2017). Shining Light on the Dark Web. *Computer*, *50*(4), 100–105. doi:10.1109/MC.2017.110 PMID:29213147

Junger, M., Montoya, L., & Overink, F.-J. (2017). Priming and warnings are not effective to prevent social engineering attacks. *Computers in Human Behavior*, *66*, 75–87. doi:10.1016/j.chb.2016.09.012

Koczkodaj, W. W., Mazurek, M., Strzałka, D., Wolny-Dominiak, A., & Woodbury-Smith, M. (2018). Electronic Health Record Breaches as Social Indicators. *Social Indicators Research*. doi:10.100711205-018-1837-z

Koyun, A., & Al Janabi, E. (2017). *Social Engineering Attacks. Journal of Multidisciplinary Engineering Science and Technology* (Vol. 4). JMEST.

Kruse, C. S., Frederick, B., Jacobson, T., & Kyle, D. (2017). Cybersecurity in healthcare: A systematic review of modern threats and trends. *Technology and Health Care*, *25*(1), 1–10. doi:10.3233/THC-161263 PMID:27689562

Li, N., Li, T., & Venkatasubramania, S. (2007). t -Closeness : Privacy Beyond k -Anonymity and -Diversity. *IEEE 23rd International Conference*, (3), 106–115. 10.1109/ICDE.2007.367856

Lord, N. (2018a). *Top 10 Biggest Healthcare Data Breaches of All Time | Digital Guardian*. Retrieved from https://digitalguardian.com/blog/top-10-biggest-healthcare-data-breaches-all-time

Lord, N. (2018b). *What is GDPR (General Data Protection Regulation)? Understanding and Complying with GDPR Data Protection Requirements | Digital Guardian*. Retrieved from https://digitalguardian.com/blog/what-gdpr-general-data-protection-regulation-understanding-and-complying-gdpr-data-protection

Loukides, G., Gkoulalas-Divanis, A., & Malin, B. (2010). Anonymization of electronic medical records for validating genome-wide association studies. *Proceedings of the National Academy of Sciences of the United States of America*, *107*(17), 7898–7903. doi:10.1073/pnas.0911686107 PMID:20385806

Loukides, G., Gkoulalas-Divanis, A., & Shao, J. (2013). Efficient and flexible anonymization of transaction data. *Knowledge and Information Systems*, *36*(1), 153–210. doi:10.100710115-012-0544-3

Machanavajjhala, A., Kifer, D., Gehrke, J., & Venkitasubramaniam, M. (2007). *L* -diversity. *ACM Transactions on Knowledge Discovery from Data*, *1*(1), 3. doi:10.1145/1217299.1217302

Martens, B., & Teuteberg, F. (2012). Decision-making in cloud computing environments: A cost and risk based approach. *Information Systems Frontiers*, *14*(4), 871–893. doi:10.100710796-011-9317-x

Martin, G., Martin, P., Hankin, C., Darzi, A., & Kinross, J. (2017). Cybersecurity and healthcare: How safe are we? *BMJ (Clinical Research Ed.)*, *j3179*. doi:10.1136/bmj.j3179 PMID:28684400

Mell, P. M., & Grance, T. (2011). *The NIST definition of cloud computing*. doi:10.6028/NIST.SP.800-145

Nakamoto, S. (2008). Bitcoin: A Peer-to-Peer Electronic cash system. *Bitcoin*, *9*. doi:10.100710838-008-9062-0

Nergiz, M. E., & Clifton, C. (2007). Thoughts on k-anonymization. *Data & Knowledge Engineering*, *63*(3), 622–645. doi:10.1016/j.datak.2007.03.009

Noether, S., Mackenzie, A., & Research Lab, T. M. (2016). Ring Confidential Transactions. *Ledger*, *1*, 1–18. doi:10.5195/LEDGER.2016.34

Olavsrud, T. (2010). *9 Best Defenses Against Social Engineering Attacks*. Retrieved December 6, 2018, from https://www.esecurityplanet.com/views/article.php/3908881/9-Best-Defenses-Against-Social-Engineering-Attacks.htm

Orito, Y., & Murata, K. (2005). Privacy protection in Japan: cultural influence on the universal value. *Electronic Proceedings of Ethicomp, 5*.

Pulkkis, G., Karlsson, J., Westerlund, M., & Tana, J. (2017). Secure and Reliable Internet of Things Systems for Healthcare. In *2017 IEEE 5th International Conference on Future Internet of Things and Cloud (FiCloud)* (pp. 169–176). IEEE. 10.1109/FiCloud.2017.50

Samarati, P., & Sweeney, L. (1998). Protecting Privacy when Disclosing Information: k-Anonymity and its Enforcement Through Generalization and Suppresion. *Proceedings of the IEEE Symposium on Research in Security and Privacy*, 384–393. 10.1145/1150402.1150499

Seale, K., McDonald, J., Glisson, W., Pardue, H., & Jacobs, M. (2018). MedDevRisk: Risk Analysis Methodology for Networked Medical Devices. *Hawaii International Conference on System Sciences 2018 (HICSS-51)*. 10.24251/HICSS.2018.414

Singhealth, T., Attack, C., Author, C. O. I. F., Jayakumar, S., Attack, S. C., Findings, C. O. I., … Url, C. D. (2019). *This document is downloaded from DR-NTU, Nanyang Technological SingHealth Cyber Attack : Learning from COI Findings*. Academic Press.

Spitzer, J. (2018). *Healthcare data breaches spike significantly in 7 years: 5 things to know*. Retrieved from https://www.beckershospitalreview.com/cybersecurity/healthcare-data-breaches-spike-significantly-in-7-years-5-things-to-know.html

Summary of the HIPAA Security Rule | HHS.gov. (2013). Retrieved from https://www.hhs.gov/hipaa/for-professionals/security/laws-regulations/index.html

Sweeney, L. (2001). *Computational disclosure control: a primer on data privacy protection*. Massachusetts Institute of Technology.

Sweeney, L. (2002). Achieving k-anonymity privacy protection using generalization and suppression. *International Journal of Uncertainty, Fuzziness and Knowledge-based Systems*, *10*(05), 571–588. doi:10.1142/S021848850200165X

Terrovitis, M., Mamoulis, N., & Kalnis, P. (2008). Privacy-preserving anonymization of set-valued data. *Proceedings of the VLDB Endowment International Conference on Very Large Data Bases*, *1*(1), 115–125. doi:10.14778/1453856.1453874

Top 10-2017 Details About Risk Factors - OWASP. (2017). Retrieved December 6, 2018, from https://www.owasp.org/index.php/Top_10-2017_Details_About_Risk_Factors

Truta, T. M., & Vinay, B. (2006). Privacy protection: p-sensitive k-anonymity property. In Null (p. 94). IEEE.

Washington, V., DeSalvo, K., Mostashari, F., & Blumenthal, D. (2017). The HITECH Era and the Path Forward. *The New England Journal of Medicine*, *377*(10), 904–906. doi:10.1056/NEJMp1703370 PMID:28877013

Weimann, G. (2016). Going dark: Terrorism on the dark web. *Studies in Conflict and Terrorism*, *39*(3), 195–206. doi:10.1080/1057610X.2015.1119546

What is the HITECH ACT? | What HITECH Compliance Means. (2009). Retrieved from https://compliancy-group.com/what-is-the-hitech-act/

Withrow, S. C. (2010). How to avoid a HIPAA horror story: The HITECH Act has expanded the financial risk for hospitals that do not meet the privacy and security requirements under HIPAA. *Healthcare Financial Management*, *64*(8), 82–89. PMID:20707266

Wong, R. C.-W., Li, J., Fu, A. W.-C., & Wang, K. (2006). (α, k)-anonymity: an enhanced k-anonymity model for privacy preserving data publishing. In *Proceedings of the 12th ACM SIGKDD international conference on Knowledge discovery and data mining* (pp. 754–759). ACM.

KEY TERMS AND DEFINITIONS

Anonymity: Anonymity and thus anonymous data is any information from which the person to whom the data relates cannot be identified, whether by the company processing the data or by any other person.

Cloud Computing: Cloud computing is a type of computing that relies on shared computing resources rather than having local servers or personal devices to handle applications.

Cyberattack: A deliberate exploitation of computer systems, technology-dependent enterprises and networks.

GDPR: General Data Protection Regulation is a new set of rules governing the privacy and security of personal data laid down by the European Commission.

Private Health Data: Is defined as individually-identifiable health data, which is exquisitely sensitive. Being linked to an individual, the private health data can only be shared with the permission of the individual.

This research was previously published in the Encyclopedia of Criminal Activities and the Deep Web; pages 763-787, copyright year 2020 by Information Science Reference (an imprint of IGI Global).

Chapter 48
Assessing HIPAA Compliance of Open Source Electronic Health Record Applications

Hossain Shahriar
Kennesaw State University, USA

Hisham M. Haddad
Kennesaw State University, USA

Maryam Farhadi
Kennesaw State University, USA

ABSTRACT

Electronic health record (EHR) applications are digital versions of paper-based patient health information. EHR applications are increasingly being adopted in many countries. They have resulted in improved quality in healthcare, convenient access to histories of patient medication and clinic visits, easier follow up of patient treatment plans, and precise medical decision-making process. The goal of this paper is to identify HIPAA technical requirements, evaluate two open source EHR applications (OpenEMR and OpenClinic) for security vulnerabilities using two open-source scanner tools (RIPS and PHP VulnHunter), and map the identified vulnerabilities to HIPAA technical requirements.

INTRODUCTION

Digital version of electronic health data improved the quality of care due to easier follow-ups, lowering cost of patient care, enabling data track over time, and making more precise medical decisions. Three types of health records are defined: (i) *Electronic Medical Records* (EMRs) refer to digital version of paper-based clinical data. The clinical data, gathered by clinicians, include information that enables the clinicians to make better medical decisions; (ii) *Electronic Health Records* (EHRs) provide a more comprehensive view of the patient's overall well-being. It contains information collected by all clinicians

DOI: 10.4018/978-1-6684-6311-6.ch048

engaged in the patient's healthcare. Therefore, information in EHRs can be shared among all involved providers; and (iii) *Personal Health Records* (PHRs) are EHRs that are controlled and accessed by the patients (EHR, 2019).

As healthcare application becomes more and more evidence-based, storing health data is becoming more important. Weak health data protection may lead to identity theft, obtaining medical care at the expense of others, ordering expensive drugs for resale, and fraudulent insurance claims (Data, 2013). Moreover, healthcare data hacks may threaten patient's health due to the change of patient's medical history. For example, if health records do not contain a correct listing of allergies, the patient could suffer serious consequences or death due to wrong prescription (Smith et al., 2010).

Compare to banks and financial institutions, patients' data has less protection. Banks are mostly equipped with two-factor authentication while healthcare applications are not. Two-factor authentication is an extra protection which includes not only username and password, but also some unique information that only the user has, such as a physical token. Furthermore, unlike bank accounts that can be locked and changed for protection, it is completely impossible to get back the compromised and disclosed health data (Oliynyk, 2016; 2FA, 2019).

In 2017, Emory Healthcare's appointment system was hacked compromising almost 80,000 patients PHI data such as names, birthdates, internal medical record and appointment information. The appointment information was unencrypted, which opened the door for hackers to obtain plain text information. According to a report (Emory, 2017), this incident is the largest breach in 2017 in the US. The HIPAA Meaningful Usage act requires that any data security breaches affecting 500 or more patients be reported to public through US Health and Human Service Office for Civil Rights' Breach Portal and the affected healthcare provider must take appropriate steps within a certain time limit, otherwise, faces further penalties. Thus, PHI leakage not only brings reputation problem for healthcare providers, but also affects patient's privacy and well-being.

The prevalence of healthcare data security breach can be observed both inside and outside USA. According to 2016 Data Breach Investigations Report (DBIR), there were 115 cases of data breach in North America during 2015. It included 32% privilege misuse, 22% miscellaneous errors, 19% stolen assets, 7% point of sale, 3% cyber-espionage, 3% crimeware, 3% web applications, and 11% other incidents. Healthcare is among the top industries vulnerable to physical theft and loss, miscellaneous errors, insider and privilege misuse, and others. Physical theft and loss is any occurrence where information or a device containing information is missing. Miscellaneous errors occur when accidental actions weaken a security attribute. Insider threats and privilege misuses refer to all unapproved or malicious use (Data Breach Report, 2016).

According to Verizon survey report, some of the reported healthcare data breaches in 2015 were as follows: In February, Anthem, a Blue Cross health insurance member-company, reported a data breach where 80 million patients were affected. In March, Premera, another Blue Cross member, reported a data breach affecting 11 million patients. In both cases, ThreatConnect (2019) announced that Chinese threat Actor "Deep Panda" was probably the attacker. Partners HealthCare, CareFirst Blue Cross and Blue Shield, MetroHealth and Bellvue Hospital reported breaches in April of 2015. In June of the same year, US Office of Personnel Management (OPM) reported mega-breaches for health insurance. The US Department of Health and Human Services reported a breach in August 2015 (Data Breach Report, 2016).

In order to maintain better healthcare, individuals must ensure that their personal health information is private and secure. Otherwise, if patients do not feel that their information remains confidential, they may not want to disclose their health information to healthcare providers, which could endanger the patient's life. Moreover, when a security breach occurs, it may lead to financial harm for healthcare providers or the patient alike (Guide to Privacy and Security, 2015).

Many security vulnerabilities remain undetected for long time (Allan, 2008). Fixing security vulnerabilities becomes more expensive when they are discovered later. Moreover, many security-related mistakes are repeated all the time. Static analysis is a method that directly examines the code of a program without executing the program. It can detect common vulnerabilities before releasing the program. Since manual static analysis takes a long time to be performed, static analysis tools are used to speed up the process of evaluating programs. Static analysis tools examine the text of a program statically, without attempting to execute it.

In this paper, we apply two popular code analysis tools, named RIPS (RIPS, 2019) and PHP VulnHunter to examine the code in OpenEMR and OpenClinic. The obtained results are then manually inspected for accuracy to form a basis of compliance with HIPAA technical requirements due to traditional web security vulnerabilities. We then check a number of HIPAA criteria for compliance within OpenEMR and OpenClinic. The initial results show that both evaluated EHRs may violate some required and optional HIPAA's technical safeguards.

The paper is organized as follows: the next section discusses related work. Next, we describe HIPAA technical requirements. We then discuss web security vulnerabilities common for web-based EHR applications. Next, we describe the static analysis tools and software we used in this work along with the results. Finally, we conclude the paper.

RELATED WORK

In this section, we describe related work and the approaches used to detect security vulnerabilities in EHR applications. Since EHR applications are traditional web applications implemented using various languages (e.g., PHP, JSP) and deployed with databases (e.g., MySQL, MSSQL, Oracle) in well-known servers (e.g., Apache), they may be vulnerable in their implementation. Attackers may exploit the vulnerabilities by providing malicious inputs and compromise the data processed and stored by EHR applications. A number of literature works have explored the magnitude of vulnerabilities present in popular and open source EHRs and checked whether EHR implementations are complying with HIPAA related acts.

For example, Smith *et al.* (2010) empirically evaluated the ability of the Certification Commission of Healthcare IT (CCHIT) to identify a range of vulnerability types. CCHIT focuses on required functional capabilities in EHR applications, such as ambulatory (with prefix AM), ambulatory interoperability (IO-AM), and security (SC).

In a prior study, the authors discussed more than 400 vulnerabilities they discovered using automated security testing tools in OpenEMR (OpenEMR, 2019). In their current work, they tried to observe the consequences of the vulnerabilities rather than finding all vulnerabilities of a particular type. The authors exploited a range of common vulnerabilities in code-level and design-level in EHR applications. Code-level refers to implementation defects and design-level refers to design flaws. Some of the consequences of these exploits were denial of service, users' login information exposure, and editing health records by any users.

A team of instructed attackers was created to target the two EHR applications: OpenEMR and ProprietaryMed. The attackers' focus was on misuse cases of the CCHIT criteria not the overall security of the applications. Misuse cases are defined as actions that are not allowed in the system and can help

Table 1. List of vulnerabilities missing in cchit criteria

Implementation Defects	
Vulnerability	**Misuse Case(s)**
SQL injection	Attacker obtains every user's username and password.
Cross-Site Scripting	Attacker causes a denial of service by rendering the home page to be blank for all future users. Attacker injects scripts that execute additional malicious code.
Session Hijacking	Attacker spoofs another user's identity. Attacker obtains unauthorized access to the system.
Phishing	Attacker obtains the victim's username and password.
PDF Exploits	Attacker executes applications on the client's computer. Attacker executes embedded applications.
Denial of Service: File Uploads	Attacker renders the web server slow or unresponsive.
Authorization Failure	Attacker creates a new user account with any access privileges the attacker desires.
Design Flaws	
Repudiation	Attacker modifies data in an untraceable fashion thus making fraud an unperceivable event to the EHR.
Lack of Authorization Control	Attacker views patient's confidential health records and personal identification information.

developers to think like an attacker. The test attack environment included OpenEMR and ProprietaryMed applications, hacking scripts with additional server, and the researchers' computer with WebScarab and Firebug. WebScarab - which is a Java-based application - was used as a proxy to execute testing attacks and record any traffic between the computers and the test servers. Firebug was used as JavaScript debugger to monitor the attacks. Firebug is a web development plug-in integrates with Firefox and enable users to edit HTML, JavaScript, and Cascading Style Sheets. Firebug is also able to executes any script live. Therefore, the researchers did not need an additional webpage for storing attacks.

In implementation defect situations, the following problems occurred while none of them had previously been exposed by CCHIT test script: SQL injection, cross-site scripting, session hijacking, phishing, PDF exploits, denial of service (file uploads), and authorization failure. Table 1 shows the misuse case(s) of vulnerabilities that has not been addressed by CCHIT.

The results show that CCHIT certification process has two failures: First, when an application meets the security requirements, CCHIT test scripts do not test the application for implementation defects. Second, some security items about patient's health records are not considered at all. It has been suggested that misuse cases are added to the manual test script to simulate the attacks. Moreover, the test scripts can be more comprehensive by launching various attacks on the host application. The manual test scripts should also include the most current list of threats.

Austin and William (2011) discussed insufficient vulnerability discovery techniques from EHR applications. Four discovery techniques were applied to EHR applications to understand when to use each type of discovery techniques. The evaluated EHR applications were OpenEMR and Tolven eCHR. The techniques were systematic and exploratory manual penetration, automated penetration, and static analysis. Penetration testing looks at the security of an application from a user perspective and examines the functionality of an application. In manual penetration testing, no automated tools are used. Exploratory manual penetration is testing an application based on tester's prior experience and it has no test plan. Systematic penetration testing is a test based on a predefined test plan. Automated penetration testing uses automated tools to speed up the process of scanning. Static analysis testing examines the code without executing the program. It can be examination of the source code, the machine code, or the object code. The authors first collected the vulnerabilities detected by each technique, then classified vulnerabilities based on being true or false positive (False positive: mistakenly label code as contain fault. True positive: when faults are correctly identified). The techniques that generated false positives were static analysis and automated penetration testing. The developers need to manually examine each potential false report to recognize if they are false positives.

Some of the detected vulnerabilities were SQL injection, cross-site scripting, system information leak, hidden fields, path manipulation, dangerous function, no HTTP Only attribute, dangerous file inclusion, file upload abuse, and header manipulation. The authors classified vulnerabilities as either implementation defects or design flaws. They empirically proved that no single technique is sufficient for discovering every type of vulnerability and also there is almost no vulnerabilities that can be detected by several techniques. Results showed that systematic manual penetration is more efficient than exploratory manual penetration in terms of detecting vulnerabilities. Systematic manual penetration was effective at finding design flaws. Static analysis detected the largest number of vulnerabilities. Automated penetration was the fastest technique, while static analysis, systematic penetration, and manual penetration were ranked in the next order respectively.

It is suggested that in case of time constraint, automated penetration is used to detect implementation defects, and systematic manual penetration for discovering design flaws. The study has the following limitations: The selected tools for representing static analysis and automated penetration is not a representative of other tools. The authors used just one tool for measuring each detection technique, while other tools might detect other types of vulnerabilities. The examined EHR applications are not representative of all other software. The classification of errors (true positive and false positive) were time consuming and error prone. Human errors can cause vulnerabilities to be neglected.

ACCESS CONTROL IN EHR

In EHR applications, access control is one of the necessary security requirements in terms of protecting patient information from being compromised. Below is some of the studies that has been done in this area.

Helms and Williams (2011) claimed that there has been little effort to evaluate access control vulnerabilities in EHR applications. Four EHR applications were evaluated based on 25 criteria related to access control. The evaluated EHRs were OpenEMR, OpenMRS, iTrust, and Tolven. The criteria were retrieved from HIPAA, Certification Commission for Health Information Technology (CCHIT) Criteria, National Institute for Standards and Technology (NIST) Meaningful Use, and NIST Flat role-based access control (RBAC). CCHIT criteria was met by iTrust but other applications were configuration dependent. OpenEMR and openMRS are able to create super user roles which make them be target of insider attack. Among all evaluated applications, none of them addressed access control during emergency time. Moreover, these EHR applications failed to allow creating roles with separation of duty. Separation of duty prevents a task to be done by just a single user. In addition, none of the certification criteria covered the implementation standards.

Oladimeji *et al.* (2011) discussed that traditional access controls are not insufficient in ubiquitous applications. They proposed a goal-oriented and policy-driven framework to mitigate the security and privacy risks of ubiquitous applications in healthcare domain. The framework captures application's security and privacy requirements and decreases the threats against those requirements. In the proposed framework, these items are modeled: (1) security and privacy objectives, (2) threats against those objectives, (3) mitigation strategies in the form of safeguards or countermeasures. The paper uses emergency response scenario to show the efficiency of the framework. It is mentioned that issues such as untimely arrival of ambulance is a real problem that could happened as a result of verbal misinformation, GPS misleading, or imprecise policies guiding. Introducing some automated mediation may lead to significant improvement. The eHealth security and privacy issues are described in 4 categories: confidentiality, privacy, integrity, and availability. The authors mentioned that there are no universal solutions to these issues that fit all ubicomp applications. Therefore, each ubicomp application needs context-sensitive evaluation of what threats need to be addressed. The authors proposed the framework based on this idea that ubicomp security and privacy are context-sensitive problems, and need to be addressed not only in infrastructure level but application level. In the proposed framework, each step leads to creation of a visual model that is used as a security and privacy requirement. These models can be used as semantically rich means of communication among requirements analysts, architects, developers and other stakeholders. The framework consisted of context definition, sensitivity characterization, risk and tradeoff analysis, and purpose-driven policy analysis.

Context definition: To establish a context for an application, there should be a specific *definition* of what security and privacy really mean in the application. To create the context, the authors used a semantics non-functional requirement (NFR) framework. In the framework, NFRs are modeled as *softgoals* to be *satisfied* or *denied*. *Sensitivity Characterization:* Protecting health data as Electronic Health Record (EHR) is a high-level protection and it's too restrictive. Therefore, for sensitive context evaluation, the authors classified data into hierarchical structure and assigned a security and privacy requirement to each level. Thus, instead of defining data as EHR, data was classified as health information (HI), protected health information (PHI), highly sensitive health information (HSHI), sensitive personal information (SPI), and personally identifiable information (PII).

The work of Tuikka *et al.* (2005) is based on systematic literature review of previous studies about patients' involvement in EHR applications. Based on this paper, patients' opinion has not been properly considered in EHR development. It is suggested that ethical values be considered in designing EHRs, and patients' access to all their records and even able to add some information to them. The paper concluded that the best representatives for the patients' needs are the patients themselves not the organizations or advocates.

Grunwel *et al.* (2016) discussed the delegation of access in EHR applications and proposed an Information Accountability Framework (IAF) to balance the requirements of both healthcare professionals and patients in EHR applications. In the framework, patients have explicit control over who access and use their information and set usage policies. The IAF framework ensures that the right information is available to the right person at the right time. To operationalize the framework, it needs to provide for a diverse range of users and use cases. For example, the requirements for delegation of access to another user on your behalf.

PRIVACY AND MONITORING OF EHR ACTIVITIES

Privacy protections apply to patient's "individually identifiable health information" (Protecting Your Privacy & Security, 2019). As medical records are digitized, patient privacy becomes a more challenging issue (Kam, 2012). A number of studies have discussed the patient privacy and the required monitoring over patient records.

In order to improve accountability of EHR applications, Mashima and Ahamad (2012) presented a patient centric monitoring system that monitors all the updates and usage of health information stored in EHR/PHR repository. The proposed system uses cryptographic primitives, and allows patients to have control over their health record accessibility. However, in this system the monitoring agent is assumed trusted.

King and Williams (2014) discussed that in EHR applications, viewing protected data is often not monitored. Therefore, unauthorized views of PHIs remain undetected. They proposed a set of principles that should be considered during developing logging mechanisms. They monitored the current state of logging mechanisms to capture and prove user's activities in the application. The authors supplemented the expected results of existing functional black-box test cases to include log output. They used an existing black-box test suite provided by the National Institute of Standards and Technology (NIST). They selected 10 certification criteria from the NIST black-box testing including demographics, medication list, medication allergy list, etc. The authors executed the 30 test cases on EHR applications. 67.8% of applicable executed test cases failed. Four of failed cases was related to viewing of critical data, showing that users may view protected information without being captured.

In order to meet HIPAA's privacy requirements, Reinsmidt *et al.* (2016) proposed an approach that provides a secure connected mobile system in a mobile cloud environment. The connection between mobile systems takes place using authentication and encryption. The protocol execution includes encryption, decryption, and key generation time. After a mobile device opens a socket with the listening server, the server responds with its public part of the DH exchange. The mobile device hashes the results with SHA-256 to calculate the symmetric encryption/decryption key. This key is used in the advanced encryption standard (AES).

Kingsford *et al.* (2017) proposed a mathematical framework to improve the preservation of patient's privacy in EMR applications during the collection of patient health data for analysis. The authors used an identity-based encryption (IBE) protocol. In the proposed framework, patient's identity is delinked from the health data before submitting to health workers for analysis. Health data is encrypted before submitting. The administrator then decrypts the submitted data. Patient's identity is delinked from submitted data in this stage. The administrator checks that only the health data (not the identity of the patient) is sent to health worker for analysis. Therefore, the identity of the patient will not be disclosed and PU's privacy is preserved.

GAP BETWEEN HIPAA REQUIREMENTS AND BREACH NOTIFICATION

Gaps between security policies and real breaches always exist in healthcare. Policies are often stated in an ambiguous manner (Kamsties, 2005; Popescu et al., 2007). Therefore, in reality not all the breaches are addressed by policies. Below is a study about measuring the breach coverage percentage by HIPAA security policies. Kafali *et al.* (2017) proposed a semantic reasoning framework to identify gaps between

HIPAA policy and security breaches. They revealed that only 65% of security breaches are covered by HIPAA policy rules. Moreover, HIPAA security policy is more successful in covering malicious misuse than accidental misuse.

In this work, we use a static analysis tool to examine an open-source EHR application. Then, we map the identified security vulnerabilities to HIPAA technical requirements.

HIPAA SECURITY REQUIREMENTS

Although EHRs result in better care, concerns of security and privacy breach always exist among digital formats. HIPAA was established in 1996 to protect healthcare coverage for individuals with lower income (HIPAA, 2012). It also provides federal protections for patient health information by specifying measures to ensure EHR confidentiality, integrity, and availability (Guide to Privacy and Security, 2015; Bowers, 2011). Table 2 shows HIPAA's technical safeguards which if not implemented will lead to fine and penalties (HIPAA Security Checklist, 2016). Some requirements are marked as addressable, which should be implemented in EHR so that PHI remains secured. Compliance with technical safeguards enables meeting other types of safeguards (e.g., providing tools and applications to check and monitor administrative security policies), and prevents unwanted incidents due to lack of compliance. For example, if a laptop having an EHR application gets lost or stolen, it would be very difficult to hack PHI data if authentication and data encryption are present.

COMMON WEB SECURITY VULNERABILITIES

Since EHR applications are deployed over the web, they suffer *from* common security vulnerabilities found in traditional web applications. These may include SQL Injection, cross-site scripting, file inclusion, HTTP response splitting, and control flow alteration. Below, we provide a brief description of these common security vulnerabilities in EHR applications.

SQL Injection

SQL injection is a code injection attack that occurs when an application does not sanitize untrusted input properly. Therefore, an attacker can inject reserved words into input fields, executes malicious SQL statements, and change the logical structures of SQL statements (Smith et al., 2010; RIPS, 2019).

Cross-Site Scripting

In a cross-site scripting attack, an attacker injects malicious code into the trusted web application that does not properly validate the user input. Therefore, a victim can run the malicious code into the browser. Cross-site scripting is a threat for users, not the application itself (Smith et al., 2010; Wassermann and Su, 2008).

Table 2. HIPAA technical safeguards

Security Rule Reference	Technical Safeguards
164.312(a)(1)	**Access Controls: Implement technical policies and procedures for electronic information systems that maintain EPHI to allow access only to those persons or software programs that have been granted access rights as specified in Sec. 164.308(a)(4).**
164.312(a)(2)(i)	Have you assigned a unique name and/or number for identifying and tracking user identity? (REQUIRED)
164.312(a)(2)(ii)	Have you established (and implemented as needed) procedures for obtaining for obtaining necessary EPHI during and emergency? (REQUIRED)
164.312(a)(2)(iii)	Have you implemented procedures that terminate an electronic session after a predetermined time of inactivity? (ADDRESSABLE)
164.312(a)(2)(iv)	Have you implemented a mechanism to encrypt and decrypt EPHI? (ADDRESSABLE)
164.312(b)	**Have you implemented Audit Controls, hardware, software, and/or procedural mechanisms that record and examine activity in information systems that contain or use EPHI? (REQUIRED)**
164.312(c)(1)	**Integrity: Implement policies and procedures to protect EPHI from improper alteration or destruction.**
164.312(c)(2)	Have you implemented electronic mechanisms to corroborate that EPHI has not been altered or destroyed in an unauthorized manner? (ADDRESSABLE)
164.312(d)	**Have you implemented Person or Entity Authentication procedures to verify that a person or entity seeking access EPHI is the one claimed? (REQUIRED)**
164.312(e)(1)	**Transmission Security: Implement technical security measures to guard against unauthorized access to EPHI that is being transmitted over an electronic communications network.**
164.312(e)(2)(i)	Have you implemented security measures to ensure that electronically transmitted EPHI is not improperly modified without detection until disposed of? (ADDRESSABLE)
164.312(e)(2)(ii)	Have you implemented a mechanism to encrypt EPHI whenever deemed appropriate? (ADDRESSABLE)

Reflection Injection Attack

Reflection is the computer ability to inspect itself and describe the properties, methods and types of objects that the user is working with. In reflection injection attack, tainted data is used as a function name which may lead to execution of arbitrary functions and unexpected behavior of the application. Reflection injection may also lead to a specific code injection (Unsafe Use of Reflection, 2019; Reflection in PHP, 2019).

File Inclusion

This vulnerability occurs due to poor input validation when an attacker is allowed to exploit external file inclusion functionality that dynamically includes local or external files. It will lead to the execution of malicious code or unauthorized access to sensitive files (File Inclusion Attacks, 2019; LFI, 2019).

HTTP Response Splitting

In HTTP response splitting attack, malicious data is embedded in HTTP response headers. HTTP response is split into two responses instead of one. This attack can lead to other vulnerabilities including cross-site scripting (Klein, 2004; HTTP Response Splitting, 2009).

Flow Control

Flow control attacks occur as a result of injecting malicious user input into the program counter (PC). Flow Control attacks are the subversion of the program execution due to tampering with program code. This vulnerability may result in execution of unintended code (Arthur, 2016; Anti-Subversion Software, 2019).

Protocol Injection

It occurs when attacker change the connection handling parameters. User tainted data may be used when selecting those parameters (RIPS, 2019).

File Disclosure

In File Disclosure vulnerability, an attacker can read local files. User tainted data is used when creating the file name that is supposed to get opened. Therefore, the attacker can read the source code and other files which might lead to other attacks (LFI, 2019).

File Manipulation

An attacker can inject code into a file or write to arbitrary files. User tainted data is used when creating the file name that is supposed to get opened or when creating the string that will be written to the file. An attacker can try to write arbitrary PHP code in a PHP file allowing to fully compromise the server (RIPS, 2019b).

EVALUATION

Applications and Tools

To find out a list of potential web security vulnerabilities, we have used RIPS (RIPS, 2019) and PHP VulnHunter (VulnHunter, 2019) tools on OpenEMR (OpenEMR, 2019) and OpenClinic (OpenClinic, 2019), two open source EHR applications currently being adopted and used in the real world. We used Windows operating system to install tools and EHR applications, and deployed Apache server and MySQL database.

OpenEMR is a PHP-based application that uses Apache as the web server and MySQL as the database server. OpenEMR is under the GNU Public License (GPL). It can be installed on UNIX, Microsoft, and Mac OS X platforms. It contains many essential features for clinical practices such as feeding data of patient (e.g., biographic data, diagnostic results, medication history) as EHR, disease management, scheduling, and electronic billing. OpenEMR is one of the most popular free EHR systems with over 7000 downloads per month. It has been downloaded more than 500,000 times since March 2005 (OpenEMR, 2019b). In this work, we scanned all 5594 files in OpenEMR.

OpenClinic is a platform independent, PHP-based EHR application which has been mainly used in private clinics and private doctors. It requires MySQL and a web server for executing PHP code (like

Apache). OpenClinic is under GNU General Public License (GPL) (OpenClinic, 2019). In this work, we scanned all 170 files in OpenClinic.

RIPS is a tool for automated identification of vulnerabilities in PHP applications. In open-source version of RIPS, PHP code is tokenized and transformed into a program model for scanning. RIPS then detects vulnerable functions that an attacker can provide with malicious inputs. RIPS detects a number of vulnerability types including cross-site scripting, SQL injection, and local file inclusion. RIPS is capable of identifying a large number of vulnerabilities, including Code Execution, Command Execution, Cross-Site Scripting, Header Injection, File Disclosure, File Inclusion, File Manipulation, LDAP Injection, SQL Injection, Unserialize with POP, and XPath Injection.

PHP VulnHunter is a static analysis tool which scans php vulnerabilities automatically. In fact, it uses a combination of static and dynamic analysis to automatically map the target application. It scans a large number of vulnerabilities in PHP web applications. PHP Vulnerability Hunter can detect the following classes of vulnerabilities: Arbitrary command execution, Arbitrary file read/write/change/rename/delete, Local file inclusion, Arbitrary PHP execution, SQL injection, User controlled function invocatino, User controlled class instantiation, Reflected cross-site scripting (XSS), Open redirect, Full path disclosure.

Results

We summarized the results of applying static analysis tools to OpenEMR and OpenClinic in Tables 3 and 4. Table 3 shows identified vulnerabilities by RIPS and PHP VulnHunter, while Table 4 provides some code examples of the detected vulnerable files.

Table 3. detected vulnerabilities found by rips and php vulnhunter in openemr and OpenClinic

Vulnerability	OpenEMR		OpenClinic	
	RIPS	VulnHunter	RIPS	VulnHunter
File Inclusion	✓	✓	-	-
Cross-Site Scripting	✓	✓	✓	✓
SQL Injection	-	-	-	✓
HTTP Response Splitting	✓	-	✓	-
Reflection Injection	✓	-	-	-
Possible Flow Control	✓	-	-	-
Protocol Injection	✓	-	-	-
File Disclosure	✓	✓	✓	-
File Manipulation	✓	-	✓	-

Tables 3 shows that Cross-Site Scripting was detected in both applications by both tools, while SQL Injection, Reflection Injection, Flow Control, and Protocol Injection were least detected vulnerabilities.

File inclusion may lead to unauthorized access and consequently alternation of PHI. This vulnerability violates HIPAA rules for Access Control (**Security rule 164.312(a)(1)**) and Integrity of the EHR application (**Security rule 164.312(c)(1)**).

Table 4. code Examples of vulnerable files in openemr and OpenClinic

Vulnerability	Code Example	Description
1. File Inclusion	require_once "sites/$site_id/sqlconf.php"; $site_id = 'default'; $site_id = $_SERVER['HTTP_HOST'];	The function *require_once* and *$_SERVER* together can cause File Inclusion vulnerability.
2. Cross-Site Scripting	echo $controller->act($_GET); $_GET = undomagicquotes ($_GET);	The function *echo* and *$_GET* together can cause Cross-Site Scripting vulnerability.
3. SQL Injection	mysql_query('USE ' . $_POST['dbName']) or die(sprintf(_("Instruction: %s Error: %s"), $sql, mysql_error()));	The function mysql_query and *$_ POST* together can cause SQL Injection vulnerability.
4. HTTP Response Splitting	header("Location: interface/login/login.php?site=$site_id"); $site_id = 'default'; $site_id = $_SERVER['HTTP_HOST'];	The function *header* and *$_SERVER* together can cause HTTP Response Splitting vulnerability.
5. Reflection Injection	call_user_func_array (array(&$obj, $func), array($var, $_POST)); function populate_object (&$job); $func = "set_" . $varname; $varname = preg_replace("/[^A-Za-z0-9_]/", "", $varname); foreach ($_POST as $varname=>$var)	The function *call_user_func_array* and *$_POST* together can cause Reflection Injection vulnerability.
6. Possible Flow Control	extract ($_GET, EXTR_SKIP); $_GET = undomagicquotes ($_GET);	The function *extract* and *$_GET* together can cause Possible Flow Control vulnerability.
7. Protocol Injection	fsockopen fsockopen(($this->ssl"ssl://": "") . $ip, $port, $errno, $error, $this->timeout): $ip = gethostbyname($domain), $domain)) ⇓ Function connecttohost($domain, $port, $resolve_message)	The function *fsockopen* and *$_GET* together can cause Protocol Injection vulnerability.
8. File Disclosure	fread $filetext = fread($tmpfile, $_FILES['file']['size'][$key]); $tmpfile = fopen($_FILES['file']['tmp_name'][$key], "r");	The function *fread* and *$_FILES* together can cause File Disclosure vulnerability.
9. File Manipulation	chmod chmod($destinationFile, 0644); $destinationFile = $destinationDir . '/' . $destinationName; function upload(&$file, $destinationDir = "", $destinationName = "", $secure = true) $destinationName = $file['name']; function upload(&$file, $destinationDir = "", $destinationName = "", $secure = true)	The function *chmod* and *$_GET* together can cause File Manipulation vulnerability.

In SQL injection attack, an attacker injects reserved words into input fields, executes malicious SQL statements, and change the logical structures of SQL statements. This vulnerability violates HIPAA rules for Access Control (**Security rule 164.312(a)(1)**) and Integrity of the EHR application (**Security rule 164.312(c)(1)**).

In cross-site scripting, an attacker can cause a denial of service by rendering the home page to be blank for all future users or inject scripts that execute additional malicious code. Therefore, authorized users may fail to access the PHI during emergency time. This vulnerability violates HIPAA rules for Access Control (**Security rule 164.312(a)(1)**) and Integrity of the EHR application (**Security rule 164.312(c)(1)**).

HTTP response splitting will lead to other vulnerabilities including cross-site scripting which may disrupt authorized access to the system and cause denial of service. This vulnerability violates HIPAA rules for Access Control (**Security rule 164.312(a)(1)**) and Integrity of the EHR application (**Security rule 164.312(c)(1)**).

Reflection injection may allow an attacker to gain access to the PHI and result in specific code injection. This violates HIPAA rules for Access Control (**Security rule 164.312(a)(1)**) and Integrity of the EHR application (**Security rule 164.312(c)(1)**).

Control flow attacks may result in execution of unintended code which could result in a denial of service. This can cause problem especially during emergency time. Control flow attacks violate HIPAA rule for access during emergency time (**Security rule164.312(a)(2)(ii)**) which is a REQUIRED safeguard.

In protocol injection vulnerability, user tainted data may be used when selecting and changing the connection handling parameters. This violates HIPAA rules for Access Control (**Security rule 164.312(a)(1)**) and Integrity of the EHR application (**Security rule 164.312(c)(1)**).

In file disclosure vulnerability, an attacker can read files. User tainted data is used when creating the file name that is supposed to be opened. Therefore, the attacker can read the source code and other files which might lead to other attacks. This vulnerability violates HIPAA rules for Access Control (**Security rule 164.312(a)(1)**) and Integrity of the EHR application (**Security rule 164.312(c)(1)**).

In file manipulation vulnerability, an attacker can inject code into a file or write to arbitrary files. This violates HIPAA rules for Access Control (**Security rule 164.312(a)(1)**) and Integrity of the EHR application (**Security rule 164.312(c)(1)**).

OpenEMR also failed to address encryption and decryption of PHIs. There were no functions such as *crypt()* for encryption and *md5()* for data hashing. This obviously violates HIPAA rule for encryption and decryption of PHIs **(Security rule 164.312(a)(2)(iv)).**

In Table 4, we show code example for vulnerabilities and describe how the presented code can lead to the associated vulnerability. An example is File Disclosure (example 8) vulnerability where $filetext variable is being used to read a file from Global variable **$_FILES['file']['size'][$key].** This value has been set in another location of the program and it has not been sanitized before file being opened. Thus, an attacker provided input file name can lead to arbitrary file opening and data disclosure.

A summary of HIPAA violated rules is provided in Table 5. The table clearly indicates that presence of vulnerability can potentially lead to HIPAA data security violation in the real world.

CONCLUSION

Given that large scale PHI data security breach occurs in the real world, it is imperative to look at the EHR system and verify their compliance with HIPAA safeguards, particularly technical safeguards. IN general, EHR applications suffer from implementation level vulnerabilities impacting HIPAA requirements. In this work, we examined two open-source EHR applications (OpenEMR and OpenClinic) using a static analysis tools (RIPS and PHP VulnHunter). Then we mapped the identified vulnerabilities to HIPAA technical requirements. Our results from this work showed that OpenEMR and OpenClinic do not comply with some of HIPAA security technical requirements. This is an evidence of the gap between HIPAA technical requirements and traditional security vulnerabilities. The future work will specify and analyze other open-source EHR applications using different static analysis tools. This is in an effort to

Table 5. hipaa rules violated by security vulnerabilities

Vulnerability	Violated HIPPA Rule(s)
File Inclusion	164.312(a)(1) and 164.312(c)(1)
Cross-Site Scripting	164.312(a)(1) and 164.312(c)(1)
SQL Injection	164.312(a)(1) and 164.312(c)(1)
HTTP Response Splitting	164.312(a)(1) and 164.312(c)(1)
Reflection Injection	164.312(a)(1) and 164.312(c)(1)
Possible Flow Control	164.312(a)(2)(ii)
Protocol Injection	164.312(a)(1) and 164.312(c)(1)
File Disclosure	164.312(a)(1) and 164.312(c)(1)
File Manipulation	164.312(a)(1) and 164.312(c)(1)

highlight some EHR application design characteristics that threaten the integrity of EHR systems and endanger patient's health and information.

REFERENCES

Allan, D. (2008). *Web application security: automated scanning versus manual penetration testing*. IBM Rational Software, Somers, White Paper.

Anti-Subversion Software. (2019). https://en.wikipedia.org/wiki/Anti-Subversion_Software

Arthur, W. (2016). *Control-Flow Security*. https://web.eecs.umich.edu/~taustin/papers/Arthur_dissertation.pdf

Austin, A., & Williams, L. (2011). One Technique is Not Enough: A Comparison of Vulnerability Discovery Techniques. *Proceedings of the 5th International Symposium on Empirical Software Engineering and Measurement*. 10.1109/ESEM.2011.18

Bowers, D. (2011). *The Health Insurance Portability and Accountability Act: is it really all that bad?* Accessed from https://www.ncbi.nlm.nih.gov/pmc/articles/PMC1305898/

Data. (2013). *The Importance of Data in Healthcare*. https://www.lumedx.com/the-importance-of-data-in-health-care-.aspx

Data Breach Report. (2016). https://regmedia.co.uk/2016/05/12/dbir_2016.pdf

EHR2. (2015). *What are the differences between electronic medical records, electronic health records, and personal health records?* https://www.healthit.gov/providers-professionals/faqs/what-are-differences-between-electronic-medical-records-electronic

EHR. (2019). *What is an electronic health record (EHR)?* https://www.healthit.gov/providers-professionals/faqs/what-electronic-health-record-ehr

Emory. (2017). *Healthcare cyberattack affects 80,000 patient records.* https://www.modernhealthcare.com/article/20170302/NEWS/170309983/emory-healthcare-cyberattack-affects-80000-patient-

FA. (2019). *An extra layer of security that is known as multi factor authentication.* https://www.securenvoy.com/two-factor-authentication/what-is-2fa.shtm

File Inclusion Attacks. (2019). http://resources.infosecinstitute.com/file-inclusion-attacks/#gref

Grunwel, D., & Sahama, T. (2016). Delegation of access in an Information Accountability Framework for eHealth. *Proceedings of the Australasian Computer Science Week Multiconference.* 10.1145/2843043.2843383

Guide to Privacy and Security. (2015). Accessed from https://www.healthit.gov/sites/default/files/pdf/privacy/privacy-and-security-guide.pdf

Halfond, W., & Orso, A. (2005). AMNESIA: Analysis and monitoring for NEutralizing SQL injection attacks. *Proceedings of International Conference on Automated Software Engineering*, 174-183. 10.1145/1101908.1101935

Helms, E., & Williams, L. (2011). Evaluating Access Control of Open Source Electronic Health Record Systems. *Proceedings of the 3rd Workshop on Software Engineering in Health Care*, 63-70. 10.1145/1987993.1988006

HIPAA. (2010). http://hipaa.bsd.uchicago.edu/background.html

Kafali, O., Jones, J., Petruso, M., Williams, L., & Singh, M. (2017). How Good is a Security Policy against Real Breaches? *Proceedings of the 39th International Conference on Software Engineering*, 530-540.

Kam, R. (2012). *Top 3 issues facing patient privacy.* https://www.healthcareitnews.com/news/top-3-issues-facing-patient-privacy

Kamsties, E. (2005). Understanding ambiguity in requirements engineering. In *Engineering and Managing Software Requirements* (pp. 245–266). Springer Berlin Heidelberg. doi:10.1007/3-540-28244-0_11

King, J., & Williams, L. (2014). Log Your CRUD: Design Principles for Software Logging Mechanisms. *Proceedings of the 2014 Symposium and Bootcamp on the Science of Security.* 10.1145/2600176.2600183

Kingsford, K. M., Zhang, F., & Nii Ayeh, M. D. (2017). A Mathematical Model for a Hybrid System Framework for Privacy Preservation of Patient Health Records. *Proceedings of the 2017 IEEE 41st Annual Computer Software and Applications Conference.* 10.1109/COMPSAC.2017.21

Klein, A. (2004). *Divide and Conquer - HTTP Response Splitting, Web Cache Poisoning Attacks, and Related Topics.* http://www.packetstormsecurity.org/papers/general/whitepaper_httpresponse.pdf

LFI. (2019). *Local File Inclusion.* https://www.acunetix.com/blog/articles/local-file-inclusion-lfi/

Mashima, D., & Ahamad, M. (2012). Enhancing Accountability of Electronic Health Record Usage via Patient-centric Monitoring. *Proceedings of the 2nd ACM SIGHIT International Health Informatics Symposium*, 409-418. 10.1145/2110363.2110410

Oladimeji, E., Jung, H., Chung, E., & Kim, J. (2011). Managing Security and Privacy in Ubiquitous eHealth Information Interchange. *Proceedings of the 5th International Conference on Ubiquitous Information Management and Communication*. 10.1145/1968613.1968645

Oliynyk, M. (2016). *Why is healthcare data security so important?* https://www.protectimus.com/blog/why-is-healthcare-data-security-so-important/

OpenClinic. (2019). http://openclinic.sourceforge.net

OpenEMR. (2019). https://www.open-emr.org/

OpenEMR. (2019b). https://sourceforge.net/projects/openemr/files/stats/timeline

PHPVulnHunter. (2019). https://thehackernews.com/2011/11/php-vulnerability-hunter-v1146.html

Popescu, D., Rugaber, S., Medvidovic, N., & Berry, D. (2007). Reducing ambiguities in requirements specifications via auto- matically created object-oriented models. *Proceedings of the 14th Workshop on Innovations for Requirement Analysis*, 103–124.

Protecting Your Privacy & Security. (2019). *Your Health Information Privacy*. https://www.healthit.gov/patients-families/your-health-information-privacy

Reflection in PHP. (2019). https://culttt.com/2014/07/02/reflection-php/

Reinsmidt, E., Schwab, D., & Yang, L. (2016). Securing a Connected Mobile System for Healthcare. *Proceedings of the 2016 IEEE 17th International Symposium on High Assurance Systems Engineering*. 10.1109/HASE.2016.53

Response SplittingH. T. T. P. (2009). http://projects.webappsec.org/w/page/13246931/HTTP%20Response%20Splitting

RIPS. (2019). *A static source code analyzer for vulnerabilities in PHP scripts*. http://rips-scanner.sourceforge.net/

RIPS. (2019b). *Re-Inforce PHP Security*. https://en.wikipedia.org/wiki/RIPS

Security ChecklistH. I. P. A. A. (2016). https://www.ihs.gov/hipaa/documents/IHS_HIPAA_Security_Checklist.pdf

Smith, B., Austin, A., Brown, M., King, J., Lankford, J., Meneely, A., & Williams, L. (2010). Challenges for Protecting the Privacy of Health Information: Required Certification Can Leave Common Vulnerabilities Undetected. *Proceedings of the second annual workshop on Security and privacy in medical and home-care systems*, 1-12. 10.1145/1866914.1866916

ThreatConnect. (2019). *Security Operations and Analytics Platform*. https://www.threatconnect.com

Tuikka, A., Rantanen, M., & Heimo, O. (2005). Where is Patient in EHR Project? *ACM SIGCAS Computers and Society, 45*(3), 73-78.

Unsafe Use of Reflection. (2019). https://www.owasp.org/index.php/Unsafe_use_of_Reflection

Vulnerability Hunter OverviewP. H. P. (2019). https://www.autosectools.com/PHP-Vulnerability-Scanner

Wassermann, G., & Su, Z. (2008). Static detection of cross-site scripting vulnerabilities. *Proceedings of International Conference on Software Engineering*, 171-180.

This research was previously published in the International Journal of Information Security and Privacy (IJISP), 15(2); pages 181-195, copyright year 2021 by IGI Publishing (an imprint of IGI Global).

Chapter 49
Electronic Healthcare Records:
Indian vs. International Perspective on Standards and Privacy

Aashish Bhardwaj
https://orcid.org/0000-0001-7618-8837
Guru Tegh Bahadur Institute of Technology, India

Vikas Kumar
https://orcid.org/0000-0002-6753-1557
Chaudhary Bansi Lal University, Bhiwani-127021, Haryana, India

ABSTRACT

Patient data is very valuable and must be protected from misuse by the third parties. Also, the rights of patient like privacy, confidentiality of medical information, information about possible risks of medical treatment, to consent or refuse a treatment are very much important. Individuals should have the right to access their health records and get these deleted from hospital records after completing the treatment. Traditional ways of keeping paper-based health records are being replaced by electronic health records as they increase portability and accessibility to medical records. Governments and hospitals across the world and putting huge efforts to implement the electronic health records. The present work explores the different aspects of health privacy and health records. Most important stakeholders, technological and legal aspects have been presented from both the Indian and international perspectives. A comparative analysis has been presented for the available EHR standards with a focus on their roles and implementation challenges.

INTRODUCTION

Every person in the world is spending a huge share of earning on healthcare services. Considering this, worldwide governments and organizations are working hard to improve the health quality and safety of their citizens or employees. WHO (World Health Organization) has surveyed that total global expenditure for health is US$ 7.3 trillion in year 2015 which is approximately 10% of GDP. This includes both public

DOI: 10.4018/978-1-6684-6311-6.ch049

Table 1. Definition of electronic health records

S. No.	Definition	Reference
1	Electronic Health Record is an information resource which is real time, secure, patient-centric and helps clinicians in decision support.	Taylor & Underwood, 2003
2	EHR is a warehouse of information regarding the health of a subject in computer readable form, stored, transmitted securely and accessed by authorized users.	International Organization for Standardization, 2005
3	EHR is a single point of care for patients and healthcare organizations which provide cost effective, errorless, safe and quality care.	Kwak, 2005
4	EHR is information in electronic form which contains the past, present and future health status or healthcare provided to subject of care.	Katehakis & Tsiknakis, 2006
5	EHR is a central database used by different persons and organizations to enter information about patients; it contains not only the clinical data but wellness data also.	Knaup et al, 2007
6	Electronic Health Record contains information related to patients ranging from files in one department to longitudinal collections of patient data.	Häyrinen, et al, 2008
7	Electronic Health Record is an object used to collaborate, learn from data and study new models from the information present in health records.	Hripcsk & Albers, 2012
8	Electronic Health Records is used to accelerate clinical research and predictive analysis. It enables prediction of drug effects and improvements in patient health.	Miotto et al, 2016

and private expenditure on health. Developed countries are spending 12%, while developing and under-developed are spending 6%-7%. (World Health Organization, 2017). In this expenditure, a big amount is spent on maintaining the record of patients, doctors, diseases, health insurance etc. (Barhoun et. al., 2019). The traditional way of maintaining paper based records in file for patients is getting obsolete, due to challenges like incomplete information, data duplication, poor security and privacy, difficulties in data migration and sharing etc. Due to all these challenges, paper based records consume a lot of time in processing the patient information. Electronic Health Records (EHR) are gaining popularity and are being used worldwide for maintaining patient records (Galli, 2018). As per the report by Energias Market Research (2019), the global electronic health records (EHRs) market in 2018 has been valued at USD 24.7 billion and the same is expected to reach USD 36.2 billion by 2025 with an estimated CAGR of 5.6%. This increase is attributed, not only to the growing demand of better healthcare services, but also to the adoption of new technologies and solutions like machine learning, data mining, artificial intelligence, clinical decision support system etc (Sisodia & Agrawal, 2019). The ultimate aim is to achieve the better productivity of healthcare system with improved patient satisfaction. EHR of a patient contains personal information like age, weight; demographics like education, nationality, religion, medical history, medication, allergies, immunization status, laboratory test results, radiology images, vital signs and billing information etc. (Trends, 2014). Many researchers have defined the EHR in different ways and some of the prominent definitions of EHR have been presented in Table 1.

Millions of patients die in hospitals throughout globe due to poor record-keeping of patient's data (Stanberry, 2011). Patient's data related to their blood sugar levels, blood pressure, allergy with certain substances etc., are not properly maintained and this leads to innocent mistakes during hospitalization (Kumar & Bhardwaj, 2020). Poor record-keeping of patients may even lead to deaths in the hospitals. EHRs offer many advantages like improved patient care (Entzeridou et al, 2018), improved care coordination (Samhan & Joshi, 2017), increased patient participation (Fragidis & Chatzoglour, 2018), improved diagnostics (Edirisinghe, 2019), patient outcomes (Ladd, 2017), practice efficiencies (Rathert et al, 2019), healthcare planning (Gold et al, 2018) and cost savings (https://www.healthit.gov/providers-professionals/benefits-electronic-health-records-ehrs).EHRs can also play a vital role in the implementation of Telemedicine projects, using telecommunication technology for treatment and diagnosis of patients. Telemedicine is having several projects running like WiLDNet (Patra et al, 2007), iPath (Brauchli et al, 2005) and Asynchronous remote medical consultation (Luk et al, 2008). It allows specialists in medical field to connect to patients in remote areas of same countries or foreign countries and get opinions for their healthcare. This is especially useful in areas with low infrastructure of connectivity but is having mobile or internet networks operating in those areas. Benefits of using Electronic health Records (EHRs) for patients can be categorized as (Stanberry, 2011; Huang et al, 2009; Bentley et al, 2008):

- **Cost Reduction:** It has been observed by Stanberry (2011) that EHRs would save around US$20 billion per year in public sector and US$30 billion per year in private sector. As patient's medical records are kept at a single location, duplicated diagnosis and testing is avoided, which saves time and cost both. Adoption of EHR could save the cost of US$ 142 billion for out-patient facilities and US$ 371 billion for in-patient facilities over a period of 15 years (https://hitconsultant.net/2012/04/03/infographic-ehr-vs-traditional-paper-records/).
- **Improved Quality of Care:** EHRs provides an improved quality of care by storing medical and diagnostic treatment records (Entzeridou et al, 2018). This provides a faster access to medical best practices as well as most recent literature for reference, leading to improved care coordination (Samhan & Joshi, 2017). This reduces medical errors by 63% and could provide improved safety for patients of Diabetes, Breast Cancer and Colorectal Cancer like diseases (Nguyen et al, 2014; https://www.healthit.gov/topic/health-it-basics/improved-diagnostics-patient-outcomes).
- **Record Keeping:** EHR systems have the flexibility to connect with other medical records for reference purpose. This helps patients to fix appointments and track down records easily, while they are changing doctors or hospitals or changing locations like cities or even countries. A study by Balestras (2017) have quoted that 79% of practitioners have improved their functionality and patient contact time through electronic prescription using EHRs.
- **Record Portability:** A patient may be transferred from one hospital to another, within a nation or anywhere in the world. With the use of EHRs, patient's records are portable and can be transferred globally anywhere for their help. This provides a good background for health worker to take care of new patient (Huang et al, 2009).

Jha et. al. (2008) have examined Electronic Health Records in seven countries and found that all of these countries have a very high priority towards electronic health. These seven countries are the United States of America, Canada, United Kingdom, Germany, Netherlands, Australia and New Zealand. More than 90% of general practitioner in four countries (United Kingdom, Netherlands, Australia and New Zealand) is having a universal use of EHRs. Germany had 40% – 80%, while the United States of America and Canada had only 10% – 30% use of EHR. The 2017 Global Market overview of EHR [https://klasresearch.com/report/global-emr-market-share-2017/1192]has found that America (North and South) is spending around$ 11.1 Billion. EMEA (Europe, Middle East and Africa) is spending around $ 7 Billion and Asia Pacific is spending $ 4 Billion on the EH systems, whereas the other countries are spending approximately $ 0.2 Billion on EHR systems.

2. INTERNATIONAL STANDARDS FOR EHR

Most hospitals throughout the world have been given significant financial independence. Taking advantage of this, a major portion of their income is generated through user's fees, sale of drugs, services for basic care and high technology diagnostics (Elloumi et. al., 2017). Governments are trying to control this with major attention to provide healthcare till last mile. For this, there has been a significant focus on the digitization work in the healthcare sector. Main emphasis is to improve the healthcare of citizens, integration of medical information across all hospitals, automated patient's data, adoption of IT services for clinical services and health management. Governments are facing difficulties due to economic resources and lack of skilled manpower. Developed countries are making use of commercial EHR systems, while the developing countries are emphasizing on open source software like HOSxp, OpenEMR and OpenVistA (Torre et. al., 2013). Table 2 compares the EHR standards of different countries with specific details.

3. PRIVACY IN ELECTRONIC HEALTHCARE RECORDS

A patient's medical records are generally shared by a number of departments in hospital like anesthesia, medicine, orthopedic, research and public domains. This places a threat to patient's privacy, when data is accessed by many actors in the system (Hodges et al, 1999). Compromise of such data related to health may lead to patient's loss of job, insurance, housing etc and may invite hatred and embarrassments in the society. Patients wish to control the access of their medical information in EHRs just like they are maintaining web accounts for banking transactions, property, university details, investments etc. Common privacy protection tools include the HTTPS, paid VPN like Air VPN, Cryptostorm, Hide Me, Express VPN, Earth VPN etc and DNS. Certainly, there is a cost involved in ensuring the privacy of electronic health records. Acquisti et al (2013) have related privacy with financial gains in two aspects. Firstly, How much is the financial gain to an individual in disclosing the private data? Secondly, how much an individual would pay to protect this private information in public? Privacy in general, has been defined by many researchers and most common definitions have been presented in Table 2.

With the large scale growth of government and private transactions, as well as the unreasonable intrusions in this 'Digital Age', privacy protection has entered a new dimension (Berman & Bruening, 2001). Haas et. al. (2011) have presented the two main aspects of privacy protection of individuals in electronic health records. Firstly, patient's data should not be disclosed to third parties as an enforced obligation and without their explicit consent. Secondly, the organization maintaining electronic health records should not set a profile of patient's health data. As privacy concern, people do not want health data to be publically available. Simplest example of maintaining privacy include: early stage of pregnancy, which people want to share only with family members and not with the friend circle. Also, people do not want to share the past history of depression with office friends. Similarly, people do not want to share the information on addiction of alcohol or drugs with anybody.

3.1 Different Aspects of Health Privacy

PwC Health Research Institute (2015) has reported that 88 percent of times, doctors get the personal data of patient without any objection during the treatment. There is no standard definition of the right to privacy, which is mainly context driven. Indian Healthcare sector is at par with International standards

Table 2. Comparison of EHR standards

S. No.	Historical / Applications	India	France	USA	China
1	Name	Electronic Health Record Standards of India	Dossier Medical Personnel (DMI)	Health Information Technology for Economic and Clinical Health (HITECH) Act	Health Information Technology (Health IT)
2	Promoter	Ministry of Health and Family Welfare, Government of India	ASIP Sante: Government Agency for health information systems	Department of Health and Human Services	Ministry of Health, Government of China
3	First Guidelines	August, 2013	January, 2011	February, 2009	2009
4	Purpose	To establish a uniform system for maintenance of EHR by hospitals and healthcare providers in India.	To improve coordination among healthcare professionals and enhance information required for patients easily.	To motivate implementation of EHR and supporting technologies in United States.	To establish healthcare system for citizens and provide medical services which are convenient and effective.
5	Role	To electronically collect health records of an individual that gets generated starting from birth to any clinical encounter and through other self care devices and systems.	To form a technical infrastructural base for e-health services from public or private authorities through voluntary adoption by patients and healthcare professionals.	To impose standards on medical and healthcare organizations in addition to those imposed by HIPAA. This ensures that privacy, reliability and accessibility of data are not compromised.	To integrate medical information across all departments in hospital, effective overall IT planning and attention of end-user requirements, needs and process reengineering.
6	Base	A set of recommendations to adopt EHR for data capture, store, view, presentation, transmission and achieve interoperability in clinical/health records.	Corporation with vendors for DMP interoperability, specification of interfaces, publication and integration of public comments for pushing forward e-health in France.	Meaningful use of EHRs throughout U.S. as a critical national goal and identifies challenges faced by healthcare executives in achieving highest satisfaction.	EHRs, regional healthcare information networks to share records, integration of diverse systems for better management and efficiency.
7	Advantages	Providing a set of international standard in achieving syntactic and semantic interoperability of healthcare delivery. This will also enable every citizen in India to visit any health service provider, diagnostic center or pharmacy with fully integrated health records.	Ownership of health information system projects, rolling out healthcare professional card, supporting public or private initiatives, agreements for international health information sharing, defining or rectifying healthcare system products and services.	It widens scope of privacy and security protections and increases potential legal liability for non-compliance. Workers are provided with higher salary, feature of regular feedbacks, emphasizing on training with full reimbursement for training expenses.	Improved health outcomes and nearly universal coverage of citizens. Also improved performance of providers yielding good quality, cost savings and greater engagements with patients. Reduce health disparity and increased access for entire China.
8	Challenges	Legacy system with mostly paper based records in multiple languages, high cost of implementation, lack of coordination among hospitals and insufficient computer literate staff.	Healthcare professional have to include DMP functionalities at the same timeline in their existing softwares as it a centralized service which can be accessed by all.	To provide electronic form of Protected Health Information (ePHI) related to individual's healthcare. Placing ePHI data on cloud or third party data centers for risk coverage.	Lack of expertise in healthcare software vendors, investment in IT, skilled workers and lack of strong change management.

in diagnosis, treatment and use of contemporary technology (Reddy & Qadeer, 2010). Right to privacy is context driven and there is no universally acceptable definition available till date. Right to privacy

Table 3. Privacy definitions

S. No.	Definition of Privacy	Reference
1	Claim of individual persons, groups or organizations to determine what extent of information about them to be communicated to others.	Westin, 1967
2	A regulation that aims to access control the flow of information to others and external stimulation to own personal gains.	Klopfer & Rubenstein, 1977
3	A condition, nobody is having any undocumented personal information of an individual which can be used in gain access in some sorts.	Parent, 1983
4	A relative and relational concept, where an individual has freedom or immunity from judgment of others which are fixed and least susceptible to change.	Introna & Pouloudi, 1999
5	Semi-honest behavior of a person in society through which personal details are not shared to every individual but to only some persons.	Lindell & Pinkas, 2000
6	Different social spheres of a person in home, public and correspondence life associated with information technologies.	Nissenbaum, 2004
7	Right to be left alone or undisturbed i.e. withdrawn from society or public interest which can cannot be shared easily to everybody in society.	Rowlingson, 2006
8	A very sensitive issue in today's information society where details are frequently available in social forms through internet and freely.	Hargittai, 2010
9	Freedom of expression and social values of human dignity which leads to harmony in self, family, society and nature making them happy.	Lieshout et. al., 2011
10	Ability of the individuals to protect their own information about themselves at every times in society with sharing information at their choices.	Werner et al, 2017

is seen as an extension of the Fundamental Right to Life and Liberty. There are different forms to right to privacy, which includes communication privacy, transactional privacy, health and body privacy. The health and body privacy includes the organs, genetic material and biological functions (Gera et. al., 2017). These includes the right of an individual to disclose the nature of disease, a woman not to be compelled to undergo a blood test, the bodily autonomy to bear children or not, the decision for termination to a pregnancy and custodial rights to the child for two individuals.

Most the governments throughout world are implementing EHR for its inherent advantages with reduced cost. Yet the citizen's confidence is not being gained due to their concerns for privacy in health and body (Hissi et. al., 2018). Indian government efforts through implementation of different regulations from time to time with growing needs of patient's privacy are shown in this section. These acts have to implement a safe sharing environment for medical records between different actors involved like patient, doctor, insurance company, lab technicians, support staff etc. As per Shah Committee report on Privacy Protection (2016), the Privacy is seen as a context of the foundation of the fiduciary relationship between a doctor and a patient. This fiduciary relationship is a mutual trust between the doctor and his patients which was established by the Indian Medical Council Act of 1952. Privacy in healthcare sector includes number of different aspects as mentioned below:

- **Informational privacy:** This includes confidentiality, anonymity and data security. The healthcare systems are managed by multitude of users for diverse purposes within and outside organization for multiple applications. Appari & Johnson (2010) recommended an access control mechanism for consideration of information security through work processes and structure in organization. It also suggests participation of patients in audits.

- **Physical privacy:** This includes modesty and bodily integrity. Yue et al, (2016) recommended that healthcare data should to be owned and controlled by patient as a personal asset. This preserves the patient's privacy and forms a valuable asset for healthcare intelligence. This also prevents any third party to conduct computation over patient's data without proper permissions.
- **Associational privacy:** This includes intimate sharing of death, illness and recovery. The new healthcare framework adapts to establish Circle of Trust (CoT) so that patients can securely obtain and manage their information (Appari & Johnson, 2010). CoT includes hospital, insurer, pharmacy and labs; provides an audit service, logs all transactional requests, enables a privacy officer to investigate any data breach incident.
- **Proprietary privacy**: This includes self-ownership, control over personal identifiers, genetic data and body tissues. The dissemination of patient's data to agencies involved in public health or to the interest of multiple stakeholders should always be concerned with the privacy of individuals and usability of released data (Appari & Johnson). It is also recommended that data remains consistent with minimal information loss.
- **Decisional privacy:** This includes autonomy and choice in medical decision making. Absence of undesired interference in making decisions, also enables the expression of autonomy. It is placed at risk while transmitting data to third party across social, spatial, temporal borders, public or private spaces. The devices used for information sharing may transmit information due to its visibility is also breach of privacy.

All these aspects of privacy bind the healthcare sector to secure individual's health information from releasing to third parties without consent or inadequate notification (Tatoian & Hamel, 2018). As such a disclose leads to embarrassment, stigmatization or discrimination. But such personal health information is permitted and does not amount to a violation of privacy in the following situations:

- During referral.
- When demanded by the court or by the police.
- When demanded by insurance companies when patient has exercised his rights on taking the insurance.
- When required by consumer protection cases, workmen's compensation cases or for income tax authorities.
- Disease registration
- Communicable disease investigations
- Vaccination studies
- Drug adverse event reporting

As per Haas et. al. (2011), As per Every patient should be able to express and should know obligations regarding disclosure to third party. Also, organizations should not be able to gain access or profiles of patients.

3.2 Prominent Stakeholders in EHR Privacy

There are different stakeholders in the privacy in electronic health records:

- **Organization:** Organizations have a corporate responsibility to protect privacy of their employees. For doing this, they should have regular monitoring and protection of data and should train the employees. Appointment of chief privacy officer is also recommended for the big organizations. Schwartz (2008) has suggested many good practices for privacy protection in organizations, including the training of employees for privacy and risk management in organization. Cavoukian et. al. (2010) has presented a maturity model for different aspects of privacy protection an organization should be equipped to take on.
- **Information Technology:** It plays an important role in protection of privacy from user input to complete life-cycle in the system. This aspect of privacy includes fitness devices and wellness programs. Importance of user representation in the system is identified by GoogleBuzz (social networking tool) and Facebook's Beacon (advertisement system). VanLieshout (2011) has found that organizations are disclosing their privacy policies to patients and are taking written consents from them or their attendants. Patients or their attendants at that point are signing it without giving due emphasis and they are left with limited options afterwards. Siljee (2015) has suggested that privacy can be enhanced by using tools like privacy icons and the interest of people in healthcare wearable products. It was found that there are two main reasons, which convince persons to wear healthcare products: (a) Recommended by their doctors, (b) Recommended by their insurance company. It was also observed that 76 percent of patients accept the recommendation of their doctors to wear healthcare products, while 68 percent of times patients are convinced for wearing a healthcare product if it is recommended by their insurance company.
- **Physical Environment:** Cavoukian (2012) has suggested that physical environments of hospitals, laboratories etc. should be privacy enhanced. The physical environment means design of sample collection rooms, operation theaters, medical practitioner observation room, and waiting hall for depressed patients etc. Cavoukian (2012) have presented a case study of Dutch Railway Company, surveying their passengers for sitting arrangements in train coaches. Persons at that point have suggested a change in sitting arrangement from four travelers facing each other to be changed. They suggested that if they are sitting one after other that is better for privacy needs. There are always suggestions to protect privacy while travelers are scanned at airport.

The other aspects related to the privacy of EHR include:

- **Location of Stored Data:** Patient should be informed about the location, where the health data is stored.
- **Access to Medical Records:** Patient should be informed about persons who can access their medical records.
- **Authorization to Third Party:** Patient should be informed about importing medical data to third party.
- **Accountability:** Patient should be informed about the accountability of the person or group of persons who are responsible in case of any privacy breach incident.

4. INDIAN REGULATIONS ON HEALTH PRIVACY

The Patient's protection of Privacy in India is ensured through seven different Acts and the important aspects have been presented as:

4.1 Medical Termination of Pregnancy Act, 1971

A woman has the right to an abortion within a bodily privacy, but autonomy and choice in decision making is not allowed. This is even not allowed to patients and their families in sex determination of the baby. In order to facilitate an abortion, a written consent from the patient is mandatory. The disclosure of such information can only be done to the Chief Medical Officer of the State. Written consent implies that patient is aware of all her options, the risks, post abortion care and has been counseled about the procedure under Medical Termination of Pregnancy Act, 1971.

4.2 Mental Health Act, 1987

The act limits the nature and extent exercised by relevant authorities for collection of information, the limitation on the collection of data and restriction on the use or disclosure of collected data. The information regarding the nature and degree of the mental disorder is issued by a doctor through medical certificates. Also no inspecting officer can disclosure the personal records of the patient under this act.

4.3 Pre-Conception and Pre-Natal Diagnostic Techniques Act, 1994

This Act was formed in the public interest for prevention of female feticide. The pre-natal diagnostic testing is necessary for a mother to follow for finding the consent of age, abortion history and family history. Under this test a woman has to reveal any family history of mental retardation or physical deformities. The Act provides a special concern for privacy and confidentiality regarding the disclosure of genetic information, Pre-Conception and Pre-Natal Diagnostic Techniques (Prohibition of Sex Selection) Act, 1994.

4.4 Insurance Regulatory and Development Authority (Third Party Administrators), Health Services Regulations, 2001

IRDA has restricted the insurance referral companies from disclosing the details of their customers without their prior consent. TPAs are bound to maintain the confidentiality of the data collected on behalf of insurance company. TPAs are required to keep this information for not less than three years. An exception exists, when TPA is asked to provide relevant information to any Court of Law/Tribunal, The Government, or any other Authority in case of any investigation carried out or proposed to be carried out against insurance company.

4.5 Indian Medical Council Regulations, 2002

Medical Council of India (MCI) has set a professional standard for medical practice, Code of Ethics Regulations, 2002. This Act limits the gathering of excessively personal information for any said procedure. Physicians have to maintain the confidentiality of patients during all the stages of the procedure. This information includes any personal and domestic details. The exception to the Act is allowed, if there is a risk to specific person or community because of a disease.

4.6 Ethical Guidelines for Biomedical Research on Human Subjects 2006

The Act provides a limitation for the information collected and its subsequent use. The privacy information includes choice to prevent their biological samples, possible current and future uses of the biological samples collected and the risk of discovery of any sensitive information. The Act provides a special concern on privacy and confidentiality, when conducting genetic family studies. The data collected can be disclosed in a court of law, if there a threat to person's life, if there a severe drug reaction or if there is a risk to public health.

5. INTERNATIONAL PRACTICES OF PRIVACY PROTECTION

Privacy is a Global concern and correspondingly, many regulations and laws have been framed by different countries to protect privacy of their citizens. This includes protection of personal data, traces of health related online and physical activities, health related data of Government, corporate and other organizations. The most important international regulations related to health privacy include the European Union's regulation for data protection (2012), United States of America's the State Alliance for eHealth (2007), the Health Insurance Portability and Accountability Act, 1996 and Australia's Privacy Act (1988).

5.1 European Union

A European Union regulation was introduced in 2012 for data protection [http://ec/europa.eu/justice/data-protection/document/review2012/com_2012_11_en.pdf]. It was implemented in all its member states of European Union, without any alteration or amendments. This included the specific risks to privacy, consisting of the profiling, sensitive data related to health, genetic material or biometric information. A regulation acts as a framework for Privacy Impact Assessments (Wright & Hert, 2012) with regard to the processing of personal data and on the free movement of such data. The regulation established that implicit consent is not enough but a need for explicit consent is required for sensitive personal data. This is because of the inherent imbalance between data subject and data controller. For example the patient and the hospital or the life sciences company conducting the research. The regulation provides a window, wherein patients can request for their data to be deleted after the treatment is finished or they are discharged. If such information is not deleted, it may be subjected to unauthorized access and misuse. This is an important step towards the creation of privacy protection environment. One more added concern is the nature and extent of consent. The consent taken for a clinical trial is not always sufficient to carry out additional research. It is not possible to do additional research, while carrying out initial research from same data collected. The data is coded adequately even then it is not allowed to be transferred outside the European Economic Area (provides the free movement of persons, goods, services and capital within European market). An additional level of data protection is required from the local data protection authority if a court outside European Union requests for disclosure of any personal data. The regulation directs the use of health data only for three purposes:

- The data can be processed in case of medical diagnosis, treatment of healthcare services, preventive medicines and where data is processed by healthcare professionals. In these cases also, it is kept under professional secrecy.
- The data can be processed under considerations of public interest for example for ensuring a high standard of quality for medicinal products, safety or services. The data can be processed under the circumstance of legitimate cross border threats to health.
- The data can be processed for the reason of public interest such as social protection.

5.2 The United States of America

The Health Maintenance and Organization Act, 1973 [https://www.ssa.gov/policy/docs/ssb/v37n3p35.pdf] was prepared keeping in view the rapid development in Information technology. The act was formed to protect the privacy of patient from new forms of threats. To implement this goal a federal regulation was implemented i.e. the Privacy and Security ruled under the Health Insurance Portability and Accountability Act (HIPAA) 1996 [http://www.hhs.gov.ocr/privacy/hipaa/administrative/statute/hipaastatutepdf.pdf] and the State Alliance for eHealth (2007) [https://www2.illinois.gov/gov/healthcarereform/Documents/Alliance%20011614.pdf]. HIPAA addresses the disclosure of a patient's personal information under various health care plans, medical providers and clearinghouses. These are primary agents involved in obtaining the patient information for purposes like: treatment, payment, managing healthcare operations, medical research and subcontracting. Under the HIPAA regulationinsurance agencies are required to ensure the implementation of various administrative safeguards such as policies, guidelines, regulations or rules to monitor and control the inter as well as intra-organizational access to data. The State Alliance for eHealth has been instrumental in creating awareness about privacy requirements in the healthcare sector and improving the efficiency of data collection and transfer.

5.3 Australia

Australia has a comprehensive law that deals with the right of privacy. An amendment to the Privacy Act 1988 [http://www.comlaw.gov.au/Series/C2004A03712] applies to all healthcare providers and was made applicable from 21st December 2001. This establishes minimum standards of privacy regulation with respect to the handling of personal information in the healthcare sector. The privacy Act includes the following practices:

- An informed consent prior to the collection of health related information is required.
- A provision regarding the information that needs to be provided to individuals before information is collected from them.
- Considerations that have to be taken into account before the transfer of information to third parties such as insurance agencies. This also includes the specific instances, wherein the information can be passed on.
- The details that must be included in the Privacy policy of the healthcare services providers Privacy Policy.
- Secure storage of the health related data
- Providing individuals with a right to access their out health records.

The Act provides for anonymity wherein individuals have the option not to identify themselves while entering into transactions with an organization. The Act also provides for restriction on the transfer of personal data outside Australia and the extent of collection of personal and sensitive data.

6. CONCLUSION

Electronic Health Records offer many advantages as compared to traditional paper based system and many countries have a strong focus for their implementation. EHRs can prove to be vital in offering the global access and portability of medical records and hence supporting the international medical care. However, still there is a lack of globally accepted EHR standards and their implementation. On the other hand, privacy concerns are very high with the development of health records. Many countries have come-up with the specific privacy and medical regulations to take care of these concerns. However, the right to privacy in healthcare sector can be effectively implemented only through the collaborative efforts of different stakeholders. This includes institutions with private and public domain, insurance companies, online servers and civil action groups. Hence, a lot of global effort is required to address these issues on EHR privacy and standards.

REFERENCES

Acquisti, A., John, L. K., & Loewenstein, G. (2013). What is privacy worth? *The Journal of Legal Studies*, *42*(2), 249–274. doi:10.1086/671754

Appari, A., & Johnson, M. E. (2010). Information security and privacy in healthcare: current state of research. *International Journal of Internet and Enterprise Management, 6*(4), 279-314.

Balestra, M. L. (2017). Electronic health records: Patient care and ethical and legal implications for nurse practitioners. *The Journal for Nurse Practitioners*, *13*(2), 105–111. doi:10.1016/j.nurpra.2016.09.010

Barhoun, R., Ed-daibouni, M., & Namir, A. (2019). An Extended Attribute-Based Access Control (ABAC) Model for Distributed Collaborative Healthcare System. *International Journal of Service Science, Management, Engineering, and Technology*, *10*(4), 81–94. doi:10.4018/IJSSMET.2019100105

Bentley, T. G., Effros, R. M., Palar, K., & Keeler, E. B. (2008). Waste in the US health care system: A conceptual framework. *The Milbank Quarterly*, *86*(4), 629–659. doi:10.1111/j.1468-0009.2008.00537.x

Berman, J., & Bruening, P. (2001). Is privacy still possible in the twenty-first century? *Social Research*, 306–318.

Brauchli, K., O'Mahony, D., Banach, L., & Oberholzer, M. (2005). iPath-a telemedicine platform to support health providers in low resource settings. *Studies in Health Technology and Informatics*, *114*, 11–17.

Cavoukian, A. (2012). Privacy by design. *IEEE Technology and Society Magazine*, *31*(4), 18–19. doi:10.1109/MTS.2012.2225459

Cavoukian, A., Polonetsky, J., & Wolf, C. (2010). Smartprivacy for the smart grid: Embedding privacy into the design of electricity conservation. *Identity in the Information Society*, *3*(2), 275–294. doi:10.100712394-010-0046-y

de la Torre, I., Martínez, B., & López-Coronado, M. (2013, October). Analyzing open-source and commercial EHR solutions from an international perspective. In *2013 IEEE 15th International Conference on e-Health Networking, Applications and Services (Healthcom 2013)* (pp. 399-403). IEEE. 10.1109/HealthCom.2013.6720708

Edirisinghe, E. D. N. S. (2019). *The Impact of electronic health record (EHR) system design determinants on user attitude towards using the system*. Academic Press.

El Hissi, Y., Benjouid, Z., Haqiq, A., & Idrissi, L. L. (2018). Contribution of New Technologies in the Relationship Between the Governance and the Social Responsibility at the Moroccan University. *International Journal of Service Science, Management, Engineering, and Technology*, *9*(3), 1–13. doi:10.4018/IJSSMET.2018070101

Elloumi, N., Kacem, H. L. H., Dey, N., Ashour, A. S., & Bouhlel, M. S. (2017). Perceptual metrics quality: Comparative study for 3D static meshes. *International Journal of Service Science, Management, Engineering, and Technology*, *8*(1), 63–80. doi:10.4018/IJSSMET.2017010105

Entzeridou, E., Markopoulou, E., & Mollaki, V. (2018). Public and physician's expectations and ethical concerns about electronic health record: Benefits outweigh risks except for information security. *International Journal of Medical Informatics*, *110*, 98–107. doi:10.1016/j.ijmedinf.2017.12.004

Fragidis, L. L., & Chatzoglou, P. D. (2018). Implementation of a nationwide electronic health record (EHR) the international experience in 13 countries. *International Journal of Health Care Quality Assurance*, *31*(2), 116–130. doi:10.1108/IJHCQA-09-2016-0136

Galli, B. J. (2018). Risks related to lean six sigma deployment and sustainment risks: How project management can help. *International Journal of Service Science, Management, Engineering, and Technology*, *9*(3), 82–105. doi:10.4018/IJSSMET.2018070106

Gera, R., Mittal, S., Batra, D. K., & Prasad, B. (2017). Evaluating the effects of service quality, customer satisfaction, and service value on behavioral intentions with life insurance customers in India. *International Journal of Service Science, Management, Engineering, and Technology*, *8*(3), 1–20. doi:10.4018/IJSSMET.2017070101

Gold, R., Bunce, A., Cowburn, S., Dambrun, K., Dearing, M., Middendorf, M., Ned, H., & Celine, M. (2018). Adoption of social determinants of health EHR tools by community health centers. *Annals of Family Medicine*, *16*(5), 399–407. doi:10.1370/afm.2275

Haas, S., Wohlgemuth, S., Echizen, I., Sonehara, N., & Müller, G. (2011). Aspects of privacy for electronic health records. *International Journal of Medical Informatics*, *80*(2), e26–e31. doi:10.1016/j.ijmedinf.2010.10.001

Hargittai, E. (2010). Facebook privacy settings: Who cares? *First Monday*, *15*(8).

Häyrinen, K., Saranto, K., & Nykänen, P. (2008). Definition, structure, content, use and impacts of electronic health records: A review of the research literature. *International Journal of Medical Informatics*, *77*(5), 291–304. doi:10.1016/j.ijmedinf.2007.09.001

Hodges, A., Byrne, M., Grant, E., & Johnstone, E. (1999). People at risk of schizophrenia: Sample characteristics of the first 100 cases in the Edinburgh High-Risk Study. *The British Journal of Psychiatry*, *174*(6), 547–553. doi:10.1192/bjp.174.6.547

Hripcsak, G., & Albers, D. J. (2012). Next-generation phenotyping of electronic health records. *Journal of the American Medical Informatics Association*, *20*(1), 117–121. doi:10.1136/amiajnl-2012-001145

Huang, L. C., Chu, H. C., Lien, C. Y., Hsiao, C. H., & Kao, T. (2009). Privacy preservation and information security protection for patients' portable electronic health records. *Computers in Biology and Medicine*, *39*(9), 743–750. doi:10.1016/j.compbiomed.2009.06.004

Introna, L., & Pouloudi, A. (1999). Privacy in the information age: Stakeholders, interests and values. *Journal of Business Ethics*, *22*(1), 27–38. doi:10.1023/A:1006151900807

Jha, A. K., Doolan, D., Grandt, D., Scott, T., & Bates, D. W. (2008). The use of health information technology in seven nations. *International Journal of Medical Informatics*, *77*(12), 848–854. doi:10.1016/j.ijmedinf.2008.06.007

Katehakis, D. G., & Tsiknakis, M. (2006). *Electronic health record*. Wiley Encyclopedia of Biomedical Engineering.

Klopfer, P. H., & Rubenstein, D. I. (1977). The concept privacy and its biological basis. *The Journal of Social Issues*, *33*(3), 52–65. doi:10.1111/j.1540-4560.1977.tb01882.x

Knaup, P., Bott, O., Kohl, C., Lovis, C., & Garde, S. (2007). Section 2: Patient Records: Electronic Patient Records: Moving from Islands and Bridges towards Electronic Health Records for Continuity of Care. *Yearbook of Medical Informatics*, *16*(01), 34–46. doi:10.1055-0038-1638520

Kumar, V., & Bhardwaj, A. (2020). Deploying Cloud Based Healthcare Services: A Holistic Approach. *International Journal of Service Science, Management, Engineering, and Technology*, *12*(1), 87–100. doi:10.4018/IJSSMET.2020100106

Kwak, Y. S. (2005, June). International standards for building electronic health record (ehr). In *Proceedings of 7th International Workshop on Enterprise networking and Computing in Healthcare Industry, 2005. HEALTHCOM 2005.* (pp. 18-23). IEEE. 10.1109/HEALTH.2005.1500373

Ladd, J. (2017). Increased EHR use has advantages, but also patient safety barriers. *Pharmacy Today*, *23*(12), 6–7. doi:10.1016/j.ptdy.2017.11.005

Lindell, Y., & Pinkas, B. (2000, August). Privacy preserving data mining. In *Annual International Cryptology Conference* (pp. 36-54). Springer.

Luk, R., Ho, M., & Aoki, P. M. (2008, April). Asynchronous remote medical consultation for Ghana. In *Proceedings of the SIGCHI conference on human factors in computing systems* (pp. 743-752). ACM.

Miotto, R., Li, L., Kidd, B. A., & Dudley, J. T. (2016). Deep patient: An unsupervised representation to predict the future of patients from the electronic health records. *Scientific Reports*, *6*(1), 26094. doi:10.1038rep26094

Ng, H. S., Sim, M. L., & Tan, C. M. (2006). Security issues of wireless sensor networks in healthcare applications. *BT Technology Journal*, *24*(2), 138–144. doi:10.100710550-006-0051-8

Nguyen, L., Bellucci, E., & Nguyen, L. T. (2014). Electronic health records implementation: An evaluation of information system impact and contingency factors. *International Journal of Medical Informatics*, *83*(11), 779–796. doi:10.1016/j.ijmedinf.2014.06.011

Nissenbaum, H. (2004). Privacy as contextual integrity. *Washington Law Review (Seattle, Wash.)*, *79*, 119.

Parent, W. A. (1983). Recent work on the concept of privacy. *American Philosophical Quarterly*, *20*(4), 341–355.

Patra, R. K., Nedevschi, S., Surana, S., Sheth, A., Subramanian, L., & Brewer, E. A. (2007, April). WiLDNet: Design and Implementation of High Performance WiFi Based Long Distance Networks. In NSDI (Vol. 1, No. 1, p. 1). Academic Press.

Rathert, C., Porter, T. H., Mittler, J. N., & Fleig-Palmer, M. (2019). Seven years after Meaningful Use: Physicians' and nurses' experiences with electronic health records. *Health Care Management Review*, *44*(1), 30–40. doi:10.1097/HMR.0000000000000168

Reddy, S., & Qadeer, I. (2010). Medical tourism in India: Progress or predicament? *Economic and Political Weekly*, 69–75.

Rowlingson, R. R. (2006). Marrying privacy law to information security. *Computer Fraud & Security*, *2006*(8), 4–6. doi:10.1016/S1361-3723(06)70408-0

Samhan, B., & Joshi, K. D. (2017). Understanding electronic health records resistance: A revealed causal mapping approach. *International Journal of Electronic Healthcare*, *9*(2-3), 100–128. doi:10.1504/IJEH.2017.083163

Schwartz, P. M. (2008). Preemption and privacy. *Yale Lj*, *118*, 902.

Siljee, J. (2015, July). Privacy transparency patterns. In *Proceedings of the 20th European Conference on Pattern Languages of Programs* (p. 52). ACM.

Sisodia, S., & Agrawal, N. (2019). Examining Employability Skills for Healthcare Services in India: A Descriptive Literature Review. *International Journal of Service Science, Management, Engineering, and Technology*, *10*(3), 63–79. doi:10.4018/IJSSMET.2019070105

Stanberry, K. (2011). US and global efforts to expand the use of electronic health records. *Records Management Journal*, *21*(3), 214–224. doi:10.1108/09565691111186885

Tatoian, R., & Hamel, L. (2018). Self-Organizing Map Convergence. *International Journal of Service Science, Management, Engineering, and Technology*, *9*(2), 61–84. doi:10.4018/IJSSMET.2018040103

Taylor, S., & Underwood, P. C. (2003). *HIMSS electronic health record definitional model version 1.0*. Academic Press.

VanLieshout, M., Kool, L., van Schoonhoven, B., & de Jonge, M. (2011). Privacy by Design: an alternative to existing practice in safeguarding privacy. *Info, 13*(6), 55-68.

Werner, J., Westphall, C. M., & Westphall, C. B. (2017). Cloud identity management: A survey on privacy strategies. *Computer Networks*, *122*, 29–42. doi:10.1016/j.comnet.2017.04.030

Westin, A. F. (1967). Special report: Legal safeguards to insure privacy in a computer society. *Communications of the ACM*, *10*(9), 533–537. doi:10.1145/363566.363579

World Health Organization. (2017). *New perspectives on global health spending for universal health coverage*. WHO.

Wright, D., & De Hert, P. (2012). Introduction to privacy impact assessment. In *Privacy Impact Assessment* (pp. 3–32). Springer Netherlands. doi:10.1007/978-94-007-2543-0_1

Yue, X., Wang, H., Jin, D., Li, M., & Jiang, W. (2016). Healthcare data gateways: Found healthcare intelligence on blockchain with novel privacy risk control. *Journal of Medical Systems*, *40*(10), 218. doi:10.100710916-016-0574-6

This research was previously published in the International Journal of Service Science, Management, Engineering, and Technology (IJSSMET), 12(2); pages 44-58, copyright year 2021 by IGI Publishing (an imprint of IGI Global).

Index

2D Gauss iterated map 464, 475-477

A

ABAC 311, 943, 952, 955, 957-960, 966-968, 1023
Access Control 24-25, 27, 31, 33, 35, 39, 41, 43-44, 46, 51, 54, 66, 69, 72, 90-91, 99, 106-107, 120, 125-126, 145, 171, 187, 194, 200, 257-259, 261, 264-265, 267, 279-280, 294, 296, 301-302, 308, 310-313, 316, 318-320, 322, 432, 456, 458, 531, 596-599, 628-629, 632, 642, 710, 713, 716, 719, 736, 749, 768, 815, 819, 825, 828, 830, 864, 871-872, 881, 900-901, 922, 924-930, 936-940, 942-945, 952-955, 957-960, 963, 966-969, 976-977, 999, 1005-1007, 1009, 1017, 1023
access control model 945, 955, 958, 960, 968-969
Accessibility 94, 103, 154, 163, 172, 186, 212, 257, 261, 280, 300, 302, 312-313, 573, 575-576, 579, 601-602, 608, 613, 628, 670, 713, 721, 790-791, 793-794, 834, 837, 855-856, 858-859, 878, 1001, 1012
Actuators 151, 155, 188-189, 240-241, 243, 246, 269-270, 617, 619-620, 673-674
AES 120, 197, 269, 282, 319, 410, 449, 452-453, 456, 458, 461-462, 647, 659, 694, 843-844, 847, 852, 864, 905, 914, 916, 920, 925, 1001
alter detection 519, 530
Anonymity 194, 385, 390, 408, 411-413, 421, 423, 425, 427, 641, 643, 814, 817, 820, 822, 827, 970, 977, 979, 985, 987, 994, 1017, 1023
Appalachia 363, 379
Application Entity 463, 648
Apps 18, 170, 184, 193, 206, 211, 337, 340-341, 346, 353, 355, 358-367, 369-372, 374, 378, 380-382, 385-397, 399-404, 406-407, 441, 446, 696, 699-700, 800, 803, 807, 831, 842
Architectures 127-128, 133-134, 140, 143, 147, 149-151, 170, 706, 712, 723, 952
Artificial Intelligence (AI) 205, 208, 213, 246, 254, 703, 819
Asset 59, 69-70, 76-77, 81, 83, 130, 137, 139, 213, 239, 309, 313, 317-318, 561, 666, 674-676, 740, 830, 840, 857, 1018
Attack 1-4, 6-12, 14-15, 18, 24, 34, 55, 61-63, 72, 75-77, 81-83, 86, 88, 108, 112, 116, 123, 173, 239, 248-249, 256-264, 267, 275, 279-282, 285, 288, 292, 304-307, 379, 383, 410-412, 421-422, 424, 432, 435-437, 463, 508-511, 534-538, 543-545, 549-552, 564-565, 567, 570, 589, 591, 619, 623-624, 674, 684, 687, 689-691, 693, 738, 743, 750, 760, 766, 768, 862, 903, 909, 911, 918, 956, 970-972, 974-976, 978-979, 984-985, 988, 993, 998-999, 1002-1003, 1006
Australia 340, 428, 430-435, 440-442, 446, 747, 805, 922, 1014, 1021-1023
Authentication 14, 17, 20, 24-27, 32-39, 42-44, 46, 49-57, 66, 70-71, 89-90, 136-137, 146, 148-149, 160, 172, 187, 195-196, 199-200, 202, 256-258, 262-265, 279-280, 285, 288, 296-297, 302, 308, 310, 312-313, 315, 322-323, 326-328, 330, 334-335, 388, 391, 408, 410-416, 420-429, 441, 462, 465-466, 472, 486, 488, 490-491, 493-495, 508, 511, 514-517, 530, 533, 536-537, 541-545, 557-559, 561, 563-566, 568-571, 590, 600, 602, 606, 617-619, 623-624, 628, 630-632, 634, 636, 638-643, 652, 659, 682, 684, 691, 696, 707, 710, 712-713, 778, 819, 821-822, 844, 847, 863-864, 880, 884, 891-893, 899, 904, 906, 929, 938, 954, 956, 976, 991, 996, 1001-1002, 1009

B

Big Data 85-86, 94, 98, 145, 205-207, 212, 217, 219, 223, 225, 241, 243, 249, 254, 271, 302, 352, 354, 366, 373, 377-378, 424, 455, 458, 461, 463, 623, 641, 659, 688, 773, 782, 819, 821, 827, 841, 902, 906, 940, 989
Biomedical 56-57, 92-93, 100, 145, 177-179, 194, 198,

251, 291, 378, 388, 403, 442-443, 446, 449-450, 454-455, 458-461, 463, 484-485, 560, 567, 569-570, 637, 642, 745, 806, 811, 813, 824, 828-829, 832, 841, 900-901, 939, 970-971, 990, 1021, 1025
Biometric Authentication 17, 20, 323, 623, 634, 638, 641
Biometric identity 31
Biometric identity management 31
Biometrics 17, 20-47, 50-58, 265, 322-323, 328, 334-335, 413, 415, 617, 622, 624, 628, 630, 632, 634-636, 638, 640-643, 844, 877
Biometrics identity 31-33, 50-51, 57-58
Biometrics identity management 31-33, 51, 58
Biometrics Models 617
Bitcoin 62, 84-88, 92, 96, 814, 833-835, 839, 841-842, 978, 980, 989, 992
Blind Watermarking 462, 484, 517-518, 530, 537, 567, 570
Blockchain 84-102, 204-212, 214-223, 388-389, 403, 434, 438, 443-446, 701, 811-842, 881, 902, 980, 1027
Blockchain Technology 84-94, 97-101, 205-206, 208-209, 212, 214-216, 219-223, 388, 403, 434, 438, 444-446, 701, 812-813, 815-816, 818-819, 821-823, 825, 827-830, 832-833, 835, 839, 841-842

C

Cardiovascular Disease 275, 379
Catalan numbers 644, 649-650, 654, 660
Challenges 15-17, 19, 32-35, 52-53, 55, 60-61, 66, 79, 82, 87-88, 92-97, 100-101, 128, 130, 136, 140, 143, 146-149, 179, 203, 206-208, 212, 220-222, 226, 229, 233, 235, 242, 269, 277, 280, 284, 289, 291, 294-295, 297, 303, 315, 320, 340, 348-350, 371, 374, 376, 383-385, 401-403, 406, 409, 428, 430-431, 436, 440, 443-444, 450, 460-461, 486, 495, 518, 570, 579, 593, 639-640, 646, 671-672, 683, 705, 745, 753, 758, 779, 782, 791, 793-794, 800-801, 803, 805, 807, 809, 811-813, 816, 823-825, 828-831, 833, 845, 872, 875, 882, 919, 924, 938, 956, 971, 1010, 1012-1013
CIA triad model 449-450
classical cryptography 279, 282, 287, 290
Clinical Trials 84, 89-90, 92-94, 98, 100, 205, 208, 222, 374, 404, 700-701, 798, 808, 816, 824-825, 827-828, 830-832
Cloud Computing 125-126, 130-131, 134, 145, 148, 151, 159, 187, 200-201, 228, 241, 249, 271, 298-300, 308, 311, 319-320, 358, 366, 383-384, 400, 409, 439, 514, 530-531, 624, 639, 683, 776, 783, 801, 844, 852, 854, 856-857, 860-861, 873-876, 878-879, 900-902, 904-905, 919-920, 938-939, 953-954, 958, 968, 971, 991-992, 994
Cloud Technology 617-618, 623, 630-631, 636, 639
Collaborative Control Theory (CCT) 243, 254
Comorbidity 379
COMPLIANCE AUDIT 706-707, 716
Compression 54, 198, 298, 375, 449-450, 452-453, 460-461, 463, 470, 534, 559, 563-564, 566, 568-569, 638, 646-650, 846
Computer Integrated Manufacturing (CIM) 240, 254
Computer Security 16, 32, 51, 58, 125-126, 424, 687, 726, 953, 968-969, 989
Confidentiality 26, 75, 91, 159, 162, 164, 172, 206, 211, 215-217, 219, 241, 249, 258, 264, 269, 296, 302, 306, 312, 316, 323-326, 359, 362, 368-369, 383, 392, 394, 397, 399, 402, 405, 412, 430-431, 433, 440, 442, 446, 450-451, 456, 458-459, 465-466, 472, 490, 537, 559, 585, 619, 623-624, 628, 630, 645-646, 666, 678, 687, 691-692, 696, 707, 709, 714, 720, 722, 725, 727, 742, 766, 775-780, 782-783, 785, 788-794, 796, 799-804, 806, 808-809, 818, 821, 845, 856, 862, 864-865, 871, 881, 903-905, 909, 918-919, 922, 924, 926, 928, 930, 937, 956, 985, 1000, 1002, 1012, 1017, 1020-1021
Congress 336-337, 340-342, 344, 347-350, 355, 395, 514, 564-565, 729, 736, 746, 919
Consumers 34, 55, 188, 193, 206-207, 232, 296, 336-338, 346, 360, 362-367, 395, 400, 428-429, 431, 433-434, 437-440, 446, 698, 844, 857, 862-863, 928, 981
Countermeasures 1-3, 12, 14, 66, 564, 589, 591, 728, 879, 970, 980, 1000
COVID 19 204-206, 208, 213, 219
Critical Infrastructures 15-16, 60-61, 63, 66-69, 71, 73, 75, 77, 80
Critical Media Industry Analysis 342, 355
cryptocompression system 449-450, 453, 459-460, 463
Cryptography 34, 101, 124-125, 136-137, 145, 199, 261, 269, 279-280, 282-284, 286-293, 309, 313, 410, 425, 452, 462-463, 484, 487-488, 518, 569, 623, 638, 640, 643-649, 655, 658-660, 677-678, 681, 683, 685-687, 689-690, 692-694, 703-705, 713-714, 746, 819, 822, 838, 845, 854, 856, 864-865, 867, 871, 873-876, 922, 924-925, 928-929, 937, 943
Cryptosystem 194, 269, 318, 452, 463, 619, 624, 677-681, 683, 687, 842, 867-871, 874, 876, 906
CSIRT 16
C-SPAN 337, 342-343, 351, 353-356
Cyber 1-7, 9-12, 14-16, 20, 30, 49, 59-61, 63-69, 71-

76, 78-79, 81-83, 93, 204, 206-207, 210, 212-214, 216-218, 223, 238-240, 242-243, 247-249, 251, 253-254, 262, 269, 272, 281-282, 286-287, 290, 336-337, 345-346, 355, 375, 382-383, 388, 405, 407, 429, 431-437, 440, 442, 444, 516, 573, 616, 634, 646, 648, 658, 687, 721, 723-725, 730, 738, 745, 749, 751-752, 759-762, 764-766, 770, 772, 775-779, 787, 830, 833, 836, 862, 978, 993
cyber incident 61, 74, 83
Cyber Security 2-3, 10-12, 14-16, 59-60, 64, 66-67, 71-73, 78-79, 81, 83, 93, 204, 206-207, 212-213, 217-218, 223, 238-239, 242, 247-249, 253-254, 262, 269, 336-337, 346, 355, 405, 407, 431-434, 436-437, 440, 442, 516, 616, 687, 724, 759, 761, 772, 775-777, 779, 787
Cyber Threats 1-2, 4, 12, 20, 59, 61, 65, 68-69, 75, 214, 240, 248-249, 388, 429, 444, 721, 751, 762, 775, 777-779, 836
Cyberattack 239, 433, 738, 751, 758, 760, 972, 994, 1009
Cybercriminals 1, 3, 8, 20, 238-239, 765, 862, 904, 971-972, 974
Cybersecurity 1, 3, 14-16, 71, 73, 75-76, 80-82, 90, 190, 204, 206, 212-213, 215, 217-220, 222-224, 239, 251-253, 268, 381-385, 387-389, 391-392, 396-397, 399-401, 403-404, 406, 428-447, 706, 712, 721, 723, 725, 731, 747-748, 750-753, 759-763, 765-766, 770-773, 829, 973, 988, 991-993
Cyber-Security 66, 204, 210, 261, 431, 437-438, 442, 444, 725, 758, 764
Cybersecurity Framework 1, 3, 14, 16, 396, 404, 761
Cybersecurity Risk 213, 396, 430, 446, 753

D

Data Breach 2, 11, 80, 183, 341, 442, 577, 674-675, 726-732, 734-740, 742-744, 746-749, 752, 759, 762, 772-773, 807, 971-973, 983, 996, 1008, 1018
data controller 792, 809, 1021
Data Hiding 486-488, 496, 516, 533, 535, 537-538, 545, 552-553, 557-559, 564, 566, 568-569, 644-645, 648-650, 652, 659-660
Data Management 84, 90-91, 205, 207-208, 219, 334, 359, 367, 371, 646, 732, 811, 817, 819-820, 825, 831, 855
Data matrix 464, 466, 471-472, 476
Data Misuse 336
Data Privacy 92, 104, 320, 336-338, 344, 346, 348, 350, 358-359, 362-363, 365, 367-368, 370-371, 386, 388, 428-429, 440, 460, 518, 616, 627-628, 723, 726, 734, 740, 742, 777, 782, 790, 793, 811-812, 816, 822, 833, 853, 878, 882, 920, 939, 952, 993
Data Protection 66-67, 79, 238-239, 339, 341, 351, 363, 374, 384, 386, 389, 397, 400, 514, 521, 529, 645, 652, 658, 723, 726, 736, 739, 742, 748, 788, 792-793, 800-802, 804-805, 809, 846, 852-854, 863, 871, 982-983, 985, 990, 992, 994, 996, 1021
data readers 103-104, 107, 123
Data Security 11, 62, 90, 171, 193, 199, 201, 211, 272, 281, 290, 310, 321, 336-337, 340, 342-343, 345-348, 350, 353, 383-384, 386-387, 404, 407, 429, 433, 453, 517-518, 521, 527, 577-578, 615, 640, 645-646, 650, 657, 659, 662-664, 674, 677, 684, 695, 722, 746, 757, 764-766, 771, 777, 779, 783, 812, 822, 826, 839, 872, 881-882, 903, 920, 922, 924, 983, 988, 996, 1007, 1010, 1017
Data Sharing 90-92, 100-101, 123, 125, 273, 296, 320, 359, 365-366, 438, 798, 801, 819, 821, 831, 841, 871, 878, 880-882, 884-891, 893-902, 919-921, 926, 939-940, 950, 954-955, 990
Data Warehouses 229, 336, 355, 990
data writers 103-104, 107
DCT 464, 466-467, 469-471, 477, 481-484, 518-519, 530, 537, 570
Decision Threshold 322
Decryption 112, 115-116, 119-120, 123, 134, 282, 285, 302, 308-309, 423, 452-453, 463, 487-488, 535, 541, 649, 678-680, 685, 695, 716, 819, 847, 864-868, 880-882, 884, 892-894, 899, 903, 905, 909-911, 914, 918, 922, 924-926, 928-929, 931-932, 934-936, 1001, 1007
Denial of Service (DoS) Attack 463
DES 75, 282, 449, 452, 456, 646, 655
DET 322, 329-333
Device 6, 9, 18, 20, 32, 48, 62-63, 71-73, 93, 136-138, 140, 153-154, 160, 163, 168-170, 172, 174, 177-179, 182-186, 188-190, 192-193, 195-197, 207, 238, 242, 251-252, 255-271, 274, 278, 280, 282, 286-288, 291, 294, 297, 299-300, 303, 306-307, 335, 338, 340-343, 345, 352, 354, 367-369, 375, 385-388, 390, 395, 402-403, 414-415, 431-432, 585, 599-600, 619-620, 622, 630, 667, 680, 684, 687, 690, 696-698, 701, 714, 717, 737, 776, 800, 812, 818-820, 838, 854, 873, 883, 888, 890, 892, 900, 962, 975, 996, 1001
Diabetes 91, 98, 166, 168, 170, 186, 192, 203, 276, 358, 360-362, 368-379, 382, 402, 404, 665, 669, 696-697, 699, 1014
Digital 11, 15, 17-18, 20, 25, 27-29, 32, 34, 37-40, 46, 49, 55, 57, 76, 84, 86, 88-89, 94, 97-98, 100, 106, 124, 126, 148, 151, 184, 187, 195, 201, 204-214, 217-224, 227, 238-239, 241, 243, 248, 254, 302,

308, 334, 338, 341-342, 351, 355, 359-362, 364, 366-367, 371, 373-377, 382, 394, 404-405, 420, 424, 428-431, 434-441, 443-444, 446-447, 450, 454, 456-457, 460-463, 465-467, 484, 486-493, 495-496, 505-506, 515-516, 518, 531, 533-538, 557-571, 574, 602, 630, 646, 648-649, 659-660, 678, 681-683, 685, 695, 699, 706-707, 721-722, 743, 751, 758, 776, 778, 801, 804, 808, 812, 818, 821, 827, 829, 831, 833-835, 841-842, 868, 876, 905, 919, 938, 950, 968, 980, 988-989, 991-992, 995, 1002, 1015
digital health technology 446
Digital Healthcare 17-18, 25, 27-28, 221, 434, 443
Digital Image Watermarking 531, 533, 538, 558, 564, 568
Digital Imaging And Communications In Medicine 456, 462-463, 646, 659-660
Digital Transformation 204, 206, 210, 212, 214, 217, 220-224, 227, 428, 430, 435, 439, 446-447, 751
Digitalization 84, 204, 207-210, 212-213, 216, 218, 221-222, 645
discourse analysis 336, 352-355
distributed collaborative environment 955-959, 966
Distributed DoS Attack 463
Distributed Hierarchical Control System (DHCS) 240, 254
Distributed Ledger 86, 89, 93, 96, 100, 206, 208-209, 214, 216, 443, 811, 813, 827-829, 835, 838, 841
Drug Supply Chain 90, 92-93, 208, 822-823, 829, 831
DWT 462, 464, 466-467, 470-471, 477, 481-484, 518-519, 531, 564

E

Eavesdropping 8, 257, 261, 264, 284, 435, 662, 689, 692, 704
ECC Barcode 200 464
edge computing 134, 151, 294-303, 306-308, 311-314, 316, 319-321
Efficiency 17-18, 33, 37, 52, 69, 85, 87, 89, 121, 123, 180-181, 219, 227, 233-236, 240, 277, 322-325, 328, 330, 364, 369, 391, 437, 446, 544, 573-575, 577, 579, 608, 613, 623, 636, 689, 696, 703, 751, 793, 812, 815, 823, 854, 864-866, 869, 871, 878, 880-882, 911, 913, 916, 937, 981, 1000, 1022
Ehealth 3, 90, 220, 272, 288, 322-323, 325-327, 330, 334-335, 435, 445, 518, 527, 530, 627-628, 638, 640, 645-646, 657-658, 682, 688, 701, 705, 725, 778, 793, 800, 802, 809, 828, 1000, 1009-1010, 1021-1022
E-Health 18, 34, 57, 67, 71-73, 75, 85, 91, 99-101, 103-109, 112, 123, 125, 177, 179, 198-199, 202, 222, 233, 404, 406-407, 428-438, 440, 446-447, 517-518, 521, 530, 563, 570, 627-628, 638, 640, 644-645, 648, 651, 658-659, 705, 772, 780, 790, 793, 800-801, 804-805, 807, 830-831, 842, 879, 881, 900-906, 911, 918, 920-921, 950-951, 991, 1024
E-Health Applications 123, 517, 530, 628, 644-645
E-Health System 34, 103-109, 112, 123, 429, 433, 651, 658, 879, 881, 904, 920
E-Healthcare Systems 295-296, 639, 902-903, 953
EHR applications 995, 997-1002, 1004, 1007
electronic health information system 790-791, 809
Electronic Health Record (EHR) 34, 44, 457, 533, 535, 616, 695, 776, 881, 995, 1000, 1008, 1024-1025
ElGamal 662, 678-681, 865, 868, 871, 874, 909, 925
Elliptical Curve Cryptography 922, 924-925, 928-929
Empowerment 430, 436, 438-439, 443, 798, 810
Encryption 7, 12, 34, 57, 63, 71, 103-104, 106-108, 110-111, 113-114, 116-117, 119-127, 134, 136, 161, 172-173, 187, 192, 194-197, 199, 201, 214, 216-217, 257, 261, 265, 279-280, 282-283, 285, 296-297, 301-302, 308-310, 312, 314-316, 318-320, 359, 362, 386, 389, 391, 397, 410, 420, 423, 433, 444, 449-450, 452-453, 455-456, 460-466, 475, 478, 482, 484, 487-488, 529-530, 532, 533, 535, 541-542, 544, 576, 585, 597-598, 600, 602, 628, 640, 643-650, 652-653, 655, 657-660, 662, 666, 674, 676-680, 685-687, 689-695, 702, 714, 716, 720-721, 727, 730, 737, 743, 777, 783, 816, 819, 822, 835, 838, 843-847, 852-854, 856, 863-868, 870-877, 880-882, 884, 888-890, 892-893, 895, 899-900, 903-907, 909-911, 914, 918-922, 924-926, 929, 931-933, 935-936, 938-940, 943, 945, 976, 978-979, 988, 1001-1002, 1007
end stage renal disease 358, 379
ENISA 3, 16, 63, 70-71, 79, 82
Equal Error Rate (EER) 322, 324
Ethical Concerns in Mobile Health 381

F

feature extraction 32, 35-36, 47, 53-55, 58, 311, 327
File Security 843-844, 852
Fog Computing 133-134, 144-145, 148, 177, 223, 294-298, 319-320, 409, 659
Food and Drugs Administration (FDA) 239, 254
forward secrecy 408, 410-413, 421, 423, 427
Fragile 501, 509, 511, 514-515, 518, 526, 533-535, 537-538, 543-545, 558, 562, 565, 569-570, 939
Fully Homomorphic Encryption 853, 866, 870-876, 921

fundus image authentication 486, 495, 511, 514-515

G

Gauss iterated map 464, 473, 475-477
GDPR 80, 83, 239, 341, 351-352, 792-793, 801-802, 809, 982-983, 985, 989, 991-992, 994
General Data Protection Regulation (GDPR) 239, 792, 801, 809, 982, 985
Geolocation 213, 340, 395, 843-844, 852

H

Health 4.0 238, 240-241, 243, 252-254
Health 4.0 (H4.0) 238, 243, 254
Health Cybersecurity 750
Health Cyber-Security 764
Health Informatics 84, 125, 143, 179, 372, 388, 397, 401, 404-405, 407, 429-431, 440, 445, 560, 614, 730, 747, 803, 806-808, 900-901, 954, 968, 1009
Health Information Systems 234, 400, 564, 645, 762, 764, 789-791, 793-794, 802, 809, 954
Health Information Technology (IT) 789, 809
Health Insurance Portability And Accountability Act (HIPAA) 27, 37, 239, 252-254, 372, 458, 576-577, 579, 593, 608-609, 613-614, 709, 723, 985, 1022
Health Monitoring System 158, 163, 169, 181, 187, 201, 688, 919, 924
Health Policy 205, 225-226, 236, 372, 401, 745, 796, 804, 807
Health Record Management 90, 829, 1012
Health Systems Management 750
Healthcare 1-4, 10-12, 14-20, 22, 25-29, 31-35, 37-40, 43-44, 46, 48-52, 55-65, 67-69, 71-73, 77-78, 80-86, 89-102, 126, 128-132, 135-136, 138-140, 143-146, 148, 150-159, 163-168, 170-183, 186-191, 193-195, 198-215, 218-223, 225-226, 229, 232-233, 235, 238-241, 248-249, 251-252, 254, 261-262, 269, 271-272, 274-281, 286-290, 294-296, 302, 311-316, 319, 322, 325, 331, 334-335, 338-340, 344, 346, 351-352, 354, 358-366, 369-371, 373, 375, 377-379, 381-384, 386-404, 406-411, 413, 423-438, 440-446, 455-458, 463, 465, 514, 517, 530, 535-536, 560, 565-566, 570, 573-581, 584-587, 590-596, 601-603, 605-610, 612-618, 623-624, 626-628, 630-632, 634, 636-640, 642, 644-646, 652, 658-659, 662-663, 668, 680-683, 685-688, 695-707, 710-711, 721-732, 734-751, 753, 757-768, 770-773, 775-783, 785, 788-800, 802-813, 815-836, 839-844, 846-847, 852-854, 865, 872-873, 877, 879, 901, 903-904, 909, 918-920, 922-924, 926, 928-930, 936-939, 942-944, 947-958, 960-961, 964, 966-969, 971-973, 976, 978, 980-981, 983-984, 988-993, 995-997, 1000-1002, 1008-1010, 1012-1015, 1017-1019, 1022-1023, 1025-1027
HEALTHCARE AND BLOCKCHAIN 89, 833
Healthcare Data 3, 10, 19, 27-28, 37, 61, 63, 80, 83, 85, 90-91, 93, 98, 102, 171, 201, 281, 290, 314, 338-339, 346, 362-363, 382-383, 387, 391, 410, 429-430, 434-435, 437-438, 440-442, 446, 617-618, 630, 685-686, 726-731, 734-735, 738-741, 743-746, 748-749, 773, 775-776, 778, 807, 811-812, 817, 820-821, 827, 831, 833-834, 842-844, 852, 854, 901, 903-904, 919, 937, 972-973, 980, 990-991, 993, 996, 1010, 1018, 1027
Healthcare Data Integrity 446
Healthcare fraud 17-18, 25, 27
Healthcare Internet of Things 150, 155, 223
Healthcare privacy and security 833
Healthcare Security 17, 64, 138, 143, 225-226, 229, 232, 615, 732, 981
Healthcare System 4, 12, 17, 25, 31-35, 37-40, 43, 46, 50-51, 55-56, 85, 94, 97, 131, 148, 150, 155, 159, 163, 165, 167, 171-174, 176, 181, 190, 193, 201-202, 223, 225, 235, 274-275, 277-278, 280, 288-290, 359-360, 362-363, 430-431, 434, 605, 627, 640, 658, 686, 698, 704, 706-707, 723, 740, 745, 775, 778-779, 791, 811-813, 815, 817, 819-820, 822, 830, 832, 836, 873, 904, 918, 924, 952, 955-958, 960, 964, 967, 991, 1013, 1023
Healthcare Systems 32, 34, 37, 51, 55-56, 85, 89, 101, 129, 131-132, 150, 152, 156, 163-167, 171-172, 175-177, 179, 181-183, 190, 194-195, 198, 200, 202, 209, 219, 248, 269, 271, 274, 276-277, 279, 281, 286, 288-289, 313, 315, 363, 637, 642, 687, 698, 704, 751, 768, 778, 785, 790, 811-813, 815-818, 821, 824, 826-827, 831, 969, 976, 1017
HFIF 576, 616
HIPAA 27, 30, 37, 61-62, 80, 83, 90, 94, 195, 239-240, 248, 252-254, 340, 346, 363, 366, 368, 370, 372-373, 376, 384-387, 389, 394-396, 399, 401-402, 405, 407, 449, 458-459, 461-462, 465, 559, 573-581, 584-586, 591-594, 596-600, 602-609, 612-616, 628, 706-707, 709-710, 716, 720, 723-725, 730, 746, 810, 942-944, 949, 980-982, 985, 988, 991, 993, 995-997, 999, 1001-1003, 1005-1010, 1022
HIPAA Compliance 90, 363, 458, 573-576, 578-580, 586, 592, 614-616, 716, 723-724, 981, 995
HISF 575, 616
HISP 575, 616

HISTD 575, 586, 590-591, 616
HL7 449, 456-457, 461-462
Homomorphic Encryption 309, 318, 530, 677, 816, 853, 865-867, 870-877, 903, 905-907, 909-911, 918, 920-921
Hospital 4, 12, 25-27, 31, 34, 51, 59-63, 67-70, 72, 75-77, 81-83, 85, 93, 104-105, 108, 183, 185, 191, 193, 195, 197, 199, 204-206, 208-210, 215, 219-220, 222, 229, 231-232, 234-236, 239, 249, 261-262, 274, 276-277, 287, 323, 326, 363, 365, 428, 430, 433-435, 437, 440, 443, 446-447, 457, 460, 465, 476, 491, 534, 543, 579-580, 592-595, 601-602, 605-613, 662-663, 680-681, 683, 688, 695, 700, 705, 730, 735-736, 738-739, 747, 749-751, 758, 760, 772-773, 775, 777, 780-781, 789-790, 792, 816, 826, 829-830, 833, 854, 879, 881, 904, 906, 944, 947, 960, 978, 989, 996, 1012, 1014-1015, 1018, 1021
Hybrid Beings 338, 355

I

ICT 3, 15-16, 61, 71-72, 85, 88, 135, 334, 402, 645-646, 779, 781, 790
Identification 18-22, 24-29, 31-37, 39-49, 51-52, 54-55, 57, 61, 63, 65, 70, 75, 80-81, 139, 141, 150-151, 179, 185, 193, 195, 198-199, 207, 216, 218, 240, 249, 254, 264, 280, 313, 322-323, 329-330, 335, 375, 378, 384, 433, 487, 489, 506, 515, 569, 586, 588, 619, 630, 635-636, 640-641, 644-645, 648, 655, 658, 691, 696, 765, 776, 819, 823, 825, 835, 873, 977-978, 985, 987, 1005
IDS 10-11, 16, 599, 601, 716, 739, 821
Imperceptibility 494-495, 501, 507-509, 511-513, 517-520, 524, 526, 528, 530, 538, 544, 552-553, 563, 646
Incident 2, 10-12, 14, 16, 59-62, 64-65, 67-68, 74, 83, 263, 607, 628, 682, 697, 711-712, 721, 736-739, 742, 744, 752, 760, 977, 989, 996, 1018-1019
Individually Identifiable Health Information (IIHI) 789, 809
inertial sensors 150, 165, 167, 170
Information Security 14, 16, 68, 71, 124, 146, 212, 217-218, 239, 251, 253, 279-280, 383-384, 387-389, 391, 396-397, 400-401, 406-407, 442, 444, 446, 449-450, 461, 463, 485, 487, 490, 530, 536, 573, 575-576, 578-582, 584, 586-587, 589-593, 595, 609, 614-616, 639-640, 647, 661, 710-711, 722-724, 727, 740, 743-746, 748-749, 753, 756-757, 759-761, 764-773, 776, 781, 793, 801, 831, 856, 859, 875-877, 901-902, 939, 945, 953, 969, 980, 988, 991, 1011, 1017, 1023-1026
Information Society 225, 646, 1024
Information Technology 18, 56-57, 78, 86, 101, 125, 177, 189, 202, 212, 215, 225-226, 228, 234, 236, 239-240, 253, 277, 293, 344, 353, 383, 387, 389, 391, 397, 400, 425, 432, 438, 440, 442-444, 515, 533, 536, 557-562, 565, 567, 571, 576-578, 580, 584-586, 593, 600, 608, 613, 615-616, 646, 659-661, 706, 709, 714, 719, 723, 749, 753, 759, 761, 765, 775, 780-782, 788-789, 791-793, 800, 802, 804, 807, 809-810, 821, 832, 837, 879, 920-921, 953, 971-972, 978, 982, 999, 1019, 1022, 1025
Integer Transform 486, 495-498, 500-502, 505, 507, 511, 514, 557
Integrity 26-28, 30, 34-35, 44, 54, 65, 71, 91-93, 134, 162, 173, 196-197, 204-205, 208, 210, 212, 214, 217-219, 241, 264, 269, 278-279, 288-289, 302-303, 306-307, 309, 312-313, 316, 323, 326, 363-364, 383, 389, 394, 397, 399, 430, 435, 437, 446, 450-451, 456, 458-459, 465, 490, 517-521, 523-524, 527-528, 559-560, 562, 564, 571, 573, 575, 579, 585, 590, 598-599, 602-604, 608, 613, 618-619, 624, 627-628, 630, 632, 635, 640, 645, 647-648, 657-659, 678, 687, 707-711, 714, 716, 720-722, 724-725, 742-743, 772, 776, 783, 816-819, 821-822, 825, 829, 845, 855-856, 859, 871, 881-882, 903-905, 911, 918, 922, 924, 926, 928, 930, 937-938, 950-951, 959, 1000, 1002, 1005-1008, 1018, 1026
Integrity Checking 71, 264, 518-520, 524, 527-528, 903, 905
Intelligent Healthcare 177, 688, 811, 820
Internet Of Medical Things 93, 148, 775-777, 782, 824, 826, 828, 832
Internet Of Things (Iot) 18, 30, 61, 85, 94, 128-129, 145-148, 150, 179, 182, 204-210, 213, 217-219, 221, 239, 254, 269-270, 335, 409, 426, 618, 663, 674, 686, 695, 704, 765, 775-776, 781, 812, 876, 922-923, 926
Interoperability 89-90, 94, 97-99, 103, 130, 154, 159, 161, 165, 207, 235, 240, 278, 299, 317, 364, 402, 456, 573, 602, 647, 721, 776, 811, 816-819, 821, 825, 828, 832, 837, 839, 841-842, 950-951, 982, 988, 997
Iomt 93, 101, 223, 268, 775-780, 782, 811, 824, 826-828, 830
Iot Devices 130, 133-134, 136-138, 151, 183, 185, 190, 192-195, 201, 238, 241, 247-248, 261, 269-272, 274, 280-281, 289-290, 295, 297-298, 302-304, 307, 315, 409, 663, 680, 685-686, 688, 695, 698, 776, 819, 873

IoT infrastructure 188, 270-271
IoT Security Issues and Challenges 128
IPS 10-11, 16, 599, 601

J

Java programming 644-645, 658
JPEG 2000 standard 449, 453

K

Keyword Privacy 103, 108

M

M2M integration 181, 188-190, 200
MA-ABAC 955, 957, 959-960, 962-966
Machine Learning 150, 174-176, 205-207, 209-210, 216-217, 219, 222, 226, 258, 300, 302, 306, 324, 334, 559, 616, 655, 668, 700, 703, 820, 827, 894, 900, 1013
Matching 20-21, 26, 32, 35-36, 40, 44, 47, 50, 52-54, 58, 200, 323, 327-329, 331, 414, 589, 821, 909
Meaningful Use 406, 573-575, 579, 584, 593, 613-614, 616, 780, 982, 999, 1026
Medical 2, 4, 10-12, 20, 24-28, 32, 34-35, 37, 39, 41, 44-45, 49, 51, 56-58, 60, 62-64, 69-73, 75, 77-80, 82-83, 85, 89-91, 93-94, 96, 98-116, 119, 123-126, 128-129, 139, 146-148, 150-164, 166, 171-176, 179-180, 182-183, 185-187, 190-193, 195, 197-198, 201-202, 206-207, 213-215, 217, 220-221, 223, 226, 229-236, 238-239, 242, 248-249, 251, 253-255, 257-258, 260-268, 272, 274-277, 279, 281-282, 287-290, 296, 302, 311, 316-320, 322-328, 330, 334-335, 337-338, 340, 346-347, 352, 360, 362, 365-367, 371-374, 376-377, 382, 384-388, 395-396, 401-404, 406-409, 411-414, 420, 422-436, 438, 440-446, 449, 453-466, 476, 478, 480-484, 486-487, 490-493, 495-496, 505, 514-521, 526, 528-531, 533-538, 541, 543-545, 557-571, 573, 616, 623-624, 627-628, 630-631, 634-635, 638, 640-642, 644-654, 656-664, 666-668, 670, 674, 682-684, 686, 688, 695-697, 699-701, 703-704, 707, 709-710, 716, 721, 723, 725-730, 732, 734-736, 738-739, 742-746, 748-749, 751-752, 754, 757-758, 760-762, 764-768, 770, 772-773, 775-783, 785, 788-791, 793-800, 803-813, 816-817, 819, 821-839, 841-844, 852-855, 865, 870, 873, 877, 879, 881, 901-904, 919, 921, 923-924, 926, 928, 931, 937-940, 942-944, 947-952, 954-958, 960-964, 966, 970-972, 977-978, 980-981, 984-985, 988-990, 992, 995-996, 1001, 1008, 1010, 1012-1015, 1017-1020, 1022-1027
medical activity 955-956, 960-964, 966
Medical Data 2, 10, 12, 34, 91, 98, 101, 103-104, 107, 123, 155-157, 159, 161-163, 172-176, 277, 279, 288-289, 296, 320, 324-325, 327-328, 362, 409, 433, 458, 517, 521, 529, 534, 536, 640, 644-646, 648-654, 657-660, 662, 668, 674, 684, 707, 723, 725, 746, 812, 816, 819, 825, 827, 830-831, 833, 839, 844, 853, 873, 877, 881, 901, 904, 924, 943-944, 950, 954-956, 970-971, 977, 985, 988, 1019
Medical Data Security 517, 640, 659, 684
Medical Image 233, 442, 444, 460-461, 464-466, 476, 478, 480-484, 486, 490, 493, 505, 515-521, 526, 528-531, 533, 537-538, 541, 558-560, 562-568, 570-571, 638, 644, 646-648, 650-651, 656-657, 660-661, 939
Medical Record 20, 26, 28, 34-35, 44, 90, 103, 106, 108-109, 111-116, 123-124, 185, 262, 352, 396, 404, 407, 514, 535, 638, 697, 776, 782, 793, 807, 824-825, 830-831, 948, 961, 964, 996
Medical Sensor Network 198, 426, 662, 666-667
Mhealth 101, 206-207, 220, 322, 373-374, 378-379, 381-382, 384-386, 388-392, 395-396, 398-407, 441, 800, 807, 810, 831
mHealth (mobile health) 810
mHealth Adoption 381
Military 45, 48, 229, 336-337, 339-341, 344-350, 352, 359, 364, 737, 923, 937-938, 973
Mitigation 3, 12, 14, 65, 67, 71, 78, 292, 383, 395, 445, 584, 594, 611, 706-707, 718, 725, 953, 984, 986, 1000
Mobile Health Framework 381
multi-biometrics system 51-53, 58
multi-keyword search 103-104, 106, 108, 119-120, 202
My Health Record 428-432, 436, 438-443, 446
My Health Records 428-433, 435-440, 445

N

National Institute Of Standards And Technology 252-253, 292, 396, 404, 452, 461-463, 616, 710, 724, 856, 945, 952-953, 989, 1001

O

obesity 358, 360-361, 366-367, 370-376, 378-379
Obstructive Sleep Apnea 360, 379
Opportunities 18, 90, 100-101, 146, 149, 152, 183, 186, 205-207, 220-222, 227, 291, 346, 360-361, 371, 401-402, 430, 440, 443, 640, 687, 700-701,

705, 733, 740, 742, 796-797, 803, 806, 828, 831, 838, 875, 951
Organizational Culture 71, 740, 754, 763, 768, 770

P

PACS 62, 70, 457-461, 463, 534, 559, 568
Pailier 662
Partially Homomorphic Encryption 853, 866-867
Patient Confidentiality 91, 394, 458, 666, 788, 790-794, 799-801
patient literacy 428
Patient Monitoring 17, 28-29, 93-94, 99, 138, 191, 202, 208, 262, 267, 382, 680, 698, 816, 826, 829, 831
Patient-Centered 430, 688, 766, 811-812, 828, 873, 881
Patient-Driven Interoperability 99, 811, 817-818, 828, 841
Personal Data 67, 80, 83, 92, 171, 200, 280, 295-296, 313, 341, 348-349, 359-360, 362-364, 367, 369, 393, 430, 432, 440, 464, 477, 482, 628, 702, 739, 747, 777, 791-793, 800-802, 809-810, 825, 842, 865, 982-985, 994, 1015, 1021, 1023
Personal Health Systems 322
personal ownership 358-359, 362-364, 367-368, 370-371
Pharmaceutical Manufacturing 832
Physical 18, 20, 25, 27, 31-33, 37, 39, 47, 51, 55, 59-61, 63-69, 71-76, 78, 82, 112, 129, 133, 136, 147, 151, 161, 167, 170, 179, 191, 197, 206, 238, 241, 246, 255-257, 259, 261, 269-271, 277, 288, 295, 298-299, 312, 323, 336, 338, 344, 360, 362, 365, 367, 370-372, 377-378, 384-385, 410, 424, 449, 456, 458, 460, 535, 591, 597, 600, 603, 605-607, 618, 620, 622, 624, 630, 632, 651, 664-670, 673, 683, 686, 689-690, 697, 700, 703-704, 708-710, 712, 716, 718-720, 725, 728, 736-738, 740, 743, 755, 778, 789, 793-794, 800, 809, 829-830, 844, 853, 855, 857, 861-863, 975, 977, 984, 996, 1018-1021
Picture Archiving And Communication System 70, 457, 463, 534, 568
Platform 42, 66, 88-89, 98, 135, 145, 149-150, 152, 154-155, 160-163, 170, 172, 183-184, 189, 199, 202, 206, 211, 217, 221, 240, 243, 247, 249-252, 323, 325-326, 334-335, 342, 355, 367-368, 382, 389, 410, 428-430, 438, 560, 676, 683, 688, 776, 797-798, 823-825, 827, 830, 841, 856, 858, 861, 878, 881, 920, 929, 940, 965, 977, 1004, 1010, 1023
Portability 27, 37, 239, 252-254, 340, 358-359, 362-364, 367-368, 370-372, 380, 384, 389, 401, 458, 465, 573, 576-577, 579, 593, 608-609, 613-614, 616, 668, 672, 676, 706, 709, 723, 821, 952, 980-982, 985, 991, 1008, 1012, 1014, 1021-1023
Preprocessing 35-36, 58, 96, 160, 270, 522-523
Prevention 14-16, 25, 28, 51, 61, 63, 65, 67-69, 78, 83, 91, 98, 131, 213, 216, 218, 241, 277, 360-361, 372, 374, 387, 395, 401, 445, 591, 595, 599-602, 708, 710-711, 731, 734-736, 740, 743-744, 807, 855, 984, 990, 1020
Privacy 6, 11, 15, 17, 25-27, 34, 37, 39, 46, 56, 60, 66-67, 71, 75, 78, 84-85, 89, 91-94, 96-97, 102-104, 108, 124, 134, 136, 146, 164, 171, 178, 193-194, 200, 202, 204-209, 211-212, 215, 217, 219-220, 223, 239, 249, 251-254, 264, 267, 269, 279, 289, 294, 296-297, 299, 301-303, 306, 309-311, 313, 316, 319-320, 322-323, 326, 336-338, 340-355, 358-359, 362-365, 367-371, 373, 375-377, 380, 384-388, 391, 393-397, 400-403, 405-412, 420, 423-424, 426, 428-436, 438, 440-445, 455, 458, 460-461, 463, 465, 518, 529, 565, 570-571, 574-576, 580, 591, 603-605, 607-608, 610, 614-619, 627-628, 630, 632, 636, 639, 646-647, 659, 662, 664, 672, 674, 678, 682, 686, 688-691, 702, 706-707, 709-711, 716, 720, 722-728, 730-732, 734, 737, 740, 742, 744-746, 748-749, 766, 770, 772, 777, 781-783, 788-794, 796, 799-813, 816-823, 825-827, 829, 831, 833, 841-842, 853, 856, 862, 865-866, 870-873, 876, 878-879, 881-882, 900-902, 904, 908-910, 918-920, 926, 937-940, 942-944, 949-954, 956, 968, 970-971, 976-977, 981-983, 985, 989-994, 996-997, 1000-1002, 1009-1013, 1015-1027
privacy preservation 639, 819, 878-879, 881-882, 901, 942, 954, 1009, 1025
Privacy Preserving 56, 178, 200, 313, 320, 617-618, 636, 827, 841, 900, 902, 920, 942-944, 953-954, 993, 1025
Privacy Protection 299, 323, 363, 395, 397, 408, 411, 423, 426, 723, 801, 805, 856, 952, 954, 985, 990, 992-993, 1015, 1017, 1019, 1021
privacy through blockchain 833
Private Health Data 429, 970, 994
professional ethics 802
Public Health Information (PHI) 878
Public Health Record (PHR) 878
Public Health Surveillance 27, 751, 794, 796, 798

Q

QKD 285, 685-687, 689-692, 694
Quality Management 225, 234, 809
Quantum Cryptography 269, 280, 283-284, 286-293,

658, 686-687, 689-690, 692-694, 703-705
Quantum Key Distribution 269, 285-286, 292, 686, 690-693, 704
quantum security 685-687, 695

R

Radio Frequency Identification (RFID) 139, 141, 150-151, 240, 254
Ransomware 1-5, 10-11, 18, 30, 59, 61-63, 81, 206-207, 214, 248-249, 253, 282, 435, 729, 731, 737-738, 743, 746, 750-751, 761, 974, 978
Regulators 239, 336-338, 342, 348, 350, 437, 439-440, 574, 578, 802, 862, 983
rehabilitation 85, 150, 165, 170, 177, 179, 251
Remote Intervention 150, 154
reversible data hiding 533, 535, 537, 559, 568
Risk 2, 10, 26-27, 66-68, 75-76, 78, 81, 89, 102, 165, 171, 183, 185, 190, 193, 195, 206-207, 210, 212-213, 216-218, 226, 235, 248, 256, 262, 264, 272, 274-275, 324, 327, 340, 343, 347, 360, 372, 376, 382, 385-386, 388, 396, 403, 430, 433-434, 436, 438, 446, 576, 578, 581, 584, 594-595, 598, 600-601, 605, 608, 611-612, 615, 618, 634, 650, 662, 706-707, 710-713, 715, 718, 721, 725, 728-730, 732, 734, 736, 742, 747, 749, 753-754, 756-758, 766-768, 770, 788-793, 799-800, 802, 807, 831, 833, 836, 842, 854, 856, 862, 942-946, 949-954, 976, 978, 980, 984-985, 988-989, 992-993, 1000, 1018-1019, 1021, 1025, 1027
Risk Assessment 67-68, 75, 386, 430, 576, 706-707, 718, 742, 944-945, 950, 953
Risk Reduction 213, 756, 942, 944-946, 949-951
Robustness 28, 52, 188, 517-521, 523-524, 526-530, 534, 537-538, 545, 564, 628, 680
RSA 269, 283-284, 308, 646-647, 659, 662, 677-678, 680, 687, 694, 864-865, 867-868, 905, 909, 919-920, 925

S

Secure 2, 4, 6-7, 9, 11-12, 14, 20, 25-28, 33-35, 37, 44, 51, 55-56, 58, 60, 62, 66, 75, 85-86, 89, 91, 93-94, 99, 106-107, 112-113, 116, 118-119, 124-126, 135, 137, 146, 160, 172, 181, 183, 187-188, 191, 193-197, 199-202, 206-207, 212, 214, 217, 219, 238, 248, 256, 259, 263-264, 267-269, 280-281, 283-290, 292, 297, 301, 309, 312, 317-320, 322-324, 326-328, 335, 345, 359, 368, 371, 382, 385, 388-389, 391, 397, 403, 410-414, 423, 425-426, 428-429, 431, 434, 436, 438, 441, 445-447, 449-450, 453-456, 459-461, 465, 472, 475, 487, 493, 516-518, 520, 527, 529-531, 533, 535, 558-560, 564, 566-567, 569, 571, 574, 578, 585, 598-601, 603, 607, 610, 614, 618-619, 623-624, 628, 630, 638-639, 641-643, 645-646, 661-662, 666, 673-674, 678, 683-694, 696, 703-705, 709-710, 717, 719-720, 723, 727, 737, 743, 777-778, 786, 812-813, 817, 819, 821, 823-826, 829-830, 832-834, 840-845, 852, 863-867, 870-872, 875-878, 880-882, 895, 899-906, 908, 918-922, 924, 926-927, 938-940, 954, 967, 975, 980-981, 983, 988, 992, 996, 1001, 1018, 1022
Security 1-5, 7, 10-12, 14-18, 21, 24-27, 30, 32-35, 37-38, 41, 44, 47, 49-52, 54-69, 71-75, 77-90, 93-94, 96-97, 103-104, 106, 108-110, 112-113, 116-117, 123-130, 134, 136-140, 143, 146-150, 161-164, 171-174, 176, 181-183, 187, 190-202, 204, 206-207, 209-215, 217-220, 222-223, 225-226, 229-230, 232-233, 236, 238-242, 247-249, 251-259, 261-265, 267-269, 272, 279-286, 288-292, 294-304, 306-313, 315-328, 335-338, 340-348, 350-351, 353-355, 360, 363, 368-369, 373-376, 382-394, 396-397, 400-413, 416, 420-421, 423-426, 428-438, 440-442, 444-446, 449-450, 453, 455-466, 473, 475-476, 481, 483-485, 487, 490-491, 493-495, 514-519, 521-522, 527-530, 534, 536, 544-545, 558-561, 563-566, 568, 570-571, 573-582, 584-612, 614-619, 623-625, 627-628, 630-631, 636, 639-643, 645-647, 649-650, 657-664, 672-674, 677-680, 682, 684-691, 695-697, 699, 703-704, 706-714, 716-728, 730-732, 734-740, 742-749, 751-754, 756-761, 764-773, 775-783, 787, 790, 792-794, 796, 800-801, 804-806, 811-812, 814-815, 818-820, 822-823, 825-827, 829, 831, 833, 835-836, 838-845, 847, 852-854, 856, 858-865, 869-870, 872-882, 884, 888, 890, 901-906, 909, 911, 913, 916-922, 924-932, 935-940, 943-946, 952-959, 967-972, 974-978, 980-985, 987-1002, 1004-1013, 1017, 1022-1026
Security Breaches 248, 281, 385, 428, 432-433, 591, 710, 758, 765-766, 768, 770, 772, 970, 996, 1002
Security Measures 1, 10, 12, 55, 85, 195, 199, 212, 218, 255-257, 264, 346, 389, 449-450, 458, 577, 585, 623, 627, 742, 856, 943-945
security of health care 181, 194
Security Risks 15, 190, 193, 251, 255-256, 265, 346, 645, 718, 721, 723, 737, 742, 756-757, 760, 764, 770-771, 800-801, 806, 826, 829, 844, 873, 969, 975, 995
sensor cloud 922-924, 927-929, 936-938

Sensors 17-18, 34, 37, 52, 54, 58, 63, 66, 70, 73, 78, 85, 93, 99, 128-129, 133-139, 143, 146, 151-152, 154-155, 158-159, 161, 163, 165-167, 170-172, 177-179, 182, 184, 186-189, 191, 194-195, 198, 201, 220, 228, 240-241, 243, 246, 269-277, 280-281, 300-303, 306-307, 311-312, 316, 324, 334, 338, 341, 369, 373-375, 377-379, 385, 404, 425-427, 454, 487, 617, 619-621, 623-624, 639-641, 643, 662-666, 668-670, 672-674, 680-684, 688, 696-699, 703-704, 819, 830, 834, 837, 853-855, 922-924, 928-929, 931, 937
SHA 843, 849-850, 911, 920
Similarity score 31, 58
Smart Contract 84, 88, 91-92, 819, 830
Smart Healthcare 128, 130-131, 135, 148, 150, 209, 223, 319, 685, 688, 823, 873, 939
Social Media 7, 14, 226-228, 347, 353, 366, 371, 386-387, 405, 454, 514, 730, 742, 779, 788, 790-791, 793-799, 802-810, 974, 979
Somewhat Homomorphic Encryption 309, 853, 866, 870, 874
Spatial Domain 449, 464-467, 470, 517-519, 522-524, 526, 530, 533, 535, 544
standard protocols 238, 240, 248, 456
Standardized 12, 14, 39, 45, 50, 93, 456, 573-575, 577-578, 580, 591-592, 608, 611, 613, 615, 663, 801, 871
Static Analysis 73, 995, 997-999, 1002, 1005, 1007
Steganography 269, 282, 427, 488, 496, 515, 557-558, 564, 569, 644-650, 656, 658-661
Supervisory Control Systems 238, 247-248, 251
Systems Management 320, 750

T

TBHM 903-904, 906-908, 910-919
Threat 1-4, 9, 14, 18, 63, 65, 67, 70-75, 78, 83, 173-174, 191-192, 212, 239, 280, 311, 345-347, 385, 412, 442, 521, 685, 693, 695, 707, 725, 728-729, 744, 751, 795, 844, 862, 872, 881, 945, 976, 989, 996, 1002, 1015, 1021
transform domain 465-467, 517-518, 522-523, 526, 530
Transformation 17, 41, 54, 150, 204, 206-207, 210, 212, 214, 217, 220-224, 227-231, 241, 428, 430, 435, 439, 446-447, 462, 467, 470, 628, 693, 751, 802, 812
Trust 2, 61, 86, 89, 91, 93, 96, 99, 182, 204, 212, 217-219, 223, 249, 258, 295, 297, 313, 369, 393-394, 396, 398-399, 404, 406, 433, 435, 462, 577-578, 617-618, 634, 636, 638-640, 642, 682, 777, 792-793, 797, 802, 816-817, 823-824, 834, 837, 844, 862, 879, 919, 938, 944-947, 949-952, 954, 974, 978, 988, 1017-1018

U

User Anonymity 408, 411-413, 421, 423, 425, 641, 643

V

Verification 20-21, 25, 31-37, 46, 49-52, 55-58, 71, 86-87, 89, 112, 126, 136-137, 172, 212, 258, 265, 268, 318, 323-333, 335, 411, 416, 420, 489-490, 514, 562, 571, 585, 619, 628-629, 632, 634, 639-641, 678, 711, 823, 843-844, 847, 880, 882, 884, 891-893, 899, 906, 911, 920, 980
Vulnerability 4, 8-9, 12, 60, 63, 79, 83, 171-173, 192, 262, 279, 289, 305, 311, 339, 345, 347, 388, 535, 584, 586, 589-592, 597, 607-608, 612, 642, 717-718, 723-725, 742, 752, 759, 834, 976, 980, 986, 988, 997-999, 1003-1008, 1010

W

Watermarking 444, 462, 464-467, 476, 483-484, 486-491, 493-496, 502, 508, 514-519, 521, 529-532, 533-538, 543-544, 557-571, 638, 640, 647, 660, 939
Wearable Sensors 18, 170, 177, 179, 373, 377-378, 385, 670, 854, 922, 937
wearable technology 341, 347, 358, 361, 372, 374, 379
Wearables 18, 161, 165, 167, 171, 180-181, 184, 187, 191, 201, 211, 273-274, 338, 350-351, 354, 356, 372, 374, 376, 404-405, 686, 699, 704, 800, 826
Web Criminality 970
whistleblowing 766-767, 770-772, 774
WiMAX 150, 165
Wireless Medical Sensor Networks 146, 408-409, 425-427, 441, 682

Z

Zigbee 136, 150, 154, 161, 164, 271, 665, 696

Printed in the United States
by Baker & Taylor Publisher Services